**Community
Development Series**

# DESIGNING FOR
# HUMAN BEHAVIOR:
## Architecture and
## the Behavioral Sciences

Edited by
**JON LANG**
University of Pennsylvania

**CHARLES BURNETTE**
A.I.A. / Philadelphia Chapter

**WALTER MOLESKI**
Environmental Research Group
Philadelphia

**DAVID VACHON**
Architect

Dowden, Hutchinson
& Ross, Inc.
Stroudsburg, Pennsylvania

**Library of Congress Cataloging in Publication Data**
Main entry under title:

Designing for human behavior.

   (Community development series, v. 6)
   Bibliography:  p.
   1.  Architectural design.  2.  Architecture--
Psychological aspects.  I.  Lang, Jon T., comp.
[DNLM:  1.  Architecture.  2.  Behavior.  3.  Environ-
ment.  BF353 D457  1974]
NA2750.D42    720'.1'9        73-22208
ISBN 0-87933-054-6

Copyright © 1974 by Dowden, Hutchinson & Ross, Inc.
Library of Congress Catalog Number: 73-22208
ISBN: 0-87933-054-6

74  75  76   5  4  3  2  1

Manufactured in the United States of America.

Exclusive distributor outside the United States and
Canada:
John Wiley & Sons, Inc.

# Series Editor's Preface

What designers propose and clients build has significant influence on human behavior. To sharpen and focus that influence is a worthwhile enterprise for several reasons.

• Documented insights can help avoid repetition and replication of earlier environmental disasters.

• Identifying ways and means to use environmental research will inevitably enrich the design processes.

• Clarifying design intentions through the rigor and discipline of the social sciences means, at the least, commanding more information than intuition alone permits.

It seems particularly appropriate that Philadelphia—which has contributed so much to better design—should again provide the place and the people to address these issues.

Richard P. Dober, AIP

# Preface

During the autumn of 1971 the Philadelphia Chapter of the American Institute of Architects, with the cooperation and support of the Franklin Institute, The Institute for Environmental Studies of the University of Pennsylvania, and the Environmental Design Department of the Philadelphia College of Art, organized a conference and exhibit on *Architecture for Human Behavior*. It was, apparently, the first conference in this country which sought to bring some understanding of environmental design research to a community of building users and practicing architects, as well as to students and draftsmen, who are typically unable to afford such learning experiences. The program of the conference was deliberately designed to help bridge the gap presently separating research and practice. It sought to assure vital communication and evaluation of recent research by having architects, many with national reputations, and informed laymen respond to researchers in the process of addressing problems with which they were familiar.

The most tangible product of the conference was the prepublished proceedings. The enthusiasm with which that collection of papers was received indicated a significant interest in the subjects covered. At the same time, it was obvious that those papers, on the one hand, had presented only an introduction to the emerging field of ecological research called *environmental psychology* and, on the other hand, had failed to communicate the implications of this field for the practice and teaching of architecture. This volume is a response to those shortcomings. It attempts to synthesize and digest recent changes in architectural philosophy which are concomitant with the development of the field of environmental psychology. It strives to do this from the viewpoint of the practicing architect and without attempting to transform him into an amateur behavioral scientist. This is not a comprehensive book on architectural theory, however, and should not be interpreted as such.

A number of important subjects in the development of a comprehensive theory of architecture are not considered in this book. It does not, for instance, deal either with mechanics or with the needs of specific types of architectural projects; nor does it cover either anthropometrics or the way in which the designed environment can provide for the physiological states required to support human behavior. It touches on theories of designing only to the extent necessary to make the discussion of social, behavioral, and psychological factors in design comprehensible.

This book is concerned with the need for environments which facilitate the behavior needed or desired by people to achieve their goals. It is concerned with the meaning that different aspects of the environment have for different people and what things tend to be known and liked. It is concerned with procedures for ascertaining what is enjoyed by people and what people find spiritually uplifting. It is thus concerned with people's needs and desires at a variety of levels of complexity and importance and is as much concerned with the traditional nonbehavioral aspects of architecture as with the overt behavioral factors whose richness has too long been reduced to a concept of simple functionalism. Above all, this book is concerned with raising the standard of the designed environment from the present level, which both architects and laymen agree is unsatisfactory, to one which meets human needs at as many levels as possible.

At best, the questions raised here, along with suggestions for ways to obtain answers, are only partial solutions to the problem of designing better environments. The problems cut across many disciplines and activities and cannot be solved by any one discipline. Questions regarding the role of governmental agencies, codes, and ordinances, real estate developers, and individual clients are among those not considered. This is not because such issues are unimportant (an analysis of any major building quickly illustrates that many design decisions are made by people other than those credited with the design) but because the main objective here is to raise the sensitivity of architects to the complex social and psychological issues to which they, by necessity, must address themselves. Without a fundamental willingness to deal with these issues and an understanding of ways they might be resolved, our buildings will continue to be partial solutions to poorly identified problems.

This book is divided into five parts. *Part One* describes some emerging issues in architectural theory and practice and points out examples of inappropriate design which have led to the identification of these issues. The intent is not to censure the designers involved; indeed, much of the work that is cited has been thoroughly scrutinized by researchers and critics be-

cause it has been designed by some of the most sensitive architects practicing today. Rather, it is to demonstrate that sensitivity alone, while a necessary condition for better design, can no longer be regarded as a sufficient condition. Similarly, it will be argued that traditional concepts of *architectural theory* are inadequate for the design tasks that architects face. It will be argued that architecture needs a theoretical base comparable to that of the social sciences if the issues that need discussion are to be considered with any rationality or if the research necessary for the progress of the profession is to be carried out. It will also be suggested that architects need to reconsider their present approaches to designing. Once these arguments have been presented, the potential contribution of the behavioral sciences to architectural theory and practice can be discussed.

*Part Two* of the book is concerned with what appear to the editors to be the fundamental processes of environmental psychology that will have an impact on architectural theory. These include the topics of formal and symbolic aesthetics, environmental imagery, and spatial behavior. These are discussed in sections entitled *perception, cognition,* and *spatial behavior,* respectively. Implied in these titles is a somewhat broader concern with psychological processes than has been traditional among architects.

*Part Three* of the book describes the methodological contribution of the behavioral sciences to architectural programming and evaluation. Ways in which one can obtain and use behavioral data are introduced, and examples of both applied and primarily research studies are presented.

This book cannot succinctly cover all the social and psychological aspects of design that are important for the architect to consider. Thus in *Part Four,* the conclusion, an attempt is made to place the objectives of this book in some retrospective framework. Some areas of interest to architects which require additional consideration are also identified.

Finally, *Part Five* is a reference bibliography designed to supplement the text. It is hoped that the books and articles included will both ameliorate the gaps in the book's discussion and whet the reader's appetite for future reading.

Environmental psychology has become so broad a

field that no single volume can begin to provide a comprehensive examination of it and its usefulness as a theoretical basis for architectural research and practice. Nevertheless, ordering and categorizing a group of papers such as those collected should not only help define the present state-of-the-art, its goals, and some of its internal problems and contradictions but should stimulate further research, more rigorous descriptions, and better explanations of the field by researchers and practitioners alike. If any of these result, then the conference, the exhibit, the original publication, and now this volume will have succeeded, and the original venture by the Philadelphia Chapter/American Institute of Architects will have been worthwhile.

There are numerous people who have aided in these endeavors. Josephine Romanach, Administrator of the American Institute of Architects/Philadelphia Chapter, David Anstrand, and Richard Dagenhart provided considerable editorial and design assistance in the production of the original conference proceedings, while Robert Brown, Patti Stem, Gunther Cohn of the Franklin Institute, Daria Bolton, Rick Smith, and Randy Simon were largely responsible for the design and construction of the exhibit. The production of this volume would have been impossible without the help of Aileen Sharp and Karen Lagosky of the Environmental Research Group in Philadelphia and the editorial assistance of Barbara Zeiders and Randy Foy. Last, but not least, a special debt of gratitude is owed to Charles Hutchinson for his continued interest and support in making this publication possible.

Philadelphia
July 1973

Jon Lang
Charles Burnette
Walter Moleski
David Vachon

# Contents

**PART ONE
EMERGING ISSUES IN
ARCHITECTURE**

# EMERGING ISSUES IN ARCHITECTURE

Strong dissatisfaction has been expressed with many recently constructed buildings and with the architectural philosophy that has produced them. This book is based on the premise that most buildings reflect the varying degrees of difficulty that the architectural profession has been experiencing in its efforts to meet the needs, values, and expectations of building users.[1] Criticism of recent architectural efforts has come from a number of sources: clients and building users, social scientists, and architects themselves. Architects have always claimed to be designing for people and thus to be interested in designing an environment that can "uplift the spirit and enhance the sense of well-being."[2] It is clear from even the most cursory glance at the manifestos of the modern masters that a desire to create environments full of "availabilities" and "opportunities" for a "rich" life is deeply rooted in architectural philosophy.[3] If the profession's critics are to be believed, however, there has been a tremendous gap between the architect's intentions and his achievements. There are many parts of the consciously designed environment which are a "sheer delight" but others which are

barren and lifeless—though they may well have been designed by the same architect. This disparity between success and failure illustrates the difficulty that architects have had in predicting the outcome of designs—their impact on people—with any reasonable probability of accuracy.

The reasons for this are diverse but have to do basically with the changing nature of the architectural client. As long as architects designed buildings for clients like themselves—that is, people with similar needs, values, and attitudes—relatively few problems arose. The probability of success declines, however, with the growing heterogeneity of client groups and the shifting of needs from those related to physiology and security toward higher-order needs of self-esteem and self-actualization.[4]

There is a need to reconsider both the traditional principles and processes of design used by architects in light of these changes. The profession as a whole remains reluctant to invest much effort in this task. Instead, as a recent critic of the current status of architectural theory points out, architects are heard to ask: "Why are people so stubborn or misguided as not to use the places and spaces we design—either not at all or in the wrong way?"[5] or "People have to be educated to appreciate the forms we make"—an education which seldom occurs.[6] The latter opinion may be valid when the forms expressed have some adaptive value to the people who use or observe them. It has no validity as long as the "arrogant assumption persists that the knowledge needed is already at the designer's command by virtue of his intuition."[7] This book is only part of a current effort to reduce reliance on untested belief systems in architectural design by expanding the theoretical and factual bases of architecture to include knowledge that is directly related to the appreciation and experience of architecture.

The objective of *Part One* of this book is to come to some understanding of why so much recent architecture fails to meet the needs of its users and to suggest ways in which the probability of success can be increased. The work of authors with different interests and different foci, the seven papers included here do not present a unified view of architecture or human behavior but do raise a host of common issues which are of major importance to the future of the profession. We can divide our discussion of these papers into three parts. In the first, we define the nature of the problem; the second, "Processes of Designing," considers new attitudes and approaches to the way architects can go about the task of programming, designing, and evaluating buildings; the third, "The Behavioral Sciences and Architectural Design," deals with the relationship between architectural practice and research and the emerging field of environmental psychology.

## THE NATURE OF THE PROBLEM

The first three papers discuss the nature of the problem itself. Authored by Howard Mitchell, a clinical psychologist and Director of the Center for Human Resources at the University of Pennsylvania, Alan Lipman, Reader in Architecture at the University of Wales, and Constance Perin, author of *With Man in Mind,* these papers help to explain the dilemmas facing the architectural profession today. They focus on interrelated problems: the first is that the architectural profession has been slow to respond to changing relationships between professional and client; the second is that most architects have a naïve belief that the physical environment is a major determinant of social behavior; and, the third is that architecture is by and large an atheoretical discipline.

An understanding of the changing roles of professional and client is important because a reconsideration of these roles will lead to a redefinition of the processes of designing and a reordering of the emphasis that architects place on different aspects of designs. The recognition of the second problem is important because it begins to explain the gap which often occurs between the architect's intentions and the manner in which a building actually works. The third problem is important because theory is a prerequisite to any understanding of a complex phenomenon.

During the past few years there has been a great deal of research which should help architects overcome the difficulties they have previously encountered in their efforts to design architecture for human behavior—that is, a truly functional architecture which will meet physiological, social, and psychological needs. This research also provides a basis for remedying the present atheoretical nature of architecture. There is first of all, however, a need to reconsider the changing nature of the client–professional relationship.

### The Client–Professional Relationship

Almost all professions have been reconsidering the nature of the client–professional relationship. Howard Mitchell reviews many of these issues in his article. It is clear that the architect's paternalistic attitudes toward building clients and users will have to change. It is also clear that relying on what people say they want is unlikely to lead to "good" solutions either, as the forlorn and almost totally unused vest-pocket park illustrated in Figure 1 indicates. The design for this park was based almost directly on what people in the neighborhood said they wanted. In a somewhat different context a well-known psychologist notes: "the whole point of designing a culture is not to build a world liked by people as they are now, but a world that people will like who live in it."[8] Most attempts at adapting citizen participation methods of planning to large-scale architectural problems have failed because they do not inform people of what alternatives are available to them and because individual representatives do not know the needs, values, and aspirations of the people they represent. There is no substitution for scientific sampling procedures, and citizen participation alone will not supply the information needed by architects for either the development of building programs or the design of buildings which fulfill the program requirements.

The problem remains. How can the sensitive architect obtain the necessary information for building programming and design to meet the diverse social and psychological needs of an increasingly heterogeneous client population? The nub of the problem is that architects lack any real understanding of the man–environment relationship and the spatial relationships which people find comfortable in different situations. This is due, to some extent, to the architect's belief that all people will perceive opportunities in the designed environment in the same way that he sees them. The failures of many recent buildings in human terms clearly illustrates that this is not so. The architect's

belief system and particularly the belief held by many architects that the physical environment is a major determinant of social behavior (a concept which has come to be known as *architectural determinism*) requires reexamination.

## Architectural Determinism

The belief that the designed environment has a major impact on social behavior is deeply rooted in the polemic of the modern movement in architecture, as Alan Lipman points out in his article. Albert Mayer once noted: "We all naïvely thought that if we could eliminate the very bad physical dwellings and surroundings of slums, the new sanitized dwellings and surroundings would almost 'per se' cure social ills. We know better now."[9] It is now clear that the probability of any behavior—spatial, cognitive, or emotional—is a complex function of a person's habits and intentions as well as factors which can be regarded as facilitators of that behavior. The intentions themselves are a function of social pres-

**Figure 1**

sures, the desirability of that particular behavior for the person or people involved, and its perceived consequences. The facilitators may be architectural in nature, but they are just as likely to be administrative, financial, or some other factor. The fallacy of the belief that architecture is a major effector of human social behavior is probably best exemplified by the housing project which has attracted the most attention in the lay press—the Pruitt-Igoe housing project in St. Louis.[10]

The Pruitt–Igoe housing project consisted of thirty-three 11-story buildings, modeled, according to Roger Montgomery, on such landmarks "in the evolution of contemporary esthetics as Le Corbusier's Unité d'habitation in Marseilles, France, and the Brown–Kock–Kennedy–Demars–Rapson 100 Memorial Drive Apartments near M.I.T. in Cambridge, Mass." The buildings had skipstop elevators which stopped only on the fourth, seventh, and tenth floors. Access to the other floors was by stairs from spacious galleries on the "stop" floors, but landings were dark and unlit. As a consequence the activities which bring neighbors to-gether were difficult. Montgomery writes:

*In 1951,* Architectural Forum *wrote glowingly about the Pruitt-Igoe project "the new plan saves not only people but money." On October 3, 1956, the* St. Louis Post Dispatch *carried news of the unprecedented $7 million remodeling effort to correct the deficiencies in the housing project that were built in when it was put up ten years ago. The gallery corridors* Forum *applauded as a "close safe playground" the tenants call "the gauntlet" an unpoliceable turf for violent youths. They will be narrowed by remodeling into conventional corridors. As many buildings as possible will be reconstructed to eliminate the skipstop elevators the professional press once praised as imaginative design.*[11]

The difference between the anticipated and actual use of the galleries is graphically illustrated in the well-known pair of photographs shown in Figures 2 and 3. A different design would not necessarily have eliminated juvenile delinquency or have created strong neighbor-like activities, but the buildings could have, as Oscar Newman suggests in his recent book,[12] provided fewer opportunities for the former and more for the latter. As it was, the tenants in the buildings found that they could not cope with the stresses of living in

**Figure 2**
**Photo credit:** *Journal of the American Institute of Planners,* **and Mac Mizuki**

**Figure 3**
**Photo credit:** *Journal of the American Institute of Planners,* **and Mac Mizuki**

the project and withdrew to a less stressful situation. The project is, at the time of writing, being partly demolished and partly remodeled. The St. Louis Housing Authority reportedly still owes $30 million in construction fees for the original project.

With the wisdom of hindsight one can ask the question: "What happened in the design of Pruitt–Igoe?" The architects were certainly well-intentioned, design principles which apparently worked well elsewhere were used, and sociologists were enlisted to provide expertise in areas about which the architects knew very little. Simply summarized, a solution appropriate for a particular group of people was provided for tenants with very different sets of needs, values, and attitudes toward housing and the use of space.

To avoid such situations in the future, greater emphasis should be placed on the identifying of potential uses and users and the latter's specific sets of behavior and needs. If this is not done, architects will go on designing playgrounds such as that shown in Figure 4, which although sensitive to a wide range of children's behavior tends to eliminate opportunities for the type of play shown in Figure 5.[13] Again, it would be simpleminded to blame only the designers. All design problems exist within a context of administrative and other requirements which may be part of the problem. Architects, however, must get away from imposing designs which they as a subculture like on people with different sets of needs and aspirations.

## Architects As a Subculture

A content analysis by Edward Wood, Sidney Brower, and Margaret Latimer of drawings of downtown renewal schemes suggests that the implicit values and attitudes of potential users were as follows:
*a high degree of formal ordering which requires the subordination of each part of the environment to the demands of a single overall composition, thus presenting an image of a highly unified society;*
*a high value placed upon "high" cultural and aesthetic tastes from the portrayal of public facilities. . . .*[14]

**Figure 4**
**Photo credit: Nanine Clay**

**Figure 5**
**Photo credit: Nanine Clay**

The values portrayed seem representative of the subculture to which most architects belong rather than representative of the variety of people who use the central areas of cities. The probability of creating lively, usable environments which meet the needs of diverse user groups is low as long as the architect depends only on his own value system in designing.

This is underscored by Amos Rapoport in his critique of the CBS building in New York, an example of "total design." The building, widely applauded in the professional press but more skeptically received by the lay press represents, according to Rapoport,

*the conflict between aesthetic design ideas, the choice of art to be compatible with the building (rather than the people), the choice of colors and plants; the prohibition against any personal objects in the building, the regulations to ensure uniformity, and the people who use the building, their resistance and struggle to express themselves in the building.*

Apart from the office of the Chairman of the Board, everything had, Rapoport continues, the "designers' meaning, the architects' meaning, the meaning of that subculture but not the inhabitants' meaning."[15] The underlying assumptions in such cases are that people are infinitely adaptable, that they will respond in the way that the architects deem appropriate, and that they will give up normal tendencies to personalize the spaces in which they work. There is little support for this belief if the ensuing conflict between the CBS management and its employees is any indication.

One of the reasons for this situation is related to the nature of architectural "theory." A detailed knowledge of human behavior, aspirations, and values has not played a prominent role in the shaping of either architectural theory or buildings. This must change.

## The Nature of Architectural Theory

The traditional focus of architectural theory has been on the relationship of the architect to the artifact he produces and thus on the ideologies and testaments of individual designers, rather than on the relationship between people (either as individuals, or in general) and the built environment. It has not focused on understanding how the environment is perceived, the meaning it has for different people in either concrete or symbolic terms, or the opportunities that different people perceive in it. Similarly, architectural education has emphasized and continues to stress learning *by* ex-

perience almost to the total exclusion of learning *from* experience. Even architectural philosophy has been characterized by the personal sensitivities of its leaders rather than by a concern for theoretical foundations for both designing and for analyzing the issues which confront the profession.

Architecture has traditionally been the last of the arts to be affected by changes in the structure of society and the cultural environment to which it contributes. The attitudes of architects both toward architecture and building users are still deeply rooted in the humanism of the Renaissance rather than in the humanism of the twentieth century. While both imply an interest in classical studies, the modern use of the term *humanism* includes the practical study of human values and the application of scientific methodology to the problems of mankind. Architects have been extraordinarily reluctant to embrace this new definition.

This fear of science has kept important questions from being asked about the nature of architecture and the nature of designing. Consequently, architects continue to favor casual and unsystematic approaches to observation and analysis. With increasing frequency, data generated in this way are inappropriate for the situations to which they are applied. The reason is simply that it is possible to develop a highly rational and internally consistent model of the world based on dubious assumptions, which, in turn, are based on biased observations. Subsequent observations as well as architectural designs are then prejudiced by this model. In her article, Constance Perin points out how crude our assumptions are about housing. While scientific effort is not free from the direction of a false model or hypothesis, it does lead inevitably to rejection of the inappropriate and to replacement by more accurate hypotheses. This is true both for theories of built form and for theories of the process of designing, which also require considerable attention.

## PROCESSES OF DESIGNING

Designing is regarded by architects as the development of a prescription for a building prior to its construction. The designed environment is essentially a man-made system of surfaces which are interposed between active and changing subsets of people and between these and the "impinging milieu." When properly con-

figured, these systems of surfaces have three functions:
1. They maintain the physiological states necessary for people to attain their goals.
2. They provide for, and allow people to perceive, opportunities for the specific patterns of behavior required to attain their goals.
3. They support, to some extent, the psychological states necessary for people to attain their goals by fulfilling certain symbolic and affective functions.[16]

A design problem, then, exists when there is a perceived difference between the existing layout of surfaces defining the environment and one which will permit its users to better achieve their objectives. The process by which this difference is resolved is called the *designing process* in this book.

*Unself-conscious* and *self-conscious* approaches to the designing process have been distinguished by Christopher Alexander.[17] Designing is usually unself-conscious in societies where there is a narrow range of environmental problems to consider and a low division of labor. The unself-conscious process is largely mimetic in that typical designs evolve by trial and error over an extended period of time. Today's situation is quite different because problems are of a larger scale and of greater complexity. Many building types now cater to a wider range of needs, there is a high division of labor, and design is done largely by professional specialists. Design today is a self-conscious process and is becoming more so.

Architects have always been extremely wary of efforts to analyze and understand their methods of designing—an uneasiness stemming apparently from a fear that analysis will hamper creativity. Recent studies of creativity and designing suggest that the opposite is true. During the past decade there has been an increasing recognition by the profession that the processes of designing can be made more explicit and thus should be the subject of increased research. The research done to date has already begun to provide a better understanding of the process and a number of normative models of the process have been published. These models can be classified into two groups: those that have drawn their inspiration from operations research and the management sciences, and those that have been influenced by analogies between design and language—the linguistic models. The paper by Jon Lang and Charles Burnette would fall into the first category and that by Christopher Alexander into the second. These approaches should not be considered mutually exclusive for they try to elucidate different aspects of the designing problems facing architects. The first focuses on the conduct of the process and the second, while addressing a broad range of issues, discusses the content of design.

## Process

Architectural problems are notoriously ill-defined. It is seldom clear exactly what the scope of the problem is and what aspects fall within the professional concern of the architect. As a result the architect is often confronting problems which are not architectural in nature; yet to proceed at all he must push toward some resolution of the need, even though he is never sure that he is attacking the problem at the appropriate level. This is particularly true as the scale of building increases.

The ill-defined character and the complexity of architectural problems are often accompanied by contradictions among physiological, activity-pattern, psychological, and technological requirements. The major constraint on design solutions is that it is impossible to identify all possibilities; life is too short. Moreover, there is no rule telling the architect when to stop searching for a better solution. It is thus impossible to ensure an *optimal* design. Fortunately, it is seldom necessary to have the optimal solution—a good-enough solution will suffice. The more creative architect is the one who can develop a better than merely satisfactory solution within a limited time. The ill-defined nature of architectural problems also makes the evaluation of different possible solutions difficult. Different people have different values and attitudes, and a good solution to some may exacerbate the problems of others. The debates which occur on architectural juries provide ample evidence of the frequent differences of opinion among people with very similar attitudes.

In addition, all architectural problems are unique except at higher levels of generalization. The traditional reliance on prototypical solutions truncates the analysis of the problem before there is any real understanding of it. What the architectural profession needs are ways of approaching the programming and design of buildings which will develop an individual architect's abilities and direct attention to the critical elements of the particular building program that an architect wishes to solve. This is what Jon Lang and Charles Burnette do in their paper "A Model of the Designing Process." The paper provides a framework for improving the architect's methodological skill so that he may enhance his creative ability. The architect is also constrained by his limited information. As continuing research provides more information, it is essential that it be organized in a form that architects find useful and that will aid, not hinder, the designing process.

## Content

Traditionally, architectural information has been condensed into an informal, often implicit and unstructured set of design principles. They are of various types. In general, their structure is something like the following:
*If situation* x *occurs, perform action* y.
Principles of this type enable a designer to make decisions on matters about which he knows very little. Principles are easy to misuse, however, because they fail to extend the architect's understanding of the relationships he is considering. Because of this, a number of attempts have been made recently to provide a device which extends the usefulness of traditional design principles by increasing the architect's understanding of the relationships they define. For example, the work of Christopher Alexander and others at the Center for Environmental Structure has resulted in the formulation of a "pattern language."[18] The language consists of statements and pictorial representations, and rules for combining them. The statements are of the general form:
*If situation* x *occurs, perform action* y *to solve problem* z.
In these statements, *"x"* is the "context" of the pattern and refers to the provision of a service or activity setting; *"y"* is the "solution," the requirements for a system of surfaces; and *"z"* refers to the problem being solved. Following is an example of a pattern statement taken from *Houses Generated by Patterns,* a set of designs and patterns for the Proyecto Experimental House in Peru:
Context:
*Any Peruvian house for large, low-income families.*

Solution:
*The kitchen is large enough to contain a kitchen table and at least 3.60 meters of counter.*
Problem:
*In a Peruvian household, the kitchen is often used by several people at once. This is especially important during a fiesta, when all the women of the family will crowd into the kitchen to help prepare food and serve guests. At such times, or if anyone is trying to eat in the kitchen there must be plenty of room in the kitchen—at least room for a table and room for three people working (3.60 meters at 1.20 meters each).*[19]
Having a data base of such information is not going to ensure responsive architectural environments; but it should go a long way toward meeting the architect's continual plea for more information. The data must, however, be applied with caution. Christopher Alexander, Sara Ishikawa, and Murray Silverstein point out a number of dangers inherent in design principles which are only partially eliminated by the development of the pattern language.[20] The major dangers are as follows:
1. The situation being faced by the designer may well be different from x in the pattern statement. In fact, there may be a tendency for the designer to pay attention to those factors of the problem situation which are similar to x and thus to assume that the present situation is the same.
2. The situation x in the statement may not, in fact, be an accurate representation of the situation in which the observed relationship between y and z occurs.

If all architectural research findings are organized into pattern languages, the designer will have an easily accessible data base. The utility of the pattern language would be further enhanced if it were developed for specific behavior types rather than building types. The added understanding that such pattern languages would give the architect should greatly enhance his creative role by making him aware of where he can express his own values and where he has an obligation to meet the requirements of the users of the building he is designing.

The paper by Christopher Alexander included in this volume is a summary of his forthcoming book. He explains the concepts introduced here in greater detail and presents a much broader look at the problem of environmental design—the need for a shared body of knowledge represented by a shared pattern language.

All this implies a commitment on the part of the architectural profession to the development and use of some language of behavioral prediction and a commitment to continuing behavioral research, which, in turn, implies that the behavioral sciences have something to offer the design profession.

## THE BEHAVIORAL SCIENCES AND ARCHITECTURAL DESIGN

Throughout history, architecture has both accommodated and constrained behavior. It is thus not surprising that there has been considerable discussion of behavioral research for architectural design. This has been particularly true since Hannes Meyer's short-lived attempts to include courses on psychology and cultural history at the Bauhaus.[21] Yet there has been great difficulty in sustaining conversation between architects and behavioral scientists.

It would be easy to dismiss this by saying that most architects feel very threatened by the challenge to their inherited beliefs, social creeds, habits of designing, and design principles that logical analysis, controlled observation, and the norms of disciplined argument and thought bring with them. The reasons are more diverse. First, architects have been highly skeptical of "scientific optimism"—the belief that advances in science will automatically improve the lot of mankind; second, the behavioral sciences examine the past to describe and explain behavior while architects have a strong future orientation; third, the words "behavior" and "behaviorism" have negative connotations for many architects; fourth, the findings of the social sciences are so diffuse and often so tentative that it is difficult to assess them; and, fifth, the traditional academic disciplines have regarded the study of the environment as incidental to their main research interests. These stumbling blocks to cooperation between behavioral scientists and architects are all beginning to disappear.

The belief in "scientific optimism" has been tempered by the recognition that scientific methodology is only useful if interesting questions are being asked and that there is a role for both inductive and deductive logic in theory building. On the part of architects there has come the recognition that the underlying mechanisms of human behavior are surprisingly stable and that it is impossible to design ideal systems without a thorough understanding of how present systems function and malfunction. Similarly, the word "behavior" is beginning to be placed in its proper perspective by architects.

*Behaviorism,* one of the major orientations in the study of learning, stresses that psychology should deal only with the observable and not with the mentalistic concepts of sensation, perception, attention, image, and will, which depend on the subjective procedure of introspectionism. Behaviorist approaches deal with "the stimuli that impinge on an organism's sense organs and the observable responses or behavior elicited as responses to stimuli."[22] The possibility of thinking of architecture in this way is attractive, but its utility has not been shown. Rather, the architectural environment presents opportunities for perception, opportunities for activities, and opportunities for emotional responses. It will not automatically elicit these.

The term "behavior" as used in this book is not restricted to observable activity patterns but includes the areas of perception and cognition that have long interested architects. The term "behavioral science" is almost a synonym for "social science" but implies a greater emphasis on the individual rather than on society. More recently there has been a similar shift from the field of *human ecology,* which attempted to include the study of the physical environment in its study of group behavior, to *environmental psychology,* which has focused more on the individual but by no means exclusively so. It is this emerging field which promises to organize the diffuse studies of interest to architects and to include the physical environment as a major component of its study program.

### Environmental Psychology

A number of reviews of environmental psychology have been written.[23] It is clear from these reviews that there is some dissatisfaction with the term "environmental psychology" and that no commonly accepted paradigm for the field has yet been developed. There is dissatisfaction with the name of the field because all psychology is environmental, and second, because the multidisciplinary nature of the field is not apparent from its title. Since this name has some general acceptance, however, it is used here.

As environmental psychology is in a preparadigmatic stage, most descriptions of the field simply describe the types of research with which it is concerned. Kenneth Craik identifies the following topics: environmental assessment, environmental perception, cognitive

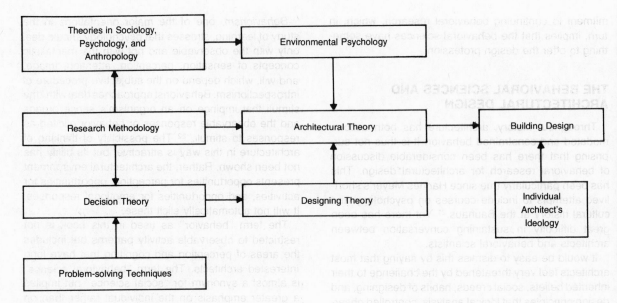

**Figure 6**
**The behavioral sciences and architecture**

**Table 1**
**The Relationship Between Fundamental Processes of**
**Environmental Behavior and the Concerns of Architecture**

| Vitruvian model of the objectives of architecture | *Delight* | | *Commodite* | *Firmeness* |
|---|---|---|---|---|
| Concerns as expressed in recent architectural philosophy | "Formal" aesthetics | "Symbolic" aesthetics | Function | Technology |
| Fundamental processes of environmental behavior | | Cognitive response ← | | |
| | Perception ⟶ | Cognition | ⟶ Spatial behavior | |

representations of the large-scale environment, personality and the environment, environmental decision making, public attitudes toward the environment, the quality of the sensory environment, ecological psychology and the analysis of behavior settings, human spatial behavior, behavioral effects of density, behavioral factors in residential environments, behavioral factors in institutional environments, and outdoor recreation and responses to landscape.[24] To illustrate the full potential of environmental psychology for architecture, another organization might be more useful. Such an organization is shown in Table 1.

Table 1 shows the relationship between the fundamental psychological processes and the concerns of architecture. Sir Henry Wotton, the British humanist, paraphrased Vitruvius in saying that the concern of architecture is to build well on the dimensions of "commodite, firmeness and delight." [25] Much modern architecture has assumed that commodite + firmeness = delight. However, if one accepts the Vitruvian model, delight seems to be composed of both "formal" aesthetics and "symbolic" aesthetics and "commodite" with spatial behavior in all its manifestations. The consideration of "firmeness" falls outside the scope of this book, unless one extends the concept to include "visual" firmeness, which seems to be more of an aesthetic question. The basic behavioral concepts with which one is concerned in thinking about these objectives are perception, cognition, and spatial behavior. *Part Two* of the book is organized around these. Again, the way people perceive, think about, and respond to the environment emotionally or spatially is governed by their physiological nature, personalities, culture, the social organizations of which they are members, and the environment itself.[26] This organization is a highly tentative one, but it does portray the areas in which architects are demanding stronger descriptive and explanatory theories of human behavior. With the increased understanding of adaptive mechanisms that fields such as *ecology* and *cybernetics* are bringing us, an increased cogency and form should be added to environmental psychology.

The potential contribution of the behavioral sciences to architecture is illustrated in Figure 6. A new architectural theory akin to the theoretical background of the behavioral sciences is foreseen. Each new building then becomes a hypothesis about the relationship of human behavior to the designed environment—a hypothesis which can only be tested by using the *pragmatic principle* of observing how it works in reality.

Two papers on environmental psychology and design conclude *Part One* of this book. The first deals with an applied situation, and the second presents an overview. Powell Lawton brings to the reader his experience as an institutionally affiliated researcher constantly evaluating the response and use patterns within a particular facility. His knowledge of how older people actually use space is a testimonial to the value of behavioral observation for design. Harold Proshansky, a psychologist and coeditor of the important reference book *Environmental Psychology: Man and His Physical Setting,*[27] then describes the range of concepts and research efforts which presently characterizes the field of environmental psychology and suggests what mutual benefits might arise from the close cooperation between architects and behavioral scientists in the study of human behavior in the physical environment.

## NOTES AND REFERENCES

1. William Michelson, "Most people don't want what architects want," *Transaction,* Vol. 5 (July–August 1968), 37–43.
2. Kenneth H. Craik, "Environmental psychology," in *New Directions in Psychology 4,* New York: Holt, 1970.
3. See, for instance, Ulrich Conrad, ed., *Programs and Manifestos on 20th Century Architecture,* Cambridge, Mass.: The MIT Press, 1970.
4. A number of architects have found the hierarchical model of human needs formulated by Abraham Maslow useful in ordering their thinking. See his article, "Theory of human motivation," *Psychological Review,* Vol. 50 (1943), 370–396. It is described in greater detail in *Part Two* of this book.
5. Constance Perin, *With Man in Mind,* Cambridge, Mass.: The MIT Press, 1970.
6. "The public still thinks in terms of conventional appearances and reasons on the foundation of an insufficient education," Le Corbusier, *Towards a New Architecture,* 1927, cited by Christian Norberg-Schulz, *Intentions in Architecture,* Cambridge, Mass.: The MIT Press, 1965. The problem is that the architect often departs from conventional models without a sound educational basis.
7. A. E. Parr, "In search of theory," *Arts and Architecture* (September 1965).
8. Elizabeth Hall, "Will success spoil B. F. Skinner?" *Psychology Today,* Vol. 6 (November 1972), 71.
9. Albert Mayer, *The Urgent Future,* New York: McGraw-Hill, 1967, 20.

10. For example, see Alex Poinsett, "Countdown in housing," *Ebony,* Vol. 27 (September 1972), 60–68.

11. Roger Montgomery, "Comment on 'Fear and house-as-haven in the lower class'," *Journal of the American Institute of Planners,* Vol. 32 (January 1966), 31–35. See also Lee Rainwater, "Fear and house-as-haven in the lower class," *Journal of the American Institute of Planners,* Vol. 32 (January 1966), 23–31.

12. Oscar Newman, *Defensible Space: Crime Prevention Through Urban Design,* New York: Macmillan, 1972.

13. Nanine Clay, "Landscapes for urban play," *Architectural Forum,* Vol. 137 (October 1972), 34–39.

14. Amos Rapoport, "Whose meaning in architecture?" *Arena/Interbuild,* Vol. 14 (October 1967), 44–46.

15. *Ibid.*

16. See also the paper by Raymond G. Studer, "The dynamics of behavior-contingent physical systems," in A. Ward and G. Broadbent, eds., *Design Methods in Architecture,* London: Lund Humphries, 1970.

17. Christopher Alexander, *Notes on the Synthesis of Form,* Cambridge, Mass.: Harvard University Press, 1964.

18. Christopher Alexander, Sara Ishikawa, and Murray Silverstein, *A Pattern Language Which Generates Multi-Service Centers,* Berkeley, Calif.: Center for Environmental Structure, 1968.

19. Christopher Alexander, Sanford Hirshen, Sara Ishikawa, Christie Coffin, and Shlomo Angel, *Houses Generated by Patterns,* Berkeley, Calif.: Center for Environmental Structure, 1969.

20. Alexander, Ishikawa, and Silverstein, *op. cit.*

21. Hans Wingler, *The Bauhaus,* trans. by Wolfgang Jabs and Basil Gilbert, Cambridge, Mass.: The MIT Press, 1969.

22. Morton Deutsch and Robert M. Krauss, *Theories in Social Psychology,* New York: Basic Books, 1965, 78.

23. In particular see Rajendra K. Srivastava, "Environmental psychology: an introduction," *Journal of Education and Psychology,* Vol. 29 (April 1971), 29–40; Craik, *op. cit.,* 1-121; and Amos Rapoport, "Some observations regarding man–environment studies," *Architectural Research and Teaching,* Vol. 2 (November 1971), 4–15.

24. Craik, *op. cit.*

25. Quoted by Alan Lipman in his paper, "The architectural belief system and social behavior," included in this book.

26. Talcott Parsons, *Societies,* Englewood Cliffs, N.J.: Prentice-Hall, 1966.

27. Harold M. Proshansky, William H. Ittelson, and Leanne G. Rivlin, *Environmental Psychology: Man and His Physical Setting,* New York: Holt, 1970.

*At the same time that the social fabric of society is being dramatically reshaped, it is creating value dilemmas for the professional. This has happened before: for architects the whole climate of building patronage changed during the Industrial Revolution. Now we are faced with thrusts towards a more participatory democratic structure where professionals find they can no longer retain traditional attitudes toward clients. Architects have traditionally taken either "pragmatic" or "egotistical" attitudes toward clients, but neither approach can create desired future environments. The pressures for change and the fact that architects are unprepared by either training or practice for the new social pressures that face them are discussed, along with the emergence of collaborative relationships between client and professional. The exact nature of these relationships, while unclear at present, does follow a philosophy of action and an ethical quality consistent with the social structures necessary for our postindustrial future. The need is clear—a greater appreciation of the needs and values of users and a more mutually trusting relationship between architect, sponsor, and user-client.*

# Professional and Client: An Emerging Collaborative Relationship

**Howard E. Mitchell**

**University of Pennsylvania**

## VALUE DILEMMAS FOR THE PROFESSIONAL

We are witnessing a period of such transition in society that its very social fabric is being reshaped. There is universal agreement among students of societal change that such periods in history challenge traditional modes of behavior of men and the operation of social institutions. On the other hand, John Gardner argues for the continuous self-renewal of our social institutions at this time,[1] while Lewis Mumford calls attention to the critical choice between further technological development and the need to give greater emphasis to human values in community development. "The notion that automation gives any guarantee of human liberation is a piece of wishful thinking," writes Mumford.[2]

For the purposes of this paper, we first focus upon the value dilemmas created for the professional by the increased movement from improverishment to abundance, from work to great leisure, from nationalism to internationalism, and from an authoritarian tradition to one that is equalitarian. Today the professional,

whether physician, lawyer, or architect is called upon to examine critically his professional life style and way of relating to his clients. Such self-assessment at transitional periods of history causes considerable anxiety in the professional's search for new meanings and purposes of his work in addition to often irrational attempts to reestablish some sense of integration. It is likewise difficult for most social institutions, as well as the individual practitioner of his craft, to adapt rationally to new modes of service delivery in the midst of rapid cultural change. Many people and institutions are prone to look for societal anchors, and they retreat defensively to traditional modes of operation.

James Peterson calls our attention to the fact that "in such periods of history, problems of values come into sharp focus, for man is a valuing being and he dwells in a world of perplexing choices." Writing from the reference point of personal counseling he says that "in such a world, counselors, who by the very nature of their work are involved with individuals in the process of choice-making, cannot afford to neglect the realm of values, for one cannot avoid becoming involved."[3]

Likewise, members of the architectural profession, who are charged with the design of the man-made environment, which leaves its impact upon all of us, are faced today with new value dilemmas and ethical considerations:

1.  To what extent should the design of the social environment be a function of a traditional alliance of architecture with the power elite?
2.  To what extent should the architectural product be the result of the creativity and technical skill of the professional alone?
3.  Should the professional be influenced by social forces related to man's need to have greater control over his behavior and destiny?
4.  Is the answer to be found in a developing collaborative relationship between professional and client which is sensitive to the winds of social change but at the same time respects the integrity of the professional?

David Oakley writes about the new movement in thought, science, and art in England as it passed through rapid changes when industrialization got underway during the third quarter of the nineteenth century:

*This was to lead to a transformed environment by the end of the nineteenth century. The whole climate of building patronage and of the kinds of buildings required was also changed. Government—local and national—the new commercial firms and the ever-expanding railways were the clients of the new age and old aristocracy of blue blood and landed gentry were fading away as commissioners of building work. . . . Architecture ceased to be the primary technology and ceased to provide the largest man-made objects to be seen in the landscape. Size and importance had tended to go together in the past and architects of Victorian England must have been confused by the new situation. When presented by tasks such as workers' housing, where great economic stringency was the rule, they came up with quite simple and advanced (for the time) solutions.* [4]

Parallel to the above period is the current postindustrial era in which designers and planners must confront a whole array of new forces. Authority and the decision-making process in all areas of human services are being challenged. These challenges are articulated in thrusts toward more participatory democratic structures, citizen input into public and social policy formulation and implementaton, community control of areas of public and private personal services, as well as consumer

rights. Today, toward the end of the period of industrialization, as at its beginning, no profession will be permitted to meet new conditions with traditional approaches.

Just as it is difficult to forecast the future, it is risky to suggest the nature of the professional's relationship to his client in the future. Nevertheless, some greater understanding of that relationship might be achieved if we examine in some detail the play of societal pressures upon the traditional role of the architect with his client. We suggest in advance that this new relationship can be characterized not only as reflecting a collaborative relationship between architect and client sensitive to social reality but also as a force for catalytic constructive social change. Architects, joined by their clients, "are on this account not mere craftsmen; their demanding role is to find ways to aid and encourage their society to speak through their buildings . . . in other words to be catalysts, or translators in the sense of the distinguished poets who perform literary achievements in another language." [5] Since architects are rarely trained for this role, we cannot expect them to play it easily or often. Moreover, the increasing awareness and availability of behavioral data makes decisions about the man-made environment more difficult.

## TRADITIONAL PROFESSIONAL ATTITUDES

James S. Ackerman, in an article with the delightful title "Listening to Architecture," suggests that most architects adopt one of two traditional positions in their contact with clients and the public: "the Pragmatic, or give-'em-what-they-want school, and the Egoistic, or give-'em-what-I-want school." [6]

The first of these approaches "is not the catalyst or translator because "em' he designs for do not represent society, but clients interested primarily in the short-range investment viability of buildings." This leads, he says, to conservative design or "fashionable modernism and the Pragmatist introjects just enough of his own concepts into a design to differentiate one building from another." [7]

The Egoist brand of architect, Ackerman goes on to say,

*gets the less hard headed clients of the same group: some discriminating, some just soft. He is the form-giver our architectural schools try to produce (and he usually teaches in them on the side)—the inheritor of the mantle of Frank Lloyd Wright, Mies van der Rohe and Le Corbusier. He and his client silently agree that a building is an isolated work of art, an inhabitable sculpture, in which the most significant ingredient is the flavor of the designer's characteristic style. . . . He is also less inclined to listen to history than the three masters mentioned above, who had an acute sensitivity to the traditions within which they worked. The Egoist is not a translator but a monologuist.*[8]

If, for the sake of argument, we accept Ackerman's two traditional types, we would be in further agreement that neither the pragmatist nor the egoist is capable of creating the humane environment we desire for the future. Indeed, in an increasingly urbanized, technological world such an environment is not only desirable but necessary for man's stability and survival. The designer who falls into one or the other of the above categories seems incapable of engaging with his clients or their world with the sharpness of perception and sensitivity required. He is unable

*to find the significant functions and aspirations of his milieu and to distinguish his own and his client's private aspirations from those of the society. Further, he needs a keen sense of tradition; to help him first to recognize in his own work what he has inherited and what he has invented—to judge whether a solution is just for its context or has crept in as a cliche or affectation—and second to realize the possible alternatives to a particular design decision.*[9]

Why then, are architects inclined to cling to traditional modes of behavior and client relationships in the face of change.

Perhaps one answer is that architects, like other professionals, have only recently become interested in integrating social and behavioral science into their practice. This is not surprising in that the members of the personal service professions have only recently become interested in social science. Whether they are social workers, doctors, nurses, or teachers, they are concerned to find out about the social background and history of their clients. They are also increasingly conscious of the fact that their own relationship with their clients is complex and that social science has many useful observations to make about that relationship. Indeed, they are beginning to recognize (1) that in social work, at least, rendering effective help to the client while remaining only intuitively sensible to social realities is no longer satisfactory, and (2) that such an attitude is rapidly becoming regarded as amounting to incompetence in all the other branches of the personal service

professions as well.[10] Although Paul Halmos writes from his British base of observations, this author feels that, similarly, most personal service workers in the United States have only recently seen the need to become more sophisticated about such social realities as political, economic, and sociological considerations. In doing so, the professional is forced to face more clearly the bases on which he makes his choices and value judgments.

Traditional modes are not only related to the professional architect's awareness and integration of social realities, but it is assumed that his attitudes toward his clients are in part a function of his relationship with his own profession—that is, his professional identifications. His relationship to his clients also reflects and determines his attitudes toward members of other professions who assume roles in helping to create the man-made environment. If the practitioner is reasonably mature and his basic personality problems have been resolved before he enters his profession, what then is the influence of his professional training on his relationships with his clients and with others who also see his clients?

The character of professional training orients the aspiring architect to those behaviors which will establish his professional identifications. The curriculum tells him (1) what the profession expects him to learn, (2) how he should carry out his role with clients, and (3) his relationship to other disciplines if he expects the rewards of the profession. It follows that if the aspiring architect is not intentionally taught alternative ways of engaging and disengaging with clients, the value of behavioral science inputs, and the usefulness of working collaboratively with related disciplines, he is prone to adopt a most parsimonious role in his professional activities and cling to the traditional. Hence the professional is able to ward off the pressures of change which affect his practice by retreating to the security of traditional roles which the profession respects.

The author recalls, in this respect, having presented behavioral data to a group of architects some years ago which demonstrated the clinical trauma experienced by young children who had not been prepared for moving from a stabilized environment to a new setting.[11] After the meeting a young architect approached me and said that although he accepted the facts as presented, he wished that I had not said them. When

I asked why, he replied, "Architecture is difficult enough having to learn about form, structure, perspective, and how to deal with ignorant clients, and now you bring in all of these other behavioral facts—it's just too much. I sometimes wish I had practiced in medieval Florence and had to present my plans only to the Medici or the Roman Catholic Church."

It is beyond the scope of this paper to speculate whether the designer's job was less difficult then than now. On the other hand, we are becoming more aware in all professions of social pressures which affect not only how we relate to clients but indeed the very definition of *client*.

Moreover, contrast the views of the architect cited above with the advice of Christian Norberg-Schulz to his fellow architects:

*The architect does not work in a vacuum. His products are solutions to problems coming from the environment, and the solutions also have a retroactive effect. We therefore have to inquire what the environment asks from the architect, or rather, what it ought to ask from him, and also how a "good" solution is defined. The architect works in "situations" which are composed in particular ways and which explicitly or implicitly pose particular questions. The situations are for instance made up of economical, political and social conditions, of cultural traditions, of physical conditions such as climate and topography, and not least of human beings who "see" the environment in very different ways.*[12]

One of the problems in effecting a professional–client relationship during periods of great change is the degree and direction to which both members of the relationship functionally select those changes which each feels are significant. It has been demonstrated in the psychology of social perception that perception is functionally selective. Investigators have pointed out "that no one perceives everything that is 'out there' to be perceived but that only certain objects play a major role in one's perceptual organization. The objects thus accentuated in perceptual organization are usually those which are functionally significant to the perceiving individuals."[13] If the professional and his clients are not tuned to the same social realities, they of course will be prone neither to respect the integrity of each other nor to develop the kind of relationship productive of a more humane environment in the future.

## SOCIETAL PRESSURES FOR CHANGE

Murray Levine and Adeline Levine provide an excellent historical account of the impact of social pressures

upon a profession. In their review of *A Social History of Helping Services* they trace not only how periods of cultural reform and conservatism have affected practitioners in clinics, courts, schools, and community organizations but suggest how these professionals might better prepare to meet the challenges of tomorrow. They argue "that helping forms arise in response to urgent social need and that the urgent social need is a product of social change."[14] When the predominant mores favor social change, people will be viewed as essentially good and productive and the cause of their problems a function of environmental conditions. Under these circumstances helping forms operate toward modifying social institutions to provide for greater personal growth and development.

Similarly, a host of societal pressures for change in the extent to which man has more direct input into the decisions that will determine his world has implications for all professionals and their relationships with their clients. Our special interest here is how the professional architect appreciates and responds to these pressures. The critical question posed here is: To what extent is the architect aware of the implications of the thrust toward participatory democracy, greater community control of public and private services, citizen participation in community development, the decentralization of urban services and consumerism for his practice, and the relationship with his clients?

It is this writer's observation that physical designers and urban planners were unprepared by training or practice for the new societal pressures which became manifest in American society in the 1960's. This cluster of phenomena that people talk about when they discuss "citizen involvement," "participation," "decentralization," and the "community revolution" has been categorized by social scientists who concentrate their efforts in this area. It is suggested that the implications for a new emerging professional–client relationship be viewed in the context of such a classification. Moreover, the very definition of "client" might be more clearly understood in such context.

Bruce L. R. Smith roughly divides these phenomena which bring decision making closer to the people into three categories: administrative decentralization, community control, and citizen involvement. The first, *administrative decentralization*, "refers to the delegation of authority from higher to lower levels within an organization or unit of government."[15] If the architect's client has been an urban Board of Education which has been decentralized, he may now have to relate to a bureaucratic unit (as clients) on another level which may be at a very different state of organization and development.

*Community control* is defined by Smith as the delegation of authority not only to lower levels within the formal government hierarchy but also to groups outside the government (usually in the form of legislative-type bodies at the local level to which administrative officials are in some sense accountable). In the extreme versions, "control" is assumed to have literal meaning, and the local unit seeks autonomy while at the same time asserting a claim to the fiscal and taxing resources of the wider community. The political implications of community control for the financial support of an architectural project is clear. Certainly the professional must expect both the approval and financing of his proposed creation to take more time.

*Citizen involvement* is the third category outlined by Smith, who states that "it refers to the variety of devices which allow the individual access to the institutions of government. "The exact relationship between citizen involvement and formal decentralization," he suggests, "is one of the great confusions in the movement."[16] The assumption is usually made that more decentralization will lead to more participation, but this runs counter to a substantial body of social science research. There tends to be less, not more, participation in small units of government, particularly in special-purpose governmental units. Citizens tend to have less knowledge of, and less interest in, matters at the precinct, ward, and borough levels than large municipal, state, and national politics. This point needs to be clearly understood because many professionals sensitive to the issues of citizen involvement are confused in their advocate role at local levels, when they find their new clients uninformed about the operation of community power in their own neighborhoods. On the other hand, numerous instances come to mind in which the important expertise of the local client is just this sensitivity, and importance is attached to the extent to which the professional recognizes this fact in their relationship.

R. M. Kramer points out that the participation stand has the most powerful impact upon the decentralization ideology. He suggests that the participatory thrust may also be divided into components. The four outlined are as follows:

1. Participation in policy making.
2. Participation in the sense of citizens as consumers of public services providing "feedback" to the bureaucracies.
3. Participation in the sense of paraprofessionals incorporated in the administration of services.
4. Participation in the sense of mobilizing new constituencies to bring pressure on politicians and administrators so as to change the power realities underlying the administrative system presumably to the advantage of marginal groups in the society.[17]

All components except the third cited above have a direct bearing upon the professional architect and his relationship with the public client. Moreover, the entire democratic thrust embodied in these trends also has made the private client more prone to have more say in what is being planned for him and his children. The latter phenomenon as it affects the individual client is not only a function of greater citizen involvement but of the more basic cultural urge toward self-expression. Perhaps this is most clearly reflected in the growing recognition by government that consumers should have a choice in the marketplace for public services and an appropriate involvement in management decision making.[18]

This recognition, of course, is not shared by all in government, nor by those outside, and the architect and planner will do well to watch closely the unfolding of this drama. Suzanne Farkas writes that the issue of urban decentralization

*is ultimately one of the most refractory issues of American intergovernmental relations. It involves the roles of many actors—national, state, regional, urban, and neighborhood —all sharing powers and functions in a complex arena. It highlights the need for national priority-setting without crippling local institutions and initiatives, and for drawing on private energies without bringing confusion to the administration of public affairs.*[18]

It is suggested in the concluding section of this paper that "the sharing-of-power" is a critical component of an emerging professional–client relationship. Arnold Schuchter provides a good illustration of the problem in this regard in making references to both the Office of Economic Opportunity (OEO) and Model Cities efforts. He writes:

*In the struggle between centralization (outmoded bureaucracy) and community control, neither side will win; both sides will lose as the resource-allocation process becomes chaotic. The problem will become more critical if and when working class and lower class representatives of the poor succeed in challenging middle class citizens and administrators who dominate both OEO and Model Cities and who tend to fit into the machinery of city hall.*[20]

A more humane future environment will not be a product of a win–lose, competitive professional–client relationship. A search for new emerging models of professional–client interaction is imperative.

## AN EMERGING COLLABORATIVE RELATIONSHIP

From the foregoing discussion it is argued that the professional of the future will find himself engaged in an even greater number of emerging relationships with his patrons or clients than in the past. The social institutions of society are in such a state of flux that it is too early to forecast all the organizational forms of tomorrow. Warren Bennis speculates that the might be "adaptive, problem-solving, temporary systems of diverse specialists, linked together by coordinating and task-evaluating specialists in an organic flux—this is the organizational form that will gradually replace bureaucracy as we know it."[21] Bennis refers to these new institiouns of the future as "organic–adaptive structures" that will replace the present bureaucracy, which was necessary in order to harness the power required of the industrial revolution. "In today's world, it is a lifeless crutch that is no longer useful. For we now require structures of freedom to permit the expression of play and imagination and to exploit the new pleasure of work."[22] It is within the context of these "organic–adaptive structures" of tomorrow that we will consider below one of the possibile emerging relationships between architect and client. These relationships may require as great a change in the practice of architecture as that witnessed two centuries ago.

*In the late eighteenth century, with the establishment of the distinct professions of Surveyor and Civil Engineer, the architect's field became still more specific; while in the present century, technical developments have introduced many more specialists into the building scene, and the architect's duties have become more important and more exacting than ever. He is still the artist working between the employer and the builder; but the "builder" no longer represents the trades of a century ago and includes innumerable technicians and specialists all of whom need his attention and understanding.*[23]

The phrase "emerging relationships" is used here because we have practically no historical experience relevant to the expected organizational arrangements required in the future society which would enable us to speak of one prototypical emerging relationship. For example, in the context of the organizational structures suggested by Bennis, an operational definition of client for any given situation is required and not a generalized expression. This definition would vary as determined by the particular role and status of the client who would be engaged in the relationship with the professional. Likewise, definition of the professional will need to be situationally determined, as the role played by the professional of the future will be more variable than at present.

Clearly society is becoming more flexible and more fluid. Within the ever changing social equilibrium in America, involving not only harmonious and cohesive integrated change but varying degrees of disequilibrium, sometimes resulting in social conflict and personal disintegration, we wish to consider some aspects of one emerging relationship. This emerging relationship, which is called *collaborative,* has a philosophy of action and an ethical quality about it, consistent with the social structures that Bennis feels is necessary for our postindustrialized future. Moreover, it seems that the collaborative relationship will also enable the architect to practice his art in sufficiently close contact with that section of humanity for which he is designing and to be aware of the impact of his building upon behavior. Frank Jenkins in his survey of professional relations and practice of architecture in England from the sixteenth century to the present day, says:

*Perhaps the most important of the architect's duties—and certainly the most essential part of the design process—ties in the interpretation of the requirements of the person who is to use the finished building. But the architect is concerned not only with accommodation, with aspect and prospect, with the servicing of the building and other readily comprehended questions; he is concerned with the right atmosphere. He must be aware of the sort of impact his building will make on the people using and seeing it, and control that impact as he sees fit.*[24]

A good example of the lack of appreciation of a new building for its functional users is Intermediate School 201 in New York City. As reported, I.S. 201 was constructed in New York City during the 1960's and won an architectural award for advanced urban school design.[25] One feature which won the architect the accolades of his profession became the focal point of objection by irate parents, resulting in a school boycott. I.S. 201 had few windows in order to reduce vandalism, but the community-control-conscious parents said that this feature in the school design was a way of cutting their children off from their environment while they were being "brain-washed." This situation obviously raises the question of who is the client in the planning of I.S. 201 and how such situations might be avoided in the future.

Following the pioneering work of Warren Bennis we foresee the increasing importance of a collaborative relationship between professional and client. The professional views himself as an active agent of planned social change and thus views his engagement with his client as a joint effort. Bennis states that the collaborative relationship built on a basis of mutual trust has the following features:

1. A joint effort that involves mutual determination of goals.
2. A spirit of industry—a reliance on determinations based on data, publicly shared.
3. A relationship growing out of a concrete, here-and-now encounter.
4. A voluntary relationship between change agent and client with either party free to terminate the relationship after joint consultation.
5. A power distribution in which the client and change agent have equal or almost equal opportunity to influence one another.
6. An emphasis on methodological, rather than specific, substantive goals.[26]

Theorizing about the nature of the architect's more collaborative relationship with his client in the future, we wish to underscore certain features from the above list. The degree to which both architect and patron see themselves engaging in a joint effort which involves a mutual determination of the design and planning goals of a project is very important. Ackerman talks about how learned faculties and trustees of universities often fail to bring to this relationship what is their distinctive responsibility. They

*fail to specify a structure which expresses the belief in and helps clarify a certain mode of learning and living together, a certain relationship to the town and its people, a certain tradition marked by notable figures in the past and present.*

*Instead, they ask for a Kahn, a Johnson, or a Saarinen, and they get a building significant as a stage in the career of these capable gentlemen. The architect cannot be expected in the course of attempting to solve the financial, legal, technical, logistic and other professional problems raised by the commission singly to deduce or to imagine the character and the aspirations of the institution; that is the responsibility of the client and the community, and it is universally evaded.[27]*

Greater citizen involvement in the decision making of the environment in the future should result in less evasion of this responsibility and should reflect the distinctive expertise of the consumers. The degree to which clients will increasingly recognize this responsibility in the collaborative relationship will be a product of its openness and bidirectional flow of communication. The open and public sharing of information is deemed another important feature of an emerging mutually trusting relationship.

Public sharing of information is defined by the context of the relationship. If we have reference to the professional engaged with a private client, we mean that all pertinent information is openly shared between them. On the other hand, if we are talking about the urban designer engaged by a client who represents a public agency or trust, then all phases of goal setting and decision making about the project should be open to the general public. This we see as a feature of a more participatory democracy in the future, but at the same time we are aware that already there are social forces at work to impede such movement. However, if a voluntary relationship has been developed which encourages a mutually satisfying spirit of inquiry and problem solving, both professional and client will be better prepared to face new issues and unpredicted problems as they arise in the relationship. "Members in both groups are not 'bound' by old expectations. Instead, they are now free to explore jointly for new solutions with the other group under the more collaborative conditions. . . ."[28]

Most importantly, the degree to which these collaborative conditions will develop will be a function of the extent to which both professional and client learn to share power. The crucial meaning of power here is in its instrumental use. By such a definition it gives the individual or group control of organizational resources and thereby control of persons. We do not have reference here to the tendency for power to become functionally autonomous and a goal in its own right. The latter use of power intensifies the relationship of power to conflict and often is a feature of traditional values held by the professional in client contracts.[29] This also characterizes the current state of disequilibrium in society as we move toward greater citizen input to decision making. In numerous instances these new thrusts have become the battleground for individuals on both sides to gain power by creating conflict rather than collaboration. The choice open to the professional, in the future, is either to resort defensively to a traditional value system in his engagements with clients or to take an active role in encouraging the development of a mutually trusting relationship. The latter approach is not only consistent with current societal trends but brings more actors into the unfolding drama of democracy.

## NOTES AND REFERENCES

1. John W. Gardner, *Self-Renewal: The Individual and the Innovative Society,* New York: Harper & Row, 1964.
2. Lewis Mumford, *The Myth of the Machine: The Pentagon of Power,* New York: Harcourt, 1964.
3. James A. Peterson, *Counseling and Values,* Scranton, Pa.: International Textbook, 1970.
4. David Oakley, *The Phenomenon of Architecture in Cultures in Change,* New York: Pergamon Press, 1970.
5. James S. Ackerman, "Listening to architecture," *Harvard Educational Review,* Vol. 39 (November 4, 1969).
6. *Ibid.*
7. *Ibid.*
8. *Ibid.*
9. *Ibid.*
10. Paul Halmos, *The Personal Service Society,* New York: Schocken Books, 1970.
11. For a fuller understanding of the psychological significance of the home to the growing child and the family see Herta Reise, *Heal the Hurt Child,* Chicago: University of Chicago Press, 1962; Marc Fried, "Grieving for a lost home," in Leonard J. Duhl, ed., *The Urban Condition,* New York: Basic Books, 1963.
12. Christian Norberg-Schulz, *Intentions in Architecture,* Cambridge, Mass.: The MIT Press, 1965.
13. David Krech and Richard S. Crutchfield, *Theory and Problems of Social Psychology,* New York: McGraw-Hill, 1948.
14. Murray Levine and Adeline Levine, "The more things change: a case history of child guidance clinics," *Journal of Social Issues,* Vol. 26 (Summer 1970), 19–33.
15. Bruce L. R. Smith, "Introduction," *American Behavioral Scientist,* Vol. 15 (September–October 1971), 3–14.
16. *Ibid.*
17. R. M. Kramer, *Participation of the Poor,* Englewood Cliffs, N.J.: Prentice-Hall, 1969.
18. We especially have in mind here the federal role in urban decentralization and citizen involvement in anti-poverty, Model Cities, and urban education programs. Arnold L. Schuchter, "Prospectives for the model cities program," *Planning 1970.* Chicago: ASPO, 1970, 72–96, provides an excellent critique of the Model Cities program in a wide-ranging article which takes into account the interplay of most of the social forces discussed here.
19. Suzanne Farkas, "The federal role in urban decentralization," *American Behavioral Scientist,* Vol. 15 (September–October 1971.)
20. Schucter, *op. cit.*
21. W. G. Bennis, K. D. Benne, and R. Chin, eds., "Collaboration and conflict," in *The Planning of Change,* 2nd ed., Chap. 4, New York: Holt, 1967, 147–191.
22. *Ibid.*
23. Frank Jenkins, *Architect and Patron.* New York: Oxford University Press, 1961.
24. *Ibid.*
25. Gertrude S. Goldberg, *I.S. 201—An Educational Landmark,* New York: Yeshiva University, ERIC Clearinghouse, 1966.
26. Bennis, Benne, and Chin, *op. cit.*
27. Ackerman, *op. cit.*
28. Bennis, Benne, and Chin, *op. cit.*
29. Robert L. Kahn and Elise Boulding, *Power and Conflict in Organizations,* Ann Arbor, Mich.: Foundation for Research on Human Behavior, 1964, 1–7.

# The Architectural Belief System and Social Behavior*

**Alan Lipman**

**The Welsh School of Architecture**

*Much architectural theory contends that architects direct social behavior through their work. The historical roots and pervasiveness of this belief are examined through consideration of the concept of "functionalism" and the writings of leading practitioners. Yet the need for studying social values and requirements does not rest on this belief and social scientists have been highly sceptical of it. The reasons for the belief in architectural determinism and the need for its successful propagation for the image and practice of the profession are described, in addition to the increasing social and administrative distance between architect and client and the designer's frustrations in meeting the needs of unfamiliar ways of life. The problem of the taste gap is also brought to the reader's attention. The belief that the designed environment manages social relationships is used by architects to reduce the tensions that arise in such situations as these. We are reminded that in aspiring to social engineering we reassure ourselves about our role in society and also follow the well-established tradition of modern architectural philosophy.*

This essay examines one aspect of contemporary architectural ideology, and offers some suggestions as to how that facet of the profession's belief system may assist practitioners to define and respond to the situations in which they find themselves. Architectural theory contends that the social behavior of building users is influenced, even determined, by the physical environment in which the behavior occurs. Thus the belief system includes the notion that we architects direct social behavior patterns through our work. This premise—the subject of my discussion here—flows from a specific interpretation and emphasis of the architectural concept of "functionalism."

Functionalism is the declared kernel of twentieth-century architectural philosophy. One of its major claims is that, in contrast to the formalistic revivalisms of nineteenth-century styles, the forms of modern architecture are, and should be, derived from the functions which buildings house. This doctrine was given its characteristic moral rationale by Walter Gropius in 1923 when he wrote: "we want to create a clear organic architecture, whose inner logic will be . . . unencumbered by lying facades and trickeries: we want an architecture whose function is clearly recognizable in the relation of its forms."[1] And writing under the rubric "Functionalism" in the *Encyclopedia of Modern Architecture,* Peter Blake states: "'form follows function' is the catchphrase that spells modern architecture. . . . [It] continues to evoke the image of modern as opposed to traditional architecture more readily than any other slogan."[2] The doctrine is phrased in more pragmatic terms in the British Ministry of Housing's "Parker-Morris" report:

*The right approach to the design of a room is, first to define what activities are likely to take place in it, then to assess the furniture and equipment necessary for these activities and then to design around these needs. . . . [These] depend on the way of life of the prospective occupiers. . . .[3]*

*Adapted from a paper published under the same title in *The British Journal of Sociology,* Vol. 20 (June 1969), 190–204. Published here with the kind permission of the author and Routledge & Kegan Paul.

**Photo credit: Roy Berkeley**

## ARCHITECTURAL DESIGN AND SOCIAL BEHAVIOR

The last quotation highlights the link between the notion discussed in this paper and the overall ideals of architectural functionalism. In what follows, I shall attempt to outline how the concept provides architects with a self-image which can promote the resolution of a dilemma currently confronting the profession.

Clearly, to establish that the notion—that is, the belief that the physical settings architects design influences social behavior—is general currency among practitioners requires empirical evidence. It requires attitude surveys of practitioners, of architectural educators, and of students, and suggests the need for content analyses of documents selected from the whole range of architectural publications. Since presenting data of this nature is beyond the scope of this report, I must rely on brief extracts from a number of statements made by designers and on the corroborative observations of some social scientists who have worked with architects.

In 1965 the Royal Institute of British Architects (R.I.B.A.) launched a series of addresses by well-known practitioners under the title "An architect's approach to architecture." Analysis of the papers[4] delivered to date (September 1967) shows that all but one of the speakers made explicit reference to the supposedly determinate role of building design in shaping the social behavior of actual or intended building users—the single "odd" man implied acceptance of the belief rather than specifically mentioning it. The tenor of the speakers' espousal of the concept can be illustrated by quoting from two of these statements of belief. Of his design proposals for the new University of East Anglia, Denys Lasdun said:

*Schools of study were to be the social and academic entities. . . . Thus the brief from the academics rightly posed the question, "How should young people live in a new University?" The design directive was inspired by this brief. Groups of not more than twelve study-bedrooms with a breakfast room were to form the basic "habitat."[5]*

Describing the plan for Loughborough University of Technology as "in many respects a summation of the ideas I have tried to express," Phillip Dowson claimed:
*Some of the places will be quiet, secluded backwaters, while others will attract a concentration of people. . . . There is a close juxtaposition of teaching and living, meeting and recreation. . . . It is upon the involvement of successive generations of students . . . that the life and vitality of the community . . . will depend. We have to provide a framework within which this organism of individuals can evolve.[6]*

If these statements are felt to be insufficiently overt, one might consider the Dutch architect J. B. Bakema's assertion that "architecture is the three-dimensional expression of human behaviour,"[7] or J. Noble's contentions in a paper intended to provide architects "with an analysis of the factors governing human reactions to the environment." Dealing *inter alia* with the phenomena of clique formation, neighborliness, and social interaction in which "the layout was the major factor determining (social) groupings," J. Noble opened with the words:

*As architects we help to shape people's future behavior by the environment we create. At all stages of the design we make assumptions about human behavior and the successes or failure of our work may depend on our ability to predict human behavior with reasonable accuracy.[8]*

Where social scientists have speculated, or conducted research which might suggest that there are possible links between spatial arrangements and social behavior (these have usually been secondary aspects of their investigations), architects have regarded these as reinforcement of their beliefs. J. Noble's paper draws on, among others, W. H. Whyte's *The Organization Man* and M. Young and P. Willmott's Bethnal Green Studies. In 1957 the psychiatrist Humphry Osmond characterized "two general qualities of buildings" by the terms "sociofugal" and "sociopetal"; he described this terminology:

*By* sociofugality *I mean a design which prevents or discourages the formation of stable human relationships. . . . Sociopetality is that quality which encourages, fosters and even enforces the development of stable interpersonal relationships such as are found in small, face-to-face groups.*[9]

Eight years later Robert Geddes, Dean of the School of Architecture at Princeton, claiming to follow Osmond's principles, commented that a building, illustrated in a paper entitled "The psychological dimensions of architectural space," observed

*the limits of size for every group . . . beyond which friendships do not form. . . . It seems likely that the frequency of involuntary, personal, face-to-face contacts is one of the most important factors in the formation of groups and informal friendships. . . . The layout . . . [has] direct bearing on the formation and maintenance of informal social groups.*[10]

Not surprisingly, perhaps, there are social scientists who are skeptical, if not incredulous, about the varying declensions which this aspect of architectural doctrine has assumed. Two such reactions are selected for mention here because they have appeared in architectural journals and express alarm about the wide acceptance of this notion among architects. Maurice Broady, a sociologist who, as a biographical note indicates, "often lectures at the Architectural Association School in London" characterizes the belief as "architectural determinism." He describes it as an assertion

*that architectural design has a direct and determinate effect on the way people behave. It implies a one-way process in which the physical environment is the independent, and human behaviour the dependent variable. It suggests that those human beings for whom the architects and planners create their designs are simply moulded by the environment which is provided for them.*[11]

In an address to the annual conference of the R.I.B.A. in 1966, F. J. Langdon, a principal officer at the Building Research Station in charge of research on human response to physical environment, echoes Broady's charge of architectural determinism. A portion of his address is devoted to the examination of this "heresy," as he calls it; he says:

*The point has recently been made that the influence of the [designed] environment has been somewhat overestimated by some architects. . . . This is a good point to make. . . . The need to study social values and requirements, and to embody the results in design does not rest on the assumption that one kind of environment makes people come together . . . while another keeps them apart.*[12]

These statements are noteworthy because they were made by social scientists in intimate contact with architects. Both appear to have felt the necessity of attempting to counter a belief which they consider to be widespread.

## PARTIES TO THE CONCEPT OF ARCHITECTURAL DETERMINISM

Three main categories and/or associations of people can be regarded as those to whom the concept of architectural determinism is directed: the public composing the society in which the profession operates, the professional fraternity, and individual practitioners.

The public constitutes the body of people for whom architects, as specialists, perform their professional services. As a professional service occupation architecture stands in a unique position vis-à-vis its public. Architectural decisions take tangible form, and are available for all to experience. Where the results of professional work are so concretely manifest, it is in the profession's interest to project certain images of professional scope and competence. Of such images the ability to influence human behavior has obvious appeal. Its successful propagation might help ensure a steady clientele, and could enhance the prestige of the profession. It could also offer a powerful argument in reconciling anomalies in the profession's extrinsic and intrinsic interests—the conflict between legitimate economic interests and the proclaimed professional concern with standing above pecuniary reward. To the degree to which architects can persuade their public that they are not wholly bound by "crude" financial considerations and are able to claim that their work provides for human satisfaction at a profound level, they may be successful in resolving this classic professional dilemma.[13]

A belief which offers the likelihood of economic stability is attractive, especially if its claims cannot be verified readily. While laymen may be aware of the effects of their social contacts and behavior, they are largely ignorant of the mechanisms by which these are achieved and sustained. Not being in a position to question the assumptions of their specialist consultants, they tend to accept their claims at face value. An example of such client–architect agreement may be seen in the case of the members of a high-ranking academic staff who accepted the notion that the layout of a university campus and the spatial dispositioning of elements within college buildings would affect interstudent, interstaff, and staff–student social and educational behavior—to the extent that they invited their architects to participate in the formulation of academic policy.[14] It seems, then, that for the profession as a whole, and for individual practitioners, belief in their role as manipulators of social behavior assures them that their work has value reaching beyond the mere provision of shelter. In this psychologically and sociologically conscious period the profession's traditional belief that it satisfies aesthetic "needs" can be extended to psychic and social "needs." Indeed, it is difficult to imagine a more gratifying belief, one which could better recompense architects for the vicissitudes of their professional activities. In this context enunciation of the belief by prestigious members of the profession—as in the R.I.B.A. series—is likely to reinforce mutual beliefs. And, as Paul Halmos indicates, sustained belief in one's professional role, even if it does not accord with fact, may well bring about a "self-fulfilling fallacy."[15]

## THE PROBLEM OF ROLE DEFINITION

Thus far I have argued that part of the architectural self-image comprises the belief that architects possess the ability to affect social relationships via their work. Why does this ideology prevail? Why do architects hold this belief? What needs does it satisfy or assuage?

Briefly, my argument is that in the need to clarify their uncertain position in the triadic relationship of artist–technologist–social engineer, architects face a salient problem of role definition. The nub of this suggestion is that today the profession operates with an unprecedented armory of technical equipment and knowledge and, in consequence, its traditional self-image as artist has been dislocated. In an effort to overcome this displacement, architects tend to lean on

their similarly traditional but relatively latent self-conception as social engineers.[16] Here, my model of the architectural self-image is one in which resources are focused in three directions to meet demands from each. In this respect Sir Henry Wotton's frequently referred to "aims of architecture" provide a convenient summary:

*In* Architecture *as in all other* Operative Arts, *the* end *must direct the* Operation.
*The* end *is to build well*.
*Well building hath three Conditions,*
Commodite, Firmeness, *and* Delight.
    —*Sir Henry Wotton, 1604*

Delight—the architect as artist—is considered to be achieved by intuitive personal gift; "firmeness"—architects as technologists, and latterly as managers—by rational analysis; and "commodite"—the products of social engineering—by social experience and insight. The ideal self-image toward which architects aspire would entail a balance of resources and demands across each dimension.[17]

The problem of role definition with which we are concerned appears to spring from technological (and concomitant organizational–managerial) pressure on architects. Since World War II, these have tended to eclipse "delight" and "commodite." In a historical study of the profession in Britain, Barrington Kaye[18] analyzed this process, and presented data which contrast it with the situation prevailing in the nineteenth century, when architect–client relationships resulted in a distortion of the profession's self-image, which emphasized "delight." He showed that the period up to about World War I was characterized by an architect–patron relationship in which the erection of "works of art" played a dominant part. Since the 1920's personal patronage has diminished, and the contemporary architect stands in a different relationship to his clients. This new relationship seems to be the core of a dilemma now facing the profession—a dilemma which impels practitioners to emphasize their social engineering claims in attempts to counter the imbalance between their ideal self-image and the actual situation.

The major force governing changes in the relationships between architects and building users is the factor which has conditioned much modern social change, population growth. The development of a mass clientele has altered the personal relationships of the past, and now architects find themselves separated from those for whom they design in two decisive ways: socially and administratively they are no longer in close contact with the mass of building users and occupants.

## SOCIAL DISTANCE

To my knowledge, systematically acquired data on the social class origins of contemporary architects do not exist, but such evidence as is available[19] indicates that there is a gap between the social and educational backgrounds of building designers and those who live in the buildings they design. In this respect today's architect differs from his pre-World War I predecessor: then *buildings* were for the masses and were not architect designed; *architecture* was commissioned by the "gentry" and the wealthy. When patronage prevailed, the architect was, or in becoming a professional he became, a member of the same—or a similar—social milieu as his patron. He was in a position to grasp the patterns of behavior of his client by virtue of shared social experience. Today this is seldom the case. Interpolation from Kaye's data indicates that while there is evidence of social differentiation in the nineteenth century, as one might expect in a patronage situation, this is not comparable with the differentiations of today. According to Kaye's analysis of the social backgrounds of nineteenth-century architects it would appear that from about 1820 building designers came from parentages among the higher occupational grades and that this has persisted, but today the equable sharing of social background by building designers and users only pertains in isolated instances. Now that architecture embraces the design of buildings for almost the whole range of social strata, differing life styles preclude shared experience.

Among those who have examined some of the effects of this differentiation (see, for example, C. Madge[20] and D. Chapman[21]), stress has been placed on the frustrations of the building occupants. Writing on the "Sociology of Housing," Chapman comments:

*The tenant of the rented house and the purchaser of the new house are rarely able to influence the design of the dwelling, even if they understood their own living habits sufficiently to do so, and as a rule they are not able to recognize the effects of dwelling design on their patterns of living. . . .*[22]

Frustration for designers flows from attempting to meet unexpressed needs arising from ways of life with which they are unfamiliar. In this situation, and given the service bias of their overall professional ideology, they are able to utilize their belief in their power to affect social behavior to justify and reinforce their altruistic objectives. The social engineering aspect of their occupational self-image offers the opportunity to meet some of the consequences of social distance by the assumption, for example, that design decisions regarding the dispositioning of spatial elements can and do determine social contacts. In addition, the nature of their conceptions of "commodite" considerations enable designers to counter reproaches that their designs may not satisfy adequately social behavioral requirements by the claim that "commodite" is operationally indefinable. And where they may feel culpable for not having realized such objectives, their own misgivings can be assuaged by this claim.

The belief can also compensate for the tensions which result from the technological preoccupations forced on architecture in recent years. Meeting mass demands for buildings appears to be impossible without utilization of the techniques of mass production and immersion in technological know-how; familiarization with techniques such as modular coordination, critical path analysis, and systematic design method is now required for an occupation which remains rooted in its craft origins. Architects can find that tension management is, to some degree, accomplished by their belief that they "manage" social relationships.

## ADMINISTRATIVE DISTANCE

The advent of a mass clientele has brought a further change in architect–client relationships: the intervention of administrative agencies standing between architects and building users. The bureaucratization of industrial society has severed the former personal contacts between those who design and those who occupy buildings; typically committees now speak for building users and prospective building occupiers. In the case, say, of local government housing it may be theoretically possible for a local community to influence the selection of sites and the planning of dwellings, but the link between individual members of that community and officially employed, or commissioned, architects is tenuous. Sheer numbers—not to speak of the likely incapacity of future tenants to formulate their requirements—make direct contact rare and highly formalized. And in the private sector of building, except for a minority of high-income groups, the situation is similar. To be effective, user requirements would have to be voiced, and responded to, *before* plans are prepared, and everyday experience suggests that prior consultation is exceptional or indirect.

In Britain, official architects—those employed by local and central government agencies—have constituted over a third of the registered architects in the country since 1949; these professionals are part of bureaucratic, and usually large-scale, organizations. The ethos of such bodies, as Weberian sociology has shown, is biased toward rational and efficient administration. Their bases for decision making are universalistic, and technical professional criteria tend to dominate so that particularistic factors tend to be suppressed. While it may be an open question whether our aspect of architectural social theory is a particularistic or a universalistic consideration, it seems reasonable to suggest that relations between official architects—the servers—and building users—the served—are impersonal and circumscribed by formal organizational contacts. This is a far cry from the relationships of the past in which personal social contacts might have justified social engineering assumptions. Private practitioners are not free of the consequences of bureaucratization. While not necessarily in their direct employment, they are increasingly commissioned by bureaucratic bodies.[23] Mass demand for buildings, and mass-productive means to meet these demands, also affect design for small-scale consumers. Such factors as the availability of standardized building components dictate that bulk ordering is best managed by larger units than individual and isolated clients. We thus find that prospective house owners tend to combine in voluntary housing associations where personal contacts between designers and individual occupants are likely to become secondary to general requirements.

By augmenting the effects of social distance, administrative distance exacerbates architectural divorce from building users. Belief that the profession aspires to, and attempts to, engineer social behavior can temper practitioners' doubts about the social value of their work. It would seem likely that for architects, their alienation from those for whom they design can be countered by the belief that despite, or perhaps because of, this separation they can determine social behavior.

## ARTISTIC AUTONOMY

Schisms in social and administrative relations may go some way toward an explication of the effect of a mass clientele on architectural practice, but it is necessary to attempt to account for the apparent diminution of the aspect of "delight" if one is to complete the argument. This can best be done by considering a major theme of Kaye's study, the concept of the "dilemma of artistic autonomy."

Earlier in this discussion, reference was made to the public nature of architectural products; at the other end of the process of building design there is a further feature which is unique to architecture as a creative activity. Unlike other arts, architecture is an occupation in which artistic communication only transpires when a design conception becomes physically tangible in the form of an actual built entity. Except for those rare instances in which architecture is practiced as a hobby, a relationship between an artist as a professional specialist and a client is a *sine qua non* of the process. Where architect–client interaction deals with "nonartistic" functional requirements such as room size, heating and ventilating standards, and the like, it is possible to design without tensions, but where the relationship impinges on stylistic and aesthetic aspects of a designer's vision he can find himself in an ambiguous position. He may insist on maintaining his artistic integrity and risk the loss of a client, or he may abandon integrity and thereby personal autonomy. Kaye contends that "it is clear that this dilemma becomes the more insupportable the more the architect thinks of his work as approaching pure art." And in the past two decades the admix of technical and scientific knowledge has constrained the scope of "pure art" in design; increasingly objective, nonintuitive criteria have become applicable, and have been applied, in fields ranging from structural engineering to the psychology of perception.[24]

Kaye argues that this factor, the increased number of official architects, and a growing acceptance of the modern "style" have combined to reduce, and even eliminate, the dilemma. Based, as they are purported to be, on functional criteria, modern architectural forms have come to be seen by architects in terms in which aesthetic aims are realized by the fulfillment of functional requirements. In striving for this fulfillment the emphasis has been on technology, and, Kaye claims, the self-image of architects has shifted away from "the creative artist expressing a unique vision, and toward that of the professional seeking to find the best possible technical solution . . . a trend in other words, away from the artist and toward the technician."[25] While, as I have already argued, "commodite" aspirations may be compensating for "firmness" preoccupations, there is no evidence of which I am aware to indicate that aesthetic aims are being abandoned by the profession. On the contrary, the doctrine of architectural functionalism is, as we have seen, inextricably bound up with aesthetic objectives. Considering the matter within the framework of this paper, one is inclined to suggest that, in terms of the relations between architects and their clients (as represented by the individuals and committees with whom they deal), Kaye's proposition that there has been a decline in the tensions involved in the dilemma of artistic autonomy is justifiable. But now tensions about aesthetic and stylistic matters have been transposed to the sphere of differences between public and professional taste.

Architects and the people with whom they deal in the agencies commissioning or employing them may share common social backgrounds, and their aesthetic values may be in some degree of accord, but this is not the case with the public at large. Now tensions are likely to be felt as a result of discrepancies between specialists' conceptions of "good" architecture and popular tastes.[26] It would seem that far from being resolved, the dilemma has been intensified—albeit in a different social context.

The taste gap may well be bridged by the mass media and public education, but for practitioners there appears to be a feeling that social "connections" must be made. One of the contributors to the R.I.B.A. series to which I have referred voiced this in the words: "the . . . essential of an approach to architecture is expressed in its briefest possible form in the two words . . . 'only connect'."[27] The desired role of social engineer could be the image most readily suited to convincing potential building users that connections are possible.

## CONCLUSION

I have attempted to describe an aspect of the architectural belief system and to outline the functions it appears to serve in defining a social role for architecture in contemporary Western societies. For architects, influencing human behavior is doing so for the betterment of the "human condition"; as Sigfried Gideon has argued, their self-assumed goal is "to reinstate basic human values."[28]

Halmos has indicated that the ethic of the personal service professions is increasingly influencing the self-image, values, and objectives of "professional workers whose calling is not in the area of the personal services."[29] It is hardly surprising that architects have responded to this ethic. From its origins in the social ideals of John Ruskin and William Morris the social aims of the modern architectural movement have included aspects which have allied it with antiauthoritarian, and even radical, social, and political forces. When the social values of such modern pioneers as Walter Gropius and Mies van der Rohe clashed with the prevailing ideology of national socialism in Germany, the authorities closed their school of design, the Bauhaus, as early as 1933.[30] During the Stalinist period modern architecture was simply nonexistent in the U.S.S.R. Writing in the *Encyclopedia of Modern Architecture* the art historian G. Veronesi described the tradition-oriented architectural movement of fascist Italy, the Noveccento Italiano, as "a dangerously suggestive constant . . . recruited from the 'reactionaries of the modern revolution' (as one of its founders wrote), or rather from the 'revolutionaries of the Facist reaction' as its critics saw it"[31] (Veronesi's parentheses).

In aspiring to social engineering, post-World War II architects are not only attempting to reassure themselves and their public that they are concerned with social welfare; they are also following an established tradition in the short history of modern architecture.

## NOTES AND REFERENCES

1. Walter Gropius, *Bauhaus 1919–1928,* Boston: Branford, 1959.
2. Peter Blake, "Functionalism," in G. Hatje, ed., *Encyclopedia of Modern Architecture,* London: Thames and Hudson, 1963, 112–113.
3. British Ministry of Housing and Local Government,

*Homes for Today and Tomorrow,* London: H.M.S.O. 1961, 4.

4.   "An architect's approach to architecture," *RIBA Journal,* Vol. 72 (1965), 184–195, 231–240, 298–304; Vol. 73 (1966), 105–115, 116–127, 155–163; Vol. 74 (1967), 191–200, 229–238, 271–280.

5.   Denys Lasdun, "An architect's approach to architecture," *RIBA Journal,* Vol. 73 (1966), 105–115.

6.   P. Dowson, "An architect's approach to architecture," *RIBA Journal,* Vol. 73 (1966), 105–115.

7.   J. J. Vriend, "Netherlands," in Hatje, *op. cit.,* 209–213.

8.   J. Noble, "The how and why of behavior: social psychology for the architect," *Architects' Journal,* Vol. 137 (1963), 531–546.

9.   Humphry Osmond, "Function as the basis of psychiatric ward design," *Mental Hospitals,* Vol. 8 (April 1957), 23–29.

10.  "The psychological dimensions of architectural space," *Progressive Architecture* (April 1965), 159–167.

11.  Maurice Broady, "Social theory in architectural design," *Arena: Journal of the Architectural Association,* Vol. 81 (1966), 149–154.

12.  F. J. Langdon, "The social and physical environment: a social scientist's view," *RIBA Journal,* Vol. 73 (1966), 460–464.

13.  This is particularly acute for private architects: professional fees are percentages of overall building costs, yet architects expect and are expected to design economically. Clients have to be convinced that their interests weigh more heavily than practitioners' self-interest.

14.  "University planning, a discussion," *Architectural Association Journal,* Vol. 80 (1965), 159–168.

15.  P. Halmos, "The personal service society," *British Journal of Sociology,* Vol. 18 (1967), 13–28; also cf. R. K. Merton, "The self-fulfilling prophecy," in *Social Theory and Social Structure,* rev. ed., New York: The Free Press, 1966, 421–436.

16.  The architectural propensity for social generalizations probably springs from the traditional approach of regarding social factors as a variable in historical stylistic changes; see Bannister Fletcher, *A History of Architecture on the Comparative Method,* London: Batsford, 1896. Le Play's place/work/folk formula is usually the basis of architecture; see *RIBA Journal,* Vol. 33 (1925), 12–18.

17.  Support for my contention that these three aspects constitute the architect's conception of his role can be found in, among others: (a) D. M. MacKinnon, "The personality correlates of creativity: a study of American architects," in *Proceedings of the 14th International Congress of Applied Psychology, Copenhagen, 1961, Vol. II,* Copenhagen: Munksgaard, 1962, 11–39; (b) G. Barry, "The place of the architect in the post-war world," *RIBA Journal,* Vol. 53 (1946), 372–376; (c) R. Llewelyn-Davies and P. Cowan, "The future of research," *RIBA Journal,* Vol. 71 (1964), 149–156; (d) Viscount Esher, "Presidential address: not a job but a role," *RIBA Journal,* Vol. 73 (1966), 500–504; (e) "An architect's approach to architecture," *RIBA Journal,* Vol. 74 (1967), 229–238.

18.  B. Kaye, *The Development of the Architectural Profession in Britain: A Sociological Study,* London: Allen and Unwin, 1960.

19.  Extrapolation from the *Observer Survey of Architects* (1964) suggests that over 70% of architects come from middle-class styles of life at school.

20.  C. Madge, "Planning for people," *Town Planning Review,* Vol. 21 (1950), 131–144.

21.  D. Chapman, *The Home and Social Status,* London: Routledge & Kegan Paul, 1965, 2–3.

22.  *Ibid.*

23.  Extrapolation from the quarterly RIBA publication, *New Commissions for Private Architects,* indicates that about one third of the commissions for private architects come from government agencies.

24.  For some indications of the range of technological and scientific enquiry relating to architecture see Llewelyn-Davies and Cowan, *op. cit.*

25.  Kaye, *op. cit.*

26.  For a report of housing estate tenants' reactions to unsightly features of their surroundings see Vere Hole, "Social effects of planned rehousing," *Town Planning Review,* Vol. 30 (1959), 161–173. For some comments on discrepancies in standards of taste as correlates of cultural and class differentials see A.S.B. Study Group No. 1, "Sociology and architecture," *RIBA Journal,* Vol. 53 (1946), 386–394.

27.  H. Morris, "An architect's approach to architecture," *RIBA Journal,* Vol. 73 (1966), 155–163.

28.  Sigfried Gideon, *Mechanization Takes Command: A Contribution to Anonymous History,* New York: Oxford University Press, 1948.

29.  Halmos, *op. cit.*

30.  Gropius, *op. cit.*

31.  G. Veronesi, "Italy," in Hatje, *op. cit.,* 155–159.

*There is a twofold purpose of theory in environmental design: first, to understand human purposes and needs in building, and, second, to provide social scientists with access into the workings of design. The theoretical position is maintained that perfect fits between whole environments and diverse people do not exist; instead, adaptations are made. The study of these adaptations—subtle as well as obvious—is therefore central. The major part of the paper focuses on one specific issue—housing size—to illustrate these questions. Housing quality depends on the extent to which interiors relate to the occupants' requirements. New housing is smaller than old: Is this due simply to the price people are willing to pay? It is argued that demand is constrained by supply. The meaning of housing size is examined and the implications of the trend to smaller housing for familial activities is discussed.*

# The Social Order of Environmental Design*

**Constance Perin**

**Resources for the Future, Inc.
Washington, D.C.**

In this paper, I first recapitulate briefly my definition of the problem of "designing for human behavior." I next dicusss data on the current size of housing in order to exemplify specific questions about accepted definitions of the universe of human behavior. Last, I ask about the role of the designer in supporting ideas about social order that fit only parts of a universe of diversity.

## THE PURPOSE OF THEORY IN ENVIRONMENTAL DESIGN

The theory of human nature for environmental design which I developed in *With Man in Mind* is meant to accomplish two purposes.[1] The first is to provide an alternative to environmental design's lack of theory vis-à-vis its human consequences. By making the latter explicit, as the aesthetic and technical levels have not, there results a clear change in the referents for designers: environmental design now shares in concern for the same human processes as psychology, anthropology, and sociology. Aesthetic and technical fields are appropriate still to the work of the design fields, to be sure: environments must exemplify the ideals of beauty and efficiency. What I intend to make clear, however, is that it is no longer possible for designers to overclaim or distort the human consequences of their work: good intentions and technical know-how are no longer sufficient for the pace and extent of the environmental changes facing us. *Why* we build as we do must become the question shared across all disciplines.

The second purpose of my theoretical approach is to provide social scientists with access into the workings of environmental design; their role of interested bystander and critic must become one of active involvement. On the one hand, we have had the rhetoric of the designer asserting that he uses man as the measure, and on the other, we have had the all-too-cogent criticism of the social scientist, speaking as he nearly always does, from the periphery, outside the action. And indeed, when he does speak, he sounds more like Everyman than a scientist; even now, all too few social scientists perceive that their professional concerns can contribute to the ideas and methods of environmental design. And so I have tried to delineate the issues that arise when designing the built environment in terms that can interest scholars in the social sciences. In so doing, I have defined the *design program*—an already accepted step in the design process —as the locus of interdisciplinary work; social scientists, following the paradigms of their fields, provide the human specifications from which the physical environment is generated.

## ADAPTIVE POSSIBILITIES AND LIMITS

In brief, my theoretical proposition sees man as an active participant in his daily environment; there is no such thing as a perfect fit between whole environments and diverse people; instead, adaptations are made, and the interesting question is the form these adaptations take as man strives to maintain and develop his sense of competence, his self-esteem, his ego. The physical environment is relevant to these strivings to the extent that it facilitates or hinders him in accomplishing those purposes with which he defines himself. His purposes—those things he finds important to do—are a function of his class, his education, his experiences, his membership in social groups, his stage in the life cycle. And so that which brings him a heightened sense of competence, a greater self-esteem, and a stronger ego is directly related to his position in the larger society. The interdisciplinary research task is, then, to find out what are the purposes—definitions of self—of the various populations to use various environments.

The study of the interface between environment and behavior is the study of those adaptations people are making to what is put in place for them to use: the monetary, psychic, situational, social, and physical adaptations. Every adaptation expresses people's values and priorities. Each one is a kind of "talking back" to the inert environment, and what prompts us to be concerned and careful is that people's capacity for making active rejoinders varies considerably, determined mostly by their position in the social system—their access to jobs, to education, to physical health, and to an old age free of financial and social insecurity. The debacle of the Pruitt–Igoe public housing project in St. Louis can be viewed not only as an incredible waste of scarce money, but also as a *human success:* the people in it talked back, effectively making their rejoinder that that particular environment demanded adaptations they refused to enter into. Studying the adaptations people make and how they feel about them should be the subject of both basic and applied research in environmental design. We must ask: How much "free variation" does the environment permit people? Where does any building or place fall on a continuum ranging from authoritarian and captive, on the one hand, to free and flexible, on the other?

We have a long way to go in preventing even those environmental and ecological crises that can readily be foreseen on the basis of even a few cases. The subtle and less visible human adaptations are of equal seriousness, meriting as intense attention as we give to environmental degradations. I contend that these subtleties are of such major importance in their human consequences that in examining them closely we may find a basis for revolutionizing our stereotyped models of building and community form. I will shortly discuss this issue in the specific terms of housing size. But, first, it is necessary to say also what my approach to theory is not.

My perspective rejects the idea that the designer deals in physical objects at all: he works out symbols representing ideas and social priorities. They are symbols requiring plumbers, to be sure, and they do populate our visible world. Their designer is not, however, a Great Inspirator putting things in place to which people respond. Nor is he prior in any way: he, too, is part of this incessantly reverberative system, and his ideas about what a place should look like and what a building should have in it are equally the consequences of his position in the total system. That position also influences the alternatives he can visualize, and because these are limited, people in different positions will find the designer's symbols unlike theirs, and wonder why his predominate.

For those reasons, we must begin to understand that there is nothing logically or formally inevitable about the physical environment as we know it historically and presently: it is entirely man-made. These man-made symbols in concrete and stone are largely ideas centered around the distribution of power and historical principles of environmental order. These two aspects often combine, such that the principles of ecological, aesthetic, and technical order are converted into moral principles of social order. These are simultaneously the source of our current bewilderment, as we find ourselves so uncomfortable with the prospect that the metaphor might work best in reverse: physical disorder as a symbol of social order. Those socially "disorderly" ideas such as self-determination, local control, and cultural diversity are not likely to give rise to the types of environmental structuring we are used to. They represent instead the opposite moral principle of shared, diffuse power as the source of authentic social order. It is also this very control by people over their lives that can bring them heightened competence and self-esteem, at another level.

When the designer tries to create aesthetic and technical order out of these human values he faces a far more difficult task than that of implementing purely formal and logical principles. When he tries, he destroys for himself and others the complacent illusion that only formal and logical principles can create symbols of social orderliness. Because concentrated power has characterized the traditional clients of environmental designers—partly because what is built is so often done on a large scale, expensively—these symbols have predominated. A new humanism will mean a new aesthetic—one that encompasses People's Parks and squatters' housing—and both require a revolution in the theory and practice of environmental design.

## THE SIZE OF HOUSES

Although so many new energies are being devoted to questioning the ways in which we dilute the quality of our environment, I have observed a gap in the discussions of housing quality. One looks in vain for evaluations of the interior livability of the houses that we have and are now getting (although there are many about their appearance), even in such focused studies as those produced in recent years by the Douglas Commission and the Kaiser Committee. At the same time, one hears much about the psychological stresses and sociological problems said to stem from high building-to-ground density or of tall buildings per se—pronouncements that come just as land prices are higher than ever before. I want to dwell in some detail on

the question of housing size and livability, first, because it is ignored in research, and, second, because it represents one of the main moral and social questions we must face—that is, how we *live* as a people. We have nowhere else to do it, breakfast after breakfast, dinner after dinner, but in our houses.

Housing price, in dollars, is the usual surrogate for housing quality, and size is never a variable apart from price. Yet much small housing is high-priced housing, and the limits of its livability cast doubts on its automatic correlation with high quality.

The question of housing quality must be stated in terms of the extent to which the interiors of housing units relate to the human requirements of their occupants. The accessible measures are the amount of floor area in a housing unit and the number of bedrooms it has, from which the number of people expected to occupy each unit can be deduced. The measures we might like to have are unavailable—for example, baselines on the extent to which housing of various sizes, layouts, and building types functionally satisfies households of various sizes, ages, income characteristics, and so on. We know almost nothing about these in a systematic way, yet the issue of "crowding" is one that produces concern from many—similarly unsystematic—points of view. Irwin Altman and Patricia Nelson's study of how doors on rooms are used, of how kitchens are lived in, and where people spend their free time inside houses is the very first holistic approach.[2]

But the ways we have dealt with the crowding of people in their everyday at-home environment are singularly limited. We know from our own experiences that new housing is "smaller" than older housing, and the U.S. Census uses a measure of more than 1.51 persons per room as its indicator of "overcrowding"—a nonsensical measure when we lack information on the size of the room. One point of departure here is the premise that a single room can be crowded when occupied by one person: crowding depends on what it is we think people do, can do, and should be able to do in their interior living spaces.

In a preliminary round of discussions of housing size with architects, builders, economists, and public officials, all did agree that it "costs too much" to provide roomy housing. Is it in fact the cost of doing so? Or is it the price put on roomy housing? If price, then what are its components? To what extent is housing size so much a symbol of social status that the *functional* need for larger housing by people no matter their income is obscured by ideology?

*Mr. Biderman. These townhouses ($15,000 to $19,500) go from a two-bedroom, one story unit of 985 square feet to a two-story three bedroom unit of 1,450 square feet.*

*Representative Widnall. Would they be too small for public housing?*

*Mr. Biderman. Oh, no. They would be too large.*[3]

This exchange exemplifies as well two attitudes I have found among these otherwise sophisticated people: first, they personalize about the question of housing size as they would be reluctant to personalize about materials, costs, and similar variables. Their conversations contain meandering personal recollections of experiences of living in different houses; but, still more baffling, my interest in learning systematically about housing size comes as a completely new idea, to which there is evident resistance. Second, they will state unequivocally that even if conditions in the United States leave something to be desired, they are better than anywhere else in the world. In tandem with that idea is the attitude that "people get what they pay for" and that poor people, especially, should be content with housing of any size. (Both political conservatives and radicals share in these attitudes, where radicals say that any roof at all will do, just get the numbers going.) Any serious research into this topic will, I suggest, have to address itself to the cultural context of housing production and consumption—its meanings as a reward or punishment, as a given over which one has little control, and as a vehicle by which people in various social positions express their beliefs about how society is and should be structured.

In economic terms, the price of housing is determined by what people are willing to pay for it; but, speaking as a noneconomist, I ask: To what extent is the demand of necessity constrained by the supply? In other words, it appears that what exists dictates "demand," and is not necessarily what is wanted or satisfactory. There's no import supply in housing, as there has been in cars, to *demonstrate* real demand. If income is allocated to buy housing of a certain size but that housing does not exist, what then?

My hunch is that the demand is there, but suppliers are building what satisfies their short-range interests; thus the housing produced is frequently a mere residual of profit in land sales and of depreciation allowances in the tax system. Housing is thrown up, as it were, as an afterthought to the more profitable land resale it entails. The housing and building codes which are supposed to guarantee the consumer's long-range interests in livability are written by the producers at worst, and unquestioned by design professionals, at best. The consumer is locked into a set of beliefs about the extravagantly high costs of producing the housing available, and I suggest that in the continued absence of reliable data about margins of profit in residential house-lot sales, it is warranted to question the extent to which that is true. We know that land prices are rising drastically and that the proportion of housing cost attributable to land has increased, but we will not be able to be clear in the analysis of housing size and the feasibility of larger houses until we begin to separate the questions of land costs from those of construction costs and housing prices. The marginal cost of adding square footage is given conversationally as about one third the original cost ($4 more per square foot at an original square foot cost of $14), and a research step I have not carried out would relate this rule-of-thumb to the asking price of comparable units of different sizes. I sought and could not find data on actual marginal costs of additional square feet. Intuitively, however, that marginal cost seems converted directly into a premium—a "feature" to be paid for at a level reflecting its scarcity. The scarcity is not so much a response to low demand for space, but more a function of the producers' rationing its supply.

## MEASURES OF HOUSING SIZE AND OCCUPANCY

I have combed readily available sources for what little data there are on the specifics of interior living space—how much there is, to be occupied by how many persons, at what costs and prices. From these limited data I find that much of the single-family housing built now has a higher room count in the same amount of floor areas as existing housing, so that more persons are expected to live in the same amount of floor area than formerly. A family of four ordinarily will occupy

**Table 1**
**Housing-Size Levels in Square Feet Related to Total Occupancy**

| | One Bedroom | | Two Bedrooms | | Three Bedrooms | | Four Bedrooms | | Five Bedrooms | |
|---|---|---|---|---|---|---|---|---|---|---|
| | Number of persons | Total sq ft | Number of persons | Total sq ft | Number of persons | Total sq ft | Number of persons | Total sq ft | Number of persons | Total sq ft |
| American Public Health Association levels for one-story house | 1 2 | 416 855 | 3 4 | 1096 1281 | 4 5 6 | 1558 1704 | 4 6 8 | 1840 | 6 10 | |
| Great Britain: Parker-Morris one-story house | 1 2 | 350 520 | 3 4 | 655 770–850 | 4–6 | 860–1060 | 4–8 | 950–1100 | | |
| U. S.: Public Housing levels | 1–2 | 550 | 3–4 | 720 | 4–6 | 900 | 4–6 | 1120 | 8 | 1320[a] |
| Douglas Commission large-family definitions | | | | | 5–6 | | 7–8 | | 9–10 | |
| Typical mobile home | | | | 660 | | | | | | |

[a]Six bedrooms: 1540 sq ft.

at least a two-bedroom unit; a family of at least five and perhaps six can be expected in a three-bedroom unit. The U.S. Census measure of overcrowding, therefore, is of no use in uncovering the facts about interior densities. (In Table 1 I have compiled a few housing-size "standards," which I prefer to call *levels* in the absence of the firm ground that *standards* suggest.)

Small housing units may not violate any existing occupancy (health) codes, but it is the codes themselves that must be called into question: they have been derived out of thin air, the consequence of inexplicit decisions by *housing producers*. No set of standards for housing has ever been created by housing consumers, and, not surprisingly, the minimum amounts of floor space per person put forward in "model" building codes turn out to be those promulgated by the International Building Officials Conference and the Building Officials Conference of America. Where are the planners and architects whose rhetoric claims "man as the measure"? Or do these codes reflect his dimensions when he is sitting still?

*Headquarters staff at ICBO (International Conference of Building Officials) indicated (November, 1968) that although their model code does not specifically permit nor prohibit it, a one-room living-room-bedroom-kitchen of 150 square feet (10 x 15) is considered acceptable for one or two persons.*[4]

Louis Winnick published *American Housing and Its Use: The Demand for Shelter Space* in 1957, to date the single study of housing space available. His analyses rested, of necessity, on the only measure available:

*The persons-per-room ratio is the principal measure of the utilization of housing space that can be derived from census data. It is clear that, in the absence of a real measurement, this ratio remains an imperfect tool for quantitative analysis though an infinite advance over a persons-per-dwelling unit ratio, which is a mere statement of household size. The PPR ratio, of course, tells us nothing of the arrangements within a dwelling unit that affect its utilization and, like any simple*

**Table 2**[6]

**Floor Area and Number of Bedrooms in New Homes (Percentage Distribution)**

| Region | Year | Floor Area (sq ft) | | | | | No. Bedrooms | | |
| | | Under 800 | 800–1199 | 1200–1599 | 1600–1999 | 2000+ | 2 or fewer | 3 | 4 |
|---|---|---|---|---|---|---|---|---|---|
| United States | 1963 | 1 | 35 | 32 | 18 | 14 | 7 | 71 | 22 |
| | 1966 | 1 | 23 | 32 | 21 | 24 | 5 | 65 | 30 |
| | 1969 | (z) | 22 | 28 | 21 | 28 | 8 | 61 | 31 |
| Northeast | 1963 | 2 | 27 | 30 | 20 | 21 | 7 | 67 | 26 |
| | 1966 | 3 | 19 | 27 | 19 | 32 | 4 | 55 | 40 |
| | 1969 | 1 | 15 | 21 | 23 | 40 | 6 | 46 | 48 |
| Northcentral | 1963 | 1 | 46 | 28 | 14 | 12 | 4 | 78 | 18 |
| | 1966 | (z) | 28 | 26 | 23 | 23 | 3 | 69 | 27 |
| | 1969 | (z) | 28 | 29 | 19 | 24 | 7 | 64 | 29 |
| South | 1963 | 2 | 37 | 29 | 19 | 13 | 7 | 77 | 16 |
| | 1966 | 1 | 27 | 36 | 18 | 19 | 5 | 73 | 22 |
| | 1969 | (z) | 24 | 29 | 21 | 26 | 7 | 67 | 25 |
| West | 1963 | (z) | 24 | 39 | 22 | 15 | 8 | 60 | 32 |
| | 1966 | (z) | 15 | 34 | 23 | 27 | 7 | 55 | 38 |
| | 1969 | (z) | 19 | 30 | 23 | 27 | 11 | 56 | 33 |

*measure, is incapable of expressing the complexity of the phenomenon it is intended to describe. The PPR ratio of a given dwelling unit represents an egalitarian allocation of a given number of cubicles within a house among its occupants. PPR is probably most open to criticism because of its inability to differentiate households of various size and composition. We have no way of demonstrating that a PPR ratio of 0.50 achieved by one person in 2 rooms is more or less satisfactory than the same PPR ratio for five persons in 10 rooms . . .*[5]

The measure of floor area is available from government and private sources, if and as it is reported: in U.S. Census publications about 20 percent of all single-family homes sold do not report it, compared to 4 to 10 percent who fail to report the number of bedrooms. At the federal level, there are no published time-series data on the floor area of units in multifamily structures.

**Table 3**

**Three-Bedroom Single-Family Houses 800–1199 Sq Ft (Percent Decrease)**

| | 1963–66 | 1966–69 |
|---|---|---|
| United States | 10 | 5 |
| Northeast | 4 | 8 |
| Northcentral | 18 | 4 |
| South | 9 | 6 |
| West | 8 | 0 |

**Table 4[7]**

| PERCENT OF HOUSES AT EACH SIZE | | | | | NUMBER OF BEDROOMS IN NEW AND EXISTING HOUSES OF EACH SIZE CATEGORY IN 1969 | | | | | | | | | | | |
|---|---|---|---|---|---|---|---|---|---|---|---|---|---|---|---|---|
| Sec 203 New | Sec 221 | Sec 203 Existing | Sec 221 | HOUSE SIZE | Two bedrooms or less | | | | Three bedrooms | | | | Four bedrooms or more | | | |
|  |  |  |  |  | New | | Existing | | New | | Existing | | New | | Existing | |
| N = 25,300 | N = 2250 | N = 67,500 | N = 27,900 | Sq ft | 203 | 221 | 203 | 221 | 203 | 221 | 203 | 221 | 203 | 221 | 203 | 221 |
| 100% | 100% | 100% | 100% |  | 1 | 2 | 3 | 4 | 5 | 6 | 7 | 8 | 9 | 10 | 11 | 12 |
| 2.9 | 6.1 | 8.5 | 20.2 | Less than 800 | 33.4 | 41.8 | 90 | 95 | 65.8 | 56 | 9.5 | 4.7 | 0.8 | 2.2 | 0.5 | 0.3 |
| 6.8 | 15.2 | 10.1 | 18.2 | 800– 899 | 14.7 | 13.9 | 66.6 | 72.7 | 85.2 | 82 | 32.9 | 27.2 | 0.1 | 4.1 | 0.5 | 0.1 |
| 13.9 | 35.1 | 14.3 | 21.2 | 900– 999 | 6.9 | 1.8 | 35.8 | 40.2 | 91.4 | 97.2 | 63 | 58.9 | 1.7 | 1 | 1.2 | 0.9 |
| 16 | 31.2 | 16.8 | 17.4 | 1000–1099 | 5.2 | 0.3 | 23.1 | 26.4 | 89.1 | 91.3 | 74.4 | 70.9 | 5.7 | 8.4 | 2.5 | 2.7 |
| 13 | 7.2 | 12.8 | 10.1 | 1100–1199 | 3.7 | 0.6 | 17.0 | 18.2 | 85.9 | 77.5 | 75.9 | 74.7 | 10.4 | 21.9 | 7.1 | 7.1 |
| 12 | 3.5 | 10.7 | 6.1 | 1200–1299 | 3.0 | 9.8 | 13.3 | 12.5 | 89.1 | 57.3 | 76.1 | 75.4 | 7.9 | 32.9 | 10.6 | 12.1 |
| 9.8 | 1.7ᵃ | 7.6 | 6.8ᵃ | 1300–1399 | 2.8 | 0.8ᵃ | 9.2 | 8.3 | 77.7 | 93.3 | 74.6 | 70.9 | 19.5 | 6.7 | 16.2 | 20.8 |
| 8 |  | 5.9 |  | 1400–1499 | 0.8 |  | 7.3 | 6.6 | 68.8 | ᵃ | 72 | 64.3 | 30.4 | ᵃ | 20.7 | 29.1 |
| 5.7 |  | 4.1 |  | 1500–1599 | 0.8 |  | 5.5 | 3.6 | 65.9 |  | 68.5 | 56.8 | 33.3 |  | 26 | 39.6ᶜ |
| 7.4 |  | 5.1 |  | 1600–1799 | 0.8 |  | 4.2 | 3.4 | 53.5 |  | 60.9 | 45.9 | 45.7 |  | 34.9 | 50.7 |
| 4.5 |  | 4.1 |  | 1800–1999 | 0.4 |  | 3.0 | 2.9 | 34.6 |  | 50 | 29.1 | 65 |  | 47 | 68 |
|  |  |  |  | 2000+ᵇ | 0.2 |  | 2.3 | 0.8 | 13.8 |  | 33.7 | 13.6 | 86 |  | 64 | 85.6 |

N.B.: The following columns add across to 100%: 1, 5, 9; 2, 6, 10; 3, 7, 11; and 4, 8, 12.

ᵃ Category is "1300 and over," FHA Tables 55a and 55b, and on FHA Tables 53a and 53b for the remaining size categories, the footnote reads: "Data not significant."

ᵇ Categories are variously "1800 and over," "1800 to 1999," and "2000 or more."

ᶜ FHA Tables 53a and 53b show 10.7 percent of total houses as "4 bedrooms or more," compared to 7.6 percent of new houses of 4 bedrooms or more, but giving no distributions of new houses above 1399 sq. ft.

## FLOOR AREA, NUMBER OF BEDROOMS, AND EXPECTED OCCUPANCY

In material submitted to the House Banking and Currency Committee in June 1971, the interpretation is made that "new homes were generally larger in later years," as a means of explaining higher average sales prices (see Table 2). Starting from the premise that a three-bedroom house will have four occupants (1300 square feet at American Public Health Association levels), or five occupants (1600 square feet), or six occupants (1700 square feet), any three-bedroom houses with less than 1300 square feet are undersized. Data in Table 2 are further analyzed in Table 3 to show that it is inaccurate to say only that "housing is getting larger," in that what must also be said is that the proportion of undersized housing relative to expected occupancy is decreasing, though much less in the last time period recorded than in the first.

Data for two federal mortgage insurance programs [Secs. 203 and 221(d)(2)] are given in Table 4. They show that more than three times as many existing as new single-family homes are less than 800 square feet, which can give rise to the interpretation that "housing is getting larger." But of those previously built homes, 90 to 95 percent appropriately have only two bedrooms or less, whereas 56 to 66 percent of new homes at this size have three bedrooms (compared to 5 to 10 percent of the existing small houses). With an additional 100 square feet—still a small house—we find that 82 to 85 percent of new housing 800–899 square feet is built with three bedrooms, compared to 27 to 33 percent of existing houses of that size with three bedrooms. Again, no more than four persons are expected to live in a two-bedroom house, whereas as many as six people are expected in a three-bedroom unit.

The trend is therefore nearly the opposite of the interpretation made without relating the number of bedrooms to total square footage: when new housing is "larger" than existing in square feet, the number of bedrooms and hence the number of expected occupants also gets larger, but not proportionately to the square feet. "More bedrooms" is not more "living space."

In the 212(d)(2) program (Table 4) there are about twice as many new houses 1000–1099 square feet as there are existing houses at that size. But nearly all these new houses contain three bedrooms (91 percent) compared to 26 percent of the existing houses at that size having only two bedrooms. In the Section 203 program, 89 percent of new housing 1000–1099 square feet has three bedrooms, compared to 74 percent (still high) of existing housing under the same program. New single-family houses under this program over 1100 square feet account for only 12 percent of the total, while they are nearly twice that (23 percent) in the existing stock. (Three persons should have 1100 square feet and four persons 1300 square feet, according to American Public Health Association levels.)

## IMPLICATIONS OF THE TREND TO SMALLER HOUSING

Data on existing houses in the 212(d)(2) program (Table 5) include a breakdown by time period built. Of this sample of 27,900 houses nationwide, only 6.6 percent were built during the past ten years. Housing built before 1929—and still in use—comprises 81 percent of the housing having 2000 square feet and over, and 14 percent of the housing with less than 800 square feet. Housing built in the last twenty years shows the opposite pattern: 2.3 percent of houses 2000 square feet and more have been built in the past twenty years, and 45 percent of the houses of less than 800 square feet have been built in the same span.

This stock will filter down only to small households, unlike the older group which is at or fast approaching obsolescence. Reinforcing this trend is the fact that about 6 percent more houses of less than 800 square feet were built in the past twenty years than in the previous twenty; for those 800–899, about 50 percent more in the past twenty than previous; and for those 1000–1199, about 33 percent more in the recent than the far past.

As we have seen earlier, housing in this middle range of floor area simultaneously expands the number of bedrooms and expected occupants per square foot. For housing larger than 1199 square feet, the last twenty years have seen only decreases—meaning that the supply of single-family housing for families of more than four persons built between 1930 and 1950 is not being replaced (at least under this government program; conventionally financed housing tends to be larger, but size-trend data are unavailable here).

**Table 5[8]**
**Floor Area in Existing One-Family Homes (Percentage Distribution)**
[Sec. 221(d)(2)]

| Year Built | Total | Floor Area (sq ft) | | | | | | | | | | | |
|---|---|---|---|---|---|---|---|---|---|---|---|---|---|
| | | Under 800 | 800– 899 | 900– 999 | 1000– 1099 | 1100– 1199 | 1200– 1299 | 1300– 1399 | 1400– 1499 | 1500– 1599 | 1600– 1799 | 1800– 1999 | 2000+ |
| 1930–1949 | 28.8 | 39.6 | 32.7 | 23.3 | 26.5 | 26.0 | 28.4 | 27.8 | 27.9 | 25.2 | 24.7 | 22.7 | 16.9 |
| 1950–1969 | 39.1 | 45.4 | 50.1 | 55.4 | 47.1 | 38.0 | 26.7 | 21.6 | 16.1 | 14.1 | 9.2 | 5.2 | 2.3 |
| (Prior to 1930) | 32.1 | | | | | | | | | | | | |
| Difference | | +5.8 | +17.4 | +32.1 | +20.6 | +12.0 | −1.7 | −6.2 | −11.8 | −11.1 | −15.5 | −17.5 | −14.6 |

The research questions merely opened up here are many. What is the correlation among the number of square feet in a housing unit, its cost to produce, and its market price? Does the consumer get what he can afford to pay for in the way of square footage? Is family size decreasing similarly? Are the home construction and the federal subsidy program meeting demand—or avoiding it with housing sizes comfortable only to the balance sheet?

The quest for housing quality is always thought, of course, to consist of the entire package of goals people have. In asking solely about housing size, "the housing bundle" is distorted, because floor space is only one of several equally important aspects of the decision to buy or rent one house and not another: the location, first and foremost; the quality of the schools; the length of the journey to work; and the safety and status or friendliness of the immediate neighborhood. Sometimes "space" is provided outside the house itself, in the form of common areas, swimming pool, recreation hall. But after the decision is made to pay a particular price for a "housing bundle," with floor area having been relegated to its proper position in a hierarchy of values or priorities—what then of the actual occupation of the housing, after the tradeoffs are made? To what extent among various populations is small size the main sacrifice? What are the behavioral tradeoffs made daily, weekly, seasonally? In the economists' terms what

externalities (costs) are imposed by the benefits to producers of small houses? How do public regulations in zoning, building, and health codes contribute to these externalities?

We do not know; the studies have not been made. We do know that there is much mobility prompted by job changes, and we also know that it is very expensive to move. We may conclude that people have to feel extremely distressed before they will pay a dollar cost to get out of small houses. Before that point is reached, in what ways are stress evidenced, and what adaptations are made, at what economic and psychological costs and benefits?

## THE HOUSING OF FAMILIAL ACTIVITIES

Household activities can be seen as but one part of the entire social system in which families are engaged. The larger system includes institutions focused around different activities: occupational, religious, consumption, educational, health. We expect that the activities within the housing unit are just as specialized. When families use their living rooms, for example, primarily as a shrine for religious objects and observances, we see clearly an example of a merging of these otherwise separate realms of the domestic and the religious. Our culture generally doesn't happen to emphasize household shrines indoors, or even in the backyard. Nor is recreation for maintaining physical fitness and health expected to be within the housing environment; and so gyms are public facilities, tennis courts are community resources, and so on.

The economies of scale for some of the things that families do, then, mean that the interiors of houses in this culture can serve a limited number of activities. Interior living spaces can be smaller, we may think, because other institutions cater to these other space-using activities. American norms view some things as rightly a public cost, borne by taxation, and others as rightly private because they have not become socially approved institutions. By what decision process have we arrived at this allocation of public resources between inside of housing and outside? One real choice not offered by the sets of stereotypes we use, whether in environmental design or in municipal budgeting, is that between larger indoor space and less outside-house space. We use outside-house spaces to justify smaller houses, in fact; hardly ever do we pose the reverse alternative.

The activities comprising family life are tied to the sizes of the indoor spaces provided. Unlike studies of factories, stores, schools, and libraries, for example, we do not make studies of the problems of crowding in interior living spaces. Instead, we put much energy into coping with it: it is a fair hypothesis that a random sampling of home-decorating articles in magazines and newspapers will show a majority of them spelling out hints for spending time and (more) money to make the most out of the least space. Visiting several single-family subdivisions in the $25–35,000 range in the sub-urbs, I noticed in the sales models that whenever possible tables had but two legs: their other ends were attached to walls, thus saving on floor space. Bedrooms for children had bunkbeds, desks and shelving hung from the walls, and a tiny patch of floor space remained. I have since heard that it is common practice for furnishings used in model houses to be scaled to seven eighths of normal size to give an illusion of more space, but I have no evidence for that.

The size of a dwelling is also a statement about the universe of activities of a household, and through the prevalence of small housing and of very high-priced large housing, that universe is being defined a priori. *Whose* definition is it?

In one respect the new emphasis on user research can co-opt us into studying questions minutely for which the real answers are in the realm of values and ideals: just because stingy space by itself may not be found to be the controlling variable in, for example, psychological stress, task performance, or intergroup cooperation, that is no reason not to evaluate it as small, cramping, inhibiting, restrictive. Indeed, once we agree to study "the effects of small housing," we accept the necessity for it in the first place; the close tolerances discovered in undersea and outer-space research represent the edges that human beings can skirt, but are they the edges we should live with, day by day?

I would like to see "minimum standards" for housing size determined by research that delineates the behavior settings of a wide variety of families, in terms of size, stage in the life cycle, values and priorities, class, and metropolitan location. In my own research, I found that people demonstrate that to do those things that are important to them, they rearrange their given environments.[9] However, one consequence of inalterably small spaces is that both adults and children are unable to work or play *cumulatively* at the same activity over time; they cannot see the consequences of what they had begun to do because the next activity, forced to occur in the same space, displaces them. What they had begun to do had to be dismantled, and they had to begin anew, the next time space was available. They begin but never complete many kinds of play and work. We must begin to learn about the long-range consequences of such subtleties as these. How do these discontinuous experiences relate to cognitive development and emotional maturation?

I observed also that families living in housing they find to be small must, in addition, make up a great many rules for family members—rules for using living rooms, the activities permissible, when noise is allowed and disallowed, and so on. The more rules, the more disputes over their infraction. The more disputes, the less family peace and harmony. The less family peace, the more turning away from the group by its members.

## LETTING AMBIGUITY IN

What does "larger housing" mean to the designer? Does it mean that he foregoes specification of every nook and cranny? That what can, does, and should occur in a dwelling is not entirely of his making? What the current trend toward built-in furnishings may save in dollars it costs in the freedom of users to determine their own behavior settings.

We have been concentrating better on users in recent years, but at the same time we should be studying ourselves as originators of the forms of the built environment. Those of us in the design professions are self-selected in several ways, and one of them is our share of the ordinary human need to order the universe, to put things in their proper place, to classify, and to sort. We can resolve some of the ambiguities of life. Environmental disorder stands as a metaphor of the unpredictable, for that which arouses natural human anxiety. By their nature, planning and design mobilize foresight to dampen realistic anxieties about the future. Designers tend to see metaphoric chaos, as it appears in objects and in their visual properties of scale, color, texture, and sequence. For people not in design, their chaos is, perhaps, more internal, less tangible, and less accessible to management. So in one way designers are fortunate in having a constructive use for their fair share of anxiety about the unknowns of life. But we must continually ask the question, as we go about our business of creating order, *whose* chaos are we taming? *Whose* discomfort about the unpredictable and the unmanageable are we decreasing?

## DISORDERLY IDEAS

A recent book by an American historian, David J. Rothman, is entitled *The Discovery of the Asylum: Social Order and Disorder in the New Republic.*[10] The book as a whole is asking and answering one basic question about the Jacksonian years in the 1820's and beyond: Why, suddenly, were institutions being constructed and supported for deviant and dependent members of the community? All at once, in contrast to the colonial period, Americans were putting up penitentiaries for the criminal, asylums for the insane, almshouses for the poor, orphan asylums for homeless children, and reformatories. Rothman finds consistent documentation that in colonial times—from settlement in the colonies through the early eighteenth century—the poor were cared for at home or with relatives or neighbors. Criminals were fined or whipped, or put in stocks—but not put behind bars for particular periods of time. The insane were left to the care of their families

and there were generally no buildings especially designed for them. There were exceptions to this general way of handling a "problem" population in the larger colonial towns, according to Rothman, but they were used only as places of last resort.

Why, then, did such institutions become the places of first resort to deal with poverty, crime, delinquency, and insanity? It is hard for us now to take such a fresh look at an innovation that we have for so long considered to be a mark of social reform and progress, but Rothman shows convincingly that, as he puts it, "there was nothing inevitable about the asylum" as a way of dealing with these ubiquitous social conditions.[11] Today, for example, out-patient health care and vocational training serve as proof that there are many alternatives available to our society.

It is the historical answers to Rothman's question that are relevant now as we deal with complex questions of social order and environmental disorder. He finds in the historical record evidence that the very independence the new Republic was intended to encourage was perceived as pernicious in its effect on society and the individual. Dreaming the impossible, being discontented with a lot assigned by birth, and redefining one's social position were seen by psychiatrists of that day to lead only to mental illness—not to liberation or rich human spontaneity or fuller spiritual development, nor even as living manifestations of the very principles behind the founding of the Republic. A social order defined by openness was not seen then to have beneficial effects. Thus it was that the asylum gained status as the best and only way to put people "right" again. Seen as a model society, it was to serve as a distinctive environment in which "to exemplify the advantages of an orderly, regular, and disciplined routine."[12] From the asylum's "moral treatment" program came also that of the penitentiary, seeing individual behavior and social relationships in terms of respect for authority and tradition, and an acceptance of a given station in society's ranks.[13] In contrast, the almshouses of colonial times were organized like households and people lived in them much as families live, working out together their mealtimes, chores, and relationships.

Rothman sees that the regimentation, punctuality, and precision of these institutions were a "rebuke to the casual organization of the household" and the informality prevailing in colonial almshouses.[14] The architectural forms of asylums and prisons expressed and reinforced the rigidities of the reformers. "The appropriate arrangement of the asylum, its physical dimensions and daily routine, monopolized their thinking."[15] Rothman attributes only the best of motives to them, however.

We can draw many lessons from his book for our work today. The first is that we must use retrospection such as his book provides in order to be alert to the meanings of our good intentions. What definitions of man do our plans for environmental order imply? Do we place people in categories without looking beyond their most superficial characteristics? This may be a useful device for simplifying our increasingly complex society, but why is that a goal at all? We should look first to ourselves to seek the reasons why we are proud to live in a country based upon "freedom with dignity," and, at the same time, constantly look for some least common denominator that obliterates our diversity and our dignity.

## CONCLUSION

The best use of the foresight of designers and planners is, I believe, to maximize the possibilities for others. It is no contradiction to design for spontaneity and for self-determination. We must learn how to define our design problems so that we can let their solutions become a collaborative enterprise. To arrive at these definitions, we must bring into the design process an explicitness about its human consequences—another way of saying that the development of theory in environmental design is essential. We must also extend outward from our drawing boards to more actively shape the values not always explicit in public policy.

There was nothing inevitable about the asylum, and there is nothing inevitable about 10-by-10-foot bedrooms. Once these ideas about people-in-and-of their environments become the principles from which we design, the forms of environmental structure will be generated not from the ideas of other times and men, but from the social order of the living present.

## NOTES AND REFERENCES

1. Constance Perin, *With Man in Mind,* Cambridge, Mass.: The MIT Press, 1970.
2. Irwin Altman and Patricia A. Nelson, *The Ecology of Home Environments,* Washington, D.C.: U.S. Department of HEW, Office of Education, Bureau of Research, 1972.
3. *Industrialized Housing,* Hearings before the Subcommittee on Urban Affairs of the Joint Economic Committee, U.S. Congress, Part 1, July 9, 1969, 36.
4. Eric M. Mood, "The development, objectives and adequacy of current housing code standards," in *Housing Code Standards: Three Critical Studies,* Washington, D.C.; Douglas Commission, Research Report 19, 1969, 4.
5. Louis Winnick, *American Housing and Its Use: The Demand for Shelter Space,* New York: Wiley, 1957.
6. Source: *Characteristics of New One-Family Homes, 1969,* U.S. Census Bureau and U.S. Department of Housing and Urban Development.
7. Source: *1969 F.H.A. Tables,* 41a, 41b, 45a, 45b, 53a, 53b, U.S. Department of Housing and Urban Development.
8. Source: *1969 F.H.A. Table,* 53b, U.S. Department of Housing and Urban Development.
9. Constance Perin, "Concepts and methods for studying environments in use," in William J. Mitchell, ed., *Environmental Design: Research and Practice: Proceedings of the EDRA3/AR8 Conference,* University of California, Los Angeles, January 1972, 13.6.1–13.6.10.
10. David J. Rothman, *The Discovery of the Asylum: Social Order and Disorder in the New Republic,* Boston: Little, Brown, 1971.
11. *Ibid.*
12. *Ibid.,* 129.
13. *Ibid.,* 133.
14. *Ibid.,* 154.
15. *Ibid.,* 134.

# A Model of the Designing Process

**Jon Lang**
**University of Pennsylvania**

**Charles Burnette**
**Executive Director**
**Philadelphia Chapter,**
**American Institute of Architects**

As the scale and complexity of architectural projects increase, so the need to reconsider the profession's traditional approaches to the process of designing becomes more evident. Most architects rely on design methods associated with the Beaux Arts tradition. Recently, architectural designing has come to be regarded as one of a family of decision-making processes. The overall designing process consists of a number of phases of activities. While there is considerable overlap among them, they can be identified as an intelligence or programming phase, a design phase, and phases involving evaluation and choice, implementation, and postconstruction evaluation. Thinking of architectural designing in this way does not imply high rationality or comprehensive ability on the part of the architect. It suggests that ordering the overall designing process focuses the architectural programmer or designer's attention on some important variables and relationships that he might otherwise miss. Models of the designing process also enable an architect to understand and evaluate the impact of new design techniques that continuing research is providing the profession.

Present approaches to designing are those inherited from the *Beaux Arts* tradition. Designing within this mimetic tradition is largely intuitive, poorly structured, and solution oriented. While this approach encourages divergent and generative thinking which can result in highly innovative design, it also increases the probability that the wrong problem will have been solved. To reduce this possibility, explicit methods of designing are beginning to emerge and are being used by architects and urban designers on an increasing scale. The aim is to bring to the attention of those involved in the process all elements of the problem in a systematic and thorough way. This involves a departure from solution-oriented approaches to designing toward problem-oriented ones. In the former the processes of analysis and synthesis are merged with the emphasis on synthesis. Problem-oriented approaches, on the other hand, emphasize the identification and descriptive analysis of the problem prior to the attempt to synthesize solutions (although attempts in synthesis may redefine the problem). The purely linear model of the designing process which frequently accompanied the solution-oriented approach has proven inadequate. The new conception of design recognizes that there is considerable feedback and feedforward in the development of any architectural solution.

Architects are finding it increasingly useful to be explicit, systematic, and problem oriented in their design approach. They are also finding it useful to develop strategies of design or models of the process before beginning a project. Research conducted on creativity suggests that the ability to formulate and use such strategies is a prerequisite for creative synthesis in fields, such as architecture, where the designer is confronted with ill-defined problems.[1]

## MODELS OF DESIGNING

Models of the designing process can be regarded as *descriptive, behavioral,* or *normative.* Descriptive models identify those actions and events that actually take place during design, behavioral models hypothesize why these activities took place, and normative models are prescriptive and state what should or normally would take place. Unfortunately, because of an unwillingness to examine the process of designing in a critical way, architects' normative models lack the sound theoretical basis that could be developed from descriptive and behavioral models. The notoriously inaccurate analyses by creative people of their own activities hampers the process of model building (and architectural education). Recent research indicates that there is a substantial difference between the actual design process and the process imagined by most architects.[2] For instance, more decision makers are usually involved than expected. Design decisions, prior to construction, are made by legislators and city planners as well as by architects and clients. Contractors make decisions during construction and users modify the building after completion. Models of designing frequently fail to recognize that each of these participants employ different values. Based on the limited research available a number of designing models have been developed.

Normative models of interest to architects can be divided into three groups:

1.  General models of decision making.
2.  General models of architectural designing.
3.  Models specific to particular problems.

An example of the second will be developed based on an example of the first. It is suggested here that such general models can form the basis for the creation of specific models for specific design problems; general models bring to the architect's attention the overall structure of the process and the activities which should form part of designing in any situation. The specific set of techniques for carrying out these activities can be chosen to meet the needs of a particular situation.

## A GENERAL MODEL OF DECISION MAKING

General models of decision making are of interest to architects because architectural designing is one of the family of decision-making processes. Different scholars have structured the process of making decisions in different ways, but there is a general consensus that it approximates that shown in Figure 1. The process involves an *intelligence* or analytical effort aimed at identifying and understanding problems, the *design* and representation of alternative solutions, the evaluation of these and the *choice* of one of them as the most desirable. Models of decision making should not be thought to be purely linear or even purely cyclic. There is considerable interaction between phases, each of which, in fact, consists of analytical, design, and choice activities; and each is, in itself, a decision-making process.

The original impetus for considering decision making in this way came from the behavioral and management sciences.[3] Engineers and operations researchers seem to have been the first designers to have become interested in such models of decision making, although the impact on the engineering profession as a whole is still low. Its impact on architectural philosophy is certainly much more recent.

## A GENERAL MODEL OF DESIGNING

There are a number of models of the designing process which correspond more or less to the structure shown in Figure 1. These models should not be considered to be mutually exclusive. They represent different ways of expressing similar events. Some have been

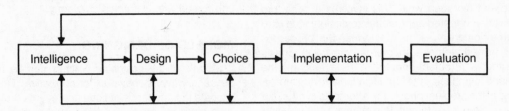

**Figure 1**
**A general model of decision making: feedback loop of a cybernetic model of decision making**

criticized by architects as implying levels of rationality and comprehensiveness beyond human capacities.

The model to be discussed here does not imply high rationality or comprehensiveness; it simply suggests that there are certain classes of activities that must be carried out if building failures are to be avoided. There is, of course, the underlying hypothesis that the more intelligently and thoroughly these activities are carried out, the more closely the building or buildings will provide for the needs of their future users. If one recognizes that the problems with many recent buildings have arisen because too little attention was paid to the needs of building users and too much to the need for self-expression on the part of the architect, the need for more comprehensive and explicit approaches to both analysis and synthesis will be seen as justified. The overall structure of such a process is presented in Figure 2 and discussed in the following pages. It parallels the work of a number of authors, being at the level of generality of Marvin Mannheim's model, and like Raymond Studer's model it is "behavior-contingent."[4]

As in decision making in general, the first phase of the designing process is one of *intelligence*. Intelligence involves both the identification and elucidation of the problem situation and the development of an architectural or building program on which the design is to

be based. The constraints under which the solution has to operate and the resources available must also be identified. In the next phase of the overall process the architect becomes concerned primarily with *design* activities. In architecture, these are characterized by sketch layouts relating first programmatic and then physical elements of the building to each other. As the designs become more concrete they are constrained by knowledge of methods of implementation. Design, the process of synthesis, is still "clouded with mystery." It is clear, however, that intelligent analysis is a necessary but not a sufficient condition for creative synthesis. The *choice* phase involves both the abstract evaluation of the alternative results of creative synthesis and the selection of one sketch design for further development. The *implementation* phase involves the production of working drawings, specifications, and other forms of technical presentation, and the actual contracting and building. It is suggested here that a final phase involving the *evaluation* of the completed building and the process of designing used should be a standard part of the architect's activities, as Michael Brill suggests in *Part Three* of this book. Without this evaluation architects will not be learning from past successes and failures.

Again, it must be constantly remembered in this discussion that the designing is not a purely linear process.

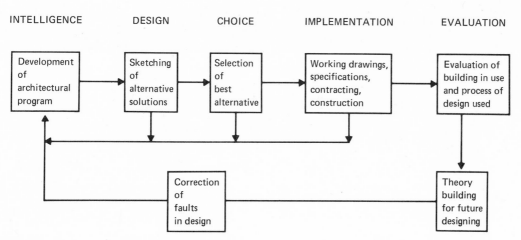

**Figure 2**
**A general model of the designing process**

In fact, it is often difficult to separate the phases of the process because of so much feedback and feedforward. Organizing the process in this way, however, focuses the attention of the architect on the overall pattern in design. It brings out and illustrates certain roles and perspectives which will be required and points out characteristic types of information needed in each phase or role.[5] To understand the full implication of considering designing in this way, a fuller description of the phases of the process, and particularly the first three phases, is necessary.

### The Intelligence Phase

The intelligence phase begins with the perception of a need (or opportunity) and ends with a detailed program of functional and psychosocial needs which the building is to meet. The perception of a need will depend on the nature of a given problematic situation and the people involved. Any number of people are likely to be directly or indirectly involved. While each individual is unique, common characteristics and interests are likely to exist. In the design of a single-family dwelling, the identification of different interests and values may not be difficult—but in large-scale architectural projects a number of groups of people with different and frequently conflicting objectives and values are likely to exist (Figure 3). At a general level the following groups of people are involved:

1. The client or sponsor of the project.
2. Nonusers affected by or involved with the project.
3. Architects and allied professionals.

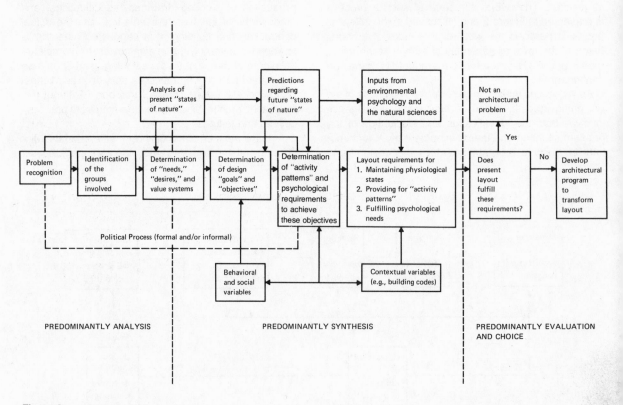

**Figure 3**
**A model of the intelligence phase. The directional arrows indicate only the main order of activities and flows of information. Feedbacks and secondary flows of information are not indicated.**

4. City officials, regulatory bodies, and the general public.
5. Contractors.
6. Users.

These groups can again be subdivided, and each subset will have a unique combination of goals and values. One of the reasons for the failures of some recent buildings and urban design projects is that groups (2.) and (6.) have been inadequately considered in decision making. If architecture is to be valid for all groups involved, it is essential that design goals should stem from an analysis of the needs, desires, and values of all participants in the process rather than only from what the design professions feel is needed.

Many leading architects have made a considerable effort to move in this direction despite hurdles such as those documented by Roger Montgomery.[6] The impact of user input on a design solution is possibly best illustrated by two designs for the East River project in Harlem.[7] The original design, shown in Figure 4, was a competition winner in 1963. A revised scheme, shown in Figure 5, was recently announced. Designed by the same architects to essentially the same building program (as far as units and services are concerned), the new proposal is very different from the original. The reason for this is simply that the new design is based on stated user preferences, while the original design was based on the theories of a number of people including those expressed by Jane Jacobs in her book *The Death and Life of Great American Cities*.[8] The success of the revised scheme remains to be seen.

A normative model of the intelligence process can be summarized as one of establishing goals and directions from needs and desires; of defining these goals in terms of available resources[9]; of identifying activity patterns and the psychological requirements for attaining a satisfying end product; and of establishing the required architectural elements to cater to these needs. The whole intelligence process is carried out in a highly political atmosphere. Carefully structured observational

**Figure 4**
**Photo credit: THE Hodne/Stageberg PARTNERS, Inc.**

**Figure 5**
**Photo credit: THE Hodne/Stageberg PARTNERS, Inc.**

studies and interviews such as those described in *Part Three* of this book can lend some rationality to the task. The techniques used in the intelligence phase may be the most immediate contribution the behavioral sciences can make to architecture.

Observational studies can lead to an understanding of behavior and the way it may be accommodated in building. Questionnaires and interviews may be used to uncover the "desires" of the people with whom (or for whom) we are designing. There are three inter-related problems inherent in the information obtained from studies of this type:

1. Information on needs and desires is obtained from a malfunctioning environment.
2. Participants do not know the full range of alternatives open to them.
3. People's circumstances, behaviors, and attitudes change.

Thus a building program cannot be based entirely on an analysis of existing circumstances. It must involve both inductive and deductive logic. To make adequate projections of alternative ways to achieve goals, the architect must have more knowledge about the way the built environment is used and the way people perceive opportunities for different behavior patterns within it than he does at present. He needs normative information which cannot be generated purely from the situation under consideration but which requires a commitment to ongoing research in "environmental psychology" and genuine efforts to assimilate and use the findings. The architect's role during the intelligence process is to make sure that the needs and desires of all participants are elucidated, that alternatives and intangibles are considered, and that the design implications of different goals are understood. His role is also to raise the level of the participants' perception of design goals from merely satisfactory ones toward better ones.

While we have stressed the need for gathering knowledge about the human needs to be met in the design of a building, the intelligence phase also involves the gathering of knowledge regarding the natural ecology of the site, financial, material, and technical resources, and future circumstances which will affect the design. Information resulting from this phase is the factual description of the elements to be related and synthesized in the design phase.

Where in the past the architect obtained information from catalogs, graphic standards, and technical consultants, in the new designing he will need, and is beginning to get, techniques to determine user preferences such as discussed by Robert Helmreich, Henry Sanoff, John Zeisel, and others in *Part Three* of this book, as well as useful compendiums of behavioral knowledge, such as Christopher Alexander's "pattern language," described in the following paper.

Yet the intelligence process is an increasingly complex one as the scale of buildings and the distance between the architect and user increases. It is made more complex by the recognition that the architect is designing for the future. What are the forces of the impinging milieu going to be in the future? Is prediction really possible? Many architects claim it is not. It seems that until we can improve our prediction techniques (perhaps along the lines which Robert Hershberger suggests later in this book), we should design for the present and allow for a range of future alternatives in our buildings. This should be reflected in both building programs and technological research.[10] While it is hypothesized here that architects should be involved in the intelligence phase of designing if building quality is to be enhanced, many architects and architectural schools treat the overall designing process as if it starts with a building program rather than with a need for a better environment. A cursory analysis of the work of architects considered by the profession to be most creative, however, suggests that their major contributions have, in many cases, really been made in intelligence rather than design activities.

**The Design Phase**

The generation of alternative solutions to an architectural program is a process about which we know very little. It is clear that it is an active and complex process of synthesis involving many simultaneously acting variables. It is an act of conceptualization, in which the elements of the problem are related and transformed to gain an overall resolution. It is not simply a collection of partial solutions to partial problems.

There appear to be at least two approaches to this act of synthesis. The first is design by habit, while the second involves the use of creative effort. The range and novelty of our problems today makes the second approach essential in more and more situations.

Architectural designing requires creative effort because design requirements are often contradictory, because decisions are not independent, and because any decision constrains those that follow. It must be recognized, however, that the design phase requires as much evaluation and choice as it does the generation of alternatives. Every time the designer draws a line, a choice has been made from a number of possibilities. One of the major difficulties in designing is that, owing to the sequential holistic nature of decision making, premature rejection of an alternative solution to part of a problem may result in a potentially worthwhile solution to the whole problem not being developed.[11] To overcome this situation it seems that decisions which impose only general constraints on subsequent decisions should be made at the outset. This implies the application of a general value system. An appropriate one should stress the goals and values of the different client groups.

The design phase begins with the analytical activities of relating the systems and components of the program and organizing them into a hierarchy of importance. In some cases details may be of overwhelming importance; in other cases the overall form may be most important. At the same time a strategy for overall synthesis should be developed. The designer should ask himself the question: What is the best approach for solving this set of problems? The attempt to answer this question may lead to the need for more data. If so, the architect would return to intelligence activities.

Moving from a set of problem statements that constitute a building program to a set of solution statements requires a "creative leap." What really is creativity? It is certainly not just high intelligence. Creative people often see a wider range of *affordances* of things or see the structure of the problem with a particular insight. Alternatively, they may also think uniquely and thus envision solutions which elude others. The goals of architectural education include enhancing the student's abilities to do these things. Increasingly this is being done through team designing, simulation of experience, and actual "clinical" experience while in school. New techniques of problem solving which integrate the results of research into creativity with roles and phases

in designing are also emerging.[12] But creative designing in architecture demands more than just novelty—it also demands a worthwhile solution. An architect's ability is constrained by his methodological skills and by the quality and quantity of his knowledge. Current research on creativity and design methodology should help improve the former, and the normative data generated through an ongoing research program in environmental psychology should help the latter. Clarification of the basic relationships between human behavior and designed environment should provide understanding needed to develop alternative solutions with confidence.

The lessons from the research on creativity seem clear: first, record all solutions and evaluate them later—premature criticism may truncate a fruitful line of development; second, look at as many different ways of solving a problem as time permits—there is a correlation between productivity and creativity. It was stated above that there is no rule to state when it is pointless to simply continue generating solutions. Time is the constraint. Therefore, it is foolhardy to regard design as an exhaustive procedure. Architects must be selective in generating alternative solutions. Ordering the critical variables helps to attain this selectivity by bringing the structure of the problem and its critical points to the architect's attention. Unfortunately, the alternative strategy is usually adopted in practice—the statement of the problem is simplified to make it easier to solve. Given this situation, it is hardly surprising that designs are so frequently lifeless and inappropriate for the people who use them.

## The Choice Phase

The choice phase involves the evaluation of possible (usually partial) solutions and the decision either that one of them best meets the program requirements or, perhaps, that none is appropriate. If the latter is the case, then the architect would return to either intelligence or design activities. If the decision is made to go ahead with one of the schemes, then the architect would prepare drawings and specifications. This again involves intelligence, design, and choice activities and frequently results in a complete reevaluation of the design itself.

Adequate evaluation and choice of a design depends on adequate prediction and understanding of the building users and their future development, as well as on the functioning of the product. One advantage of an explicit designing process is that it helps counteract the tendency to use only one value system—usually the architect's and/or sponsor's—in evaluation. Even with adequate evaluation techniques, however, the choice of the best alternative may be difficult. Different designs may perform similarly or have very different strengths and weaknesses. Even if one solution appears best, the final arbiter's global attitudes may make any evaluation completely irrational. It is for this reason, and to avoid premature truncation of the search for alternative solutions, that it is useful to differentiate clearly between design and choice phases.

The performance of designs can be evaluated in several ways. They can be analyzed logically, they can be subjected to experimentation, or the performances they support can be simulated. The first of these is the traditional way.[13] The second is usually only feasible on a partial basis through prototype construction. The third tends to be piecemeal and skeletal when used only for the evaluation of circulation, queuing, and physical problems. Gaming simulations, however, may deal with the overall problems, attitudes, and experiences in such a way as to offer behavioral insights.

## The Implementation Phase

It is not our intention to dwell on the problems of implementation here. One of the hypotheses behind the presentation of a model of the design process is that if the intelligence, design, and choice phases are carried out thoroughly, the problems traditionally associated with implementation will be lessened. If one extends the concept of implementation to include the production of working drawings and specifications as well as construction, then there appears to be some utility in following Herbert Simon's suggestion and regarding it as a decision-making process in its own right.[14] It certainly consists of analysis, synthesis, and decision making, and it is clear that knowledge of implementation problems constrains and influences the intelligence, design, and choice phases. It is as significant to study the behavior and communication of those

who carry out the building process as it is to study those who will inhabit and use the finished product.

## The Evaluation of Product and Process

As a profession, architects have woefully neglected the systematic evaluation of completed buildings in terms of both their use and their performance. Neither do they critically examine the process by which they were achieved. Unless this situation is changed, the evolution of architectural theory will be seriously hampered. Architectural periodicals are replete with photographs and comments on recently completed buildings. These hardly constitute a true evaluation because they rely on unstructured personal observations that frequently result in conclusions that are unique to the critic. Carefully structured observations and judicious surveys using adequate sampling techniques combined with an understanding of their use are necessary if any progress is to be made.

## IMPLICATIONS FOR RESEARCH AND PRACTICE

Designing is a process considerably more complex and more contradictory than architects have previously admitted it to be. It also requires a more disciplined effort than most have devoted to it. New techniques are necessary to help handle the complexity and contradiction in problem definition, design, choice, communication, implementation, and evaluation.

An examination of recent architectural research indicates that many new designing tools are being developed.[15] There are new methods of representing decision processes, many programs in computer-assisted design, and many techniques for the enlightened management of effort. At the present many of these techniques should be applied with caution. Many of them have been borrowed from disciplines such as mathematics and operations research, and their utility for architectural designing has not been clearly demonstrated. There has already been a reaction to such borrowings on the part of many architects. This is due partly to the conservatism of the profession; yet even the most ardent supporters of new design methods grant that new techniques often seem more involved with their own internal aesthetics than with improving architecture. It would be unfortunate if the reaction to such research on the process of designing were to send us willy-nilly back to architecture's failing procedures. At a time when many architects feel threatened by new techniques, however, it is essential that new procedures be evaluated carefully before they are widely heralded.

One of the advantages of the model presented here is that continuing methodological advances can be placed in an overall perspective. It should also enable the architect to understand, structure, and critically examine his own design efforts. It should lead him to understand where he has a free hand to express himself and where he has an obligation to meet the constraints imposed upon him. Looking at design in this way also helps the architect to perceive the limitations of his knowledge about the relationship between man and environment. The potential contribution of environmental psychology can be enhanced by bringing to the attention of researchers the questions of interest to architects. This can only occur with a better understanding of how buildings work and the process by which they are designed. It also makes clear that architects need better means for organizing the social and psychological information they require for designing.

## NOTES AND REFERENCES

1. Much of this research is reviewed by Gary T. Moore and Lynne Meyer Gay in *"Creative problem solving in architecture—a pilot study,"* University of California, Berkeley, Department of Architecture, 1968.
2. Clare Cooper and Phyllis Hackett, *Analysis of the Design Process at Two Moderate-Income Housing Developments,* Berkeley, Calif.: Center for Planning and Development Research, University of California, 1968.
3. See in particular Herbert A. Simon, *The New Science of Management Decision,* New York: Harper & Row, 1960.
4. Marvin Mannheim, "A design model: theory and application to transportation planning," in G. Moore, ed., *Emerging Methods in Environmental Design and Planning,* Cambridge, Mass.: MIT Press, 1970; Studer, *op. cit.*
5. Charles H. Burnette, *The ARC System: A Functional Organization for Building Information,* P.B. 177 839, Springfield, Va.: National Bureau of Standards, Clearinghouse for Federal Scientific and Technical Information, November 15, 1967.
6. Roger Montgomery, "Comment on 'Fear and house-as-haven in the lower class'," *Journal of the American Institute of Planners,* Vol. 32 (January 1966), 31-35.
7. "New York, N.Y.," *Architectural Forum,* Vol. 134 (May 1971), 43–44.
8. Jane Jacobs, *The Death and Life of Great American Cities,* New York: Random House, 1961.
9. There is considerable confusion over the use of the terms "goals" and "objectives"; some authors completely reverse the definitions used here.
10. See Harold Horowitz, "The program's the thing," *AIA Journal,* Vol. 47 (May 1967), 94–100, for a statement on what information a "thoroughly detailed architect's program" should contain.
11. Barclay G. Jones, "Design process and decision theory," in Marcus Wiffen, ed., *Teaching of Architecture,* Washington, D.C.: The American Institute of Architects, 1964.
12. Charles H. Burnette, Gary T. Moore, and Lynn Simek, "A role oriented approach to creative problem solving by groups," in Wolfgang Preiser, ed., *Environmental Design Research Proceedings of the Fourth International EDRA4 Conference,* Stroudsburg, Pa.: Dowden, Hutchinson & Ross, 1973.
13. Sami Hassid, "Systems of judgment of architectural design," in *New Building Research,* Washington, D.C.: National Academy of Sciences and the National Research Council, 1961.
14. Simon, *op. cit.*
15. Some of these comments were made by one of the authors, Jon Lang, in a review of the most interesting collection of papers on design methodology, *Emerging Methods in Environmental Design and Planning,* ed. by Gary Moore, Cambridge, Mass.: The MIT Press, 1970. The review appeared in the *New York Planning Review,* Vol. 14 (Winter–Spring 1972), B-1.

*The fundamental problem of design is to create environments which are real. Something that is real in this sense has no pretensions; it is direct and simple. How can one make cities more real? Cities are not built by just a few people but by millions. How can each person share in this sense of the real? To be able to answer these questions, this paper first defines a whole or real environment, and then explains both how we can see our environment as an integral part of ourselves, and how millions of acts of building can achieve a coherent whole. Every environment is formed from combinatorial systems of images which are defined as* pattern languages. *The patterns we use today are unwhole and thus cannot be used to create whole environments. It is possible, however, to create pattern languages which are whole and which any person can use to create environments which are themselves whole and real. All builders of the environment can gradually come to share a common pattern language.*

# An Early Summary of "The Timeless Way of Building," 1970*

**Christopher Alexander**

**Center for Environmental Structure
Berkeley, California**

What is the fundamental problem of environmental design? It is to create an environment which is real, utterly real. The Alhambra, a tiny gothic church, an old New England house, an alpine village, an ancient Zen temple—what is it that they have in common? They are beautiful, ordered, harmonious—yes, all these things. But especially, and what strikes to the heart, they are utterly real. By comparison, the works of modern architecture and the developments in modern cities are mostly not real. Does anyone really want to live in a house of glass and steel and concrete unless he is trying to prove he understands modern architecture? For me these buildings are unreal and false, like people who are not fully real.

What is something which is real? It accepts itself; it is true to its own nature; it has no pretensions; it is whole, and that means only that it must be direct and simple. It is the simplest thing in the world to make something which is real; yet it calls on the utmost inner resources to do it. In order to be that simple, I must be able to throw away all superimposed ideas; I must first see myself, and my own feelings, so clearly that

I can then enter into a situation outside myself and see that clearly too.

This book started simply as a part of my own struggle to make buildings more real. But then, of course, even if I myself succeed in making a few small places real, that is almost nothing compared with the vastness of our environment as a whole. How will it

*I have been working for almost ten years on a book which is called *The Timeless Way of Building*. It will be published at the end of 1974, by Oxford University Press. The following summary, written in 1970, is different from the full work in many details, but its overall spirit and intent are already reflections of the full work. The book itself will be published as Volume 1 of a series of three books, by the members of the Center for Environmental Structure. Volume 2, *A Pattern Language,* and Volume 3, *The Oregon Experiment,* will also be published in 1974. The following statement will appear at the beginning of all three books: "This is the first (second, third) of three books which describe an entirely new attitude towards architecture and planning. The three books, and others which will follow them, are intended to present a complete working alternative to our present ideas about architecture, building, and planning—an alternative which will, we hope, gradually replace current ideas and practices."

ever be possible for the entire environment, all the places we live in, to be entirely real also? Of course, no one person can help the reality of a city by a few individual acts of design; so I began to wonder if there was any way in which this quality of being utterly real could ever find its way into the city at large, and into all the houses, of all the people who live in it.

To make the city real—real for all the people who live there—that is a problem of design also—but not the kind that you can do with a pencil. If it was fully real, the city would be immensely orderly—but not with a visible, straightjacketed order—more with a kind of subterranean order, like the order you can feel in a man who is at peace. How would it be possible for this kind of order to find its way into a city?

I realized right away that the city is not built by a few people who could graciously give this kind of order to it. A city could only become real if all the millions of people in the city, whose acts of building and design create and re-create the city constantly, could all be suffused by this kind of reality; and this, of course, could only happen if each one of them could do what I want to be able to do myself—to make places which are utterly real.

So I saw, then, that the task of giving the city coherence and order, as a whole, meant simply that every single person living in the city—not just a few architects —could share this same sense of the real, and could create it: in short, that any person in society could do what the greatest architects and Zen masters have always dreamed of. Is this impossible? I do not think it is. I began to see that the problem of giving this ability to all the people in society was exactly the same as the problem of giving it to myself; since if I could find a way to give it to myself, then anyone else could have it too.

These two threads run throughout the book. On the one hand, the book is my own effort to find a way of making buildings which are more real. On the other hand, there is the larger question: since my own designs, or anyone else's, are just a few drops in an ocean, what guarantee is there that our environment will ever be real and coherent as a whole?

This second, and larger question is a much greater intellectual challenge than the smaller one. In scientific terms, it is rather like the classic problem of biology: *How are the growth and repair of billions of individual cells in an organism coordinated to make the organism whole at every stage of its development?* For the environment: *How can millions of personal acts of building cooperate in such a way that the environment which they create, though changing constantly, is coherent, whole, and real, as a totality, at every moment of its life?*

This problem cannot be solved until we have answers to three questions:

1. What exactly is an environment which is whole and real? And under what conditions will an environment become whole?
2. How can we see our total environment as a single whole, in which the larger-scale layout of forests and roads, the location of building, the design of houses, and the detailed design of windows in the houses, are all part of one great integrated picture?
3. How can the millions of personal acts of building which create the environment be coordinated to produce a coherent whole, without totalitarian control, in a way that leaves each individual free, and personal?

At present, we do not know how to answer any one of these questions. These are the questions which I try to answer in this book. To answer them, the book has three main parts.

The first part deals with the question of wholeness. It has three sections. First, I define the concept of a "whole" environment as one which allows all the people in it to become whole as persons, by their own efforts. Then I describe the process by which an environment gets formed, and show that every environment, whether whole or unwhole, is always formed from combinatorial systems of images, which I call *pattern languages*. Finally, I show that when the patern languages which the builders of an environment use are private and unwhole, as they are today, it is inevitable that the environment which they generate will be unwhole. To make our environment whole, we must find a way to share our pattern languages, and a way to make them whole.

In the second part of the book, I try to show how we can build a sharable pattern language. First, I define the concept of an explicit pattern, and define a sharable pattern language as an ordered system of explicit patterns. Second, I define such a language as whole when it covers every feature of an environment, and has the capacity to generate a whole environment; I show that a language can become whole, gradually, by the piecemeal evolution of its individual patterns. Third, I show that any person, not just a designer, who uses a shared pattern language which is whole can use it to create environments which are whole and real.

In the third part of the book I describe the evolutionary process by which all the builders of an environment can gradually come to share a pattern language which is whole. First, I show, in practical terms, how the creation, evolution, and use of a whole pattern language can pass gradually from the design profession into the hands of all members of a society together. Second, I describe the fact that the communal creation and evolution of a shared pattern language is the evolution of a culture: our attempt to evolve a picture of a way of life in which we can be whole. And last, I restate the central change of attitude which all this requires. Design is not merely the creation of individual objects: it is genetic—its purpose to create genetic processes from which a whole environment can grow, just as a plant grows from a seed.

Now comes a more detailed summary, chapter by chapter. I have written one paragraph to summarize each chapter. By reading the paragraphs in order, you can get an idea of the whole book. In the finished book, each paragraph will also appear, in bold type, at the head of its chapter.

## PART ONE: WHOLENESS

### Section 1: The Concept of a Whole Environment

The book begins with the fundamental idea that any system, whether it is inorganic, a living organism, or a society, can be whole, or less whole. Wholeness is not an extrinsic criterion, but intrinsic: The wholeness of a system, and the process of becoming whole, is different for every system; it is a process of becoming true to its own nature, a kind of self-consistency. A system is whole when it is at one with itself, and when all the forces which emerge from its own nature are in balance. A system which is fully whole is utterly real: the less whole it is, the more unreal.

An environment which is whole is one which allows each person to become whole, by his own efforts. A person can only become whole in an environment which

is whole. This follows directly from the previous definition. Since most of the forces which occur in an environment are the ones which people experience inside themselves, and since these forces are not in balance unless people are themselves whole, it follows that an environment is whole only if it allows people to become whole; and that a person cannot become whole, except in an environment which is whole.

Finally, I show that a whole environment will always have the geometry of nature. There will be infinite variety: each part of it, at every level, will be unique; yet, as it is in nature, this variety will be of the most simple kind. Like a forest, or an ocean, it will have far-reaching morphological laws, repeated infinitely many times, but always differently combined—and just as every leaf and every wave are different, every place will be unique.

### Section 2: How Is an Environment Formed, in Fact?

Before asking how we can make our environment whole, we must first find out how an environment, in fact, is formed.

I begin with the idea that every environment, large and small, is the three-dimensional embodiment of a culture. It is an arrangement of culturally defined categories in space—where each category defines an activity, or place, or thing, and its associated human behavior. This definition of an environment includes the geometry of the purely physical objects in the environment, but also includes the organization of social institutions—since the activities which define each social institution are themselves always anchored in space. The categories of space inside a house embody the culture of its family; those in a city embody the culture of its people.

The morphology of an environment is given to it by a system of endlessly repeated spatial relationships among its spatial categories: its morphological laws. What makes different environments recognizable as London, Paris, an English house, a Japanese garden, an American gas station, is given to them by their particular collections of morphological laws. And even the unique qualities that any one particular English house has are given to it by the unique interaction of the same morphological laws.

Every environment gets its morphology from millions of personal acts made by its builders; and these acts are themselves guided, exclusively, by the combination of images which the builders already have in their heads, at the time of the act. This is true at every scale of an environment; it has been true for all environments in history; and it remains true for all environments today.

When we examine these combinatorial systems of images, closely, we find that they are exactly like human languages. Both are systems which allow a person to produce an infinite variety of unique combinations, by means of his own creative act. For this reason, I call these systems *pattern languages*. An ordinary language such as English allows you to create an infinite variety of one-dimensional combinations of words, called sentences. A pattern language allows its users to create an infinite variety of three-dimensional combinations of activities, places, things, and called environments.

The system which allowed a traditional barn builder to build barns was a pattern language. The knowledge which allowed a traditional Japanese farmer to design his own house, the citizen to participate in the creation of a medieval city, the knowledge which created the Georgian terraces and squares of London, all were pattern languages. Today's developers, freeway builders, and city governments, all have their pattern languages. And the same is true for every architect and city planner: Frank Lloyd Wright, Aalto, Le Corbusier, Mies van der Rohe have all created their designs by using pattern languages. And you, yourself, also create your designs by using a pattern language.

## Section 3: Why Our Environment Isn't Whole Today

Going back now to the definition of wholeness, it is easy to show that our own environment today is not whole. Although there are one or two corners of modern cities which are whole, there is no city on earth today which is whole as a totality. On the other hand, many traditional environments were whole: entire villages, buildings, and their details. Since traditional environments and today's environment *both* get their morphology from the pattern languages used by the people who build them, the reason for the difference must lie in the pattern languages.

What is the peculiarity which pattern languages have today that makes our environment unwhole? The

answer is: An environment can only become whole if the pattern languages which its builders use are themselves whole, *and this can only happen if these languages are shared*. In today's society, almost all the pattern languages at work are either private, or highly specialized: they are not shared. So long as this state of affairs continues, it is quite impossible for the environment ever to become whole. To prove this, I now define five conditions which must hold in any environment which is to become whole.

1. All the deepest society-wide psychological needs must be taken into account: the inner needs associated with birth, infancy, childhood, teenage years, family life, old age, and death. So long as pattern languages are private, many of these deeper social and psychological needs are not reflected in the environment, because no one private language has responsibility for the whole.

2. Human feelings, climate, engineering, social problems, ecology, transportation, economics, must all be integrated. They can only be integrated if it is possible to express the contribution which each one makes to the environment in comparable terms. So long as they are expressed in specialized terms, neither one man, nor any team, can put them together.

3. Each person needs access to a shared pool of experience. A person whose pattern language is private must rely entirely on his own experience, and cannot possibly know, or foresee, all the different possible kinds of failure that can occur, even in a simple building; so his buildings will inevitably be full of mistakes.

4. One hundred percent of the acts of building which make the environment must contribute to its wholeness. Today, architects and ecologists, who are perhaps most concerned with wholeness, build less than 5 percent of our environment.

5. The environment must be built by the people who live in it. So long as pattern languages are specialized, great parts of the environment will be built by mass processes. These mass processes must inevitably lead to endless sameness, and will be utterly insensitive to the local variation and uniqueness of each place, each family, each person.

In a traditional society, all five of these conditions are satisfied. That is why the action of the pattern languages at work in a traditional society made the environment whole. But in today's society, not one of these five conditions is satisfied. So long as the pattern languages which people use stay unwhole and private, these conditions must stay unsatisfied, and the environment must inevitably stay unwhole.

Yet the definition of a whole environment tells us that we cannot become whole in an environment which is not whole. The conclusion seems inescapable. For our own sake, if we ourselves—you and I—want to become whole, we must somehow find a way of sharing our pattern languages so that the environment can be whole again.

## PART TWO: A PATTERN LANGUAGE WHICH IS WHOLE

### Section 1: A Pattern Language Which Can Be Shared

In this first chapter, I described a sharable language in outline. It is a system of explicit patterns, so organized that all the patterns relevant to any given context can be obtained in the order most appropriate for design, and then combined, by simple combinatory operations, to form a whole.

The most important elements of the language are the patterns themselves, which correspond to the rules of grammar in a natural language. Every pattern is essentially a re-usable design idea for the environment. Anyone who has an idea about the design of the environment, and tries to express his idea in such a way that someone else can reuse it, will find that he has to define three things: The problem which this "idea" solves; the range of spatial arrangements which solve this problem; and the range of contexts in which it makes sense to re-use this "idea." In short, anyone who tries to express a design idea in such a way that someone else can re-use it, will find himself creating something which is a "pattern" exactly like the patterns in traditional pattern languages.

Patterns can be stated equally well for the human details of buildings, the overall layout of a building, ecology, large-scale social aspects of urban planning, regional economics, structural engineering, building construction. In this chapter I include examples of explicit patterns at all these scales: the distribution of subcultures in a region, the layout of major roads, the organization of work groups in an industry, the arrangement of trees at the edge of a forest, the design of a window, the planting of flowers in a garden. A sharable pattern language is organized so that it can include all patterns, at all scales, within a single framework.

Although precise, each pattern is a fluid image which does no violence to the uniqueness of the designs in which it appears. It is the carrier of the spirit and the feeling of a particular kind of spatial order; but it will appear in a slightly different concrete form, every time it appears, according to the way that it is combined with other patterns.

Finally, every pattern is always tentative. It is a current "best guess"; it will change constantly, and improve cumulatively, under the impact of fresh evidence. In this sense, patterns play the same role in environmental design that hypotheses have played in science.

### Section 2: The Wholeness of a Pattern Language and the Balance of Individual Patterns

We cannot share our patterns, or improve them cumulatively, without a shared moral principle to judge them by. The only moral principle common to all individual values is the morality of wholeness.

I define a pattern language as whole if its use will generate a whole environment. But a language is not created all at once; and it cannot be made whole at once. It evolves slowly, by a piecemeal process, one pattern at a time. A language can therefore only become whole if we can find a way of making sure that individual patterns always get improved in such a way as to increase the wholeness of the language and of the environments which that language generates.

A pattern contributes to the wholeness of an environment only if that environment contains a system of conflicting forces, and if this pattern is able to bring these forces into balance, without creating new imbalance among other forces. I call such a pattern *balanced*.

The concept of a balanced pattern is directly related to the concept of a whole environment. I have already defined a whole environment as one in which people can become whole. In a whole environment, the stresses which a person experiences are ones which challenge him, which extend him, and which he can ultimately cope with. An environment is unwhole when a person experiences conflicts which are beyond his capacity. These unresolvable conflicts do not challenge him. They merely reduce his capacity to cope with further conflicts, and so lead to a spiraling deterioration in which he becomes less and less able to cope with conflicts, and less and less able to grow.

It is easy to see that every balanced pattern makes life more full, since it sustains people in their effort to become whole. But since every unresolved system of conflicting forces reduces people's capacity to cope with further stress, the balanced patterns are not merely pleasant; they are essential. An environment cannot be whole unless all of its patterns are balanced, down to the last detail.

The wholeness of a pattern language and the balance of its patterns are subtle questions, but they are questions of fact. Of course, there can be a great variety of different languages which are all whole—as many as there are cultures—and the ability to cope with conflict varies from person to person even within a culture. However, the balance of a pattern and the wholeness of a language do not depend on subjective estimates of what ought to be, or personally stated goals. The ultimate test of any pattern, or any language, is its reality.

## Section 3: Using a Pattern Language to Create New Designs

A person with a whole pattern language can create any part of the environment. He can equally well contribute to the planning of a city, design his own house, or remodel a single room, because in each case he knows all the relevant patterns, he knows how to combine them, and he knows how the particular piece he is working on fits into the larger whole. He does not need to be an "expert" to do this. The expertise is in the language. Any normally creative human being can use a pattern language to design an environment which is whole.

The creative power of a pattern language hinges on the ordering of patterns in the language, and on the integrative ability common to any normal human mind.

I show that, for any set of patterns, there is an order which allows you to take the patterns one at a time, and build up a coherent mental image of a design which contains them all.

A language is so organized that a person who has a particular context in mind can obtain all the patterns appropriate to the context from the language, in the order most suitable for combination. This ordered set of patterns, in the proper order, is called the *sublanguage* for that context. Every culture has its own language which defines the total environment for that culture. Every subculture in a culture, and every institution in a culture, has its own sublanguage, a sublanguage of the language for that culture. And every particular building problem, because it has a unique client and a unique context, itself has its own unique sublanguage, again a sublanguage of the language for the subculture it belongs to.

A person who uses the language for a given context will be able to build up a three-dimensional design appropriate to that context, simply by combining the patterns in his mind. The order given by the sublanguage will make the image of the design come together by itself, in the person's mind; he will not even need a pencil, except to put the finished design down on paper.

Each design created by a person who uses a language will be different. It will be different, because each design is created by the interaction of the language with a specific local context. And if two people use the same language, for the same context, the two designs will still be different—because each person will create combinations that are unique to him.

The geometry of a design created from a language which is whole will be like the geometry of nature: a subtle multiplicity of patterns, in which no one pattern stands out more clearly than another, many many patterns balanced against each other, all simultaneously visible and present, yet no one dominant. In a perfectly conceived whole, every single part of the design, at every scale, and every gap between the parts, will be both whole in itself and part of some greater whole.

Finally, although it is true that anyone can use a pattern language to create a whole environment, the language will never create wholeness automatically. The patterns in the sublanguage for a given context give a rough idea of the relationships which that environment needs in order to be whole; but the sublanguage cannot ever be complete. Every combination of patterns creates new circumstances; so the use of the language always depends, in the end, on your ability to bring the spirit of the patterns into situations for which patterns don't exist—on your intuitive knowledge of the difference between what is real and what is not real. Your ability to know the real, in a given context, may start with the language: but once you know the language, you must always go beyond the language.

## PART THREE: EVOLUTION

### Section 1: The Evolution of a Society-wide Language Which Is Whole

In the second part of the book, I have described a kind of pattern language which can be shared, and have shown that anyone can use a language. However, so far, this sharable pattern language is still a theoretical construct. Now the question is: What practical steps must be taken, to make this theory work? I have shown that an environment cannot become whole until all its inhabitants are actively involved in the evolution and use of a shared pattern language. How can a whole language evolve? And, above all, how can it evolve in a way which leaves each person free, not deluged by a mass of impersonal information, and not diminished by a system which he did not create?

It requires a dual process, partly public, partly personal. On one hand, individual patterns may be published through normal channels of publication. The full presentation of patterns, the criticism and debate concerning patterns, evidence concerning the validity and testing of patterns, may be collected in archives in various libraries, offices, universities, and other centers.

On the other hand, it is essential that each person feels that his language is personal, and "his." For this reason, the public archives themselves will never be used, directly, to design buildings: They will merely be sources, from which each person creates his own personal language. To make your own pattern language, you create it, literally, for yourself, by re-creating every single pattern in your own personal way. You may draw

upon the archives, or upon someone else's language; but every pattern in your language will be yours, even if someone else invented it, and even if a thousand other people share it, because you create the version which is yours. This is just what happens when we learn our mother tongue. The rules of grammar and meaning are not given to us predigested: we re-create them for ourselves, in our own minds, so that for each of us, our language is both personal and shared.

The beauty of this arrangement is the following. Without any monolithic, totalitarian, or centralized control, the shared personal languages which people have will gradually evolve towards greater and greater wholeness. The good patterns will spread widely; the bad patterns will eventually drop out. The mere existence of a common format for patterns is enough to guarantee widespread sharing, and a slow evolution towards wholeness.

This evolution of a sharable pattern language creates a natural framework for learning and research, since all learning and research which really helps the design of the environment is concerned either with the evolution of individual patterns, or with the process of combining them. As more and more people publish their intuitions, and ideas, in pattern form, the archive languages will gradually contain patterns on all the problems which occur in the environment.

As languages evolve, the barriers between professions will disappear. Each designer who uses a language will have, at his command, all the intuition and design knowledge of ecologists, structural engineers, architects, planners, transportation engineers, economists, sociologists, and psychologists. He will be like a modern Renaissance man.

Finally, the distinction between professional designers and nondesigners will disappear altogether. When all the intuition and knowledge needed to build environments is embodied in a language, every person in society will be able to design any part of the environment. Everyone will be a designer.

An environment will be fully whole when it reaches this last stage. Only then, when each place is designed by the people who know it best, will each place have the proper balance of generic patterns and local uniqueness.

## Section 2: A Pattern Language As a Picture of a Way of Life

In early times, the city was an image of the universe —its form a guarantee to each person who lived there of a whole and coherent picture of a way of life. A pattern language too is a coherent picture of a way of life. It shows each person his relationship to the forces which occur in him, his culture, and the nature which surrounds him.

A pattern language is, in short, a picture of a culture. And each personal version of the language is a work of art: a personal effort, by each person, to create a single picture of his culture which fits together and makes sense of life. If all of us, together, try to create such personal languages, and share them, then the evolution of our shared language will be a continuous communal effort, by all of us, to create an integrated picture of a future way of life, in which all of us can, communally, be whole.

And then, at this stage, when each of us has his own personal version of a language which is shared, there is some hope that the fundamental problem of environmental design may be solved. From millions of personal languages which all embody a shared urban order, there is some hope that a shared urban order can emerge: A new urban order—in which not only buildings will be there, but all the architecture of community, no leftover space, every spot useful for life, ordered by common consent, created not by a design elite, but by the harmony of thousands of acts, all working with a common intent.

## Section 3: What Then Is Design?

All this requires a fundamental change of attitude.

If you want to make a living flower, you do not build it physically with tweezers, cell by cell; you grow it from the seed. If you want to design a new flower, you will design the seed and let it grow. The seeds of the environment are pattern languages. The only serious way of influencing the environment is through the pattern languages from which it grows. If you want to improve your own ability to design, improve your pattern language. If you want to influence the larger environment, plant your ideas in the pattern languages which other people use. In the end, the only way we can possibly hope to create a whole environment is to join hands, and together create a pattern language which will be the seed of our environment.

*One trouble with the institution has been the leveling of all individual needs to one prescription, that is, a long hallway with dayrooms and nurses stations, regardless of whether it is an adolescent, an octogenerian, an alcoholic, or a schizophrenic who is being treated. It is suggested that design should seek to maximize the congruity between the individual and the environment rather than seek an "ideal solution" that would fit all people of a given class, that behavior explained by the physical environment is very rare, and that most people judge structures by how well they make important life tasks achievable. To the less-competent disadvantaged group that form all institutional populations, the environment, whether purely physical, social, or regulated by people, is likely to be more significant in their daily lives than it would be to the noninstitutionalized person. Experience in the Philadelphia Geriatric Center is related to the architectural considerations of institutional location, dispersion of spaces, patient personal and social space, staff space, and other concerns.*

# The Human Being and the Institutional Building

**M. Powell Lawton**

**Philadelphia Geriatric Center**

Institutions have a habit of existing for themselves and not for people. They have a bad name for very good reasons, and everyone should support those whose aim is to humanize them. Let us not forget, however, that institutions do have a purpose and that we cannot afford to throw out their legitimate purposes with their faults. Mental hospitals and institutions for the elderly have changed greatly in recent years, but in an interdependent way. Since 1960, the population in state and county mental hospitals has decreased from 520,000 to 340,000, while the population in nursing homes and homes for the aged has increased almost 50 percent, from 510,000 in 1963 to 780,000 in 1967. Part of the change has involved the direct transfer of many thousands of elderly patients from state hospitals to nursing homes. The newest thing in the geriatric world today is called "alternatives to institutionalization," yet the percentage of all older people in institutions has grown from 3.8 percent to almost 5 percent since 1960. The Scandinavian countries have been years ahead of us in developing services for the elderly, yet Sweden has a much higher rate of institutionalization than we have—in the neighborhood of 8

percent. In short, while we may redefine appropriate types of treatment and the target population for the treatment, it is clear that society will always have a need for the institution, and we had therefore best devote ourselves to doing what we can to improve, rather than scrap, the model.

In trying to talk about the common meeting ground of behavioral science and the design professions, it has been found helpful to reason from human needs and capability to structure, utilizing hard data wherever possible, but realizing that if one waited for all the data to come in, we would wait forever. Therefore, an attempt will be made to make it clear when experimental facts support suggestions.

We shall look at several general principles underlying this complex area of man–environment transactions, and then proceed to deal analytically with the design implications of knowledge in the behavioral sciences for several types of institutions. The first principle is that design should seek to maximize the congruity between the individual and the environment, rather than seek an "ideal solution" that would fit all people of a given class. To state that old people differ among themselves as much as people of any age sounds very obvious. Yet, one repeatedly hears such assertions as, "Old people prefer. . . ." One implication of the search for congruity is that diversity of structure, as well as person, should be the rule. One problem with the institution has been the leveling of all individual needs to one prescription, that is, a long hallway with dayroom and nurses' station, regardless of whether it is an adolescent, an octogenarian, an alcoholic, or a schizophrenic who is being treated. Institutional planners have shied away from the idea of individual, rather than "average," need as the major determinant of structure, in part because it is probably more expensive to build for diversity. On the other hand, this cannot be the whole story. A significant part is the human need to think in stereotypes, to seek simplistic solutions. Data is not yet available relating good outcomes to specific combinations of man–made environments and personality types, but there is evidence suggesting, for instance, that negative aggressive, mildly antisocial older people do better in institutions,[1] or in specialized treatment programs[2] than do more conforming, docile people.

A second important point to make is that it is very difficult to speak as if one factor causes another in the complex set of interrelationships that form an institution. A change in the physical structure of a ward may very well occasion many behavioral changes, but the behavioral changes themselves may be minimized by counteractive behavior, or they may be directed in a feedback loop toward the physical environment in such a way as to modify it. Perhaps one of the most important aspects of this systemic view of behavior is that the physical environment very rarely acts as unilaterally as it does, for example, in a flood. The actual environment is in constant interaction with the human beings defining or managing space, and the human object thus defined may participate actively in the use of modification on the space. In short, it appears that behavior explained solely by environment is very rare—it is almost impossible to build a structure that demands a single, unvarying behavior unless it goes beyond the threshold of human coping.

## ADAPTATION TO ENVIRONMENTS

Another basic premise of this personal approach to behavior and environment is the conviction that most people judge structures by how well they make important life tasks achievable. Constance Perin[3] has argued persuasively, using some pilot study data as evidence, that visual aesthetic judgment is rarely the basis for people's evaluations of their physical environments. Unquestionably, there is a threshold effect on both ends of the scale: a structure may be ugly or beautiful enough to affect significantly one's outlook on occasion. The fact is, however, that one of our most human characteristics is our ability to adapt to a wide range of stimuli, and to become aware of the stimuli only when their value departs significantly from the level to which we have become accustomed. It could be argued further that this capacity to shut out awareness of aspects of the environment is essential to our ability to cope with the everyday tasks of life. By far the greatest part of our behavioral lives is devoted to coping with only tiny aspects of our physical surroundings—sustained consciousness of larger segments of the environment would make impossible our performance of instrumental tasks.

No attempt to downgrade the aesthetic criterion for design generally is intended, but rather to emphasize that the criterion of self-perceived competence may well become increasingly relevant as competence becomes more difficult to achieve. The aesthetic experience may be enjoyed most fully when one's general level of competence is high enough to perform most tasks adequately, with energy expenditure and attention levels either moderate or distributed over time as to allow "time out" for actively sought varied experience. This suggestion is related to what has elsewhere been the "environmental docility" hypothesis.[4] According to this view, as competence or status of any kind decreases, the probability becomes greater that behavior will be influenced by environmental constraints or facilitators. The most intelligent, the healthiest, the wealthiest, have most options available, and can literally manipulate their environments most easily. Conversely, the mentally retarded person may be dependent on community resources for his sustenance, the disabled may avail themselves only of recreation that is within their own block, and the impoverished inner city resident can participate only in activities that take place within the safety of daylight. Thus, to the disadvantaged groups that form all institutional populations, the environment, whether purely physical, social, or physical-controlled-by-people, is likely to be more significant in their daily lives than to the more competent noninstitutionalized person. If this docility hypothesis is true, and there is some empirical evidence supporting it, careful attention to the design of the institution could have a significant influence on the well-being of the resident.

The final general point to be emphasized is that an ecological view of institutional treatment inevitably leads one to a disability-oriented approach to design. Ogden Lindsley has referred to "the prosthetic environment" as one designed to compensate for failures in individual performance.[5] This compensation it would then appear should lead to a heightened appreciation of one's own competence and ultimately be therapeutic, in the sense of permanently raising the level of performance. Frequently, however, the therapy lies solely in the person's internal perception of himself performing competently, the external prosthesis being required permanently to maintain behavior. Thus, institutional design requires us to produce (1) permanent behavior-maintaining structures, (2) structures that will exercise latent healthy behavior that may be learned for permanent use (rehabilitation), and (3) structures that will allow for freedom of operation and an expansion in scope of healthy aspects of the individual (self-realization). This triple function of the institutional environment leads us back to the principle of congruity: not only do different people need different environmental solutions, but even the same individual's differing competencies may require prosthetic, therapeutic, and self-realizing aids.

Concerning oneself only with questions of relevance to the above three functions of institutions (that is, ignoring cost, engineering, and aesthetic considerations), time can be spent discussing some possible translations of behavioral-science knowledge into design suggestions.

## THE LOCATION OF INSTITUTIONS

Differing therapeutic philosophies have led to different choices of institutional locations. There is some evidence that a more cohesive social network develops as more of the total life of a community is located within the bounds of the setting. The more physically isolated the setting, the more likely that all important activities will be centered within, rather than without. Some of the best private psychiatric institutions have been located far from the outside community, under the theory that they can design a better therapeutic community of their own than could be obtained by encouraging more frequent exchange with the community. In general, however, this is a dying concept of treatment. Even in institutions for the elderly, current therapeutic philosophy aims at establishing all possible links with the community, including use of institutional facilities by community residents as well as inpatients, and combining rehabilitative and terminal-care patients. Thus a central location might not only provide better access to community resources, but would encourage continued exercise in coping with the environmental and social stresses of the world at large. The alternative, a self-sufficient intrainstutional subsociety, has the advantage of reducing stress and encouraging the development of standards for behavior more appropriate to the treatment group. This alternative may be desirable if the population is permanent. For example, given the goal of providing a home for people during their final years, it may suit many people best to have the norms for active good citizenship established by their age peers in their housing environment, rather than applying inappropriate young-adult norms of activity, community participation, and so on. In this case, we take the risk of reinforcing the estrangement between "inmate" and community dweller, and perpetuating society's negative stereotypes. Taking such risks seems clearly contraindicated with respect to the mental hospital. Constant, measured practice in dealing with societal stress is critical to rehabilitation, especially for the younger mental patient. Older people, as they became less mobile, make less use of community facilities, so that in the case of nursing homes and homes for aged, less central location is possible, so long as travel distance for staff, relatives, or other outsiders does not become too great. On the other hand, for substantial numbers of people who live in specially built housing for the elderly, engagement with life in general may depend on proximity to community social, recreational, and life-sustaining resources (Figure 1). They clearly need a central location to maintain function.

There are, of course, situations where it is vitally

**Figure 1**
**Housing situated where it is almost impossible for interaction with the community**

necessary to filter out some environmental stimuli. An unsafe neighborhood is good for no one. Drug traffic into mental hospitals is an increasing problem. Although both problem and solution may be more personal than structural, locations of drug traffic are generally known, and might be avoided in considering a proposed location.

## WITHIN-INSTITUTION DISPERSION OF SPACES

The older mental hospital, in keeping with the "asylum" tradition and the value placed upon rest and retreat, typically was built away from population centers, with many acres of ground and wide separations among buildings. Many such preserves still exist, frequently encroached upon by urban sprawl but with ample space for new building. Thus one still has the option of locating new buildings at varying distances from existing ones. New construction where land is less plentiful has no

such range of choice, but one still must decide whether to build a large building for many treatment purposes or a smaller building for a specialized purpose. Psychological knowledge can help with two major questions involved in these small-scale locational questions —the ideal distance between patient and resource, and the relative virtues of a homogeneous versus a heterogeneous patient population.

For the physically able person, distance is not a major limiting factor in the use of resources. While we all may experience the inertia of distance, if we need medical care badly we will travel for it. But disability may cause increased resistance to seeking out activities distant from where one lives. Research clearly indicates that the likelihood of using a senior center, or of seeing friends, decreases with the distance from them, even when the older person is in relatively good health. Despite the clarity of these research findings, a number of planners insist on producing housing for older people without recreation, dining-room, or medical clinic services on the site, lest too-easy access erode independence. In fact, federal housing policy has made it very difficult for a housing sponsor to include such services in housing. There is, however, room for both types of housing. Research at the Philadelphia Geriatric Center fails to indicate any decrease in independent functioning attributable to on-site services. It has been found, however, that housing environments that offer such services recruited tenants who were somewhat less inpendent to begin with. Therefore, the planner should realize the possibility, as well as the converse—that housing with no services will initially be populated by relatively independent older people. However, this observation simply underlines that fact that such housing should cater to a variety of types of people. Each person should be matched to an environment congruent with his needs.

Within institutions for less-competent older people, even shorter distances assume great importance. Institutional architecture can be identified by its long halls, and the relatively long walks necessary for patients to go about their business. Even the staff is subject to the distance effect. Research in the ward for mentally impaired aged at the Philadelphia Geriatric Center shows that the major staff activity node in a very traditional building is around the nurses' station, with a steady decrease in staff members' presence as one moves farther down the hall. For the most limited geriatric patient, services must be provided very close to his habitual location or they will not be used.

It is clear that there is such a thing as too-great clustering, and too-great dispersion of activity spaces. An individual's tendency to stay put more than is healthy may be counteracted by placing his resources at an optimum distance consistent with his competence. There are few physically well psychiatric patients who cannot walk some distance to work assignments or recreational activity. Much would seem to be gained by deliberately locating these features some distance from buildings where younger adults live, but within, or close by, buildings where physically ill or geriatric patients live.

The second aspect of intrainstitutional dispersion of space concerns the decision to house or not house different treatment populations in physical proximity to one another. There has been considerable discussion,

though surprisingly few empirical studies of, the effects of treating elderly and young-adult, senile and intact, adolescent and adult, or schizophrenic and sociopathic patients, together. The little bit of research evidence that we have tends to favor integration, though the findings are by no means conclusive. On the other hand, institutional administrators are likely to attempt to segregate wherever feasible, since administrative problems are fewer where one set of procedures fits most patients. One is led to suspect, then, that an "infection" process can occur if individuals having too wide a range of pathology are housed or treated together. Grossly senile behavior is very anxiety-arousing to residents of moderate to good mental status; a true sociopathic personality will victimize psychotic patients of low competence; children and adolescents housed in apartment buildings with substantial concentrations of elderly people are very destructive to the older person's feeling of security. Thus, we may generalize that segregating extreme groups protects those of lowest competence and relieves those of average or better competence of the fear of contagion. Within the much wider band above the low extreme, however, there is evidence that mixing can provide helpful models for the less competent, and helping roles for the more competent.

The architect will often be told that finely detailed segregation of treatment groups is best from a psychiatric point of view. He should interpret this generalization to read "from an administrative point of view," and operate under the assumption that it is the extreme disadvantaged groups that need physical separation and a particularly prosthetic design.

Sometimes the decision is made to design a special-purpose unit close to, but not within, a general treatment unit. This proximate-but-not-intimate situation may be ideal in that it separates the extreme group, but affords a resource that the more competent person knows will be available when and if he comes to need it. This is exactly the situation in the case of Geriatric Center's apartment building and nursing home. Although the two are side-by-side, the apartment dwellers are careful not to engage in activities at the nursing home, or to go near it, unless absolutely necessary. Yet, when interviewed as to their feelings about being on the same grounds with a nursing home, they say very explicitly that they don't like it but feel secure knowing they can move next door if they become more impaired. Similarly the state of Ohio and the Columbus Housing Authority are joint sponsors of a "Golden Age Village" located on a mainstreet corner of a mental hospital's grounds. The housing is far enough from hospital buildings to allow both tenants and the public to dissociate it from the hospital. Yet a quarter of the tenants are recently discharged mental patients relearning the art of independent living while availing themselves of supportive services provided by the hospital. They know that if they cannot sustain themselves, there is a prepared route back to a more protected situation.

## BUILDING TYPE

There has been much debate about the merits of high-rise versus ground-floor living. Our research has failed to document the existence of any substantial displeasure with high-rise living among elderly tenants, even those moving from rural parts of a county into a high-rise building in a small city. While too-great dispersion has the many disadvantages noted earlier, healthy older people living in low-rise and detached homes do not seem to object to the distances.

There are no reliable data on the relationship of size to satisfaction of tenants or residents of institutions for the elderly. There is research indicating that small size of patient population may be associated with higher patient discharge rate, but there are no studies of size of single building in relation to a quality criterion.

In line with the importance of distance as a mediator of much behavior of disadvantaged people, the proximity of living units to one another is the single most important determinant of friendship formation, whether in housing, homes for aged, or hospitals. Thus, the high-rise building places units maximally close to one another; tenant competence being equal, there are more social relationships among high-rise than among detached-unit tenants.

## PATIENT PERSONAL SPACE

Robert Sommer has discussed at length the meaning of personal space, including space in institutional life.[6] He finds a clear need for both private and shared space, and notes that these needs vary with age, degree of competence, what one is used to, and perhaps other factors. A large number of people have been surveyed recently regarding their wishes for a private, as compared to a shared room, should they be in a home for aged. College students could not imagine being without a roommate, but among people not in institutions, a steadily higher number preferred single rooms through middle age, and a high rate was maintained through old age. Interestingly enough, substantially fewer institutionalized older people who were sharing rooms at the time expressed a wish for a private room. At one home, however, once it was announced that many single rooms would be available in a new building, *all* subjects with roommates expressed the wish for a single room. The lesson to be learned is that perhaps those aforementioned subjects who seemed satisfied with their roommates may have been constrained by the effects of institutionalization and lowered competence to act submissively and to sacrifice, or adapt to the lack of, basic human needs. An interesting paradoxical finding regarding private mental hospital rooms was provided by William Ittelson, Harold Proshansky, and Leanne Rivlin.[7] They actually found *more* social behavior in single than in multiple-bed rooms. Patients sharing a room rarely occupied the room together during the day; rather, it was treated as a one-person retreat, rotating among its occupants. By contrast, the single room-occupant sometimes used the room as a private retreat, but at other times invited others for social purposes.

The absence of single rooms in all but the most expensive mental hospitals at least partly reflects the conclusion that mental patients do not have the same needs as others. While there is no strong empirical evidence, it seems reasonable that providing spatial privacy would help to humanize the mental hospital. The loss of the sense of self has been described as a central phenomenon among both the institutionalized and the mentally ill. Self is partially defined by belongings, personal space, and props such as mirrors and pictures of significant people. Some of these features may be built into institutional rooms, thus coercing administrators into enduring the extra trouble required by their presence.

These bits of information suggest that for many patients, geriatric or psychiatric, some private space is a very desirable option to have. The survey done at our Center does suggest a slight tendency for residents from a working-class background to prefer shared space more than middle-class residents, perhaps resulting from past experiences of adaptation to less privacy. Also, people were somewhat more likely to think they would like a roommate if they were in poor health, because they could call on them for help. The coming generation of older people will be far more used to privacy than the present one. Preferences of the generation that invented the commune, however, remain to be seen.

One aspect of the single room that may be different from the sheer need for privacy is that one's room is frequently the locus of everyday, solitary, self-maintaining and recreational tasks. Dressing, care of one's wardrobe, grooming, and housekeeping are normal activities carried out in a bedroom. Expressive tasks such as reading, listening to music, hobbies, or recreation may also be performed there. No research evidence tells us whether these activities are more frequent, or better performed, by occupants of single- or multiple-occupant rooms. However, it seems at least reasonable to ask whether there will be greater motivation to perform such tasks when the space is one's own. Even if more than one person must occupy a room, it is possible to design it in such a way as to maximize the demarcation of one's own territory as compared to someone else's. Furniture dividers may be used for this purpose. Built-in furniture may also denote an area either private or shared. For example, a bank of closets running along a single wall may give the most efficient use of space, but this arrangement makes totally impossible the incorporation of personal-belonging space into a truly personal area. Far to be preferred is the clustering of space for everything belonging to a single individual into an area distinguishable from someone else's. Room decorations and movable furnishings might also be used to distinguish among room occupants.

## PATIENT SOCIAL SPACE

A pioneer characterization of social space was made by Humphrey Osmond in his concept of sociopetal versus sociofugal space.[8] Sociopetal space is an area whose structure encourages social interaction, whereas its opposite, sociofugal space, separates or isolates people. While there are few empirical data to support the idea that space itself mandates behavior so clearly, there is much to support the notion that some rooms and areas are associated with higher human population and level of social interaction than others. The major social spaces of institutions are lobbies, halls, explicitly designated social areas, and outdoor spaces. Some qualities that define these areas as social are their use as traffic ways, their location near centers of activity, the presence of markers such as seats, TV sets, or other equipment, and their names, such as "dayroom," "community room," and so on. Since a social disability is almost always present in any institutionalized population, social spaces are central to any prosthetic or therapeutic program. Most professionals are willing to assign positive value to social interaction. This point of view is accepted, with the limitation that large-scale social behavior and total privacy be thought of as end points on a continuum. The ideal situation would be one where several options are available, and where both the patient and the therapeutic personnel have some input into the choices made by the patient. A description of social design problems in each of the major space types follows.[5]

### Lobbies

A lobby into which a building entrance leads is frequently a densely populated institutional area. The lobby of the Haverford State Hospital buildings designed according to the Osmond sociopetality principle sometimes constitutes an embarrassment to the theory. Three major spaces were designed in the building—private, small social, and large social—and a small lobby connects the building entrance with this tripartite space. Unfortunately, it is frequently the small, incidental lobby that is full of people, rather than the explicitly designated social spaces. Anyone who has ever visited an institution will instantly recognize this tendency to cluster near entrances where traffic is heavy. This "sitting-and-watching syndrome" is very distasteful to many administrators and some go so far as to remove chairs from such areas and forbid "loitering" there. From a psychological point of view, it is clear that watching other people behave may for some impaired patients be their substitute for actual participation. If we can make value judgments that assign higher value to more complex behavior, then we may agree that watching a varying stimulus field is more desirable than watching an unvarying one, such as the blank walls of a bedroom. This attraction to areas of activity may also bring people who are more competent. The simultaneous presence of two or more people being a precondition of social interaction, it seems desirable to capitalize on any means of aggregating individuals. The lobby is, where allowed administratively and structurally, the center of the social life in housing for the elderly. A hesitant recommendation can be made that every institutional building have a lobby through which most building traffic must go, provided with ample seating, both fixed and movable, from which patients can see others come and go. Such an arrangement can make personnel sitting ducks for the aggressive patient who is determined to watch for the hard-to-find doctor or the elusive administrator. This may, however, actually be a good way of being accessible at scheduled times, when coupled with other means of planning for in-office time.

## Halls

Long halls have been a tradition forever in institutions, though the Kirkbride plan made an attempt to break the monotony with wall offsets. In addition to visual monotony, patients may have a substantial problem of orientation where every doorway looks alike, every floor looks alike, and where there are confusing aspects like mirror-image wings and wraparound hallways. Osmond feels that the ceiling lighting, its reflection on an overpolished floor, and the diminishing perspective at the end of the long hall feed the anxieties of paranoid patients. Sometimes lighting and color value are so poor as to constitute a physical hazard to locomotion. Finally, the sheer length may be an architectural barrier for the disabled person who cannot expend the energy to traverse it, or face the anxiety of the unknown at the other end. Very careful stopwatch-and-tape measure studies have indicated clearly the greater amount of staff transit time involved in hospitals with linear, as opposed to circular, plans. It is therefore dif-

ficult to understand why the long hall continues to dominate institutional construction. The Philadelphia Geriatric Center's original building has long halls and a shortage of satisfactory common space. Therefore, the center of much activity is the hallway, which is probably a positive feature, since there is little other space for either engaging in activity or watching it (Figure 2). But it would be much better from a socially prosthetic point of view to arrange patient rooms around four sides of a rectangle, leaving the center space for (1) traffic, (2) staff space, such as nurses' station, and (3) patient activity, all of which may be watched from rooms or chairs along the periphery. The Center is engaged in planning a building with these features for grossly impaired elderly patients. On the other hand, the long hallway is more tolerable for less-impaired patients, particularly those who are off the ward much of the day. Where a structure is burdened with this design, smaller changes may be made to counteract the corridor's negative qualities. Some of Walter Moleski's students from the Philadelphia College of Art designed hall alteration projects at our Center that included the construction of alcoves, the introduction of light from sources other than the ceiling, and use of furniture for conversational grouping at intervals along the hall.

## Social Areas

The concepts of sociopetal space and behavior watching may be applied to explicit social areas as well as to lobbies or hallways. Every natural traffic pathway is a potential supplier of encounters which can become interactions. Therefore, the social space located at the far end of a hall, or even halfway down the hall, from the entranceway has part of its therapeutic function diluted. Many housing sites for older people have the good idea of building a small social space on each floor to encourage intimacy among floor residents. Our experience has been that their location on floors other than the main floor is a disadvantage. Unless some scheduled activity is held there, they are underused. When they are on upper floors and at the end of hallways, they are almost totally wasted space. An ideal use of such space is seen in the Ohio Golden Age Village, where the residents of each floor are

**Figure 2**
**Photo credit: Elias Vassiliades**

served meals in an area in front of the elevators. The area is separated by a half-wall from the main corridor and is available for use the rest of the day. Some housing for the elderly has used the top floor, with a grand view of the surrounding area for social or activity space. The necessity of taking the long elevator trip, and loss of the opportunity to watch people come and go, as on a ground floor, are deterrents to full use. In accordance with the principle of person–environment congruity, however, it must be noted that every environment has its scattering of people who seek out these sparsely populated common spaces; every institutional building should contain at least one such low-use area for these people.

The less competent the individual to be served, the more clustered must all space be to maximize activity participation. However, one can see this principle applied in extreme form in many mental hospital wards so constructed and administered that all patients are taken from their rooms in the morning to a dayroom, where all activities, such as they are, take place. For patients who must spend much of their time in a small area, an attempt should be made to avoid sensory deprivation by varying the area as much as possible. Separate dining areas should be built, perhaps adjoining the dayroom, but clearly separate from it, and with distinctive furnishings. Either the dayroom or the dining room would thus be usable for recreation as well, preferably with furniture and physical props that are portable and which would clearly denote "activity time."

## OUTDOOR SPACES

Many of the observations regarding indoor social space apply to outdoor space (Figure 3). Visitors arriving at an institution may feel uncomfortable when observed by patients sitting outdoors; however, they can tolerate such scrutiny, and it provides excellent entertainment for the curious. The same phenomenon may well be a source of tension for patients who feel very sensitive about being observed. Housing tenants frequently complain that they must run the gantlet of nosy and gossipy residents who keep close tabs of one's coming and going. Within the limits of security, such people might be allowed to use a noncentral entrance.

Some sites have the option of orienting buildings

or outdoor spaces toward local resources that may have some interest or aesthetic value. A busy street, a children's playyard (very carefully screened against physical entry), or even a factory may have some sitting-and-watching value. Outdoor seats are relatively cheap—though they could certainly use some design improvements—and the chance should be provided.

Outdoor security is a major concern of patients or tenants in any urban institution. In addition to obvious measures such as locked doors and security guards, structural security may be increased by placing outdoor sitting or activity areas within view of major traffic. A corner formed by building shape is desirable, since there is a certain amount of security inherent in the curiosity of people looking out of their windows (Figure 4). If staff space is located so that they look out on outdoor areas from where they sit in their offices, a

considerable gain is achieved. The best within-building security is obtained by forcing all visitors to enter through a lobby monitored by staff and tenants.

## INSTRUMENTAL ACTIVITY SPACE

Reference has been made to the importance of private territory in facilitating some self-maintenance behaviors. Some instrumental activities may be performed, or must be performed, in other areas. Skills such as cooking, laundry, and sewing need to be exercised to be maintained. The architect can do much to make it possible to engage in these activities by building in spaces for these activities. It is particularly desirable to locate them so that they open into patient areas, rather than staff areas. Otherwise there is a very real danger that the staff may annex them or over-control their use.

**Figure 3**
**One form of outdoor seating allows people to observe each other and people using natural pathways, but does not forcibly orient them to each other at closer distances.**

**Figure 4**
**Good outdoor security in a high-crime area. The seating nestles in the building's L shape, surveillance occurs from staff offices, no neighborhood pathways run through the area and a low fence separates it from a sidewalk (not shown).**

Instrumental tasks for men are more difficult to maintain. Shops are likely to be underutilized, though very useful for those who have both the skill and the interest. However, when designing purely service and maintenance areas, the architect might always bear in mind the possibility that a patient might find a work assignment there. Thus, additional safety measures befitting patient status might provide meaningful time use for an occasional patient.

The sheltered workshop appears to be a very useful way of providing training, meaningful time use, and spending money for many patients. These spaces are frequently best designed, and remodeled where necessary, to suit the specific tasks that are performed there. The work performed may be either solitary or cooperative, and the work spaces must be designed accordingly. Individual work is best performed in clearly marked, individual space; sometimes there may even be dividers shielding the view of one person's work from his neighbor. On the other hand, the workshop situation may be used to enhance social functioning. In these instances, tasks must be found where one operation depends on a prior operation by another, or where two people are required to perform a task. In these cases, ample space for all people involved is needed, and thought given to how they are oriented to each other: face-to-face, side-by-side, at right angles, and so on.

## STAFF SPACE

The evidence seems to be clear that there is more staff–patient interaction when the nurses' station is open rather than closed, and located centrally rather than peripherally. Whatever the original reason for the locked-door, glass-enclosed station, maximum permeability of nursing station–patient area boundaries seems indicated today. Contact is also increased by locating staff offices in corridors opening onto patient space. A favorite ploy to decrease the proportion of time a mental health professional spends with the patient is for him to have two offices: a pleasant office near his colleagues but distant from the patient area, and a less pleasant office on or near the ward.

Naturally, staff must have ways of shutting off contact with patients or other staff. However, this should be controlled administratively, for the most part. In the case of the nurses' station, the exposed part of the station should have built into it many spaces for the most time-consuming activities—desk space, chart space, and so on. However, human needs also demand some time offstage—back regions such as a medication preparation area, toilet, and lounge may open off the exposed station.

## ENVIRONMENTS FOR SPECIFIC DISABILITIES

For the most part, prosthetic functions have been discussed under appropriate topics above. However, brief comments about special problems may be useful.

### Disorientation

A frequent symptom among brain-damaged older people is the inability to locate themselves in time, space, or with reference to other people. Special attention might be paid to throwing into relief differences among segments of buildings. Each patient's room could be painted in different colors, nonrepeating patterns could be built into floors, ceilings, or wall decorations, distinctive graphics could be used to designate staff offices, elevators, toilets, dining rooms, and so on. Clocks and calendars should be large and unequivocal, and special care should be taken to denote the days of the week, special holidays, and seasons of the year. Multiple sensory channels could be used—auditory time signals, or announcements about locations, in addition to visual stimuli, for instance. Orientation to self is aided by mirrors, personal belongings, frequency of naming, and other techniques.

### Sensory and Other Deficits

In populations likely to have impaired hearing or vision, it is easy to think of ways to amplify appropriate stimuli. On the other hand, intellectual deficits are more difficult to deal with, though a general rule would be to minimize the complexity of the stimulus and the fineness of discriminations to be made before knowing how to behave. There may well be a point where the provision of environmental prosthetics produces such a complex stimulus field as to confuse any of us.

## Designing for the Adolescent

Segregation from older adults seems to be the first rule, and there are many who feel that the teenager should not be housed with young or middle-aged adults for institutional treatment. The institutionalized adolescent not only has major problems, but he frequently has poor impulse control and can be physically and mentally harmful to others. At best, exuberance, and at worst, destructiveness may tax the best of facilities. There really must be special construction to discourage access to utility lines, broken glass, and so on. Both private and shared living space should be provided, since there are always some who need each type. There has been a tendency to assume that the adolescent does best when housed in a dormitory sleeping a large number of people. In units observed this has uniformly worked badly, from the point of view of such diverse considerations as mass destructiveness, preservation of dignity, or obtaining enough sleep.

These are only a few examples of designing with disabilities in mind. In review one becomes doubly aware of how scant the hard evidence is. It is hoped, however, that the many assertions and armchair arguments may lead some who have the chance to observe structures in use to check them out empirically.

## NOTES AND REFERENCES

1. B. T. Turner, S. S. Tobin, and M. A. Lieberman, "Personality traits as predictors of institutional adaptation among the aged," *Journal of Gerontology,* 1971.
2. M. H. Kleban, E. M. Brody, and M. P. Lawton, "Personality traits in the mentally impaired aged and their relationship to improvements in current functioning," *The Gerontologist,* Vol. 11 (1971), 134–140.
3. Constance Perin, *With Man in Mind,* Cambridge, Mass.: The MIT Press, 1970.
4. M. P. Lawton, "Ecology and aging," in Leon A. Pastalan and Daniel H. Carson, eds., *Spatial Behavior of Older People,* Ann Arbor, Mich.: Institute of Gerontology, University of Michigan, 1970.
5. O. R. Lindsley, "Geriatric behavioral prosthetics," in R. Kastenbaum, ed., *New Thoughts in Old Age,* New York: Springer, 1964.
6. Robert Sommer, *Personal Space: The Behavioral Basis of Design,* Englewood Cliffs, N.J.: Prentice-Hall, 1969.
7. William H. Ittelson, Harold M. Proshansky, and Leanne G. Rivlin, "Bedroom size and social interaction in the psychic ward," *Environment and Behavior,* Vol. 2 (December 1970), 255–270.
8. Humphry Osmond, "Function as the basis of psychiatric ward design," *Mental Hospitals,* Vol. 8 (April 1957), 23–29.

72

*The relationship of environmental psychology and the design professions is clarified, first, by a brief overview of environmental psychology—introducing issues, methods, and concepts of the field; second, by the specific consideration of some basic misconceptions regarding its nature and scope and its relationship to the design professions; and, third, by the presentation of ways in which environmental psychology can make significant and important contributions to those who face the formidable task of designing man's physical world. The important contributions which design professionals could make in return through the explication of their behavioral knowledge is recognized. Caution is voiced regarding the measurement methods, reliability, and transferability of behavioral information. Finally, it is suggested that some architects should engage in research in collaboration with behavioral scientists, particularly if architects are to become cognizant of the unintended consequences of the buildings they design.*

# Environmental Psychology and the Design Professions

**Harold M. Proshansky**

**City University of New York**

The title of this paper is quite benign. Don't be misled by it. I have more in mind than the seemingly simple task of describing the role of environmental psychology for the design professions. Perhaps the title should have been longer: "The Role of Environmental Psychology for the Design Professions: Setting the Record Straight." Or perhaps the shorter title of "Facts and Fancies About Environmental Psychology." In any event my intention is to expose—and thereby substitute fact for fiction—the exaggerations, misconceptions, and indeed, in some instances, sheer nonsense about the new emerging field of environmental psychology, particularly in its relationships to the design professions.

To do this I have divided my task into three parts. First, I will attempt to give you my capsule version of environmental psychology. Clearly one must have some blueprint of the nature and scope of this field before it is possible to discuss facts versus fancies. Following this brief overview of the field, I will then consider specifically some of the more basic misconceptions attributed to the nature and scope of environmental psychology in its relationships with the design professions. Finally, I will suggest a number of ways in which environmental psychology can make significant and important contributions to those who face the formidable tasks of designing and redesigning man's physical world—the architect, city planner, interior designer, landscape architect, and so on. This will have provided "an overview aimed at providing the practicing architect with a frame of reference for understanding the field and using the information emerging within it."

One caution before this overview begins. It is just as possible and indeed it is a fundamental requirement, that architects and other design professionals present to environmental psychologists a frame of reference for understanding what they do, what conceptions and methods they employ, and what they need and expect from environmental psychologists. The success of environmental psychology as a newly emerging field of behavioral science will depend to a large measure on a mutual or two-way relationship between it and the design profession. I will have more to say on this later.

Environmental psychology is concerned with people,

**Photo credit: Laurence Fink**

design, content, organization, and meaning. More specifically, environmental psychology asks questions about rooms, buildings, neighborhoods, hospitals and hospital wards, houses, apartments, museums, schools, automobiles, aeroplanes, theaters, beds, chairs, urban settings, vacation areas, natural forests, and other settings of varying scope.

## Behavior in Psychiatric Settings

Having defined the field and operationalized it by listing a variety of settings that are the focus of its concern, let us turn to a description of some specific investigations carried out in conjunction with the Ph.D. Program in Environmental Psychology at The City University of New York. A major study recently completed concerns the influence of ward design on patient and staff behavior in psychiatric settings. Such questions as how patients and staff use the space in psychiatric wards, and whether there is regularity over extended periods of time in their use of this space have been asked and investigated.[1] The method employed is *behavioral mapping:* it establishes by means of systematic and sustained observations what people in the ward are doing, where they are doing it, for how long, and with whom, if anybody.[2] Wards varying in organization and design have also been compared, and in fact the nature and organization of one room in a ward was changed to determine its impact on the previously established spatial utilization pattern of this ward.[3] Did the difference make a difference? It did. Refurnishing and reorganizing a poorly furnished and underused solarium not only increased activity in the solarium, but changed the extent and nature of activities in other parts of the ward. We observed what we now refer to as the "conservation of behavior." Whereas the change in the solarium caused a corner of the main corridor used for isolated standing by various patients at different times to be less available for this purpose because of increased traffic, the "standing area" appeared in another part of the ward following the change.

Make no mistake; at this stage in the development of a program of research in environmental psychology, highest priority is given to research strategies that leave the events and settings intact, rather than to those that

places, and the behavior and experiences of these people in relation to these places. Stated more formally, it raises theoretical questions about and undertakes empirical research into the relationships between the physical environment and human behavior and experience. At this point one should be made acutely aware of what is meant by the "physical environment." It does not mean the physical stimuli of traditional psychology, that is, light, sound, temperature, and so on, nor even the integration of these basic physical stimuli with others such as shape, color, and density into specific physical objects. The "physical environment" means the *complexity* that constitutes any physical setting in which men live, interact, and engage in activities for either brief or extended periods of time. And if we consider which physical settings have been given the highest theoretical and research priorities because of the nature of modern industrial societies, then it must be evident that at the center of the environmental psychologist's concern with the physical environment is the *built environment:* its evolve highly sophisticated and indeed complex methodologies in search of the "right problem." On the other hand we by no means reject the laboratory approach if it permits us to view physical environmental "happenings" close up, without distorting them to any degree, as a means of evolving hypotheses or developing ideas about what is important in these real-life settings for human behavior. Let me illustrate this by describing a laboratory-designed "novel-environment" room—a dark room with a series of mirrors with electronically controlled surface contours, strobe lights, and pulsating sounds associated with each mirror. The mirrors, lights, and sounds can be sequenced and coordinated in a variety of patterns by the experimenter. To some degree the room permits us to duplicate the continuing "novelty" of sights and sounds experienced by the inner city resident or shopper. Given this room we have investigated how people behave in and describe novel environments, and the relationships between these behaviors and descriptions and the social interaction conditions under which they experience the room, that is, alone or in a group.[4]

Research in other psychiatric settings such as a children's psychiatric hospital is also being done. This research is quite rare. Thanks to fortuitous timing, Leanne Rivlin and Maxine Wolfe[5] had the opportunity to study the *evolution* of space utilization patterns in hospitals, particularly in terms of the *intended* versus the *actual* use of the new facility. Beginning with a set of predictions about the ultimate use of the space based on the architect's intentions in designing it, and the hospital director's conception of how it could be used therapeutically, the children were observed from the *first* day of occupancy through the next two weeks, all during the day for the fourteen days. We then returned for a full week's observation, first, two months after the opening of the facility, and then after a six-month period. Thus we were able to trace the "spatial life history" of the hospital during the first year of occupancy.

## Space Utilization Patterns

Given the special purpose of this paper and space limitations, it is not my intention to go into the findings of our investigations. But having said this much about the Rivlin and Wolfe study, I ought to at least answer the question of whether specific space utilization patterns evolved. Quite clearly they did. In this particular instance, within two months the house (or living area) changed from its active use as an area for social interaction to one for withdrawal with a decline in its social function, even though it was clearly designed for a variety of both private and small group activities. At the root of such changes are the reciprocal interrelationships involving the design of the building or its particular areas, its intended therapeutic program, and the one which actually evolves. Other studies of this psychiatric facility are in process with attention being given to such questions as the effects of age differences on the use of space and the relationships among such factors as pathology, group size, and space utilization.

Now let us consider two quite different physical settings in which systematic research is being done. Urban transportation has become a major human problem in the 1970's, not just in terms of speed, safety, and efficiency, but also from the viewpoint of people's other needs, for example privacy and comfort. There is not one but two crises confronting modern man in his urban setting: a crisis in human dignity as well as in human life. With new subway lines being built in New York City, for example, research has investigated how subway riders use the stations and what they expect, are satisfied with, and are dissatisfied with in their experience with this means of travel.[7] The second setting I want to draw your attention to is the school, and more particularly the open school or open classroom, that is, the school without fixed classrooms. During the last decade such schools have sprung up in many places in the United States on the assumption that the "learning situation" under these conditions will facilitate the educational process, because it will be more responsive to the individual needs, talents, and proclivities of each pupil. Our research in this setting is just getting underway.

## Housing and Human Behavior

By way of completing this description of the kind of research that is going on in environmental psychology, it is important that the significance of the "house and home" is pointed out. A major aspect of the urban dilemma is the question of what kind of housing for what kind of people for what kind of purposes.

Much has been written about neighborhood settings, high-rise housing projects, segregated versus mixed income housing, the physical and social dimensions of the urban slum, community planning and satisfaction, site planning for urban redevelopment programs, and any number of other housing related issues. Far, far less research has been done about user needs, expectations, and experiences with respect to new housing, particularly in attempts to change the face of the inner city by systematic relocation of low- and middle-income groups. And almost no research has been reported on how families use space in the setting of their own home, and what consequences it has for day-to-day relationships and interactions with each other.

As part of the research program at the City University of New York, the attitudes and expectations of low- and middle-income groups being relocated as part of an urban redevelopment program in a city outside of New York City are being studied. The efforts with respect to systematic research into housing and human behavior are being greatly increased, particularly with respect to the general question of what constitutes community satisfaction for homeowners or apartment dwellers in urban and suburban settings.

To give some flavor of what previous research has produced in the area of housing and human behavior, it would be worthwhile citing some of the 24 generalizations listed by William Michelson in his review of research with respect to this problem.[7] These generalizations are tentative, but they do rest to a larger or smaller degree on systematic data. Space permits the mention of only a small number here, seriatim without further discussion:

1. People with "cosmopolitan" life styles desire more physical separation from neighbors and place less emphasis on proximity to facilities and services than do people whose interests are "local."
2. Direct access to the outside maximizes control in child raising under conventional parent–child relationships.
3. Self-contained housing units minimize parent fostering of children's inhibitions.
4. Adults, before and after raising children (as well as those who are childless) frequently rate centrality (i.e., access to consumer goals and services) more highly than people with growing chidren.

5. The percentage of income that people will spend on good quality housing varies primarily according to education.
6. High neighborhood densities seem more related to social pathologics than crowding within dwelling units, but its effect is mediated by personal and cultural factors.
7. Completely random placement of working-class residents among middle-class neighbors results in an isolation of the former rather than in any intended, positive result.

An overview of the field of environmental psychology would not be complete without some reference to its organizing theoretical concepts. It would be ideal if an elaborate theoretical structure for understanding human behavior and experience in relation to physical settings existed but it does not. What theory exists is fragmentary, and not always useful in terms of deriving testable hypotheses. This is to be expected, and not only because environmental psychology is such a relatively new field of inquiry. Psychologists, sociologists, and other behavioral scientists are only now beginning to ask what the implications are for the nature and design of physical settings of the many theoretical conceptions they have evolved to explain human behavior and experience in relation to psychological, social, and cultural variables.

Added to this are two other factors that preclude anything more than an exploratory, inductive empirical approach rather than the use of an encompassing theoretical system even for a given problem area, for example hospital design. First, the behavioral sciences, individually and collectively, leave much to be desired in terms of their present theoretical development, although such development is actually taking place. And second, and perhaps more importantly, is the fact that if given psychological conceptions of human behavior and experience have implications for the design of space, then clearly, the concepts and principles that the design professions use in designing the built environment must have implications for human psychological and social processes. If given physical dimensions such as distance, form, density, complexity, boundary, and others are employed in creating this environment, then apart from other considerations, these too must be examined in terms of their meaning and consequences for the way people act and feel in given physical settings.

## Cognitive Structure

If one considers the various physical settings referred to in the discussion above, then a number of organizing concepts immediately suggest themselves. First, and perhaps most critical, is the concept of "cognitive map," or said more simply, "image of a place." Only in recent years, has it been noted that people develop selective and unique conceptions of the cities in which they live, the schools and hospitals they frequent, the routes they take to work, and so on, and that these in turn influence how they use, move about in, and indeed feel about the space. The more embracing concept of "cognitive structure," which can be defined as the beliefs, values, precepts, and attitudes an individual has about actual and potential physical settings, seems preferable. Clearly, as a function of cultural background, age, sex, social class, occupation, and other factors, cognitive structures relevant to given physical settings will vary, and it is on the basis of such variations that the design professions may derive an improved basis for the environments they create. Privacy, of course, is an important conception in the thinking of environmental psychologists. Oddly enough, while it is a human need with many dimensions, it has received almost no attention from behavioral scientists. And all this notwithstanding the fact that in the setting of the home, school, business office, the hospital, and other institutional settings the need for privacy looms as a paramount factor in the relationships among individuals.

## Territoriality

The concept of "freedom of choice" has also been evoked at the City University of New York as a basis for understanding the influence of physical settings on human behavior—both in terms of overt action and inner process.[9] Patently, any setting must have the facilities and be designed to permit certain activities to go on and thereby allow the individual not only to make his choice but realize it. The fact, for example, that a faculty member has his own room at home in which he can be alone if he so desires is of no help if other individuals are freely permitted to move in and

out of this room. As Alexander Kira points out, only the bathroom has a lock on it in most American homes, thereby allowing children and parents to guarantee that at least there they can actually maintain visual and, to a degree, auditory privacy.[10] It is also important to remember that a crowded dayroom, ward, or apartment also reduces each individual's freedom of choice not only with respect to privacy, but with respect to where he can sit, engage in particular activities, or even just watch TV.

Freedom of choice implies that the individual can exert some control over his physical setting, and in this regard we are confronted with the growing concern over *human territoriality*. Individuals not only lay claim to "privacy" for themselves as corporeal objects, but for the things they own, the spaces they occupy, and their so-called "personal effects." The personal pronoun "my" in the sense of "my room," "my desk," "my chair at the table," "my neighborhood," "my sheet," "my file," "my papers," and so on, implies more than legal or normative ownership. These objects, spaces, and places are extensions of the individual's self—they may be elements of his self-identity—and in this sense he and only he can determine who besides himself—if anyone at all—will use them, change them, or even view them. It is in this sense that I have recently written about "place-identity," that aspect of the person's self-identity represented by actual and desired physical settings that help to establish who he is and what he is.

It should be evident that territoriality is as much a group concept as it is an individual concept. Group function and process is facilitated, indeed can only be effective over time, if group members can satisfy their desires for "a place" both *for the group* and for themselves as individuals. To the extent that a group expects, wants, and needs a particular physical setting for their own, to this degree will the effectiveness of group function and process depend on the satisfaction of its territorial aspirations. The street corner of the delinquent gang, the clubhouse of a teenage girls' club, and the corner of the dayroom of the somewhat healthier psychiatric patients, reflect the desire for territoriality in human groups. But within such groups—and in those that endure over a longer period of time, for example the family, the individual's own need for controlling his "piece" of the environment is no less important. Group functions and process depend on it in the sense that given group members must reign over certain physical areas if group tasks and functions are to be realized. Leadership is indeed expressed by putting the leader at the head of the table; and putting the secretary at his side subtly expresses the meaning and nature of this role. That mothers and wives have final authority over the kitchen—at least in some homes—expresses this same principle.

This completes an overview of the field of environmental psychology. Of course this has only been a rough pencil sketch, but with enough detail so that one should have a reasonably clear picture of it—clear enough so that you can relate it to your own concerns about the role of human psychological and social process in designing physical settings. If this has not occurred, then perhaps the remainder of this discussion will provide the additional clarification needed. Let us turn now immediately to some misconceptions and distortions about the role of environmental psychology in relation to the design professions. Here then—to put it simply—is what the field is *not* nor can ever be in this respect.

## MISCONCEPTIONS AND DISTORTIONS

The primary value of environmental psychology for the design professions *does not lie* in its capacity to measure human behavior, attitudes, values, and desires. Some architects and indeed some environmental psychologists view the field solely as a kind of specialized market research approach for finding out what people want, expect, or are willing to settle for by way of a house, a new park, the design of a classroom, and so on. Following the usual query: "What are the users' needs?" or "How much privacy do you think they want?" comes the request of us that if we don't know, could we measure these behaviors and find out.

Clearly environmental psychologists do in fact carry out such survey research, but this indeed is a minor aspect of the role of environmental psychology for the design professions. As a matter of fact any psychologist or sociologist trained in survey research can carry out this function. The fundamental significance of environmental psychology for the design professions lies in its potential capacity to provide a body of knowledge —conceptual and empirical—for understanding the relationships between human behavior and experience and the built environment.

Obviously it is undesirable to "throw out the baby with the bath water." Environmental psychologists are quite skilled in measuring the behavior attitudes, interests, values, and perceptions of individuals in relation to physical settings, and indeed this is an important aspect of their research and perhaps even of their contributions to the design professions. But here, too, there tends to be a misconception on the part of some design profession people, and perhaps even of some environmental psychologists.

There is a tendency to attribute more than can be delivered by such measurement. Quantification is an important aspect of the behavioral sciences, but not to the extent achieved by the physical sciences, particularly when what is being measured are what people want, think, feel, and believe. True, design people depend to a large degree on intuition and "feel," but the demand from environmental psychology for precise answers with respect to specific behavioral questions can only be approximated rather than achieved. The instruments we derive are of limited validity and reliability, and, as such, repeated measurement with a variety of measurement techniques is what we need to increase the certainty of our predictions.

Let us consider where the real problem lies in the measurement of the individual's perceptions, attitudes, needs, and values about given physical settings. Hopefully, the design professions will not find this out the hard way, the way many social psychologists did in the 1940's and 1950's. What they found out was that, because one can easily measure via questionnaire and other measurement techniques the social, economic, political, or religious attitudes of groups of individuals, doesn't necessarily mean that these individuals hold such attitudes, and if they do that they are significant in influencing how they perceive, think, or behave in given situations. In other words, people very easily answer questionnaires or interviewers in terms which are immediate to the situation and helpful to the interviewer. More than a few environmental psychologists have learned through their research that unlike specific social attitudes, the attitudes, feelings, perceptions, and even values people have about physical settings can be vague, sometimes nonexistent, and quite often reflective of immediate events. Even when clear they may compete with other values, attitudes, and perceptions, and indeed can change with critical changes on the social scene.

One cannot simply rush into measurement regardless of the quality of the instruments. The measurement of behavior or attitudes or values must occur as part of a larger research context in which one first determines who the respondents are, how relevant the physical setting is for them, what other factors, for example, group pressures, may be related to their responses to questions about this setting, and perhaps most important, how aware they are of what is happening relevant to an existing or changing physical setting. Let us consider this in another way. What people "want" is not always what they may need from an objective point of view. But even assuming that what they want is what they need, this would only be true if their knowledge and experience about housing, for example, or any physical setting were adequate.

The third misconception of what environmental psychology can do for the design professions is perhaps the most important. If the focus of architect's concern and that of the environmental psychologist is the influence of the physical environment on behavior and experience, then it is very important that one realize from the beginning that this influence is limited. A principle can be stated: the more complex the behavior or experience that is the focus of our concern, the more likely that there will be a variety of factors influencing it, physical, social, psychological, and so on, and the less likely the physical environment will be a major factor in this respect. Thus it is one thing to ask how the design of a home may increase or decrease interaction between husband or wife, and quite another to suggest that you may want this design to limit the number of arguments they have, or for it to ensure that they will always be in love.

The term used in the behavioral sciences in considering the relative influence of a set of causal factors on behavior is *variance*. To attribute too much variance to the physical environment as opposed to social, cultural, historical, and psychological variables is to ignore the complexity of human behavior on the one hand

and the total environment on the other. How much of the variance is attributable to physical space and its design is an empirical question that only systematic research can answer. Whether it is little or great is beside the point. A full understanding of human behavior on the part of the behavioral scientist requires the study of man's physical environment—and whether or not the design professions make demands on us. Indeed psychologists would still make demands on architects in order to achieve such understanding through systematic research.

## ENVIRONMENTAL PSYCHOLOGY TODAY

Now let us turn to a positive definition of the role of environmental psychology in relation to the tasks of the architect, city planner, or designer. In defining this role here, there should be little possibility of misinterpretation in the light of the above remarks about the nature of environmental psychology.

Beginning with the obvious, the field of environmental psychology is new and clearly at a rudimentary level of development. However, there are available some findings and more importantly, space-related theoretical conceptions and orientations that can be useful to the design professions. For the designer, architect, or city planner who finds himself increasingly confronted with physical-setting questions about what people want, how they will react, and what they expect, such existing data and theory—little as it may be—can serve as a backdrop against which he can at least make educated guesses in the attempt to resolve design problems or make design decisions. Make no mistake, I am not suggesting a "behavioral handbook" for the design professional to refer to when he is seeking specific questions for a given setting. I am suggesting that he at least consult the existing literature and talk to environmental psychologists as a basis of meeting his own concerns about the "human element." As has already been suggested, this will at least give the designer some reasonable basis—if not a sound empirical one—for his design decisions.

For the members of the design professions who are concerned with human behavior as a factor in the design of physical settings, the next specification of the role of environmental psychology for these professions is probably not necessary. But this specification is critical for the many, many more members of these professions who are not so concerned. A broad, general, but crucial function that environmental psychology can and should have for the design professional is to make him aware of the implicit assumptions he makes about human behavior and experience when he does in fact create physical settings for particular purposes. In effect—like it or not—all design professionals to some degree are behavior oriented, at least on an implicit level, when they design a given space. The assumptions they make are by no means trivial. They involve conceptions of what persons need, want, and are able to cope with as far as the nature of a given physical setting is concerned. There is nothing wrong with making assumptions. There is, however, a great deal wrong if these assumptions remain implicit and therefore also remain unexamined and unquestioned if not untested. In part, this failure of the design professions to consider the many implicit assumptions they make about human behavior and experience is understandable. The task of being a design professional is difficult enough with all of the forces that operate on the practicing architect —the client and what he wants, economic considerations, legal questions, political and other governmental restraints, and so on. On the other hand, with an ever-increasing population living in urban settings amidst an incredibly expanding technology, the design profession as a whole has no choice but to come to grips with human behavior and its underlying needs and values in relation to physical settings.

Perhaps what is needed is the model characteristic of such other professions as medicine and engineering. Most architects should practice, but some others should quite definitely engage in research in collaboration with behavioral scientists. Increasingly, people in the design professions—as in the case of the use of new disease-fighting drugs by the medical profession—must worry about the unintended as well as the intended consequences of the built environments they design.

This brings me to a fundamental issue. The design professions can only begin to consider the implicit assumptions they make about people as reflected in the spaces and places they create or design for them if it is realized that an inherent part of their task is to evaluate their design efforts. Unless in selected

instances architects are willing to return to the physical setting after it has been designed and is operating, then indeed nobody will ever know whether the assumptions that are made about people's behavior in relation to space—explicit or implicit—have any validity. It is difficult to find more than a few instances of such evaluation. Clearly this is a task which is a "natural" for the collaboration of the design professions and environmental psychology.

Let us now turn to the fourth and final dimension of the role that I think environmental psychology can play in relation to the design professions. Actually it is a role dimension which can only be realized if one recognizes and accepts what was stated much earlier in my paper: that the street that connects environmental psychology and the design professions must be a two-way street. This is necessary if for no other purpose than evolving from the environmental psychologist's point of view a theory and body of knowledge of space-related behavior. Such a theory must depend on what architects can tell environmental psychologists about the various principles, concepts, and assumptions they use in the design process itself. It may well be that your guiding conceptions may have significant implications for what is important behaviorally in people with respect to how they view, use, and modify physical settings.

But it is necessary to go further, and it is at this point that I would emphasize the final role dimension of the environmental psychologist. It is my contention that most architects, designers, and planners have a wealth of "unrefined" data and ideas about people in relation to physical space and its organization which has yet to be tapped in any systematic fashion. It is the fact that most architects are continually involved in the design process in relation to a variety of "clients" who are either private individuals, institutional leaders, or government administrators, which are the sources of these "unrefined data." To the extent that environmental psychologists can elicit from architects this array of experiences, and use them as a basis for formulating hypotheses and testing them, to this extent will each group make contributions to each other. As a researcher interested in the development of a behavioral theory about given physical settings, I want all of your significant experiences, the pet ideas you arrived at out of these experiences, and indeed the hunches you have about what people want or don't want, believe or don't believe, accept or don't accept with respect to the nature and use of their physical setting.

If it is true that each of us carries around an implicit theory of human personality or behavior based on continuing experiences, and which we use to gauge and evaluate people when we first meet, it is probably no less true that architects, designers, and planners have built into this theory something about people in relation to places and spaces. The value of having these "theories" out in the open is not merely as a source of hypotheses for the environmental psychologist, but this process of "exposure" would in all probability reveal the implicit assumptions about people and their behavior that underlie the architect or designer's approach to designing space.

Perhaps the title of this paper should have been: "The Roles of Environmental Psychology and the Design Professions for Each Other."

## NOTES AND REFERENCES

1.  William H. Ittelson, Harold M. Proshansky, and Leanne G. Rivlin, "The environmental psychology of the psychiatric ward," in Proshansky, Ittelson, and Rivlin, eds., *Environmental Psychology: Man and His Physical Setting,* New York: Holt, 1970.

2.  William H. Ittelson, Leanne G. Rivlin, and Harold M. Proshansky, "The use of behavioral maps in environmental psychology," in Proshansky, Ittelson, and Rivlin, *op. cit.*

3.  Leanne G. Rivlin, Harold M. Proshansky, and William H. Ittelson, "Changes in psychiatric ward design and patient behavior: an experimental study," *Transactions of the Bartlett Society* (1972–72).

4.  Lucille Nahemow, "Research in a novel environment," *Environment and Behavior,* Vol. 3, (March 1971), 81-102.

5.  Leanne G. Rivlin and Maxine Wolfe, "The early history of psychiatric hospital for children: expectations and reality," *Environment and Behavior,* Vol. 4, No. 1 (1972), 33-72.

6.  Gary H. Winkel and D. Geoffrey Hayward, *Some Major Causes of Congestion in Subway Stations,* Report to Transit/Land Use Working Committee, Environmental Psychology Program, City University of New York, May, 1971.

7.  William Michelson, *Man and His Urban Environment: A Sociological Approach,* Reading, Mass.: Addison-Wesley, 1970.

8.  Ittelson, Proshansky, and Rivlin, *op. cit.*

9.  Harold M. Proshansky, William H. Ittelson, and Leanne G. Rivlin, "Freedom of choice and behavior in a physical setting," in Proshansky, Ittelson, and Rivlin, *op. cit.*

10. Alexander Kira, *The Bathroom: Criteria for Design,* Ithaca, N.Y.: Center for Housing and Environmental Studies, Cornell University, 1966.

# PART TWO
# FUNDAMENTAL
# PROCESSES OF
# ENVIRONMENTAL
# BEHAVIOR

Photo credit: Ron Partridge

# FUNDAMENTAL PROCESSES OF ENVIRONMENTAL BEHAVIOR

If there is to be any collaboration between behavioral scientists and architects in coming to an understanding of the effect of the designed environment on human behavior, then there must be some common understanding of the meaning of the term "environment" and some agreement as to the nature of the psychological processes involved in the man-environment interaction. Although these concepts are being continuously refined, it is possible to outline our current understanding of them here.

The key attribute in any definition of "environment" is that "environments surround."[1] It is important to consider that man is both the center of *his* environment and an integral part of *the* environment; therefore, an individual affects and is affected by his environment. W. Ross Ashby wrote: "Given an organism, its environment is defined as those variables whose change affects the organism and those variables which are changed by the organism's behavior."[2] Thus the environment cannot be considered as merely a container for human activity, but also as an integral part of a pattern of behavior.

## PSYCHOLOGICAL PROCESSES

Psychological processes play a functional role in enabling man to adjust to or achieve mastery over his environment. Three processes—perception, cognition, and spatial behavior—are particularly important in understanding man's behavior in the environment. *Perception* is the process of obtaining or receiving input, *cognition* is the throughput function involving the processes of thinking, remembering, and feeling, and *spatial behavior* denotes the output manifested in an organism's actions and responses. Other processes—motivation, affect, and development—modify the way in which we perceive, think about, and behave in the environment.

Behavioral patterns are established through the unity of motives, percepts, and actions.[3] Behavior can be considered to be a goal-directed attempt by an organism to satisfy needs that are perceived and cognitively organized. The purposiveness of behavior has long been accepted by most psychologists as its significant determinant, affecting not only a person's activities but also his perceptions and mental processes. A person will select whatever information is appropriate to his needs and will remain relatively unaware of irrelevant features of the external world.[4] He will then organize this information to achieve his goals. If an environment does not offer the potentials for achieving his goals, a person can reorganize it, he can move to a new environment, or he can learn new behavioral responses. Similarly, when an individual is faced with a new situation in which his established behavioral responses are inadequate, he may exercise the same options. Man's cognitive abilities to learn and give meaning to environmental experiences allow him greater control in fulfilling needs.[5]

## Motivation

Since behavior is directed toward satisfying needs, the motivational aspects of behavior must be understood as a fundamental concept in designing for human behavior. Motivation, like so many other complex variables, has many definitions. In essence, it is the process of arousing action, sustaining activity in progress, and regulating the pattern of that activity.[6]

A *need* has been described as a force in the mind that organizes perceptions, cognition, and behavior to transform an existing, unsatisfying situation.[7] Needs have their basis in both the physiological, psychological, and sociological aspects of behavior. Hunger, fatigue, and thirst are physiologically based. Needs such as sex, self-preservation, and maternal behavior have a physiological base, but admit individual exceptions. Aggression, self-assertiveness, and flight have a physiological base that comes under strong social and cultural constraints. Other needs, such as those for affiliation, have no physiological component.

A framework by which need satisfaction can be viewed is offered by psychologist Abraham Maslow.[8] He suggests that human needs can be arranged in hierarchical fashion—strongest-level needs taking precedence. His hierarchy, in descending order is as follows: *physiological needs,* such as hunger or thirst; *safety needs,* such as security and protection from physical and psychological harm; *belonging* or *love needs,* which concern the relationships of responsive, or affectionate, and authoritative needs; *esteem needs,*

or those needs of an individual to be held in high evaluation by self and others; *actualization needs,* representing the desire to fulfill one's total capacities; and *cognitive and aesthetic needs,* such as the thirst for knowledge or the desire for beauty. While this classification is a very simplified model from which individuals may vary enormously, it does provide a basis for thinking about the needs which buildings fulfill.

Much recent architecture has been more successful in meeting physiological needs than it has social and psychological needs. Social and psychological needs involve symbolization and imagery and can only be satisfied if the designer understands the mental processes that give rise to them.

## The Behavioral System

In addition to purposiveness of behavior, there are other characteristics of an individual which influence the processes of perception, cognition, and spatial behavior. Everybody is a participant in an ongoing *behavioral system,* defined by the individual's physiological capabilities, his personality, the social group of which he is a member, his values, and his environment. Following Talcott Parsons,[9] these are labeled "organism," "personality," "social group," "culture," and "environment," respectively, in Figure 1.

The organismal component of the behavior system is important because the physiological abilities of an individual affect not only the way he perceives the environment but also how he thinks about it, and how he can use it. This is particularly true if there is any loss of sensory abilities. The designer must recognize that different levels of skill and intelligence, mental and physical capacities, require different environmental layouts and different presentations of environmental information.

An individual's personality is what makes him psychologically unique and colors the way he looks at the world, the way he thinks about it, and the way he behaves in it. Carl Jung introduced a twofold classification that has become part of our everyday language: extrovert and introvert. The *extrovert* lives according to external necessities and the *introvert* stresses his own subjective values. In defining whether a person (or a group) is an extrovert or an introvert, one has

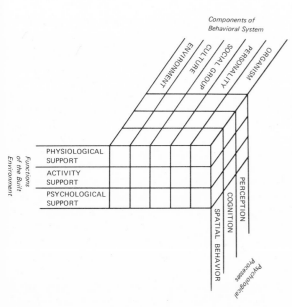

Components of
Behavioral System

ENVIRONMENT
CULTURE
SOCIAL GROUP
PERSONALITY
ORGANISM

*Functions
of the Built
Environment*

PHYSIOLOGICAL
SUPPORT

ACTIVITY
SUPPORT

PSYCHOLOGICAL
SUPPORT

PERCEPTION
COGNITION
SPATIAL BEHAVIOR

*Psychological
Processes*

**Figure 1**
**Architectural view of the fundamental concerns of
environmental psychology**

to consider two dimensions—(1) the manner in which
a person reacts to the environment, and (2) the manner
in which he acts on it. A surprisingly small proportion
of the population is either introvert or extrovert in both
dimensions.[10] Thus in defining architectural goals, one
faces a dilemma because people select environments
in terms of the image of themselves that they wish
to portray rather than for what they are. Carl Jung refers
to this as the *persona,* which shapes the face we show
to the world and serves as a protection of the inner
man.

The social group component of behavior in Parson's
scheme refers to those processes that bind individuals
into groups and those interactions which take place
among the members of groups. An individual is a
member of many groups, the nature of which depends
on his interests and stage in the life cycle. The groups
influence not only his actions but also the way he perceives the world and what he thinks about it. His status
and perception of his own role and that of others are
particularly important factors.

The cultural component of behavior denotes those
aspects of behavior that are controlled by the value
orientation of a group of individuals. Culture has been
defined as "the configuration of learned behavior, and
results of behavior whose elements are shared and
transmitted by members of a particular society."[11] Culture influences behavior through the process of
socialization, by which language, traditions, norms,
values, expectations, and sanctions are taught. Cross-
cultural studies have shown the effects of culture on
perception,[12] cognitive representations,[13] and behavioral patterns.[14]

Not only are perceptions, cognitive representations,
and spatial behavior affected by organismal, personality, social group, and cultural factors but by physical-
environmental factors as well. This has been largely
neglected by behavioral scientists. People are products of a physical environment as well as a social
environment.

*Everything man does is associated with the experience of
space. Nothing occurs, real or imagined, without a spatial
context, because space (along with time) is one of the principles organizing systems for living organisms. Proxemics
deals with man's use and structuring of space, particularly
the unconscious patterns that deeply influence life.*[15]

It is interesting to note that architects, in their designs,
often reflect the patterns of the environment in which
they grew up.

## The Function of the Architectural Environment

In *Part One* of this book, it was pointed out that the
architectural environment functions in three ways: it
maintains the physiological states necessary to sustain
behavior; it provides the necessary behavior settings;
and it supports psychological states through the use
of symbols. In each of these functions there is a perceptual, a cognitive, and an action component. Not only
must the environment be perceived as being potentially
capable of supporting the required behavior, but the
user must realize this and know how to use the environment; and, finally, the environment must actually support the required activity.

Figure 1 ties the goals of design, the fundamental
psychological processes related to them, and
behavioral system characteristics of the client group(s)

into a three-dimensional matrix. The matrix provides some order to a complex set of ideas. It also relates the focus of this book—on the processes of perception, cognition, and spatial behavior— to the client inputs and the design outputs which are beyond the scope of this book.

## PERCEPTION

Perception, it was stated above, is the process of obtaining or receiving information from the environment. Any individual attends to certain elements of the environment and not to others. The effective environment depends on the constraints of one's perceptual systems—the nature of the individual as an organism.[16] In addition, what one attends to in the environment depends on one's personality,[17] one's membership in a social group, one's culture,[18] and the environment in which one usually operates.[19] It is clear that while the potential environment is the same for an architect and his clients, the effective environment may be very different.

It is surprising that the psychology of perception has not attracted the attention of architects to a greater degree, and it is surprising that the subject of architecture has aroused so little interest among psychologists. The visual organization of architectural forms, rhythms, proportions, and the use of light and illumination as expressive factors in formal organization have long been the concern of architects. Yet there is no common agreement among architects about these matters, and architectural theories of visual organization remain the province of art historians and students of style. At the same time, a number of architects have indeed turned to the psychology of perception to clarify their thinking on design and architecture. The modifications that theories of perception have undergone during the past thirty years have aided this process.

One of the major modifications has resulted from the challenge that atomistic and structuralist theories of perception have received from Gestalt theory and more recently from the transactionalist school and the theory of information-based perception.[20] A number of factors emerge from current research which should have an impact on our thinking about design—indeed, some architectural philosophers have always thought in these terms.

One of the factors has been the abandonment of the belief in stimulus determination: the assumption that perception is largely or completely determined by the characteristics of external stimulus. We now talk in terms of "stimulus information" to which people can attend, but we must remember that different people must attend to different aspects. The implication for design is that principles of design must recognize these differences. This is essential if architects are to meet their clients' personal needs.

While our basic neural circuitry for making attending adjustments to what there is to be perceived is built in by the time of our birth, our experiences shape what we attend to. Jean Piaget's work suggests that the ability to select, abstract, and organize information grows as a child matures.[21] It is through experience that we learn to identify the variables which provide more and more information about the world. William James gives the example of the improvement in ability to differentiate between different types of wine with practice.[22] This must not be confused with the accrual of associations. It is a process of progressive "differentiation," accompanied by the organization of these differences and relationships in memory. The question for architecture is: Have architects developed a set of principles of differentiation and selection unique to the profession or are they shared by others? Are they derived from common stimulus information from the environment or are they arbitrarily defined and learned? A look at some of the developments in perception theory helps to clarify these issues.

In a very perceptive paper, William Ittelson notes three major contributions to recent perceptual theory.[23] These are, first, that action plays a major role in obtaining information from the environment; second, that we seek information for some purpose; and, third, that there is a difference between object and environmental perception. These three contributions are associated with Egon Brunswick, Adelbert Ames, and James J. Gibson, respectively. Each of these factors brings our attention to some important architectural issues.

In the first place, there has always been an awareness on the part of architects that it is through movement that we perceive works of architecture. When an observer moves, the entire environment goes through a perspective transformation. Yet this is very often neglected in design. This is a pity, for, as people such as Philip Thiel[24] and Gordon Cullen[25] point out, much of the interest in the environment stems from the way in which these transformations take place. Basic design courses in schools of architecture focus too much on two-dimensional design. This is one of the issues that Jon Lang, Assistant Professor of Urban Design at the University of Pennsylvania, raises in his paper "Theories of Perception and 'Formal' Design," included in this book.

Our movement through the environment is also purposive. What we attend to depends on our motivations. Philip Thiel has noted two extremes in the way people attend to the environment. At one end of the scale is the level of attention characteristic of the tourist and, at the other end, a level characteristic of the habitué.[26] In a recent article Amos Rapoport and Robert Kantor suggest that we design environments which are ambiguous—ambiguous in the sense that they have different types of information and different meanings for the attention of different users.[27] The same position has been taken by Robert Venturi, whose designs often have one level of meaning intended for the user and another for the "cognoscenti."[28] It is also worth noting that people perceive opportunities for behavior of which the designer is unaware. This is not necessarily bad, although signs such as that shown in Figure 2 are symptoms of the discrepancy.

"Environments surround." It is possible to consider buildings or even cities as objects; indeed, many of our aesthetic theories do, and it is certainly the way buildings are displayed in the architectural press. More appropriately for its users, however, one can consider the physical environment as a nested set of spaces.[29] To get to know these spaces, one explores, and builds a mental "map" of them. With this we touch on the topic of environmental imagery, which is discussed below. Nonetheless, it is worth noting here that the environment consists of varieties of information specific to different perceptual systems, a factor largely ignored by architectural theorists and, too frequently, by designers.

Steen Eiler Rasmussen has a number of chapters devoted to the nonvisual environment in his book *Experiencing Architecture.*[30] "Environments are always multimodal," notes Ittelson.[31] The richness of environmental experience is due to this variety. Much of this information is redundant in the sense that we

**Figure 2**

perceive that something is on fire by seeing it, by smelling it, by hearing it, and by feeling its heat. This redundancy heightens our experience of the phenomenon. If the multimodal nature of perception is neglected in design, positive visual experiences may be accompanied by negative sonic ones, for example. Concert halls are not the only place where this type of incongruity should be avoided.

The factor that relates this discussion of perception to the later discussion of spatial behavior is that environments are encountered in relationship to an activity. The *atmosphere* or *ambience* of a place such as that shown in Figure 3, is as much a function of this activity as the role of light and illumination and other aesthetic qualities. Ittelson refers to the relationship between events and setting as "systemic" and suggests that the recognition of these relationships is one of the major factors in environmental perception. It should be in environmental design as well.

There are other factors in visual perception that have long interested architects. One of these is in the area of visual illusion and visual refinement. All architects

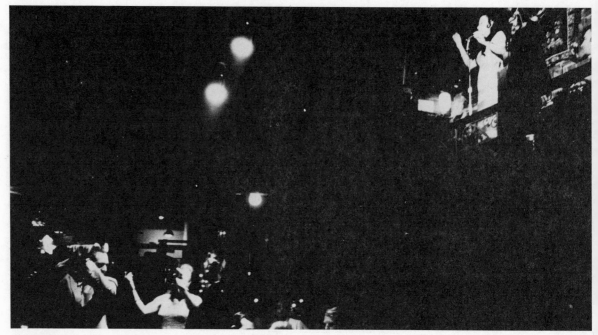

**Figure 3**
**Photo credit: Elliott Kaufman**

know of the many refinements made on buildings during the classical Greek period to correct optical illusions, and the illusion of depth that Palladio achieved in the permanent stage of the *Teatro Olimpico* (see Figure 4). There are also other types of illusions, some of which are of interest to the architect.

It is possible to differentiate between *objective* and *subjective* illusions. Illusions of the first type are caused for example, by contradictory information from artificial sources, refraction and reflection, and obscure combinations of information in geometrical drawings. Illusions of the second type, on the other hand, arise from deficiencies in perception caused by such things as aftereffects of neural excitation and the internal excitation of the neural system. There is a backlog of research on objective illusions and a number of books on their application in architecture.[32] Architects know considerably less about subjective illusions.

Subjective illusions result from unusual conditions such as staring at a source of stimulation for too long. Examples are aftersensations of light and color, where

for some physiological reason excitation occurs after the stimulation has ceased. A number of disturbing figures such as the McKay rays, shown in Figure 5, appear to be of this type. Whatever the reasons that these figures appear to be so disturbing, the effect should be considered when repeated patterns of the same type are used. Edward T. Hall points out that disturbances of this type can make people "acutely uncomfortable." He cites the example of a dry goods store where the combination of glare from fluorescent lights coupled with the "intense stimulation" of the peripheral field of vision by stacks of produce made shoppers feel uncomfortable.[33]

There are other types of illusions such as the variety of drug-induced hallucinations. There has even been some experimentation by architects with the use of hallucinogenics. In one study the objective was to increase an architect's awareness of how mental patients may perceive the environment.[34]

It becomes clear from a short review like this that the three papers in this part dealing with perception—

**Figure 4**

"Theories of Perception and 'Formal' Design," by Jon Lang; "The Gestalt Psychology of Expression in Architecture," by David Levi of the New School of Social Research; and "Psychological Factors in the Use of Light and Lighting in Buildings," by Geoffrey Hayward of the Environmental Psychology Program at the City University of New York—provide only a glimpse of the potential knowledge that can be gained from a study of environmental perception. Yet these papers do present a point of departure for "aesthetic theory." At the same time they neglect the question of "pleasingness" and "interestingness" on which there has been considerable research by such people as Daniel Berlyne[35] and Russell Eisenman.[36] Correlations have been found between "complexity" and "pleasingness" and personality characteristics. Much of this research has focused on object perception and, while interesting in itself, it has not provided architects with a conceptual framework more advanced than that provided by George Santayana[37] almost eighty years ago. Henry Sanoff's paper "Measuring Attributes of the Visual Environment," which appears in *Part Three* of this book,

represents an attempt to come to grips with the variables which influence interestingness and pleasingness.

Architects, as visual artists, are interested in the processes of visual perception. Much of architectural philosophy has been full of insight into the process. The multimodal nature of the perceptual processes must, however, be better understood, and the architectural profession needs to examine afresh its basic principles. As Harold Proshansky points out in his article in *Part One,* however, the flow of information between architect and psychologist has to be in both directions. Much of Kandinsky's work seems to have preceded the work of Gestalt psychologists.

## COGNITION

Cognitive psychology is concerned with the workings of the mind. It has traditionally focused on the issues of symbolic knowledge, feeling, thinking, remembering, learning, and mental development rather than on the phenomenal issues which have dominated the study

**Figure 5**

of perception or the observable human responses which characterize studies of spatial behavior.

The research on the processes of cognition can be ordered in terms of the structure shown in Figure 1 of this section. Studies on the relationship between the physiology of an organism and environmental cognition include those on neurobiological functions, the development of cognitive abilities,[38] and the effect of either perceptual or neural impairment on the thought processes.[39] There are many studies on personality, group membership, and culture—and their effect on environmental cognition. There has been research showing that the styles in which people relate to the environment are fairly stable and enduring dimensions of one's personality.[40] This is reflected in the way an individual is predisposed to perceive his environment.[41]

The social influence on environmental cognition is twofold; first, during the whole process of socialization an individual is taught not only appropriate roles but the appropriate times and places to act these roles; and, second, a person encounters a setting within a social context. Similarly, the meaning of a setting is partly a function of culture.[42] Cross-cultural comparisons show that mental representations of the environment differ for people from different cultural backgrounds.[43] Finally, the physical environment influences our cognitive processes to some extent. This is particularly true of the environments in which we grow. It is clear from this brief overview that a complex web of relationships determines our emotional and other responses to the environment.

The psychic and mental states which result from man's interaction over time with his physical settings thus belong to the area of cognition. Even though they are usually expressed in symbolic terms, such feelings as the experience of beauty, the comfort of home, and the satisfaction produced by the color of the room still require a theory of cognition for their explication. Concepts like those of the *ego*, the *id*,[44] and the *archetype*[45] have helped to explain both rational and irrational behavior and have helped to build general ideas of how people aggregate their experiences into images of themselves and their surroundings—as the paper "The House as Symbol of the Self," by Clare Cooper, Assistant Professor of Landscape Architecture of the University of California at Berkeley, suggests.

An individual's preference for one environment over another introduces the problem of the measurement of preference and meaning for the architect. In his paper, Robert Hershberger, Associate Professor of Architecture at Arizona State University, discusses meaning in architecture and introduces a tool by which affective responses to environmental scenes may be systematically identified and so aid an architect to understand his client's preferences. Both Clare Cooper and Robert Hershberger focus on overall feelings and their manifestations rather than on the actual content, structure, or process of cognition.

These issues of mental content and function become manifest when one attempts to recall or express knowledge of previously experienced environments. The study of symbolic coding, memory, and thinking relative to the environment has been increasing rapidly since Kevin Lynch published his seminal book *The Image of the City,* in 1960.[46] A general review of this area of study is offered by David Stea, Associate Professor of Architecture and City Planning at UCLA, in his paper "Architecture in the Head—Cognitive Mapping."

A concern for the mental representations of the environment must lead to questions regarding how such images are acquired and how this learning might be influenced through the design of the environment. Thus the vast amount of research in developmental psychology done by such men as Heinz Werner, Jean Piaget, and Jerome Bruner becomes a necessary aspect of the study of environmental cognition. An introduction to cognitive development, the use of such knowledge as a guide to design, and a preliminary theory relating useful distinctions in thought to environmental form is offered in the paper "The Mental Image and Design," by Charles Burnette, now Dean of the School of Architecture at the University of Texas in Austin.

While all these papers, and the various domains of cognitive psychology that they represent, seek to relate the environment to thought, they do not offer models of the process of cognition itself. Some knowledge of how the mind receives, processes, stores, and produces environmental information is necessary if perception and human behavior are to be related in a continuous process.

There have been continuing efforts to describe how the processes of the mind might work. As a result of recent developments in psychology,[47] linguistics,[48] computer sciences,[49] and problem solving,[50] there has been a growing sophistication in the ability to model thinking processes and to test such models against human performance. This work tends to view cognition as an information-processing problem which can be modeled in computational terms.[51] Of particular interest is the recent work of Herbert A. Simon and his colleagues.[52].

In their operating model of cognition, inputs from the peripheral sensing and encoding (perceptual) mechanisms compete with internally generated information for temporary storage in a short-lived and very small immediate memory. This small-capacity, short-term memory functions to regulate or *buffer* the sensory input to a second and larger system called an *acquisition memory*. This intermediate system provides the discrimination and familiarization functions used to build representations of the information supplied by the immediate memory. The intermediate central-processing memory supports the recognition, discrimination, and conceptualization functions of thought for up to a few hours, and may be viewed as the working memory of current thought. A third-level component, a permanent memory, which is essentially unlimited in size, constitutes the long-term repository for the images produced by the intermediate memory.

This three-level computational model of the mind can closely simulate human cognitive performance. For example, at the level of the intermediate memory, stimulus encodings are serially scanned for differences under the control of an adaptive attention-focusing strategy. Other strategies function to assemble cue tokens into images and to reference other images in the net, doing so in a manner just adequate for successful performance. Images, even subnets assembled in this way in the intermediate memory, are transferred on a low-priority basis to the permanent memory and reprocessed there to consolidate them into a useful and relevant form—a very slow procedure that may take days.

Such models cannot be ignored by those who study environmental cognition. The ability to experiment directly with such models could be a very powerful tool for the architect. The simulation of such things as spatial knowledge,[53] metaphorical thinking, imagination, and the permutations of individual models of environmental preference, in addition to creative form generation and problem-solving communication,[54] are potentially productive areas of research.

The information-processing model of cognition also provides for the direct simulation of learning and thinking strategies relative to the environment and designing. Indeed, such strategies as those identified by Jerome Bruner and his colleagues in their studies of concept attainment[55] can be modeled in the form of computer subroutines with which to process the structured content of memory.

Herbert Simon has noted that once any such strategy is selected, the course of search through the image of possibilities for the problem's solution probably depends on the structure of the data more than on the characteristics of the problem solver.[56] However, the selection of strategies does reflect the individual's intellectual skill in manipulating this structure and his flexibility in changing his mode of attack.[57] Problem-solving thought depends not only on an individual's repertoire of relevant categories and symbols but on his ability to recognize this relevance. He must be able to search through both his "intermediate" and permanent memory and assemble the combination of concepts appropriate to the solution of his problem. To do this, he must have a repertoire of strategies for manipulating concepts as well as some executive control over the choice, sequence, and application of these strategies.

There are a great many symbolic tools such as mathematical logic, style, and methods of designing which can assist the individual in his management of both conscious and unconscious thought. While verbal language is the most important, the ability to think visually and to make conscious use of environmental imagery to help structure memory has always characterized thought. For example, when books were rare and orators were forced to train their memories, mnemonic techniques based on environmental imagery were developed to assist them. We have a description of this process from Quintillian:

*In order to form a series of places in memory, a building is to be remembered, as spacious and varied a one as possible . . . not omitting statues and other ornaments with which the rooms are decorated. The images by which the speech is to be remembered are then placed in imagination on the places which have been memorized in the building. This is done as soon as the memory of the facts require to be revived, all these places are visited in turn and the various deposits demanded of their custodian.*[58]

Thus the training of memory in Quintillian's time relied on an image of an environment, subordinate images within it, and some idea of the path. These roles of environmental imagery are discussed in more detail in the paper by Charles Burnette. Other systems to assist recall also typically used spatial associations and sequential devices to reinforce memory traces of interest, and much of therapeutic psychiatry is concerned with the structure of such associations and their relationship to behavior. While the individual's habits of mind, his style of thinking, and his perceptions are structured by his physiology and experience in the environment to form personal strategies or habits of mind,

they are often guided by the formal tools of thinking such as language, art, and mathematics. The thought processes are also guided by general attitudes, ideals, purposes, and motives such as those described by Abraham Maslow and outlined earlier in this section. There is a growing body of knowledge and work concerned with these overall controls of emotion, affective response, and cognition. Role playing, gaming, group-think, and problem-solving methods are becoming important means by which the environmental designer may elicit an understanding of the working of his client's mind as well as of his own.[59] General strategies for the creative generation of ideas such as brainstorming, free association, direct analogy, and the use of metaphors,[60] once reasonably well understood, can become as much a function of the design of the environment as of any other language of symbolic communication. Disneyland is a case in point.

Thus while the workings of cognition have one basis in the physiology of the organism and another in the stimulus sources of the environment, they also refer to the accumulated symbolism of language, culture, and society. If their significance is to be understood, however, it is important to remember that the environment, in both its physical and cultural aspects, constitutes the source of information and the ultimate test of its adaptive use by the organism. To study cognition is to study the events between this source and its testing.

The papers by Clare Cooper, Robert Hershberger, David Stea, and Charles Burnette included in this book are all motivated by the desire to better understand the relationship between the environment and the processes of thought. They have been ordered to reflect a progression of inquiry from questions concerning basic psychic identification to abstract theories instrumentally useful in environmental design. The objective is to stimulate the consideration of how we have knowledge of the world and how we use this knowledge to adapt to the circumstances of the social and physical environment.

## SPATIAL BEHAVIOR

It has been suggested that one of the objectives of architectural design is to create spatial layouts which will provide for the activity patterns required by a set of building users to achieve their goals. This involves an understanding of movement patterns, human physical dimensions, and the far more subtle uses of space such as for territory and settings for interaction between people. In recent years the work of Robert Sommer, Edward T. Hall, and others has provided architects with a better understanding of *personal space*[61] and *proxemics*.[62] These do not fully explain, however, the relationship between a physical setting and the activity patterns taking place within it. While activity patterns are relatively easy to establish, it is important to understand the complex system of behavioral components which underpin them. Without this understanding, it is easy to fall into the trap of designing for an ongoing but malfunctioning pattern of activities.

Although some of our activity patterns can be described as the result of some process of habituation, they are, in fact, purposive actions. A person will scrutinize the environment for, in Louis Kahn's terms, "availabilities" for achieving his goals. If a physical setting hinders or does not support a goal-directed activity, an individual will reorganize the situation by changing the physical setting, changing his relationship to it, or by adapting his activity within the setting. Behavior is neither totally determined by the physical environment nor does it exist without reference to its spatial context. The physical setting can support some behaviors and discourage others; if the motive for reaching some goal is strong enough, the individual will adapt his behavior or the setting to fulfill that need. If neither of these options are possible, a highly stressful situation will develop.[63]

There are two useful units for analyzing human spatial behavior. One, *activity systems,*[64] is primarily concerned with the organization of the sequence of activities taking place in a setting; the other, *behavior settings,*[65] with the relationship between the setting and a recurring pattern of behavior. Activity systems, or *streams of behavior,* consist of meaningful discrete *episodes* (akin to Louis Kahn's concept of *inseparable parts*). These episodes, when found to serve similar purposes, can be grouped into a classification of activities. The activity system, then, consists of a sequence of activities having the same context in some specific order and temporal rhythm.[66]

Behavior settings are viewed as the natural units of behavior in our day-to-day lives. These settings have

spatial and temporal boundaries circumscribing a "standing pattern of behavior." The layout of the setting affects the standing pattern of behavior (Figure 6). We are not sure of the extent of this effect, as Maxine Wolfe and Harold Proshansky of the Environmental Psychology Program at the City University of New York point out in their article "The Physical Setting as a Factor in Group Function and Process." Nevertheless, behavioral settings are useful units of analysis for architects because they cause the designer to think about the human activities taking place in a setting, rather than in terms of rooms. William LeCompte, a psychologist at the University of Houston, draws on his research experience to discuss "Behavior Settings as Data-Generating Units for the Environmental Planner and Architect."

Spatial behavior is very much affected by the physiology, personality, social group membership, and culture of an individual and the environment in which he operates. *Ergonomics,* the discipline relating human physiological processes to the performance requirements of work tasks, and *anthropometrics,* which involves the detailed anatomical measurements of the human being, are both concerned with human physiology and behavioral capabilities.[67] The increased vocalism of groups of handicapped people is bringing home to the architect the need to consider physiological capabilities in the design of all buildings.

The literature on the relationship between personality and spatial behavior falls into three categories: studies that deal with the general nature of personality and spatial behavior; studies that are involved with pathology; and studies relating to the satisfaction of personal needs. The first group has shown that a person's attitudes toward space can be explained by his personality traits,[68] and that there is a correlation between physical environment and the development of personality and the ability to cope with change.[69] Many studies have been carried out in hospitals, particularly psychiatric hospitals. They have shown that territorial behavior and dominance characteristics are correlated,[70] and that there is a relationship between environmental ambiguity and feelings of anxiety in schizophrenic patients.[71] These studies have utility in developing concepts about "normal people"—Robert Sommer's concept of personal space developed from his studies in psychiatric hospitals. The third group

**Figure 6**
**Photo credit: Arthur Anderson**

of studies has shown that correlations exist between personality constructs and the search for variety,[72] and that needs for privacy are related to personality components.[73] There are thus many studies on personality systems and spatial behavior patterns, but they need some theoretical construct to bring them together.

When in the presence of others, an individual is guided by the specific rules that define the situation. Psychologist Irwin Altman has proposed a model of interaction based on social roles and the physical environment.[74] The model describes social interaction or interpersonal behavior as a dynamic system. The participants initially determine situational properties on the basis of past experience. From this initial definition of the situation, participants select appropriate behaviors and role relations and then integrate the use of *environmental props* with *self-markers* to form a complex behavioral pattern. As the interaction continues, adjustments are made which, in turn, redefine the situation. Maxine Wolfe and Harold Proshansky discuss

some of these matters in their paper "The Physical Setting as a Factor in Group Function and Process." In particular, they focus on the issue of freedom to choose when to participate in group life and when to withdraw.

Cultural systems affect spatial behavior by establishing norms and value orientations which guide behavior. Edward T. Hall, Professor of Anthropology at Northwestern University, pioneered the study of the cultural context of spatial behavior. His paper, "Meeting Man's Basic Spatial Needs in Artificial Environments," is a synthesis of his ideas for architects. Amos Rapoport discussed the relationship between culture and spatial living patterns in his book *House Form and Culture*.[75] This theme is also expressed by John Zeisel in his paper "Fundamental Values in Planning for the Non-paying Client," which appears in *Part Three* of this book. Another aspect of cultural system, that of social organization and its structuring of spatial behavioral patterns, is discussed at length in another paper that appears in *Part Three* —"Behavioral Analysis and Environmental Programming for Offices," by Walter Moleski.

The environmental factors which affect spatial behavior range from climatic conditions to the structure of the physical environment itself. The latter, only, is considered in this book. It is discussed on two levels —behavioral settings and territory. William LeCompte's paper discusses the relationship of setting to ongoing spatial behavior. Both Edward T. Hall and Robert Sommer, on the other hand, focus on understanding how the physical space that an individual occupies becomes part of his behavioral repertoire.

What, then, is the effect of the physical environment on spatial behavior? Harold Proshansky, William Ittelson, and Leanne Rivlin offer some assumptions based on our present knowledge.[76] It is worthwhile outlining some of these here. Since certain activities are carried out in a specific place, at specific times, characteristic behavior patterns for those settings can be identified. Because an individual, although limited, has a choice of behavior, there will be a diversity of behavior in a setting. Since a setting is not bounded by time, administrative decisions will cause variability in behavior settings over time. By including other people, activities, and nonfixed objects in the setting, it becomes a dynamically defined situation open to change by the occupants. Changing any part of the setting will have varying effects on all other parts, and will result in changes to the characteristic behavior patterns for that setting. When a change is incompatible with the ongoing behavioral pattern, the behavioral pattern will reappear at a different time and place. All the components of the behavioral system—physical, social, cultural, and administrative—define and are defined by the nature of their interrelationships; a change in one will not only affect the others, but will, in turn, be affected by them. Therefore, the environment and the behavioral system are unique at any given time and place, and are unique for each individual. The final point that Proshansky, Ittelson, and Rivlin make is that the surroundings remain neutral and will enter into awareness only when they deviate from some adaptive level. However, although neutral, a setting influences the spatial behavior of its occupants.

Since spatial behavior is directed at satisfying human needs, a large portion of environmental research has been concerned with the issue of needs. Only the fundamental concepts have been considered here. It must be pointed out, as Robert Gutman and Barbara Westergaard state in their paper in *Part Three,* that

*Concepts like personal space and territoriality point to presumed basic needs and are intended to have implications for the design of the environment. In fact, however, these concepts do not help us design the environment any more than knowing that men need food to survive enables the nutritionist to prescribe a diet or a chef to prepare a menu.*

Robert Sommer, now Chairman of the Department of Psychology of the University of California at Davis, also expresses some reservations on the utility of these concepts for architectural programming and design in his paper "Looking Back at Personal Space." The quality of the physical environment has more to do with the fit between the whole behavioral and psychological program than just the way people relate to each other in space. The editors of this book feel that, while the concept of personal space is still useful in understanding certain interior design problems, particularly those involving seating arrangements, it is not the basic unit for design. Other factors such as adaptability, the ability to personalize space, and catering to ongoing patterns of behavior are just as important. "To some extent these are administrative decisions to be made when a building is complete, but, to some extent, the physical environment must allow personalization without damage, particularly if there is a reasonable turnover in population."[77] Edward T. Hall includes in his paper an "empirical anthropological checklist" of items which should be considered when designing a building. This checklist should prove very useful to the architect and architectural student because it brings the important factors to consider in spatial design to the attention of the designer.

The factor to remember when considering the relationship between architectural design and spatial behavior is that the relationship is not a closed one but one that is dynamically organized around the satisfaction of human needs. This support should be provided in part through perceptual cues identifying opportunities for desired behavior in the environment. It is also necessary for the architect to consider the importance that a person's concept of his environment has for his behavior; an individual uses this concept to analyze what his behavioral possibilities are. At the same time, buildings have to function in the future, so architects have to understand and allow for changes in behavior. Very seldom will the architectural environment cause major changes in social behavior, however; rather, these are more largely determined by changes in the social and cultural context in which architecture occurs.

*Part Two* of this book thus brings together eleven papers which deal with perception, cognition (including affect), and spatial behavior. The objective is to provide a broad introduction and survey of the current understanding which the behavioral sciences can bring to the traditional goals of architecture. As is true for each part of this book, the papers do not present a unified stance or total agreement on theoretical questions. As a group, however, they provide considerable insight into the processes of environmental behavior. Without this insight it will be difficult to design for human behavior.

## NOTES AND REFERENCES

1. William H. Ittelson, "Perception of the large-scale environment," paper presented to the New York Academy of Sciences, April 13, 1970.
2. W. Ross Ashby, *Design for a Brain: The Origin of Adaptive Behavior,* London: Chapman & Hall, 1954.
3. Gardner Murphy, *Personality: A Biosocial Approach to Origins and Structure,* New York: Harper & Row, 1947.
4. *Ibid.*
5. Harold M. Proshansky, William H. Ittelson, and Leanne G. Rivlin, eds., *Environmental Psychology: Man and His Physical Setting,* New York: Holt, 1970.
6. P. T. Young, "The role of hedonic process in motivation," in M. R. Jones, ed., *Nebraska Symposium on Motivation,* Lincoln, Nebr.: University of Nebraska Press, 1955, 193–238.
7. H. A. Murray, *Explorations in Personality,* New York: Oxford University Press, 1938.
8. Abraham Maslow, *Motivation and Personality,* New York: Harper & Row, 1954.
9. Talcott Parsons, *Societies,* Englewood Cliffs, N.J.: Prentice-Hall, 1966, Chap. 2. See also William Michelson, *Man and His Urban Environment: A Sociological Approach,* Reading, Mass.: Addison-Wesley, 1970.
10. Russell Ackoff and Fred Emery, *Purposive Systems,* Chicago: Aldine-Atherton, 1972; see Chap. 8 in particular.
11. Ralph Linton, *The Cultural Background of Personality,* New York: Appleton-Century-Crofts, 1945.
12. Marshall H. Segall, Donald T. Campbell, and Melville J. Herskovits, *The Influence of Culture on Perception,* Indianapolis, Ind.: Bobbs-Merrill, 1966.
13. R. Maurer and J. C. Baxter, "Images of the neighborhood and city among Black-, Anglo-, and Mexican-American children," *Environment and Behavior,* Vol. 4 (December 1972), 351–388.
14. Edward T. Hall, *The Hidden Dimension,* Garden City, N.Y.: Doubleday, 1966.
15. Edward T. Hall, "Proxemics and design," *Design and Environment,* Vol. 2 (Winter 1971), 24–25, 58.
16. Warren Brodey, "The other than visual world of the blind," *Ekistics,* Vol. 28 (August 1969), 100–103.
17. C. R. Rogers, *Client-Centered Therapy,* Boston: Houghton Mifflin, 1951.
18. Benjamin L. Whorf, *Language, Thought and Reality,* Cambridge, Mass.: The MIT Press, 1956.
19. Segall, Campbell, and Herskovits, *op. cit.*
20. See Kurt Koffka, *Principles of Gestalt Psychology,* New York: Harcourt, 1935; William H. Ittelson and Hadley Cantril, *Perception: Transactionalist Approach,* Garden City, N.Y.: Doubleday, 1954; James J. Gibson, *The Senses Considered As Perceptual Systems,* Boston: Houghton Mifflin, 1966.
21. Jean Piaget and Barbara Inhelder, *The Child's Conception of Space,* New York: Humanities Press, 1956.
22. William James, *The Principles of Psychology,* New York: Holt, 1890.
23. Ittelson, *op. cit.*
24. Philip Thiel, "A sequence-experience notation for architectural and urban spaces," *Town Planning Review,* Vol. 32 (April 1961), 33–52.
25. Gordon Cullen, *Townscape,* London: The Architectural Press, 1962.
26. Philip Thiel, "The tourist and the habitué: two polar modes of environmental experience, with some notes on an 'experience cube,'" July 1964 (mimeographed).
27. Amos Rapoport and Robert Kantor, "Complexity and ambiguity in environmental design," *Journal of the American Institute of Planners,* Vol. 33 (July 1967), 201–221.
28. Robert Venturi, *Complexity and Contradiction in Architecture,* New York: Museum of Modern Art, 1966.
29. Gibson, *op. cit.*
30. Steen Eiler Rasmussen, *Experiencing Architecture,* Cambridge, Mass.: The MIT Press, 1959.
31. Ittelson, *op. cit.*
32. For instance, see M. Lukiesch, *Visual Illusions, Their Causes, Characteristics and Applications,* New York: Van Nostrand Reinhold, 1922.
33. Edward T. Hall, "Seeing and believing," *Architectural Review,* Vol. 144 (August 1968), 117–118.
34. Kyoshi Izumi, "LSD and architecture," Human Ecology Program, University of Saskatchawan, 1967 (mimeographed).
35. Daniel Berlyne, *Conflict, Arousal and Curiosity,* New York: McGraw-Hill, 1960.
36. Russell Eisenman, "Pleasingness and interesting visual complexity: support for Berlyne," *Perceptual and Motor Skills,* Vol. 23 (1966), 1167–1170.
37. George Santayana, *The Sense of Beauty,* New York; Dover, 1955 (New York: Scribner's Sons, 1901).
38. Gary T. Moore, "Elements of a genetic–structural theory of the development of environmental cognition," in William J. Mitchell, ed., *Environmental Design: Research*

and Practice: Proceedings of the EDRA/AR8 Conference, University of California, Los Angeles, January 1972, 30.9.1–30.9.13.

39. M. Powell Lawton, "Ecology and aging," in Leon A. Pastalan and Daniel H. Carson, eds., *Spatial Behavior of Older People,* Ann Arbor, Mich.: Institute of Gerontology, University of Michigan, 1970.

40. Kenneth H. Craik, "Assessing environmental dispositions," a contribution to a symposium, "Assessing environmental contexts of behavior," American Psychological Association, Washington, D.C., 1969.

41. Donald Appleyard, "Notes on urban perception and knowledge," in John Archea and Charles Eastman, eds., *EDRA2: Proceedings of the Second Annual Environmental Design Research Association Conference,* Pittsburgh, Pa., October 1970.

42. Amos Rapoport, *House Form and Culture,* Englewood Cliffs, N.J.: Prentice-Hall, 1969.

43. Florence Ladd, "Black youths view their environment: neighborhood maps," *Environment and Behavior,* Vol. 2 (June 1967), 75–99.

44. Sigmund Freud, *The Complete Psychological Works of Sigmund Freud,* London: Hogarth, 1959.

45. Carl Jung, *Psychological Types,* New York: Harcourt, 1924.

46. Kevin Lynch, *The Image of the City,* Cambridge, Mass.: The MIT Press, 1960.

47. George Miller, E. Galanter, and K. Pribram, *Plans and the Structure of Behavior,* New York: Holt, 1960.

48. Noam Chomsky, *Syntactic Structure,* The Hague: Mouton, 1957.

49. Edward Feigerbaum and Julian Feldman, eds., *Computers and Thought,* New York: McGraw-Hill, 1963.

50. Alan Newell, J. C. Shaw, and Herbert A. Simon, "Elements of a theory of human problem solving," *Psychological Review,* Vol. 65 (1958).

51. Walter Reitman, *Cognition and Thought,* New York: Wiley, 1965.

52. Newell, Shaw, and Simon, *op. cit.*

53. Thomas Moran, "The cognitive structure of spatial knowledge," in Wolfgang Preiser, ed., *Environmental Design Research, Proceedings of the Fourth International EDRA Conference,* Stroudsburg, Pa.: Dowden, Hutchinson & Ross, 1973.

54. Charles Burnette, "The organization of information for computer aided communication in architecture," Ph.D. dissertation, University of Pennsylvania, 1969.

55. Jerome Bruner, Jacquelin Goodnow, and George Austin, *A Study of Thinking,* New York: Wiley, 1965, 1.

56. Herbert A. Simon, *The Sciences of the Artificial,* Cambridge, Mass.: The MIT Press, 1969, 30.

57. J. B. Carroll, *Language and Thought,* Englewood Cliffs, N.J.: Prentice-Hall, 1964.

58. Frances Yates, *The Art of Memory,* Chicago: University of Chicago Press, 1966.

59. Charles Burnette, Gary Moore, and Lynn Simek, "A role oriented approach to creative problem solving by groups," in Wolfgang Preiser, ed., *Environmental Design*

*Research, Proceedings of the Fourth International EDRA4 Conference,* Vol. 1, Stroudsburg, Pa.: Dowden, Hutchinson & Ross, 1973.

60. See W. J. J. Gordon, *Synectics,* New York: Collier, 1961; W. J. J. Gordon, *The Metaphorical Way,* Cambridge, Mass.: Porpoise Books, 1971; and, G. M. Prince, *The Practice of Creativity,* New York: Harper & Row, 1970.

61. Robert Sommer, *Personal Space: The Behavioral Basis of Design,* Englewood Cliffs, N.J.: Prentice-Hall, 1969.

62. Edward T. Hall, *The Hidden Dimension,* Garden City, N.Y.: Doubleday, 1966.

63. This was essentially the situation at the Pruitt–Igoe project in St. Louis. The adaptive behavior was to abandon the project.

64. F. Stuart Chapin, Jr., "Activity systems and urban structure; a working schema," *The Journal of the American Institute of Planners,* Vol. 34 (January 1968), 34.

65. Roger G. Barker, *Ecological Psychology: Concepts and Methods fcr Studying the Environment of Human Behavior,* Stanford, Calif.: Stanford University Press, 1968.

66. Chapin, *op. cit.*

67. See Clifford T. Morgan, et al., *Human Engineering: Guide to Equipment Design,* New York: McGraw-Hill, 1963; and Henry Dreyfuss, *The Measure of Man: Human Factors in Design,* 2nd ed., New York: Whitney Library of Design, 1967.

68. Michael Balint, "Friendly expanses—horrid empty spaces," *International Journal of Psychoanalysis,* Vol. 36 (1955), 225–241.

69. S. R. Maddi, "Exploratory behavior and variation seeking in man," in D. W. Fiske and S. R. Maddi, eds., *Functions of Varied Experience,* Homewood, Ill.: Dorsey Press, 1961.

70. Aristide Esser et al., "Territoriality of patients on a research ward," in Proshansky, Ittelson, and Rivlin, *op. cit.*

71. Harold F. Searles, *The Non-Human Environment in Normal Development and Schizophrenia,* New York: International Universities Press, 1960.

72. Maddi, *op. cit.*

73. Nancy Marshall, "Personality correlates of orientation toward privacy," in John Archea and Charles Eastman, eds., *EDRA2: Proceedings of the Second Annual Environmental Design Research Association Conference,* Pittsburgh, Pa., October 1970.

74. Irwin Altman and E. E. Lett, "The ecology of interpersonal relationships: a classification system and conceptual model," in E. McGrath, ed., *Social and Psychological Factors in Stress,* New York: Holt, 1970, 177–201.

75. Amos Rapoport, *House Form and Culture,* Englewood Cliffs, N.J.: Prentice-Hall, 1969.

76. Harold M. Proshansky, William H. Ittelson, and Leanne G. Rivlin, "The influence of the physical environment on behavior: some basic assumptions," in Proshansky, Ittelson, and Rivlin, *op. cit.*

77. Amos Rapoport, "Whose meaning in architecture?" *Arena/Interbuild,* Vol. 14 (October 1967), 44–46.

*Our present theories of basic design have borrowed more from theories of psychology, particularly Gestalt theories of perception, than any other area of architectural theory. Current models of basic design were formulated by the Bauhaus masters and have been unaffected by recent findings which are changing our understanding of the processes of perception. At the same time present formulations of basic design have been criticized heavily. This paper suggests a reformulation of basic design principles to recognize our added understanding of how we perceive the environment. It hypothesizes that the added conceptual clarity that such a reformulation will bring to "formal" aesthetics will be reflected in an enhanced quality of the visual environment.*

# Theories of Perception and "Formal" Design

Jon Lang

**University of Pennsylvania**

The architect is, in part, a visual artist. So is the sculptor. The architect's work, however, is more closely constrained by economic, social, structural, and other requirements; his approach to form is different. The architect attempts to meet a set of objectives which seem appropriate from an analysis of the problem he faces. Many of these objectives are visual in character. It is hardly surprising, therefore, that architects have long been interested in visual perception and that current theories of "basic design" have borrowed heavily from the psychology of perception. Walter Gropius expressed the reason quite succinctly: "if we can understand the nature of what we see and the way we perceive it, then we will know more about the potential influence of manmade design on human feeling and thinking."[1] Current theories of basic design (for which we owe an intellectual debt to the Bauhaus masters) draw particularly heavily on Gestalt psychology, which evolved contemporaneously to the Bauhaus.[2]

Recent expressions of interest in the processes of perception cover the spectrum of perceptual research and theory. The concern here is restricted to what one recent author calls the "formal" aspects of basic design rather than the "symbolic.":

*Formal aesthetics deals with proportions, rhythms, repetition, formal cohesion, consistency, etc. Symbolic aesthetics on the contrary employs such epithets as 'honest', 'truly modern': or in the case of Palladio 'barbarian' versus 'good' or again with Ruskin and Pugin, 'pagan' versus 'christian'.*[3]

The concern of this paper is with theories of perception, with formal issues in design as considered and introduced to students in many basic design courses today, and with the misfit between perception theory and basic design theory. Basic design, as it is taught and discussed in the literature, has been heavily criticized for a number of reasons.[4] These include the inappropriateness of the subject matter for architects and the failure to keep pace with current research on the psychology of perception. Probably most importantly, it has been recognized that the most creative architects amoing us do not think about formal issues in the terms specified by most basic design theorists. Despite recognition of the situation little effort has been made to reformulate basic design theories.

The reasons for this appear to be twofold. In the first place, architectural theorists appear to be more intent on building ideological positions than understanding the processes of perception. In the second place, there are mutually contradictory theories of perception in psychology and philosophy that enmesh the architect in controversies irrelevant to his purposes. As long as the first situation prevails, perceptual psychology will have little to offer the designer because perception theory attempts to describe and explain phenomena and not state what is good or bad.

In order to reduce the theoretical confusion for architects an attempt is made here to distinguish among theories of perception. This should provide a coherent theoretical context from which design principles may be extracted. A greater conceptual clarity on the part of architects should, if recent studies are accurate, lead to an enhanced design quality relative to formal perception.[5]

## THEORIES OF PERCEPTION

Various people have classified theories of perception in different ways. It is possible to divide theories of perception into four broad categories, as follows:
1. *Empiricism,* as defined by the work of such people as Helmhotz, Titchner, American functional psychologists such as Carr, and the transactionalists such as Adelbert Ames, Hadley Cantril, and William Ittelson.[6]
2. *Rationalism and nativism,* as exemplified by the work of Emmanuel Kant, Jean Piaget, and Noam Chomsky.[7]
3. *Gestalt Theory,* as developed by Kurt Koffka, Wolfgang Köhler, and Max Wertheimer.[8]
4. *Information-based perception theory,* as developed by psychologists such as James J. Gibson and Eleanor J. Gibson.[9]

Empiricism, rationalism and Gestalt theories suggest that perception is sensation based. Environmental stimuli are said to arouse the senses, and the sensations so aroused are integrated in some way into a perception.

The sensation-based theories of perception attempt to deal with the supposed units of perception, sense data, and to explain how these are put together in the brain. Physiologists attempted to discover the fundamental sensations and their receptor elements; psychologists, the laws by which these elements were combined. All other qualities for which there were no

receptors would be fabricated out of these basic sensations, and other qualities would be brought to mind by association. The different sensation-based theories of perception suggest different models for this process. In contrast, information-based perception theory focuses not on how the data identified with the object of perception are delivered in an organized way but on the discovery of how we process phenomenal information and the relationships that come to exist within it. The existence of sensory experience is not denied, but patterns within the entire context provided by ambient light is said to be the basis of visual perception rather than the defining qualities of particular sensations.

Architects have drawn on or been intrigued by different theories of perception—particularly those from the empiricist and Gestalt schools. In the mid-nineteenth century Alexander Jackson Downing, more interested in symbolic than formal aesthetics, drew on the "laws of association," formulated by John Locke, the British empiricist, almost three hundred years earlier, to suggest that certain styles of architecture were appropriate for certain building types.[10] This represents an attempt to rationalize an ideological position. More recently, the transactionalist school of empiricists has attracted the attention of architects.

The transactionalists emphasize the privacy of each individual's perceptual world. Thus what is perceived is a function of an individual's life history, motivations, and values. Individuals, they say, create their own world: an *assumptive* one, of objects, people, and events out of *transactions* with the environment. Greater experience increases the probability that the world we see is the same as the "real" one. The experience comes from seeing the consequences of action.[11]

During the 1940's a number of architects were intrigued by the transactionalist position and particularly the experiments of Adelbert Ames in which different combinations of objects all resulted in the same perception when seen from a particular point through a peephole. Walter Gropius wrote: "widely different materials caused the same pattern on the retina of our eyes and resulted in the same sensation . . . and [therefore] the sensation did not come from the material in the environment, but from us. It comes from prior experience."[12]

A certain amount of speculation as to what the architect *should* do, given the transactionalist position, can be found in the architectural literature.[13] The transactionalists, however, have had little to say about "formal" design issues. Perhaps the main contribution of the transactionalist school has been to make us aware that different people attend to different things in the environment, based on their own experience, education, and purposes. Architects have been educated to attend to certain formal relationships, and these have become extraordinarily important to our polemics. These will not necessarily be the relationships which are attended to or regarded as important by other people.

Of the sensation-based theories of perception, Gestalt psychology has attracted the most sustained interest of architects and artists since its formulation in the 1920's. Perception, as suggested by Wertheimer, Koffka, and Köhler, is more than an assemblage of independent point sensations—it involves whole shaped regions. They were thus interested in pattern, and pattern is what interests architects. An understanding of Gestalt psychology requires an understanding of its concepts of *form, isomorphism,* and *field forces*.

Form is fundamental. Köhler wrote: "our view will be that, instead of reacting to local stimuli by local and independent events, the organism responds to the pattern of stimuli to which it is exposed."[14] Gestalt psychologists set out to discover the rules that govern the appearance of shapes and forms. Forms, they suggested, stand apart as closed and structured elements of the world. They have the quality of figure in a "figure–ground" relationship and draw strength from their structure and degree of closure. The experimental research on the perception of form is extensive. The list of factors that Gestalt theorists suggest as influencial in the perception of shape have had a profound impact on principles of formal composition in basic design.

The concept of *field forces* was adapted from physics.[15] All forces, activity, and behavior occur in some field of environment. Forces in the visual field, as in mechanics, have an area of application, a direction, and a magnitude. The state of the field is a resultant of all the forces acting in the field. "Action" stems from disequilibrium or lack of balance and tension between forces. "Inaction" stems from a state of equilibrium and

homogeneity. To explain this, Koffka hypothesized that a relationship exists between the neuropsychological field, which includes the nervous system and psychological phenomena, and direct experience. To explain the relationships between the behavioral field of percepts and the nervous system, Koffka turns to the concept of isomorphism.

*Isomorphism* is a term describing the congruence of the organization of underlying neurological processes and forms of the perceptual experience. Several Gestalt theorists speculated about the types of neurological organization that would account for the way perception is organized. The application of isomorphism is summarized in the following quote from Köhler: "experienced order in space is always structurally identical with a functional order in the distribution of underlying brain processes."[16] These processes account for the fact that a perception is not a copy of the retinal image. An as yet unsettled controversy, however, arose over the role of immediate perceptual organization in comparison to the role of past experience for explaining errors in form perception (such as those that occur in optical illusions). The empirical observations of the Gestalt theorists do seem to provide useful information on how a subject learns to discriminate between particular patterns. These are, suggests Gibson, learned discriminations, and a theory to explain them is necessary.[17]

Gibson's information-based theory of perception has attracted the interest of a number of architects during the past decade because it appears to account more easily for the facts of perception and complexity in the environment as discovered by the observer.[18] Instead of describing how punctate sensations are organized and enriched from memory to comprehend the environment, this theory attempts to answer the questions of how we know the environment and the relationships that exist within it and how we learn, with greater experience, to discriminate among objects and among qualities. This is in complete contrast to the research effort of the sensation-based theorists whose goal it is to learn more about the sensations one can experience. Gibson suggests that the eye registers ambient light—the point of departure for his theory of visual perception.

*Ambient light* is that which arrives at a station point,

such as the eye, reflected off the surfaces of the world. It has different intensities in different directions, for the surfaces which compose the environment have different reflectances, given that they face different directions and are made of different materials. The ambient light arriving at a point is called the *optic array* at that point.[19] This is somewhat similar to the approach to perception manifested in perspective geometry—a system of rules for representing the three-dimensional world on a two-dimensional surface.

An optic array, in geometric terms, is a set of light rays converging at the eye. The array has a pattern which is in correspondence to the environment. For the observer there is *potential* information in this array. It becomes *effective* if the observer attends to it.

The optic array is structured by the differences in the intensity of the ambient light. These transitions provide information about the world, for they correspond "to the layout, the chemical and structural composition, and the illumination of the solids, liquids, and gases of the environment. That is, they depend on the edges, corners and other irregularities of reflecting surfaces."[20] If these are the basis for perception of the visual world, and for many designers the basis of design, then maybe our theories of architecture should deal with them more explicitly. Our theories have too long been based on Wassily Kandinsky's points, lines, and planes. We must get away from thinking about the design of "forms" and think more about the design of *layouts,* the entire aspect of an environment which will result in a particular optic array for a given observer in a given place.

Gibson also suggests that the flux of optical stimulation contains all the information that is necessary for visual perception.[21] Thus the primary learning experience in visual perception is not that of making associations with elemental forms but of differentiating smaller and smaller differences in qualities, features, and dimensions of variation. *Perceptual learning thus consists of attending to variables of stimulation not responded to before*. In many ways this was required by the Bauhaus educators, who constantly strove to bring the attention of students to different materials, shapes, and textures so as to provide designers with a richer vocabulary.[22] The conceptual background for these exercises, however, was often lacking, and conceptual clarity, as noted previously, is a prerequisite

for creative design if recent critics are to be believed.

There is another factor that makes knowledge of information-based perception theory important to architects. This is its stress on movement in the comprehension of the environment. Slight movements yield changes in the optic array. Perspective geometricians knew this, and architects and artists have known it for a long time. Yet too often we design a "frozen" static world simply because our graphic techniques of orthographic projection represent such a world. A number of architects, recognizing that much of our interest and pleasure in the world stems from the way in which changes take place as we move through it, have attempted to go beyond this static conception.[23] Basic design should be more concerned with these transitions and transformations of the world as we move through it than it is at present.

To understand how best to consider "formal" issues in basic design and how the application of Gibson's concepts to present theoretical formulation might change them requires a consideration of traditional approaches to "formal" aesthetics. A review of the present approach to basic design will also provide an opportunity to review the contribution of one sensation-based theory of perception, Gestalt psychology. Once this has been done, the impact of Gibson's theory on the concepts of basic design can be discussed.

## TRADITIONAL APPROACHES TO "FORMAL" THEORY IN BASIC DESIGN

Current theories of basic design vary in content and scope. There are, however, major similarities which make it possible to represent them by a general model. All the discussions of basic design begin with the consideration of basic elements and then deal with the organization of these into visual compositions in much the same way as sensation-based theories deal with the processes of perception.[24]

The simplest unit of design—the basic element—is considered to be a dot. The simplest composition is a single dot in the middle of a square picture plane. When there are two dots on a piece of paper, tension is said to exist between them. This tension is said to have a magnitude and a direction, so it is described as a "psychological force." Dots can be accumulated

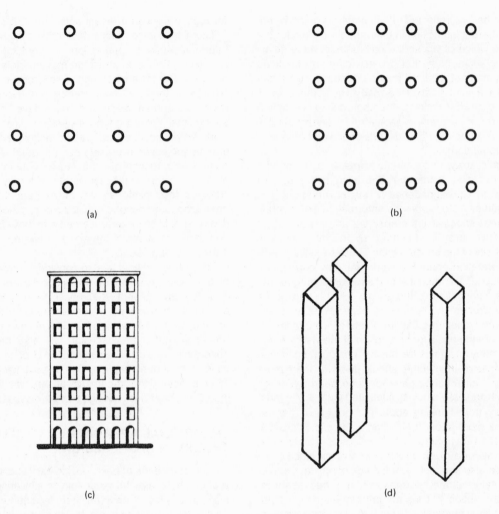

**Figure 1**
**The Gestalt theory law of proximity**

to form textures or composed in such a way as to create a variety of tensions and energies.[25]

Dots can be chained together to form a line which has direction and contains energy, which is said to appear to travel along its length. Kandinsky says that a line occurs when an external force is applied to a point. Different thicknesses of line are described as having different associations; a broader line is said to be bolder than a narrower one and a zigzag one exciting. Thus more traditional theories of basic design

quickly get into the expressive qualities of such formal elements. Lines, like dots, can be grouped together, and different combinations of lengths and widths express rhythms and beats. In sum, the dot and the line in the context provided by the Gestalt field of forces provide the fundamental "vocabulary" of basic design.[26]

Formal aesthetics also draws heavily on Gestalt theory, particularly the "laws of organization," because architects find it useful to consider the optical characteristics which tend to be seen together as a spatial configuration. The Gestalt "laws" of proximity, similarity, continuance, and closure are particularly important to "formal" theory.

"*Proximity* is the simplest condition of organization."[27] Objects which are close together tend to be grouped together. According to Gestalt theory the relative closeness offers the strongest tendency to interconnection between sensory units. In Figure 1 (a) it is possible to see the rows or columns with equal ease. In Figure 1(b) the dots are closer together horizontally and the rows tend to be seen as units. This can be extended to the architectural examples in Figures 1(c) and 1(d).

Proximity, however, often yields to other factors involved in perceptual organizations.[28] If elements have *similar* qualities, they are said to tend to be tied into stable relationships. The similar qualities may be ones of size, color, values, textures, and contours. In Figure 2(a) the lines appear to be related because they are similar. In Figure 2(b) the organization is weaker, although the proximity is the same. Figure 2(c) illustrates an architectural example. Here masses 1, 2, and 3 appear to be more powerfully related than masses 4, 5, and 6, although the latter group has its elements more closely spaced. Some basic design theorists suggest that the competition between the forces of similarity and proximity can lead to "vital experience in plastic tension."[29]

The law of *good continuance* is illustrated in Figure 3. It states that the arrangement of figure and ground that has good continuance will be seen the most easily. Thus in Figure 3(a), line 1 appears to run through, behind, or in front of line 2. It is more difficult to perceive the organization shown in Figure 3(b). Julian Hochberg illustrates the law with the diagram shown in Figure 3(c).[30] The pattern is almost always seen as a sine wave and not as a series of adjacent areas, as shown in Figure 3(d), which is what one would expect from another law of organization, *closedness,* which states that areas with closed and clearly defined contours tend to be seen as figures more easily than those without. Gyorgy Kepes suggests that the most potent application of the concept of good continuance is in, "binding together heterogenous elements."[31]

The law of *closure* states, according to Köhler, that optical units tend to be shaped into closed compact wholes by the forces of organization.[32] In other words, almost completed figures tend to look whole. In Figure 4 we tend to think of all the shapes as closed units. The openings or gaps in the figures seem to be either unimportant or very unimportant, depending on our focus of attention. In his concern with space, the architect is frequently concerned with principles derived

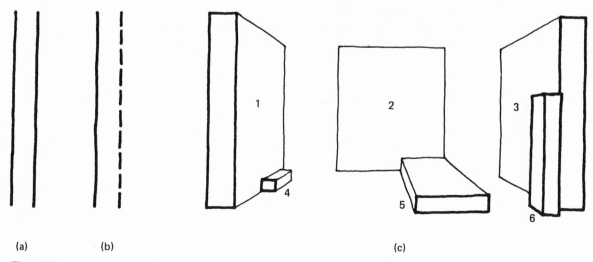

(a)               (b)                                        (c)

**Figure 2**
**The Gestalt theory law of similarity**

from the law of closure. Heinrich Wolflin suggests that there have been two contrasting attitudes towards closure in architectural history. The one he calls the "classic," in which closure is well defined by enclosing elements, and the "baroque," where it is more loosely defined.[33] The attitude one should take depends on the task at hand and the design objectives one is attempting to meet.

Governing all these laws is the *law of Pragnanz,*

*Perception of unity does not require a strict adherence to all Gestalt laws at the same time; a contrast in one area (which goes against perceptual expectations and therefore disrupts the unity) may be compensated for by harmony in another. Architects are thus at a liberty to choose from a (limited) range of formally unifying devices. Therefore, although formal architectural principles show a far greater consistency over the centuries than symbolic ones, they are not always the same principles despite their common psychological roots.*[35]

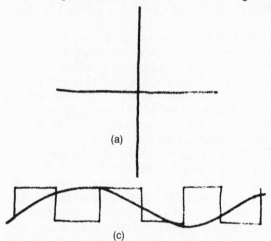

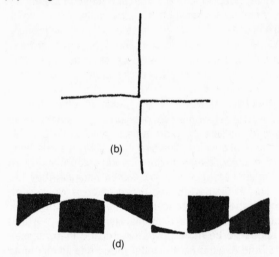

**Figure 3**
**The Gestalt theory law of good continuance**

which states that the "psychological organization" will always be as "good" as the prevailing conditions allow. According to David Katz, "good" figures have the following characteristics: symmetry, inclusiveness, unity, harmony, regularity, conciseness, and "maximal" simplicity.[34] Maximal simplicity occurs when a form possesses the fewest articulated elements required to maintain the structure. Thus parts have a degree of "essentialness" to the whole. Some are necessary to maintain the form, others merely enhance it.

It is clear from extensive experimentation that simple regular forms with repetitous elements are easiest to perceive. If critics are to be believed, architects have striven too much for simplicity and the strict application of Gestalt rules. The result is often monotony. Contrast and variety are frequently desirable, and the laws of Gestalt psychology can be flaunted to achieve these. Luning Prak notes:

The very brief review above is a fairly typical representation of the way formal aspects of design are dealt with in much current basic design theory. Such theory deals with the visual world as a set of points, lines, and planes extended into the third dimension. The attempt is made to provide a value-free basis for the consideration of formal composition in design. The application of the principles is, of course, value laden. The problem is that it does not take opaque planes into account in an explicit way. The main difference between space, as defined by information-based perception theory, and geometrical space is the recognition that opaque surfaces hide other surfaces. If the fundamental condition for environmental perception is an array of illuminated surfaces, maybe the way to consider formal issues in environmental design is to consider the surface as the basic unit of design rather than a dot.

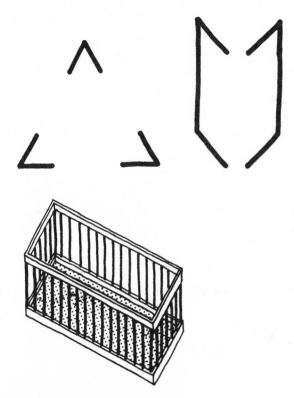

**Figure 4**
**The Gestalt theory law of closure**

## OPAQUE GEOMETRY AND BASIC DESIGN

A number of the modern masters seem to consider the designed environment as a system of surfaces which are interposed between collections of human participants and between them and the impinging milieu. Surfaces are the means for creating environments. They provide the physiological support needed for life and delimit the behavior settings which support social systems. They also carry meaning in themselves. Architectural theory should be concerned with surfaces as they respond to each of these capacities. Basic design is concerned primarily with the last. It should be concerned with surfaces, contours, textures, edges, and enclosure.

The fundamental types of surfaces are illustrated in Figure 5.[36] They are (a) the planar, the convex, and the concave surface, (b) the closed continuous surface, and (c) the elongated object. Surface layouts consist of combinations of these basic types. When two surfaces are immediately adjacent, there will be a "crack" delineating the junction. If separated, there will be a gap. A crack in a surface will appear as a line in the optic array. It will not be the same as a contour, because intensity of texture on each side of the line will be the same. The types of surfaces mentioned above are not specified with reference to a point of observation. Except for the bare interior of a windowless room, some part of the surface layout is always hidden. This will depend on the point of observation and will change as the point changes. For this reason edges are important. For occlusion—that is, the hiding of part of the environment by a surface—there must be some type of edge. Some of the types identified by Gibson are shown in Figure 6.[37] The implication is that one views which of two surfaces is closer to the observer, without any ambiguity, in the three-dimensional world by the stimulus information for occlusion and not by *closure*—the tendency to complete a form, as the Gestalt theorists suggest. The concept of closure is more useful in two-dimensional designing than in dealing with the three-dimensional world of the man-made environment. Thinking in terms of occlusion will add conceptual clarity to three-dimensional design and focus the architect's attention on the phenomena that actually exist in the world.

Other variables which should be considered as basic elements of visual design are textures and contours. Texture or the "fine structure" of surfaces specifies the physical character of a material. In other words, if a patch in the optic array has texture, it is perceived as a physical element in space. If not, it specifies only the medium—air. Transparent surfaces are only perceived if they reflect a virtual image or have dust on them or distort the view through them, as a number of people who have attempted to walk through plate glass have discovered to their dismay. The kind of texture in a patch in the optic array is fairly specific to the substance of the surface in the world. An object is perceived as hard or soft, solid or liquid, rough or smooth with a high degree of accuracy. These qualities all have meaning and utility to the observer.

A contour in the optic array is defined as an "abrupt intensity transition" in the texture.[38] It may specify either

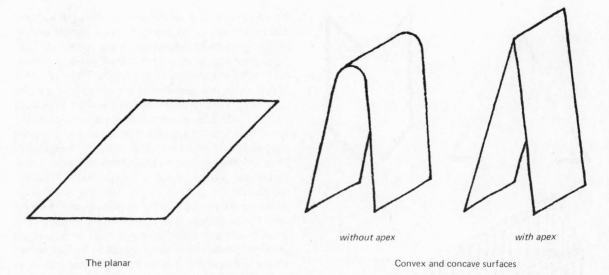

*without apex*                    *with apex*

The planar                    Convex and concave surfaces

(a)

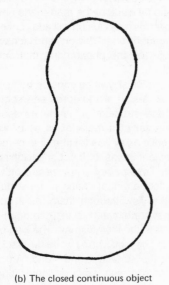

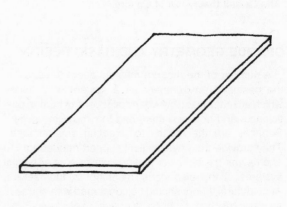

(b) The closed continuous object            (c) The elongated object

**Figure 5**
**Some basic surfaces**

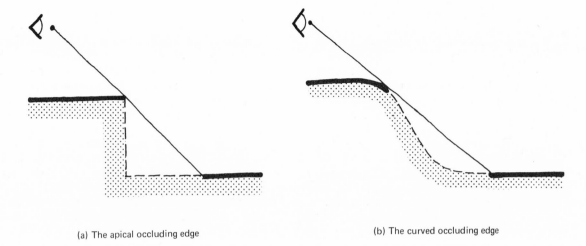

(a) The apical occluding edge                (b) The curved occluding edge

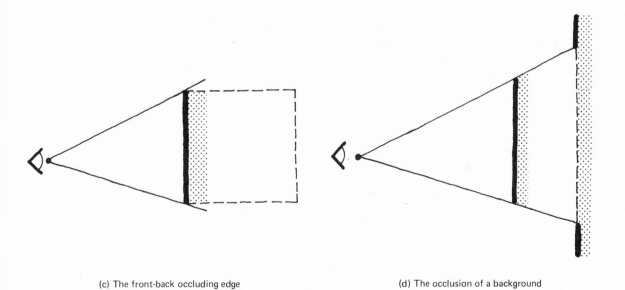

(c) The front-back occluding edge            (d) The occlusion of a background

**Figure 6**

an edge of some sort or the change in pigment on a surface. If the contour is blurred, it corresponds to either a cast shadow on a flat surface or an attached shadow on a curved surface. A closed contour is ambiguous. The figure–ground illusions that form the basis for so much research in Gestalt psychology demonstrate this. In the three-dimensional world, however, such illusions do not exist. If a closed contour in the optic array has texture within it and not on the outside, it specifies an object.

Contours and texture density provide us with information about distances and angles of surfaces in the world.[39] A contour at which texture density approaches infinite density specifies great distance; degrees of one-way compression of optical texture specify the slant of a surface in the world. This is usually accompanied by the foreshortening of contour, as in perspective drawing, and the effects are difficult to separate. Changes in texture density also specify edges and corners in ways specific to each. Contours and textures thus provide us with much information about the "formal" relationships of the architectural world. If one accepts that the Gestalt laws of organization are learned procedures of perceiving relationships, then the design principles derived from them should focus more on surfaces, contours, and texture than on the elements of geometry used to represent them.

Conceptual clarity can also be added to the traditional architectural concept of "space" if one thinks of it explicitly in terms of opaque geometry. There are two extreme types: (1) open unenclosed space, and (2) completely enclosed space. Examples of the two types are obvious. The first seldom occurs in reality, but the situation is approximately exemplified by the prairie or being on a raft at sea. The second is exemplified by a windowless room. Between these two extremes we have various degrees of enclosure: space partially enclosed by occluding objects such as partitions, walls, screens, and trees. In architecture and urban design there is not only the space within a building but also the space between buildings that is important. All of these are enclosed by surfaces of some sort or other. They may be the natural elements of the landscape or man-made barriers.

The movement of the observer through the adjacent and nested set of spaces that constitute the man-made environment involves transformations in the optic array.[40] Movement through the environment can be passive or active and can be at very different speeds. We attend to different types of information in the optic array when we travel through it at different speeds or with different purposes. Yet, in designing, we too infrequently consider how the formal relationships which appear in an architectural drawing will appear as we move through the environment. The sequence of experiences becomes important, and the way the optic array transforms and the way certain elements remain the same are important. A number of elements have been made to develop notations for sequence experience design.[41] Possibly the most interesting aspect of these are the factors in the visual world which are identified as important for design.

The point being made here is that the student of architecture should attend more to the variables of opaque solids. Surfaces, contours, textures, and the way the optic array transforms when people move through the environment should be regarded as the basic variables of "formal" design. Perceptual learning is a process of differentiation—of an increasing ability to attend to smaller and smaller differences in the optic array. The process of education in basic design courses does not draw the attention of the aspiring architect to the variables which are the basis of perception in the three-dimensional world; rather it educates him to produce abstract and largely two-dimensional frozen art.

## CONCLUSION

A frequent criticism one hears of architecture is that many buildings look better on paper than in reality; students are criticized for making patterns on paper rather than thinking about how the building will appear in reality. That this occurs is not surprising because present formulations of basic design derived from the philosophy of art are more suitable for abstract two-dimensional art, as Kepes recognizes, than for environmental design. Thinking in terms of lines and points is not the way many of the most creative architects of the modern movement seem to think. Thus it does not seem appropriate for students to be introduced to architectural design in this way. Ecological optics can provide a framework for courses in basic design that is conceptually clear.

Of course, formal aesthetics as discussed in this paper is a very limited way to discuss the subject of design. The description here leaves out the fact that surfaces and shapes have meaning. This paper has dealt with only the surfaces and textures themselves but not with the meaning.

Different psychologists have dealt with meaning in different ways. It is a broad subject because there are many different levels of meaning. Gibson, in his book *Perception of the Visual World,* identifies six levels.[42] First is the primitive concrete meaning of things: the way surfaces look as if they can be walked on or grasped or pulled. The second level comprises "use" meanings, such as food objects and toy objects. At the third level we have the meanings of instruments and machines. Fourth are the "values and emotional meaning of things." Fifth, we have a level of meaning exemplified by signs, and sixth, by symbols. In architectural philosophy these would all be subsumed under the rubric of symbolic aesthetics by authors such as Prak.[43] Any theory of architecture has to deal with both formal and symbolic aesthetics as well as the behavioral factors which fall outside the scope of this paper.

## NOTES AND REFERENCES

1. Walter Gropius, *Scope of Total Architecture,* New York: Harper & Row, 1943; Walter Gropius, "Design topics," *Magazine of Art,* Vol. 40 (1947).
2. See Paul Overy's biography, *Kandinsky: The Language of the Eye,* New York: Praeger, 1969, ftn. 3, p. 49.
3. Luning Prak, *The Language of Architecture,* The Hague: Mouton, 1968, 5.
4. See, for instance, Peter Lloyd Jones, "The failure of basic design," *Leonardo,* Vol. 2 (April 1969), 155–160.
5. An interesting study that relates conceptual clarity to design ability is that by D. Canter, J. Johnson, and J. M'Comisky, "Familiarity with architectural concepts and academic achievement of architectural students," *Perceptual and Motor Skills,* Vol. 27 (1968), 871–874.
6. The early development of theories of perception is described in E. G. Boring, *Sensation and Perception in the History of Experimental Psychology,* New York: Appleton-Century-Crofts, 1942. See also Julian Hochberg, *Perception,* Englewood Cliffs, N.J.: Prentice-Hall, 1964. For the transactionalist theory see William H. Ittelson and Hadley Cantril, *Perception: A Transac-*
*tionalist Approach,* Garden City, N.Y.: Doubleday, 1954.
7. Of particular interest is Jean Piaget, *The Child's Construction of Reality,* New York: Basic Books, 1964.
8. Wolfgang Köhler, *Gestalt Psychology,* New York: Liveright, 1929; Kurt Koffka, *Principles of Gestalt Psychology,* New York: Harcourt, 1935.
9. James J. Gibson, *The Senses Considered as Perceptual Systems,* Boston: Houghton Mifflin, 1966; Eleanor J. Gibson, *Principles of Perceptual Learning and Development,* New York: Appleton-Century-Crofts, 1969.
10. John William Ward, "The politics of design," in Laurence B. Holland, ed., *Who Designs America?* Garden City, N.Y.: Doubleday, 1966, 57–58.
11. Ittelson and Cantril, *op. cit.*
12. Walter Gropius, *Scope of Total Architecture, op. cit.,* 22.
13. For example see "Form still follows function," *Progressive Architecture,* Vol. 28 (December 1947), 20.
14. Köhler, *op. cit.*
15. Koffka, *op. cit.,* 39.
16. Köhler, *op. cit.,* 39.
17. James J. Gibson, *Perception of the Visual World,* Boston: Houghton Mifflin, 1950.
18. Gibson, *The Senses Considered As Perceptual Systems, op. cit.*
19. *Ibid.,* 13; see also James J. Gibson, "Ecological optics," in *Vision Research,* Vol. 1 (1961), 253–262.
20. Gibson, "Ecological optics," *op. cit.,* 259.
21. *Ibid.*
22. Hans Wingler, *The Bauhaus,* tr. by Wolfgang Jabs and Basil Gilbert, Cambridge, Mass.: The MIT Press, 1969.
23. Gordon Cullen, *Townscape,* London: The Architectural Press, 1962; Philip Thiel, "A sequence-experience notation for architectural and urban spaces," *Town Planning Review,* Vol. 32 (April 1961), 33–52.
24. See, for instance, Maurice De Sausmarez, *Basic Design: The Dynamics of Visual Form,* New York: Van Nostrand Reinhold, 1964.
25. See Rudolf Arnheim, *Art and Visual Perception,* Berkeley, Calif.: University of California Press, 1954.
26. De Sausmarez, *op. cit.,* 20.
27. Gyorgy Kepes, *The Language of Vision,* Chicago: Paul Thiebold, 1944, 45.
28. *Ibid.,* 47.
29. *Ibid.*
30. Hochberg, *op. cit.,* 86.
31. Kepes, *op. cit.,* 70.
32. Koffka, *op. cit.,* 164.
33. Heinrich Wölflin, *Principles of Art History,* tr. by M. D. Hottinger, New York: Dover, 1950.
34. David Katz, *Gestalt Psychology: Its Nature and Significance,* New York: Ronald Press, 1950.
35. Prak, *op. cit.,* 10.
36. See also James J. Gibson, "The perception of surface layouts, a classification of types," November 1968 (dittoed).

37. *Ibid.*
38. James J. Gibson, "A list of ecologically valid meanings in a stationary optic array," January 1968 (dittoed).
39. *Ibid.*
40. James J. Gibson, "Memo on motion," October 1968 (mimeographed): See also James J. Gibson, "Visually controlled locomotion and visual orientation in animals," *British Journal of Psychology,* Vol. 49 (August 1958), 182–194.
41. Philip Thiel, *op. cit.;* Lawrence Halprin, *The RSVP Cycles: Creative Processes in the Human Environment,* New York: Braziller, 1969.
42. Gibson, *Perception of the Visual World, op. cit.,* 198–199.
43. Prak, *op. cit.*

# The Gestalt Psychology of Expression in Architecture

**David Levi**

**New School for Social Research**

*Gestalt psychologists, particularly Rudolf Arnheim, suggest that "expressive qualities" are bound in some way to particular configurations in our experience. This is true of the class of forms experienced through the visual modality. Visual shapes are experienced as having expressive qualities which can be used in the visual organization of architectural form and therefore should form part of every architect's vocabulary. In reality architects cannot avoid using expressive qualities and should use them to deliberately avoid the communication of unintended visual qualities. Expressive qualities also have a social function. Examples such as the Chrysler Building are analyzed and important variables identified.*

Perhaps more than any other approach currently being developed, that of Gestalt psychology seems to bear the largest promise for the arts. The Gestalt approach has actually been employed mainly in regard to artistic works created for the visual modality—especially painting and sculpture. It seems clear that the application of this approach in the arts is only in its initial phase. Nonetheless, the groundbreaking research of Professor Rudolf Arnheim well attests to the fruitfulness of such efforts.[1]

Since attempts to increase the relevancy of psychology for the arts are in their infancy, we have no developed psychology of architecture which can guide our efforts at this point. We can, however, attempt to specify those aspects of Gestalt psychology which seem to make it suitable for furthering our understanding of the arts. Such an attempt is presented here, beginning with some general considerations, and proceeding to applications in architecture and the other arts.

## EXPERIENCE

As is true of the artist, the psychologist is concerned with our direct experience. The nature and facts of our direct and immediate experience provide both origin and direction for psychological research. Here "direct experience" is taken to mean, simply, the world and ourselves as they appear. In this regard, thinking a thought and perceiving a chair are entirely comparable events—they are occurrences within our direct experience. As long as we approach our experience uncritically, we must accept and record all aspects of it, without judgment. While it is true that in our explanations we go beyond direct experience, this cannot be done without initially giving adequate concern to this experience. Both Wolfgang Köhler[2] and Kurt Koffka[3] have stressed the importance of this point.

With the determination to rely on our experience in setting and attempting to resolve problems, another central feature of the Gestalt approach requires mentioning. Perhaps the most striking general feature of our experience is its organization. Regardless of which aspect of our experience is considered, we are confronted by configurations variously occurring in relation. For example, let us consider my visual experience of the room in which I am sitting. Spread before me is an array of objects—mostly furniture. A table is in front of a chair which is, in turn, in front of a bookcase. The same table and chair are beside a couch. A mirror is above the couch; there is a wall behind the couch; and so on. Perception of things as behind, before, above, beside, and so on, are examples of the immediate experience of relation. Neither calculation nor deliberation is required for me to know that the mirror hangs above the couch. That relation of "above" is given in my perception of them. Each of the "things" which appear as before me is itself an established, organized entity. The table to my left appears as a single, unified thing. Its legs appear as belonging to it—not to the carpet on which it rests. It is seen as an extended structure having shape, internal unity, and definite location with regard to other extended structures. A concern with unified wholes in experience is characteristic of Gestalt psychology. Indeed, the word "Gestalt" could be rendered in English as "configuration" or "form."

For examples of organized wholes occurring in relation, we need not confine ourselves to the visual modality. Consider our everyday experience of speech. While listening to the utterances of another person, we experience a more or less continuous flow of words which will themselves seem to occur in different groupings. This experience contrasts with the discontinuous oscillations in the atmosphere between speaker and listener. Even though they can be analyzed into smaller units, sentences come to us as single structures. A sentence hangs together even though its terminal phoneme may follow its initial sounds by a considerable time.

Given the organized character of experience, two possible directions are suggested. On one hand, we could inquire further regarding the determinants of configurations within experience. This would turn us toward experimentation on the conditions responsible for the establishment and/or alteration of wholes in experience. The laws of perceptual organization, among Max Wertheimer's pioneering contributions, exemplify the basic findings within this direction.[4] The second possibility would allow us to take the structure of experience for granted. We might then explore the qualities of such forms as they are experienced. The latter alternative is the direction of investigation which promises to be an important link between psychology and the arts. The remainder of this work will be a discussion of whole properties.

## WHOLE PROPERTY

Generally put, "whole property" refers to qualities which are bound in some way to the occurrence of a particular configuration in our experience. Our concern will be with a type of whole property—namely, "expressive qualities." Christian von Ehrenfels presented the first extensive account of whole qualities and established two basic facts regarding whole properties.[5] First, a whole quality (therefore expressive properties, too) depends upon the occurrence of extended structures in experience. It seems that the nature of the structure itself is of major importance in determining the whole properties experienced. This leads us to the second fact—that whole properties are transposable. We can apply considerable alteration to extended wholes without destroying their whole properties. It seems important for the whole properties that the structure itself should not be altered. For example, even though we change its color and its brightness dramatically, a visual shape remains recognizable as the "same." A red circle and a yellow circle are not identical. Nonetheless, we can see them as the "same," especially if their diameters are equal. Here, the whole property of shape is being transposed between two different visual experiences. This dependence on structure and the possibility of transposition are also true of expressive qualities. An example from everyday experience can clarify this notion.

## EXPRESSIVE QUALITIES

Suppose that we come to observe the manner in which a particular person is walking along the street. He is walking slowly, his shoulders drooped slightly forward, head down. It is easy to see that such a person is depressed or down-and-out. The different aspects of his gait and posture constitute, in our visual experience, a particular spatial and temporal configuration or pattern. The particular articulation of this pattern being what it is (a "slow droopiness"), we then experience before us a depressed person moving along the street. To be somewhat more accurate, had we seen a person proceeding in such a way, probably the most outstanding quality (as a visual pattern) manifest would be his depression. We might secondarily notice his rate of motion and posture. We must first experience the person in a particular form of motion in order to experience him as depressed. In other words, the impact of seeing the individual walking in this fashion (the impact of a pattern structured in this way) is our experience of him as depressed. Seeing the walking person as depressed is an example of an expressive quality coming to us in visual organization.

When discussing the phenomena of expressive qualities, it should be emphasized that we are not concerned with empathy. It can be noted in this regard that it was not I, the observer, who was depressed—thus unfairly seeing the pedestrian as an example of my mood. Likewise, it was not necessary to observe his movements, recollect how I feel when moving, and then decide "He is depressed." No calculation was required to find that this individual *appears* depressed. This is what is meant by asserting that expressive qualities are in our experience and that they are experienced as properties of certain wholes.

Experience in our daily routine is rich in expressive qualities. But our experience of expressive qualities is by no means confined to encounters with human beings. Work done by R. Heider and M. Simmel[6] and A. E. Michotte[7] demonstrates this well. In both these experiments, subjects report their experience of simple geometric shapes which have been animated. Shapes having particular movements were consistently described in terms indicative of expressive qualities. Little triangles can be experienced variously as angry or afraid, depending upon the form of the perceived movements. This illustrates once again our assertion that expressive qualities are properties of experienced wholes.

One more example can further demonstrate the ubiquity of expressive qualities in experience. Upon listening to a song, I am impressed with how lively and bouncy its melody sounds. Again, it is not I who am "lively" and "bouncy"; these terms are descriptive of certain aspects of my auditory experience. The melody itself is lively. This "liveliness" is an expressive quality. Experiencing the melody as lively is contingent upon my perception of the articulated melodic form. The melody comes to me as sounding lively because I experience it as a whole which is articulated in a certain way. The particular pattern of crescendos and decrescendos, the specific array of accented beats, the pattern of pitch changes, all set a definite tempo—all of these evolving simultaneously give rise to the melody as an organized experience and constitute its articulation.

## ARTISTIC CREATION

Thus far, in considering the Gestalt approach within psychology, we have emphasized experience and the multiplicity of organization, patterning, and form to be found in experience. In accordance with Arnheim's work,[8] we have emphasized expressive qualities as being properties of organized wholes. The emphasis on expressive qualities, presented within this context, appears to be a prime means for advancing our understanding of art (including architecture) and its creation.

Although it was perhaps implicit in our examples, let us now attempt to make explicit and justification for an emphasis on expressive qualities. Two truisms can serve as a starting point. First of all, art (in the broad sense) is created by human beings for human beings. Second, art works (excepting, of course, the explicitly verbal arts such as literature, poetry, dramatics, etc.) have significance but without functioning in the referential way characteristic of words. There is no language (in the usual sense of the word "language") employed in creating and appreciating art works. An artist is concerned, foremost, with the fashioning of an object (or in the case of composers and choreographers, an operation) to be experienced by himself and others.[9] The art object, or art performance, is created for its effects on experience. Manipulation of the formal characteristics of the object, or operation, becomes the artist's method for determining various aspects of the experience of an observer. Since an artist is essentially interested in patterning some aspect of the observer's experience, it follows that some considerations regarding the nature of experience could be most useful in furthering the artist's goal. That experience tends toward organization (as discussed above) is generally a fundamental assumption of artistic creation. Obviously, the properties attendant upon such experienced forms are also within the domain of an artist's legitimate concerns.

This complicates the task of artistic creation considerably. Not only must an artist be technically adept (that is, in possession of the skills required for constructing the form or planning the operation), but he must also be attuned to the experiential properties, especially the expressive qualities, which he stands to manipulate. Arnheim[10] has emphasized the dangers in any artistic training which neglects sensitizing the artist to expressive qualities in experience. He makes the additional point that this danger, of neglecting experiential properties, is particularly great in such highly technical forms as architecture. Training in geometric analysis and construction techniques cannot ensure proper cognizance of expressive qualities.

## ARCHITECTURAL EXPRESSIVE QUALITY

Architectural forms can be assessed simply as another class of forms experienced through the visual modality. Therefore, we can investigate the expressive qualities of such forms. Below, several architectural forms will be discussed with regard to expressive qualities as a further illustration of the Gestalt approach as outlined above.

Arnheim[11] compares the semicircle to the parabola as visual forms. The semicircle appears rigid and contained, while the parabola appears dynamic and directed. Arnheim indicated that their comparative appearances are in keeping with the complexity of their respective defining conditions—namely, the circle having a single limiting condition (the locus of all points equidistant from a given point) versus the two conditions limiting a parabola (the locus of all points equidistant from a line and a point outside a line). The shapes reflect the forces bringing them into organized form— the semicircle appears relatively static, the parabola more dynamic (Figure 1).

Arnheim considers these two forms independently, and separately from each other. Nonetheless, such an

**Figure 1**

**Figure 2**

**Figure 3**

analysis can serve to illuminate the expressive qualities attending a form in which semicircle and parabola are both incorporated and contrasted. Let us consider New York City's Chrysler Building—particularly the upper portion. The building literally soars; it does not appear to rest on the ground so much as it appears to push forcefully into the air (Figure 2). This soaring quality is an expressive quality. As such, we can further our understanding of it by discussing the articulation of its form. Seen from the side, the overall shape of the building's top portion is that of an elongated and sharpened point. Although conveying a definite direction, points do not in and of themselves, appear as soaring—observe a pencil point (or for that matter, the upper portion of the Empire State Building) for an example of a nonsoaring point. In our examples above, we have attempted to understand the nature of an expressive quality by reference to the kind of form (i.e., the particular articulation of the form) manifesting the quality. The apex crowning the Chrysler Building is articulated

into a series of curves. From the base to the tip of the apex, the curves gradually change from semicircle to parabola to spire. Since the apex is finished in a reflective metal, each curved shape is distinctly apparent and is easily seen as a single "outside" surface. In terms of the above comparison, there is a clear transition from a static and rigid form to a tense and dynamic form. Furthermore, this transition occurs within a visually unified form. We are suggesting that it is the experience of this change united in a single form (i.e., the experience of the apex as a form articulated in this way) which is responsible for our experience of the expressive quality of "soaring."

Another building, a view of which is presented in Figure 3, will present us with a quite different architectural form to consider. Taken as a whole, this form has a quite ominous, almost sinister, character about it. Its quality is definitely threatening. Again, considering the articulation of this form can provide us with a greater understanding of this experience. For one thing, the building is strikingly solid in appearance. There is a large central mass wedged between two smaller, but equally solid, vertical masses. The central mass protrudes over the sidewalk. Likewise, entrance to the building is possible only between two vertical masses and under a smaller horizontal mass, which seems pressed into place by its vertical neighbors. There is something potentially crushing about the way these large, heavy-appearing masses are arranged. There is no apparent support for the protruding central mass, as well as the apparent pressure exerted between the two vertical masses (and hence over the entrance). A sense of controlled force dominates our experience of these masses. Both "powerful" and "ominous" qualities seem to derive from the apparent tension between the comprising masses of this form.

That the forms appear so solid seems to derive from two features of their structure. First of all is the surface texture—the outside walls are rough, uneven and virtually unbroken. Second, the contours or edges of the building are not sharply or clearly defined: the corners are bluntly formed by the meeting of concrete slabs. The rough texture and blunt edge tend to act against any experience of surface as separable from volume. The outside of the building is seen as the result of precariously arranging some very large concrete blocks —rather than as the result of having folded a continuous sheet in this particular way.

Simply by way of contrast to the above two examples, a brief third example will be offered. Figure 4 presents an angle view of the New York University Library. If observed for a short time, it shows an eerie, almost undulating, quality. Although rather enormous, this structure appears quite flat. In our examples above, analysis has revealed the important role, first, of sharp contours, then, of blunt contours as important for the expressive effect of different architectural forms. In this example the central edge, facing us, is completely indistinct. The varying textures comprising the building's surface seem to have thoroughly masked this contour. This flat and eerie quality seems largely dependent upon the role of a completely indistinct contour in the context of an otherwise well-defined shape. It is really difficult to determine whether the angle which we are viewing points out toward us or in away from us. The flatness seems related both to the strangely shaded

**Figure 4**

surface and to the masked contour. The overall effect is that of a rather unstable appearing shape having an eerie quality.[12]

## ARCHITECTURAL IMPORTANCE

Our emphasis has been primarily on the structural importance of contour and texture. However, it would be possible to have followed Arnheim further and to have considered the role of proportion in architectural form. For example, in the second architectural form treated above, a concern with proportion would have led us to consider the relative sizes of its masses as possibly of expressive importance. Alexander Walton[13] as also outlined other avenues from which one can approach architectural forms. He has given attention to the relative dominance of the horizontal or vertical directions as well as to the amount of internal repetition of detail.

Two other reasons can be given for the importance, architecturally, of expressive qualities in experience.

**Figures 5 and 6**
In considering the form of the Sydney Opera House, one is struck by the dominance of the roof and its "billowing" expressive quality. However, if we view the form of its geographical context, a quite different impression is conveyed. The placement of this form in this context (i.e., a harbor) is rather a good example of using an architectural form thematically. The general feeling of being-propelled-over-water thus emerges as a theme in the interaction of this form with its context.

The first reason is actually a negative statement of much that has been offered above. Being a specialist in the creation of certain kinds of visual forms, the architect really cannot avoid the use of expressive qualities. In other words, an architect has the choice of designing his forms so as to create certain expressive forms deliberately—or of simply engineering a physical structure and allowing its experiential qualities to be what they will (i.e., unintentional manipulation of expressive qualities). Unfortunately, the latter alternative seems very frequently the one taken. Any American city is likely to be oversupplied with examples of buildings which have been designed with no regard for expressive qualities. The extensive tracts of public housing, in the South Bronx for example, are prime instances of this. These buildings form row after row of brown, brick shoeboxes. They contribute substantially to the unnatural, and certainly uninviting, landscape of this area. It seems that much of the contemporary building which is "faceless" or simply "ugly" has resulted from an insensitivity to the expressive qualities of experienced forms.

The second reason expressive qualities are of architectural importance pertains to a social function performed by expressive qualities in architectural forms. We have noted above that the arts, excluding the verbal arts, employ no conventional language. This does not necessarily entail the conclusion that such art works are thus mute and self-contained. For example, it is not surprising to learn that the massive building shown in Figure 3 is an armory. Given that we have the extra-architectural knowledge of what an armory is, the visual experience of this form definitely emphasizes certain nonbenign aspects of this institution. That is, we can find a kind of congruence between the "ominous" and "powerful" qualities of the form and our knowledge concerning the social functions of it as an armory.

The Chrysler Building, despite its beauty, does not seem in any obvious way congruent with the social functions of the business ethic. Although the building itself does soar, we might resist concluding that Chrysler (as a corporation), too, soars above them all. Here, our extra-architectural knowledge of corporations is not congruent with the expressive quality of this corporation building. We are not arguing that architectural forms *ought* to manifest expressive characteristics consonant with their larger social functions. Rather, we are suggesting that this is certainly a possibility. Clearly, some of the greatest architectural works available to us are instances in which expressive qualities have been skillfully, and deliberately, shaped in accordance with the larger social meaning of a building. For example, the Reims Cathedral (and much genuine Gothic architecture) reveals both incredible sensitivity to expressive qualities and firm insight regarding their relation to certain religious themes. It is not possible that every building could so brilliantly unite expressive qualities and social meaning. Nonetheless, at least some thought should be given to the expressive character of a form before it is more or less permanently established in the public domain.

## CONCLUSION

Obviously, the history of architecture is replete with instances in which an architect has relied heavily on expressive qualities in arriving at an architectural form. Anytime an architect is guided by careful attention to his own experience of form, expressive qualities of these forms will undoubtedly influence his resulting creation. Louis Kahn is a contemporary architect whose works display a sensitivity to expressive qualities. However, it seems that something would be gained if the notion of expressive quality were explicitly included among the tools of all those in the architectural arts. A slightly altered view of the architect's problem would emerge.

The general role of an architect as creator of building forms would remain much the same. Two important sets of requirements would still be seen as governing the particularities selected for architectural forms. On the one hand are the physical–technical requirements. The particular architectural form must be possible given the materials, engineering techniques, locale, and budget available. On the other hand, we have the functional requirements. It must be possible for people to carry out certain anticipated activities in the structure. Obviously, allowing for both these requirements does not uniquely or completely determine what form a building will take. It is in getting some more specific guidelines for form determination that expressive qualities can be used creatively. This seems to demand a somewhat playful attitude on behalf of the architect. He should attempt to vary the architectural forms he is considering purely as a means of exploring their expressive qualities. By taking seriously the expressive qualities of experienced forms, the architect stands in a position where he is capable of altering the character of the environment in which we live. In a sense, this is proposing a third class of requirements for consideration by the architect in the execution of his art—a class of experiential requirements.

## NOTES AND REFERENCES

1. Further references to Arnheim's work appear below.
2. Wolfgang Köhler, *Gestalt Psychology,* New York: Liveright, 1929.
3. Kurt Koffka, *Principles of Gestalt Psychology,* New York: Harcourt, 1935.
4. For example, see Max Wertheimer, "Principles of perceptual organization," in D. Beardslee and M. Wertheimer, eds., *Readings in Perception,* New York: Van Nostrand Reinhold, 1958.
5. Köhler, *op. cit., 102–104.*
6. R. Heider and M. Simmel, "An experimental study of apparent behavior," *American Journal of Psychology,* Vol. 57 (1944), 43–59.
7. A. E. Michotte, "The emotional significance of movement," in M. Arnold, ed., *The Nature of Emotion,* Baltimore: Penguin Books, 1968.
8. For example, Rudolf Arnheim, "The Gestalt theory of expression," *Psychological Review,* Vol. 56, No. 3 (1949); Rudolf Arnheim, "Perceptual and aesthetic aspects of movement response," *Journal of Personality,* Vol. 19 (1951), 265–281.
9. Although the architectural form has utilitarian functions as well, it seems quite justified to consider it primarily as an artistic form.
10. Rudolf Arnheim, "From function to expression," *Journal of Aesthetics and Art Criticism,* Vol. 23 (1964), 29–41.
11. Rudolf Arnheim, *Art and Visual Perception,* Berkeley, Calif.: University of California Press, 1954, 363–364.
12. Worthy of mention is the fact that the effects discussed in these examples are actually more compelling when the buildings are viewed firsthand.
13. Alexander Walton, *Architecture and Music,* Cambridge, England: Heffer & Sons, 1934.

*The effective use of light has been the traditional hallmark of an aesthetic experience in architecture. Yet there is little real understanding of the use of natural light or artificial lighting to enhance the human experience of architecture. Architects need to be concerned with design objectives and concepts of implementation. Different settings require different design goals. Three types of research offer insights to the architect: human engineering, psychological correlates, and global responses to the environment. In drawing on this research, it must be noted that (1) lighting requirements are not static although architects often design for them as if they are, and (2) questions of control, personalization, and choice are very important.*

# Psychological Factors in the Use of Light and Lighting in Buildings

**D. Geoffrey Hayward**

**City University of New York**

It is indisputable that light is a necessary condition for living, and that it needs to be an integral part of any design process. That is, people in most societies rely more on visual perception than on other perceptual systems to obtain information about the environmment and their relation to it. Such a state of affairs has significant consequences for a design process. For example, the quantity and quality of light available in any setting lends structure to our experience and has a strong effect on human emotions, communication, and behavior. Also, it is significant that the effective use of light has been the traditional hallmark of an aesthetic experience in architecture (Figure 1): "imagine the surprise and animation experienced when a sunbeam shining through the stained glass window in a cathedral, wanders slowly through the twilight of a nave and suddenly hits the altarpiece. What a stimulus for the spectators."[1] Such dramas of space, light, and symbolism are not available simply at the flick of a switch (although at great expense and with great ingenuity they can be approximated). More importantly, they are arrived at by a careful consideration of human purpose and experience and through the understanding of how both

**Figure 1**

planned and unplanned illumination can give structure and inspiration to our everyday experiences.

Few architects and fewer building owners have any real understanding of how the luminous environment can be orchestrated to enhance human experience. Even the buildings of the best architects have blinding glares, tortuous rhythms, disturbing patterns, no responsive controls, and no recognition of the marvelous ambience of natural light and its role in linking people to the rhythms of the universe. Most architects appear to be concerned with a building as a static object to be artifically lit for a single purpose rather than as a variable setting responsive to human needs, purposes, and aspirations.

How, then, does one go about conceptualizing the role of light in the context of a design process? Does one merely follow conventional rules of thumb for lighting systems? Are novel lighting effects necessary? Are they always warranted?

Essentially, there are two sets of concepts which are important here. These concepts are also important in almost every other aspect of a design process: they are the *objectives* and the *implementation concepts*.

The objectives are developed by the designer and are the root formulation of the design scheme: they may be manifestations of the designer's intuition, specific client requirements, or both. Thus this first set of concepts is basic to any critique. The most inspiring and useful designs are those which grow from explicitly formulated objectives which are responsive to the variety of people affected by them. This is as true with light as for any other part of the design.

Implementation concepts are those which concern particular design parameters in relation to the objectives of the design process. Obviously, the use of the second set of concepts presumes the formulation of the first set. Also, the implementation concepts are crucial to the architect's communication:

*Only by manipulating the physical properties of his environment—heat, air, light, color, odor, sound, surface, and space—can the architect communicate with his client at all. And only by doing it well, i.e., meeting all man's requirements, objective and subjective, can he create buildings which men may find beautiful.*[2]

Thus, the "success" of a design depends on the designer's ability to provide for human needs and purposes through the implementation of stated objectives.

What are these implementation concepts? Do they employ specific criteria to account for human needs during a lighting design process? Yes, there are criteria available—even more than the number available for an acoustic or thermal design process. However, the collection of criteria for light is neither well organized, nor readily understandable, nor is that collection adequate in explaining phenomenological or behavioral responses to illumination. There are descriptive conventions and measures such as foot candles, foot lamberts, lumens, and illuminance; yet it is not sufficient to know such things as the intensity, spread, or color of light from a lamp nor even the light reflecting value of a color, texture, or material. These descriptors have not been tied to a useful theory of perception, affect, and experience, and they are only beginning to be organized in a way that guides designing. The mammoth task which has not been achieved is the integration of these measures with design objectives for particular kinds of settings. Hence, the architect has to rely on his own experience; successes and failures are largely a function of his own objectiveness and acuteness of observation and his ability to project these observations to space which is yet to be built.

The inadequacy of our present understanding of illumination in architecture stems from an incomplete consideration of human purpose and experience as well as a lack of systematic study of various design parameters as they influence human behavior. For example, it is not always sufficiently clear that different criteria are appropriate for different reasons. Common sense would tell us that "task performance" is an inappropriate set of criteria for a chapel (except, perhaps, for the podium), and "orientation" may not be crucial in one's own home, although these same constructs are important in libraries and large department stores, respectively.

Several preliminary principles may serve to point up the complexity of the problem of establishing lighting design concepts:

1. Requirements for illumination in particular spaces must be based on the activities being designed for as well as the intended psychological and visual experiences which are desired in those spaces.

2.  Different kinds of activities, design objectives, states of mind, times of day, and so on, may very well require different illumination or even different systems of illumination.
3.  Light is a phenomenon which we usually take for granted: we are usually unaware of the nature of light in a space until we are forced to attend to it. Therefore, it is not only the phenomenological experience but also the nonphenomenological, the overt behavioral, the unconscious influences that are important. It is extremely difficult, then, to anticipate design requirements from a set of experiences which cannot be expressed, which are not usually felt, and for which we cannot state our explicit needs and preferences.
4.  A design process must always come to terms with a series of alternatives before implementation. In lighting design one should consider the *possible alternatives* of intensity, direction of light, color rendition, and so on, when the program is being developed. Anticipating the consequences of those alternatives is crucial, and difficult.
5.  Variation in discrete requirements and variations within a changing context of behavior, purpose, and preference should be taken into account as early as possible.

Some clarification of these complex issues is possible through a more detailed discussion.

## DIFFERENT SETTINGS, DIFFERENT GOALS

There are often several, not necessarily concurrent, human purposes to be served in a given physical setting, and several lighting solutions may be required. For example, in stores, lighting is important for the display of merchandise; it can also make circulation paths more readily apparent and attractive, provide the means for shoppers to orient themselves, and generally assist attendants in carrying out their tasks. These different needs can be met in different ways. However, if one perfectly even, nondirectional, diffused lighting system were installed, the achievement of all these purposes might well be reduced. The designer must select and make use of various means available to him to enhance the necessary environmental messages. Some of these depend on light, but color, form, texture, pattern, and spatial organization are among other means available.

In any event the differential use of light can enhance the functional, phenomenal, and symbolic experience of any environment and reduce or increase its apparent complexity and ambiguity. It can be a source of perceptual strain or it can reduce it.

What is of great importance is that there are different activities and different psychological states of mind which must be accommodated, sometimes in different settings, sometimes in the same setting. Any given lighting scheme may not be appropriate in a different setting, and even the same criteria may not be appropriate to evaluate lighting schemes in different settings. Or, if some criteria are appropriately applied across different settings, then perhaps the range of measures for one criterion may vary from setting to setting. For example, fast-food places maintain high levels of illumination to increase customer turnover, while soft lighting in bars has been used to keep the turnover down, which is "good business" in each case. These applications of level of illumination consider neither the relaxed digestion of food nor a reasonable consumption of alcohol.

Since recurring types of buildings and space roughly characterize (perhaps too roughly) different human activities and purposes, each new combination presents a new problem in analyzing the goals of the setting and the likely consequences of intended lighting schemes. The designer needs to consider the range of man–environment transactions to identify which are essential and which are secondary relative to the setting being designed.

Sometimes the relationship of goals and activities to particular settings seems to be relatively straightforward: when designing lighting for a factory, one is likely to be concerned with task performance and fatigue. When designing a space for meditation, mood, reverence, and mysticism are likely to be more important. At other times it is not so clear. Different goals and activities may overlap and compete for lighting requirements. However, there are times when one has cause to wonder if the straightforward relationships are all that clear. A friend once designed a lighting scheme for a space in a large mansion that was to be converted into a church. He proposed to complement the dark, warm wood-paneled walls without disturbing the overhead wooden beams which added to the character of the space. He also proposed to concentrate most of the light on the altar with minimal, largely peripheral light in the nave itself. In his absence from the congregation, however, a local contractor entered the picture and installed several rows of bare, cool, white fluorescent lamps to provide an even 30 foot candles for the entire space! The tubes were suspended directly from the overhead wooden beams. There is no mysticism or reverence in bare, cool, white tubes, and this is certainly one instance when the limitations of using foot candles as a criterion of illumination should have been recognized.

Variations in activities and requirements over time may also seem like common-sense considerations, but they are usually forgotten. Different lighting schemes may be desirable to complement different brightnesses of daylight, different weather conditions, different temperatures, different frequencies and qualities of human activity, or for different times of the day. However, most of these changing conditions are ignored because the relationship of illumination to them is not understood or they are not thought to be worthwhile.

For a moment, though, consider the importance of different influences as a function over time. Participants in an office have had to *turn off* the light fixtures when their orientation changed from specific tables to one end of the room. A presentation at one end was an extremely uncomfortable experience in the light of the previous group interaction. Furthermore, the goals, activities, and requirements in a setting may change gradually or even drastically from day to night. A dining area with exposure to daylight may be a very different place in the evening from what it was at lunchtime. Task performance, orientations, moods, the sense of place, and so on may warrant different lighting requirements. For orientation, focal points may be initiated, changed, or eliminated. For mood, illumination levels may serve different purposes, and have different meanings. In dormitories it is not unusual for some spaces to be lounges by day and quiet study areas by night. Different populations of people, with different preferences, may be attracted to the setting and engage in different kinds of activities. In all, the requirements of different goals and activities may lead to many different lighting schemes, not only in different settings, but in the same setting over time and space.

The requirements of particular activities and human needs should be the important determinants for a light-

ing design process rather than the formal or customary scheme for buildings of a certain type. Unfortunately, any individual's knowledge is limited relative to the settings, activities, goals, and consequences of alternative lighting systems. No one can be expected to be knowledgeable about the entire range of activities and typical building types. Therefore, attempts to develop comprehensive sets of criteria for the specification of appropriate lighting schemes are of great interest.[3]

The existing comprehensive surveys of lighting systems and lighting requirements are also important in describing the phenomenon of light. For instance, understanding the linear nature of light is fundamental to understanding how one perceives the environment. Light selects information from the environment according to spatial location and relative to the light source, in that those things out of line from the light source are not conveyed while those things in direct or reflected line with it are conveyed. Light also structures information from the environment in that forms recede and surfaces cohere according to the incidence with which light strikes the form in the environment and according to the nature of the surface on which it falls.

In addition to the nature of light, the functioning of the eye is also important. Normal functioning of the eye requires directional illumination to be accompanied by an appreciable surrounding brightness. Under the sun and clear sky conditions at least 20 percent of the horizontal surface illumination is due to this surrounding brightness, while the entire illumination in overcast sky conditions is, of course, due to it. If the brightness of a surface is excessive in particular directions (criteria are available for this judgment), then our vision in these directions is subjected to major visual discomfort and disability which we know as "glare." Consequently, the brightness of a light source or an object relative to its individual surroundings has a great deal to do with visual comfort. Research has shown that comfortable seeing conditions are found when this brightness ratio lies between 1 and 3.[4]

Yet many architects argue that this information is totally inadequate in that it does not tell anything about how people feel about the luminous quality of the settings in which such tasks are performed nor does it explain such subtleties as the lighting in Notre Dame du Haut at Ronchamp (Figure 2). The fact of the matter is that achieving an understanding of light and illumina-

**Figure 2**
**Photo credit: Elliott Kaufman**

tion requires a multidisciplinary effort that covers the multiplicity of purposes for which we use light in architecture.

The diversity of specializations interested and involved with light and lighting is helpful in this respect, as each participant in a multidisciplinary effort is obligated to see the issues from other perspectives. Thus an engineer may begin to explore the question of what illumination or distribution of it might lead to "cheerfulness," and a psychologist may begin to explore the kinds of conditions for which "sparkle" is important. Most significantly, a multidisciplinary effort offers the potential of understanding the psychological experience of users in a manner which allows its application directly to a design process.

## WHAT RESEARCH HAS TO OFFER

Research in lighting comes from a number of sources and disciplines: engineers, psychologists, architects, opthalmologists, color consultants, and others have contributed to this body of research. As might be expected, this variety of interests presents a diversity and sometimes even an incompatibility of goals, methodology, and language. For example, the goal of an architect may be to design a low-cost, efficient lighting system, while the goal of a psychologist may be to develop psychological assessment techniques for different conditions of illumination. As a consequence the architect may seek analytical information on the characteristics of a particular lighting fixture, while the psychologist is seeking to assess the environment as a whole. Their descriptive conventions may be unrelated. Despite these differences, interdisciplinary contributions to an understanding of illumination and its potential effects are both necessary and compelling.

*At least three general classifications of research work have important implications for a lighting design process: human engineering, psychological correlates and global responses to the environment.* Each of these characterizations has applicability to the wider range of issues in architectural design.

In human engineering research, man is considered as a system of interrelated sensory mechanisms with the receptors for each sense needing certain conditions for optimum performance. Most studies have been carried out in laboratories in experimentally controlled conditions and in static settings with a focus on single activities. Much of the research has concentrated on the visual task. Such work has had a long and successful history in clarifying the nature of visibility, sensitivities of the eye, and visual performance in general. Deriving principles from their research, investigators have iden-

**Table 1[10]**
**Psychological Responses to Color**

| Color | Psychological Response |
| --- | --- |
| Red | exciting, stimulating, defiant, contrary, hostile, hot, passionate, active, fierce, intense, happy, sometimes irritating |
| Blue | calm, peaceful, soothing, tender, secure, comfortable, melancholic, contemplative, subduing, sad, dignified, restful |

tified factors such as illumination level, brightness, contrast, glare, sparkle, veiling reflection, and spectral quality. It has been demonstrated, for example, that contrast (the comparison of object reflectance with background reflectance) so greatly affects visual acuity, and visual performance (speed and accuracy) that, in many circumstances, contrast in visual task is more important than level of illumination.[5] Other research has demonstrated that performance under low illumination with certain color-rendering qualities can be as good as performance under higher illumination with poor color rendition.[6] These studies are only representative of a vast number of investigations which are reviewed in the *IES Handbook*.[7]

The research on psychological correlates focuses more on human values, associations, and learned relationships to light and color effects. Correlates usually have limited applicability outside the boundaries of particular societies, regions, age groups, or settings for which they are formulated, and they are related to trends in fashion and aesthetics. It is essential to know what these correlates are if designs are to complement the life styles of those for whom they are intended. Builders, architects, and advertising consultants have commonly based decisions on their beliefs about these correlates—for example, that landscapes are pleasant and that yellow packages won't sell.

Investigations of psychological correlates of different types and degrees of illumination are considerably less numerous than studies of color. These are not, of course, independent.[8] One study noted differential responses, including anxiety, arousal, subjective temperature perception, and degree of comfort, to red, white, and blue light.[9] Others have produced lists of psychological responses to different colors. A list of such responses to red and blue is given in Table 1.

Some architects believe that color choices should be based on personal preference. Others point out that in some cases these may not be the most appropriate. For instance, when designing for people with mental or psychological disorders there may not be a direct relationship between preferred and "therapeutic" colors.[11]

There are many "laws" for designing successful color schemes—for example, "complementaries are often used together as a balance of opposites." It has even been suggested that complementary colors have not only a visual effect but also have an effect on activity. For example, "red may be suited to produce the emotional background out of which ideas and action will emerge; in green these ideas will be developed and the ideas executed."[12] Although there is considerable research and speculation on the psychological correlates of color, there are often startling divergencies in conclusions. Norman and Scott note the differences in opinion regarding color preferences among the mentally retarded: "schizophrenics according to Mosse prefer yellow: to Birren, blue, while Warner says they do not like green and yellow, an antipathy they share with manic depressives."[13] Such investigations have usually arrived at such conclusions in one or both of the following ways: color schemes that have been found to exist with some frequency are assumed to be the ones that *should be* recommended; or architects are used as judges and their conclusions are accepted as statements of fact. It is hardly surprising that such differences of opinion exist.

Although individual designs need not be geared to the median of other color schemes, studies of normative responses to color and studies of acceptable and unacceptable color schemes are useful in anticipating the likely consequences of proposed schemes.

The third line of research focuses on the technical aspects of lighting and more global responses to the way the environment is lighted. These studies have used multidimensional scaling of several environments that have the same purpose. For example, one investigation had architectural students rate a series of ten libraries on several semantic scales.[14] Results indicated that several attributes of the environment were being responded to with some consistency: level of illumination, room luminance, general glare and glare from individual fixtures, distribution of light, colorfulness, naturalness of color, color of light, modeling, fixture arrangement, and others. These results, however, need to be tempered by the knowledge that semantic scales themselves identify the attribute to be judged. Also, the students for this research were observing and not studying at the time (which is one way of dealing with principle 3, stated earlier). Many such methodological questions arise in studies like these. However, this research has produced examples of consistently rated environments and lighting schemes. Extremes are easily identifiable and specific objections can lead to recommendations for future designs. For example, a consistently low rating for a particular arrangement of fixtures may lead to its disuse in similar situations.

One other series of invesigations has also used multi-dimensional scaling to elicit broad dimensions of the response to environment. Specifically, one room was equipped with several different lighting schemes which were varied through six conditions.[15] In contrast to the previous investigation this research used many rating scales which were not identifications of particular attributes,[16] and then dimensions of response were constructed from a factor analysis of those ratings. It is interesting to note that the investigators were able to identify such dimensions as "evaluative," "perceptual clarity," and "spaciousness" for illumination, which are on the same order as the global responses to environment in a larger context.

One of the hazards of using research data for design is that many apparent conclusions are actually artifacts of the research situation itself. This may be due to unusual experimental conditions, interpersonal expectations, suspiciousness of the experimenter's intent, desire to report what is wanted by the experimenter, lack of sensitization to pretest conditions, and experimenter bias.[17] Conclusions may also be specific to the research situation, as when one uses subjects from an unrepresentative population. Using subjects who are not in familiar surroundings, or who are not engaged in the activities which are usually performed in particular settings, further complicates the analysis of research data. As such, one may look to research for answers only to find that poorly conducted investigations have produced new problems and misleading results. Improved sensitivity to these possibilities and the inclusion of several disciplines in a research team can help correct these problems.

## CHANGE AND NOVELTY IN THE ENVIRONMENT

One of the common assumptions built into large-scale lighting systems is that lighting requirements are static. Indeed, as Walter Gropius noted, this is often the argument for artificial rather than natural lighting

sources.[18] Consequently, most lighting systems either function in the way they were initially designed or they don't function at all. The on–off option is the only possible change. Small wonder that one gets fatigued in any setting over long periods: it may not be the work itself which is tiring but rather the static position of ones body and the monotony of the visual environment over time. Taking an occasional walk to someone else's desk or making trips to the water cooler and the bathroom serve the function of relieving fatigue. One's body changes metabolic rates, and one's eyes escape the work-surface illumination.

In point of fact, variation in experience is the *normal* condition of human behavior. This variation serves "in the organism's development, in its interaction with the environment, and in the effective experiences of man."[19] To deny this variation by designing a constant visual environment is bound to produce undesirable consequences.

One prominent example of how variation in lighting produced change in human behavior is the classic example at the Hawthorne plant of Western Electric, where experiments were undertaken to investigate the effects of a variety of practices and environmental conditions on the performance of employees.[20] For lighting, a test room was selected and initial performance measures were recorded. Then the level of illumination was increased. Lo and behold, performance increased, too. Again the level of illumination was increased, and again performance increased. In fact, this occurred several times until the illumination level was up to about 200 foot candles—unheard of in the 1930's—and each change had produced an increase in performance! The experiments had apparently confirmed a direct relationship between the level of illumination and the level of performance until someone decided to reverse the process. The level of illumination was decreased by the previous increment, and performance increased again! No matter what change was introduced, there was a consequent increase in performance. The investigators ultimately concluded that it was not the light, per se, that was influencing performance, but rather the fact that the employees were aware of some special attention by the management, and they worked harder; the "message" was merely perceived through light. Apprehension of messages through light is as old as the sun and the moon.

Yet human behavior is not related to changes in stimulation along simple dimensions. The complexity of the relationship is pointed up when, for example, one notes that a change in stimulation may produce results which would have been unanticipated from a prior knowledge of behavior under similar stimulation. Furthermore, attention and behavior—especially exploratory behavior[21]—are influenced by novelty, complexity, incongruity, and surprisingness. At least some of these stimulus variables should be included in a visual environment if continuing interest is expected.

There are some obvious possibilities that one could draw upon to introduce desirable variation in the visual environment. For example, daylight changes during the course of the day and fades out completely in the evening. The changing color, direction, and quality of daylight can be used to good advantage for introducing variety. However, that is not to say that one merely adds windows, thereby creating novel effects. There needs to be some consideration given to the direction of light that one wants to admit, the surfaces upon which the daylight will be incident, the materials through which it will be transmitted or reflected, the possibilities of excessive heat and glare being introduced as a consequence of daylight, and so on.

Variation in intensity, and sparkle, and the existence of shadows, may also produce interesting effects as many architects have shown. Often, pieces of sculpture in outdoor gardens reflect light in unique ways. Changing daylight can introduce dazzling effects which can attract one's attention repeatedly. These effects are very stimulating and much of the excitement derives from their ever-changing character.

Despite the strangely uninteresting sense of these pieces at night, it would be a mistake to try to artificially reproduce the natural effects produced by daylight. Recreating the sun, having fixed shadows, fixed reflections, and so on is lamentable in its unreality. It ranks alongside fake fireplaces—with the light "dancing" around on the "logs"—as a manifestation of a completely misunderstood experience.

## CONTROL, PERSONALIZATION, AND CHOICE

Although much of the thought about the effect of lighting systems on people is concerned with morale, performance, interest, and fatigue, the psychological construct of motivation can be of great potential value to the design of the luminous environment. In terms of high and sustained motivational states, control, personalization, choice, and interpersonal relationships may be more important than physical attributes of an environment. It has been pointed out, for example, that "in any situational context, the individual attempts to organize his physical environment so that it *maximizes* his freedom of choice."[22] Unfortunately, totally designed or bureaucratically controlled environments inhibit significant transactions between man and the environment, thereby stifling personal reorganization of space and disallowing any significant range of choices. Such inhibitive systems assume that we are almost always designing for large, anonymous populations rather than for people who are expected to act intelligently and creatively. Even though most people, at one time or another, have reasonable and legitimate reasons for making changes in their environment, they are rarely allowed to do so. They cannot personalize their spaces. Apparently, the environment takes on greater importance than the people who use it, within the context of some sets of rules and norms. Other assumptions are that chaos will ensue if individuals are allowed some opportunity for transaction with the environment and one another, that chaos is bad, and that transaction with the environment requires some kind of special knowledge which can not be given out to just anyone. If, however, variation in experience is healthy, then it makes sense to allow people some opportunity for control and choice so that they may regulate or use the environment in a way which is most appropriate for themselves, acting individually and in concert. This regulation may be influenced by their preferences, activities, moods, or by their stimulation seeking, and it may focus on type and quality of stimulation as well as quantity. Even in the case of large lighting systems, such regulation or use would be possible by reducing the scale of control of those systems. A much more responsive and appropriate environment as well as a new means of territorial communication would be created if each person were provided with something as simple as a dimmer to control the amount of light in his or her work area. Interestingly, the creation of an appropriate environment would then become a *process,* responding to changes in activity, mood, amount of daylight, and so on, if these items are salient changes for the individual. Even if the dimmers were only used infrequently, the levels to which they were regulated would have been determined by each individual's needs and sensitivities. This kind of arrangement would better approximate a more useful and stimulating environment.

## WHEN FACED WITH DESIGN SITUATIONS

Although a great deal of attention still needs to be directed towards a better understanding of psychological factors in lighting, there are several sources available which provide information about light and its use in architecture. These sources focus more on the "human engineering" aspects of design than on the other two areas of interest to architects, namely, psychological correlates and the more global responses to the environment.

The use of natural and artificial light should certainly be regarded as an integral part of design and not something which is considered once the shell has been designed. It should form an integral part of programmatic, schematic, preliminary, and final design development. Evaluation and testing of the environmental effects taking place should be conducted at each stage to monitor the potential success of the products and process.

Identification of the needs and potentials for illumination relative to the activities and goals being planned for should be one of the first steps in architectural programming. It is also here that research should be useful, especially in understanding how people might evaluate their needs in different situations, and whether intended psychological states of mind are likely to be fostered by the proposed environment and its scheme of illumination. The development of requirements for a lighting scheme should grow from the needs of the people and activities to be accommodated. Such lighting scheme requirements can be considered as the beginnings of a performance specification, which would include the following:
1. The analysis of activities and tasks.
2. The desirable spatial illumination (including relationships with other spatial variables such as form, texture, color, and direction).
3. Illumination for variety and novelty if not dysfunctional to design objectives nor to the needs of people in particular settings,
4. Provisions for regulations and control of the scheme by individuals.

## NOTES AND REFERENCES

1. Walter Gropius, *Scope of Total Architecture,* New York: Collier, 1962, 41.
2. James Marston Fitch, "The aesthetics of function," *Annals of the New York Academy of Sciences,* Vol. 128, (1965), 706–714.
3. Cf. John Flynn and Samuel Mills, *Architectural Lighting Graphics,* New York: Van Nostrand Reinhold, 1962; Robert A. Boyd, "The luminous environment," in *School Environments Research 2: Environmental Evaluations,* Ann Arbor, Mich.: Architectural Research Laboratory, University of Michigan, 1965, 105–129; John Flynn and Arthur Segil, *Architectural Interior Systems: Lighting Air Conditioning, Acoustics,* New York: Van Nostrand Reinhold, 1970.
4. Boyd, *op. cit.*
5. Sylvester K. Guth, "Lighting research," *American Industrial Hygiene Association Journal,* Vol. 23 (1962), 359–371.
6. E. Rowlands, D. L. Loe, I. M. Walters, and R. G. Hopkinson, "Visual performance in illuminance of different spectral quality," paper presented at C.I.E. Conference, 17th Session, Barcelona, Spain, 1971, Paper 71.36.
7. *IES Handbook,* 5th ed., New York: Illuminating Engineering Society, 1972.
8. The interdependence of light and color became perfectly apparent to me one day when I was attending a lighting demonstration that introduced several different types of illumination into the same test room. As the light changed from one system to the next, my brown socks changed to gold to a horrible green to a yellow brown. I asked myself: "What color are these socks, *really?*" The question, of course, needs to be answered in terms of the available illumination.
9. Robert M. Gerard, *"The differential effects of colored lights on psychophysical functions,"* Ph. D. dissertation in psychology, University of California, Los Angeles, 1958.
10. *Environmental Criteria: M.R. Preschool Day Care Facilities, Architecture and Environmental Design,* Texas A & M University, no date (ca. 1972), 28.
11. Kenneth Bayes, *The Therapeutic Effect of the Environment on Emotionally Disturbed and Mentally Subnormal Children,* London: The Gresham Press, 1967, 33–34.
12. *Ibid.*
13. *Ibid.*
14. Hugo G. Blasdel, "Multidimensional scaling for architec-

tural environments," in William J. Mitchell, ed., *Environmental Design: Research and Practice; Proceedings of the EDRA3/AR8 Conference,* University of California, Los Angeles, January 1972, Paper 25.1.

15. T. J. Spencer, J. E. Flynn, O. Martyniuk, and C. Hendrik, "Rating scales, factor analysis, and multidimensional scaling as procedures for investigating lighting: progress toward development of a general design evaluation system," in Wolfgang Preiser, ed., *Environmental Design, Research, Proceedings of the Fourth International EDRA4 Conference,* Stroudsburg, Pa.: Dowden, Hutchinson & Ross, 1973.

16. For example, ratings were solicited on a scale between such pairs as pleasant–unpleasant, sociable–unsociable, focused–unfocused.

17. R. Rosenthal and R. L. Rosnow, *Artifact in Behavioral Research,* New York: Academic Press, 1969.

18. Gropius, *op. cit.,* 41.

19. D. W. Fiske and S. R. Maddi, *Functions of Varied Experience,* Homewood, Ill.: Dorsey Press, 1961, Preface.

20. F. J. Roethlisberger and William J. Dickson, *Management and the Worker,* Cambridge, Mass.: Harvard University Press, 1939.

21. Fiske and Maddi, *op. cit.*

22. Harold M. Proshansky, William H. Ittelson, and Leanne G. Rivlin, "Freedom of choice and behavior in a physical setting," in Proshansky, Ittelson, and Rivlin, eds., *Environmental Psychology: Man and His Physical Setting,* New York: Holt, 1970.

*In this paper doubts are expressed about the traditional survey techniques used in ascertaining the meaning of "house." The psychological theories of Carl Jung suggest another approach. His most significant contribution to the understanding of the human psyche are the concepts of collective unconscious, the archetype and the symbol. These concepts are discussed and the most basic of archetypes —self—is identified. The house reflects how man sees himself. Examples from contemporary architecture are presented, and it is shown that in poetry, literature, and dreams, houses are invested with human qualities. Jung's theories of dreams, that is, his concept of the unconscious, are used to interpret the symbolic meaning of "house" in dreams. The house is also seen as sacred, giving man a fixed point of reference to structure the world about him. The location of the threshold is symbolic of how people relate to the rest of society; the hearth also has special meaning. Cities have been built in the image, either conscious or unconscious, that people have of the world.*

# The House as Symbol of the Self*

**Clare Cooper**

**University of California at Berkeley**

## INTRODUCTION

My work of the last few years comprised sociological surveys of people's responses to the designs of their houses and communication of the resultant guidelines to architects. But I have experienced a nagging doubt that I was merely scratching the surface of the true meaning of "the house." There seemed to be something far deeper and more subliminal that I was not admitting, or that my surveys and investigations were not revealing. The exciting personal discovery of the work of the psychologist Carl Jung has opened a door into another level of my own consciousness which has prompted me to consider the house from a wholly different viewpoint. This paper is a tentative initial exploration into the subject.

The reader must expect no startling, all-embracing conclusion; there is none. This is a speculative think piece and is deliberately left open-ended in the hope that it will motivate the reader, and the author, to think further and more deeply in this area.

## JUNG'S CONCEPTS OF THE COLLECTIVE UNCONSCIOUS, THE ARCHETYPE, AND THE SYMBOL

Three of the most significant contributions of Carl Jung to the understanding of the human psyche are the concepts of the *collective* unconscious, the archetype, and the symbol. Sigmund Freud postulated an *individual* unconscious in which are deposited the suppressed and repressed memories of infancy and childhood. Theoretically, the psyche keeps these memories in storage until they are reawakened into consciousness by the medium of the dream, or its waking equivalent, free association.

Initially embracing Freud's theories, Jung became increasingly dissatisfied as his studies of persistent motifs in his patients' dreams and fantasies, and in primitive mythology and folk tales, revealed what seemed to be *universal* patterns which could not be accounted for solely by the theory of an *individual* unconscious. He began to postulate the theory of an individual unconscious plus a universal or collective unconscious linking man to his primitive past, and in which are deposited certain basic and timeless nodes of psychic energy, which he termed *archetypes*.

Jolande Jacobi has termed the archetype "a profound riddle surpassing our rational comprehension."[1] It precedes all conscious experience and therefore cannot be fully explained through conscious thought processes. Perhaps one of the simplest analogies is that offered by Jacobi of a kind of "psychic mesh" with nodal points within the unconscious, a structure which somehow has shaped and organized the myriad contents of the psyche into potential images, emotions, ideas, and patterns of behavior. The archetype can only provide a potential or possibility of representation in the conscious mind, for as soon as we encounter it through dreams, fantasies, or rational thought, the archetype becomes clothed in images of the concrete world and is no longer an archetype: it is an *archetypal image* or *symbol*. As Jacobi has written:

*Man's need to understand the world and his experience in it symbolically as well as realistically may be noted early in the lives of many children. The symbolic imaginative view of the world is just as organic a part of the child's life as the view transmitted by the sense organs. It represents a natural and spontaneous striving which adds to man's biological bond a parallel and equivalent psychic bond, thus enriching life by another dimension–and it is eminently this dimension that makes man what he is. It is the root of all creative activity. . . .[2]*

If we can think of the archetype as a node of psychic energy within the unconscious, then the symbol is the medium by which it becomes manifest in the here and now of space and time. Thus a symbol, although it has objective visible reality, always has behind it a hidden, profound, and only partly intelligible meaning which represents its roots in the archetype.

Although impossible for most of us to define or describe, we are all aware of the existence of something we call "self": the inner heart of our being, our soul, our uniqueness—however we want to describe it. It is in the nature of man that he constantly seeks a rational explanation of the inexplicable, and so he struggles with the questions: What is self? Why here? Why now?

In trying to comprehend this most basic of archetypes—self—to give it concrete substance, man grasps at physical forms or symbols which are close and meaningful to him, and which are visible and definable. The first and most consciously selected form to represent self is the body, for it appears to be both the outward manifestation, and the encloser, of self. On a less conscious level, I believe, man also frequently selects the house, that basic protector of his internal environment (beyond skin and clothing) to represent or symbolize what is tantalizingly unrepresentable.

The French philosopher Gaston Bachelard has suggested that just as the house and the nonhouse are the basic divisions of geographic space, so the self and the nonself represent the basic divisions of psychic space.[3] The house both encloses space (the house interior) and excludes space (everything outside it). Thus it has two very important and different components; its interior and its façade. The house therefore nicely reflects how man sees himself, with both an intimate interior, or self as viewed from within and revealed only to those intimates who are invited inside, and a public exterior (the *persona* or *mask,* in Jungian terms) or the self that we choose to display to others.[4]

Most of us have had the experience of moving from one house to another, and of finding the new abode initially strange, unwelcoming, perhaps even hostile. But with time, we get used to the new house and its quirks, and it seems almost as though it gets used to us; we can relax when we return to it, put our feet up, become ourselves. But why in this particular box should we be ourselves more than in any other? It seems as though the personal space bubble which we carry with us and which is an almost tangible extension of our self expands to embrace the house we have designated as ours. As we become accustomed to, and lay claim to, this little niche in the world, we project something of ourselves onto its physical fabric. The furniture we install, the way we arrange it, the pictures we hang, the plants we buy and tend, all are expressions of our image of ourselves, all are messages about ourselves that we want to convey back to ourselves, and to the few intimates that we invite into this, our house. Thus, the house might be viewed as both an avowal of the self—that is, the psychic messages are moving from self to the objective symbol of self—and as a revelation of the nature of self; that is, the messages are moving from objective symbol back to the self. It is almost as if the house–self continuum could be thought of as both the negative and positive of a film, simultaneously.

## THE HOUSE AS SYMBOL-OF-SELF: EXAMPLES FROM CONTEMPORARY ARCHITECTURE

Man was a symbol-making animal long before he was a toolmaker: he reached high degrees of specialization in song, dance, ritual, religion, and myth before he did in the material aspects of culture. Describing the rich symbolism of the man-made environment in part of Africa, Amos Rapoport notes:

*Among the Dogon and Bambara of Mali every object and social event has a symbolic as well as a utilitarian function. Houses, household objects, and chairs have all this symbolic quality, and the Dogon civilization, otherwise relatively poor, has several thousand symbolic elements. The farm plots and the whole landscape of the Dogon reflect this cosmic order. The villages are built in pairs to represent heaven and earth, and fields are cleared in spirals because the world has been created spirally. The villages are laid out in the way the parts of the body lie with respect to each other, while the house of the Dogon, or paramount chief, is a model of the universe at a smaller scale.[5]*

Rapoport concludes significantly that "man's achievements have been due more to his need to utilize his internal resources than to his needs for control of the physical environment or more food."[6]

It would seem that there is an inverse relationship between technological advances and the cultivation of symbol and ritual. For so-called civilized man, the conscious recognition of the symbolism of what we do, how we live, and the houses we live in, has been all but lost. But if we start to delve beneath the surface, the symbolism is still there.

In a recent study of how contemporary California suburbanites chose their homes, Berkeley sociologist Carl Werthman concluded that many people bought houses to bolster their image of self—both as an individual and as a person in a certain status position in society.[7] In one large suburban development near

**Figure 1**
**Photo credit: Mitchell Payne**

San Francisco, for example, he noted that extroverted, self-made businessmen tended to choose somewhat ostentatious, mock-colonial display homes, such as in Figure 1, while people in the helping professions, whose goals revolved around personal satisfaction rather than financial success, tended to opt for the quieter, inward-looking architect-designed styles conforming to current standards of "good design," such as that in Figure 2.

In the contemporary English-speaking world, a premium is put on originality, on having a house that is unique and somewhat different from the others on the street, for the inhabitants who identify with these houses are themselves struggling to maintain some sense of personal uniqueness in an increasingly conformist world. On the other hand, one's house must not be too way-out, for that would label the inhabitant as a nonconformist, and that, for many Americans, is a label to be avoided.

The house as symbol-of-self is deeply engrained in the American ethos (albeit unconsciously for many),

**Figure 2**
**Photo credit: Mitchell Payne**

and this may partly explain the inability of society to come to grips with the housing problem—a problem which is quite within its technological and financial capabilities to solve and which it persistently delegates to a low level in the hierarchy of budgetary values. America is the home of the self-made man, and if the house is seen (even unconsciously) as the symbol of self, then it is small wonder that there is a resistance to subsidized housing or to the State's providing houses *for* people. The frontier image of the man clearing the land and building a cabin for himself and his family is not far behind us. To a culture inbred with this image, the house–self identity is particularly strong. In some barely conscious way, society has decided to penalize those who, through no fault of their own cannot build, buy, or rent their own housing. They are not self-made men.

Numbers of studies in England, Australia, and the United States have indicated that when asked to describe their ideal house, people of all incomes and backgrounds will tend to describe a free-standing, square, detached, single-family house and yard. For example, in a recent survey of 748 men and women in thirty-two metropolitan areas in the U.S. 85 percent said they preferred living in a single-family house rather than in an apartment.[8] It is difficult to say whether the attachment to this form is the form itself, or the fact that it subsumes territorial rights over a small portion of the earth, or the fact that apartments can rarely be owned. But we do know that almost universally the image of the high-rise building for family living is rejected. An apartment is rarely seen as home, for a house can only be seen as a free-standing house-on-the-ground.

One could argue that people have been conditioned to want this through advertising, model homes salesmanship, and the image of the good life portrayed on television. To a certain extent this must be true, but these media are in turn only reflecting what seems to be a universal need for a house form in which the self and family unit can be seen as separate, unique, private, and protected.

The high-rise apartment building is rejected by most Americans as a family home because, I would suggest, it gives one no territory on the ground, violates the archaic image of what a house is, and is perceived unconsciously as a threat to one's self-image as a separate and unique personality. The house form in which people are being asked to live is not a symbol-of-self, but the symbol of a stereotyped, anonymous filing-cabinet collection of selves, which people fear they are becoming. Even though we may make apartments larger, with many of the appurtenances of a house, as well as opportunities for modification and ownership, it may still be a long time before the majority of lower- and middle-income American families will accept this as a valid image of a permanent home.[9] It is too great a threat to their self-image. It is possible that the vandalism inflicted on high-rise housing projects is, in part, an angry reaction of the inhabitants to this blatant violation of self-image.

The mobile hippie house-on-wheels is another instance of a new housing form greatly threatening people's image of what a house—or by implication, its inhabitants—*should* be. The van converted to mobile home and the wooden gable-roofed house built in the back of a truck are becoming common sights in a university community such as Berkeley and drop-out staging grounds, such as San Francisco. It is tempting to speculate that this house form has been adopted by hippies, not only because of its cheapness as living accommodation, but also because its mobility and form are reflections of where the inhabitants are in psychic terms —concerned with self and with making manifest their own uniqueness, convinced of the need for inward exploration and for freedom to move and swing with whatever happens. Hippies view themselves as different from the average person, and so they have chosen to live in self-generated house forms—converted trucks, tree-houses, geodesic domes, Indian teepees—which reflect and bolster that uniqueness.

It was perhaps to be expected that eventually the establishment would react. In February 1970, the city of Berkeley passed an ordinance making it illegal to live in a converted truck or van; the residents of these new houses mobilized and formed the Rolling Homes Association, but it was too late to prevent the ordinance from being passed.[10] When others too openly display the appurtenance (clothes, hair-styles, houses) of a new self-image, it is perceived as a threat to the values and images of the majority community. The image of the self as a house-on-wheels was too much for the establishment to accept.

Even the edge-of-town mobile home park occupied by the young retireds and the transient lower middle class is somehow looked down upon by the average American home owner as violating the true image of home and neighborhood. A person who lives in a house that moves must somehow be as unstable as the structure he inhabits. Very much the same view is held by house owners in Marin County, California, about the houseboat dwellers in Sausalito. They are "different," "Bohemian," "nonconformists," and their extraordinary choice of dwelling reflects these values.

The contrasting views which people of different socioeconomic classes in the U.S. have of their houses reflects again the house as a symbol-of-self in a self –world relationship. The greater are people's feelings of living in a dangerous and hostile world with constant threats to the self, the greater is the likelihood that they will regard their house as a shell, a fortress into which to retreat. The sociologist Lee Rainwater has shown that this image of the self, and of the house, is true for low-income blacks (particularly women) in the ghettoes and housing projects of this country.[11] With increasing economic and psychic stability (and in some cases, these are linked), a person may no longer regard his house as a fortress-to-be-defended, but as an attractive, individual expression of self-and-family with picture windows so that neighbors can admire the inside. Thus, for many in the middle-income bracket, the house is an expression of self, rather than a defender of self. The self-and-environnment are seen in a state of mutual regard, instead of a state of combat.

The fact that the decoration of the house interior often symbolizes the inhabitants' feelings about self is one that has long been recognized. It has even been suggested that the rise in popularity of the profession of interior decorating is in some way related to people's inability to make these decisions for themselves since they're not sure what their self really is. The phenomenon of people, particularly women, rearranging the fur-

**Figure 3**
**Photo credit: Mitchell Payne**

niture in their house at times of psychic turmoil or changes-in-self, is a further suggestion that the house is very intimately entwined with the psyche.

The pregnant woman—in a very special psychological and physiological state of change—is especially likely to identify with the house, both in dreams and in reality:

*Sudden compulsive urges to do thorough house cleaning seem common among pregnant women. They are, on the one level, practical attempts to prepare for the coming baby; but when the house is already amply clean and delivery is impending, there may be a second, more significant level. The woman may be acting out her unconscious identification of the house with her own body. She may feel that if she cleans out the house and puts everything in order, she is in some way doing something about that other living space, the "house" of her unborn child. For her, it is an object rather than a word, which has taken on secret meanings.*[12]

An interesting contemporary development is the interior decoration of the urban commune. In a number of examples in the Berkeley–Oakland area visited by the author, it was very noticeable that the bedrooms, the only private spaces of residents, were decorated in an attractive and highly personal way symbolic of the self whose space it was, as shown in Figure 3. The living rooms, the communal territory of six or eight or more different personalities, however, were only sparsely decorated, as exemplified by the one in Figure 4, since, presumably, the problem of getting agreement on taste from a number of disparate and highly individual selves was too great to overcome. Interestingly, the more normal family house may display an opposite arrangement, with bedrooms functionally but uninterestingly decorated, and the living room, where guests and relatives are entertained, containing the best furniture, family mementos, art purchases, photos, and so on, and representing the collective family self. The only exception to this pattern may be the teenager's room—highly personalized as a reflection of his struggle to become an individual with a personality separate from his parents.

In a recently published study of living rooms, Edward Laumann and James House have found that

**Figure 4**
**Photo credit: Mitchell Payne**

the presence or absence of certain objects are good if not perfect clues to status and attitudes. It is the living room rather than any other room in the house which provides these clues because

*The living room in the area where "performances" for guests are most often given, and hence the "setting" of it must be appropriate to the performance. Thus we expect that more than any other part of the home, the living room reflects the individual's conscious and unconscious attempts to express a social identity.*[13]

For example, they looked at a random sample of 41 homes from among 186 respondents (all of which were one-and-two-family home dwellers in Detroit) who had annual incomes over $15,000 and presumably had enough money to decorate any way they wanted. They found that those with a traditional decor—French or Early American furniture, wall mirrors, small potted plants and/or artificial flowers, paintings of people or still lifes, clocks—tended to be the white Anglo-Saxon establishment, occupying occupations and status positions similar to their fathers. Those with a more modern decor, characterized by modern furniture, wood walls, abstract paintings, solid carpets, and abstract designed

curtains, tended to be upwardly mobile, non Anglo-Saxon Catholics whose families had migrated to the United States from southern and eastern Europe after 1900.

*The* nouveaux riches *have a strong need to validate their new found status, yet they are not acceptable socially by the traditional upper classes. Since their associations do not clearly validate their position, they turn to conspicuous consumption. . . . The* nouveaux riches, *then, spurn the style of the traditional upper class in favor of the newer fashions. This serves a double purpose: to establish their tastefulness and hence status, while symbolically showing their disdain for the "snobby" traditionals.*[14]

The findings of this study of decorative styles of living rooms seem to tie in well with the result of Werthman's study of choices of house styles, for in both cases there appears to be a strong correlation between the style selected and the self-image of the consumer. The house façade and the interior design seem often to be selected so that they reflect how a person views himself both as an individual psyche, and in relation to society and the outside world, and how he wishes to present his self to family and friends.

These are just a few examples of how the house-as-self linkage becomes manifest in individual and societal behavior and attitudes; no doubt the reader can add many more instances from his personal experience. The thesis is not a new one: but it seems that the Jungian notions of the collective unconscious, the archetype and the symbol, may offer a useful conceptual structure to tie these examples together. Since the house–self symbolism seems to arise again and again, in many disparate settings, and since there appears to be little conscious sharing of this phenomenon, it seems reasonable to suggest that it is through the medium of the collective unconscious that people are in touch with an archaic and basically similar archetype (the self) and with a symbol for that archetype that has changed little through space and time (the house). Perhaps we can comprehend the essence of the house–self analogy more easily by looking at evidence from literature, poetry, and dreams —forms of expression that may get closer to true unconscious meanings than sociological surveys or similar empirical investigations.

## THE HOUSE-AS-SELF AS MANIFESTED IN LITERATURE, POETRY, AND DREAMS

One doesn't have to look farther than the very words that are sometimes used to describe houses—austere, welcoming, friendly—to see that we have somehow invested the house with human qualities. In a book describing his experiences while cleaning and repairing a country cottage to live in, Walter Murray wrote:

So I left the cottage, swept if not yet garnished, and as I looked back at it that quiet evening with the sunset all aglow behind it, it seemed that somehow it was changed. The windows were clean, and the soul of a house looked out of its eyes; sweet cottages peep, old houses blink and welcome. Now Copsford, which had at first defied, gazed after me at least as an acquaintance, and months later was even friendly. But I never knew a smile to wrinkle the hard corners of its eyes.[15]

Although one might perhaps sneer at its cute anthropomorphizing of the environment, it is passages such as this which reveal what may be profound and barely recognized connections with, and projections onto, that environment.

In her introspective autobiography, written in the form of a diary, Anais Nin saw quite clearly both the security and sustenance that can ensue from living in a house

that reflects one's own self-image, and the phenomenon of projecting onto the home one's inner fears and anxieties:

When I look at the large green iron gate from my window it takes on the air of a prison gate. An unjust feeling, since I know I can leave the place whenever I want to, and since I know that human beings place upon an object, or a person, this responsibility of being the obstacle when the obstacle lies always within one's self.

In spite of this knowledge, I often stand at the window staring at the large closed iron gate, as if hoping to obtain from this contemplation a reflection of my inner obstacles to a full, open life. . . . But the little gate, with its overhanging ivy like disordered hair over a running child's forehead, has a sleepy and sly air, an air of being always half open.

I chose the house for many reasons.

Because it seemed to have sprouted out of the earth like a tree, so deeply grooved it was within the old garden. It had no cellar and the rooms rested right on the ground. Below the rug, I felt, was the earth. I could take root here, feel at one with house and garden, take nourishment from them like the plants.[16]

In a short passage from a popular newsmagazine description of the German writer Günter Grass, the image of his style of writing, his way of working, his clothes, and the house he lives in—all reflect the inner character, the self, of this man:

Grass is a fanatic for moderation. He is a moderate tne way other men are extremists. He is a man almost crazy for sanity.

Balance is Grass's game. He is in love with the firm, the tangible. He has a peasant's instinct for the solid ground, an artisan's feeling for materials. His West Berlin home –described by one visitor as "a god-awful Wilhelmian house"–is solid as a fort. The furniture is reassuringly thick-legged. The floors are bare. There are no curtains. In lean, wrinkled, absolutely undistinguished clothes –open necked shirts are the rule–Grass walks from room to room with workmanlike purpose. He looks like a visiting plumber who has a job to do and knows quite well that he can do it.[17]

The notion of house as symbol of mother or the womb is one fairly common in literature, and indeed has been the inspiration of a number of organic architects who have tried to re-create this safe, enclosed, encircling feeling in their designs. In the following fictional account, we see how the house takes on a symbolic maternal function in response to the fear of the man within and the storm outside:

The house was fighting gallantly. At first it gave voice to its complaints; the most awful gusts were attacking it from every side at once, with evident hatred and such howls of rage that, at times, I trembled with fear. But it stood firm. . . . The already human being in whom I had sought shelter for my body yielded nothing to the storm. The house clung to *me, like a she-wolf, and at times I could smell her odor penetrating maternally to my very heart. That night she was really my mother. She was all I had to keep and sustain me. We were alone.*[18]

Here, in the unusual circumstances of a storm, one can see how this human, protective symbol of the house might well be conceived. But what of ordinary circumstances? How does the house-as-self symbol first begin to take root? Undoubtedly, one must look for the roots in infancy. At first, the mother is its whole environment. Gradually, as the range of senses expands, the baby begins to perceive the people and physical environment around it. The house becomes its world, its very cosmos. From being a shadowy shell glimpsed out of half-closed eyes, the house becomes familiar, recognizable, a place of security and love.

The child's world then becomes divided into the house, that microspace within the greater world that he knows through personal discovery, and everything that lies beyond it, which is unknown and perhaps frightening. In a sense, the child's experience reflects the assessment of known space as made by preliterate societies. As Mircea Eliade has written:

*One of the outstanding characteristics of traditional societies is the opposition that they assume between their inhabited territory and the unknown and indeterminate space that surrounds it. The former is world (more precisely, our world), the cosmos; everything outside it is no longer a cosmos but a sort of "other world," foreign, chaotic space, peopled by ghosts, demons, foreigners. . . .*[19]

As the child matures, he ventures into the house's outer space, the yard, the garden, then gradually into the neighborhood, the city, the region, the world. As space becomes known and experienced, it becomes a part of his world. But all the time, the house is home, the place of first conscious thoughts, of security and roots. It is no longer an inert box; it has been experienced, has become a symbol for self, family, mother, security. As Bachelard has written, "geometry is transcended."

In the following poem, written by a child of 12 years, the notion of the family house being a special place of security and love to which the child anxiously returns after school, is feelingly evoked.

### O JOYOUS HOUSE[20]

*When I walk home from school,*
*I see many houses*
*Many houses down many streets.*

*They are warm comfortable houses*
*But other people's houses*
*I pass without much notice.*

*Then as I walk farther, farther*
*I see a house, the house.*
*It springs up with a jerk*
*That speeds my pace;*
*I lurch forward*
*Longing makes me happy,*
*I bubble inside.*
*It's my house.*

As we become more ourselves—more self-actualized, in Maslow's terms—it seems that the house-as-symbol becomes even less tied to its geometry. A writer quoted by Bachelard describes his house thus:

*My house is diaphanous but it is not of glass. It is more of the nature of vapor. Its walls contract and expand as I desire. At times, I draw them close about me like protective armor. . . . But at others, I let the walls of my house blossom out in their own space, which is infinitely extensible.*[21]

The symbol has become flexible, expandable according to psychic needs. For most people, the house is not actually changeable, except by such measures as opening and closing drapes and rearranging furniture to suit our moods. For one French poet, these alternate needs of expansion and contraction, extroversion and introspection, openness and withdrawal were made physical realities in the design of his dream home—a Breton fisherman's cottage around which he constructed a magnificent manor house.

*In the body of the winged manor, which dominates both town and sea, man and the universe, he retained a cottage chrysalis in order to be able to hide alone in complete repose. . . . The two extreme realities of cottage and manor . . . take into account our need for retreat and expansion, for simplicity and magnificence.*[22]

Perhaps the suburban home buyers' yen for both an opulent façade with picture-window view and colonial porch and for a private secluded den is a modern manifestation of this need.

A recent news story suggests, in somewhat startling fashion, what may be strong evidence for the significance of house or home to the psyche:

*When both his parachutes failed in a recent jump from a plane 3,300 feet above the Coolidge, Ariz. airport, sky diver Bob Hall, 19, plummeted earthward and hit the ground at an estimated 60 m.p.h. Miraculously, he survived. A few days later, recovering from nothing more serious than a smashed nose and loosened teeth, he told reporters what the plunge* had been like: *"I screamed. I knew I was dead and that my life was ended. All my past life flashed before my eyes, it really did. I saw my mother's face,* all the homes I've lived in [italics added], *the military academy I attended, the faces of friends, everything."*[23]

Surely, the fact that images of "all the homes I've lived in" flashed through the mind of a man approaching almost certain death, must indicate a significance of that element of the physical environment far beyond its concrete reality.

If we start to consider the messages from the unconscious made manifest through dreams, we have even more striking evidence of the house-as-self symbol. Carl Jung in his autobiography describes quite vividly a dream of himself as house, and his explorations within it.

*I was in a house I did not know, which had two storeys. It was "my house." I found myself in the upper storey, where there was a kind of salon furnished with fine old pieces in rococo style. On the walls hung a number of precious old paintings. I wondered that this should be my house, and thought, "Not bad." But then it occurred to me that I did not know what the lower floor looked like. Descending the stairs, I reached the ground floor. There everything was much older, and I realized that this part of the house must date from about the fifteenth or sixteenth century. The furnishings were medieval; the floors were of red brick. Everywhere it was rather dark. I went from one room to another thinking, "Now I really must explore the whole house." I came upon a heavy door and opened it. Beyond it, I discovered a stone stairway that led down into the cellar. Descending again, I found myself in a beautifully vaulted room which looked exceedingly ancient. Examining the walls, I discovered layers of brick among the ordinary stone blocks, and chips of brick in the mortar. As soon as I saw this I knew that the walls dated from Roman times. My interest by now was intense. I looked more closely at the floor. It was on stone slabs, and in one of these I discovered a ring. When I pulled it, the stone slab lifted, and again I saw a stairway of narrow stone steps leading down into the depths. These, too, I descended, and entered a low cave cut into the rock. Thick dust lay on the floor, and in the dust were scattered bones and broken pottery, like remains of a primitive culture. I discovered two human skulls, obviously very old and half disintegrated. Then I awoke.*[24]

Jung's own interpretation of the dream was as follows:

*It was plain to me that the house represented a kind of image of the psyche—that is to say, of my then state of consciousness, with hitherto unconscious additions. Consciousness was represented by the salon. It had an inhabited atmosphere, in spite of its antiquated style.*

*The ground floor stood for the first level of the unconscious. The deeper I went, the more alien and the darker the scene*

became. *In the cave, I discovered remains of a primitive culture, that is the world of the primitive man within myself—a world which can scarcely be reached or illuminated by consciousness. The primitive psyche of man borders on the life of the animal soul, just as the caves of prehistoric times were usually inhabited by animals before man laid claim to them.*[25]

Jung describes here the house with many levels seen as the symbol-of-self with its many levels of consciousness; the descent downward into lesser known realms of the unconscious is represented by the ground floor, cellar, and vault beneath it. A final descent leads to a cave cut into bedrock, a part of the house rooted in the very earth itself. This seems very clearly to be a symbol of the collective unconscious, part of the self-house and yet, too, part of the universal bedrock of humanity.

Jung, unlike Freud, also saw the dream as a possible prognosticator of the future; the unconscious not only holds individual and collective memories but also the seeds of future action. At one period of his life Jung was searching for some historical basis or precedent for the ideas he was developing about the unconscious. He didn't know where to start the search. At this point he started having a series of dreams which all dealt with the same theme:

*Beside my house stood another, that is to say, another wing or annex, which was strange to me. Each time I would wonder in my dream why I did not know this house, although it had apparently always been there. Finally came a dream in which I reached the other wing. I discovered there a wonderful library, dating largely from the sixteenth and seventeenth centuries. Large, fat folio volumes bound in pigskin stood along the walls. Among them were a number of books embellished with copper engravings of a strange character, and illustrations containing curious symbols such as I had never seen before. At the time I did not know to what they referred; only much later did I recognize them as alchemical symbols. In the dream I was conscious only of the fascination exerted by them and by the entire library. It was a collection of incunabula and sixteenth century prints.*

*The unknown wing of the house was a part of my personality, an aspect of myself; it represented something that belonged to me but of which I was not yet conscious. It, and especially the library, referred to alchemy of which I was ignorant, but which I was soon to study. Some fifteen years later I had assembled a library very like the one in the dream.*[26]

Thus here in another dream Jung sees an unexplored wing of the house as an unknown part of himself and a symbol of an area of study with which he would become very absorbed in the future, and which permitted him to expand his concepts of the transformation of the self.

From many house dreams I have collected, two will suffice here to further emphasize the point. In the first one, the dreamer had, in reality, just lost a close friend in an auto accident. She reports the dream thus:

*I was being led through a ruined house by a tall, calm man, dressed all in white. The house was alone in a field, its walls of rubble, the layout and doorways no longer visible. The man guide led me slowly through the house pointing out how it used to be, where rooms were connected, where doorways lead to the outside world.*

*My interpretation of this dream is that, the tall man is a part of me, maybe my masculine, strong, calm side, and he is pointing out that despite the fact that my self-life-house appear to be in ruins right now, due to my shock and grief at A's death, there is part of me that calmly and clearly will know how to find my way through the chaos. It was a very comforting dream at a time of great stress.*

In another dream, the dreamer was in reality under much pressure from students and colleagues in his academic job. He described his dream thus:

*There was a house, a large English stately home, open to the public to look at and traipse through. But on this day, it was temporarily closed, and visitors were disappointedly reading the notices and turning away. I was in the basement of the house, sorting through some oil paintings, to see if there was anything there of value.*

With the aid of a therapist, skilled in the interpretation of dreams, he saw the following message within the dream:

*I need to 'close up shop,' take a vacation from all the pressures and human input I'm experiencing right now, and have time to sort through some ideas in my unconscious (the basement of the house) to see if any are of value in guiding my future direction.*

Returning to Jung's autobiography, he describes how, later in his life, he made manifest in stone the symbol which had at times stood for self in his dreams. He describes how he yearned to put his knowledge of the contents of the unconscious into solid form, rather than just describe them in words. In the building of his house—the tower at Bollingen on Lake Zurick—he was to make "a confession of faith in stone":

*At first I did not plan a proper house, but merely a kind of primitive one-story dwelling. It was to be a round structure with a hearth in the center and bunks along the walls. I more or less had in mind an African hut where the fire, ringed with stone, burns in the middle, and the whole life of the family revolves around this centre. Primitive huts concretise an idea of wholeness, a familial wholeness in which all sorts*

*of domestic animals likewise participate. But I altered the plan even during the first stages of building, for I felt it was too primitive. I realized it would have to be a regular two-story house, not a mere hut crouched on the ground. So in 1923 the first round house was built, and when it was over I saw that it had become a suitable dwelling tower.*

*The feeling of repose and renewal that I had in this tower was intense from the start. It represented for me the maternal hearth.*[27]

Feeling that something more needed to be said, four years later Jung added another building with a tower-like annex. Again, after an interval of four years, he felt the need to add more and built onto the tower a retiring room for meditation and seclusion where no one else could enter; it became his retreat for spiritual concentration. After another interval of four years he felt the need for another area, open to nature and the sky, and so added a courtyard and an adjoining loggia. The resultant quanternity pleased him, no doubt because his own studies in mythology and symbolism had provided much evidence of the completeness and wholeness represented by the figure four. Finally, after his wife's death, he felt an inner obligation to "become what I myself am," and recognized that the small central section of the house

*which crouched so low and hidden was myself! I could no longer hide myself behind the "maternal" and "spiritual" towers. So in the same year, I added an upper storey to this section, which represents myself or my ego-personality. Earlier, I would not have been able to do this; I would have regarded it as presumptuous self-emphasis. Now it signified an extension of consciousness achieved in old age. With that the building was complete.*[28]

Jung had thus built his house over time as a representation in stone of his own evolving and maturing psyche; it was the place, he said, where "I am in the midst of my true life, I am most deeply myself." He describes how:

*From the beginning I felt the Tower as in some way a place of maturation–a maternal womb or a maternal figure in which I could become what I was, what I am and will be. It gave me a feeling as if I were being reborn in stone. It is thus a concretisation of the individuation process. . . . During the building work of course, I never considered these matters. . . . Only afterwards did I see how all the parts fitted together and that a meaningful form had resulted: a symbol of psychic wholeness.*[29]

In examining at some length Jung's own reflections on the house as dream-symbol, and the building of his own house as a manifestation of the self, we are not just examining one man's inner life; hopefully, there is something here of the inner symbolism of all men. Jung, perhaps more than any other thinker or writer of this century, has fearlessly examined his own unconscious and delved into a great range of disciplines which together aided him in his quest to build a theory of the unconscious and the self.

We must return again to Jung's concept of the collective unconscious. It should be possible if his notion of an unconscious stretching through space and time beyond the individual is correct to find comparable indications of the house-self linkage in places and times far removed from contemporary Western civilization If there is indeed an archetype self, then perhaps in other places and times, the house has become one (though not necessarily the only) symbol for that indefinable archetype in the physical world. For, as Jung has confirmed with ample evidence, the older and more archaic the archetype, the more persistent and unchanging the symbol.

## MAKING SPACE SACRED

In the opening chapter of his book *The Sacred and the Profane: The Nature of Religion* entitled "Sacred Space and Making the World Sacred,"[30] the noted historian of religion, Mircea Eliade describes how for many preliterate societies, space was not homogenous; inhabited parts were seen as sacred while all other space around was a formless, foreign expanse. In settling a new territory, man was faced with both a horizontal expanse of unknown land, and a complete lack of vertical connections to other cosmic levels, such as the heavens and the underworld. In defining and consecrating a spot as sacred, be it shrine, a temple, a ceremonial house, man gave himself a fixed point, a point of reference from which to structure the world about him. In doing so, he consciously emulated the gods who, many believed, created the world by starting at a fixed point —for example, an egg, or the navel of a slain monster—then moving out to the surrounding territory. As Hebrew tradition retells it: "The Most Holy One created the world like an embryo. As the embryo grows from the navel, so God began to create the world by the navel and from there it spread out in all directions."[31] Through finding a sacred space, generally with the aid

of signs or the revelations of animals, man began to transform the shapeless, homogeneous chaos of space into his world.

Once located, the sacred space had to be consecrated, and this very often took the form of a construction which had at its center a pillar, pole, or tree. This was seen as a symbol for the cosmic axis and the means by which communication was made possible from one cosmic level to another. Whether seen as a ladder, as in Jacob's dream, or as a sacred pillar, as worshipped by the Celts and Germans before their conversion to Christianity, the vertical upright was an almost universal symbol for passage to the worlds of the gods above and below the earth.

Having created a sacred place in the homogeneity of space, man erected a symbol for the cosmic axis and thus centered this place at the Center of the World. But, Eliade maintains, there could be many Centers of the World, and indeed the Achilpa people of the Arunta tribe of Australian aborigines always carried the sacred pole with them so as not to be far from the Center or its link with other worlds. The religious man of fixed settlements, although he knew that his country and village and temple all constituted the navel of the universe,

*also wanted his own house to be at the Center and to be an "imago mundi". . . . (He) could only live in a space opening upward, where the break in plane was symbolically assured and hence communication with the "other world," the transcendental world, was ritually possible. Of course the sanctuary—the Center par excellence—was there, close to him . . . but he felt the need to live at the Center always. . . .[32]*

Thus it was that the house, like the temple and the city, became a symbol of the universe with man, like God, at its center and in charge of its creation. The house, like the temple or shrine, was sanctified by ritual.

Just as the entrance to the temple was, and still is, regarded as the dividing line between the sacred and the profane worlds and is suitably embellished to ward off evil spirits which might attempt to enter the inner sanctum, so the threshold of the house is regarded as one of the most important dividing lines between inner private space and the other public world. Even if few living in the Western World would admit today to a belief in household spirits, there are still parts of the world where there are strong beliefs about how the house should be entered (right foot first among country dwellers in Finland, Syria, Egypt, and Yorkshire), and the custom of carrying the bride over the threshold is widespread throughout the world and has been recorded since ancient Roman times. Among contemporary city dwellers, the sanctity of the threshold is still revered by such behavior as removing one's hat and wiping one's shoes before entering the dwelling, or in Arab houses, by removing one's shoes. In China, the orientation of the door toward the south, and in Madagascar toward the west, are examples of the importance of a felicitous orientation of the door to the cosmos.[33] Among orthodox Jews, the Commandments are attached to the doorpost of the house, for they have been ordered: "Thou shalt write them on the posts by thy house and on thy gates" (Deuteronomy VI: 9). In northern England working class districts, the daily routine of polishing the front door knob and whitening the doorstep is a further contemporary example of special, almost ritualistic, attention paid to the threshold.

The location of the threshold varies in different cultures,[34] and it may well be that this location vis-á-vis the outside world is symbolic of how the people as individuals relate to the rest of society. In the American house, the front yard is generally unfenced and part of the streetscape, and may be viewed as semipublic territory; the real threshold to the house is the front door itself. This may reflect an American interpersonal trait of openness to strangers and of (initial at least) friendliness to people they hardly know. In England, however, the fenced front garden with a gate puts the initial threshold at some distance from the house itself, and is probably symbolic of the greater English reserve at inviting strangers into their houses and at opening up to people before they know them very well. The compound of a Moslem house puts the threshold even more forcibly and deliberately at some distance from the house, and reflects the extreme privacy required by individuals, particularly women, from strangers and neighbors.

Traditionally one of the principal tasks of the woman of the house was to keep the hearth fire perpetually burning. Lord Raglan in his study of the origins of the house[35] suggests that the hearth was originally conceived as a microcosm of the sun. Cooking took place

outside, or in a separate building, and the sacred hearth was seen as a parallel to the sacred flame in the temple, not something to be cooked on, but a symbol of the sun which must never be allowed to go out for fear the sun itself would go out.[36]

It is probable that fire existed before man built his first dwellings. Pierre Deffontaines has suggested that the house originated as a shelter for this sacred fire that must not be allowed to go out.[37] Among the ancient Greeks the sacred fire was first enclosed in a special precinct, which later was surrounded by the living quarters of the family. The dwelling thus came into existence to protect the fire, and the Greeks maintain it was the sacred hearth that inspired man to build the house. In the houses of northern China, the kang, a large central hearth of brick and earth, is thought of and referred to as "the mother of the dwelling." Deffontaines reports that until recently in houses in rural Sardinia, the hearth fire was kept perpetually alight and only extinguished when someone died, for the period of mourning. The belief that the house had its traditional beginning in the protection of fire is still maintained in Madagascar, where fire must be the first item brought into a newly completed dwelling.[38]

The hearth was, until very recently, still the focus of family life in England, where wives left behind by their soldier husbands in World War I were enjoined to "keep the home fires burning." Although central heating is becoming more and more common in England, and antipollution laws prevent the burning of coal in open fires in most parts of the country, many families have replaced the perpetual hearth with an electric heater displaying artificial smouldering "logs." It is not easy, after many centuries of veneration of the hearth, to replace it overnight with concealed hot air vents and to feel that something of the home has not been lost. An interesting parallel reported in the *San Francisco Chronicle* in May 1971 told of the demolition of a soup kitchen in the Mission District where the only item to be saved for incorporation in a new old men's hospital was the much loved symbolic hearth.

The ritual of keeping the hearth alight because it represents the sun can be termed a cosmic ritual. Such rituals are based upon the belief that one can affect the macrocosm by acting upon a microcosm. There are many indications that temples of various faiths have been built as symbols of the universe, with the dome or high vaulted roof as symbolic of the heavens, and the floor symbolic of earth below. Raglan reports "in the rituals of the Pawnees the earth lodge is made typical of man's abode on earth; the floor is the plain, the wall the distant horizon, the dome the arching sky, the central opening, the zenith, dwelling place of Tirawa, the invisible power which gives life to all created beings."[39]

Since one of the most widespread primitive beliefs about the creation of the world was that it originated from an egg, so many of the first cosmic manifestations in temples and houses were round or spherical in shape. Lord Raglan has suggested that an original belief in the world as circular began to be replaced by a belief in the world as square, and starting in Mesopotamia and Egypt, and spreading later to China, India, Rome, North America, and Africa, the temple and the house as cosmic manifestations began to be built on a square or rectangular plan, instead of a circular one.[40] People as far apart as the Eskimos, Egyptians, Maoris, and tribes of the North Cameroons believed that the sky or heavens were held by four corner posts which had to be protected from decay or damage, and whose guardian deities had to be placated by ritual. The weathercock on the roof, which is believed in parts of England to crow to wind spirits in the four quarters and ward them off, is one of the few contemporary western manifestations of the ancient cosmic significance of the square and the four cardinal points.

In most parts of the world, the rectangular house predominates today, but the circular shape has often been retained in the form of the dome for religious or important secular buildings (for example, city hall, the state capitol, the opera house), recalling much earlier times when the circle had specific cosmic significance.

To summarize Raglan's thesis, he suggests that house forms were derived from the forms of temples (the houses of the gods), and symbolize man's early beliefs concerning the form and shape of the universe. Drawing conclusions from his studies of myth and folklore, rather than buildings, Eliade comes to similar conclusions.

*By assuming the responsibility of creating the world that he has chosen to inhabit, he not only cosmicizes chaos but also sanctifies his little cosmos by making it like the world of the gods. . . . That is why settling somewhere—building a village or merely a house—represents a serious decision, for the very existence of man is involved; he must, in short, create his own world and assume the responsibility of maintaining and renewing it. Habitations are not lightly changed, for it is not easy to abandon one's world. The house is not an object, a "machine to live in"; it is a universe that man constructs for himself by imitating the paradigmatic creation of the gods, the cosmogony.*[41]

## THE SELF-HOUSE/SELF-UNIVERSE ANALOGY

It seems that consciously or unconsciously, then, many men in many parts of the world have built their cities, temples, and houses as images of the universe. My contention is that somewhere, through the collective unconscious, man is still in touch with this symbolism. Our house is seen, however unconsciously, as the center of *our* universe and symbolic of *the* universe. But how does this connect with my earlier arguments regarding the house-as-symbol-of-self? Primitive man sees his dwelling as symbolic of the universe, with himself, like God, at its center. Modern man apparently sees his dwelling as symbolic of the self, but has lost touch with this archaic connection between house–self–universe.

The phenomenon of dreaming or imagining the self as a house—that package outside our own skin which encloses us and in which we feel most secure—is perhaps the first glimmering of the unconscious that the "I" and the "non-I" are indeed one and the same. As Alan Watts has so eloquently written in the *The Book; On the Taboo Against Knowing Who You are,*[42] the notion that each individual ego is separate (in space) and finite (in time) and is something different from the universe around him is one of the grand hoaxes of Western thought. Although virtually impossible for most of us nonmystics to grasp in more than a superficial way, this knowledge of our indivisibility from the environment is buried deep within the collective unconscious and becomes manifest symbolically (often without our recognizing it) in fantasies, flashes of intuition, dreams, poems, paintings, and literature.

The so-called mentally ill may in fact be more closely in touch with these lost connections between self and environment than any of us realize. After a long career working with schizophrenics, Harold Searles noted:

*It seems to me that, in our culture, a conscious ignoring of the psychological importance of the nonhuman environment exists simultaneously with a (largely unconscious) over-dependence upon that environment. I believe that the actual importance of that environment to the individual is so great that he dare not recognize it. Unconsciously it is felt, I believe, to be not only an intensely important conglomeration of things outside the self, but also a large and integral part of the self. . . .*[43]

*The concreteness of the child's thinking suggests for him, as for the member of the so-called primitive culture and for the schizophrenic adult, the wealth of nonhuman objects about him are constituents of his psychological being in a more intimate sense than they are for the adult in our culture, the adult whose ego is, as Hartman and Werner emphasize, relatively clearly differentiated from the surrounding world, and whose development of the capacity for abstract thinking helps free him . . . from his original oneness with the nonhuman world.*[44]

Perhaps it is the so-called normal adult who, having been socialized to regard self and environment as separate and totally different, is most out of touch with the essential reality of oneness with the environment, which small children, schizophrenics, preliterate people, and adherents of certain Eastern religions understand completely. There are certain religions, for example Buddhism, that regard the apparent separation of the individual and the universe as a delusion. My contention is that in thinking, dreaming, or fantasy-ing about self and house as somehow being inextricably intertwined, as being at some level one and the same thing, man may be taking the first step on the path towards what Zen adherents would term enlightenment. He is ridding himself of the delusion of the separation of man from his environment.

## CONCLUSION

If there is some validity to the notion of house-as-self, it goes part of the way to explain why for most people their house is so sacred and why they so strongly resist a change in the basic form which they and their fathers and their fathers' fathers have lived in since the dawn of time. Jung recognized that the more archaic and universal the archetype made manifest in the symbol, the more universal and unchanging the symbol itself. Since self must be an archetype as universal and almost as archaic as man himself, this may explain the univer-

sality of its symbolic form, the house, and the extreme resistance of most people to any change in its basic form.

For most people the self is a fragile and vulnerable entity; we wish therefore to envelop ourselves in a symbol-for-self which is familiar, solid, inviolate, unchanging. Small wonder, then, that in Anglo-Saxon law it is permissible, if necessary, to kill anyone who breaks and enters your house. A violation of the self (house) is perhaps one of man's most deep-seated and universal fears. Similarly, the thought of living in a round house or a houseboat or a mobile home is, to most people, as threatening as is the suggestion that they might change their basic self-concept. A conventional house and a rigidly static concept of self are mutually supporting. Perhaps with the coming of age of Reich's Consciousness III generation, and the social movements (civil rights, women's liberation, human potential movement, etc.) which are causing many to question the inviolate nature of old self-concepts, we can expect an increased openness to new housing forms and living arrangements, the beginnings of which are already apparent in the proliferation of communes and drop-out communities.

This long statement on house-as-symbol-of-the-self brings me back to my original problem: how to advise architects on the design of houses for clients who are often poor, whom they will never know, let alone delve into their psychic lives or concepts of self. I have no pat answer, but if there is some validity to the concept of house-as-self, we must learn ways—through group encounters, resident-meetings, participant observation, interviews—of empathizing with the users' concepts of self, and we must devise means of complementing and enhancing that image through dwelling design. If in new housing forms we violate this image, we may have produced an objective reality which pleases the politicians and designers, but at the same time produced a symbolic reality which leaves the residents bewildered and resentful.

Certainly, one area that every architect involved with house design can and should investigate is his or her own biases based on images of self. Bachelard, in his very thought provoking study *The Poetics of Space,* suggests somewhat fancifully, that along with psychoanalysis, every patient should be assisted in making a topoanalysis, or an analysis of the spaces and places which have been settings for his past emotional development. I would go further and say this exercise should be required of every designer. He or she should begin to understand how present self-images are being unconsciously concretized in design, and how scenes of earlier development (particularly childhood between the ages of about 5 and 12) are often unconsciously reproduced in designs in an effort, presumably, to recall that earlier often happier phase of life.

In the past few years, as a teacher in the College of Environmental Design at Berkeley, I have had students draw, in as much detail as they can remember, their childhood environments. After an interval of a few weeks, they have then drawn what for each of them would be an ideal environment. The similarities are often striking, as also are the similarities they begin to observe between these two drawings, and what they produce in the design studio. The purpose of the exercise is not to say that there is anything wrong with such influences from the past, but just to point out that they are there, and it may well be to his advantage as a designer to recognize the biases they may introduce into his work.

In the field of man's relationship with his environment, the type of approach which might be termed intuitive speculation seems to have been lost in a world devoted to the supposedly more scientific approach of objective analysis. As Alan Watts has speculated, this emphasis on the so-called objective may indeed be a sickness of Western man, for it enables him to retain his belief in the separateness of the ego from all that surrounds it. Although certain objective facts have been presented in this paper, it is hoped by the author that its overall message is clear: allow yourself to be open to the consideration of relationships other than those that can be proved or disproved by scientific method, for it may well be in these that a deeper truth lies. Perhaps no one has stated it more eloquently than Watts, and it is with a quotation from his *Nature, Man and Woman* that I will end this paper:

*The laws and hypotheses of science are not so much discoveries as instruments, like knives and hammers, for bending nature to one's will. So there is a type of personality which approaches the world with an entire armory of sharp and hard instruments, by means of which it slices and sorts the universe into precise and sterile categories which will not interfere with one's peace of mind.*

*There is a place in life for a sharp knife, but there is a still more important place for other kinds of contact with the world. Man is not to be an intellectual porcupine, meeting his environment with a surface of spikes. Man meets the world outside with a soft skin, with a delicate eyeball and eardrum and finds communion with it through a warm melting, vaguely defined, and caressing touch whereby the world is not set at a distance like an enemy to be shot, but embraced to become one flesh, like a beloved wife. . . . Hence the importance of opinion, of instruments of the mind, which are vague, misty, and melting rather than clear-cut. They provide possibilities of communication, of actual contact and relationships with nature more intimate than anything to be found by preserving at all costs the "distance of objectivity." As Chinese and Japanese painters have so well understood there are landscapes which are best viewed through half-closed eyes, mountains which are most alluring when partially veiled in mist, and waters which are most profound when the horizon is lost, and they are merged with the sky.* [45]

## NOTES AND REFERENCES

1. Jolande Jacobi, *Complex, Archetype, Symbol in the Psychology of C. G. Jung,* New York: Pantheon Books, 1957.
2. *Ibid.,* 47.
3. Gaston Bachelard, *The Poetics of Space,* Boston: Beacon Press, 1969.
4. For the purposes of this paper, we will accept the Jungian view of "self," which he saw as both the core of the unconscious *and* the totality of the conscious and the unconscious. To illustrate with a diagram:

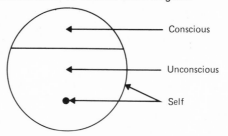

5. Amos Rapoport, *House Form and Culture,* Englewood Cliffs, N.J.: Prentice-Hall, 1969, 50.
6. *Ibid.,* 43.
7. Carl Werthman, *"The social meaning of the physical environment,"* Ph.D. dissertation in sociology, University of California, Berkeley, 1968.
8. William Michelson, "Most people don't want what architects want," *Transaction,* Vol. 5 (July–August 1968), 37–43.
9. The urban rich accept apartments because they generally have a house somewhere else; the elderly seem to adapt well to apartments because they offer privacy with the

possibility of many nearby neighbors, minimum upkeep problems, security, communal facilities, etc.; and for mobile young singles or childless couples the limited spatial and temporal commitment of an apartment is generally the ideal living environment.

10. A similar ordinance was passed in San Francisco in March 1971.

11. Lee Rainwater, "Fear and house-as-haven in the lower class" *Journal of the American Institute of Planners,* Vol. 32 (January 1966), 23–31, and *Behind Ghetto Walls,* Chicago: Aldine-Atherton, 1970.

12. Arthur Colman and Libby Colman, *Pregnancy: The Psychological Experience,* New York: Herder and Herder, 1971.

13. Edward Laumann and James House, "Living room styles and social attributes: patterning of material artifacts in an urban community," in Laumann, Siegel, and Hodges, eds., *The Logic of Social Hierarchies,* Chicago: Markham, 1972, 189–203.

14. *Ibid.*

15. Walter J. C. Murray, *Copsford,* London: Allen and Unwin, 1950, 34.

16. Nin, Anais, *The Diary of Anais Nin, 1931–34,* New York: Harcourt, 1966.

17. "The dentist's chair as an allegory of life," *Time* (April 13, 1970), 70.

18. Henri Bosco, *Malicroix,* as quoted in G. Bachelard, *The Poetics of Space,* New York: The Orion Press, 1964, 45.

19. Mircea Eliade, *The Scared and the Profane: The Nature of Religion,* New York: Harcourt, 1959.

20. Richard Janzen, from Canada, in *Miracles: Poems by Children of the English-Speaking World,* collected by Richard Lewis, New York: Simon and Schuster, 1966. © 1966 by Richard Lewis. Reprinted by permission of Simon and Schuster.

21. George Spyridaki, *Mort Lucide,* as quoted in Bachelard, *op. cit.,* 51.

22. Bachelard, *op. cit.,* 65.

23. "The pleasure of dying," *Time* (December 4, 1972), 44–45.

24. Carl Jung, *Memories, Dreams and Reflections,* London: Collins, The Fontana Library Series, 1969, 182–183.

25. *Ibid.,* 184.

26. *Ibid.,* 228.

27. *Ibid.,* 250.

28. *Ibid.,* 252.

29. *Ibid.,* 253.

30. Eliade, *op. cit.*

31. *Ibid.,* 4.

32. *Ibid.,* 43.

33. Pierre Deffontaines, "The place of believing," extracted from "Géographie et religions," in *Landscape,* Vol. 2 (Spring 1953), 26.

34. Rapoport, *op. cit.,* 80.

35. Lord Raglan, *The Temple and the House,* London: Routledge & Kegan Paul, 1964.

36. In most parts of the world, cooking was one of a number of activities (others included childbirth and death) which could not take place within the house.

37. Deffontaines, *op. cit.,* 26.

38. *Ibid.*

39. Raglan, *op. cit.,* 138.

40. *Ibid.,* 158.

41. Eliade, *op. cit.,* 56–57.

42. Alan Watts, *The Book: On the Taboo Against Knowing Who You Are,* New York: Macmillan, Collier Books, 1966, 43.

43. Harold F. Searles, *The Nonhuman Environment in Normal Development and in Schizophenia,* New York: International Universities Press, 1960, 395.

44. *Ibid.,* 42.

45. Alan W. Watts, *Nature, Man and Woman,* New York: Random House, Vintage Books, 1970, 80–81.

# Predicting the Meaning of Architecture

**Robert G. Hershberger**

**Arizona State University**

*The most difficult task facing the architect is to accurately predict how client–user groups will comprehend and use buildings. This will depend on the meaning the designed environment has for people. Architecture has representational and responsive meanings. Representational meanings take the form of percepts, concepts, and ideas; responsive meanings can be affective, evaluative, or prescriptive. The second is dependent on the first. The various types of meaning are described and explained with examples. Recent research results indicate that people with different educations and geographical backgrounds perceive different meanings in the same buildings. Current research is attempting to come to a greater understanding of these differences so that architectural design can be improved from the viewpoint of both architects and users.*

## PREDICTION IS THE PROBLEM

It is my belief that the most difficult task facing practicing architects is to predict before construction how client-user groups will comprehend and use buildings. It is, of course, easy enough to predict. What is difficult is to predict correctly with consistency. This is especially true for the increasingly pluralistic client–user groups for whom architects now design. It is difficult enough to design buildings which satisfy the needs and interests of people whose backgrounds are similar to those of architects. It is difficult in the extreme to satisfy client —user groups with different socioeconomic and ethnic backgrounds or groups with special age, health, or mobility problems. If the architect attempts to empathize with, or intuitively relate to, these groups, he is likely to err. He is likely to attribute environmental values, needs, and interests to such groups which in fact they do not have. He is likely to design environments which at best compromise the aspirations of the user group and at worst are intolerable for them, as with the Pruitt–Igoe Housing Development in St. Louis.[1] Yet an ever increasing number of architectural commissions, especially those financed by various governmental agencies, are directed toward such client–user groups.

If we come to achieve excellence of building design for these diverse client–user groups, it will not be said, as it has been said of the great classical architecture of Greece, that this excellence was possible because the buildings were designed in an era when all segments of society—architects, leaders, citizens—shared a common system of values. Rather, it will be because theoretical understanding of man–environment relations, research, and "clinical" skills will be developed to such an extent that the particular environmental values, needs, and interests of the client–user groups will be discovered and employed to predict how they will comprehend and use various combinations of form and space.

## COMPREHENSION AND USE

The research of a number of social scientists, and my own research thus far, has been directed toward the comprehension (or meaning) of architectural environments. While we are also interested in the use of these environments, we recognize that the architectural environment cannot be used, except in the most primitive sense, in the absence of meaning.[2] It is not ordinarily possible even to get into a building unless one "recognizes" that a wood panel approximately 3 feet wide by 7 feet high with a knob at one edge and hinges at the other is a door (an object which one can open to pass through). Use of a 3- by 7-foot panel of wood as a door is not automatic. It depends on meaning, which in turn depends on experience. Would an Eskimo or South Sea Islander automatically understand its use? If the doors were placed side by side along a wall or at the entrance to a building, would an Englishman, accustomed to driving on the left side of the road, choose the right door and tend to turn right upon entering as would his American counterpart?[3] It is hard to say. If the Englishman were to choose the left door and turn left, it should make a difference in the design of buildings for Englishmen!

In fact, many of the prediction problems which architects face everyday are of great importance. How does an Anglo architect predict the way in which minority groups will perceive, understand, and use public housing designed for them? Clearly, most public housing in urban areas is continuing testimony to the tremendous lapse of in-feeling, or empathy, that C.I.A.M. architects such as Walter Gropius and Le Corbusier had when they proposed high towers set in green fields as a solution to the housing of our urban poor—if, indeed, they actually thought it would work for them. But even if not, what about the many architects who have designed so much of the housing around the country? And the seriousness of the problem does not begin and end with public housing. What about predicting the comprehension and use of our designs for prisons, mental institutions, housing for the elderly, preschool facilities, and college dormitories? Will the architect's knowledge of and empathy for ("anecdotal evidence and folklore wisdom," says Kenneth Craik[4]) the occupants of those buildings allow him to make consistently accurate predictions about responses to what he designs? I think not. In the absence of better information, however, this is what the architect tries to do. Sometimes he succeeds. Quite often he fails. And failure is not a trivial matter. Collectively, the whole population considered, mistaken, inefficient, or unpleasant experiences in buildings account for a tremendous loss of time and energy, and equally important, for loss of personal satisfaction with life, for feelings of insecurity, hostility, and even rage. Occasionally they account for serious accidents or loss of life; witness

the many people who have walked through floor-to-ceiling glass doors or windows, believing them to be open. In many cases the problem occurs because the user did not attribute the same meaning to an architectural form or space as the architect had intended. Hence his comprehension and use of the architectural environment was not as expected.

## ARCHITECTURAL MEANING

In what ways, then, can architecture be meaningful? What theoretical understanding of meaning should an architect have to set the stage for accurate predictions? I would maintain that there are two essential categories of meaning of which the architect should be aware.[5] The first might be classified as representational meaning, the second as responsive meaning. In *representational meaning,* the architectural environment is known, in that it, and anything to which it refers, is represented in the human organism as a percept, concept, idea, or whatever (Figure 1). We "see" the rectangular object, "recognize" it to be a door, "feel," the coolness of the bronze knob, and so on. The second, or *responsive meaning,* consists of internal responses to the already internal representations. These responses might be affective, evaluative, or prescriptive in nature: "tinglings" in our spine, "feelings" of disgust or contempt, "thoughts" about the value of the represented environment, or "ideas" concerning what should be done about it.

This conceptual understanding is of great importance to architects because, unlike the model of meaning advanced by the psychologist Charles Osgood,[6] it states that where the environment is concerned, there are two distinct kinds of meaning and that the second is *dependent* on the first. If groups of people differ greatly in their representations of a specific architectural environment, there is little to be gained by comparing the responsive meanings of the groups, because the responses will not be to the same stimulus! If an Anglo architect looks at a "deteriorating ghetto" and sees dilapidated, unpainted old buildings and dirty streets, while Black residents see their neighbors' homes in all of their particulars and streets active with children at play, there is little reason to compare responses with what was represented. It is similar to sex differences: "a tastefully decorated living room is a meaning-

ARCHITECTURAL MEANING

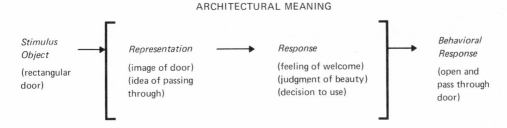

**Figure 1**

ful arrangement of sets to women who belong to the same group and who are aware of the art of decorating a room. Men are likely to look at the room as a set, to see it as one thing, and to respond to the overall effect."[7]

The duality of meaning (representational and responsive) is also important with regard to predicting behavior. The architect must first have a good understanding of the representations which the users of his building will actually form. Then he must learn how the users will react (feelings, emotions, valuations, prescriptions, etc.) to what they have represented. By considering both, the architect should be able to make reasonable estimates of the way people will behave in his building—not to mention how they will feel.

## TYPES AND LEVELS OF ARCHITECTURAL MEANING

Within the two broad categories of architectural meaning, representational and responsive, there are several subcategories of meaning which can be usefully differentiated relative to architectural prediction. With regard to representational meaning, two major categories can be isolated: presentational and referential. With regard to the responsive phase, three types of meaning can be isolated: affective, evaluative, and prescriptive.[8] These types of meaning will be discussed in the following sections.

### Presentational Meaning

The notion of presentational meaning given here is similar to that advanced by Suzanne Langer in *Philosophy in a New Key* under the heading "presentational form."[9] Forms, architectural forms in this case, present themselves to the viewer, hearer, feeler, and so on, directly and to a large extent simultaneously (nondiscursively). The forms are not acting as signs, because the representation evoked is not of all or any previously experienced forms or various other remote or imagined objects or events, but of the observed form itself. The representation usually is not verbal, in the sense that we say to ourselves, "My, isn't that complex, or large, or powerful." It is more likely to be iconic, the representation being structurally similar to the observed form. With our internal representation we separate the object from its context (field), perceive its shape, texture, color, and so on, realize its status relative to us and other objects, and categorize it according to known objects and events. We become aware of the attributes or qualities of the object or event, at least those which are in some way relevant to us.

The most basic level of presentational meaning is the recognition of form. We might see (represent) this shape:

and realize that it belongs to a category of shapes such as:

Generally, we take the next (referential) step and think to ourselves: "triangle." With more complex shapes we may, of course, simply stay at the perceptual level of categorization, having no words with which to categorize the form. We might also immediately sense or categorize forms with regard to such things as apparent size, organization, strength, texture, spaciousness, and

potency. This second level of presentational meaning involves categorization at the descriptive or adjectival level, rather than the naming or nominal level.
Finally, we might realize by size, intensity, texture, and
so on, that the object is close or far away. We realize
its status relative to ourselves.

On the surface it would seem that there would be
little difference between various groups of people with
regard to presentational meaning. However, even here,
what we represent depends on our experience.[10] If the
past experience with forms on the part of an architect
and a user group differ markedly, they may not even
see the same object. The architect might attend primarily to the shape of an object, while the user group might
attend to its status, size, or color. If this happens, and
the architect is unaware of it, he will be hard pressed
to design appropriately for the user group.

### Referential Meaning

Some forms are more important with respect to the
representations they bring to mind of objects and events
other than themselves. These forms act as signs or
symbols of other objects or events. Perfect examples
of such forms are *words*. The representation of the
form of the word itself is trivial relative to the representation which it evokes—its meaning.[11] Even with regard
to the forms of architecture, however, there is often
a strong referential importance. Doors, to continue the
previous example, within a rather wide range of size,
shape, color, and texture, evoke representations of
(make reference to) the activity of "passing through"
to most observers. The characteristics of a door might
also be used by the observer to form an "idea" of such
things as the personality of the architect who designed
it or his attitude toward the owner. In any such instance,
the door is not seen as an object, but rather as referring
to something else (Figure 2).

The levels of referential meaning are, in fact, very
numerous and account for many of the difficulties which
architects experience in predicting user responses to
their buildings. The most fundamental level of referential meaning is recognition of use. In order to operate, to
move about, to function in a building, it is of primary
importance that the spaces, forms, and colors of the

Figure 2

**Figure 3**
**Photo credit: Elliott Kaufman**

building be recognized in terms of use. Even if an architect "intends" that some objects in a building not be recognizable in terms of use, whoever occupies the building probably will not be willing or even able to accept them on those terms. This applies both to human and building use. A house should communicate to the user that it is a place where it is possible for a family to live, to eat, to sleep, to move about—human uses. It should also communicate that it will not fall down and will keep out bad weather—building uses. If it fails in either respect, it is not likely to be appreciated or used as intended by the architect.

It is also possible for an architect to communicate the purpose of the forms and spaces which he designs. It is only too easy to remember seeing an object which was easily recognizable as a chair, but which looked so uncomfortable that we hardly dared sit on it. One purpose, then, for sitting down is to rest—a physiological purpose. Such meaning can be communicated. Another purpose might be psychological. A big, high-backed, overstuffed chair might be sat upon not only for comfort but also to create a feeling of security. A chair might also indicate a social role or status, as for instance with father's chair, grandma's rocker, the preacher's chair, or the king's throne.

Values can be expressed or referred to in architecture relative to the forms themselves, the use and purpose of the forms, and independently of either. With regard first to symbolizing forms which are valued of themselves, we look both to those forms which are most often employed, and to those forms on which the most attention is lavished. Every period of history seems to have had its favorite forms, just as most architects seem to have theirs. Domes, arches, towers, galleries, axes, and cantilevers have all been highly valued at one time or another.

The example of a stairway can be used to trace all of the types and levels of meaning previously discussed and to demonstrate how architectural forms can be used to indicate the value of various purposes. First, to be identified as a stairway, an object must look as if it can be used in a functional way to step up or to step down upon in a sequence of body movements—a human use. It must also look as if it will withstand a person's weight and the wear of time—a building use. If it is to be used, it must show that it is possible for a person to go from one level to another—a physical purpose. Were it made very wide, it might indicate that many people could use it at one time—a social purpose. If it were placed in a prominent position, as in an opera house, it might indicate the psychological purpose of allowing one to observe the crowd while descending the stairs. By its size, prominence of location, and perhaps by elaborate and lavish design, it could also indicate the value that is attached to this purpose. Should a grand staircase be placed in a prominent location in a private residence, it might express a cultural value independent of purpose: "to possess a grand staircase is to consume conspicuously."[12] Similarly, if the staircase has been designed with soft sinuous lines, delicate detailing, and soft white carpet, it might symbolize grace or femininity; that is, it would likely cause the user to attribute such qualities or values to it (Figures 3 and 4).

In the case of architectural prediction, the distinction between *presentational* and *referential* meaning is of considerable importance. If an architect attends primarily to the presentational meaning of what he designs (form, color, status, etc.) while user groups attend primarily to the referential meaning (use, purpose, or value), the architect and the users are likely to differ strongly in their affective, evaluative, and prescriptive responses; and the architect is likely to err with his prediction of user group responses to his buildings. The possibility, of course, increases with decreasing rapproachment between the architect and the user, which tends to be the case in those situations involving client–user groups who differ from the architect relative to socioeconomic, ethnic, age, health, and mobility characteristics.

## Affective Meaning

Once our representations are formed, we ordinarily have further internal responses relating to our representations. One of these responses has been referred to

**Figure 4**
**Photo credit: Elliott Kaufman**

as *affective meaning*.[13] Our representations may excite us, please us, bore us, sicken us, or do a myriad of other such things. Our feelings and emotions are thus brought into play. We see a building of unknown use and purpose, but whose formal properties simply delight us. The building has just the right combination of lines, colors, textures. Or in walking through a city, we come around a corner and see a combination of shapes, shades, and shadows which takes our breath away. We are affected by the forms themselves. On the other hand, we may stand before an exceedingly handsome but apparently heavy carved door and be thrilled by the ease with which it opens. We are affected by the use of the form. Or we may sit in a chair whose form has excited us considerably and be angered by its lack of comfort. Indeed, it is often the discrepancies between representation and actuality which affect us most. The same can be said of purpose and value; we see a magnificent columned building and discover that it is a dime store, and are both disappointed and annoyed.

Affective meaning is also learned response based on experience. Unlike autonomic responses it varies widely between individuals who are similar physiologically. A building which excites a layman may bore an architect and vice versa. An underground room may affect an Arab in a completely different way than it would a German.[14] If the architect is not intimately acquainted with the cultural values of the users of his buildings, he is not likely to be able to predict how his design will affect them. The same is true of evaluative meaning.

## Evaluative Meaning

A second type of meaning which comes in response to our representations, and perhaps also to affective meaning, is *evaluative meaning*. Such meaning has to do with our immediate feelings and emotions toward it. We might look at a building, be excited and even pleased by our representations of it, and yet on reflection conclude that it is really a boring and unpleasant building. For example, we might react initially to its presentational meaning (i.e., formally), but then to its referential meaning (i.e., functionally). Values, criteria, standards, or attitudes which we possess through previous experiences are brought to focus on our representations, and considering them we conclude that the building is pleasant, unpleasant, beautiful, ugly, novel, common, or whatever. Here our purposes and values are central. A tourist, for instance, will judge buildings and cities on criteria entirely different from those of a native. Similarly, a maintenance man will evaluate the details of a building differently than will an art historian. Many an architect involved in renovation of an existing building has found that "change orders" largely reflect the values of the maintenance men. Prediction is, of course, made doubly difficult because architects do not very often design for homogeneous groups. There are almost always several different user groups with conflicting goals, interests, and activities which must be sorted out and reckoned with. It may not be possible to produce a design which will satisfy all users. If not, however, it would be to the architect's credit to know who will not be satisfied, so other than architectural means could be employed to compensate these users.

## Prescriptive Meaning

Having represented the situation, been affected by our representations of it, evaluated both our representations and their affect, we decide what to do. This is *prescriptive meaning*.[15] Ordinarily such meaning relative to architecture is not as pointed as in discursive language, where a prescription (command, entreaty, directive) is explicitly given: "No left turn." Architecture is usually prescriptive in the sense that something is made possible or convenient by an arrangement of forms. The person is led to conclude that he should not go to the left, but follow the wider and more gentle walk to the right. Nevertheless, the meaning involved is prescriptive of what action should be taken. Prescriptive meaning is thus a "disposition to response," in much the same sense as discussed by Charles Morris[16] and Roger Brown.[17] It is also the only type of meaning which can be so labeled and thus proves itself insufficient as a complete definition of meaning. Admittedly, this type of meaning might prove adequate for persons interested only in behavior. It is certainly of importance to architects who hope their buildings will be used as intended.

Prescriptive meaning is most often accountable to all of the previously mentioned levels of meaning. It is not enough to recognize the form alone to act. A person must at least recognize the use. But purpose also enters, since a building may not be intended for some people's use. The value placed on a building by society might also influence the user's actions, whether he walks or runs, whether he behaves reverently or indifferently. But this depends also on whether the user shares the values of society. The immediate affect will also likely temper the user's decisions. Finally, in light of all his representations, affects, and evaluations, the user will decide what to do, and do it. Whether the user's behavior will be as intended by the architect will depend on how well the architect predicts the whole range of meaning which the user will attribute to the building.

## PREVIOUS RESEARCH EFFORTS AND IMPLICATIONS

My initial research in this area focused on whether or not architects do, in fact, comprehend the architectural environment differently than laymen, for either the representational or responsive levels of meaning and, if so, to discover to what this difference should be attributed.[18] An experimental design was formulated, therefore, in which graduating student architects at the University of Pennsylvania were compared with nonarchitects and prearchitects at the same institution relative to their attribution of meaning to selected architectural environments. The prearchitects served as a control group whose responses, if similar to the architects and not to the nonarchitects, would demonstrate the importance of personality or preprofessional experience.

The methods of this reaseach are fully reported elsewhere.[19] Suffice it to say that there were more pronounced differences between the Penn architects and Penn nonarchitects in their comprehension of the architectural environments. Because the prearchitects were similar to the nonarchitects in most comparisons, it was evident that the professional education of the architect groups had a great deal to do with their way of comprehending the architectural environment. If the results could be generalized to architectural education as a whole, the implications would bid ill for the architect's predictive powers. The architect might be one of the *worst* persons to predict how laymen, the users of his buildings, would represent and respond to what he designs. In addition, because the groups compared at Penn were very similar in nearly all respects—ethnically, educationally, geographically, agewise, and economically—a person can only wonder about the vast differences which might pertain when these other factors are considered.

## RESULTS OF RECENT RESEARCH

My research has continued to be directed toward the end of improving the architect's ability to make preconstruction predictions (1) by making further comparisons of the environmental comprehension of different groups of people, (2) by considering problems relating to the adequacy of various media to represent the architectural environment, and (3) by attempting to develop a comprehensive set of semantic scales applicable to designed environments. Relative to the first point, my most recent study was easily accomplished.[20]

Prearchitects at Arizona State University were compared with prearchitects at the University of Pennsylvania on their attribution of meaning to an identical group of buildings. The objective of this phase of the research was to determine if major geographical (and hence cultural?) differences could account for as many differences in the comprehension of the architectural environment as had the architects' education.

It was discovered that geographical separation of these two educationally similar groups did indeed account for as many differences in the attribution of meaning as had the educational differences in the Pennsylvania study. Here again, if the results were generalizable to population groups other than prearchitects at the two schools, it would suggest that individuals living in one geographical area might be very poor predictors for people living in other geographical areas.

The other recently completed studies were methodologically oriented—specifically directed to improving the researcher's ability to study the problems of prediction.[21] The first two of these studies dealt with the problems of representing the architectural environment by photographic media. The first, a pilot study, simply compared the responses of matched groups of respondents for color and black and white slides for identical building examples. The black and white slides were, however, of somewhat inferior quality, having been reproduced from the color originals. This study was followed by a larger study comparing single color slides, multiple color slides, color film, black and white film, and black and white television with real environments. The architectural environments considered were various examples of housing. While the results are not yet completely evaluated, it appears that judgments relating to single color slides are generally nearer to judgments made in actual environments than those made for any of the other media. It is, of course, crucial to discover media substitutes for real environments so that meaningful studies can be made without having to transport respondents to the variety of environments needing to be studied—a nearly impossible task.

Additional recent studies focus on the development of a short set of semantic differential scales which fully cover the presentational, affective, and evaluational areas of architectural meaning. The first group of twenty scales was developed by reviewing a number of research efforts utilizing semantic scales[22] and extracting lead scales for dimensions which had previously appeared. A further analysis of the proposed set of scales has just been completed.[23] In this study, nine distinct dimensions of meaning and one subordinate dimension have been found to account for the majority of the scales proposed in the earlier study. Some questionable areas of scale selection remain, however, such that further study is needed. Reducing the almost infinite number of possible scales to a comparatively small yet comprehensive group is mandatory to make it possible to study large numbers of architectural environments economically without sacrifice to the various types and levels of meaning important to architects and users alike.

## CURRENT RESEARCH

The thrust of my research is now directly focused on the problem of prediction. George McKechnie, an environmental psychologist at Arizona State University, and I plan to explore how well architects can predict the meanings which specific minority groups attribute to various examples of public housing, including public housing designed by the responding architects themselves. We hope to discover what personality or experience variables tend to correlate with successful prediction of user responses. We also hope to develop a research instrument which architects can employ directly in practice to compare a profile of their own responses and predictions with the attributions of meaning recorded by client–user groups. In order to establish the validity of the instrument, we plan to conduct postconstruction evaluations to determine if use of the research instrument correlates with improved user satisfaction with the designed environments.

## CONCLUSIONS

This article has set forth what I consider to be the central challenge to the architectural designer—namely, to improve his ability to predict, before construction, the comprehension and use of his buildings by client–user groups and thus to improve his ability to design for these groups. Solid background information about architectural meaning and a sense of the importance of prediction problems relative to architectural meaning have been provided; and if studies such as the one finally proposed can be accomplished, a basis for improving architectural design from both the architect's and the user's point of view will also have been provided.

## NOTES AND REFERENCES

1. W. L. Yancey, "Architecture, interaction and social control: the case of a large scale public housing project," *Environment and Behavior,* Vol. 3, No. 1 (1971), 3–21.
2. Charles E. Osgood, G. Suci, and P. H. Tannenbaum, *The Measurement of Meaning,* Urbanda, Ill.: University of Illinois Press, 1957.
3. Gary Winkel and Robert Sasanoff, "Approach to an objective analysis of behavior in architectural space," Architectural Development Series, University of Washington, College of Architecture and Urban Planning, 1964.
4. Kenneth H. Craik, "The comprehension of the everyday physical environment," *Journal of the American Institute of Planners,* Vol. 34 (January 1968), 29–37.
5. Robert G. Hershberger, "A study of meaning and architecture," Ph.D. dissertation, University of Pennsylvania, *Dissertation Abstracts,* 1969, 30 A, 2435 A; Robert G. Hershberger, "A study of meaning and architecture," in Henry Sanoff and Sidney Cohn, eds. *EDRA1: Proceedings of the First Annual Environmental Design Research Association Conference,* Raleigh, N.C., 1970.
6. Osgood, Suci, and Tannenbaum, *op. cit.*
7. Edward T. Hall, *The Silent Language,* Greenwich, Conn.: Fawcett, 1966.
8. Hershberger, "A study of meaning and architecture," in Sanoff and Cohn, *op. cit.*
9. Suzanne Langer, *Philosophy in a New Key,* Cambridge, Mass.: Harvard University Press, 1942.
10. James J. Gibson, *Perception of the Visual World,* Boston: Houghton Mifflin, 1950.
11. P. H. Tannenbaum, H. K. Jacobson, and E. L. Norris, "An experimental investigation of typeface connotations," *Journalism Quarterly,* Vol. 41, No. 4 (1964), 65–73.
12. Robert W. Kennedy, *The House and the Art of Its Design,* New York: Van Nostrand Reinhold, 1959.
13. C. K. Ogden and I. A. Richards, *The Meaning of Meaning,* New York: Harcourt, 1923.
14. Edward T. Hall, "Quality in architecture," *AAUW Journal,* Vol. 60, No. 4 (1967), 164–165.
15. Charles Morris, *Signs, Language and Behavior,* New York: Braziller, 1955.
16. *Ibid.*
17. Roger Brown, *Words and Things,* New York: The Free Press, 1958.
18. Hershberger, "A study of meaning and architecture",

Ph.D. dissertation, *op. cit.*

19. *Ibid.*

20. Robert G. Hershberger, "Architecture and meaning," Journal of Aesthetic Education, Vol.4, No. 4 (1970), 37–55.

21. Robert G. Hershberger, "Predicting the meaning of designed environments," paper presented at the Annual Meeting of the Western Psychological Association, San Francisco, April 21–24, 1971.

22. Joyce A. Vielhauer, *The Development of a Semantic Scale for the Description of the Physical Environment,* Ann Arbor, Mich.: University Microfilms, 1965; John B. Collins, *Some Verbal Dimensions of Architectural Space Perception,* Ann Arbor, Mich.: University Microfilms, 1970; Kenneth H. Craik, "Environmental display adjective checklist," Institute of Personality Assessment and Research, University of California, Berkeley, Spring, 1966; David Canter, "The study of meaning and architecture," Building Performance Research Unit, University of Strathclyde, Glasgow, May, 1968; Robert G. Hershberger, "A study of meaning and architecture," Ph.D. dissertation, *op. cit.*

23. Robert C. Cass and Robert G. Hershberger, "Further toward a set of semantic scales to measure the meaning of designed environments," Arizona State University, 1972.

# Architecture in the Head: Cognitive Mapping

**David Stea**

**University of California at Los Angeles**

*The idea or image of a building is as important as the building itself. Cognitive maps are mental descriptions of the environment. One cannot understand spatial behavior without an understanding of how maps are acquired and used. There is no one-to-one correspondence between the "real" and "imagined" world, but there is some stability in the correspondence between the two. Cognitive maps are acquired through direct or mediated (i.e., second-hand via books, television, etc.) perception over time. One should avoid confusing the process with the techniques of assessing it. The study of cognitive mapping is concerned with how stabilized, fully formed impressions come to be, how mapping takes place in the brain, and the form and content of the maps as represented in graphic or verbal descriptions (i.e., the input, the throughput, and the output). Differences in output are associated with differences in experience, which refers back to differences in the elements to which attention is paid.*

*"He's got the whole world in his head"—from an article on David Brower of the Sierra Club.*[1]

A young school girl in the Soviet Union, blind from birth, draws a near-perfect map of her home from memory—only the windows are missing.[2] A blind graduate student in psychology draws an outline map of the United States superior in almost all respects to those produced by his sighted counterparts in geography.[3] Workers in a hospital offered a choice between two paths from one place to another, objectively equal in length, estimate the path that passes outside the building to be twice the length of the one entirely interior.[4] Institutionalized psychotics, asked to "draw their ward," produce a variety of sketches which, in some cases, correspond to their psychoses: they range from disconnected verbal statements to elaborate plans, totally bereft of doors and windows.[5] Meanwhile, back in the world of people abnormal in a different way (too small in size to matter), children at the age of 2½ are found to identify objects in aerial photographs eight years before they are "supposed" to be able to accomplish this feat.[6]

To misquote the historian Arnold Toynbee, "history itself is unimportant—what is important is what people *think* history is." One would not go so far as to say,

concerning the above examples, that "architecture and urban design are unimportant—what is important is what people *think* the products are, or will be." It *is* true, however, that the idea or image of a building is as important as the building itself: "there are two kinds of space, one physical and one conceptual."[7] People who have never actually viewed the Parthenon can provide descriptions, verbal or graphic, dependent upon things they have read and pictures they have seen. People who have visited the building can provide other descriptions, perhaps quite different. The important point is that neither set of descriptions may be very "accurate," but they are nonetheless real to the persons who have provided them. The architect and urban designer are aware of some of the impressions they are creating, but many of these go beyond "joy," "delight," "a sense of space," or other generalities commonly used in describing buildings. The impressions formed, research indicates, are far more specific than this; many of these "images," as they emerge in what we may call *environmental descriptions,* are so precise as to be almost palpable. But their precision is of a different order than that of the piece of urban enviroment thus described; it appears to follow its own set of laws. We are still in the process of trying to discover these laws; thus what is provided in the following pages is not a set of prescriptions to architects, but rather a progress report of an expedition into another little-known region of that dark continent inside man's head.[8] We shall try to say something about those entities that constitute impressions of the designed environment, under the assumption that the architect and urban designer want to know and need to know about a line of research that may someday be able to answer the question: What does a building or an urban setting *really* mean to the user?

## COGNITIVE MAPS AND COGNITIVE MAPPING

In his article entitled "The Mental Image of Architecture," Charles Burnette states:

*In addition to their role as a mental setting for thoughts of action, environmental images function to organize our perceptions, permit us to code, structure and store visual and spatial information and directly mediate and regulate our responses to the things we see. By allowing us to recognize, select, register and conserve particular aspects of our unique personal experience in the world these schematizations constitute the enduring reality which we construct from the phenomena of direct perception. . . . As a mediate pattern in the two way interaction between the observer and the environment [the image] can also help clarify the nature of style and individual tastes. . . . It provides a fundamental reference system for symbolic expression, communication, interpretation and meaning.[9]*

The essential nature of environmental images is well expressed in these few words. In another sense, however, the above description goes beyond the idea of an "image" as expressed in psychology[10] or planning.[11] I will use the term "cognitive maps" to refer to this more comprehensive class of "mental" phenomena, and "cognitive mapping" to refer to the process by which these maps, these mental descriptors of the environment, are generated. "When we refer to a cognitive map we mean that the individual has information about his environment that extends beyond what he can perceive at the moment."[12]

But why discuss cognitive maps at all in a book on architecture? The behavioral phenomena with which architects are concerned have been endowed with very different labels: territoriality,[13] personal space,[14] home range,[15] behavior settings,[16] and so on. Most of the

reports in the existing literature, however, deal with the ways in which behaviors related to territoriality, personal space, and so forth, are *manifested,* and not with how they come to *be*. A fundamental question, in other words, is: How is the "knowledge" of space and things in space acquired such that the behaviors referred to above appear as consistent, reliable phenomena within a given culture or subculture? How is it that they are manifested in a predictable fashion within a physical environment of a given design, and in certain situations of social exchange?

Typically, in most of our investigations, we deal with the "full-blown" phenomenon, describe it, research it, tally it, graph it, and discuss what it suggests in terms of future research. But we do not ask about its origin. What controversy exists over such concepts as territoriality thus becomes largely polemical. Such writers as Robert Ardrey[17] hold, on little direct evidence, that territoriality in man is largely or entirely instinctive; others, such as S. M. Lyman and M. B. Scott,[18] imply that territorial expression in civilized man is primarily learned. S. Kaplan[19] refers to the large overlap between "knowing" and territory. In academia, we speak of a stock of ideas as a man's "territory"; it is also, quite clearly, his expertise, his knowledge, and, in our society, his claim to identity. It is not just his knowledge of his spatial field, but his knowledge of his intellectual field as well (some professors use spatial mnemonics to help them remember points in a lecture) which is, as we say, cognitively mapped. "Knowledge" here is used in a generic sense, referring to that information unconsciously learned as well as that which is consciously acquired.[20]

Thus we are concerned with one aspect of the human–environment interface: with an environment which is rich, diverse, uncertain, and overwhelmingly informative; and with a human being having a limited capacity for holding information and limited time to make decisions, who is capable of storing in his brain the nature of events and objects repeatedly encountered, and who groups information into classes which are categorical[21] and schematic.[22] One kind of stored information consists of *networks* of mental representations, or images, of recurring objects and events, and these networks come close to what we term cognitive maps. But we know something more about these maps: we have reason to believe that they are evolutionarily adaptive and therefore pervasive, featuring in the spatial orientation of all humans and highly mobile animals[23]; that they are learned but largely untaught[24]; that they depend upon more than simple visual –motor coordination (since they also appear in the blind)[25]; that the capacity to utilize them develops with development of the organism[26]; that they have a neurophysiological basis[27]; and that the neurophysiological basis is likely to be more strongly represented in one hemisphere of the brain than in the other.[28]

The foregoing are the findings of a number of careful investigations. But to *think* about spatial thinking, to cognize the cognitive map is in reality quite a difficult task. There is no one-to-one correspondence between the "real" world and the imaged world; indeed, if one were capable of entering into the head of the observer, one would find a spatial representation the likes of which are found only in the world of science fiction.[29] Shapes and sizes are distorted; spatial relationships are altered; distances not only deviate from reality but depend upon direction of measurement.[30] In some areas, detail is impoverished, in others augmented,[31] until the result may appear to resemble Middle Earth much more than Planet Earth. But through it all runs a certain internal coherence, some of it idiosyncratic to the cognizing individual, and some of it characteristic of his group (ethnic, socioeconomic, or whatever) as a whole. This we know because of the *output:* what the person tells us, verbally or graphically, about his environment. Sometimes, we know a wee bit about the *input* as well, that is, the information upon which he is acting. But we have only the sketchiest of knowledge about the mapping process itself, the throughput, how things are being transformed or transduced within the head of the individual. We cannot go inside his head, and even if we could, we would not be able to "read" what was inside. Our knowledge and our technology is, as of now too limited, too primitive. But we can make some shrewd guesses about the grosser aspects of what is going on in the brain (cortical functioning), and these are referred to later in this article.

The traditional views of learning, as developed within academic psychology, shed little light upon the above process, partly because it seems absurd to assume that spatial learning, of two- or three-dimensional spaces, occurs by the processes of simple contiguous association, which are still at the base of most views of learning. Here, we adopt the view stated many times and expressed most recently by David Stea and James Blaut[32] that there are several forms of learning, each governed by its own set of laws. Perhaps much of what we shall call "nondimensional"learning.[33] can be handled within the contiguity framework of traditional stimulus–response psychology. "Dimensional" learning involves the acquisition of information explicitly or implicitly, literally or figuratively, distributed in space. Acquisition of knowledge of those things which are literally and explicitly distributed in space can be termed "geographical learning," with "geographical" used to represent a range of scale from the architectural through the global. It is to this kind of learning that the terms "cognitive mapping," "imaging," and the formation of "schemata" apply. More strongly,

Cognitive mapping is the fundamental process by which spatial information is acquired, coded, stored, decoded, and applied to the comprehension of the everyday physical environment.

Mapping is an interactive or transactive process; it cannot occur without some direct experience in the manipulation of environmental objects or their surrogates in space, or of oneself in the environment.[34] But such experience, such response to environments, is of a very different order than that allowed for in stimulus–response psychology. How, for example, could one describe the acquisition of the knowledge of "home range" in animals as a simple series of stimulus–response connections? Only if we *always* assume the existence of a restricted system of pathways and further assume that the learning of each path occurs as the solution to a single, isolated problem, can we explain what otherwise would appear to be dimensional learning in this nondimensional way. Indeed, much geographical learning in Western cities, especially among those whose movement is restricted in one way or another, may occur in this manner. But one cannot thus explain how the user of a house manages to find his way among rooms he has never visited in the order in which he now traverses them, any more than how a citizen knows the geographical configuration of the towns in his state, some of which he has never visited. Even less can we explain the behavior of animals defending the invisibile boundaries of their territories or avoiding places of danger in their home ranges as the result of the learning of a series of stimulus–response connections. An animal which had to learn the spatial distribution of attractive and dangerous things in its physical environment in so atomistic a way would have scant chance of survival.

Let us consider an example of such spatial learning in an animal, in a "natural" setting. Such a setting is to be differentiated from the highly controlled, and, hence, also highly constrained situation of the psychological laboratory.[35] It is inherent in the nature of spatial learning situations that the subject, the animal in this case, must at some point be left free to wander at will, to chose one path among many; it is equally as inherent in the nature of the laboratory situation that the subject cannot wander at all in any way not predetermined in the experimental design, lest control be lost. The laboratory situation gains precision at the expense of realism; the natural setting represents the reverse. We are often faced with a choice between results which are fuzzily meaningful or precisely meaningless.

Suppose we free an ordinary domestic cat from the confines of the laboratory and set him free to "do his thing," which appears to be environmental familiarization, territorialization, and establishment of home range, in roughly that order, within a fairly run-of-the mill work of architecture—an ordinary residence, for example. It is undeniable that his sensory experience is different from ours: he sniffs, for instance, more than we do, and what he sees is generally at an eye level but inches above the floor. Most among us have had the experience of moving a cat to a new house, of sealing up all the available exits during his first day of residence, and of witnessing his disappearance a few minutes after completing the job. Our *Umwelt*[36] of possible exits is different from that of the cat, as is our way of integrating them with the layout of the house as a whole. Our goals, too, are different. To accomplish the goals enumerated at the beginning of this paragraph, the cat rapidly samples his new environment, establishing "means–end relationships"[37] in a perfectly shameless display of teleology.

No aimless wanderer, he. It is hard to imagine that a cat would live very long who carried about no "schema" telling him, in general, where certain things were likely to be found, who had to stroll about until it encountered goal objects or places by accident. It seems equally hard to imagine that his complex neural network, or our even more complex neural net, would fire only in simple linear chains, incrementally established. Recent statements on "holograms in the head"[38] make it even more difficult to accept so simplistic a notion, much less believe that something so involved as a cortical hologram would be necessary to represent simple chain-like learning. Undoubtedly, associative learning enables one to build up one's first cognitive maps, developmentally speaking; to establish the early stages of each succeeding one; and, thereafter, to extract segments of it. Thus, it is true that "the perception of the environmental circumstances leads (by association) to possible next alternatives, and from them to possibilities still further down the road."[39] But it also appears true that such association is only a part of the total picture.

We have been talking largely about learning environments which are fixed in space. When we talk about generalization of environmental learning to new environments, the need for another explanatory system becomes even more evident. The behavioral phenomena associated with "personal space"[40] have been formulated with regard to cultural groupings rather than location, for example, but are always expressed spatially. Other phenomena, too, tend to be generalizable over a variety of settings: consider notions of privacy, concepts of environmental quality, preferences for environmental design, and characteristics of "the urban experience."[41]

## COGNITIVE MAPPING: PROCESS AND TECHNIQUE

One problem with establishing an understanding of cognitive mapping has been the confusion between the process itself and the techniques for assessing the process. One would most surely not *define* architecture in terms of drawings, done at a certain scale and with a fixed relationship among the various views. A definition of urban imagery as a system of paths, edges, districts, nodes, and landmarks would be equally misleading. This is not to deny that the processing system in the head *may* in fact classify things in this way; it is only to say that what we have now are categories imposed upon the data by the investigator, rather than biological or cognitive givens—as good and as meaningful as these categories may have been as a starting point, it is unfortunate that they have become equated with the cognitive mapping *process* in the minds of many individuals.

There are other techniques, also, somewhat less well known. In addition to unaided graphic representation (freely-drawn maps), open-ended verbal description, and responses to specific survey-type questions, these include drawings done on outline maps,[42] drawings using predetermined and pretaught symbol systems,[43] aerial photo interpretation,[44] and toy play.[45]

And, again, what about architecture—the architecture inhabited by cats, rats, and people? As urban design is not simply architecture on a grand scale, so architecture is not simply urban design in miniature. But some parallels exist. Architecture is often treated as visible form, but it is not merely visible; it is also "legible" and "imageable."[46] Even Kevin Lynch viewed urban imagery primarily as a visual phenomenon, but there is more to the image. A cognitive map gives primacy not only to those things which are visually prominent, but to things which are important for historical, economic, political, and other reasons. Thus the focal point of an architectural composition may or may not be something visually prominent. Ought it to be? That question can only be answered by the designer and his client. *Will* it be? That is determined by the users:

*Since much of design, particularly architectural and engineering design, is concerned with objects or arrangements in real Euclidean two-dimensional or three-dimensional space, the representation of space and of things in space will necessarily be a central topic in a science of design. From our (understanding) of visual perception, it should be clear that "space" inside the head of the designer or the memory of a computer may have very different properties from a picture on paper or a three-dimensional model.*[47]

We should be able to quote numerous instances of extensive research done at the architectural scale. But there is little to point to, in spite of the fact that much has been done at the level of the neighborhood, the district, the city, the metropolis, the urban region—even the nation. Thus the only response to a part of the charge under which this article was written—"the examples (used) or the applications (suggested) should be aimed at architects interested in the design of buildings

and their immediate environs"—can be, at the present time, that few such examples and applications exist. Why? There are many reasons. In part, it is because American architects have chosen to work with psychologists interested in other approaches—largely a "no choice" situation, since almost all psychologists interested in cognitive mapping are in the Soviet Union. Of their work, few English translations are in existence.[48] Also, beyond the first "splash," architects were somewhat less intrigued by cognitive mapping than were people in other disciplines: planning and geography, for example. Finally, we were all faced with the issue posed by Jane Jacobs in her discussion of "the kind of problem a city is."[49] It is not, she says in her discussion of Dr. Warren Weaver's three stages of development in the history of scientific thought, a problem of simplicity or one of disorganized complexity; it is a problem of organized complexity, more difficult than either of the other two. The psychologist interested in perception uses a single subject under strict laboratory control, reducing things to a problem of simplicity. The geographer considers large aggregates of spatial or population units, using a model of disorganized complexity.[50] Because these two approaches are easier, those working at the architectural scale have treated architecture as a simple problem or as one in disorganized complexity. It is neither. Architecture is no more a purely perceptual stimulus than a geographical entity. The traditional "models and boards" presentation is no more effective in energizing the cognitive map of the potential user than is a sophisticated stochastic model at describing this map. In studying architecture, therefore, as in many studies of urban behavior, we are often dealing with problems of organized complexity. Thus, it is not that there are no exemplars of cognitive mapping at the architectural scale. Rather, our tools are too primitive or too blunt; it has been too difficult to study these exemplars.

The architect interested in buildings alone can stop here. The architect interested in *aggregates* of buildings or in urban design may well find something of utility in what follows.

Contributions to cognitive mapping can be grouped into the three categories already indicated: studies of inputs, throughputs, and outputs. Clearly, the vast majority of the work done to date has been in the last-named category, an attempt to analyze the outputs of users of architectural and urban environments via their graphic and verbal representations, with occasional—very occasional—attempts to infer what input data or processes going on within each individual have produced these results. No attempt will be made to give an exhaustive description of all research in this category; rather, only a sampling of some recent work will be attempted. But it can be argued that the architect does not fully understand the significance of the outputs he occasionally views unless he also comprehends a little about input and throughput aspects of the process. Hence, we will treat these too, *albeit* rather briefly.

## The Input to Cognitive Mapping

What the designer sees is not only the output of a complex process, it is generally the stabilized impression of a fully formed adult member of the society. How, then, did these stabilized, fully formed impressions come to be?

First, they developed phylogenetically:

*A "primitive sense of place" presumably could be demonstrated in most higher animals, since an ability to find one's way about within one's range, find food or prey, and return to nests, protected places, or whatever, would be a necessary condition for survival. However, aside from the Primates, most mammals mainly find their way about by olfactory cues, outside of the immediate environment. Bats and Cetacea also use echo-sounding and are hence perhaps more dependant on audition than vision. . . .*

*My feeling is that the rise of man was dependent on a much enhanced "sense of place," or rather, awareness of the "map" of an extended range, based mainly on visual cues or landmarks, to which was joined at perhaps an early date in the hominization process, a proto-language system for the further encoding of landscape cues, directions, and landscape information.*[51]

Second, they developed ontogenetically. At one time, it was firmly believed that the young child was completely incapable of larger-than-perceptual scale spatial learning before the age of about 10. Recent work,[52] however, indicates that the majority of such learning is probably complete before school-entering age. Another belief was that complete perceptual development (comprehension of microscale spaces) must necessarily precede any form of sophisticated spatial learning (comprehension of meso- and macroscale spaces). Again, our results are indicative of rather the

opposite situation: much spatial learning appears to precede perceptual learning on a smaller scale. Some of the reasons why this should not be at all surprising are suggested by G. Hewes,[53] Eleanor J. Gibson,[54] and T. Bower.[55]

Both of the above are inputs antedating by millenia, in the first case, or decades in the second, the period in which the practicing architect is most interested: the present. What of that stage immediately preceding or at the very beginning of a new environmental experience?

Little has been done on this, partly because a rigorous study would require the performance of experiments, controlling the nature of a person's experiential history prior to entering a new situation. However, while we clearly cannot control *all* of an adult human's prior spatial experience, we *can* vary, and even control to some extent, his prior information, set of expectations, or instructions concerning a situation he is about to enter. A very preliminary attempt to study the effects of limited information upon urban imagery was made with secondary school teachers in a field seminar held in Brazil.[56] A less experimental, but more exhaustive study of prior influences upon environmental expectations was that presented by David Handlin, who has taken a fresh look at what is meant by "housing," more particularly, upon

*the development of the single-family detached house as the ideal setting of American domestic life. . . . In the first part of the nineteenth century the detached house, its objects and furnishings, became a source of metaphor and imagery, a universal language that everyone was interested in and understood. It superseded in part the vocabularies of religion and farming.*[57]

Small wonder that, with such forces working, it is incredibly hard to break down the concept that a home is always a house.

Handlin's essay illustrates another way to look at the problem. If we cannot experimentally vary the conditions antecedent to an environmental experience, we can perhaps examine preexisting (or concomitant) information fields. A. Kreimer[58] was concerned with the controversy over high-rise buildings in San Francisco which reached its height in 1970–1971, and is still strong. Kreimer was concerned with the question of how public opinion—that is, images of the city of San Francisco, what it was and what it ought to be—were shaped by information in newspapers. She examined the mythologies of progress, high rise, and so forth, the resident and tourist images of the city, and the messages conveyed by the media via words, drawings, and photographs, concluding that the effect of (often fabricated) environmental imagery is frequently stronger than that of "objective" statistics.

## The Throughput in Cognitive Mapping: The Brain

Whatever the nature of cognitive mapping, its fundamental locus is the same as that of all other cognitive processes: that "great raveled knot" in our heads. This "knot," as all of us learned in high school biology, is divided into two hemispheres, connected by tracts called *commisures*. For many years, it was assumed that the two hemispheres replicated each other's function in perception, affection, and cognition; thus fibers emanating from the right eye terminate in the left hemisphere, while those emanating from the left eye terminate in the right hemisphere, and so on. However, recent evidence suggests that the two hemispheres have markedly different cognitive functions, with the left hemisphere specializing in nondimensional verbal or "propositional" thought, linear and logical, "that analyzes, orders, proves and reasons through fragmentation rather than simultaneous consideration," and the right hemisphere specializing in dimensional spatial or "appositional" thought, *Gestalt* in nature.[59] If this view holds up, we must prepare to reconsider our twofold division of thought into concrete and abstract, and allow for at least three primary modes: concrete, nonspatially abstract, and spatially abstract. That there exist distinctively spatial forms of cognition has long been recognized in pathology. Systematic loss of geographic orientation occurs frequently in brain-injured patients, so frequently that it is used as means of diagnosing brain injury. One of the most remarkable forms that these spatial–geographic disorientations take is called Gerstman's syndrome, and involves an individual losing most of his capacity to find his way about a once-familiar environment. There is the example of a Londoner, who as a result of a head injury lost the ability to commute to and from his job.[60]

The above suggests a cortical *locus* for spatial thinking. *How*, neurophysiologically, such thinking occurs is quite another problem. The idea of "holograms in the head" has already been presented; interestingly, it appeared almost simultaneously in three papers.[61] Holograms, one of the few well-known nondestructive products of laser technology, create three-dimensional images of objects that can be walked around and examined from all sides. T. Bower[62] described the nature of imagined objects in just this way; K. H. Pribram[63] suggested that it is an extremely good model for the way in which the central nervous system actually functions. S. Kaplan[64] has suggested another model, quite compatible with Pribram's, based upon what the internal hookup must be for the organism to be behaviorally capable of doing just what it does.

## The Output of Cognitive Mapping: Cognitive Maps

What follows is a representative sample of "output" studies of potential interest to urban designers, rather than an exhaustive review of the cognitive mapping field. Many of the studies in this area[65] have followed in the footsteps established by Kevin Lynch (see also Charles Burnette's article in this volume) and, since they are by now relatively well known, will not be reviewed here. Few of these have seen practical application in the urban design field. The exceptions include the work of Donald Appleyard on the new town of Ciudad Guayana, Venezuela,[66] and Kevin Lynch's consultation to the Department of City Planning in Los Angeles.[67] The latter includes some most remarkable image maps of Los Angeles, much more striking than those presented in Lynch's original book on imagery.[68] These demonstrate that the "known area" of the inhabitants of one portion of the city is perhaps a thousand times as extensive as that of inhabitants of other, poorer areas. This was a finding in a later and quite similar study of Los Angeles[69] and in an earlier and quite different study of black adolescents in Roxbury, Massachusetts.[70]

The latter study provided data concerning individual conceptions of boundedness. In a study performed in the Republic of Mexico,[71] an attempt was made to elicit conceptions of boundedness by having subjects draw or describe the boundaries of (1) their neighborhoods, (2) the center of the city, and (3) the city as a whole. The responses for a given part of a particular city were

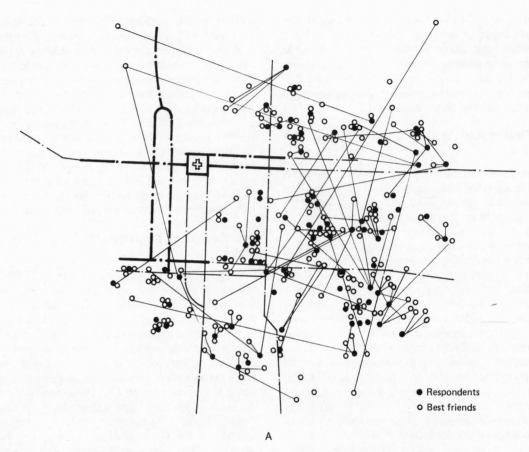

A

**Figure 1**
**(a) The pattern of linkages between the location of each person interviewed in the Raleigh Model Cities Project and the location of her three best friends. (b) The composite "cognized" neighborhoods defined by combining a variety of linkage patterns with drawn or described boundaries. The weight of the line indicates the degree of confidence that it is in fact a division between areas.**

then aggregated with all drawn boundaries plotted on the same outline map of the area. Since bounded areas differed both in size and location, the resulting agglomerate was often a group of overlapping sets, resembling a very complex Venn diagram. In most cases these sets had a clear *union* or envelope, representing all areas included by at least one respondent, and an intersection, representing all areas included by at least one respondent, and an intersection, representing that area included by all respondents. We attempted

to discover when this intersection coincided with known or supposed "central localities."

In many of the colonies drawn in Mexico City, the intersection was the Plaza. The intersections of boundaries of "El Centro" supported the contention of several planners that the Center had moved away from its traditional, or historic locality. In Guanajuato, a dispute existed concerning the number of centers in the city; some maintained that there was one center, others that there were two. Our study revealed three.

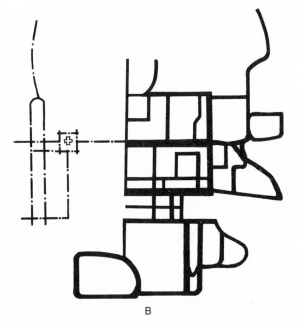

B

Such techniques can be combined with other approaches to strengthen the results or confirm the cognitive mapping output. Thus, in connection with the Model Cities Program, a study was made of the neighborhood structure of the major black ghetto in southeast Raleigh, North Carolina.[72] Here, the use of multiple criteria for boundary definition was explored. In addition to indicating perceived or cognized boundaries on a base map, each respondent was asked to indicate the locations of the following:
1. The neighborhood center,
2. Three best friends,
3. Closest relatives.
4. Primary shopping place,
5. Place of work,
6. Major neighborhood organizations,
7. Previous residences,
in reference to his own current residence. It was then possible to draw links from his home to each of the above and to aggregate the resulting collections of links, as shown in Figure 1(a). Subgroups or subcollections were formed such that the number of links within subgroups was maximized and the number of links between or among subgroups minimized. The technique employed was visual, but computer programs to perform this task already exist.[73] Any or all of these could then be aggregated to produce "neighborhoods" defined by one or more criteria, as shown in Figure 1(b).

Since the early work of Kevin Lynch,[74] at least two major advances have occurred in cognitive mapping research. The first involves recognition of a simple fact with which architects have become quite concerned: the responses of various subgroups of our population to a given environment are different; that is, there seems to exist no "universal aesthetic." The study of Mexican cities described above divided the populations surveyed by age, income, place of residence in the city, and length of residence. The "visual environment" of Los Angeles presents a variety of urban images; one can compare the view of the predominantly Chicano population of Boyle Heights with that of the predominantly WASP population of Westwood. Other studies have explored sex differences. J. Everitt[75] found that the home ranges described by a group of West Los Angeles housewives were decided differently from those of their husbands, being smaller in scale. There are implications in the above, perhaps, for the urban designer's concept of "neighborhood." P. Orleans and S. Schmidt obtained a similar difference in another study of Los Angeles residents: while the mapping *abilities* (or inabilities) of husbands and wives were substantially the same, they differed in the *kinds* of information they chose to include in their image maps. Wives are more likely to construct their own reference systems rather than using "objective" coordinates, and, even more important to the designer, display more consciousness of "point" detail.

Ethnic and occupational group differences are often even more striking. Inhabitants of highly segregated black and Italian ghetto areas in Worcester, Massachusetts, described their images of their own and each other's areas in an unpublished study. For either area, there was virtually *no* correspondence in the imagery of the two groups. In another similar study[76] blacks, police, and planning students were asked their images of Watts, Los Angeles, and its priorities. Again, no correspondence appeared among the various groups.

The other advance has involved the introduction of new techniques for assessing the output side of cognitive mapping. D. Wood's[77] most imaginative doctoral dissertation criticizes the freely drawn map as being insensitive to what the respondent to a survey really knows. In his research in London, Paris, and Rome, Wood and his associate Robert Beck taught a group of adolescent tourists a graphic language for mapping, one which was apparently quite successful in eliciting rich and varied graphic responses. Even more recently, L. Conner and E. Ritter[78] described the extension of the technique of "toyplay," originally applied to the study of cognitive spatial development in children,[79] to the study of cognitive mapping in adults. Their concern is a study performed by Peter Orleans with a group from a selected census tract in Santa Monica, California. Orleans presented his subjects with an outline map of Santa Monica, only the streets being indicated. Balsa wood miniatures of landmarks and nodes in the Santa Monica area were placed next to corresponding names and symbols on a prepared list. The problem was one of evaluating residents' knowledge of their area as indicated by placement of the models. It was unique to this study that two kinds of knowledge of the area were evaluated—locational and relational. The first involved absolute location, the second the location of models relative to one another. While the final results of this study are not yet available, it is notable for its innovations in technique. One of the many drawbacks to the freely drawn map is that many people—even very educated people—are quite simply reluctant to draw. Some flatly refuse. For whatever reason, "playing with toys" has an intrinsic appeal, even to adults.

## CONCLUSION

To be useful, a cognitive map must "predict" something—it is not enough to have a network of images; images of our present surroundings must be associated with images of those objects and events likely to come next. Similarly, to be useful to the environmental designer, cognitive mapping research must predict the behavior—whether it be overt responses or impression formulation—of the individuals experiencing designed environments. To date, however, most research has been descriptive; it describes how people are responding to an existing environment, but says little, directly, about how they might respond to a new environment in the future. And it is the latter issue in which the architect and urban planner are most interested.

But much of the research has been cumulative, and we now know something about the lawful nature of "maps in the head." Perhaps we are entering a new era in this emerging subfield of environmental behavior. Architects began their search for relevant information on human behavior with an extended flirtation with the psychology of perception; finding that what psychologists study under the heading "perception" is rarely what the architect is really interested in, they expanded their horizons, and with it their willingness to deal with those larger-scale behavioral phenomena so frequently ignored by laboratory psychology. The study of urban imagery began in the design disciplines, and came of age as cognitive mapping under the benevolent wing of "the new geography." The prodigal can now return. We hope that it will.

## NOTES AND REFERENCES

1. Arnold Hano, "He's got the whole world in his head," *West* (*Los Angeles Times*) (April 13, 1972), 16–19.
2. F. N. Shemyakin, "Orientation in space," in *Psychological Science in the USSR,* Vol. 1, Washington, D.C.: Office of Technical Services, 62–11083, 1962.
3. R. Dennis, personal demonstration, 1969.
4. Gerald Davis, personal communication, 1967.
5. Rajendra Srivastava, personal communication, 1966.
6. James M. Blaut and David Stea, "Studies of geographic learning," *Annals of the Association of American Geographers,* Vol. 61, No. 2 (1971), 387–393.
7. John B. Calhoun, "Space and the strategy of life," paper presented at meeting of the American Association for the Advancement of Science, Dallas, Texas, 1968.
8. The author of this paper is not the originator of all the ideas contained within it. Some of the contributors to cognitive mapping work are listed here in the footnotes; others, whose contribution to my own thinking make them worthy of additional mention include Jeremy Anderson, Jim Blaut, Roger Downs, Peter Gould, Gordon Hewes, Steve Kaplan, Peter Orleans, Warren Tenhouten, and Denis Wood.
9. Charles Burnette, "The mental image of architecture," in Charles Burnette, Jon Lang and David Vachon, eds., *Architecture for Human Behavior,* Philadelphia: Philadelphia Chapter/AIA, 1971, 66.
10. R. Holt, "Imagery: the return of the ostracized," *American Psychologist,* Vol. 19 (1964), 254–264.
11. Kevin Lynch, *The Image of the City,* Cambridge, Mass.: The MIT Press, 1960.

12. S. Kaplan, "Cognitive maps in perception and thought," in R. M. Downs and D. Stea, eds., *Cognitive Mapping: Images of Spatial Environments,* Chicago: Aldine-Atherton (in press).

13. David Stea, "Space, territory and human movement," *Landscape,* Vol. 15 (Autumn 1965), 13–16.

14. Robert Sommer, *Personal Space: The Behavioral Basis of Design,* New York: Prentice-Hall, 1969.

15. J. Anderson and M. Tindal, "The concept of home range: new data for the study of territorial behavior," in William J. Mitchell, ed., *Environmental Design: Research and Practice: Proceedings of the EDRA3/AR8 Conference,* University of California, Los Angeles, January 1972.

16. Roger G. Barker and Paul Gump, *Big School, Small School,* Stanford, Calif.: Stanford University Press, 1964.

17. Robert Ardrey, *The Territorial Imperative,* New York: Atheneum, 1966.

18. S. M. Lyman and M. B. Scott, "Territoriality: a neglected sociological dimension," *Social Problems,* Vol. 15 (Fall 1967), 236–249.

19. S. Kaplan et al., *Knowing Man: Towards a Human Environment* (in press).

20. Kaplan writes: "knowing is being able to see it in your head, to think about it a lot, to imagine it, to wonder about it, to feel it. Sometimes knowing something is to be able to say it, but often what one can say is so little of what one knows, and often what one says is so far from what one really feels. Knowing is being able to figure out what it is when you have seen only a little bit. Knowing is being comfortable and familiar and being able to guess what might happen next and what you would do about it if you had to. Knowing is having lots of choices about how to get somewhere, and if you go part way wrong to find your way without starting over again. Knowing is not getting lost, and not even having to worry about that," *Ibid.*

21. Jerome S. Bruner, "On perceptual readiness," *Psychological Review,* Vol. 64 (1957), 123–152.

22. Fred Attneave, "Transfer of experience with a class schema to identification-learning of patterns and shapes," *Journal of Experimental Psychology,* Vol. 54 (1957), 81–88.

23. G. Hewes, personal communication to James M. Blaut, 1971.

24. Blaut and Stea, *op. cit.*

25. Shemyakin, *op. cit.*

26. R. A. Hart and G. T. Moore, "The development of spatial cognition," in Downs and Stea, *op. cit.*

27. Kaplan, "Cognitive maps," *op. cit.*

28. J. E. Bogen, J. F. Marsh, and W. D. Tenhouten, "A theorem of cognitive functioning and social stratification," unpublished MS., University of California, Los Angeles, 1970; J. E. Bogen, R. De Zuro, W. D. Tenhouten, and J. F. Marsh, "The other side of the brain, IV, the A/P ratio," *Bulletin of the Los Angeles Neurological Societies,* Vol. 37 (April 1972), 49–61.

29. The reader to whom this is an intriguing notion will enjoy reading Edwin A. Abbott, *Flatland: A Romance of Many Dimensions,* New York: Barnes & Noble, 1963. Although this book originally appeared in the 1880's, its message to environmentalists remains strong, even today.

30. David Stea, "The measurement of mental maps: an experimental model for studying conceptual spaces," in K. R. Knox and R. G. Golledge, eds., *Behavioral Problems in Geography: A Symposium,* Northwestern University Studies in Geography 17, 1969.

31. Donald Appleyard, "Styles and methods of structuring a city," *Environment and Behavior,* Vol. 2, No. 1 (1970), 100–117.

32. David Stea and James M. Blaut, "Notes towards a developmental theory of spatial learning," *EDRA2:* in John Archea and Charles Eastman, eds., *Proceedings of the Second Annual Environmental Design Research Association Conference,* Pittsburgh, Pa., October, 1970.

33. Human verbal learning, for example, has traditionally been studied within experimental psychology largely through the use of "nonsense syllables" as the material to be learned.

34. R. Held and J. Rekosh, "Motor-sensory feedback and the geometry of visual space," *Science,* Vol. 141 (1963), 722–723.

35. M. E. P. Seligman and J. L. Hager, "Biological boundaries of learning (the Sauce-Bearnaise syndrome)," *Psychology Today,* Vol. 6 (August 1972), 59–61, 84–87.

36. J. Von Uexkull, "A stroll through the world of animals and men," in C. H. Schiller, ed., *Instinctive Behavior,* New York: International Universities Press, 1957 (originally published in German in 1934).

37. E. C. Tolman, "Cognitive maps in rats and men," *Psychological Review,* Vol. 55 (1948), 189–208; E. C. Tolman, "A psychological model," in T. Parsons and E. A. Shils, *Towards a General Theory of Action,* Cambridge, Mass.: Harvard University Press, 1951; E. C. Tolman, *Behavior and Psychological Man: Essays in Behavior,* Berkeley, Calif.: University of California Press, 1958.

38. K. H. Pribram, "The brain," *Psychology Today,* Vol. 5 (September 1971), 44–48, 89–90; Philip R. Westlake, "The possibilities of neural holographic processes within the brain," *Kybernetik,* Vol. 7 (1970), 129–153.

39. Kaplan, *Knowing Man: Towards a Human Environment, op. cit.*

40. Edward T. Hall, *The Silent Language,* Garden City, N.Y.: Doubleday, 1959; Edward T. Hall, *The Hidden Dimension,* Garden City, N.Y.: Doubleday, 1966.

41. Stanley Milgram, "The experience of living in cities," *Science* Vol. 167 (March 13, 1970), 1461–1468; Stanley Milgram et al., "A psychological map of New York City," *American Scientist,* Vol. 60 (March–April 1972), 194–200.

42. J. Everitt, Ph.D. dissertation, University of California, 1972.

43. D. Wood, Ph.D. dissertation, Clark University, 1972.

44. Blaut and Stea, *op. cit.*
45. L. S. Mark, "Modelling through toy play: a methodology for eliciting topographical representations in children," in Mitchell, *op. cit.*
46. Lynch, *op. cit.*
47. Herbert A. Simon, *The Sciences of the Artificial,* Cambridge, Mass.: The MIT Press, 1969.
48. B. G. Anan'yev and B. F. Lomov, eds., *Problems of Spatial Perception and Spatial Concepts,* Moscow: Izdatel'stvo Akademil Pedagogicheskikh Nauk RSFSR, 1961; *Psychological Science in the USSR, op. cit.*
49. Jane Jacobs, *The Death and Life of Great American Cities,* New York: Random House, Vintage Books, 1961.
50. A photograph of a multiple-car accident in a recent article on traffic flow bore the caption "An experimental confirmation of asymptotic instability" (D. C. Gazis, "Traffic flow and control: theory and applications," *American Scientist,* Vol. 60 (1972), 414–424.
51. Hewes, *op. cit.*
52. Blaut and Stea, *op. cit.*
53. Hewes, *op. cit.*
54. Eleanor J. Gibson, "The development of perception as an adaptive process," *American Scientist,* Vol. 58 (1970), 98–107.
55. T. G. R. Bower, "The visual world of infants," *Scientific American,* Vol. 215 (1966), 80–92.
56. David Stea, "Some notes on orientation," paper presented at the meeting of the New England and St. Lawrence Valley Geographical Society, Bridgewater, Mass., 1968.
57. David P. Handlin, "The detached house in the age of the object and beyond," in Mitchell, *op. cit.*
58. A. Kreimer, "The building of the imagery of San Francisco: analysis of the high-rise controversy," unpublished MS., University of California, Berkeley, 1971.
59. Bogen, Marsh, and Tenhouten, *op. cit.*
60. Hewes, *op. cit.*
61. Pribram, *op. cit.,* Stea and Blaut, *op. cit.,* Westlake, *op. cit.*
62. G. H. Bower, "Analysis of a mnemonic device," *American Scientist,* Vol. 58 (1970), 496–510.
63. Pribram, *op. cit.*
64. S. Kaplan, "Cognitive maps in perception and thought," in Downs and Stea, *op. cit.*
65. D. De Jonge, "Images of urban areas, their structure and psychological foundations," *Journal of the American Institute of Planners,* Vol. 28 (1962), 266–276; John Gulik, "Images of an Arab city," *Journal of the American Institute of Planners,* Vol. 29 (1963), 179–198.
66. Appleyard, *op. cit.*
67. C. S. Hamilton et al., *The Visual Environment of Los Angeles,* Department of City Planning, Los Angeles,1971.
68. Lynch, *op. cit.*
69. Peter Orleans, "Differential cognition of urban residents: effects of social scale on mapping," in Downs and Stea, *op. cit.*
70. F. C. Ladd, "Black youths view their environment: neighborhood maps," *Environment and Behavior,* Vol. 2, (June 1970), 74–99.
71. D. Stea and D. Wood, *A Cognitive Atlas: The Psychological Geography of Four Mexican Cities,* Mexico, D. F.: Instituto Nacional de Bellas Artes, Cuadernos de Arquitectura (in press).
72. Henry Sanoff, unpublished MS., North Carolina State University, 1969.
73. Christopher Alexander, *Notes on the Synthesis of Form,* Cambridge, Mass.: Harvard University Press, 1964.
74. Lynch, *op. cit.*
75. Everitt, *op. cit.*
76. T. Berg, P. Hatanaka, and B. Crowe, unpuslished MS., University of California, Los Angeles, 1971.
77. Wood, *op. cit.*
78. L. Conner and E. Ritter, "An investigation of methods for judging cognitive mapping ability," unpublished MS., University of Denver, 1972.
79. Blaut and Stea, *op. cit.;* Mark, *op. cit.*

*The nature and function of the mental image which people hold of architecture and their environments are discussed in terms of three important roles which these images play: as an abstract framework for organizing behavior; as functional patterns in the mediation of thought; and as the symbolic basis of language and communication. The sequence of cognitive development in infancy is described to suggest how such mental images come to exist. To demonstrate that such knowledge of cognitive psychology may be used to clarify and reinforce the imageability of an environment, the reasoning and design for an actual setting organized to have a deliberate reinforcing effect on the mental developent of children is presented. A theory which relates the imageability of an environment to stages of cognitive development and problem-solving thought as well as to recurring distinctions in architectural theory is put forward. It is intended as an epistemological tool for the description, communication, and analysis of the relationship between the environment and thought and as the basis for a universal, flexible, and operational language for use in design.*

# The Mental Image and Design

**Charles Burnette**

**Executive Director**
**Philadelphia Center,**
**American Institute of Architects**

## INTRODUCTION

This paper is presented in three parts. The first reviews the nature and function of mental *images* which people hold of the built environment. It describes three roles which these environmental images play in thinking and suggests a new perspective on questions of taste and style.

The second part describes the development of an environment designed to have a deliberate effect on the mental development of children. This is one of the first projects to apply knowledge of developmental psychology in the design of an environment. It is presented to show that it is possible to design in a manner which complements mental development and to demonstrate the use of a universal lanaguage which can be employed to strengthen the imageability of a design.

The third section outlines a theory of recurring distinctions which are held to be operative in thought, perception, and behavior. The theory reflects the stages of cognitive development and is related to certain imageable aspects of the environment. It offers a normative, synthesizing model which can be used for the description, communication, and analysis of man–environment relations.

These three sections of the paper are intended to inform the reader about the roles of mental imagery, to present a possible environment designed as a complement to these roles, and to suggest the basis of a theory relating the physical environment and its representation in the mind.

## THE NATURE AND FUNCTION OF MENTAL IMAGES

### The Cognitive Component of Behavior

Many of the studies in the emerging field of environmental psychology deal with behavior that can be observed. To explain this behavior, it is necessary to systematically reveal the mental schematizations by which people orient and guide themselves. The reason for this is that people have some plan in their minds, some program to direct their behavior and to adapt it to meet the situations which they encounter. In everyday language we refer to such mental programs for behavior as "intentions," "purposes," and "plans." Psychologists have termed such mental organizations *"schemata"*[1] and have developed concepts such as *"mental set"*[2] and *"productive thinking"*[3] to help describe how they operate in thinking.

The mental image, or abstract vision, of the environment which we "anticipate" for our actions is a necessary part of the ability to plan behavior. A pilot cannot act to control the flight of his plane, nor a driver the movement of his car without some spatially organized "idea" which relates him to the machine and the machine to the world. Similarly, to function at a place in a room, in a building, in a city, in the country, and in the world we depend on mental images of these environments, related to one another and to the activities which we conceive. Kevin Lynch in his seminal book *The Image of the City* illustrates the behavioral role of environmental images. He relates the story of an expert desert guide who, accustomed to using the faintest of cues when crossing the desert in sandstorms, used the same cues on clear days when his destination could be seen straight ahead.[4] He also notes that Eskimos and Polynesians, who live in relatively featureless environments, have developed great sensitivity and range in their spatial images.

In contrast to the impoverished visual fields of the Eskimo, Polynesian, or desert guide, our highways, cities, and buildings contain a surplus of unintegrated visual features and signs. Most buildings for multiple occupancy offer images which tend to contradict or confuse behavioral tendencies. For example, entrance lobbies, elevators, and hallways (or expressways, highways, and roads), where the potential variety of behavior is greatest, are simplified, frustrating freedom of movement. Conversely, places which require particular identification, such as doorways (or houses) are typically differentiated only by name, color, or number rather than by a striking visual form along a memorable path. As a consequence, we are forced to develop metric schemata such as travel time, distance, street number, floor number, and directions such as "three doorways on the left" to guide our movements.

Such metric schemata may provide functionally sufficient codes to get us to our destinations, but there is ample reason to believe that they reduce the richness and quality of our experience. Indeed, it has been shown that the richness and quality of our environmental experience directly influences the character and utility of our comprehensions of the world. As Donald Appleyard notes, the environmental images of subway riders are notoriously fragmented.[5] Most of us are like the subway riders, limited in the possible behaviors and activities that we imagine by our inability to form a memorable picture of the places through which we pass. The "Bauhaus" education of architects encourages this lack of behavioral significance in our environments because it teaches us to remove much of the decoration that gives distinguishing features to the spaces we design. Instead, we are encouraged to make anonymous settings that force attention to the material, the view, and the process of assembly. The prevailing habits of life, personal aesthetics, or cultural traditions are virtually ignored. Perhaps more than in any other period of architectural history, the "modern movement" has deemphasized paths of movement through space to favor a static view of the environment and one which emphasizes the massing of elements. Louis Kahn's recent dictum "the road wants to be a building" and Robert Venturi's appreciation of the architecture of the "strip" have helped to join the path to architecture in our minds. Nevertheless, we have a long way to go before the "path" is actually clear for all of us and the behavior we can imagine is enriched by an image of the environment in which it might occur.

## The Mediating Role of Mental Imagery

In addition to their role as mental settings for thoughts of action, environmental images function in the mediation of our perceptions. They permit us to code, structure, and store visual and spatial information, and they mediate and regulate our responses to the things we see. By allowing us to recognize, select, register, and conserve particular aspects of our personal experiences, the mental images which we have constitute the enduring reality which we can construct from the phenomena of direct perception.[6] Over time, they become the measure of the significance of our immediate environment to our lives as well. Lynch describes the process as follows:

*The environment suggests distinctions and relations and the observer—with great adaptability and in light of his own pur-*

**Figure 1**

*poses—selects, organizes and endows with meaning what he sees. The image so developed now limits and emphasizes what is seen, while the image itself is being tested against the filtered perceptual input in a constant interacting process.*[7]

The characteristics of a physical object which result in the formation of a strong image in any observer have been identified through field reconnaissance and interviews of people in Boston, Los Angeles, and Jersey City.[8] Lynch's analysis of the data from this study led him to identify five types of elements by which people form their image of the city. These are "nodes," points or intensive foci which people may come to, enter, and leave; "paths," or channels of movement; "edges," or boundaries which break or contain the continuity of form; "districts," domains or areas which have recognizable identity, character, or form; and "landmarks," or points of reference which are external to the observer and are singled out for purposes of identification, structuring, or orientation (Figure 1). These elements can be referred to by a designer to enhance the imageability of both cities and buildings.

The concept of the mental image as a mediated pattern in the two-way interaction between the observer and the environment can also help clarify the nature of style and individual tastes. Indeed, Herbert Simon's statement that "style is one way of doing things chosen from a number of alternative ways"[10] is complemented by the notion that style can be appreciated as an affective and powerful schematization which is easily recognizable because of its distinctive characteristics. Styles help us to organize our perceptions of architecture by providing a reference framework of imageable elements and relationships which help us to reduce and code the information which we will remember. Architects know from experience that a sense of style is manifested by favoring those things which correspond to or directly engage personal "taste."

Similarly, the experience of beauty can be appreciated as a more or less close match between a well-formed and preferred mental image and what we see. The inspirational quality of beauty can also be appreciated in terms of energy resulting from freeing up of a mental drive toward an ideal coding. Psychologists have referred to such energy, drives, or tensions in terms of directed thinking, the motivation to complete a thought, or, more recently, identified them with the concept of "cognitive dissonance," which Leon Festinger defines as "a state of affairs which occurs whenever two ideas are in marked conflict as when one is presented with an objective fact that appears to undercut a favorite belief."[11] People strive to reduce such cognitive conflicts by changing their attitudes, by seeking more information, or by restructuring or interpreting the information that is available to them. We adapt to the world by changing our behavior, the focus of our attention, or by changing our mental image of the world. Sometimes people also rid themselves of conflicting information by suppressing or ignoring it, by displaying neurotic behavior such as aggression, paranoia, or withdrawal, or by attempting as good designers to solve the problem at its sources. The controversy which surrounds the work of Robert Venturi, one of the few architects who has accepted the mental image, the taste, and preference of others as a directive for his design is indicative of the difficulties which most architects have in adjusting their own image of how a building should work to the image others hold of "good" architecture.

Despite evidence that a "good environmental image gives its possessor an important sense of emotional security and allows him to establish a harmonious relationship between himself and the world"[12] and a personal confirmation that each individual's image of good architecture is a function of his unique experience in the world, architects often ignore the taste of their clients. While we recognize that the image of good architecture which architects have results from the emphasis on sensual organization, spatial experience, and symbolic form in their education, we must recognize that this imagery is not related to the experiences and tastes of the people who use the buildings architects design. Thus it is increasingly important that architects search for the means to recognize, understand, and reinforce or transform the mental images which people hold of architecture. It is noteworthy that almost all research related to the questions of environmental imagery in areas as far-ranging as housing, mental health, and recreation, has been supported by public funding and reflects the growing public and scientific concern for ecology, social justice, and environmental quality rather more than a professional concern by architects for the taste and mental well-being of their clients.

## The Basis of Language and Communication

While functional intentions, taste, and the experience of beauty may be understood to arise and result from a mediating interaction of mental imagery and the world, the communication of these things between people is possible only to the extent that such schematizations are shared. Fortunately, while "each individual creates and bears his own image . . . there seems to be substantial agreement among members of the same group,"[13] and such agreement has been held to be a foundation of community.

The third role which the mental image of architecture and the environment plays in the lives of people is that it provides a fundamental reference system for symbolic expression, communication, interpretation, and meaning. We "read" the meaning of iron bars or open gates, of stone or glass, and understand a man by being in his home because architecture presents itself not only as settings for behavior or a physical object to perceive but also as a manifestation of what men think. Symbolic meaning has always been transmitted through the physical form of architecture.

John Summerson, in his book *The Classical Language of Architecture,*[14] outlines the sophistication in the meaning of formal elements which developed within the Greco-Roman Style, while Bernard Rudofsky,[15] Christopher Alexander,[16] and others have noted the broad popular understanding which prevailed in the enduring forms of anonymous native architecture. These two cultural patterns illustrate both the potential benefits and dangers of a fixed symbolic language for architecture. An elaborate system of meanings available only to the educated assured that the classical tradition remained the almost exclusive possession of the professional or dilettante. Conversely, when meaning resided with the common man in anonymous architecture, there was little chance for variety and change. Both exclusive sophistication for its own sake and a lack of variety and range should be avoided. In the recent history of architecture, following the classical tradition, we have developed particular meanings and reinforced styles within our profession and foisted them on the public. We are only just beginning to recognize the lesson of anonymous architecture: the need to appreciate, correlate, and synthesize the images of all building users in the interests of legibility, emotional harmony, and cultural significance. Robert Venturi is an example of an architect who consciously attempts to synthesize meanings drawn from architectural history with those found in the popular culture. However, the profession as a whole has not adequately explored or understood the cultural impact of styles. By failing to stabilize and reinforce culturally significant environmental images, the profession may be guilty of creating significant amounts of disorientation, anxiety, and confusion. Fortunately, architectural researchers such as Robert Hershberger are beginning to explore the effects of different experience and training on the meanings which different groups attribute to the same architectural forms.[17]

Donald Appleyard has noticed that people use operational, mediating, and symbolic representations to talk about their environment; these modal biases appear in perception and can come to constitute enduring dispositions manifested by personality differences and characteristic behaviors of different types of people (as for instance those of an athlete, artist, and mathematician).[18] Talcott Parsons has suggested that such patterns become institutionalized in society.[19]

Thus the three roles of imagery which I have so far discussed come to be embodied in our thoughts, our instruments, our lives, and our culture, communicating through them all.

## DESIGNING TO THE MENTAL IMAGE

If architects are to discover how to design to fulfill or change the mental image which people have of desirable architecture, it is as important for them to understand how these images come into being as it is to recognize their pervasive role in behavior, in perception, and the symbolic processes. Since it is in infancy that we first begin to build the cognitive foundations of later life, it is necessary to consider how mental development occurs and how the imageability of the environment can nourish this development. We need to learn more about how the perceptions of infancy influence those of adult life, while developing the understandings which will help us improve the relationship between the designed environment and thought.

Recent studies have established the importance of environmental influences for learning during the first 18 months of life.[20] They have also established the fundamental dominance which this period has for later learning and development.[21] Indeed, the stages of mental development of infancy are elaborated throughout childhood, remaining to manifest themselves in the working through of any process of thinking.[22] It is therefore essential that those who seek an understanding of the relationship between the environment and thinking should study developmental psychology.

Psychologists such as Heinz Werner, Jean Piaget, and Jerome Bruner have determined that mental development builds from direct sensorimotor activity in concrete physical settings to the symbolic coding and cognitive manipulation of abstract thought. Werner has recognized three successive levels of development and termed them "sensorimotor," "perceptual," and "contemplative,"[23] while Bruner has noted that children pass successively through three modes of representing the environment. He calls these "enactive" (images recalled as actions), "iconic" (images recalled in terms of their formal and physical properties), and "symbolic" (images recalled through labels, cures, and associations).[24]

Werner's and Bruner's categories parallel the roles of mental imagery that I have discussed and indicate their sequence of acquisition as first behavioral, then mediational, and finally linguistic. The literature on cognitive development also confirms Kevin Lynch's statement that the "environmental image has its original purpose in permitting purposeful mobility."[25] Further, it has been shown that the first mediations which bring order to this organically motivated activity are of a topological kind; that is, relations such as proximity, separation, succession, closure, and continuity are recognized before fixed configurations, distances, angles, or the like. Christian Norberg-Schulz suggests that the first topological laws familiar to us from Gestalt psychology are "relatively simple schematizations mainly based upon the topological schemata described by Piaget."[26] In other words, both Piaget and the Gestalt psychologists appear to agree as to the fundamental basis for the later organization of thought. It is also significant that these initial organizing principles were derived primarily from the study of visual perception, what we would term the iconic mediation of the outside world. Finally, Norberg-Schulz suggests that through perception and the process of mediation "the child learns to construct the world as a system of similarities, connect the things recognized with particular places and situate them in a more comprehensive spatial totality;"[27] he learns to recognize pattern, and recall and reference an environmental image.

This basic sequence of cognitive development has also been characterized as going from the concrete to the abstract, from the fused to the differentiated, from an organic egocentrism to a logical perspectivism, and from an immediate, unstable attention span dominated by environmental stimuli to the functional flexibility with stability of language.[28] Thus the life of the mind begins with the adaptive organic activity and ends in relatively fixed symbolic fragments. If man's adaptive competence is to be assisted by the environment, architects should take this progression into account and design environments appropriate to the stages of development of the human beings for whom they are intended. Similarly, if environmental learning is to be evolutionary and major disorientation avoided, the imageability of the environments for infants should connect in some fundamental way to the environments they will experience in later life.

To demonstrate that designing based on such knowledge of cognitive developments is possible, I shall first describe the reasoning and design of an actual physical setting organized to have a deliberate effect on the mental development of children. Second, a correlation between highly imageable classes of visual form and the stages of cognitive development will also be proposed. Third, a hypothesis that there is a sequential acquisition of certain highly imageable classes of forms will be put forward for experimental verification. Finally, I shall outline the basis for a new theory of architecture, one which lends an operational humanistic interpretation to the distinctions of classical architectural theory.

## Cognitive Development

A more detailed appreciation of infant development is needed to inform design. Piaget tells us that mental development begins with functional reflex actions such as sucking, touching, and so on, in which the child mentally attends to a single action as an isolated event. He suggests that during the first months of life, the universe presents neither permanent objects, nor imageable space, nor measurable time interconnecting events, nor forces at work beyond those of the organism.[29] The child lives in a world of his own fragmented actions. His original "purposeful mobility" is motivated by deep biological needs responsive to sensory stimuli. This sensorimotor activity soon becomes schematized as a process having continuity as the child acquires the ability to follow, to project, or rediscover coherent movement or sensations, and to control his own body movement in response, as in the grasping of a rattle. With progress in the coordination of sight and movement underway, the baby then learns to coordinate mental fragments into a single system, showing signs that he recognizes things which belong together. The infant then becomes able to intercoordinate these groups and conceptualize the world beyond the field of perception to some degree. He remains limited to immediate objects of his perception and their causal extensions. For example, he will cry when a ball rolls out of sight and attempt to retrieve it.

In this final stage of the initial stage for the "acquisition of perceptual invariants" (each stage is integrated and amplified by succeeding stages), reciprocal relations are established among and between bodies in space. The child becomes able to direct his search and to combine mental representations without having to directly perceive the phenomena. For example, he anticipates the direction from which his mother will appear. With this ability, the infant acquires a sense of himself as an object and an actor in the world. As Piaget says, the basic organization of reality has occurred "to the extent that the self is freed from itself and so assigns itself a place as a thing among things, an event among events."[30] The infant's intelligence is sufficient to make sensorimotor language and representation possible and the universe becomes substantial and spatial, causal and temporal. He can enter the realm of symbolic communication and abstract thought.

## The Design Program

This description of mental development provides the program for the design of an infant learning environment in that it suggests physical possibilities which complement the sequence. The design which has resulted provides the new-born infant with a crib place containing well-formed and distinctive stimuli, each in its own location and each possessing a distinct and related movement to attract attention. For this design, the following stimulus elements were chosen: soft round finger pockets with pulsing bottoms, an oscillating line linking elements, a vertical panel subject to rotation, a textured deformable area, a vertical shaft with liftable rings on it, and an opening or portal at which an adult would normally appear to attend the child. These objects are not arbitrary but anticipate, at the level of initial experience, the larger forms of the infant learning landscape and forms which recur over and over in the world beyond. Since the elements of the crib are merely instances of significant classes of forms, physical expressions of the same archetype may be substituted while the formal significance continues to be reinforced. On the other hand, both the location and the number of elements at any one time are limited. Location is fixed in order to reinforce the child's prior experience, by confirming his expectations in a given place. Evidence which suggests that initial perceptions might be closely related to schemata of body movement is also supported by fixed locations in that the child must physically move his body to attend to each stimulus. Through both confirmed expectations and related body movement, the infant is encouraged to develop schemata of movement. Similarly, the number of stimulus elements is limited for the purpose of maximizing differences between elements in terms of their forms, touch, and movement, and in order to gain correspondence with the organism's capacity for short-term memory (within seven plus or minus two distinctions).[31] In the crib place containing these stimulus elements, the organically motivated, egocentric, and active response of the infant to the individual stimuli is further recognized in the design of the elements themselves.

The second stage of development (characterized by the continuity of recognition limited by attention span and complexity of the stimuli, and tending to the construction of a coherent representation of the isolated perceptions acquired in the first stage) is reinforced by scaling the crib place to the limited sensorimotor domain of the infant. This domain is bounded in order to contain the visual field and provide it with a stable background against which stimulus elements and movement within the crib may be holistically perceived. Thus the infant is helped to concentrate on the limited number of elements and to locate them in a space related to himself. Once he has a coherent representation of this space, he is ready to identify it by name and symbol. It is most important to note that the partially closed environment is only one of many spaces the infant is experiencing (car, carriage, house, etc.). However, it is scaled for him and easy for him to explore physically and to comprehend. In no way is it to be thought of as an isolation chamber in which the infant is to stay or a programmed box in which the infant is controlled through stimuli. Rather, it functions like a room with functioning openings reminiscent of doorways and windows and elements more akin to objects in a landscape than to functional furniture. As the infant assimilates the organization of this partially closed environment, its openings provide him opportunities to discover the organization of the partially concealed phenomena beyond. He attempts mentally to follow these outside events, and as he does so he is given motivation for his complementary capacity to crawl. As he experiences his crib place from both inside and outside, it becomes both an object in an environment and an environment *per se* (Figure 2).

Thus the child is helped to acquire the "object concept" both for himself and the crib place in that he is either inside and identified with it or outside and

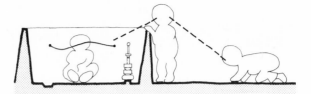

**Figure 2**

therefore related to it. Subsequently this nesting place becomes a node in the path or route representation which he soon develops.[32] The domocentric or home-based image which older children typically manifest as the basis for their first fixed reference system in the larger world is naturally anticipated by this experience.[33]

In this regard the infant's crib place is situated in a landscape composed of other distinctive places which he can visit and learn in the manner of his own "home." Thus his spatial universe is enlarged and his sense of self as actor in a stable world inhabited by other actors is reinforced.

Fully locomotive at about 18 months of age and able to link words to mental representations of objects in his experience, the infant enters the realm of symbolic meaning and communication. This capacity for apprehending objects symbolically is fostered in the design of the environment by reintroducing the elemental forms of the crib place at a new and larger scale, that of the infant learning landscape.

## The Infant Learning Landscape

The infant learning landscape was designed to provide a day-care setting for twenty infants from 4 weeks to 18 months in age. The forms of the crib place have been introduced as nesting places or identifiable homes containing four cribs and an adult caregiver. Each is provided with a changing station (surrogate bathroom). Each is sufficiently distinct in its spatial quality to allow a comprehensive range of spatial experiences in the landscape to facilitate the separation of active and sleeping infants and to allow study of the effects of various spatial settings on the behavior of both infants and caregivers. These nesting places are the dominant features of the landscape, just as the sense elements are the objective foci within the crib places; both belong

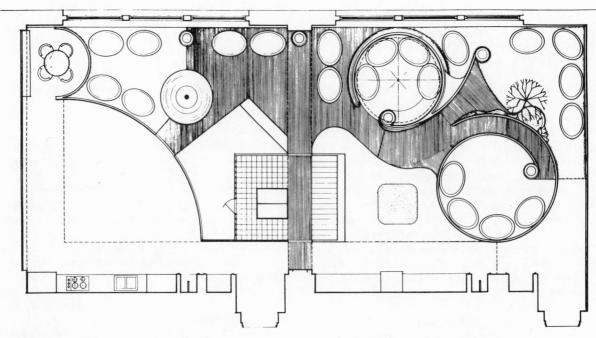

**Figure 3**
**Durham infant learning environment**

to the same classes of form, reinforcing one another and the archetype they symbolize. These archetypes correspond to Lynch's imageable classes: the node—points of intensive foci which people may come to, enter, or leave—is interpreted three-dimensionally as archetypal house, or symbolic cave; the path—or channel of movement—is interpreted as the archetypal road, or symbolic river of life; the edge or bound-

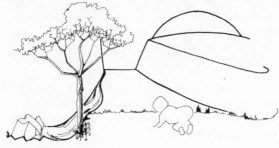

**Figure 4**

ary—which breaks or contains the continuity of experience forms—the archetypal wall, or the symbolic horizon; the district—domain or area with a recognizable character, organization, or texture—becomes the archetypal plain, symbolic of natural earth; finally, landmarks or points of reference external to the observer are interpreted as the archetypal tower symbolic of the mountains. Thus Lynch's empirically supported distinctions are seen in the archetypal forms which have been manifested throughout the history of architecture and symbolic forms and which rest deep in man's psychic and mythical history.[34]

Beyond these deeply meaningful associations, the form places in the infant learning landscape are designed to manifest the larger world of buildings, cities, and land forms. Following is a description of the landscape that will clarify this interpretation (see Figure 3).

In the top left of the plan of the two conventional schoolrooms which will contain the landscape is a nature place of organic forms and textures, containing a growing tree, a rock, and water course symbolic of the country and recreation (Figure 4). Its oval crib places range against the corner walls and a sick bed is sheltered near at hand.

From this place, a road rises and then falls to pass the opening to a cave-like space, a quiet domed place of mystery, social intimacy, and passiveness which provides a sociopetal reinforcement, symbolic of the council chamber or sacred place (Figure 5).

Opposite from the entrance to this cave-like sepulchre the road rises to a high withdrawn space giving a view of the whole (from the top of the mountain as it were). This space provides the infant with a chance to objectify and reinforce his image of the landscape as a whole. From this cluster of relatively organic forms a hard surfaced "road" symbolic of the highway and serving as the actual channel of movement for both toddlers and adults extends toward the places of great socialization and work. Its sometimes curving and eventually straight form reinforces the line of movement it represents, while allowing for places along the way to entertain, delay, and inform the toddler.

One turn in the road leads through a walled hard-surfaced enclosure filled with man-made artifacts and toys symbolic of the work place or factory. This geomet-

**Figure 5**

rically regular, Euclidean space is organized to present increments, intervals of movement, patterns, and measures to reinforce the development of abstract, rational, coordinative thought (Figure 6).

The other fork of the road passes a tower functioning as a totem, a landmark, marking the place of greatest socialization, the eating area. Besides this traditional

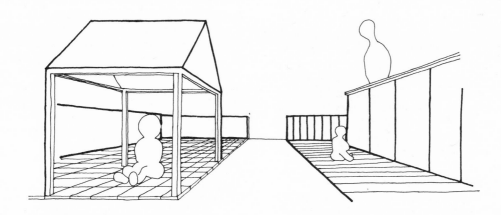

**Figure 6**

function as an orienting landmark or reference marker for a place of meeting, the tower symbolizes man's achievement vertically and his individuality in a sociofugal form reinforced by the mound on which it stands (Figure 7).

Individual prowess and dramatic physical achievement is reinforced by incorporating ascending musical notes culminating in a bell at the top which an enterprising infant may, with some difficulty, learn to ring. All the spaces and forms are reinforced by appropriate sounds, textures, and colors. For example, the cacophonic sounds, strong colors, and hard surfaces of the walled work place are differentiated from the melodic sounds, warm colors, and varied textures of the nature setting.

The form places are also differentiated in the way they reinforce sensorimotor skills in that different physical behavior, a different purposeful mobility, is required by each form place. The form and use of the road offer an example of the implications for behavioral learning contained in the environment. An infant not yet able to crawl placed near the edge of the road may first discover a difference in texture between the hard surface of the road and the adjoining form. At this "edge," a curving line reminds him of a similar but oscillating line in his nesting place. Perhaps, with the memory of movement or a tracing of the line by fingers, the infant may move with the line, discovering sooner or later that movement is easier on the hard surface. As the basic capacity to crawl develops and the road is learned as the easiest surface on which to crawl, the infant may become aware that others find the road convenient, too. A careless adult or unseeing toddler may step on a finger or cross the path with a pull toy. As the linear flow of movement encouraged by the path form is assimilated, the infant should begin to grasp the sociology of the highway—stay to one side, look ahead, don't veer to one side without looking back—a pattern of behavior and understanding that may later save his life.

Similar behavioral reinforcement (and the degree of architectural determinism at the level of infant learning is a worthwhile question) is designed into each form place and their relations one to another. In this respect, the landscape provides an experimental setting through which to examine the effect of systematic variations

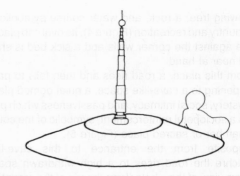

**Figure 7**

in the environment on mental development as well as behavior, personality, and socialization. It is also, depending on the use to which it is put, a physical hypothesis which can be tested, one which presents for verification as to its effect a sensorily organized, highly imageable, and symbolically rich environment, scaled to the infant and manifesting knowledge of his mental development. It is not, as most nurseries and day-care facilities today, a conventional adult-scaled room filled with unintegrated furnishing, designed to make child care less demanding of adults, and miscellaneous toys, designed to serve narrow and uncoordinated learning tasks. Instead, such an infant learning landscape as is here proposed might fulfill four of the goals desirable in educational day-care facilities today: it would invite the infant to extend himself toward greater confidence and competence in the exploration of his surroundings; foster development of a coherent, cognitive model of the larger world; encourage strong social relationships with adults and other children and for staff; and provide surroundings that are rich in content as well as functional.

## A THEORETICAL FRAMEWORK

Based on consideration of the process of cognitive development, environmental form, and architectural theory. A model is proposed which integrates Lynch's

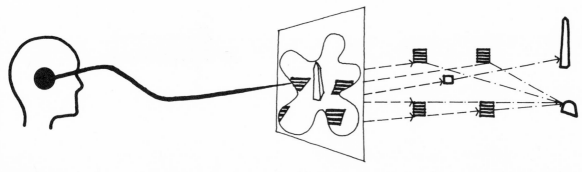

**Figure 8**

elements, classical archetypes, and symbolic forms as a basis for a theory of the imagery of man-environment relations.

In this model, it is suggested that the correspondences among these elements, archetypes, and forms identify important primitive classes of a symbolic highly imageable language or code, and that the sequence of their acquisition is first the egocentric node, then the action continuous path from the egocenter, then the edge boundary or surface of the object acted upon. These formal concepts derived from concrete experience become the foundation for the abstractly organized spatial relationships of the area or district, and, finally, the landmark emerges as the fixed symbolic reference point by which this relational image is known (Figure 8).

Such a sequential acquisition accords with our understanding of cognitive development as proceeding from organic activity to symbolic thought, from concrete to abstract, from fused to differentiated, and from immediate change to functional flexibility with stability

over time. These correspondences may be simply characterized by the mapping of this ontogenesis of cognitive development onto Lynch's elements (Figure 9).

This mapping of the sequence of cognitive development onto Lynch's elements is given in terms which model the distinctions of problem-solving thought. This is consistent with the knowledge that the stages of mental development manifest themselves in the working through of any process of thinking. Similar distinctions may characterize the roles which individuals play in groups engaged in problem solving.[35] They also imply a characteristic type of information associated with each role[36] (Figure 10).

These information types and roles provide a basis for formal information systems as well as the language-like framework for organizing thought and communication. This extended behavioral and descriptive interpretation of the correspondence between the ontogenetic progression of mental development and visually imageable elements of the environment also

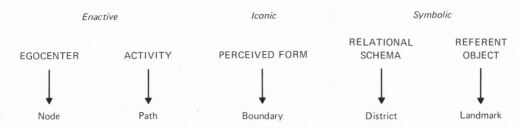

**Figure 9**

| USER | DOER | FORM GIVER | ORGANIZER | RESOURCE |
|------|------|------------|-----------|----------|
| Regulatory | Procedural | Presentational | Relational | Designative |

**Figure 10**

provides the operational and analytical capacities necessary to an integrated theory relating behavior, environment, and thought.

More specifically, the scheme can provide a significant descriptive analytical tool with which to explore and communicate the man–environment relationship. In this it integrates the distinctions of classical architectural theory with the current concerns for human behavior and thought. Thus the concepts of mass, surface, and space, the activity setting, and movement channel become mapped onto distinctions that form the descriptive basis of deductive method in science, as well as onto the three archetypal forms and symbolic images of architecture (Figure 11).

The correlation of these distinctions with the sequence of cognitive development suggests a hypothesis regarding the sequence of acquisitions of visual forms, while the suggested correspondence between information types, roles, and visually imageable forms offers a theory regarding the development and organization of memory, perceptual operations, and language. (In this it parallels Noam Chomsky's generative grammar and current related work in semantics.[37]) Thus the value of this correlation rests on an epistemological model as well as on its implications for use in experimental analyses and practical communication.

For environmental psychology, however, the model brings the concept of the activity setting and the movement channel into a structured and primary relationship to the traditional object concepts of architecture, doing so in an operationally useful way.

To give some indication of its power to accommodate and clarify important understandings, a brief recapitulation of the various correspondences is helpful. For example, Lynch's concept of the node, identified with the archetypal concept of the cave or home, and the egocentric, organic meaning from cognitive development accords with the concept of the "house as symbol-of-self," as Clare Cooper suggested earlier in this book. Similarly, as a point locus for primary sensorimotor activity, the node is the symbol for the "place," of an "activity setting" which is only meaningful in terms of the user and his satisfaction. This may be related to

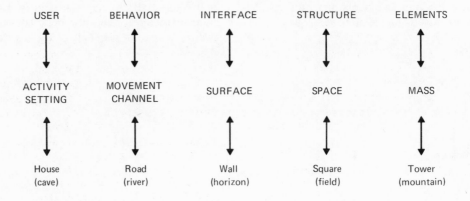

| USER | BEHAVIOR | INTERFACE | STRUCTURE | ELEMENTS |
|------|----------|-----------|-----------|----------|
| ACTIVITY SETTING | MOVEMENT CHANNEL | SURFACE | SPACE | MASS |
| House (cave) | Road (river) | Wall (horizon) | Square (field) | Tower (mountain) |

**Figure 11**

the affective pursuit of the ideal of happiness.

Just as the node and the egocenter of the user are one with the concept of house and cave, so the "path" and the continuity of behavior which it manifests are one with the concept of the road, the river, and functional activity. This class of correspondence may be related to the ideal of efficiency: the appropriate use of energy.[38]

Both classes of concepts, those identified with the "node" and those identified with the path, partition the enactive, organism-dominated domain described by Jerome Bruner.[39]

Similarly, a correlation is seen between the concept of the edge or boundary and that of mediated form, and the wall, horizon, or surface which is the reference for visual perception. This schematization is complemented in Jon Lang's paper on "Theories of Perception and 'Formal' Design." The formal and the physical properties of surfaces and the phenomena of their mediation correspond with Bruner's iconic domain of thought and may be seen in relationship to the process of recognition and the ideal of beauty, as well as the psychology of the creative mind.[40]

In Bruner's final symbolic domain of thought, dominated by the intellect, Lynch's "district" serves as the image for abstractly known relational schema, ideas of structure, organization, and space. That the concepts of space are abstract and relational has been held to be an important attribute of environmental perception[41] as well as intellectual systems such as mathematics, language, and music. Thus the intellectual idea of goodness of fit between one abstractly modeled schema and another characterizes conceptual activities such as design and is the basis for notions of their validity.

Last, Lynch's landmark element identifies a class shared by any singular referent for thought, any symbol, or objective element. Thus the architectural concept of mass and the archetypal form of the tower share an operational objectivity in thought as abstractly known facts, or as selected symbol, respectively. As objects of thoughts, any symbolic element in the mind must be verifiable in the real world if the organism is to consciously adapt to an external reality (and attain the happiness of the node–self class). Consequently, the scientific ideal of truth is identified with the distinctions of this class.

While the general value of the theory as a tool for the integration of knowledge should be evidenced by the above, a special unsolicited instance of it is provided by Christian Norberg-Schulz in his presentation of the constructs of space which we use to orient and adapt to various aspects of the environment. Norberg-Schulz notes:

*We have so far distinguished between five space concepts; the pragmatic space of physical action, the perceptual space of immediate orientation, the existential space which forms man's stable image of his environment, the cognitive space of the physical world and the abstract space of pure logical relations. Pragmatic space integrates man with his natural organic environment, perceptual space is essential to this identity as a person, existential space makes him belong to a social and cultural totality, cognitive space means that he is able to think about space, and logical space, finally, offers the tool to describe the others. The series shows a growing abstraction from pragmatic space at the "lowest" level to logical space at the top, that is, a growing content of 'information.' Cybernetically, thus, the series is controlled from the top, while its vital energy rises up from the bottom.[42]*

All interpretation of these concepts consistent with the theory would characterize them as pragmatic, functional, existential, logical, and symbolic in that order, rather than as given by Norberg-Schulz. This analysis represents the use of the distinctions of the theory as a comprehensive set of descriptive perspectives consistent with stages of thought and mental focus. The utility of the theory as an outline of descriptive exposition and analysis is suggested.

## CONCLUSION

This brief outline does no justice to the full implication of the line of reasoning it suggests. Nor does it adequately suggest the usefulness of this model of cognitive development as a normative framework for integrating and structuring large quantities of information.[43] The theory has proven to be an epistemological model of real utility to the author and one which offers the advantage of a linguistic flexibility applicable to both physical environments and the cognitive world which is the individual's prevailing reality.

This model has been outlined here in relationship to the design of an infant learning environment in order to suggest that architects who relate their design to knowledge of cognitive psychology may find themselves involved in a universal linguistic system not founded on historic styles or geometric combinations, but on human experience with, and understanding of, architecture. They will discover a new conceptual foundation for architecture that embraces symbolic content and meaning as well as the traditional notions of form, function, and technology, or mass, surface, and space.

## NOTES AND REFERENCES

1. George Miller, E. Galanter, and K. Pribram, *Plans and the Structure of Behavior,* New York: Holt, 1960.
2. Max Wertheimer, *Productive Thinking,* New York: Harper & Row, 1959.
3. Jerome Bruner, Jacqueline Goodnow, and George Austin, *A Study of Thinking,* New York: Wiley, 1956.
4. Kevin Lynch, *The Image of the City,* Cambridge, Mass.: The MIT Press, 1960, 130.
5. Donald Appleyard, "Notes on urban perception and knowledge," in John Archea and Charles Eastman, eds., *EDRA2: Proceedings of the Second Annual Environmental Design Research Association Conference,* Pittsburgh, Pa., October 1970.
6. Jean Piaget quoted by Christian Norberg-Schulz, *Existence, Space and Architecture,* New York: Praeger, 1971, 17.
7. Lynch, *op. cit.,* 6.
8. *Ibid.,* 9.
9. *Ibid.,* 46.
10. Herbert Simon, "Style in design," in Archea and Eastman, *op. cit.*
11. Leon Festinger, *A Theory of Cognitive Dissonance,* New York: Harper & Row, 1957.
12. Lynch, *op. cit.,* 4.
13. *Ibid.,* 7.
14. John Summerson, *The Classical Language of Architecture,* London: British Broadcasting Corporation, 1963.
15. Bernard Rudofsky, *Architecture Without Architects,* New York: Museum of Modern Art, 1964.
16. Christopher Alexander, *Notes on the Synthesis of Form,* Cambridge, Mass.: Harvard University Press, 1964.
17. Robert G. Hershberger, "A study of meaning and architecture," in Henry Sanoff and Sidney Cohn, eds., *EDRA1: Proceedings of the First Annual Environmental Design Research Association Conference,* Raleigh, N.C., 1970.
18. Appleyard, *op. cit.,* 98.
19. Talcott Parsons, *Societies,* Englewood Cliffs, N.J.: Prentice-Hall, 1966.
20. Jean Piaget, *The Child's Construction of Reality,* New York: Basic Books, 1954.
21. *Ibid.*
22. J. B. Carroll, *Language and Thought,* Englewood Cliffs., N.J.: Prentice-Hall, 1964.
23. Heinz Werner, *Comparative Psychology of Human Development,* New York: International Universities Press, 1948.
24. Jerome Bruner, *Toward a Theory of Instruction,* Cambridge, Mass.: Harvard University Press, 1966, 44.
25. Lynch, *op. cit.,* 124.
26. Norberg-Schulz, *op. cit.,* 18.
27. *Ibid.,* 17.
28. Roger Hart and Gary Moore, "The development of spatial cognition, a review," Place Perception Report 7, The Environmental Research Group, 529 South Wabash Avenue, Chicago, Ill, July 1971, 7-17.
29. Piaget, *op. cit.,* xii.
30. *Ibid.,* 211.
31. George Miller, "The magical number $7 \pm 2$, some limits in our capacity to process information," *Psychological Review,* Vol. 63 (1956), 81-97.
32. Hart and Moore, *op. cit.,* 7-59.
33. *Ibid.*
34. Charles Burnette, "Toward a theory of technical description for architecture," in Sanoff and Cohn, *op. cit.*
35. Charles Burnette, Gary Moore, and Lynn Simek, "A role oriented approach to creative problem solving by groups," in Wolfgang Preiser, ed., *Environmental Design Research, Proceedings of the Fourth International EDRA4 Conference,* Vol. 1, Stroudsburg, Pa.: Dowden, Hutchinson & Ross, 1973.
36. Charles Burnette, "A linguistic structure for architectonic communication," in Gary Coates and Kenneth Moffat, eds., *Response to Environment,* Raleigh, N.C.: Student Publication of the School of Design, North Carolina State University, Vol. 18, 1968.
37. Noam Chomsky, *Current Issues in Linguistic Theory,* The Hague: Mouton, 1964.
38. Russell Ackoff, "The ideals of science and society," in *Scientific Method,* Chap. 15, New York: Wiley, 1962.
39. Jerome Bruner, R. R. Olver, and P. M. Greenfield, eds., *Studies in Cognitive Growth,* New York: Wiley, 1966, 1-67.
40. Harold Rugg, *Imagination,* New York: Harper & Row, 1963.
41. William H. Ittelson, "Perception of the large scale environment," paper presented to the New York Academy of Sciences, April 13, 1970.
42. Norberg-Schulz, *op. cit.,* 11.
43. Charles Burnette, "The design of comprehensive information systems for design," in Archea and Eastman, *op. cit.*

# Behavior Settings as Data-Generating Units for the Environmental Planner and Architect

**William F. LeCompte**
**Hacettepe University***

This paper describes an ecological framework for the study of human behavior and indicates its relevance for the professional involved in the modification of the social and physical structures surrounding the individual. The behavior-setting unit and the behavior-setting survey are introduced as fundamental concepts in a data-collection system for generating systematic and precise information on the human environment. Coupled with the use of such units and methods is a theoretical perspective, one basic tenet of which is the notion of "levels of analysis." The validity of individual and environmental levels is not questioned in this approach, but an essential interdependency between them is suggested by many studies. Illustrative research is presented on a number of behavior-setting ingredients such as physical boundaries, behavior objects, and population size that function to set parameters for individual behavior and experience. These data argue for the designer of environments to adopt a variety of perspectives toward his task and to collect systematic data on the interface between behavior and environment.

## INTRODUCTION

Behavior settings occur at the interface between the individual and his environment. They are thus relevant for both social scientists and design professionals. Yet, all too often, representatives of these fields stand back to back at this juncture, the psychologist peering intently downward into the lives of individuals while the architect gazes raptly upward at the structures built to provide for behavior. A reluctance to recognize the common ground of both disciplines assures tunnel vision, a readiness to label conceptually incommensurate material as "irrelevant," and a mindless circularity in theory construction.

The vulnerability of the perspective of both disciplines is revealed dramatically when buildings are used by their inhabitants in ways which the architect did not anticipate and when individual behavior changes suddenly and unexpectedly as a person crosses the boundaries of behavior settings. Because such data tend to be embarrassing, it has been easier for the architect to use nonbehavioral criteria for evaluation and for the psychologist to apply statistical or experimental methods to control for "error" variance. The ultimate loser, in the long run, seems to be the human race,

to which laboratory techniques of behavioral control are blindly applied and around which the homogenization of the built environment becomes ever more apparent. Place a stranger in residental areas of London, Washington, Paris, and Ankara as the writer has been placed on a recent trip, and he will have a difficult time deciding which capital he is now visiting. The standing joke among consumers of packaged tours which culminates in the punch line "If it is Tuesday, this must be Rome" may speak as much for the increasing uniformity of the architectural environment as for the tour or the attitude of the tourists. It is difficult to place buildings such as that shown in Figure 1 in a particular context. Even Alvin Toffler, in a book devoted to describing the diversity of the "super industrial state" and extolling the consequent increase in individual freedom, is forced to admit the standardization of the architectural environment.[1]

The promise of research into the settings for human behavior is that it will confront the investigator with quantitative and precise data from a different perspective and thus challenge him to develop a wider understanding of his field in relation to others. For the psychologist

*On leave from the University of Houston.

**Figure 1**

it presents a view of man from the *outside,* as subject to situational pressures which are often coercive and have strong effects on his behavior. For the urban planner or architect, it presents a view of his social system or physical structure from the *inside,* in terms of systematic patterns of behavior displayed by the inhabitants. In either case, the data should contain a few surprises, depending on the extent to which the investigator is committed to his previous perspective.

## THE BEHAVIOR-SETTING UNIT

When a professor posts a written course announcement, a minister prepares for a Sunday worship service, or a physician schedules a meeting with his hospital team to review his patients, each person is acting to assure the existence of a behavior setting. In each case, a sequence of activity with other people is planned in which recurrent patterns of behavior with appropriate objects are combined in complex ways within clearly defined spatial and temporal boundaries. Roger Barker and Herbert Wright have designated the term "behavior

setting" to apply to such complex combinations of behavior and milieu.[2] From a sampling of editions of a weekly, small-town newspaper, they have shown that community behavior settings receive as many references as do individuals. This and similar findings suggest that the vast majority of a person's actions take place within ecologically defined units; behavior settings provide the stages within which our lives are acted out.

Similar to other basic units in science (cells for the biologist or planets for the astronomer, for example) behavior settings exist independently of the investigator. They have a reality of their own. For scientific purposes, however, a more precise, quantifiable definition of the unit and especially the level of interdependence between units is needed. How does one know, for example, when he is dealing with two discriminable parts of the same behavior setting as opposed to two distinct entities? The distinctions seem clear enough in the examples of the college course, the Sunday worship service and the hospital chart round presented above, but even in these cases one must determine whether two meetings of the same group generate separate settings or whether they are different occurrences of the same setting.

For this purpose, Barker has developed tests of structure and of interdependence between possible behavior settings. The structural test consists of a set of defining criteria, without which an entity cannot qualify as a behavior setting. A setting must have one or more *extraindividual patterns of behavior and milieu,* with the milieu being *circumjacent* to and *synomorphic* with the behavior patterns.[3] If we take the terms in this definition singly and in order, it can be seen that each points to a specific attribute of a setting. The term "extraindividual" denotes the operational fact that the setting is not dependent on any single person or object. The professor, minister, or physician in the examples cited above may not be able to attend the setting he has announced or prepared, but in all probability a substitute will be found and the event will occur as planned. Similarly, no single object or location is usually indispensible for the setting. It is the entire configuration that counts and, while the presence or absence of parts may make a difference in the way in which the setting functions, they do not ordinarily prevent the occurrence of the setting. The term "circumjacent milieu" refers

**Figure 2**
**Photo credit: Elliott Kaufman**

to the physical and temporal boundaries of a setting. Every behavior setting is distinct, set apart from other settings in time and space. The test of this attribute is to note that boundaries surround the actions of the people in the setting and that only highly conventional methods of penetration into these activities are permitted; one ordinarily must appear at the right doorway in the right time in order to be a participant.

Finally, the "synomorphic" nature of the relation between milieu and behavior must take place. *Synomorphic* means "similar in structure." The boundaries and the internal parts of a setting are not randomly or arbitrarily arranged, but rather display an "essential fittingness" with the extraindividual pattern of behavior within the setting. This attribute is most important for the designer of environments to understand, as it relates directly to his own concerns. The Sunday morning worship service occurs between 10:30 and 11:30 on that day at a specific location; furthermore, the arrangements of the pews inside the room (milieu) are placed to seat the listening congregation (behavior) to

face the pulpit (milieu) and the preaching minister (behavior). Any other arrangement is less appropriate, and the *soma,* or physical structure of this behavior setting, is not synomorphic with those of the hospital chart round or the college course. Thus the physical props surrounding and supporting behavior are a critical defining attribute of the setting. A similar analysis can be made of the classroom shown in Fig 2.

Barker's test for interdependence between two entities, each of which has the defining attributes of a behavior setting, is dynamic. The test asks, in a quantified fashion, the degree to which independence exists among seven different dimensions or ingredients of behavior settings. If ratings of percentage of overlap between behavior settings are high on activities, inhabitants, leadership, space, time, objects, and behavior mechanisms, the two entities qualify as distinct behavior settings. If the ratings are low, indicating a great amount of overlap in these dimensions, the two entities are classified as parts of the same behavior setting. The quantitative index on which the ratings are summed is labeled "*K*," and the precise cutting point at which two entities are declared to be two independent behavior settings is $K = 21$. A more detailed account of the procedure for making interdependence ratings is available elsewhere[4]; it is sufficient to note here that the effects of these structural and dynamic tests are to unitize an environment of interest into well-defined, equivalent behavior settings with a known amount of interdependence between them.

The procedures described above have shown an astonishing degree of generality to different types of human environments. They have been successfully applied, for example, to small communities,[5] large and small high schools,[6] parts of large communities,[7] churches,[8] and hospitals.[9] In all these cases the reliability of unitization procedures, where reported, have been high enough to more than meet the canons of scientific respectability. In the two reported studies of reliability of the interdependence ratings, 89 and 95 percent agreement was reached between field researchers operating independently on discriminations at the $K = 21$ cutting point.[10]

In summary, the concept of the behavior setting as a complex unit providing the context for individual human behavior has been introduced as a scientific unit by Barker and his coworkers. Through the operation of tests for defining structural attributes and for determining the degree of interdependence between settings, the behavior setting can be transformed into a fundamental scientific unit for the investigation of many different types of human environments.

## THE BEHAVIOR-SETTING SURVEY

Once the basic process of unitization of the environment has been completed, the systematic description of behavior settings can begin; here, the investigator is limited only by his own interests, ingenuity, and income for research. The number of countable phenomena on which data may be generated is nearly infinite. Comparisons have been made between parts of one environment, with the same environment at different times, and between different total environments. Typically, a survey year is taken as an appropriate interval for data collection in order to iron out fluctuations caused by the turnover of inhabitants, seasonal var-

iation, and other short-term factors. Representative items for data collection have included information on the following categories:

1. *People* (Who goes here and why? Who has control over the setting?)
2. *Size Characteristics* (How many person-hours are spent here? What is the physical size of the setting? How often and for how long does the setting occur?)
3. *Objects* (What type and how many behavior objects are used? What are the possibilities for stimulation, response, and adaptation?)
4. *Action Patterns* (What activities happen here? How novel or repetitive are the things that people do?)

Whatever items are included in the process of data collection, every setting is surveyed individually. Knowledgeable informants may be requested to provide information about the setting, such as personnel reports and announcements of meetings, and a considerable amount of time may be spent on direct observation. The sample of all settings is both a strength of this method, since it avoids the problems of sampling, and a weakness, since it makes it difficult to approach some environments.

## THE DEVELOPMENT OF ECOLOGICAL MEASURES

The effect of forces on the individual in a setting is now fairly well documented; indeed, many aspects of human behavior have been found to vary less across samples of individuals than across the settings that they inhabit within a single day.[11] The consistency of these findings across a variety of environments and subjects creates a need for an adequate classification scheme of behavior settings in order to better understand the kinds of settings in which human behavior is distributed. In addition, the researcher who is interested in comparing environments is aided by formal classifications and empirical indices that may tell him what areas are over- or underrepresented in the environment of interest.

Consider, for example, the research on "total" institutions, that is, environments that are inhabited by a subject population on a 24-hour-a-day basis. Such efforts have typically produced reports that are rich in qualitative description and correspondingly poor in qualitative analysis, with the result that different types of total institutions cannot be easily compared. The methods of the behavior setting survey, however, provide a systematic description of an environment in terms of precise, comparable, and quantitative indices. In a recent investigation of a rehabilitation hospital,[12] it was suspected that much of the interpersonal conflict among the staff derived from high population density. The effects of crowding are well known in ecological research, especially from animal studies, but the problem in the present case was to develop an index that would permit a quantitative comparison between the entire treatment environment and a normal community. This was accomplished with the Occupancy Time Index (OT), defined as the total number of hours spent in a setting by all of its inhabitants during a survey year. For example, the hospital setting "Treatment Area in Physical Therapy" included 89 positions for all types of inhabitants during the 1968–1969 survey year. Summing the time spent by individuals in these positions on an average day and multiplying by the total number of days on which the setting was open for business produced a total OT for this setting of 26,475 hours.

The total OT for all of the 122 behavior settings in the hospital was 1,316,185 hours. Fortunately, comparable data were available for a small midwest community,[13] indicating that the inhabitants occupied 884 behavior settings in the community during the 1963–1964 survey year for a total of 1,884,004 hours. By division, then, it can be seen that the average OT per setting is approximately five times greater in the hospital than in the community, indicating quite high population density.

For comparisons of selected population subgroups in an environment, a number of indices can be computed from behavior-setting survey data. A relatively simple measure of visibility, for example, is provided by the Territorial Range Index (TR), defined as the percentage of the total number of settings in which at least one position exists for the group in question. For instance, in the treatment environment of the hospital, physicians had the highest TR with positions in 55 percent of the total number of settings while vocational counselors had the narrowest TR, with 24 percent.

A more useful index for studying population subgroups combines the notion of breadth in the TR index with the concept of depth of penetration into important positions of power or control over the setting's activities. Setting survey data provide for this type of analysis by discriminating between *members* and *performers* within the settings. The former represents a customer, an onlooker, or a member of an audience, while the latter is typified by leaders and active functionaries within the setting, both of whom have greater control than members over the activities that occur. The degree to which a given population subgroup occupies performer positions testifies to the functional importance as well as to the visibility of that group. Barker has applied the label "Pied Piper index" to the percentage of the total number of performer positions which are occupied by the average member of a given population subgroup.[14] The allusion to the mythical piper of Hamlin is apt, for the index expresses the amount of damage that would be done to the social environment if the members of that group were suddenly piped away. Thus, the adolescents in the town of Midwest, Kansas, were found to have nearly twice the importance to the town than did their counterparts in the town of Yoredale, England, the respective Pied Piper indices being 0.34 and 0.19.

## THE PARADOX OF POPULATION SIZE

Perhaps the most investigated single ingredient of behavior settings to date is the number of people; data from many different sources have focused on the relationship between the number of inhabitants of a behavior setting and the opportunities for the average inhabitant to enter and participate in the activities of the setting. In his theory of behavior settings, Barker[15] has expressed this relationship in terms of the degree of *mannedness* of the setting. An *optimally manned* setting has just enough inhabitants to fill the required positions within the setting, whereas an *undermanned* setting has more positions of importance than it has people. An *overmanned* setting, on the other hand, has more available people than it has positions. Consider, for example, a baseball team with 7, 9, and 11 members; in the first instance, the team is undermanned, in the second, optimally manned, and in the third, overmanned. The consequences of these population states for the individual has been hypothesized to be a linear decrease in motivation to enter and take part in the setting's activities as the degree of mannedness increases.

The most convenient way of testing the accuracy of this prediction in field research has been to select a single type of behavior setting and gather data on the involvement of inhabitants through a wide range of setting sizes. Thus, for example, industrial absenteeism was found to correlate significantly with the size of the working group in factories and in coal pits as the size of the operation varied through a tenfold range. Similarly, in voluntary organizations, percentage of attendance at Rotary club meetings and at church worship services decreased significantly as the population size of the settings increased.[16] In a carefully selected sample of churches varying in size but of the same denomination, Alan Wicker[17] confirmed the latter results and found in addition that the amount of money pledged to the church per member also decreased as church membership increased. In all these cases, powerful forces operate in the large settings to keep the people coming in; large factories and coal pits have personnel departments, Rotary clubs have membership secretaries, and large churches have personnel on the staff to assist and contact members. Despite these forces, however, attendance decreases and absenteeism increases as the operation increases in size. In a systematic comparison of students at large and small high schools, Barker and Gump[18] reported that, as the average number of students in nonacademic behavior settings increased from 10 to 105, the mean number of extracurricular activities reported by graduating seniors dropped from 21.5 to 9.6. The latter study was replicated by L. L. Baird[19] with a national sample of over 21,000 high school seniors, and the same inverse relationship between school size and student activity was found.

Before completing this review of findings related to setting size, some studies indicating changes in *psychological* characteristics of inhabitants as a function of participation should be presented. Until now, the discussion has centered on observable, behavioral characteristics of the statistical group. Behavior-setting theory also predicts systematic changes in the mental furniture of individuals as a function of exposure to an environment consisting of undermanned settings. E. P. Willems studied the "sense of obligation" in individual high school students with reference to participating in and helping with school activities.[20] Sense of obligation refers to a personal, subjective disposition on the part of an individual that he "ought to" or "must do" something. Both potential dropouts and regular students in large and small high schools were asked about their reasons for attending school activities, and their verbal responses were coded for the strength of their sense of obligation. The study was repeated after a four-year interval and on both occasions the results indicated a much stronger sense of obligation in both regular and marginal students in the smaller schools. A number of other studies relating participation to psychological characteristics, such as "personal responsibility" and "cognitive complexity,"[21] have reported results similar to those of Willem's investigation. Apparently, participation generates deep psychological effects in persons, in ways that the culture tends to value positively.

These data, taken together, point to the illusion of size; as one walks through the wide halls of the large school, gazes at a magnificent cathedral, or admires a new office building or factory, the tendency seems almost irresistible to assume that the inhabitants of such edifices must have richer, more meaningful lives than people who inhabit smaller, less impressive structures. Yet the line of research just reviewed shows clearly that if the criterion is the level of commitment, involvement, or participation of the *average* inhabitant, the less meaningful lives are to be found in the more imposing structure. Here, then, is one of the surprises of behavior-setting research. When seen from an outside perspective, the larger settings are clearly more impressive and induce a sense of obligation in their inhabitants; when approached from an inside view, these same structures actually involve their inhabitants less, supporting a more behaviorally threadbare existence.

Because these investigators have been more interested in contrasting undermanned with optimally manned settings, less data than is desirable have been generated about the consequences of long-term exposure to overmanned behavior settings. To the degree that one values versatility, involvement, and participation as a life style, however, it seems safe to conclude that in today's overpopulated world the ecological opportunity to realize such values may be minimized. One challenge for the architect and environmental planner could be to attempt to create social and physical structures in which the inhabitants have a chance to participate in behavior settings where the ratio of population to positions of importance is close to 1. A possible example of such a structure is the college-within-a-college program, where the number of semiautonomous, replicated structures on the same campus presumably provides for smallness in the midst of bigness. Students who enroll within one of the smaller units may have more of the quality of the small-school existence than would be possible in an undifferentiated school of the same size. This example is merely potential, however, because no data have been collected on the *actual* ratio of performers to inhabitants within such structures. The theory of behavior settings indicates that the critical index is the ratio between the two; merely providing smaller units in terms of absolute populations is of little value unless the number of performer positions does not decrease as rapidly as the number of inhabitants. Thus, in one case known to the writer, two high school units were built on the same campus but the number of teams participating in athletic events or the number of students sent to district music festivals was not correspondingly doubled. The opportunities of the average student to fill important performer positions may well have been the same as if only one school had been constructed.

## THE PHYSICAL INGREDIENTS OF BEHAVIOR SETTINGS

The behavior setting as a complex, naturally occurring unit of the human environment depends for its definition as much on physical features as it does on patterns of social activity or on population. Unfortunately, many psychological theorists in the past have neglected or ignored the patterned nature of the physical environment, and their methods of research have tended to shatter or dismantle the organization that does exist.[22] In behavior-setting research, however, both the assumption that objects and behavior are synomorphically related and the method of including all the settings act to preserve the patterning in an intact fashion. The assumption of synomorphy implies an interdependence between behavior and objects, such that if one of the terms changes, the other can be expected to change also. The methods of the behavior-setting survey, in turn, cast a fine-meshed net across an environment of interest, so that sequential or concomitant changes in the functioning of two or more settings can be discovered and traced. These points are quite congruent with the emerging field of environmental psychology[23] and lead to important research, some examples of which will be presented.

First, however, an initial classification of environmental objects is necessary in order to distinguish between two separate functions. It is clear from the definition of behavior settings that some objects function to form spatial boundaries, while other objects serve to support the pattern of activities that take place within them. In the former case, the objects exist in a circumjacent relation to behavior; that is, the boundary objects surround behavior, while in the latter case, behavior surrounds the object.

Consider the difference between walls and fences as opposed to cups and ashtrays. In the former cases the environmental objects signal boundaries, that is, the end of one setting or subsetting and the beginning of another. Such unit-signaling objects are often involved in territoriality and tend to be ambiguous in that they seldom signal cues for appropriate behavior. In contrast, the latter two objects tend to induce standardized patterns of behavior that are quite specific and distinct from each other. In fact, inappropriate use of the latter set of objects provides the social environment with a cue for making dispositional attributions to the person (what kind of person, for example, uses both of the latter objects as receptacles for cigarette ashes?). The greater behavioral specificity of objects within settings means that they often occupy the center of our perceptual field, whereas boundary objects seldom occupy the forefront of our awarness. Both types of objects, however, generate stimuli for releasing certain behavior patterns and inhibiting others; because of synomorphy, changes in either boundary or behavior objects might be predicted to lead to changes in the behavior of setting inhabitants.

Research evidence with regard to changes in behavior objects leading to modification of behavior is scattered, but quite suggestive. An early study by Maslow and Mintz[24] found that college students produced different ratings of a set of photographs of human faces, depending on whether the room in which the ratings were made contained "beautiful" or "ugly" behavior objects. N. L. Mintz[25] further reported that the ratings were stable over a three-week period, with no evidence of adaptation to the "beautified" environment. A field study by William Ittelson, Harold Proshansky, and Leanne Rivlin[26] investigated the behavioral effects of comfortable seating in the solarium of a mental hospital ward. Two months after the changes were made, increases in a number of categories of behavior were observed, testifying to the effectiveness of the environmental change. Fortunately, the investigators had surveyed other settings in the ward as well, and the total data tell a somewhat different story. The category of "isolated, passive behavior" was actually unchanged in frequency of occurrence before and after the change in the solarium, but its location had largely been changed from the hallway into a dayroom, the appearance of which had presumably not been altered. Thus the interdependency of parts of the molar environment was dramatically revealed. On a more molecular level (that is, within setting studies of behavior objects), the work of Sommer provides a paradigm.[27] In general, research into the effects of behavior objects seems to have a fair start, but to be lacking in systematic or theoretical interest at present. The incredible frequency of object transactions in daily life may discourage investigators from such systematic attempts, but it certainly underlines the importance of such knowledge. To the writer's knowledge, no one has followed up the startling report of Schoggen, who found that three normal children in an average day transacted a total of 6,654 times with 1,950 different social and nonsocial behavior objects. With such staggering frequencies it is small wonder that subjects in so-called sensory deprivation situations (i.e., behavior objectless settings) behave in bizarre ways![28]

Two studies seem to provide leads into the function of objects as boundary or unit-signaling devices. Based on the notion that boundary objects in behavior settings emit background stimulation continuously that serve mainly to provide a context for the target, or focal stimuli in the setting, two predictions seem reasonable: (1)

adequate boundary objects will not be clearly perceived or recalled, but may provide a context that affects the judgments of those target stimuli,[29] and (2) inadequate boundary objects will motivate the inhabitants of settings into taking some relevant action either to strengthen the boundaries or to change the setting. In other words, inadequate boundaries create an unstable ecological situation and lead to change, if it is possible.

Regarding the latter prediction, William LeCompte[30] reported three cases of clearly inadequate boundaries among 122 behavior settings in the treatment environment of a rehabilitation hospital. All the areas concerned qualified as $K = 21$ behavior settings despite such structural defects. A replication of the setting survey three years later revealed dramatic evidence of structural change in two of three cases. One setting had been transformed into a veritable fortress, two others had merged into a common space, and only the boundary between two treatment areas remained unstable. These structural changes occurred despite overwhelming evidence of physical stability in most of the other settings. Apparently hospitals, once constructed, are truly tortoise-like in their rate of change.[31]

Support for the first prediction is found in an experimental study of attitudes toward mental illness.[32] Introductory psychology students were randomly assigned to one of three behavior settings, where they participated in a group drawing followed by a discussion of the product. After the discussion, a standardized attitude scale was administered, providing scores on seven different dimensions of attitude toward mental illness and mental patients. The control setting was placed in a lounge on the university campus, a hospital setting in the day center of a large Veterans Administration hospital, and a community setting in the living room of a large house located in a residential section of the city. In both the hospital and the community settings, students interacted with mental patients, but in all other characteristics (i.e., furniture, activities, apparatus for the drawings) the settings were the same. The results indicated that only the students in the community setting reported significantly favorable attitudes. The hospital and control setting attitude scores were not significantly different from each other. These differences appear to be the result of the different cues emanating from the boundaries of the community setting.

This study is an application of Alan Wicker's concept of "behavior–environment congruence" in reverse.[33] Presumably, the cues surrounding the hospital setting were congruent with the students' expectations, whereas the milieu surrounding the community setting contained no such deviancy-signaling cues (e.g., high fences, guards, institutional buildings, etc.) but rather contained cues that were congruent with normal behavior. Therefore, the lack of synomorphy between the normal boundary objects in a residential community and the presence of mental patients in the setting led to a modification of the students' beliefs and attitudes.

## IMPLICATIONS FOR DESIGN AND EVALUATION

Perhaps the most direct use of the material in behavioral ecology at the present time is as a systematic and explicit set of procedures by which individual behavior can be studied in its relation to a physical or social structure. The methods presented earlier, by focusing on the behavior setting as a basic unit, have generated interesting and coherent analyses of many behavior–environment relations. Clearly, the research that has been cited represents a bare beginning and illustrates primarily the directions in which it is possible to go. Even as such, however, these examples serve to illustrate the power of the method and of the underlying perspective to which they are tied.

One of the fundamental tenets of this perspective is the notion of levels of analysis. Phenomena at the levels of individuals, behavior settings, and the more inclusive environment are all seen as incommensurate and subject to their own laws; yet events at one level are also causally affected by the parameters of another level. Thus the ratio of number of inhabitants to positions of importance a behavior-setting index, has profound effects on the psychological functioning of individuals. Similarly, the physical ingredients of behavior settings have a direct effect on the individuals within them. Since this situation seems inevitable, the most rational approach would appear to be for the environmental professional to adopt a variety of perspectives toward his task. Information from a behavior-setting survey

may be useful initially in providing systematic data on user behavior and in suggesting possible behavioral effects of proposed modifications. Such data can then provide a quantitative and precise baseline against which the effects of the design can be assessed.

Such an approach was used quite effectively in the study of the mental hospital ward presented earlier.[34] A more sophisticated variant of the same plan, involving repeated ecological surveys over regular intervals, is currently in progress at the Texas Institute of Rehabilitation and Research.[35] The advantage of repeated surveys over time is that the data points become increasingly stable and change can be calibrated more precisely.

It may seem as if the argument for generating data through ecological methods takes the reins out of the hands of the designer, but such an interpretation is grossly inaccurate. Far from becoming the slave of a data-generating system, the planner or architect has a potentially powerful tool with which he can assess the probable consequences of a decision. The research on population size does not tell the planner to keep his settings small; instead, it says that if one wants versatility, participation, and involvement, a small setting tends to maximize these characteristics. On the other hand, if one values excellence in one activity over a mediocre performance in many activities, specialization over versatility, depth over breadth, then a high ratio of inhabitants to performer positions and large settings would be desirable. Parents who hope that their son will become another Van Cliburn or Bobby Fischer should avoid environments with many undermanned settings. The child will never find the time to practice the piano or study chess problems. Thus, as the man says, "You pays your money and you takes your choice." As the data become available, the consequences of those choices will become increasingly clear and explicit, but the choices will still be there.

## CONCLUSION

This chapter has attempted to present what might be regarded as a way of coping, psychologically, with the concept of "place." It has been written with the conviction that, until adequate translations of the dimensions of "places" into behaviorally relevant terms is accomplished, their effects on the individual will remain inscrutable. Without such knowledge the most common location may affect man in unpredictable ways. With such information and the methods that produce it, rational planning of places becomes possible, and we may no longer be victimized by our own ignorance.

The promise of behavior-setting research can be fulfilled if environmental and behavioral professionals both recognize the need for interdisciplinary research in their own respective fields. The proposal is not for a new discipline, another island to dot the proliferating map of scientific specialties, but for a bridge to span the gap between islands. If constructed, the view from such a bridge may surpass what can be seen from either point of orgin.

## NOTES AND REFERENCES

1. Alvin Toffler, *Future Shock,* New York, Random House, 1970.
2. Roger G. Barker and Herbert F. Wright, *Midwest and Its Children,* New York: Harper & Row, 1955.
3. Roger G. Barker, *Ecological Psychology: Concepts and Methods for Studying the Environment of Human Behavior,* Stanford, Calif.: Stanford University Press, 1968, 18–26.
4. Barker, *op. cit.,* 40–46.
5. Barker and Wright, *op. cit.*
6. Roger G. Barker and Paul Gump, *Big School: Small School,* Stanford, Calif.; Stanford University Press, 1964.
7. Robert B. Bechtel, "A behavioral comparison of urban and small town environment," in John Archea and Charles Eastman, eds., *EDRA2: Proceedings of the Second Annual Environmental Design Research Association Conference,* Pittsburgh, Pa., October 1970, 347–353.
8. Alan Wicker, "Size of church membership and members' support of church behavior settings," *Journal of Personality and Social Psychology,* Vol. 13 (1969), 278–288.
9. William F. LeCompte, "The taxonomy of a treatment environment," *Archives of Physical Medicine and Rehabilitation,* Vol. 53 (1972), 109–114.
10. Barker, *op. cit.;* and William F. LeCompte, "The treatment environment of a comprehensive rehabilitation facility," paper presented at the American Psychological Association Annual Meeting, Washington, D.C., 1969.
11. See M. Ashton, "An ecological study of the stream of behavior," master's thesis, University of Kansas, 1964; Barker and Wright, *op. cit.;* W. F. LeCompte and E. P. Willems, "Ecological analysis of a hospital: location dependencies in the behavior of staff and patients," in Archea and Eastman, *op. cit.,* 236–245; H. L. Raush, I. Farbman, and L. G. Llewellyn, "Person, setting and

change in social interaction, II," *Human Relations,* Vol. 13 (1960), 305–333; and E. P. Willems, "The interface of the hospital environment and patient behavior," *Archives of Physical Medicine and Rehabilitation,* Vol. 53 (1972), 115–122.
12. William F. LeCompte, "Behavior settings: the structure of the treatment environment," in William J. Mitchell, ed., *Environmental Design: Research and Practice: Proceedings of the EDRA3/AR8 Conference,* University of California, Los Angeles, January 1972, 4.2.1–4.2.5.
13. Barker, *op. cit.*
14. Roger G. Barker, "Ecology and motivation" in M. R. Jones, ed., *Nebraska Symposium on Motivation,* Lincoln, Nebr.: University of Nebraska Press, 1960, 1–49.
15. Barker, *Ecological Psychology* and "Ecology and motivation," *op. cit.*
16. William F. LeCompte and Roger G. Barker, "The ecological framework of cooperative behavior," paper presented at the American Psychological Association Annual Meeting, Chicago, 1960.
17. Wicker, *op. cit.*
18. Barker and Gump, *op. cit.*
19. L. L. Baird, "Big school, small school: a critical examination of the hypothesis," *Journal of Educational Psychology,* Vol. 60 (1969), 253–260.
20. E. P. Willems, "Sense of obligation to high school activities as related to school size and marginality of students," *Child Development,* Vol. 38 (1967), 1247–1260.
21. W. J. Campbell "Some effects of high school consolidation," in Barker and Gump, *op. cit.,* 139–153; Alan W. Wicker, "Cognitive complexity, school size and participation in school behavior settings," *Journal of Educational Psychology,* Vol. 60, (1969), 200–203.
22. Roger G. Barker, "Wanted: an eco-behavioral science," in E. P. Willems and H. L. Raush, eds., *Naturalistic Viewpoints in Psychological Research,* New York: Holt, 1969, 31–43; William F. LeCompte, "The physical object in psychological theory: a case of tunnel vision," (in press).
23. Harold M. Proshansky, William H. Ittelson, and Leanne G. Rivlin, *Environmental Psychology: Man and His Physical Setting,* New York: Holt, 1970.
24. Abraham H. Maslow and N. L. Mintz, "Effects of esthetic surroundings, I," *Journal of Psychology,* Vol. 41 (1956), 247–254.
25. N. L. Mintz, "Effects of esthetic surroundings, II: prolonged and repeated experience in a 'beautiful' and an 'ugly' room," *Journal of Psychology,* Vol. 41 (1956), 459–466.
26. William H. Ittelson, Harold M. Proshansky, and Leanne G. Rivlin, "The environmental psychology of the psychiatric ward," in Proshansky, Ittelson, and Rivlin, *op. cit.,* 419–439.
27. Robert Sommer, *Personal Space: The Behavioral Basis of Design,* Englewood Cliffs, N.J.: Prentice-Hall, 1969.
28. Schoggen's work is described in Barker and Wright *op. cit.*

29.  H. Helson, *Adaption-Level Theory,* New York: Harper & Row, 1964.

30.  William F. LeCompte, "Behavior settings: the structure of the treatment environment," in Mitchell, *op. cit.*

31.  H. McLaughlin, J. Kibre, and M. Raphael, "Patterns of physical change in six existing hospitals," in Mitchell, *op. cit.,* 12.6.1–12.6.8.

32.  D. A. Stembridge and William F. LeCompte, "Attitude changes after brief encounters with mental patients in residential and institutional environments," in Mitchell, *op. cit.,* 12.7.1–12.7.6.

33.  Alan W. Wicker, "Processes which mediate behavior–environment congruence," *Behavior Science,* Vol. 17 (1972), 265–277.

34.  Ittelson, Proshansky, and Rivlin, *op. cit.*

35.  S. E. Vineberg, "Symposium on the rehabilitative habitat and the behavioral ecology," *Archives of Physical Medicine and Rehabilitation,* Vol. 53 (1972), 101–102.

*No small group can function adequately, and achieve its goals, if the physical setting interferes with and precludes normal social interaction. Whereas it is true that group density, for instance, affects interaction, the physical layout also makes a difference to this relationship. In situations where there is group life, such as the home, camp, reformatory, or hospital, the ability to exercise freedom to experience or not experience group life is important; freedom of choice, in general, is not only a function of social systems—that is, what groups will and will not permit—but also of the physical setting. Design must therefore provide for both individual and group expression of the need for privacy and territoriality. Because it is not yet known to what degree physical layouts are important in sound group function, additional study of the physical environment is strongly indicated.*

# The Physical Setting as a Factor in Group Function and Process*

Maxine Wolfe and Harold Proshansky

City University of New York

This article is concerned with how physical settings have consequences for group function and process. If the group, in effect, is to serve as an agent of change, then those factors that maximize or minimize group function and process—of which we postulate the physical setting is not an unimportant one—will determine the extent to which the goal of individual change is achieved. In what respects, then, is the physical setting significant in group function and process, and therefore in the effectiveness of the group as an agent of change?

The response to this question can only be general. Clearly, to answer it in specific terms would require that we be asked about a particular kind of group, attempting to produce certain kinds of changes in certain types of individuals to achieve certain kinds of ends. In the present discussion we only consider those general factors with respect to *any* physical setting that have implications for the effectiveness of group function and process. And even at this level our "principles" are tentative since there are little data, if any, upon which we can draw. We wish we could point to a body of literature for the reader to examine in terms of this problem, but we can't. It doesn't exist as yet.

Let us start with the obvious, and perhaps even with what is trite. No small face-to-face group can function adequately, and therefore achieve its goals, if the physical setting interferes with and precludes normal social interaction between or among its members. An important question, therefore, is: can the physical setting and its dimensions accommodate the members of the groups in relation to the number of individuals, what they will be doing, for how long, and toward what end? Given a specific amount of space, increasing group density has been shown to have adverse effects on the types and frequency of social behavior. J. B. Calhoun has described the development of a "behavioral sink" in the living pens of Norway rats, reared in the laboratory under high-density conditions. Four interconnecting cages were designed so that two of the four pens would have a higher probability of use. As members of the group began spending a large amount of time in these pens, and specifically in one of the two, other neighboring groups were attracted to that place. The resulting large number of rats in that space was accompanied by a variety of sexually and socially deviant behaviors, including the dissolution of maternal behavior and marked social withdrawal.

Increasing group density in a constant amount of space has been shown to affect human behavior, as well. C. Hutt and M. J. Vaizey[2] observed, recorded on film, and rated the behavior of normal, brain-damaged, and autistic children in a 27.5- by 17.5-foot playroom. The children were observed in three different-sized play groups: small (6 or less), medium (7 to 11), and large (12 or more). The normal children became significantly more aggressive in the large group and showed progressively and significantly less social interaction with increasing group size, although they did not withdraw to the boundary of the room. There were different effects of increasing group size for the autistic and brain-damaged children. Brain-damaged children showed increasing aggression and destructiveness as group size increased, engaged in most social interaction, and spent least time on the periphery when playing in the medium-sized group. The significant findings for the autistic children were that they spent most of their time in social interaction in medium-sized groups, confining their interactions in large groups to the adults who were present. As density increased, these children spent significantly more time at the boundary of the room.

One aspect of social interaction in relation to the physical setting deserves special emphasis. Social interaction depends on nonverbal communication as well as verbal communication, that is, on facial expressions and body gestures and positions. The work of R. L. Birdwhistell,[3] P. Ekman,[4] Erving Goffman,[5] and others makes it quite evident that we communicate and receive the "meaning of the other" by what we see as well as what we hear. Visual and spatial configurations—where the other sits, how far, in what position, in what contexts, over what periods of time, carrying out (or not carrying out) what movements, gestures, and expressions—depend to some degree on the properties of physical setting in which the interaction occurs. Of critical importance in understanding child –adult interactions, whether at home, in school, or in any other context, are just such configurations. The differences in physical size, in the ability to articulate verbally, and in the skill necessary to manipulate physical objects in the setting—all suggest that visual and spatial configurations must play a vital role in their communication with each other.

The implications of the research and conceptions we described above are clear. The fact is that in the 1970's questions as to whether there is enough room, whether group members can hear each other, or whether the group can indeed be accommodated for long periods of time are by no means unimportant. Whether at the university, the public school, the general hospital, the industrial setting, or the psychiatric facility, the problem of adequate space and its facilities and the effects of such problems on human behavior loom as a significant issue, and the need for additional research is clearly indicated.

To state, as some of the existing small-group literature does, that twelve or ten is the optimum number for a face-to-face discussion group—as compared, let us say, to six or eight or sixteen—fails to specify under what kind of physical conditions. B. Steinzor[6] found that seating arrangement was one of the factors determining the individuals with whom one was likely to interact in a small face-to-face group. In circular seating arrangements of groups with approximately ten members, when one person stopped speaking someone opposite rather than alongside the first speaker was next to speak. Steinzor attributed this effect to the greater physical and expressive value a person has for those sitting directly opposite him in a circle. Subsequent research has indicated that the "Steinzor effect" is influenced by leadership style in the group[7] and may be a function of the amount of eye contact which is desirable in such settings.[8] In a paper on small-group ecology, Robert Sommer[9] has summarized and reviewed the literature relating spatial arrangement to group processes. We will not elaborate further here except to state that clearly, while there are physical limits to the number of people that can function in a face-to-face group, below this limit effectiveness will depend on—among other things, of course—the nature and quality of the physical setting, as we suggested above.

## GROUPS AS AGENTS OF CHANGE

Now we turn to some significant issues that raise questions about particular aspects of physical settings in which groups function as agents of change. These

**Photo credit: Arthur Anderson**

issues will constitute the remainder of our discussion in this article.

The self-identity of every individual has elements of place in it—or as we have said elsewhere, all individuals have a "place-identity." They remember, are familiar with, like, and indeed achieve recognition, status, or occupational satisfactions from certain places. Whether we are talking about "the family home," "the old hangout," "my town," or some other place, it should be obvious that physical settings are also internalized elements of human self-identity. Let us go even further. We are socialized not just to eat, drink, sleep, work, make love, and relax in certain ways but *in certain places,* in which certain conditions are accepted as necessary if not sufficient.

While little attention is usually paid to this spatial or physical environment aspect of self-identity, it is implicit in many problem areas that constitute the field of psychology. Nearly every major approach to child development speaks about the child differentiating himself from his environment. From Jean Piaget's point of view, specifically, development of cognitive function-

ing stems from the infant's interaction on a sensori-motor level with his physical environment and gradually, through this process, developing a stable concept of himself in relation to this environment.

In the case of the emotionally disturbed child, a central aspect of symptomology is the relationship of the child to his environment. It is generally agreed that schizophrenic children display an inability to come to terms with external reality, confusing it with their own private world; these children are unable to differentiate themselves from the social and physical environment and show a desire for sameness of objects and environment.[10] It is not unusual for the schizophrenic child to have an unpredictable response to visual stimuli, for instance, a peculiar preoccupation with a light or surface texture, an intense fear—or an equally strong liking—for a commonplace object.[11] While the basic factor in the therapy of such children is usually a specific type of social relationship, many psychologists have stressed the importance of the physical environment in aiding the therapeutic process. Thus H. Alt[12] has described the basic principles in the planning of facilities at a residential treatment center for disturbed children.

B. Berenson[13] is one of the few investigators who has dealt experimentally with the effects of the physical setting on the behavior of the emotionally disturbed child, and specifically with the role of this setting in establishing the child's self-identity. He found, for example, that there was a significant change in the appearance and behavior of a group of emotionally disturbed and near-delinquent girls when each was provided with a mirror near her bed; previously there had been only one mirror in the washroom used by all the girls. The mirror, according to Berenson, served to define the "personal space" of each girl and thereby helped to provide them with a sense of who they were individually.

In general, conceptions of the qualities of the physical environment that will provide the proper therapeutic milieu for the disturbed child are of a speculative nature, most often based on the experiences of persons dealing with these children.[14] As a result there are conflicting views about the nature of the environment that will be therapeutically effective. For instance, while there is some general agreement on the necessity to avoid ambiguity in building for emotionally disturbed children (i.e., spaces and rooms should be clearly defined), a minority view held is that a deeper familiarity results when it takes the child time to learn about or understand a space or building.[15] Bruno Bettelheim favors planning of residential facilities in which dorms, classrooms, and recreational facilities are close to each other because such an arrangement helps to establish a sense of security and reduce anxieties about separation.[16] In contrast, other investigators believe that school and home areas should be separated from each other so that conditions are nearer to those experienced by the normal child.[17] Even in relation to the desired number of children in a bedroom, it is difficult to find agreement. Kenneth Bayes cites a variety of viewpoints, ranging from recommendations of four to twelve in a room.[18] As we might expect, each viewpoint is supported by convincing arguments, but without the benefit of empirical research to support these arguments.

Some other dimensions of space in relation to building for the disturbed child that have been discussed are proper room size and shape,[19] the types and arrangements of furniture which should be used in a children's psychiatric setting,[20] and the extent to which the disturbed child will adjust to a change in his environment.[21]

While most of these views are speculative in that there is relatively little research to support them, it is clear that all of them express two basic assumptions either implicitly or explicitly:

1. The physical environment is a significant factor in the development and maintenance of the self-identity in the child,
2. The physical environment, therefore, can be used as a therapeutic tool, or as part of the therapeutic process, in aiding disturbed individuals, particularly the disturbed child.

Given these assumptions and the views which emerge from them, a host of questions arises about groups as agents of change. All these questions, however, can be reduced to two major issues.

First, to what degree do physical settings in which change groups operate meet the particular needs and expectancies of the individuals involved? We are not talking about meeting simple biological needs but the individual's identity needs. Can a hospital ward or a discussion room provide the same sense of familiarity, importance, and satisfaction that the individual received in the natural settings of his day-to-day existence. Of

course, the natural settings of his day-to-day existence may have negative as well as positive meaning for the individual, but clearly they can't be all negative. Furthermore, what sense of satisfaction or security can the individual derive from a group setting that is so unfamiliar or alien to his previous experience that he has little with which to identify?

In some of our work with psychiatric wards in general hospitals in New York City, we have raised the question of whether the shift from a crowded ghetto apartment in a slum area to a sleek, pastel-colored, charmingly furnished modern ward or semiprivate room is as beneficial as those of us who take the latter for granted have assumed. Does such a change necessarily have positive consequences? We are not so sure because we have found that when ghetto children are assigned to a two-bed room with just enough space, they sometimes move in a third child and thereby reduce their free physical space to almost nothing. We have seen this occur even when a much larger bedroom (accommodating four) next door could easily be used by these children.[22]

Let us direct a more fundamental but related question to those who work in and with groups as agents of social change. To what extent can we expect lasting changes in behavior, attitudes, feelings, and values induced in special "therapeutic" or "change" settings? Is the "retreat," or the therapeutic summer camp, or the special group therapy room, the place to induce change in individuals who will return to their old day-to-day physical settings? Harold Proshansky, in a chapter on the development of intergroup attitudes, has noted that while intergroup contacts may be quite effective in modifying ethnic attitudes, it is also true that such changes tend to be confined to the particular contexts in which they occur, rather than being generalized to a variety of settings.[23] Successful school integration may lead to more positive attitudes toward black schoolmates, yet not toward blacks in general, or even toward these schoolmates in nonschool contexts. Of course the question we have raised necessarily goes beyond the issue of the nature of the physical setting. Individuals return not only to familiar places, but to old relationships, conflicts, and activities. Yet, we cannot ignore the possibility that the mere removal of the group or the individual to a special setting for "self-examination" may induce situation-bound effects just because a special setting is involved. Intervention programs designed to bring about social and individual change in ongoing, familiar settings, such as community located half-way houses for drug addicts and psychiatric patients, reflect an attempt to overcome this problem by effecting meaningful change.

It is important to note that even in special settings—for example, the reformatory, camp, hospital, and others, where individuals spend considerable periods of time—group activities are carried out in still other especially designated settings. In other words, the person is asked to leave his now familiar room, bed, ward, bunkhouse, or even classroom, to interact with others in another, new special group setting.

## LIVING IN A GROUP

We would like at this point to examine in greater detail the events that characterize *life* in a group. The groups we have in mind are those in which individuals in a hospital psychiatric ward, a prison cell, an army compound, a classroom, a summer camp, spend considerable periods of time with each other. To a greater or lesser degree they live together in the sense of the members of a family living together. Within these contexts more specific groups emerge either through design, in order to accomplish certain tasks, or on a spontaneous and informal basis. In many instances the goals involved are attempts at inducing change in the individual.

A simple principle can be stated: other things being equal, the effectiveness of group function and group process in effecting change will depend on the extent to which the individual not only has the freedom of choice to experience group life, or not experience it, as he sees fit, but also on the ability of the individual *to exercise* this choice when he has it.

We would all agree that to induce change by coercion, group pressure, punishment, or surveillance—if indeed change is ever possible by these means—is not likely to produce lasting change. We also know that change is more likely to occur when the individual's group membership is something he desires because it satisfies certain specific needs, including the satisfactions he derives from playing certain roles and having particular experiences in this group.

But the effectiveness of any group in terms of the satisfaction it brings to the person depends upon the satisfaction of other needs that are invested in his sense of being (perfectly or imperfectly) a separate and autonomous individual. If a person has a need to affiliate, love, and be loved, and the need to seek a host of satisfactions from others including the sheer joy of being with others, he also has a cluster of needs that involve the freedom to be alone, to remain anonymous, and indeed to escape the setting of the group. Physical space then must not only facilitate group function and process through maximizing and optimizing the conditions of social interaction, it must also allow the person the possibility of human *privacy*.

Privacy is a human need with many dimensions; yet it has received almost no attention from behavioral scientists. The need to be alone, to think out problems, to create, to engage in fantasy, to reconsider, "to lick one's wounds," to plan the next steps, to "recharge one's psychic battery," or to enjoy the solitude of just being alone express some of the aspects of the person's need for privacy. If individuals have to learn how to function in groups, to be aware of the importance of group goals, the needs of others, and to separate these from their own nongroup relevant or egocentric interests, then *groups* must in turn learn to recognize the need for autonomy and more specifically for privacy in each of its members. To function as an effective group member, the individual must first be able to function as a person in his own right. This means that the group setting must provide the conditions that facilitate the latter in order to guarantee the former.

Space limitations do not permit us to analyze the various forms which the desire for human privacy may take. Being alone may extend from literally being alone or away from human contact as, for example, the individual who takes a long walk into the country to escape the sight, or even the conscious presence, of others, through being alone in one's room at home or in the office, to simply withdrawing in the presence of others by not listening or responding to them. Even in the case of the dyad involving passing acquaintances, friends, or members of the immediate family, somehow or another A "gets the message" that B may be sitting, standing, or working right next to him, but he would prefer "to be alone" by not having to listen or say things to A.

Human privacy, however, is not only an individual need, but, if we may also use the same term, a "group need," or perhaps said more accurately, a condition to be met by groups at various times if group function and process are to be effective. Clearly, the presence of other nearby groups, intrusions by others in the physical setting of the group, the failure of a group to have "its place" to meet—particularly when a group is first being formed, emotionally charged over a given issue, or involved in intragroup conflict—all raise questions concerning physical space and the group's need for privacy.

But as environmental psychologists we must stress the fact that not only must individuals and groups have freedom of choice with respect to their privacy, but the physical setting must afford them the opportunity to exercise this freedom. In effect, space must be designed and administered with this objective in mind.

Thus, in our psychiatric ward studies the distribution of activities in one-, two-, and three-bed rooms, and larger, were compared.[24] In the small rooms it was found that the activities are more evenly distributed over the entire range of possible activities, although *social activity* is relatively more frequent and *isolated passive behavior* is relatively less frequent. It would seem that the patient in this room perceives the whole range of possible behaviors as open to him. He feels free to choose from this range, and in fact to choose more or less equally from among all these possibilities.

On the other hand, the patient in the larger rooms tends to perceive the range of options from which he can choose as severely limited, as evidenced by the fact that he was more likely to engage in isolated passive behavior than in anything else. He spent from two thirds to three fourths of the time in his room lying on his bed either asleep or awake. It would appear then that the small rooms provide the patient with a considerable freedom of choice in what he does in his room, whereas the large, multiple-occupancy room limits freedom of choice and almost forces him into isolated passive behavior.

It is clear that "privacy" has its negative aspects also. In many therapeutic settings, one aspect of therapeutic philosophy is to encourage patients to interact with others. Thus design or administrative policies which allow private places to become a refuge or an escape—including a multiple-occupancy room, as we noted above—may be reinforcing exactly the behavior which one would hope to change. We stress both design *and* administration because spaces may be used in a variety of ways and the decisions as to their use are generally administrative. In the children's hospital we have described, for example, the house area which was clearly designed for a variety of private, small group, and larger group activities began to serve as a refuge because hospital policy and programming became so structured that the child's choice was to join a group in some other place or be alone in the house. In a short time, the house became a refuge, a place for withdrawal, a place to contain children who were acting out, and since it was physically remote from other areas of the hospital, there was practically no opportunity for a child to be on the periphery of a group while withdrawing. Thus the "environmental message," both physically and administratively, so to speak, was, "If you won't join us, then withdraw to the house." There were no other options.[25]

We haven't developed the concept of "freedom of choice" in relation to physical space very much in this discussion, although a more detailed discussion is available.[26] Here we would only like to emphasize its importance in terms of understanding human behavior—both in terms of overt action and inner process—in relation to a physical setting. Freedom of choice is not only a function of social systems and their normative features—what groups permit and don't permit—but also of the nature of the physical setting. Patently, a setting must have the facilities and be designed to permit certain activities to go on, thereby allowing the individual not only to make his choice but realize it. The fact that a room is available for an individual to be alone if he so desires is of no help if other individuals are allowed to move in and out of this room. And, in contrast, a room designed for social use, as we described above, will not be used that way if hospital policy fosters its use as a place of withdrawal or containment. As Alexander Kira points out, only the bathroom has a lock on it in most American homes, thereby allowing children and parents to guarantee that at least there they can actually maintain visual and, to a degree, auditory privacy.[27] It is also important to remember that a crowded dayroom, ward, or apartment also reduces each individual's freedom of choice not only with respect to privacy, but with respect to where he can sit, engage in particular activities, or even just watch TV.

Group function and process is facilitated, indeed can only be effective over time, if group members can satisfy their desires for "a place" both *for the group* and for themselves as individuals. To the extent that a group expects, wants, and needs a particular physical setting for their own, to this degree will the effectiveness of group function and process depend on the satisfaction of its territorial aspirations. The street corner of the delinquent gang, the clubhouse of a teenage girls' club, and the corner of the dayroom of the somewhat healthier psychiatric patients reflect the desire for territoriality in human groups. But within such groups—and in those that endure over a longer period of time, for example the family—the individual's own need for controlling his "piece" of the environment is no less important. Group functions and process depend on it in the sense that given group members must reign over certain physical areas if group tasks and functions are to be realized. Leadership is indeed expressed by putting the leader at the head of the table; and putting the secretary at his side subtly expresses the meaning and nature of this role.

Territoriality is critical, however, for each group member—aside from his assigned roles. He must almost literally find his "place" in the group if meaningful face-to-face interaction is to occur. More importantly, having "his place" not only helps to establish the validity of his membership in the group, but it permits him to exercise control over at least his part of the physical environment. Again, it is important to point out the significance for human individuality and autonomy of the person's sense of and claims to "my room," "my chair," "my house," and "my neighborhood." To the extent that the individual's self-esteem is threatened in other ways, to this degree will he lay claim to what is his territory and the objects in it.

## CONCLUSIONS

We have said enough about the physical setting and group function and process as a means of change. We will conclude with a number of generally integrative statements about our analysis in relation to the field of environmental psychology. First, what we have presented are ideas and hypotheses rather than data, for as yet no real data exist. Let us, however, put these hypotheses in their proper perspective. In no sense are we suggesting that physical settings are responsible for a great deal of the variance that accounts for how groups function and whether or not they are effective change agents. No, we do not believe that if you design the right kind of homes for young married couples that none of them will ever get divorced. How much of the variance is attributable to physical space and its design is an empirical question that only systematic research can answer. But whether it is a little or a great deal is beside the point. A full understanding of human behavior whether in groups or otherwise requires the study of man's physical environment. This is the task of the social sciences regardless of whether or not we are facing an "environmental crisis." It is time to reverse figure and ground. We can no longer afford to view the physical setting as a backdrop against which social, psychological, and biological factors influence behavior and its development.

If there is an urgency in the study of man's physical environment and its consequences for behavior, then it is important to recognize that there is not one environmental crisis, but two. There is the crisis of human life and the consequences of air, water, food, soil, and still other kinds of pollution and contamination. But there is also a crisis in human *dignity*. This is the failure to consider the effects that the designs of our cities, buildings, rooms, furniture, cars, and recreation facilities have on the structure and functioning of the individual, or perhaps better said, the quality of his existence.

In our judgment, the crisis in human dignity is no less real than the crisis in human life. Its reality in many instances, however, is far more subtle and it has as yet to evoke any real concern. What camouflages the crisis is the fact that to some degree modern technology views man in mechanistic, object-like terms. Of greater importance are two assumptions which are made to rationalize the lack of concern about what physical space, its properties, organization, and uses do to people. The first is that individuals are highly adaptable, which is indicated if they neither complain consistently or manifest other overt signs of difficulty. Somehow or another people adapt to the crowded subways, inadequate office space, improperly designed furniture, congested streets, incredibly high noise levels, and even more serious conditions of the physical environment. The second assumption rests on the first. If people adapt—as evidenced by no obvious or manifest difficulties including verbal complaints—then the designed environment has had no *real* negative effects on the growth and continued existence of the person.

It is these assumptions which make it a simple matter to regard the influence of the urban setting on man's behavior and growth as a low priority consideration in planning living sites, designing equipment, and organizing his day-to-day physical existence. The importance of the physical environment in these respects is overlooked not just in a short-term but also a long-range sense. The question becomes: Which price is being paid or will eventually be paid for this adaptability? Our responsibility is to look for not just its patent, manifest effects, but its subtle consequences. As in the case of modern medicine we will have to ask what are the long-range as well as short-term side effects on man of the various attempts to reorganize, improve, speed-up, and streamline his physical existence.

The crisis in human life engendered by the modern urban environment has to some degree brought the self-deceiving assumptions about man's adaptability into question. Intil they are completely rejected, the crisis in human dignity is likely to grow and provide its own set of catastrophes in the years to come.

## NOTES AND REFERENCES

1.  J. B. Calhoun, "Population density and social pathology," *Scientific American,* Vol. 206 (1962), 139–148.
2.  C. Hutt and M. J. Vaizey, "Differential effects of group density on social behavior," *Nature,* Vol. 209 (1966), 1371–1372.
3.  R. L. Birdwhistell, *Kinesics and Context,* Philadelphia: University of Pennsylvania Press, 1970.
4.  P. Ekman, "Communication through nonverbal behavior; a source of information about the interpersonal relationship," in S. S. Tomkins and C. E. Izard, eds., *Affect, Cognition and Personality,* New York: Springer, 1968, 390–442.
5.  Erving Goffman, *The Presentation of Self in Everyday Life,* Garden City, N.Y.: Doubleday, 1959.
6.  B. Steinzor, "The spatial factor in face to face discussion groups," *Journal of Abnormal and Social Psychology,* Vol. 45 (1950), 552–555.
7.  G. Hearn, "Leadership and the spatial factor in small groups," *Journal of Abnormal and Social Psychology,* Vol. 54 (1957), 269–272.
8.  Michael Argyle and Janet Dean, "Eye contact, distance, and affiliation," *Sociometry,* Vol. 28 (1965), 289–304.
9.  Robert Sommer, "Small group ecology," *Psychological Bulletin,* Vol. 67 (1967), 145–152.
10. W. Goldfarb, *Childhood Schizophrenia,* Cambridge, Mass.: Harvard University Press, 1961.
11. G. Stroh and D. Buick, "Perceptual development and childhood psychosis," *British Journal of Medicine and Psychology,* Vol. 37 (1964), 291–299.
12. H. Alt, *Residential Treatment for the Disturbed Child,* New York: International Universities Press, 1960.
13. B. Berenson, *Environmental Design for Mental Retardation,* Washington, D.C.: The U.S. Public Health Service, 1968.
14. Alt, *op. cit.;* Bruno Bettelheim, *Truants from Life,* New York: The Free Press, 1955.
15. Kenneth Bayes, *The Therapeutic Effect of the Environment on Emotionally Disturbed and Mentally Subnormal Children,* London: The Gresham Press, 1967.
16. Bettelheim, *op. cit.*
17. P. W. Penningroth, *Programs for Emotionally Disturbed Children,* Washington, D.C.: U.S. National Institute of Mental Health, 1963.
18. Bayes, *op. cit.*
19. Bettelheim, *op. cit.*
20. A. D. Sorosky, N. I. Roger, and P. F. Tanguay, "Furnishing a psychiatric unit for children," *Hospital and Community Psychiatry,* Vol. 20 (1969), 234–246.
21. Bayes, *op. cit.;* W. Goldfarb and N. L. Mintz, "The schizophrenic child's reaction to time and space," *Archives of General Psychiatry* (1961), 535–543.
22. Leanne G. Rivlin and Maxine Wolfe, "The establishment of activity patterns in a new children's psychiatric hospital," *Environment and Behavior* (in press).
23. Harold M. Proshansky, "The development of intergroup attitudes," in L. W. Hoffman and M. L. Hoffman, eds., *Review of Child Development Research,* New York: Holt, 1966.
24. Harold M. Proshansky, William H. Ittelson, and Leanne G. Rivlin, *Environmental Psychology: Man and His Physical Setting,* New York: Holt, 1970.
25. Leanne G. Rivlin and Maxine Wolfe, "The early history of a psychiatric hospital for children: Expectations and reality," *Environment and Behavior,* Vol. 4 (1972), 33–72.
26. Proshansky, Ittelson, and Rivlin, *op. cit.*
27. Alexander Kiva, *The Bathroom: Criteria for Design,* Ithaca, N.Y.: Center for Housing and Environmental Studies, Cornell University, 1966.

202

*Observations on the part of the author, in collaboration with Dr. Humphry Osmond, as to the use of space by patients in Saskatchewan hospital wards have led to a differentiation between the concepts of sociopetal and sociofugal space. The former provides opportunities for interpersonal interaction, while the latter tends to keep people apart. The contribution of other behavioral scientists is also reviewed to place into perspective the author's research on "personal space"—the emotionally charged space bubble around people. The concept of personal space is also compared to concepts of "territory" and "jurisdiction." Some reservations are expressed as to the utility of these concepts for architectural programming and design because the quality of the physical environment has more to do with the fit between the whole behavioral and psychological program than just the way people relate to each other in space. The main conclusion to be drawn from the research on personal space is that we need to place more emphasis on variety, flexibility, and "personalization of space." In the long run, the utility of this research will depend on whether buildings constructed according to these findings are better than buildings built in complete ignorance of them.*

# Looking Back at Personal Space

**Robert Sommer**

**University of California at Davis**

Until recently it was fashionable to generalize from animal spatial behavior to that of humans. Robert Ardrey's *The Territorial Imperative* was tremendously popular with undergraduates and the mass media.[1] When it came to research with humans, there was a growing literature of exotic and unusual environments such as submarines, antarctic research stations, isolation chambers, and space capsules,[2] but very little seemed to be known about the effects of ordinary apartments, offices, streets, and parks. Social scientists were uninterested in the effects of the physical environment. While psychologists spoke about a grand ball game played between heredity and environment, the term environment referred mainly to child-rearing practices. In view of the lack of reliable data, it was understandable that some writers should borrow concepts and findings from research with animals or from esoteric settings.

At the same time, design professionals were becoming aware that many of their buildings were not meeting the occupants' needs. The era of the direct architect –client relationship had ended. Now the client was more likely a corporation board or public agency whose members would not themselves be occupying the structure that was being designed. Architects were remote from the people for whom buildings were being designed. This erosion of a direct relationship with their consumers led architects to search for information *about* consumers. Who was better qualified, some designers reasoned, to tell them about human spatial needs than social scientists and even psychiatrists? The call went out from architectural schools throughout the country for men in white coats to tell designers about human spatial needs so that buildings might be designed in accorddance with them.

Some of us responded to the call and spent a great deal of time either telling architects how little was known and that more research was necessary before we could say anything, or summarizing the work with animals and isolation chambers, or else repeating a litany of the few available studies (mainly concerned with mental hospitals and college student housing), but these seemed irrelevant to the designer who wanted information on a specific housing development for the elderly or a day-care center for a ghetto neighborhood. The questions came faster than the answers. Though the long-range potential for fruitful collaboration between designers and social scientists seemed excellent, the short-run collaboration was frustrating. A number of

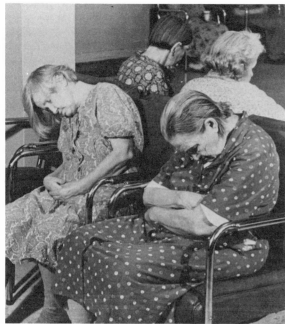

**Figure 1**
**Patients who were seated side-by-side and back-to-back found it very difficult to converse, and most of them eventually gave up.**

**Figure 2**
**These two schizophrenic patients reserved personal space on the same small bench facing away from one another.**

us wrote articles expressing reservations about being able to meet the high expectations placed on use by designers.[3,4] The impetus behind these articles was the feeling that we were being asked the wrong sorts of questions and that we should be out generating behavioral data rather than attempting to generalize on the sparse data that presently existed.

## EARLY STUDIES OF CHAIR ARRANGEMENTS

I had been turned on to the field by Humphry Osmond, a brilliant psychiatrist who was then superintendent of a large mental hospital in Western Canada. It was apparent to both of us that the architecture of the hospital did nothing to help our patients and in fact was probably detrimental to their mental and physical health (Figures 1 and 2). The long bare corridors, the sterile institutional appearance of the lounges, the drab dormitories, and

bathrooms which lacked even the most basic rudiments of privacy, all of these seemed inimical to the patient's recovery. With Dr. Osmond fortuitously stationed at the helm of this obsolete institution, it was possible for us to systematically look at the building's architecture and to systematically alter things which we felt were particularly bad. In this effort we were joined by several creative architects including Kyo Izumi and Arthur Allen. My first modest effort was directed at the large impersonal lounges. To use Dr. Osmond's term, these seemed *sociofugal,* since the rows of straight-backed chairs against the wall discouraged interaction.[5] In some wards we found four chairs around each pillar, each chair oriented in a different direction. Certainly one would not expect much interaction in this arrangement, and in our research, we found very little. After establishing a baseline level of interaction, we moved the chairs into a more *sociopetal* arrangement—that is, an arrangement designed to foster human interaction. The arrangement we selected involved the chairs being placed around small tables in a good conversational arrangement. Although it is hardly surprising now to report this, we found that this more than doubled the amount of conversation between the patients. Magazine reading went up twentyfold because the tables now provided places on which magazines could be stored.

This study fascinated me for several reasons. For one thing no one had mentioned the physical environment in all my years of graduate work in psychology. None of my professors had ever spoken about the effects of houses, office buildings, parks, or even schools or hospitals on their occupants. To see whether this had been a local shortcoming of the schools I attended, I went back and looked in the available social science literature and found the same lacuna in information. The reasons for this lack of interest in the physical environment still puzzle me. Sigmund Freud was very insistent about the requirements for an analytic chamber, even specifying the angle at which the analyst should sit vis-à-vis the patient. I felt sufficiently motivated, however, to devote the next fifteen years of my life to the area of environmental psychology.

This study of chair arrangements led me to examine other institutional settings to see what effect they had upon their occupants. I undertook naturalistic observations in airports, cafeterias, schools, parks, and even beer parlors[6] to see how the arrangement of people affected the kind of interaction that took place. I soon became aware that while natural observation was a valuable tool it would have to be supplemented by experimental studies of a more basic kind in order to specify the variables that were operating. More specifically, I decided to undertake some basic studies of human spatial behavior. It seemed necessary to know how close together people sat or stood when they had some freedom of choice and see how this was related to what they were doing. This research has been greatly developed by the work of more recent investigators, and I cannot do justice to all the various studies in a brief review. I can add that such a review was possible six years ago when I did summarize the state of the research,[7] but the burgeoning number of studies precludes it at this time. Other social scientists approached spatial behavior from very different standpoints, and it is reasonable to speak of a division of labor between us. Edward Hall emphasized space as a silent language and as an aspect of communication.[8,9] His special province was cross-cultural differences in the use of space. Erving Goffman, a brilliant observer of the social scene, looked upon space usage as an aspect of a normative system of social regulations.[10] He reminded us that Emily Post and Amy Vanderbilt had discussed space use in social settings long before any of us. Hans Esser was one of the earliest of the psychiatrists to examine human spatial behavior from an ethological standpoint.[11] What differentiated Esser from previous workers who had used animal concepts was Esser's insistence on data rather than metaphor.

## PERSONAL SPACE

Empirical research revealed that there were many different sorts of spatial behaviors that were being confused with one another. My earliest work had focused on personal space or the emotionally charged space bubble around each individual which is regarded as private and personal. An invasion of personal space produced signs of tension or withdrawal, either psychological in the forms of some compensatory mechanisms such as averting eye contact or actual withdrawal from the scene. I differentiated personal space from territory which had a specific geographic referent. From the biologist H. Hediger, presently the curator of the Zurich Zoo, I adopted personalization and defense as the criteria of territoriality.[12,13] A territory was therefore a specific geographical area that had been personalized by an individual and would be defended by him against unwanted intrusion. The concept of territoriality had a long and respected history and literature in the biological sciences. Later, the concept of *jurisdiction* was added to the list as referring to a temporary territory whose occupancy is legitimized only for prescribed periods.[14] The janitor will have jurisdiction over the classroom after the teacher and students have left for the day. Interestingly enough, the power of the custodian has reached such awesome proportions in some schools that the reverse if often perceived as the case; that is, the classroom really belongs to the custodians, and it is the teacher and the students who have temporary jurisdiction over it.

Personal space was studied in a variety of ways, both by my students and by other researchers. One common method was to observe people interacting in public settings and then measure how far apart they stood or sat. This generally confounded personal space, the soap bubble around each individual, with interaction distance or social space which can be conceived of as a soap bubble around an entire group. It has been demonstrated that people will walk around an interacting group rather than through them. Occasionally when circumstances require an individual to walk between two conversing individuals, it is done in a very stilted way, as if one is walking over an imaginary barrier and looking straight ahead to avert any eye contact. Probably the most frequent method used to investigate the boundaries of personal space has been the invasion method. Here the investigator gradually approaches a person to find out where signs of approach discomfort generally begin. This method was used quite successfully by Nancy Felipe Russo[15] in a library situation. Dr. Russo approached students sitting in the library and sat at a distance that violated the customary spatial norms of leaving an empty chair between students. Various sorts of compensatory devices were used by the students whose personal space was invaded. Frequently a student placed his hand on his ear and faced away from Dr. Russo, or the elbows went out in a defensive posture. Rarely did the student react verbally to the invasion. Other studies using the same method found that the status of the invader influenced the sort of defensive responses and flight reactions that occurred. It was also found that personal space was not a round kind of bubble but rather some kind of an hour glass with less space at the side of the body and more in front. Edward Hall had demonstrated that the space bubble varies in size from one culture to another: northern Europeans generally stood and sat farther apart during conversation than people from Latin countries. Anxiety tended to increase the distance between people. Students who had been told that they had done poorly on an experimental task sat farther away from the instructor than those told they had done well. Introverts tended to sit and stand farther away from an experimenter than did extroverts. Many other relationships of this sort were found and they are summarized elsewhere.[6,16,17]

Glen McBride[18] used the galvanic skin response (GSR) as an index of emotionality. The GSR picks up changes in skin conductivity that relate to stress and emotional behavior. McBride placed college students in a chair from which they were approached by both male and female experimenters as well as by paper figures and nonhuman objects. It was found that GSR was greatest when a person was approached frontally, whereas a side approach yielded a greater response than a rear approach. Students reacted more strongly to the approach of someone of the opposite sex than to someone of the same sex. Being touched by an object produced less of a GSR than being touched by a person.

A similar procedure without the GSR apparatus was used by Michael Argyle and Janet Dean,[19] who invited their subjects to participate in a perceptual experiment in which they were to "stand as close as possible to see well" to a book, a plaster head, and a cutout life-sized photograph of the senior author with his eyes closed and another photograph with his eyes open. Among other results, it was found that the subjects placed themselves closer to the eyes-closed photograph than the eyes-open photograph. A more recent study, by G. W. Evans and R. B. Howard,[20] compared three different reactions to invasions of personal space—the person's performance on an information task, skin conductivity (GSR), and the subject's rating of personal discomfort on a series of polar adjective scales (e.g., comfortable–uncomfortable). Evans and Howard found that spatial invasions impaired performance on the information task, raised GSR level, and produced ratings of greater discomfort on the adjective checklists, provided the subject was not totally absorbed in the information task. The modest correlations among the three response measures led the authors to suggest the use of several different methods of monitoring response to spatial discomfort rather than a single measure.

## PERSONAL SPACE AND ARCHITECTURAL DESIGN

When I did this research originally, I believed that it would be of use to architects. Since architects were concerned with designing spaces and this research was concerned with space, there *must* be something useful

**Figures 3, 4, and 5**
A modern veterans' hospital as seen from the exterior and the interior. Such architecture leaves little room for flexibility or personalization.

**Figure 6**
Students who are working on separate tasks, such as these students who are using an empty classroom for evening study, arrange themselves so as to avoid eye contact.

**Figure 7**
The fixed arrangement of built-in furnishings in a dormitory room gives virtually no privacy to the students when they study. Generally, one student waits until his roommate has departed before studying himself.

in it for architects. Looking back I think this assumption was, if not unwarranted, at least overoptimistic. I do not believe that the personal-space bubble is a logical unit in architectural design. It may be an interesting and useful concept for architects to have around for conceptualizing interaction spaces, but I would not like to see buildings designed with personal space used as some kind of a standard or unit of measurement. Besides, it soon became apparent that the important questions at the interface between design and behavior dealt with issues and concepts more complex than interaction distance. The quality of the space and its amenities have little place in the personal-space literature. The important questions in school design relate to the fit between the educational program and the building, not to the distance between students' desks or between students and teacher. It seemed necessary to look at the methods of architectural programming in relation to user behavior if we are going to improve the fit between buildings and user behavior. These questions

have led me away from the small-group studies into broader questions of environmental awareness and the evaluation of designed environments from the standpoint of user satisfaction.[21]

I think that the main value of the personal-space concept in architecture has been the lesson of individual and situational differences in spatial needs. From the architect's standpoint this puts greater weight on such design values as variety, flexibility, and personalization in contrast to the designs shown in Figures 3, 4, and 5. In our research in college libraries, for example, we found that there is no such thing as an ideal reading area for all library patrons. Some students felt that they could study better out in the public reading room where they were stimulated by the sight of other people reading, while others wanted to study together in small rooms (Figure 6), and still others wanted to hide themselves away in the library stack area. No single module would suit the needs of all these library patrons. The same conclusion was found in our work on airport waiting areas. Some travelers preferred the present sociofugal arrangement of the terminal with all the chairs bolted together and facing the same direction in straight rows, much like a schoolroom, although without the teacher's desk in front. Travelers who waited in groups of three or four, such as the family waiting for a son to return home or two couples traveling together, however, found the present arrangements awkward for sustained conversation.[22] The solution is both a variety of different sorts of waiting spaces and some flexibility within them. Both the library and the airport patrons wanted some sense of place, some indication through the architecture and decor of where they were and what was happening. When we studied facilities occupied for longer periods such as college dormitory rooms, the need for individual personalization was readily apparent. Students resented built-in desks, lockers, and book cases which could not be moved or altered to meet unique individual needs (Figure 7). The students wanted to be able to express an individual identity in the room through posters, decorations, and even repainting the room to fit mood and personality. On my own campus we were able to arrange for dormitory residents to obtain paint and brushes from the Housing Office to paint their rooms. Some designs for dormitories were far better suited to this kind of personalization than others where every poster or picture hung on the walls left a scar or mark to trouble the custodians.

## CONCLUSION

In conclusion, I look back upon the personal-space research with a sense of nostalgia. It was fun to do and it made a contribution, if not to the design fields, at least to the social sciences in bringing environmental considerations into theories of social psychology. The social sciences have finally discovered the physical environment, and there are all the marks of institutionalization to prove it. There are several journals devoted to the interface between environment and behavior *(Design and Environment and Environment and Behavior),* Ph..D. programs in environmental psychology (City University of New York), architectural psychology (University of Utah), man–environment relations (Pennsylvania State University), the social and behavioral aspects of architecture (University of Califor-

nia at Berkeley), and psychological geography (Clark University). At the undergraduate level there are entire colleges devoted to environmental issues (University of Wisconsin at Green Bay and Huxley College at Western Washington State) and numerous environmental studies programs springing up. Most of the larger schools of architecture and planning now import a social scientist to teach a course in environmental psychology if they do not have a resident social scientist for this specific purpose. In terms of these marks of legitimacy, the field has made great strides. One task still remains before the field and its practitioners can consider themselves fully legitimate. This involves the empirical demonstration that buildings designed with the help of social scientists are more satisfying to their occupants than buildings designed without the help of social scientists. This seems a rather elementary requirement for a field with a strong research orientation but it is a task that still remains to be done. It will mean that psychologists and sociologists will have to be involved in actual design projects from start to finish and even longer to complete the necessary postoccupancy evaluation. There will never be an honest field of environmental psychology if it is restricted to federally financed research grants on general issues. This is a sure-fire formula for coming up with results that are interesting rather than helpful. What does it mean to the prospective designer of a college residence hall to know that students are likely to select their friends from among people in adjacent rooms. I should add that this is a genuine finding that has been documented in a number of separate studies. This is no guarantee, however, that its implications for designers are readily apparent. At the least, someone must help to translate such behavioral findings into terms and applications that have some meaning to designers. I leave open the possibility that this finding has no practical use whatever in designing a new dormitory. On the other hand, I am certain that it does have implications for the resident advisor who counsels students in the dormitory. If a student is in difficulty, the advisor might want to approach the students in the next room who are most likely to know him. Many of the findings of environmental psychology will have more relevance for the management of spaces than to the initial design process. We will be able to sort out these considerations when we actually apply social science methods in an experimental way on actual design projects. This cannot come from surveys of what people want or from observations of what people do or from lists of needs people have or from summaries of the literature on small-group behavior. The presence of social scientists in university schools of design is certainly a healthy development. The next step is for them to become involved in actual design projects where their insights and findings can be applied and the outcome observed in a systematic way. A few years ago it was necessary for social scientists to preach to architects about the value of research and the importance of user behavior in the design process. Now it is up to social scientists to demonstrate that fruitful collaboration results in better buildings, more functional city parks, and more humane cities.

## NOTES AND REFERENCES

1. Robert Ardrey, *The Territorial Imperative,* New York: Atheneum, 1966.
2. N. H. Burns, R. M. Chambers, and E. Hendler, *Unusual Environments and Human Behavior,* New York: The Free Press, 1963.
3. R. Gutman, "The questions architects ask," *Transactions of the Bartlett Society,* Vol. 4 (1965–66), 49–82.
4. Robert Sommer, "Confessions of a psychologist," *Royal Architectural Institute of Canada Journal* (August 1962), 47–51.
5. Humphry Osmond, "The relationship between architect and psychiatrist," in C. Goshen, ed., *Psychiatric Architecture,* Washington, D.C.: American Psychiatric Association, 1959.
6. Robert Sommer, *Personal Space: The Behavioral Basis of Design,* Englewood Cliffs, N.J.: Prentice-Hall, 1969.
7. Robert Sommer, "Small group ecology," *Psychological Bulletin,* Vol. 67 (1967), 145–152.
8. Edward T. Hall, *The Silent Language,* Garden City, N.Y.: Doubleday, 1959.
9. Edward T. Hall, *The Hidden Dimension,* Garden City, N.Y.: Doubleday, 1966.
10. Goffman, Erving, *Behavior in Public Places,* New York: The Free Press, 1963.
11. A. H. Esser et al., "Territoriality of patients of a research ward," in Joseph Wortis, ed., *Recent Advances in Biological Psychiatry,* Vol. 8, New York: Plenum Press, 1965.
12. H. Hediger, *Studies of the Psychology and Behavior of Captive Animals in Zoos and Circuses,* London: Butterworth, 1955.
13. H. Hediger, *Man and Animal in the Zoo,* London: Routledge & Kegan Paul, 1970.
14. P. D. Roos, "Jurisdiction: an ecological concept," *Human Relations,* Vol. 21 (1968), 75–84.
15. Nancy Felipe and R. Sommer, "Invasions of personal space," *Social Problems,* Vol. 14, No. 2 (1966), 206-214.
16. Albert Mehrabian, *Silent Messages,* Belmont, Calif.: Wadsworth, 1971.
17. Michael Argyle, *Social Interaction,* Chicago: Aldine-Atherton, 1969.
18. G. McBride, M. G. King, and J. W. James, "Social proximity effects on GSR in adult humans," *Journal of Psychology,* Vol. 61 (1965), 153–157.
19. Michael Argyle and Janet Dean, "Eye contact, distance, and affiliation," *Sociometry,* Vol. 28 (1965), 289–304.
20. G. W. Evans and H. R. B. Howard, "A methodological investigation of personal space," in William J. Mitchell, ed., *Environmental Design: Research and Practice: Proceedings of EDRA3/AR8 Conference,* University of California, Los Angeles, January 1972.
21. Robert Sommer, *Design Awareness,* San Francisco: Rinehart Press, 1972.
22. Robert Sommer, "The lonely airport crowd," *Air Travel* (April 1969), 16–22.

*Man's behavior is the result of a continuous evolutionary process. Studies of animal behavior demonstrate the limitations of man's adaptability. An organism's behavior depends a great deal on where it is in relationship to its territory. Western man exhibits strong spatial behavior. A distinction is made between fixed-feature, semifixed-feature, and dynamic space. The first is enclosed space, the second consists of the physical objects of the environment, and dynamic space consists of the personal bubble of space that surrounds every individual. There are four or five zones of dynamic space which depend on culture, an individual's personality, and his status in his own social system. Finally, a checklist of items to consider in designing man's spatial layout is provided.*

# Meeting Man's Basic Spatial Needs in Artificial Environments

Edward T. Hall

**Northwestern University**

## SCIENTIFIC INVESTIGATIONS OF THE EFFECT OF SPACE

Since Darwin it has been generally accepted that man's body is the result of a continuous evolution from lower and less complex forms of life. It is only in recent years, however, that a few scattered specialists have recognized that man's behavior is also the result of a continuous evolutionary process.[1] Our lack of knowledge about behavior in its early forms has obscured the continuities that exist. Recent studies in animal ecology have taught us much that was not known before, and it is becoming increasingly clear that there are important attributes of human nature that appeared before man became man. This new knowledge suggests that although man is one of the toughest, most adaptable organisms on this earth, there are limitations on what he can do with himself.

One of these limitations is man's sensitivity to crowding. A recently publicized study of city dwellers revealed that only 18 percent of a representative sample were free of emotional symptoms, while 38 percent were in need of psychiatric help, and 23 percent were seriously disturbed or incapacitated.[2] It is doubtful that all these disturbances can be traced to personality disorders in the parents or explained by poverty or culture conflict. Scientific investigation of population fluctuations in lower forms of life and detailed studies of man's handling of microspace all point to the fact that there is a close relationship between the health and happiness of any species and the space which is available to it.

### Territoriality in Animals

Systematic study of territoriality (how animals use space) is recent. Publication in this field began only fifty years ago with the appearance of H. E. Howard's *Territory in Bird Life*.[3] Since that time the number of studies published on territoriality has been so great that practitioners in the field complain they can no longer keep up.

From these investigations we have learned that the way an organism behaves depends a great deal on where it is in relation to its territory. Paul L. Errington[4] has shown that small mammals who have not yet established a territory are more vulnerable to predation than those who have a territory. It has also been demonstrated[5] that wild animals in a zoo may not even survive the move to a new cage or pen. Moreover, when animals are restricted in their use of space, they become stupid.

Many animals are bound in space just as the planets are bound in the solar system. They are restricted to a home range, and limits are placed on how close they can come to their fellows and how far they can stray before losing contact with the group.

The zoologist H. Hediger[6] pointed out that a piece of land or a section of space was probably the first thing that living organisms took possession of and defended even against their own kind. He has outlined five basic functions which are performed by territoriality:[7]

1. It ensures the propagation of the species by regulating population density.
2. It keeps animals within communication distance of each other so that food and danger can be signaled.
3. It coordinates the activity of the group and holds the group together.
4. It provides the individual with a known terrain— places to learn, places to play, places to escape to, and safe places to hide.
5. It provides a framework in which things are done.

Western man exhibits the same quality in his boundary markers and laws of trespass, in the distinctions he makes between public and private property, and in his strong feelings about the sacredness of the home (Figure 1).

## Crowding and Population Control

Lack of space can be a life and death matter for lower forms of life. During the last few years several important studies have been published which show that when animals are overcrowded, stress develops, and the results are far-reaching and often lethal. These studies have upset the widely held notion that predators are the primary cause of population control in lower life forms. The evidence indicates instead that population growth is self-limiting and self-regulating.[8] Apparently what happens is that when the population reaches a certain critical point, the animals' internal mechanisms, working through the pituitary adrenal–cortical and the pituitary adrenal–gonadal systems, reduce resistance

**Figure 1**
**Photo credit: Edward Vaivoda**

to stress, and fertility is lowered. These mechanisms are brought into play prior to the point when population growth would destroy the environment.[9,10]

## Man's Sensitivity to Crowding

Men are not animals, and obviously their responses are much more complex than those of other mammals. Yet in many ways their physiological and endocrine makeup is similar, especially in those key areas which are involved in the response to stress. The effect of stress from crowding on man has been demonstrated only indirectly. We have no firm data which span several generations, but the information we do have points in the same general direction as the studies of lower animals.

We are indebted to the thorough and detailed sociology of the French for the first concrete data on crowding as such. The Chombart de Lauwe's,[11] a sociologist–psychologist husband and wife team, after years of studying French workers' families, came to the conclusion that crowding was one of a number of significant contributing variables in social pathology.

## The Influence of Space on Mental Health

Many perceptive observers from different fields have noticed the relationship between space and mental health.[12] L. Linn observed that "crowding increases disturbed behavior" in mental patients. "Conversely the more floor space per patient, the fewer the number of outbursts."[13]

E. O. Hauser in an article written a few years after World War II noted: "the dug-outs under downtown Stockholm are fitted with mobile 'panic screens' which would divide them into cozy rooms less likely, say psychologists, to induce mass hysteria."[14]

The zoologist H. Hediger commenting on World War II orphans said: "the well meaning care given in beautiful and spacious community rooms turned out to be insufficient. All kinds of psychological deficiency symptoms kept on appearing, until the idea of dividing up the room . . . was adopted." He observed that different people react in different ways to space:

*Russians from the Steppes who were confined in Switzerland during the Second World War felt very unhappy among the mountains which to them seemed sinister and oppressive. A similar eerie feeling of being oppressed, eventually becoming intolerable, is familiar to Europeans forced . . . .to penetrate into the tractless primeval forests of Central Africa. After a few days, even thoroughly well balanced men usually feel more or less depressed, and only regain their spirits when they see the light of day or reach open paths. The opposite is true of the Pygmies. For them, the open landscape is sinister and unbearable.*[15]

M. E. Linden recently observed that "human social adjustment . . . consists in discovering the 'perfect distance'—not near enough to constitute a nettling irritation nor far enough to result in isolation. . . . In most instances the establishment of such 'perfect distance' is exactly parallel to the development of good mental health."[16]

The knowledge of what crowding does to people has been put to practical and effective use by various specialists in the field of mental health. In France the psychiatrist Paul Sivadon[17] has used a revolutionary concept of milieu therapy in treating schizophrenics. Instead of placing a patient who is in panic in restraints or in a box, he gives him larger and larger rooms until the world stops "closing in on him."

In Canada an ingeniously contrived series of studies in the geriatrics ward of a hospital demonstrated that the arrangement of furniture in the ward had a deep influence on the amount of talking and interaction betweenthe patients. Dr.Humphry Osmond,[18] former Superintendent of Saskatchewan Hospital, coined two words to describe two basic kinds of spatial arrangement: "sociofugal" space, which is space that forces people apart, and "sociopetal" space, which pulls people together. Back-to-back benches, for example, are sociofugal, and the old-fashioned drug store booth is sociopetal. Because the patients were apathetic despite cheerful surroundings, Osmond thought something might be gained by altering the space. Robert Sommer,[19,20] after observing furniture arrangements associated with the maximum number of conversations, rearranged the furniture in the ward around small tables, changing the space from sociofugal to sociopetal. The number of conversations among previously apathetic patients doubled.

## Space As Communication

There are many differences in the layout of rooms, buildings, cities, and towns. Man's responses to these are not haphazard. Vincent Kling has noted that there are "happy spaces and gloomy ones."[21] The job of the anthropologist is to isolate the significant variables at work here: What spacial cues cause people to feel that some spaces are "happy" and some "gloomy," and how does space mold their behavior in different contexts?

My own research[22] has revealed that microspace can be viewed as a special form of communication.[23,24,25,26] Although this communication is consciously manipulated by some people, more often than not the individual is not consciously aware of what he is communicating. Both his reactions to space and the way he uses space are largely taken for granted; that is they are "out-of-awareness." The way people space themselves says much about their relationship (Figure 2).

**Figure 2. The way people space themselves says much about their relationship.**

These investigations as well as the previously mentioned ecological, sociological, and psychological studies indicate that man, like the other vertebrates, moves within the framework of highly patterned spatial systems. The name "proxemics" has been chosen for this field of study because of the word's familiar Latin root, indicating things which are near or next to something.[27]

Proxemics subsumes three different treatments of space. These are fixed-feature, semifixed-feature and dynamic space.

## Fixed-Feature Space

Enclosed space is fixed-feature space. This varies from culture to culture and situation to situation within a culture. Winston Churchill once observed: "we shape our buildings and later they shape us."[28] The basic soundness of his observation has been borne out by a number of recent scientific studies. Osmond's and K. Izumi's[29] investigations as well as those of A. Baker, R. L. Davies, and P. Sivadon[30] have called attention to the importance of hospital design in the treatment of psychotic patients.

Good design may be even more important in dwellings and offices where most people spend the greater parts of their lives. In a current study[31] I have been examining office space as an inducer and reliever of stress in man. Preliminary results indicate that office size is of crucial importance to man's comfort, productivity, and general well-being.

There is a close relationship between a man's office, his status, and his ego. In the United States the boss almost always has the biggest office, and most executives know in an intuitive way that when one man in the organization gets moved to a larger office, he is on the way up. In the course of interviews I have discovered several instances of executives having walls moved a few inches in order to equalize the size of two offices.

Moving a man from a large to a small office in an out-of-the-way corner of the building is as clear an indication that he is a failure as reducing his salary. A well-known publisher used to use this technique as a way of getting men to resign whom he did not want to fire. Recently I learned of a firm that deliberately designs its offices to make its executives look good,

and as a result is able to pay less than the going rate for its top positions.

In general, the layout of buildings is planned without awareness of individual or organizational space requirements. Not long ago two large organizations in New York built new buildings. They might as well have traded their old buildings. Organization A, which had been occupying a building where there was easy communication between offices, designed its new building so that people were sealed off from each other in the mistaken notion that the staff wanted the prestige of private offices. By contrast, organization B, which had been located in a building where communication was extraordinarily difficult, planned its new building with the purpose of facilitating the accessibility of staff members to each other. In drawing up plans the firm had been willing to spend well over a year discussing the communications features with each department.

Individual space needs are rarely understood or taken into account. For example, I have observed that American research scientists may need room to expound when developing ideas. The expository tone of voice is hard to take at close range; yet current bureaucratic practice is to allot people offices in accordance with their rank in the organization, and administrators are prone to determine the size of a scientist's office by his status and pay rather than by his frequent need to hold forth. In fact, the recent failure of a large-scale industrial research laboratory can be partly explained by the fact that the offices were so small that the scientists could not get far enough away from each other.[32]

Lots of space is not always desirable. Robert Sommer[33] has pointed out that there can be too much space, too little space, or the wrong kind of space, and that each of these conditions is affected by the number and kind of people using the space and the tasks being performed. A few years ago a study[34] was made of student study habits at three Eastern colleges. It was found that an inverse relationship exists between the size and desirability of study rooms. Eighty percent of the students preferred small study spaces, and 85 percent preferred to study alone. What students wanted most was privacy and an environment where they could control the heat, light, and ventilation. An interesting sidelight to this study is the resistance of college administrators to giving students individual study space.

Possibly this can be explained by the fact that an administrator who has spent many years working his way up to a private office responds primarily to the status value of private space and finds it hard to be objective about student preferences on study space.

## Semifixed-Feature Space

Semifixed-feature space, as the name indicates, consists of physical objects in the environment which can be moved about so that people are able to increase or decrease their association with others and control the general character of their transactions. They do this principally by means of the furniture. It has been found that certain kinds and arrangements of physical objects facilitate interaction between people or groups of people, and certain kinds tend to discourage such interaction (Figure 3).

Sommer[35] when he was at the University of Alberta carried out an extensive series of studies on the use of table space. He discovered that around a square or rectangular table most interaction is likely to take place corner-to-corner rather than face-to-face or side-to-side. Moreover, if the distance across the table is too great, people simply will not converse. These experiments suggest that long rectangular tables tend to foster the development of cliques at the ends of the table and to isolate those sitting toward the middle. Such an arrangement may be desirable for the administrator who must chair a meeting composed of factions that he does not want to come to blows.

Other studies have dealt with the effect of physical barriers on friendships. J. T. Gullahorn[36] discovered that when filing cabinets were placed beween rows or subgroups of office workers, interaction between rows of workers decreased, but within the subunits interaction increased. Robert Blake[37] found a similar result when he compared the number of friendships made in open barracks at an air force base with the number made in the closed cubicle type of barracks. Those who lived in the open barracks made more acquaintances, but the interaction of those in the closed cubicles was more intense.

Furniture is not always treated as movable. The Chinese treat it like the walls so that to move one's chair may be taken as an affront to the host. In this instance,

**Figure 3**
**Photo credit: Roy Flamm**

semifixed-feature   space   becomes   fixed-feature space.[38]

## Dynamic Space

Finally, there is the personal bubble of space that surrounds every individual: dynamic space. People affect their communications with others by the way they handle this space. They press close or stand aloof. Each spatial arrangement sends a different message.

Systematic study of dynamic space is recent. Simmel,[39] Sommer,[40] and C. Winick and H. Holt[41] have published on this subject, and a few related investigations have been undertaken on the effect of anxiety on man's perception of space.[42,43,44,45] My own observations include both transcultural and intracultural studies in the United States.[46,47,48,49,50]

These studies show that man, like other forms of life, is not limited to one boundary, his skin. He has several boundaries, space envelopes that expand and contract depending upon circumstances. There are four, possibly five, of these envelopes, which range from the closest most intimate zone out through the personal, social, and public zones. The size of each envelope, the activities and relationships allocated to each, and the receptors used to distinguish when boundaries have been crossed depend on at least four interlocking complex variables: the culture, the individual's personality, his status in his own social system, and how he is feeling toward others at the moment.

For example, two American businessmen of equal status who share the same North European subculture can usually interact more successfully if they avoid much touching or breathing on each other. An upper middle-class couple from the Eastern seaboard who do not know each other very well will stand so that they can see each others' faces clearly; however, they will not stand so close that they are inside the zone where heat and smell from the other's body can be detected easily and where facial features are distorted. To cross this border would signify that they had changed from an impersonal relationship to an intimate one.

## Cultural Differences

Man's personal distance varies from culture to culture[51,52]; each has a characteristic use of space. These differences cause a considerable amount of marginally felt discomfort, irritation, and even misunderstanding between people. People with a short personal distance will seem "pushy" to those whose personal distance is longer. Conversely the person with a long personal distance will appear cold, aloof, and standoffish to those with a short personal distance simply because they cannot approach such a person closely enough to become involved.

In general, middle-level Arabs, Japanese, and people with a Spanish colonial heritage can comfortably occupy much smaller spaces than Americans. This is because the personal-space bubble is smaller for these groups. Two men from the Middle East who want to discuss a matter of mutual concern must stand close enough to touch each other and to smell and feel the heat from each other's bodies. This proximity and combination of sensory inputs would arouse a hostile reaction in the average American male, or he would give the situation an intimately sexual interpretation.

People from different cultures will react in different ways to the same enclosed space. A colleague of mine discovered that his basement recreation room seemed gloomy and oppressive to Arab guests; they wanted to leave immediately. However, the room was "sehr gemutlich" to the Germans who came, and they could hardly be persuaded to leave. These responses are significant not only because they are different but also because the people involved could not tell why they felt the way they did. As I have indicated previously, most peoples' spatial responses are outside their conscious awareness.

Space that is sociofugal (pushing people apart) for one culture may be sociopetal (pulling people together) for another culture. Americans have great difficulty carrying on a conversation across a room. They may make a few remarks from this distance, but if the conversation is to continue they usually move closer together. Yet in the mountain villages of Lebanon and Syria the accepted way for men to converse casually in the evening is to sit far apart across the room.

## Space Patterns

It is probably safe to assume that there are no people in the world without well-developed patterns associating the man, the space, and the activity in some way. The English, for example, have strong proprietary feelings about their homes, but they are apt to be puzzled by the American's emphasis on his office. In England if a man is worth anything, his office is where he *is*. He doesn't depend on his surrounding work space to give him status, nor must his setting match his rank as it does in the United States. Thus it is thoroughly consistent with English culture that the members of the House of Commons have *no* offices.

In the United States, on the other hand, a man must achieve unusually high status before he can dissociate his work from a given spot. Unless he is at the very top, a person who has no office and works at home risks being categorized as "uncertain" or "unreliable"; his status is considered marginal. In America one's office is an indication of one's rank.

There are many of these patterns, and they vary from culture to culture. Every group of people has a characteristic way of organizing and structuring its space.

## CREATING AN ARTIFICAL ENVIRONMENT FOR MAN

Viewed casually in his natural habitat the twentieth-century American might be mistaken for a soft, somewhat pampered organism who could not survive a week in the wilds on his own. In his daily trek to and from his office, he is protected from the elements at all times, except perhaps for a few moments each day spent waiting for buses. It is difficult to realize that this sheltered creature is one of the toughest, most adaptable organisms on this earth. The form and functions of his body, his mental and emotional makeup, the cultures he has produced—all are the culmination of hundreds of thousands of years of evolution. In fact he is a product of his past.

This past was long and incredibly hazardous. There are features of it which should be taken into account by anyone engaged in creating artificial environments. First, man has always been a social organism. In the period before the development of agriculture, social groups were small; it has been estimated that there were probably not more than fifty to sixty individuals in each. Moreover, there was a generous amount of space for everyone, apparently 5 to 10 square miles per person.

In addition, tool making, close and distant vision, flexibility in the choice of roles open to individuals within the group, well-developed capacities for play at all ages, dependence on learned behavior (in contrast to innate behavior), and territoriality are characteristic of all men. The last of these is basic. Man specializes his use of space and associates space and time with *function, rank, activity,* and *affect.*

Thus any artificially created environment, if it is to satisfy man's nature, should contain not only variety but surprises. It should provide opportunities to continually engage man's great and inventive brain. It should present him with constant challenges.

The following questions are provided as an empirical anthropological checklist of items to be considered in designing environments for men. They are based on the combined observations of a great many cultures, studies of man's evolutionary past, and man's responses to culture as such. The checklist is not exhaustive, and the reader may wish to make additions on the basis of other experience.

## General Requirements

1. *Does the layout of space reflect the relationships among activities?* The more closely related that activities are functionally, the closer they should be in space. This is not merely for convenience; the layout of space can often point up relatedness that might not otherwise be obvious.

2. *Has an inventory been made of all activities and a time and place allocated for each?* A temporal–topological map should be created, based on the function of each activity. However, it would be advisable to draw this map without reference to materials or convention so that the true relationships become a matter of record. If it becomes necessary to separate related functions because of operational requirements or for reasons inherent in the design system, these separations should be compensated for by added communications.

3. *Are unrelated activities separated?* It is important to separate unrelated activities as much as possible so that they do not interfere with each other accidentally. In Little America, Paul Siple discovered that such a separation was *basic* and a mandatory requisite to the successful operation of a mission in the Antarctic.

   A useful model to follow is the microgeography of the dispersal of functions in the human body. The gathering of information, supplying of food, defense, and the disposal of wastes are functions performed by all organic units.

   In general, these functions should be separated from each other in space. If this is not possible, interference can be avoided if they are separated in time. Separation in both dimensions is preferable. Our present cities do not satisfy the separation requirement in any but a few respects. Traffic of all types is mixed as is breathing and the effluents of cars and factories.

## Human Requirements

1. *Have places been provided for all of man's space needs?* A study of the past shows that the first property an organism had was the space around it, and it can be demonstrated that nearly all organisms have territoriality of one kind or another. In

man this is highly developed, even though the forms vary from culture to culture.

2. *Has a place been provided which each citizen can call his own?* All societies have some provision for privacy even if it consists of no more than turning one's face away from the group and being left alone. It is important to provide for a variety of privacy options, including available open spaces outdoors.

3. *Has a variety of spaces been provided for meetings of different-sized groups?* For most cultures there is provision for large spaces in which the entire group can meet. Today's cities do not provide anywhere near the required number of meeting spaces. Moreover, it is important that spaces in which smaller groups can meet are also available, although the number and distribution of these has not been scientifically fixed.

4. *Are there enough landmarks?* Landmarks perform many functions, one of which is to identify meeting places. They are particularly desirable when large numbers travel to the meeting place from widely separated points. The landmarks can be practically anything that is readily imaged as well as identifiable, provided there is sufficient waiting space around it. In general, meeting places should be located on an avenue between work, eating, and recreation areas.

5. *Are there variations in light intensity, color, acoustics, and the olfactory environment?* In the past man was subject to a great variety of sensory inputs—extremes of hot and cold, light and dark, dryness and dampness. In order to create an environment approaching the one man evolved in, fluctuations in the environment should be provided. Making these variations at random so that they are unpredictable would seem to be preferable to the bland, unchanging environments of today's world.

6. *Have acceptable forms of peripheral stimulation been provided?* In a great many cultures people have devised various means of stimulating the peripheral nerves, such as the Finnish sauna bath and Japanese, Korean, and Arab massage. The widespread occurrence of this practice in such varied cultures indicates that there may be a basic need for stimulation of this sort. Does the environment make provisions for this need?

7. *Are work spaces the right size and character?* Every individual carries around with him a series of space bubbles in which various activities take place. The size of these bubbles varies with temperature, ambient noise level, the individual's emotional state, and the culture he was brought up in.

Work spaces should not be so large that people are isolated from each other, nor should they be so small that people are brought into too much contact. Control over screening of the senses is an important option since not only do jobs vary but people even within a culture have quite different needs.

8. *For intercultural installations, have the space differences in fixed-feature, semifixed-feature, and dynamic space been taken into account?*

9. *Have light and shadow been used to provide variety in the apparent size of the enclosure?* Highly lighted walls will make rooms appear larger. On the other hand, if overcrowding is unavoidable, the experience will seem less severe if light levels are lowered. The apparent explanation for this is that if temperature and noise level are held constant, a reduction in visual detail has the effect of increasing perceived distance.

10. *Have open spaces been provided to rest the eyes?* Accommodation convergence of the eye diminishes after 16 feet. An environment that does not provide open spaces to rest the eyes may ultimately strain one of the most highly evolved organs of the body.

11. *Is there variety in visual tasks?* People commonly overlook the fact that in the past man had a great deal of variety every day in his visual tasks. The physiology of the eye's retina reflects this past. There are three readily identifiable areas of the retina: the fovea, the macula, and the peripheral area. Each of these performs a different visual function, and each requires stimulation.

The centrally located *fovea,* which is made up of approximately 25,000 closely packed cones, subtends an angle of approximately 1° of the visual arc. Foveal vision is limited in area and extremely fine grained. Surrounding the fovea is the lozenge-shaped macula, which is composed predominately of cones but with the cones more widely dispersed than in the fovea. The *macula* subtends a vertical visual arc of approximately 3° and a horizontal visual arc of 12°. It is used for clear vision, and because of its predominant axis it enhances horizontal scanning. In the *peripheral area* of the retina there is a greater proportion of rods (which are not color sensitive) to cones. There is also a change in the way the rods and cones are connected to the nerve cells. In the fovea there is one nerve fiber for each cone; at the periphery of the retina there are a number of receptor cells for each nerve fiber. This neuronal arrangement enhances the perception of visual detail in the central portion of the eye and the perception of movement in the peripheral areas. On the other hand, overstimulation of the peripheral field as occurs in stores in which narrow aisles are created by stacked merchandise can make people nauseous (particularly women).

12. *Have man's social needs been provided for?* Man is a gregarious animal, and he needs a variety of roles. An inventory of roles should be created which makes it possible for every member of the group to be dominant at some time or other. The following relationships should be included in the basic inventory or roles: (1) individuals working alone; (2) peers working together; (3) peers working together as a team; (4) superordinates and subordinates working together; (5) individuals working as teachers; (6) individuals working as students.

Space to accommodate all these relationships should be provided.

13. *Is there opportunity for individuals to learn in a variety of contexts?* Man's humanness is due in great part to his massive brain and his reliance on learned behavior as a means of adapting to his environment. Providing people the opportunity to continue intensive learning is one way of giving them a sense of accomplishment. This is particularly important in restricted settings of the type now encountered in many of our larger cities. The city itself can be viewed as a large and never exhausted teaching machine—how much has this feature been taken into account?

14. *Do recreational activities offer opportunity for several kinds of play?* Play does not appear until late in the phylogenetic scale, and its precise function has not been determined. However, it is apparently essential for learning, socialization, and defense.

Play activities should be provided for the following categories: individuals, small groups, and large groups. Play can also be categorized as active, passive, and nonparticipating. A grid with these three along one coordinate and the first three categories along another coordinate yields nine play combinations. As many of these combinations as possible should be provided for.

## NOTES AND REFERENCES

1. Anne Roe and George Gaylord Simpson, *Behavior and Evolution,* New Haven: Yale University Press, 1958.
2. Leo Srole, T. S. Langer, and S. T. Michael, *Mental Health and the Metropolis,* Vol. I, New York: McGraw-Hill, 1962.
3. H. E. Howard, *Territory in Bird Life,* London: John Murray, 1920.
4. Paul L. Errington, "The great horned owl as an indicator of vulnerability in the prey populations," *Journal of Wildlife Management,* Vol. 2 (1938), 190.
5. H. Hediger, *Wild Animals in Captivity,* London: Butterworth, 1950.
6. H. Hediger, "The evolution of territorial behavior," in S. L. Washburn, ed., *Social Life of Early Man,* New York: Wenner-Gren Foundation for Anthropological Research, 1961.
7. *Ibid.*
8. John J. Christian, "Phenomena associated with population density," *Proceedings of the National Academy of Sciences,* Vol. 47, No. 4, 428–449.
9. John J. Christian, V. Flyger, and D. E. Davis, "Factors in mass mortality of a herd of sika deer," *Chesapeake Science,* Vol. 1 (1960), 79–95.
10. Edward S. Deevey, "The hare and the haruspex: a cautionary tale," *The American Scientist,* Vol. 48, No. 3 (1960), 415–430.
11. Paul Chombart de Lauwe, *Famille et habitation,* Paris: Centre National de la Recherche Scientifique, 1959.
12. Robert Sommer, "Space and mental health," unpublished MS.
13. L. Linn, *Handbook of Hospital Psychiatry,* New York: International Universities Press, 1955.
14. E. O. Hauser, "Does Sweden dare stay neutral?" *Saturday Evening Post* (August 31, 1951), 26.

15. H. Hediger, *Study of the Psychology and Behavior of Animals in Zoos and Circuses,* New York: Criterion Books, 1955.

16. M. E. Linden, "Some psychological aspects of rescue breathing," *American Journal of Nursing* (July 1960), 971–974.

17. A. Baker, R. L. Davies, and P. Sivadon, *Psychiatric Services and Architecture,* Geneva: World Health Organization, 1959.

18. Humphry Osmond, "The historical and sociological development of mental hospitals," and "The relationship between architect and psychiatrist," in C. Goshen, ed., *Psychiatric Architecture,* Washington, D.C.: American Psychiatric Association, 1959.

19. Robert Sommer and H. Ross, "Social interaction on a geriatrics ward," *International Journal of Social Psychology,* Vol. 4 (1958), 128–133.

20. Robert Sommer, *Personal Space, The Behavioral Basis of Design,* Englewood Cliffs, N.J.: Prentice-Hall, 1969.

21. Vincent Kling, "Space: a fundamental concept in design," in Goshen, *op. cit.*

22. Edward T. Hall, research conducted under grants from the National Institutes of Health and the Wenner-Gren Foundation.

23. Edward T. Hall, "Proxemics—the study of man's spatial relations and boundaries," in *Proceedings of the New York Academy of Medicine, Wenner-Gren Foundation Conference on Medicine and Anthropology,* New York, 1963.

24. Edward T. Hall, *The Hidden Dimension,* Garden City, N.Y.: Doubleday, 1966.

25. Edward T. Hall, "Proxemics," *Current Anthropology,* Vol. 9 (1968), 2–3.

26. Edward T. Hall, "Proxemics and design," *Design and Environment,* Vol. 2 (Winter, 1972), 24–25, 58.

27. Hall, "Proxemics," *op. cit.*

28. Kling, *op. cit.*

29. K. Izumi, "An analysis for the design of hospital quarters for the neuropsychiatric patient," *Mental Hospitals,* (April, 1957).

30. Baker, Davies, and Sivadon, *op. cit.*

31. Research in progress on social space.

32. In the instance cited a tourist court purchased to handle expansion of personnel proved more satisfactory to the scientists than space created for them.

33. Sommer, "Space and mental health," *op. cit.*

34. The Committee for New College, *Student Reactions to Study Facilities—with Implications for Architects and College Administrators,* Amherst, 1960.

35. Robert Sommer, "Studies in personal space," *Sociometry,* Vol. 22, No. 3 (1959), 247–260.

36. J. T. Gullahorn, "Distance and friendship as factors in the gross interaction matrix," *Sociometry,* Vol. 15 (1952), 123–124.

37. Robert Blake et al., "Housing architecture and social interaction," *Sociometry,* Vol. 19 (June, 1956), 133–139.

38. Paul Linebarger, personal communication.

39. Georg Simmel, "Discretion," in Kurt H. Wolff, ed., *The Sociology of Georg Simmel,* New York: The Free Press, 1950, 326–329.

40. Sommer, "Studies in personal space," *op. cit.*

41. C. Winick and H. Holt, "Seating positions as non-verbal communication in group analysis," *Psychiatry,* Vol. 24, No. 2 (1961), 171–182.

42. Harold Searles, *The Non-Human Environment in Normal Development and Schizophrenia,* New York: International Universities Press, 1960.

43. U.S. Naval Radiological Lab., *Preliminary Report on Shelter Occupancy Test,* 3-17 (USN Roh-TR-418), 1959.

44. Warren J. Wittreich, M. Grace, and K. B. Radcliff, Jr., "Three experiments in selective perceptual distortion," in F. Kilpatrick, ed., *Explorations in Transactional Psychology,* New York: New York University Press, 1961.

45. Edward T. Hall, *The Silent Language,* Garden City, N.Y.: Doubleday, 1959.

46. Edward T. Hall, "The anthropology of manners," *Scientific American,* Vol. 192, No. 4, 85–89.

47. Hall, "Proxemics—the study of man's spatial relations and boundaries," *op. cit.*

48. Edward T. Hall and William Foote Whyte, "Intercultural communication: a guide to men of action," *Human Organization,* Vol. 19 (Spring 1960).

49. Edward T. Hall, "The silent language in overseas business," *Harvard Business Review* (May–June 1960).

50. Hall, *The Silent Language, op. cit.*

51. Hall, "The anthropology of manners," *op. cit.*

52. F. L. Dimick and D. Fransworth, *Visual Acuity Tasks in a Submarine,* New London, 1951.

**PART THREE
OBTAINING AND
USING BEHAVIORAL
INFORMATION**

Photo credit: Elliott Kaufman

# OBTAINING AND USING BEHAVIORAL INFORMATION

Architects have always used the same basic techniques as the behavioral scientists to gain information about the world. The difference, however, has been that the architect has carried out his investigations in a casual manner—casual in the sense that insufficient discipline has been applied to the observation of situations and interviewing of people, and very little time and effort allotted for the task. As Alan Lipman points out in *Part One* of this book, the social, and very often administrative, gap between architect and client has increased and become more complicated, making this subjective and intuitive process of determining human needs inadequate. Therefore, new systematic and disciplined approaches to both the generation and application of objective information are required.

It is evident that the complexity of today's environmental problems compels the architect to focus on the applicable resources of other disciplines to develop methods of obtaining and applying appropriate information. It is wise to remember, however, that behavioral scientists have always been deeply concerned as to the validity of their methods of investigation[1]; furthermore, the "nature of behavior suggests that the method one uses to inquire into it affects the behavior itself."[2]

This caution must be remembered in the design of any approach to programming and evaluation and also in reflecting on the data which is obtained. Architects need to develop techniques suited to their own particular purposes. It is hoped that this presentation of research methodology will suggest some avenues of development while pointing out some techniques now in use.

If the designer is to place any relevance on the information that he uses for predication, he must be able to judge the adequacy of the research that obtained it by evaluating the reliability of the research design and methods and by judging its applicability to the issues being confronted. To do this, the architect must understand the particular nature of man–environment studies and the methodological problems involved in investigating the relationships between the physical setting and the people and activities it accommodates. It is to these two needs that *Part Three* is addressed —the discussion of methods of obtaining and using behavioral information in the architectural design process. This part is divided into two sections: the first deals with the problems of research design and techniques and the second with the issues of programming and evaluation.

## RESEARCH METHODS

The purpose of conducting research is to uncover new information that is relevant to and reliable for the solution of problems. The techniques used to arrive at this new information should be based on the scientific method, whose two important facets are that decisions (1) are reached objectively, and (2) can be replicated by other investigators. Thus research must follow a systematic procedure. Although this procedure consists of interrelated and sometimes simultaneous events, they have a logical order: formulation of the problem; establishment of research design; selection of measurement procedures; collection of data; analysis and interpretation of findings; application of information to a problem.[3] The formulation of the problem makes it concrete and explicit. The success of research, regardless of its focus and goals, depends on the researcher's having a clear idea of what he is seeking.

The formation stage consists of several interrelated steps: the statement of a hypothesis, the definition of concepts, and the establishment of operations to be used. The establishment of the research design refers to the arrangement of procedures, methods, and instruments to be used for the collection and analysis of data in a way that realizes the aims of the research. Steps in this stage consist of specifying the type of data required, selecting the data-gathering techniques, and determining measurement and statistical procedures for analysis of the data. Data collection is the actual systematic procedure of gathering information by either observation, questionnaires, interviews, or experimentation. Steps in this stage consist of developing and pretesting the instruments and using them to gather the information. After the data are collected, they must be analyzed and interpreted. The purpose of the analysis is to summarize the collected information by statistical methods, to make decisions with respect to the hypotheses, and to provide solutions to problems. The final stage is to link the data to other available information or to relate them to a particular problem through a theoretical construct. Using this brief summary of the research method as a model, we can examine the nature of man–environment studies to determine the most effective means of establishing reliable information for the environmental design process.

The phenomena that are to be researched and the purpose of studying them directly influence the formulation of the problem and the research design. The selection of issues to be studied, the sequence of research activities to be performed, and the selection of methods to obtain and analyze data are all dependent upon criteria related to the purpose of the study. The main thrust of most man–environment studies is problem oriented and thus attempts to relate ongoing behavioral patterns to particular settings. There are two significant categories of purpose—conceptual and programmatic. A conceptually oriented purpose generates studies in terms of principles and theoretical concerns which seek to understand and predict a wide range of environmental occurrences. Conceptual studies are concerned with the investigation of general classes of phenomena that may be applicable across many specific settings and activities. A study whose purpose is to obtain information for programming has a solution orientation and implies an action context for the solution of a specific problem. These categories are not always distinct nor mutually exclusive, for basic research can offer information useful in solving everyday problems, and applied research can produce insights into theoretical issues.

Since research design is strongly affected by the phenomena under study, it is essential to look at the issues that environmental behavioral scientists can legitimately explore. William Michelson, in his provocative work *Man and His Urban Environment: A Sociological Approach,* offers the following criteria for concepts that relate the physical environment to behavior.[4] The first consideration is that the investigations concern the physical attributes of the environment and not its social attributes. This point should be obvious in that this area is the one in which the architects can successfully intervene. The second consideration is that the phenomena to be studied should reflect social and behavioral patterns, for the problem is to understand the physical environment in terms of the ongoing behaviors and activities taking place within it. The third criterion for man–environment studies is that they should relate to the man-built environment in that the final product is architecture. The fourth consideration is that the chosen phenomena should be relevant to all levels of form because all levels of the environment, whether a room, a building, a group of buildings, or a city, have an effect on the behavioral patterns of the users. The fifth consideration is that the chosen phenomena systematically integrate lower levels of environment with higher levels; it is important that the environment be considered as an integrated system. The final criterion is that the phenomena be measurable; otherwise, no systematic knowledge of the environment can be generated or communicated.

Since there is a strong relationship between the questions to be answered and the methods used to arrive at these answers, an understanding of the type of information that can be sought becomes a critical element in environmental research. According to Harold Proshansky, the field of environmental psychology at this stage in its development must rely heavily on studies that are descriptive or exploratory in nature and not on studies that have causal hypotheses. The concern of man-environment studies must be in uncovering the dimensions and specific properties of the relationship between behavior and the physical setting in which it takes place.[5] The purpose of an exploratory investigation is to gain familiarity and to achieve new insights into the phenomena being studied; such investigations are characterized by flexibility in design, which permits the freedom necessary to observe changing events. Descriptive studies are those whose purpose is to identify and portray characteristics of the phenomena and to determine their frequency of occurrence; this type of study is organized to be accurate with a minimum of bias and a maximum of reliability. A third type—causal hypothesis studies—enables researchers to make inferences about causality by asking why a particular event takes place; its significant feature is the control of variables within an experimental construct.[6]

Another consideration in man–environment research is that it should be conducted in the actual physical setting that is of concern, if at all possible. To accomplish this without destroying the integrity of the setting and disturbing the activities taking place, the study must use field research methods that are nonexperimental in design. These two conditions not only limit the type of research possible, but also how it may be carried out. Neither implies, however, that environmental research be carried out without regard for scientific method or that data-gathering instruments and measurements should be unstructured. It simply requires that research design be organized in a manner that permits the objectives of the study to be reached.

## Data Gathering

To develop a data-gathering process, the source of the relevant information must first be determined; then, a method can be devised to tap that source. Since man is involved both mentally and physically with the environment, the sources to be tapped are those which are in the individual's mind and the actions of the individual in the environment. Man's mental involvement manifests itself in an individual's perceptions and mental images of the environment, his attitudes and belief systems regarding it, and his preferences and goals concerning it. Man's physical involvement manifests itself in his activity patterns and social interactions within the environment and his organization of the physical setting. Since no single method can reach both sources of information, a wide range of psychological and sociological techniques becomes applicable, depending upon the issue under investigation. Each of these techniques has strengths and weaknesses, and the researcher must anticipate these in the research design.

Since the reliability of research depends on the instrument used to obtain and measure data, it is important to establish the properties of a good instrument. First, a good instrument must measure what the investigator wants. Second, it must be reliable, giving consistent measurements. Third, it should measure by a ratio scale having an absolute zero and equal intervals. Fourth, it must be precise, measuring with a known sensitivity. Fifth, it must be convenient to use. Sixth, it has to ensure objectivity by providing the possibility of ascertaining the way in which the instrument measures.[7] Using these properties as a reference, data-collection techniques can be examined as to their relevance in man–environment research.

Three basic techniques normally available to social scientists are survey, observation, and experimentation. Each has validity and application in man–environment studies. The selection of the correct means of obtaining information is based on the type of research being performed, the research question being raised, the phenomena being studied, and the limitations placed on the study.

Survey techniques perform best when used to obtain

information about an individual's mental involvement with the environment. In addition, survey techniques have historically been used to obtain data about populations and to gather initial data cheaply and quickly. These techniques are explained in the paper "Surveys, Questionnaires, and Interviews," by Ronald Goodrich, a research psychologist at Bronx State Hospital. The paper that follows, "Measuring Attributes of the Visual Environment," by Henry Sanoff, Professor of Architecture at North Carolina State University, demonstrates the use of the questionnaire approach and the semantic differential scale for obtaining information about user preferences for visual environments.

Survey techniques have come under strong criticism because of several inherent weaknesses. These include the assumption that the respondent can verbalize his responses to the environment, the limitations of some respondents' intellectual capabilities to respond to complicated phenomena, the lack of awareness about the effect of the environment on behavior, the overemphasis on self, and prejudice which favors the known and familiar. To overcome these weaknesses, several modified techniques have been developed and used successfully in exploratory and descriptive studies by employing nonverbal responses and having the respondents draw the setting in question.[8] Techniques that obtain a large volume of information inexpensively involve asking respondents to chart their daily activities on aerial photographs of their communities[9] or to log their daily activities on a time-budget chart.[10] Another pencil-and-paper technique that has uncovered valuable information is the semiprojective game. In this technique, hypothetical situations are set up in which the respondents are forced to make decisions about options open to them.[11] While survey techniques have inherent weaknesses, variations can be developed that can cope with the respondent's inability to articulate a response to the environment. If used properly within their limitations, they can be valuable research tools.

Observation techniques have been most productive in obtaining information as to how people behave in and experience their environment. The strength of observation techniques is that it is possible to record and measure the behavioral patterns in the actual setting in which they occur at the time of their occurrence.

To be successful, however, observations should be planned systematically around clear, concise concepts and recorded with valid and reliable techniques. There have been a number of systematic observation methods employed in man–environment studies varying from simply following subjects through downtown areas to more precisely formulated techniques such as "behavioral-setting surveys," explained by William LeCompte in *Part Two* of this book, and behavioral mapping.[12] New technologies have increased the potential of observation techniques; some researchers have used films,[13] television,[14] and stop-motion still photography[15] to record events. Designers have also developed techniques to describe environmental experience by making systematic notations of environmental characteristics and movement through space.[16,17,18] These are quite different from the observation techniques described by Arthur Patterson, social psychologist teaching at Pennsylvania State University, in his paper "Unobtrusive Measures: Their Nature and Utility for Architects." In the paper, "The Evaluation of Environments: Behavioral Observations in an Undersea Habitat," Robert Helmreich, Acting Chairman of the Department of Psychology at the University of Texas, describes another systematic, unobtrusive technique used to collect and record behavioral data. It is important to reflect that observation techniques are dependent upon the issues being studied and the situation in which the behavior occurs. Observation as a technique also has some built-in weaknesses, including the effect of being observed on behavioral patterns, the lack of explanation of the purpose and meaning of the observed behaviors, the potential for observing adaptive behavior in a dysfunctionate setting, and the ability to observe only current behavioral patterns. Even with these apparent weaknesses, observation is still the most reliable method of obtaining information about the ongoing behavioral patterns in a physical setting.

As an approach, experimentation, which employs techniques to manipulate and control variables as a means to study causal relations, has seldom been used in environmental research because experimentation does not easily lend itself to the phenomena being studied or to the type of information being sought. Experimentation, however, as discussed in the paper

"Experimental Methods in Environmental Design Research," by Robert Bechtel, Director of the Environmental Research and Development Foundation, has a viable place in methodologies for use by environmental researchers. The most successful experimental approaches have been the so-called nonexperimental[19] or quasi-experimental[20] techniques in which observations have been made in the actual setting without having all the variables controlled by external means. Simulation also has shown promise as a technique for investigating hypothetical situations that cannot be duplicated in real-life situations; an example of this is the placing of an individual in a novel environment to judge his responses and perceptions to it, thus gaining an understanding of the perceptual process.[21]

It becomes evident that research designs which employ a single method of gathering data will leave out significant data. To understand the whole picture of the individual's involvement with his environment, there must be understanding of the individual's mental set in relation to his spatial behavioral patterns. For information to be useful in the design process, it is not enough to know only what behaviors occur but also to know why they occur and their significance and meaning. To accomplish this, more than one data-gathering technique should be used. In a study to develop information for the design of office furniture systems, the research design combined observations recorded by stop-motion photography with information obtained through interviews with the subjects explaining the purpose of their activities.[22] Through the combination of these techniques, the shortcomings of each were offset, and a more complete picture of the occurrence developed.

## Data Analysis

A final point to consider in research methodology is the interpretation and application of research. First, it is important not to misuse research by jumping from raw data to conclusions without the proper analytical techniques or by confusing the recording of information with its interpretations. If there is to be any continuity in the study, or reliable information generated, the techniques that are to be used in the analysis must be planned in relation to the concept being studied before any information is collected. Statistical methods are normally employed in the analysis of research. Descriptive statistics allow the reseacher to draw a general picture from the data and to make predictions about individuals within groups in terms of the variable under study, while inferential statistics permit the researcher to go beyond his data to make inferences about a larger population, to test hypotheses about populations, and to tell him how safe these predictions are. Within behavioral research endeavors, there is a wide variation in the need for statistical procedures. There exists, however, a preference for simplicity in statistical analysis; the methods for achieving this are best explained in books devoted to that subject.[23] It is critically important that architects who plan to use behavioral information have a consumer's knowledge of statistics and be completely familiar with the significance and validity of that information.

Techniques other than statistical analysis have been used successfully in environmental research. These techniques have been used singly and in combination with mathematical statistics. The most common of these is *sociometric analysis,*[24] which is concerned with the spatial description of social interaction. This type of analysis can be used to determine the location of individuals, as well as to test an individual's social position in a group, cohesion within the group, and neighborhood patterns. Its significance to environmental research is that it makes spatial references to behavior and individuals in a setting. The next method, *content analysis,*[25] involves the study of attitudes and beliefs by analyzing what people say about the subject under investigation in typical communication media such as newspapers, conversations, and meetings, or in atypical communication media such as drawings and sketches. The advantage of this type of study and analysis over questionnaires is that true feelings are more likely to be expressed outside an experimental situation. Another method of analyzing data is through the use of a *matrix*[26] to establish relationships between alternatives not easily differentiated. It systematizes and records data by three methods: rank ordering of set alternatives, visual mapping, and establishing relationship values. The matrix can be used with either mathematical entries or graphic entries.

The relevance of environmental research is not to

accumulate a body of unrelated facts and discrete "bits" of information, but to organize this information into meaningful theoretical constructs. The primary objective of a holistic research approach is to develop typologies of systems by identifying the type of system and by noting similarities to and differences between other like systems. Assumptions in holistic research include that the system is central and bounded, that it has an identifiable state of determination, and that it consists of an internal operation with all significant variables and an external environment. The relationship among the elements determines the outcome of the system, although there may be effects by external factors. Only through a holistic synthesis of information can a significant framework be developed for the design of the environment.

## PROGRAMMING AND EVALUATION STUDIES

The designing process has been described as comprising five classes of activities: *intelligence,* those activities directed at formulating the problem; *design,* those activities involved with developing solutions; *choice,* those activities concerned with selecting the solution; *implementation,* those activities involved with constructing; and *evaluation,* those activities directed to testing the solution in use. In the traditional practice of architecture, the primary concern of architects has been directed toward the design and implementation stages, while intelligence has received scant attention and evaluation has been totally ignored. Since the nature of architecture is rapidly changing and the scope of problems escalating, the intelligence and evaluation phases are gaining significantly in importance. Pointing to the necessity of architectural programming, Raymond Studer and David Stea have referred to the "designer's dilemma," which is that

*He must make this design decision involving more people emitting more complex behaviors, more communications, more knowledge about what is required, and more complex means for finding solutions. Having traditionally functioned in an artistic framework, the environmental designer finds himself generally operating outside the scientific community; as one consequence, his knowledge of the techniques for objectively analyzing and organizing complex systems is miniscule.*[27]

In discussing the lack of evaluation in the design process, psychologist Robert Sommer states:

*The lack of evaluational data not only causes the neglect of good design features, and encourages an attitude of novelty for its own sake, since no one knows what items are good or bad, but it also results in the perpetuation of bad design solutions. Reinventing the wheel for each problem is bad enough, but reinventing a square or lopsided wheel is even worse.*[28]

Because of this new emphasis on these two areas of designing process, the editors of this book feel that it is necessary to address a section of the book to the issues involved with programming and evaluation. For the sake of clarity, the term *programming* will be used to mean the intelligence phase of the design process presented in *Part One.* In very general terms, programming is the process of generating criteria for the design of facilities or buildings. The term *evaluation* will be used for the process of testing design criteria and the design solution for its acceptability in terms of user satisfaction and programmatic requirements.

Programming and evaluation are significant in the design process because these are the areas in which the behavioral sciences and architecture can gain from collaboration. Through the use of research techniques and the incorporation of behavioral information, programming can more fully describe the problem by stating the underlying needs of the building. In addition to aiding in the solution of the environmental problems, programming and evaluation serve two other important functions. By clearly identifying the goals of the project, the program establishes a means for testing the designer's assumptions in the design allowing him to learn from his successes or to benefit from his failures, thus increasing his capabilities and effectiveness as a designer. The second benefit derived from an explicit programming and evaluation process is that both add to knowledge about the relationship between the physical setting and its behavioral patterns. Explicitly stated goals for a design can be tested to unlock significant aspects of the problem. As Harold Proshansky stated earlier in this book, "most architects, designers, and planners have a wealth of 'unrefined' data and ideas about people in relationship to physical space and its organization, which has yet to be tapped in any systematic fashion." Programming and evaluation provide the means to tap this source.

Because of the issues and techniques involved, programming and evaluation work both independently and interdependently. Not only does programming provide criteria for design, it also specifies performance characteristics of the new building or facility to be tested in the evaluation stage. Evaluation, in addition to testing design decisions and validating programming information, generates new information for future programming endeavors. These processes are dynamic; they are constantly adjusting to changing environmental demands and never reaching a final, completed stage because they always generate new information and constantly test it. The essential difference between programming and evaluation lies in the relationship of the variables that are tested by each. In programming, human behavior is considered to be the cause and the physical setting the effect, while in evaluation, the physical setting is viewed as the cause and human behavior, the effect.

## Programming

John Summerson states: "the programme as a source of unity is, so far as I can see, the one new principle involved in modern architecture."[29] This points to the significance which programming has for achieving a solution to environmental problems. The purpose of programming is to prevent and correct recurrence of environmental problems and to predict the spatial and environmental needs of a project based on the requirements of the user, the user's activities, and the administrative goals. The purpose of the program is to predict those environmental conditions that are supportive and responsive to the user's activity patterns.[30] To be relevant, these projections are constrained by an economic framework that is related to the construction process, the resources of the client, and the time constraints.

Environmental problems appear as a dysfunction between the physical setting and the activities of its users. Misfits between physical settings and activity patterns can be caused by improperly designed settings that fail to appropriately accommodate the activities or arise through changes in environmental needs. Changes in activities, in the quantity of activity, in the equipment and components within the setting, in the policy of administration of the setting, and in the attitudes of the users can require a design solution. Particular environments also have problems that stem

from their specialized function. Since the purpose of programming is to propose criteria for the solution of environmental problems, it follows that the first order of activity in programming is to uncover and state the problem.

To propose a solution for environmental problems, programming seeks criteria in two general areas: goals and user requirements. Goals are the reason why a facility or building should exist. The user requirements determine the conditions which the facility should support and are expressed by the user's activities and characteristics. Programming criteria must be directly useful in the designing process, as pointed out in the paper by Robert Gutman and Barbara Westergaard. To be useful, criteria must be bound by the problem the design is intended to solve and be in some definitive form. If the criteria are not bound by the problem and are not definitive, they become too general to be useful.

Programming should investigate the environmental needs and establish criteria in five interrelated systems: objectives, activities, environment, building, and resouces.[31] The system of objectives provides the context for the activities that will take place and the aims which the facility is to fulfill. The activity system specifies behavior and interactions which will achieve the objectives of the facility. The environmental system consists of operational requirements that support the activities in terms of sociophysical attributes. The building system consists of physical elements that are set up by the environmental system. Finally, the resource system consists simply of those costs that will be incurred in the solution of the problem, in terms of each of the preceding systems.

## Concerns in Programming

Since programming should not be considered as a simple operation, several areas of concern should be discussed. The first of these involves the responsibility for the program (also, the responsibility for the evaluation). The standard architectural service agreement between owner and architect[32] states that the client has the responsibility to provide programming information. This, however, is not in the best interests of the architect, the client, or the project. Without a doubt, the architect should be actively involved in the process. Sociologist Robert Gutman states: "the profession should put out more effort to convince the client and the user that every building project demands a close scrutiny of values, goals, purposes, and present mode of social organization, according to which clients and users conduct their own affairs."[33] Since this statement also implies that the programming process is becoming more involved and requires expert help, architects will have to collaborate with behavioral scientists and other programming specialists to unravel the complexity of environmental problems. This has been aptly pointed out by Benjamin Evans and Herbert Wheeler in *Emerging Techniques 2: Architectural Programming,* published by the A.I.A.:

*After examining programs and talking to programmers, it became apparent that good programming stems from the programmer's prior experience. It results from the programmer's capability and competence to use standard procedures and systematic practice as well as data banks and feedback information, which is indicative of his sensitivity in a specified building type area.*[34]

Three aspects of the communication in the programming process cause problems. The architect must make his information needs known. This is important even if he is to do the programming himself, but doubly important if he is to utilize the services of a behavioral scientist who will probably be unfamiliar with the design process. The second area of concern in communication is that the programmer must rely on the user's ability to articulate his environmental needs. This suggests that the programmer must have knowledge of the user's past experience, his ability to verbally articulate his needs, and methods that can uncover nonexpressed needs. The final communication problem is one of information flowing from the programmer to the architect; the programmer must communicate the criteria in a well-organized and relevant manner which enlightens the architect but does not confuse him.

The complexity of the environment requires the programmer to make selective determination of the problem and to establish a hierarchy of problem needs. If one is to consider the number of variables in the environment, the activities taking place within it, and the changes caused by time, the problem of programming would be unsolvable with current problem-solving capabilities. Since all activities cannot be considered, the programmer must consider only the most important criteria for the solution of the problem. The selection of variables to be studied should be made according to the consideration of those activities considered most important by the user, those activities that are most affected by the design of the building, and those activities that will affect the design of the building. The choice of areas of study can be determined by the users if they have relevant experience or by the architects and programmers based on theoretical positions, observed behavior, previously obtained information, and analysis of existing buildings.

In the initial planning of programming activities, equal study must be given to as many variables as possible to prevent biasing. After the process begins and information is obtained that can show the relative importance of variables, weighting should be placed on those having the greatest importance and be explicitly expressed. Thus, if tradeoffs are made, they can be done within a hierarchical framework.

## Program Format

Two recently developed concepts are capable of being used as the basis for transmitting behavioral information in appropriate detail to the architect. These are "pattern language" and "performance characteristics." Pattern language has been described in the introduction to Christopher Alexander's paper in *Part One.* Performance characteristics describe the characteristics of settings for human activities by specifying what is needed in environmental terms and how much of it is wanted. Performance characteristics make use of a descriptive scale that goes from one quantity to its opposite with no value judgments implied at either end of the scale. For example, a scale would be one between spaces which draw people together (sociopetal) and those which have the effect of separating them (sociofugal), with incremental points between those two considerations.[35] Both performance characteristics and pattern languages have been used in programming endeavors. The pattern language has been used by Christopher Alexander to determine characteristics for multiuse service centers for communities[36] and in studies by others for banks and architects' offices.[37] Performance characteristics have been utilized by Michael Brill and Richard Krauss in the development of a "Planning Aid Kit" for Community Mental Health Facilities[38] and as described in this section by Walter Moleski, Director of the Environmental Research

Group, in his paper "Behavioral Analysis and Environmental Programming for Offices."

## Programming Process

Programming comprises several explicit steps. After reviewing many programming procedures used by both architects and programming consultants, the authors of *Emerging Techniques 2: Architectural Programming*[39] have distilled a model of interrelated steps:
1. Establish aims and goals.
2. Collect, organize, and analyze data.
3. Uncover and develop concepts.
4. Establish needs.
5. Develop problem statements.

This procedure is very similar to the programming procedure stated by John Zeisel, Assistant Professor in Sociology of Design, Harvard University, in his paper "Fundamental Values in Planning with the Nonpaying Client."

These procedures are related to the professional's role as the generator of the programming. Michael Brill and Richard Krauss[40] developed a procedure in which the user participates directly in the development of planning criteria. The procedure involves an active discussion between the planning group, consisting of the users of the facility and the staff that operates it; the professional consultants, such as architects, medical professionals, or management consultants; and a third group of public authorities who oversee the facility. In this process the planning group only has the authority to develop criteria; the professionals and officials act only in an advisory capacity. Steps in this process are as follows:
1. Select and unite participants.
2. Articulate the problems.
3. Select courses of action.
4. List activities.
5. Prescribe performance characteristics.
6. Design settings.
7. Evaluate feedback.

## Evaluation

The purpose of evaluation is to investigate whether or not the design has satisfactorily solved the environmental problem. Since we design in a world of limited knowledge, states Henry Sanoff, "architecture should be defined as a cybernetic process of moving toward control systems and feedback rather than a vision of an ideal state."[41] This statement shows the importance of evaluation as a feedback and feedforward mechanism that increases our knowledge of environmental problems and their solutions. Evaluation studies compare intended use with the actual use of a facility, the level of user's comfort and adaptation, the frustration of a user's desired activities and the recognizability of the intended environmental image. Evaluation can be considered in terms of short-term evaluations and long-term evaluations. Short-term evaluations focus on the solution within a narrow period of time after its completion and provide immediate feedback to the designer. Long-term evaluations take place over a period of time in which the building is investigated with regard to the evolution of spatial activities and the changing patterns of society. The problem with evaluation studies is fully discussed by Robert Gutman, Professor of Environmental Sociology, Rutgers University and Class of 1913 Lecturer in Architecture at Princeton, and Barbara Westergaard, research associate in the Department of Sociology at Rutgers, in their paper in this section, "Building Evaluation, User Satisfaction, and Design."

The process of evaluation can be outlined as follows:
1. Statement of the objectives which the designer has to satisfy.
2. Identification of limits of satisfaction.
3. Examination of available evidence as to the effects of a departure from the objective.
4. Specification of criteria for a simple measurement which would indicate level of satisfaction.
5. Collection and analysis of data.
6. Preparation of evaluation report.

Michael Brill, president of BOSTI and Chairman of the Department of Architecture, State University of New York at Buffalo, in his paper also in this section "Evaluating Buildings on a Performance Basis," argues for the use of the performance concept to give these procedures validity.

## CONCLUSION

"The load of the policy-maker is not necessarily lightened by the knowledge of user values. . . . Yet, this knowledge may enable him to plan more intelligently and to encompass the needs of diverse user groups in the design solution."[42] This statement by psychologist Robert Sommer clearly indicates that the purpose of using behavioral research as a tool in the design process is not to reduce the role of the architect but to allow him to become more innovative in fulfilling his role. The role of programming as an active part of the design process is to permit the architect to delve more deeply into the problem in search of a solution and to clearly state the client's, the user's, and his own intentions prior to beginning the design process. Evaluation performs the role of providing feedback to the design process so that the architect's search for solutions is an ongoing process in which he builds on each preceding step. It is important to stress that behavioral information will not present the architect with some miracle solution; it is still the architect's role to evaluate the program and to creatively give it form in architectural terms. As architect Louis I. Kahn has stated, "I believe that the architect's first act is to take the program that comes to him and change it . . . to put it into the realm of architecture, which is to put it into the realm of space."[43]

## NOTES AND REFERENCES

1. Harold M. Proshansky, "Methodology in environmental psychology: problems and issues," *Human Factors,* Vol. 14, No. 5 (1972) 451–460.
2. Harry Grace, "Behavioral science adequacy for the purpose of design," Grace Associates, Santa Monica, Calif. 1971 (mimeographed).
3. Claire Selltiz, Marie Jahoda, Morton Deutsch, and S. W. Cook, *Research Methods in Social Relations,* New York: Holt, 1959.
4. William Michelson, *Man and His Urban Environment: A Sociological Approach,* Reading, Mass.: Addison-Wesley, 1970, 38.
5. Proshansky, *op. cit.*
6. Selltiz et al., *op. cit.*
7. David Canter, "On appraising building appraisals," *Architects' Journal* (December 21, 1966), 881–888.
8. Sim Van der Ryn and Murray Silverstein, *Dorms at Berkeley: An Environmental Analysis,* Berkeley, Calif.: Center for Planning and Development Research, University of California, 1967.
9. William Michelson, "Selected aspects of environmental research in Scandinavia," *Man—Environment Systems* (July 1970), 2.
10. William Michelson, "Time budget research," in Wolfgang Preiser, ed., *Environmental Design Research: Proceedings of the Fourth International EDRA4 Conference,* Stroudsburg, Pa.: Dowden, Hutchinson & Ross, 1973.
11. Henry Sanoff, "Activities gameboard," *Techniques of Evaluation for Designers,* Raleigh, N.C.: Design Research Laboratory, School of Design, North Carolina State University, 1968, 58–59.
12. William H. Ittelson, Leanne G. Rivlin, and Harold M. Proshansky, "The use of behavioral maps in environmental psychology," in Proshansky, Ittelson, and Rivlin, eds., *Environmental Psychology: Man and His Physical Setting,* New York: Holt, 1970, 658–668.
13. S. Carr and D. Schissler, "The city as a trip: perceptual selection and memory in view from the road," *Environment and Behavior,* Vol. 1 (June 1969), 7–35.
14. Albert Scheflen, personal communication.
15. Robert Propst, "The human performer in the machine-related office," *Environmental Planning and Design,* Vol. 8 (January–February 1970), 25–31.
16. Philip Thiel, "Notes on the description, scaling, notation and scoring of some perceptual and cognitive attributes of the physical environment," in Proshansky, Ittelson, and Rivlin, *op. cit.,* 593–619.
17. Lawrence Halprin, "Motation," *Progressive Architecture,* Vol. 46 (July 1965), 126–133.
18. Donald Appleyard, Kevin Lynch, and John Myer, *The View from the Road,* Cambridge, Mass.: The MIT Press, 1964.
19. H. M. Blalock, Jr., *Causal Inferences in Nonexperimental Research,* Chapel Hill, N.C.: University of North Carolina Press, 1961.
20. D. Campbell and J. Stanley, *Experimental and Quasi-Experimental Designs for Research,* Skokie, Ill.: Rand McNally, 1966.
21. Lucille Nahemow, "Research in a novel environment," *Environment and Behavior,* Vol. 3 (March 1971), 81–102.
22. Propst, *op. cit.*
23. G. A. Ferguson, *Statistical Analysis in Psychology and Education,* New York: McGraw-Hill, 1966.
24. G. Lindzey and E. F. Borgatta, "Sociometric measurement," in G. Lindzey, ed., *Handbook of Social Psychology,* Vol. 1, Reading, Mass.: Addison-Wesley, 1959.
25. G. Fellman and B. Brandt, "A neighborhood a highway would destroy," *Environment and Behavior,* Vol. 2 (December 1970), 281–301.
26. Sanoff, *op. cit.*
27. Raymond Studer and David Stea, "Architectural programming, environmental design and human behavior," *The Journal of Social Issues,* Vol. 22 (Winter 1964).
28. Robert Sommer, *Design Awareness,* San Francisco, Calif.: Rinehart Press, 1972.
29. B. H. Evans and C. H. Wheeler, *Emerging Techniques 2: Architectural Programming,* Washington, D.C.: The American Institute of Architects, 1969, 10.
30. Michael Brill and C. H. Masterson, "Some thoughts on the direction of user requirements research," The American Institute of Architects, Washington, D.C., 1972.
31. Thomas Markus, "Optimization by evaluation in the appraisal of buildings," in John Archea and Charles Eastman, eds., *EDRA 2: Proceedings of the Second Annual Environmental Design Research Association Conference,* Pittsburgh, Pa., October 1970.
32. "Owner-architect agreements," in *Architect's Handbook*

*of Professional Practice,* Chap. 9, Washington, D.C.: The American Institute of Architects, 1966.

33. Robert Gutman, "The sociological implications of programming practices," *Building Research,* Vol. 6 (April-June 1969), 26.
34. Evans and Wheeler, *op. cit.*
35. Brill and Krauss, *op. cit.*
36. Christopher Alexander, Sara Ishikawa, and Murray Wilverstein, *A Pattern Language Which Generates Multi-Service Centers,* Berkeley, Calif.: Center for Environmental Structure, 1968.
37. F. Duffy and J. Torrey, "A progress report on pattern language," in Gary Moore, ed., *Emerging Methods in Environmental Design and Planning,* Cambridge, Mass.: The MIT Press, 1970, 261.
38. Michael Brill and Richard Krauss, "NIMH planning aid kit," 123rd Annual Meeting, American Psychiatric Association, San Francisco, Calif., May 12, 1970.
39. Evans and Wheeler, *op. cit.*
40. Brill and Krauss, *op. cit.*
41. Sanoff, *op. cit.*
42. Sommer, *op. cit.*
43. Jan C. Rowan, "Wanting to be: the Philadelphia School," *Progressive Architecture* (April 1969), 132.

*In this paper, the author presents an information-assessment strategy which provides a means for defining the overall problem of research and for organizing the information-gathering process. This strategy defines the purpose of the research, the respondent's characteristics, the environmental set, and the techniques to be used. Survey techniques are discussed, and the advantages and limitations of each type are presented. Considerations for questionnaire design are given: these include format, question content, question wording, and question order. Questions of the nonverbal response type are discussed as a means to uncover information not easily verbalized. Scales are presented as a method of systematizing responses. In survey research it is important that consideration be given to obtaining creditable responses relevant to the question under study.*

# Surveys, Questionnaires, and Interviews

**Ronald J. Goodrich**

**Environmental Research Group**
**Philadelphia, Pennsylvania**

## INTRODUCTION

Of the many techniques and strategies developed by social scientists to gain useful behavioral information, some of the most commonly used techniques are surveys, questionnaires, and interviews.[1] These methods are concerned with the assessment of attitudes, preferences, and opinions and have particular utility for the design-oriented person involved in programming and evaluation of the designed environment. Attitudes are inferred from what a person says about an object, from the way he feels about it, and from the way he says he will behave toward it. To what extent one's expressed attitude is consistent with his actual behavior is not an easy problem to answer. Behavior is determined not only by what people would like to do, but also by what they think they should do (social norms), by what they usually do (habits), and by expected consequences of their behavior. Thus there is no simple relationship between attitude and behavior. As a noted researcher of attitude formation and change, M. Fishbein, has stated,

*After more than seventy-five years of attitude research, there is still little, if any, consistent evidence supporting the hypothesis that knowledge of an individual's attitude toward some object will allow one to predict the way he will behave with respect to the object. Indeed, what little evidence there is to support any relationship between attitude and behavior comes from studies showing that a person tends to bring his attitude in line with his behavior, rather than from studies demonstrating that behavior is a function of attitude.[2]*

Attitudes alone, then, do not predict behavior. Attitudes, together with social norms and habits, do, and the greater the consistency among them, the greater will be the consistency between attitude and actual behavior. Despite the problems involved, a knowledge of the user's attitudes, opinions and preferences is indeed important for the successful completion of a design project. This paper is predicated on that assumption and will discuss the problem of information assessment for environmental needs relating to the procedures of programming and evaluation.

## AN INFORMATION-ASSESSMENT STRATEGY

The first step in an attempt to collect information for programming or evaluation is the development of an information-assessment strategy. The assessment strategy provides a means for defining the overall problem and for organizing the gathering of information in such a way as to make it efficient, effective, and useful. Unorganized information is no information at all. In developing this assessment strategy, many questions must be asked, and these will serve to define the problem at its various levels. The purpose of the information-gathering activity must be delineated, along with the type of data required, its relevance for the intended use, and the most appropriate methods for the collection of the information.

Initially one must ask a series of "what" questions. What is the overall purpose of gathering the information, and what will be its use? Will it be used for programming, evaluation, research, or for immediate implementation? Answers to these questions will suggest practical limitations, such as time and money, and will also set criteria for selecting and eliminating information. Only in reference to a stated goal and intended use can realistic judgments be made regarding the collection of information. In this context, one can ask: what kind of information is needed? For example, in a study conducted for a large company interested in behavioral programming for new office space, we judged it important not only to gain information about the personnel's relationship to their present space, but information about the social environment, communication patterns, and levels of supervision.[3] These factors, we felt, were influential in a person's perception of his immediate working environment. The determination of the kind of information needed will often dictate the type of responses most appropriate for that need. In some situations an open-ended question may produce rich, informative responses, which in other instances are simply too ungainly to code and develop into useful results. Some decision has to be made before assessment begins to guard against such pitfalls and to be certain that the information is useful for its intended purpose.

Another consideration is the relative importance of each piece of information obtained. Practical limitations often require that some information be eliminated, and so criteria must be set for this purpose. If several methods of information gathering are to be employed, judgments will have to be made concerning the efficiency and economy of each method, as well as the relative importance of the information gained.

Once the problem has been defined and the kind of information determined, the question becomes: What specific information is needed? General categories are developed, as well as general question areas within each of the categories. In programming an office space, for example, one might want to know about work flow. A number of questions would be necessary—for example: To whom does each person pass his work? From whom does he receive it? Is all or some work involved? Must he visit other departments? Does he work as an individual or part of a team?[4] It is often helpful at this stage in strategy development to begin to sketch out specific questions in each category. These can then be refined or eliminated as the organization of the material progresses.

Next, some decision must be made regarding the best way to obtain the information needed. What techniques or combinations of techniques will be used? Should one interview? Use a questionnaire? Observe? These questions can be answered only within the context of our earlier questions. If one must obtain specific information from large numbers of people, then the questionnaire is often the most appropriate method. It saves time and money, assures comparison across categories, and is relatively easy to administer. An interview, on the other hand, provides more detailed information and can often elicit unexpected information. The interaction in the situation also allows for clarification and interpretation of meaning.

Another question which must be asked concerns the intended use of the information, once it is gathered. Many excellent research ideas and worthwhile projects have been abandoned because this question was not answered adequately before assessment began. Sometimes a huge mass of data is jettisoned and the job proceeds without it, simply because the data is unwieldy and unorganized. One way to approach the question of the use of the information is to consider the needs of the principal user of the material. Will he be an architect or interior designer? What will he do with the material? In this context, too, how refined must the information be? Are statistical counts and summaries adequate, or is more discrete information needed? The data in the output report must be organized to be useful and should be organized in categories which the principal user will find useful.

Another series of questions asks: Who?—defining the respondent class. The immediate question is whether everyone in the given population is to be assessed or whether a sample will be used. Often this question is answered by project requirements or by a client's needs, though there is usually some flexibility. This is an implicit tradeoff situation where the assessor must weigh the amount, type, and precision of the information required against limiting constraints of time, money, and effort. As a rule, the larger the number of people who are potential respondents, the more economical it becomes to use a sample. A *sample* is a representative fraction or subgroup of the larger respondent class. It must possess the same characteristics as the larger group, and care must be taken to avoid bias. Detailed guidelines for sampling may be found in any standard research text, such as C. Selltiz.[5]

In defining the respondent group, one must consider not only how many people will be assessed, but who will supply the best information. Should it be the primary user, or are there others, such as visitors, who should be included? Are there organizational differences where different members will prescribe different requirements? Is there some inherent organizational structure which can be used to advantage?[6] Frequently, the answers to these questions will indicate that various techniques be employed. For example, in a project involving programming for a large firm, a structured interview proved the most effective means for gaining a general overview of the functioning of each department as well as providing a context for more specific user-need information obtained from all personnel. The interviews were brief (from one half to three quarters of an hour), were conducted with managers having more than five people working under them, and were consistent, as the structured interview ensured that all interviewers would obtain similar information. These interviews and the questionnaire data complemented each other and were nonredundant enough to be efficient and time-saving.[7] For purposes of programming, decisions must be made as to which people at which levels of the organization have the best possible information. The view from different levels often produces entirely different perceptions of needs and problems, and assessment techniques must build in as a means to ensure that all perspectives are being included in the data.

The next question to consider is: Who will do the assessment? This may seem at first to be a trivial problem, as anyone can ask questions and obtain answers. Anyone can write a questionnaire and administer it. In the same way, anyone can, with some drawing skills, draw up building plans. The problem, then, is whether they will have any meaning. In behavioral assessment, considerable skill is required in order to gain useful data which is unbiased, but perhaps even more critical is the problem of interpretation of the information once it has been gathered.[8] The quality of information one elicits can seriously limit the possibilities for interpretation and application. It should be remembered, too, that the user will want to interpret the data he receives, so that recommendations concerning the design or program should consider this factor. Even the best-managed and best-gathered behavioral data may be misused as a result of subsequent interpretations and decisions which ignore behavioral implications or consequences.

Another aspect of assessment-strategy development is the question: Where?—defining the environmental set. The assessment should take place in convenient, private, comfortable, and possibly neutral territory if maximum results are to be achieved. Confidentiality of information is usually important and should be guaranteed by the surroundings and general atmosphere. If a group is being assessed with a pencil-and-paper technique, precautions should be taken to discourage interaction between members of the group; monitoring may be required. Interviews must often be conducted on site, so that a trained interviewer will attempt to attain the full cooperation of the respondent as his primary consideration. Another question which asks "where?" considers the place which is being assessed. Traditionally, attitude assessment and social surveys have presented the stimulus as part of the question so that the person responds by indicating some level of preference.[9]

Nonetheless, although it is certainly still possible to measure attitudes, preferences, and opinions of one's existing environment, the design-oriented practitioner is often faced with the task of projecting such information for a newly designed or hypothetical space. Some stimulus must be presented to gain a response, and it must be done in such a way to assure that all respondents are indicating preferences to the same stimulus. Usually, instead of asking for a response to some concept of space, an image of it must be presented. Even then, the difficulty arises that various respondents may select different aspects of the image as the basis for their preferences. The saliency of elements can change as a result of experience within a given space. A small apartment may be initially preferred for the amount of light entering through the windows, or the view, when six months' living experience in it may alter the initial judgment when it is found to have inadequate space.

Furthermore, often what a person thinks about a space is often inconsistent with the way he responds when actually in the space. In addition, people often cannot make the implicit jumps in scale which some environmental assessment techniques demand. For example, a woman might show strong preference for a dark shade of blue, yet be unable to live with it when her walls are painted that color. Still another difficulty involved is the tendency for people to respond to novel stimuli in terms of their previous experience, even though there appears to be a bias in our society to respond favorably to anything new, regardless of other considerations. The part/whole problem presents another consideration. Even using some standard spatial stimuli allows the person to respond only on the basis of his visual input. When actually in the space, however, other sensory systems come into play. So, too, with environmental elements.

Other steps in the strategy deal with the issue of relevance, as the researcher or assessor must evaluate his assessment against some type of validation criteria. Another problem concerns the definition of behavioral possibilities, a difficult problem area for any assessor. Here one must consider not only the range of possible preferences, but also the presentation of information which is out of a person's normal experience, in order to permit the respondent to make an adequate judgment. This is a particular concern when doing programming. In assessing the needs and preferences of people behaving in poorly designed spaces, how can one convey that the new design will not only be an improvement, but that it might be something beyond their imaginations? When asked about privacy, for example, employees in one study thought in terms of floor-to-ceiling walls or partitions. To suggest that there might be other alternatives was meaningless to most of them.[10]

Once the assessment strategy has been developed to this point, one confronts the question: How? What are the actual techniques to be employed? The mechanics necessary to carry out the task most effectively must be determined, as well as the means for handling the resultant information. Behavioral and social scientists investigating human behavior have developed many useful methods and techniques. Alternatives available to the assessor might include observation, both structured and nonstructured, the utilization of available data of various types, projective or other indirect approaches, questionnaires and interviews. While all of the methods have value for certain situations and undoubtedly the best solution is to use several in concert, the most commonly used techniques for programming and evaluation are the interview and the questionnaire survey. As the target data here involve the attitudes, perceptions, beliefs, opinions, and expectations of the respondents, the interview and questionnaire both serve as a means for obtaining this type of information as other methods cannot. While there are criticisms which can legitimately be leveled at these two techniques, the experienced assessor will be cognizant of these and will design his strategy taking into consideration the limitations inherent in his chosen methods.

## TECHNIQUES

The interview is a relatively quick and effective way of gathering a large body of information. It is flexible and can be carried out on doorsteps, in offices, or even by telephone. Better control of the sample can be maintained, and less effort is necessary on the part of the respondent than in many techniques. The interview can be structured, following a predetermined set of questions, or unstructured, allowing for a free flow of information.Questions can be closed, where the respondent is given a choice of several categories; or they can be open-ended, where the person is encouraged to elaborate and amplify his responses. There is considerable latitude in the length of time involved. An interview provides the opportunity for clarification of ambiguous or conflicting information, and there is less danger of misinterpretation. At the same time, the skilled interviewer is able to estimate the validity of the material he is obtaining, as he observes how the information is given as well as what is being said. Another advantage is that the interview places the respondent in a situation involving social interaction, which could have relevance to behavior in real-life situations.

Conducting the interview is frequently an overlooked skill. The interviewer's task is not only to present and record the questions, but to elicit thorough, accurate, and unbiased information. To do this, it is necessary to establish rapport with the respondent, making him feel at ease, and developing a smooth, free-flowing, nonthreatening dialogue. Also important is that the interviewer be personable, direct, and demonstrate an appropriate level of interest and involvement with the respondent. He must lead the interview, gently but firmly returning to the subject matter if digressions occur. The skilled interviewer does not evaluate responses, nor should he permit his own values or aesthetics to be known.[11]

The interviewer can be a source of serious bias, even where precautions have been taken to avoid biasing. He may unintentionally smile, nod agreement, or write responses for only a certain class of questions. Studies have shown that nodding approval for a selection of verbal responses tends to reinforce that type of response, eliciting them more frequently than when the task is administered without the reinforcing nod.[12] Such biases can be minimized through practice and effective training. Orientation of the interviewer must provide him with an understanding of the purpose of the interview and the type of information being obtained. Thus he can probe more deeply when necessary, reducing ambiguity and misunderstanding.

Assuming a skilled and competent interviewer and a well-constructed interview, the next consideration is the practical one of the recording of the information. While small tape recorders might appear to be useful and unobtrusive, their presence often constrains the free flow of material and inhibits the establishment of rapport between the interviewer and respondent. Such devices also introduce another step into the process, as the material must be transcribed and coded from the tape. Writing the information on a form or taking notes is less obtrusive and fulfills the coding requirement. It allows the interviewer to record only pertinent, valuable data. Generally, the information resulting from an interview is rich and unambiguous. A good interviewer has clarified the material, elicited additional information, and eliminated redundant information.

The questionnaire can be used as an alternative technique to the interview, or more profitably, in conjunction with it. One of its advantages which makes it so widely used is that it is relatively inexpensive and enables the researcher to obtain information from a very large number of people. Far less skill is needed to administer a questionnaire, as long as clear directions and explanations accompany it. The standardized nature of the questionnaire affords some measure of uniformity from one situation to another. Though the instrument is always subject to interpretation by the respondents, regardless of careful attention to avoid this difficulty, the information obtained is easily coded and permits comparison between individuals. Still another advantage of questionnaires is the possibility for the respondent to remain anonymous, should the situation require it. As a person fills out a questionnaire, he is also afforded the opportunity for a more considered response, since the pressure of the immediate response of the interview is absent.

Questionnaires and interviews have particular utility in environmental research in that they are a more efficient and less expensive means of obtaining data in many situations, and in some, are the only means of obtaining data. While observations have been noted as being more reliable in gathering information about people's actual behavior in a physical setting,[13] there are certain limitations in the process. It is obvious that one must be able to observe behavior while it is happening in order to have a reliable observation study; however, there are cases where this is either impossible or inefficient. Such a case might be a natural disaster or some other crisis, such as one study on prisons which endeavored to learn about behavior during a riot.[14]

To observe behavior under these conditions, it is necessary to be present at a unique and unpredictable moment in time. It is clear, then, that to obtain information about such events, the most efficient manner is to question people who have been involved at the time. A similar situation exists in collecting information about past behavior patterns of the users of an environment, as well as other historical types of data. Another area in which survey studies are obviously best suited involves the opinions and expectations of a population. These studies ask questions about what people think of an environment or what they may expect from a building. Questionnaire studies have also served as a viable means of obtaining explanations of observed behavior when used in conjunction with observational techniques.[15] What is sought by this type of study is information concerning why people are behaving in a particular manner. This has importance in research in that there are the possibilities of observing adaptive behavior or behavior which has some underlying and unobservable cause. To obtain information about a respondent and his background is simple; one need only to ask him.

Furthermore, questionnaires can also provide a significantly useful means of generating information about alternative solutions to a design problem. By asking the user to evaluate certain solutions or to make a selection from various possibilities, the designer may have sufficient data to arrive at alternative solutions. The final area of utility for survey techniques is the feasibility of obtaining a large body of introductory information through the use of techniques such as a time/activity log, [16,17] in which the respondent keeps a daily record of his activities, where each took place, and with whom they took place. This type of study is finding increasing usefulness in environmental research.

## QUESTIONNAIRE DESIGN

We now turn to the survey instruments themselves. The interview schedule, used in formal interviewing by a trained interviewer, will involve requirements which are somewhat different from that of a self-administered questionnaire, where an untrained respondent must use the document unaided. The interview schedule format is designed for the convenience of the interviewer, as well as convenience in processing the information obtained. Ease in editing and coding can be built into the schedule, and it should be designed so that the interviewer may proceed smoothly and logically from one subject area to another. While the presence of an interviewer affords the opportunity for any necessary explanations of questions as well as clarification of responses, the overall design of the interview schedule must consider that, in many instances, more than one interviewer will be involved; yet standardization remains a critical factor. Only with prudent planning is it possible

to assume that the information elicited is comparable from interviewer to interviewer and from respondent to respondent.

Self-report questionnaires or inventories, on the other hand, must contain specific instructions on how the form is to be used and how the questions are to be answered. A cover letter or some other form of advisement is required to inform the respondents of the nature of the inquiry, how the questionnaire is to be used, and the ultimate purpose for obtaining the information. The questions themselves must be as unambiguous as possible, stated in simple terms, and kept to a minimum. Coding procedures, such as precoding the number of card columns in which the answer will be keypunched is ancillary to the main task of obtaining accurate responses and should not visually confuse the respondent. The layout of the questionnaire should be clear and legible, with bold type, capitals, or underlining used to enhance these qualities.

Since information is being obtained by asking questions, question content must be considered in light of the information being sought by the researcher. This factor becomes critically important for environmental research because of the complexity of the phenomena being assessed. Questionnairing has particular value for environmental research because it is the best way of obtaining information about what a person knows, believes, and wants. It also permits a respondent to describe past behaviors, to explain current behavior, and to predict future behaviors. Question content can be considered, for purposes of discussion, in the categories of the type of information being sought.

Information categories can be divided into two general concepts, factual or objective questions, and opinion or subjective questions. Factual questions seek out objective information that the respondent knows or to which he has access. Information elicited in this category concerns the respondent and his characteristics, his actions in the environment, social interactions with others, and explanations of his behavior. Opinion questions uncover subjective information about what the respondent believes, his feelings, his standards of action, and the reasons behind his beliefs.[18] Therefore, the design of the questions must reflect these two distinctive areas of information and be able to produce responses that are credible. Some information is best obtained by asking for it in explicit terms; other information may require that inferences be made from indirect questions. When making decisions about question content, other considerations are also involved, such as the necessity for a question, whether one or several questions are required, the specificity and concreteness of the wording, and possible biasing of responses.[19]

Another aspect of questionnaire design involves the actual wording of the questions, and to a great extent, effectiveness in this area depends upon the common sense and past experience of the questionnaire designer. It is crucial that each question be clear and readily understood by all respondents, with elimination of ambiguity and professional jargon. One must also ask whether all available alternatives are presented, whether the frame of reference is comprehensible to the respondents, and whether there are any misleading elements contained in the questions. It is important to avoid wordings which may be objectionable to the respondents in any way, emotionally loaded, or "leading." Language should be simple, direct, and appropriate for the respondent group. Items should be sequenced so that there is a natural progress from one to the next; yet one must guard against having one response influence subsequent ones. Questions should not be grouped in such a manner that a tendency is developed to respond in a particular way. The content of the question is to communicate, not to confound, opinionate, or educate. Still another underlying consideration must be to determine the best way that a respondent can answer a particular question. Can the information best be obtained by a short written response, by a checkoff answer such as multiple choice, or a scaled response? In addition, it is important that the responses be uniform and adequate for their intended purpose.

In discussing the question content of questionnaires and interviews, one tends naturally to think along the lines of traditional types of questions and responses. However, in recent years other forms of items have been developed, many with visual aids,[20] and a number of these are particularly suited for data collection in environmental research. These approaches permit the circumvention of the restrictions sometimes presented by total reliance on verbalized responses. One useful technique involves requiring a respondent to plot on a map or chart his movements through a particular segment of his environment.[21] Quite different information may be obtained in this manner to such questions as: Where do you do your shopping? or Where are your friends located? than when a person must verbalize his answer. Some environmental studies have included the presentation of diagrams of arrangements of the environment, with respondents selecting their favorite or ordering their preferences.[22] Again, such responses may vary considerably from written or oral descriptions of the same material. Useful data has also been obtained by requesting that the respondents give their response to a certain environmental stimulus in visual terms, through drawings.[23] Other drawing tasks, frequently and usefully employed, ask the person to construct a map of some portion of his environment.[24] Photographic aids can be valuable in assessing environmental preference data, especially as many people find it difficult to translate verbal material into visual images unaided.[25] In one study, subjects were asked to rate visual attributes of a photographed environment along an adjective scale.[26] Another use of photographs has been a choice situation, where the respondent gives his opinions of meaning along a semantic differential scale.[27] The same type of item might involve drawings and illustrations.[28] Three-dimensional drawings of elements have been utilized in environmental studies, such as the presentation of various gameboards from which the respondent makes a selection.[29] Still another technique involves a dimensional model of a specific environment, with the respondent manipulating movable components into his concept of an optimal arrangement.[30]

In attempting to measure behavior and assess information about behavior, social scientists have developed instruments for collecting standardized measurable data. Scales and indices are significant for this reason because they provide quantitative measures that are amenable to greater precision, statistical manipulation, and explicit interpretation on a specified dimension. In this approach, the respondent does not describe himself directly along the dimension in question, but reacts to statements relevant to it. A numerical scale can be used if it can be reliably assumed that there is an underlying psychological continuity which the respondent can realistically act upon as he rates the concept. Face validity is usually asserted for such a scale. As a rule, before constructing a new scale for use in a questionnaire, it is important to survey the literature to ascertain whether an appropriate scale is already available to measure the variables in question.

*The general rule is: use the available scale if it has qualities of validity, reliability, and utility (and in that order of priority). With such a scale, comparative and cumulative research is possible. The need to develop a new scale can almost be considered a disciplinary failure unless the variable represents a factor never before considered for measurement.*[31]

Several investigators have been concerned with attitude scaling and have developed such techniques as the Thurston Equal Appearing Interval Scale,[32] Likert Type Scale,[33] and Guttman Scale Analysis.[34] The study of individual differences and personality assessment has developed scaling techniques that could have use in environmental analysis; these are Q-sort descriptions,[35] Thematic Potential Analysis,[36] and symbolic metaphoric equivalents.[37] Both attitude and personality scales require considerable experience and sophistication in their construction. Therefore, simpler forms of scaling might be more appropriate for architectural programming and evaluation. Adjective,[38] activity[39] and mood[40] checklists are potentially very useful in these endeavors because of their brevity, use of everyday language, wide application, ease of response, and adaptation to analysis. Adjective checklists function by having the respondent check off from a list of adjectives those that describe an environment, either actual, proposed, or fantasied. To describe the actual or potential activity of a setting, a similar technique may be used; the variation is that a list of verbs would be used rather than adjectives. A mood checklist can be employed to describe a respondent's impression of an environment's ambience and atmosphere and his feeling toward it. The *Semantic Differential Rating* utilizes a series of seven-point bipolar rating scales to measure the meaning of an object or environment by evaluation, potency, and activity components.[41] In an attempt to construct these scales, the reader is directed to more detailed and sophisticated literature.

## CONCLUSION

Attitude questionnaires, opinion surveys, and evaluation of preferences and beliefs are widely used in programming and evaluation for design problems, and

through them one can gain much vital information about human behavior and habits, certain modes of action and thought, and professed desires and expectations. These implements can be sophisticated and produce a wealth of information. However, there are certain limitations involved in the use of survey methods, and the designer should be aware of these.

To a great extent, survey techniques have been overused and have been misused to gather information which is more appropriately sought by other means, such as information about actual behavior in physical settings. There are other inherent weaknesses in survey methods as well. Often, measured attitudes and behavior in real-life situations are not synonymous, because people in situations have many forces and constraints acting on their behavior which cannot be measured by an attitude questionnaire. What people profess to prefer or desire is often not what they really choose—the Edsel, for example. Then too, there is a question of higher-order priorities; the fact that people may want segregation in schools does not imply that facilities are designed to achieve that end. In addition, many researchers in the environmental field have begun to raise serious questions about simply transferring techniques that have been developed to study other problems to this new area, which has very different problems. People answering questions and stating preferences are responding in terms of their past experience, including their environmental experience.

Depending upon the kind of information being sought, questionnaires and survey techniques have shown utility and effectiveness, used singly or in conjunction with other methods of obtaining data. In using survey methods, it is critically important that the design of the instruments be carefully and knowledgeably developed, and that their implementation be in accordance with scientific method.

## NOTES AND REFERENCES

1. The theoretical basis of behavioral measurement and the collection of behavioral information have been refined over the years. It is not the purpose of this paper to review the literature in this area, but several useful books are available to the interested reader. *Social Surveys:* these techniques have been developed primarily by sociologists to obtain extensive data from large numbers of people; D. Miller, *Handbook of Research Design and*

*Social Measurement,* New York: David McKay, 1970. *Attitude questionnaires:* the study of attitudes and their measurement have been extensively developed by psychologists; A. N. Oppenheim, *Questionnaire Design and Attitude Measurement,* New York: Basic Books, 1966. *Interviewing:* the problems and process of the face-to-face interview have been of concern to behavioral scientists in general; R. L. Kahn and C. F. Cannell, *The Dynamics of Interviewing,* New York: Wiley, 1957, and H. Hyman, *Interviewing in Social Research,* Chicago: University of Chicago Press, 1954.

2.  M. Fishbein, ed., *Readings in Attitude Theory and Measurement,* New York: Wiley, 1967.

3.  Environmental Research Group, "Federal Reserve Bank of Philadelphia," Philadelphia, 1970 (mimeographed).

4.  Environmental Research Group, "Atlantic Richfield Company, Eastern Region," Philadelphia, 1971 (mimeographed).

5.  Claire Selltiz, Marie Jahoda, Martin Deutsch, and S. W. Cook, *Research Methods in Social Relations,* New York: Holt, 1959.

6.  See, for example, Walter Moleski and Ronald Goodrich, "The analysis of behavioral requirements in office settings," in William Mitchell, ed., *Environmental Design: Research and Practice: Proceedings of the EDRA3/AR8 Conference,* University of California, Los Angeles, January 1972.

7.  Environmental Research Group, "Atlantic Richfield Company," *op. cit.*

8.  Q. McNemar, *Psychological Statistics,* New York: Wiley, 1969.

9.  For a discussion of the use of this technique as part of environmental research see Kenneth Craik, "The comprehension of the everyday physical environment," *Journal of the American Institute of Planners,* Vol. 34 (January 1968), 29–37.

10. Environmental Research Group, "The assessment of an open plan and new work station concept by Interspace Incorporated," Philadelphia, 1972 (mimeographed).

11. Hyman, *op. cit.*

12. J. Matarazzo and A. Weins, *The Interview,* Chicago: Aldine-Atherton, 1972.

13. Harold M. Proshansky, "Methodology in environmental psychology: problems and issues," *Human Factors,* Vol. 14, No. 5 (1972), 451–460.

14. F. D. Moyer and E. E. Flynn, "A total system methodology which develops environments for corrections," in Mitchell, *op. cit.*

15. Proshansky, *op. cit.*

16. William Michelson, "Time budget research," in Wolfgang Preiser, ed., *Environmental Design Research, Proceedings of the Fourth International EDRA Conference,* Stroudsburg, Pa.: Dowden, Hutchinson & Ross, 1973.

17. Sim Van der Ryn and Murray Silverstein, *Dorms at Berkeley: An Environmental Analysis,* Berkeley, Calif.:

Center for Planning andDevelopment Research, University of California, Berkeley, 1967.

18. Selltiz et al., *op. cit.*

19. Common sense, informational ordering of priorities and ethical considerations must govern the final decision of inclusion or exclusion into the form.

20. For a review of "environmental display" techniques, see Craik, *op. cit.*

21. F. Stuart Chapin, Jr., "Activity systems and urban structure: a working scheme," *Journal of the American Institute of Planners,* Vol. 34 (January 1968), 11–18.

22. William Michelson, *Man and His Urban Environment: A Sociological Approach,* Reading, Mass.: Addison-Wesley, 1970.

23. Lucille Nahemow, "Research in a novel environment," *Environment and Behavior,* Vol. 3 (March 1971), 81–102.

24. F. C. Ladd, "Black youths view their environments: neighborhood maps," *Environment and Behavior,* Vol. 2 (June 1970), 52–73.

25. R. M. Craun, Jr., "Visual determinants of preference for dwelling environs," in Henry Sanoff and Sidney Cohn, eds., *EDRA1: Proceedings of the First Annual Environmental Design Research Association Conference,* Raleigh, N.C., 1970.

26. Henry Sanoff, "Measuring visual attributes of the physical environment," in Sanoff and Cohn, *op. cit.*

27. Robert G. Hershberger, "A study of meaning and architecture," in Sanoff and Cohn, *op. cit.*

28. David V. Canter, "An intergroup comparison of connotative dimensions in architecture," *Environment and Behavior,* Vol. 1 (June 1969), 37–48.

29. Henry Sanoff, *Techniques of Evaluation for Designers,* Raleigh, N.C.: Design Research Laboratory, School of Design, North Carolina State University, 1968, 58–59.

30. Robert Propst, *The Office: A Facility Based on Change,* Ann Arbor, Mich.: Herman Miller, 1968.

31. Miller, *op. cit.*

32. L. L. Thurstone and J. Chave, *The Measurement of Attitudes: A Psychological Method and Some Experiments with a Scale for Measuring Attitude Toward the Church,* Chicago: University of Chicago Press, 1929.

33. R. Likert, *A Technique for the Measurement of Attitudes,* New York: Columbia University Press, 1932.

34. S. A. Stouffer, *The American Soldier: Measurement and Prediction,* Princeton, N.J.: Princeton University Press, 1950.

35. J. Block, *The Q Sort Method in Personality Assessment and Psychiatric Research,* Springfield, Ill.: Charles C. Thomas, 1961.

36. William Michelson, "An empirical analysis of urban environmental preferences," *Journal of the American Institute of Planners,* Vol. 32 (November 1966), 355–360.

37. F. Barron, "Psychology of imagination," *Scientific American,* Vol. 199 (1958), 150–166.

38. H. G. Gough and A. B. Heilbrun, Jr., *The Adjective Check-*

*list Manual,* Palo Alto, Calif.: Consulting Psychologists Press, 1965.

39. Craik, *op. cit.*
40. B. Nowlis, "Research with this mood adjective checklist," in S. S. Tomlins and C. E. Izard, eds., *Affect, Cognition and Personality,* New York: Springer, 1965.
41. Charles E. Osgood, G. Suci, and P. H. Tannenbaum, *The Measurement of Meaning,* Urbana, Ill.: University of Illinois Press, 1957.

*To alleviate poverty in the visual environment, knowledge of perceptual phenomena is necessary to bring the designed environment into equilibrium with human systems. The aim of this paper is twofold: to assess the relation between visual satisfaction and complexity, ambiguity, and novelty, and to develop a model which can be utilized by designers to describe desirable attributes. The experiment described focuses on the ordering of visual attributes through the use of bipolar semantic differential scales. Two groups, experts in design and research and planning students, were asked to describe an ideal environment and to rate visual displays on these scales. The results show that there is ambiguity inherent in our language and strong value association with the connotative meaning of words. There appears to be a dichotomy between what the architects conceive of as "ideal" and how they rate actual visual displays. "Interest" and "satisfaction" are positively associated with affective judgments of the environmental displays described as novel, dynamic, stimulating, bold, serious, and individual. Also, attributes of preferred environments are described as complex, stimulating, sensuous, dynamic, and so on.*

# Measuring Attributes of the Visual Environment

**Henry Sanoff**

**North Carolina State University**

It is generally accepted that man's behavior is influenced by the environment in which he lives. The environment is multidimensional and includes both a social and physical component. Within the latter are spatial attributes of the environment which contribute to the shaping of the individual's style of life.

Our vernacular past is rich with visually satisfying environments whose development was based on a leisurely sequence of growth. Today, development is rapid and changes come swiftly; urban environments alter their character within a few years. The population increase and a mania for speed outweigh consideration of quality, resulting in environments created with very little forethought. With increasing urban development and a commensurate loss of aesthetic quality, the environment becomes monotonous, impersonal, and standardized.

Today, people experience very little more than paving, sidewalks, building walls, and advertising signs. Rarely is visual satisfaction experienced and, as a result, the individual's aesthetic sensitivity remains unawakened. Man perceives the visual world and responds to it through the areas of his potentialities that have been made functional by environmental stimulation. The life experiences determine what part of one's genetic endowment is enriched with functional attributes. There is also evidence indicating that individuals have a requirement for sensory intake of appreciably varied perceptions and that an extreme lack of external stimulation can have deleterious consequences.

Only recently has concern for quality in the environment been emerging. There is a growing awareness that some form of conscious influence over the physical environment's visual appearance is necessary. People are coming to accept the need for some sort of public regulation to preserve inherited environments and avoid extreme incongruity, particularly if visually satisfying new communities are to be achieved in the future. There is, however, little precise agreement on what the appropriate methods of aesthetic regulation should be. Many approaches have been tried to date,[1] often with unforeseen results; for example:

1. "Look-alike" regulations, seeking to enforce uniformity in a neighborhood, seem to foster monotony.
2. "No-look-alike" regulations, intended to compel variety, produce chaos.

Indirect influences have been exerted by authorities

other than just ad hoc public groups. Descriptions of what constitutes visual appeal by the Federal Housing Authority are related to the qualities of simplicity, harmony, and refinement. They define *simplicity* as freedom from complexity, intricacies, and elaborateness; *harmony* as a result of a pleasing arrangement of well-proportioned elements or as when there is such accord between the various parts of the composition that the effect of unity is produced; *refinement,* sometimes termed "good taste," is characterized by freedom from ostentation and by restraint in design.

The underlying premises of these regulations tend to be restrictive, while the aesthetic assumptions are based on prejudice. Perceptual "goodness" is largely haphazard rather than intentional, since few attempts have been made at developing a theoretical framework based on the visual impact of the environment. Designers of man's environment have had little more to rely upon as a basis for their decisions than their own intuitive responses to the environment. Though the designer today may be dissatisfied with the appropriateness of his solution, he is still unable to predict its consequences with any degree of accuracy. The criteria for the design of the visual environment have not been based on a systematic analysis of the user's perceptions, but on the intuitions, formalized into heuristics, of a group of aesthetically inclined individuals.

Freedom from imitating eclectic and ineffective forms was initiated by twentieth-century aesthetic philosophies. There are at present, however, no viable control mechanisms to prevent visual disorder or monotony despite the growing awareness of the need for them, nor does there appear to be a consensus as to the appropriate design prescriptions for overcoming dissatisfaction with the environment. As the patterns of the urban fabric become more monotonous or chaotic by design and public regulation, the possible rewards of stimulation diminish. To alleviate the visual poverty in the environment, knowledge about perceptual phenomena is necessary to increase sensitivities to the interrelation between human behavior and the physical environment. As A. E. Parr succinctly states, "the variety inherent in the natural environment has been succeeded by a far smaller selection of much more vigorously repetitve forms which has recently been reduced to even greater uniformity by explicit architec-

tural doctrine. A loss of diversity, particularly in the visually perceived environment, is one universal, and still continuing trend in the transition from virgin country to city streets."[2]

René Dubos, indicating that "we must shun uniformity of the environment," states that the present "creeping monotony" can be overcome by "creating as many diverse environments as possible."[3] Though his concept of environment is holistic in nature, the observations appear to be appropriate for many environmental circumstances. While diversity in the designed environment can give rise to sensory stimulation, a more homogeneously uniform environment may discourage any sensory arousal. Therefore, judgments of satisfaction with the physical environment are manifestations of aroused visual stimuli sustaining the interest of the perceiver.

Knowledge of man's visual comprehension of his physical environment is primarily the responsibility of *environmental psychology,* a science which may be defined as the psychological study of behavior as it relates to the everyday physical environment.[4] How people perceive their everyday physical world, the distinctions they make about it, and the significant factors affecting comprehension are all questions of great importance to architects and urban designers and require immediate attention. It seems evident that knowledge of the perceptual responses elicited by visual stimuli can be gained through the use of psychological theory and testing techniques. Experimental psychologists have conducted many laboratory studies using controlled visual stimuli and their corresponding responses. D. E. Berlyne's experiments in complexity and novelty led him to conclude that the more complex the stimuli the stronger the investigatory reflex elicited.[5] He also states that diversity, complexity, novelty, and ambiguity in a composition are conditions which lead to "arousal" and "attention."[6] Order, organization, symmetry, and repetition keep arousal within moderate and tolerable bounds. An aesthetic product has to accomplish two things: (1) gain (and maintain) the attention of an audience, and (2) keep arousal within limits. D. O. Hebb describes the stimulus field as "requiring some familiarity, yet some novelty to sustain the interest of the perceiver."[7] Carl Pfaffmann states that sensory stimulation plays a significant role in motivating as well as guiding behavior—"in controlling behavior for the pleasure of sensation," as he says.[8]

According to much of the literature of experimental psychology, the primary conditions for human sensory stimulation associated with visual environments are that the environments be continual, varied, and patterned.[9] There also exists a body of experimental literature to justify that nonfulfillment of any of these conditions produces stress and will ultimately become intolerable. Studies dealing with various forms of sensory deprivation demonstrate conclusively the need for continuity and novelty.[10] They indicate that exploratory behavior regarding novelty seeking, fantasy, and preference for moderately nonredundant figures over highly redundant ones begins when there is not enough visual information available.

The above findings and observations relate directly to the principles of good design and to the concept of "good Gestalt" as a proper end for the process of design.[11] A good Gestalt requires a high degree of internal redundancy, that is, predictability or syntactical coherence. Good Gestalt is also the absence of deviation from a predicted pattern. The less information needed to define a given organization, the better it qualifies as a good Gestalt. However, the many experiments that deal with complexity and novelty disqualify good Gestalt as a design principle because it tends towards states of diminishing novelty in the environment. Valuable as these studies are, their focus is extremely limited. They do, however, suggest possible avenues of approach.

The awareness of the need for greater perceptual interest in the physical world has recently been expressed by David Stea,[12] Francois Vigier,[13] Amos Rapoport and R. Kantor,[14] and many others. Thus the approach herein presented is predicated on the notion that physical forms are no longer ends in themselves, but means employed to bring the designed environment into equilibrium with human systems.

The problem then is to determine peoples' affective response to architecture or environmental perception—that is, how people perceive their environment. Studies of environmental perception involve four groups of variables—observers, modes of observation, environments, and attributes of environments. The experiment described in this paper focuses on the visual attributes of the environment, isolating all other stimulus inputs, such as auditory or olfactory, in order to ascertain the degree to which judgments based only on visual attributes will influence visual satisfaction. The intent is to open up avenues of exploration for the systematic analysis of responses relating to the visual environment. The specific aims of the experiments are (1) to assess the relation between visual satisfaction and complexity, ambiguity, and novelty,[15] and (2) to develop a model which can be utilized by designers to describe the desired attributes.

Before any assertions can be made, a common vocabulary among designers must be constructed, particularly if the terms are to be used for guiding designers to achieve complexity, ambiguity, and novelty in the physical environment. In order to make diagnostic predictions of useful accuracy, a fund of systematic empirical knowledge concerning stable relationships between descriptive characteristics of environmental displays and evaluative criterion indices has to become available.[16]

## THE EXPERIMENT

There are, generally, two ways in which we can examine the structure of the physical world, that is, two fundamental operations for sorting out meaningful relations among words: contrast and grouping. Attributes can be isolated so that the physical world can be ordered with respect to the attribute. Or, alternatively, descriptions can be made in terms of collections of similarities of attributes. This experiment focuses on the ordering of attributes, though it is well recognized that other associative techniques could be developed in future experiments.

Assessment techniques can be used to permit expressions of varied and subtle reactions to environmental phenomena via adjectival descriptions of the images they evoke. The encoding instrument used in eliciting descriptive judgments is based on a technique that uses a bipolar scale of attributes in the form of a semantic differential.[17]

In order to identify these attributes for study, an ad hoc list was drawn from the terms most frequently used by designers in their judgments and descriptions of the environment. The properties selected for analysis incorporate a consensus of opinions about visual attributes; however, the list is by no means exhaustive or comprehensive. It undoubtedly reflects a professional bias, since the properties were identified by professional designers. The words involve a considerable range of meaning varying with time, place, and context of perception and with the background and experience of the respondent.

Listed below are the polar nouns and adjectives incorporated in the testing instrument. R. F. Terwilliger demonstrates by the "free association and semantic differential"[18] that the accuracy of the rating scale is dependent upon the degree of ambiguity of the descriptor and, as the number of definitions of a word increases, its ambiguity increases. It is, therefore, assumed that the selection of less ambiguous words will be an important factor in determining the subject's reaction to the word. Thus the selection was based on previous findings as well as probabilistic assumptions.

Noun and adjective pairs used in the semantic differential scale are as follows:

simplicity–complexity
stimulating-sedative
harmony-discord
roughness-smoothness
ambiguity-clarity
formal-informal
symmetry-asymmetry
boldness-unobtrusiveness
interest-boredom
hardness-softness
individual-universal
unity-variety
austere-sensuous
novel–common
satisfaction-frustration
paradoxicality-comprehensibility
exhilarated-depressed
high-low
peaceful-disruptive
static-dynamic
ordered-disordered
uniform-divergent
tense-relaxed
calm-violent
intimate-distant
like-dislike

Several of the terms used to denote properties were value-laden. To many, symmetry has a negative and asymmetry a positive connotation. Novel may be viewed more favorably than common; static and dynamic seem to be bad and good, respectively. An attempt was made to include "objective" words, though they, too, have different values, depending on the attitudes of the respondents and their images of visual satisfaction.

In spite of the emotional significance of the words selected, any replacement would invalidate comparative analysis in future experiments and alter an unknown portion of responses. This technique can elicit a large number of specific judgments about a complex aesthetic stimulus through a forced-choice protocol. Responses along the scale between each pair of terms indicate the direction and intensity of each judgment, while permitting a wide discrimination of choice. Through controlled associations, connotative and denotative judgments of the visual world were made. The relative strength of these attributes as they affect judgments of satisfaction, then, becomes of prime interest.

Descriptions of the attributes of an "ideal" environment were elicited from thirty experts (architects) in research and design (Group 1, Figure 1) and thirty graduate students in planning (Group 2, Figure 1), utilizing the descriptive attribute scale on a seven-point continuum. (The architects represented a national sample drawn from the Environment and Behavior Directory.)

Results from the two groups of respondents differed substantially.[19] Group 1 displayed an unusual degree of neutrality while Group 2 was more varied in its responses. Clustering from Group 2 appeared to be symmetrical around each concept. The consistent invariance of Group 1 may be imputed to be the designers' paradigm, where the environment is a balance of positive and negative factors. The student group responded in a more predictable manner.

The same two groups were subsequently requested to describe Environmental Displays *a, b, c,* and *d* (see Figures 6–9 at the end of this article), using the identical DAS (Descriptive Attribute Scale). The photographs displayed four different residential settings that varied in architectural style. The intent was also to test the sensitivity of the instrument, that is, to see if the seman-

## Group 1 (Architects)

## Group 2 (Students)

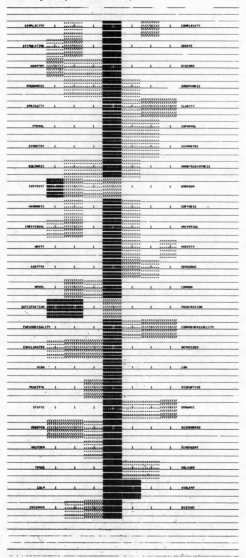

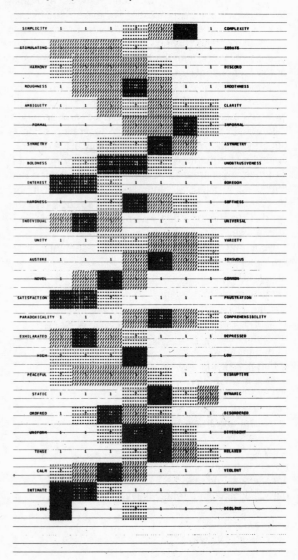

**Figure 1**
**Descriptions of the ideal environment**

## Group 1 (Architects)

## Group 2 (Students)

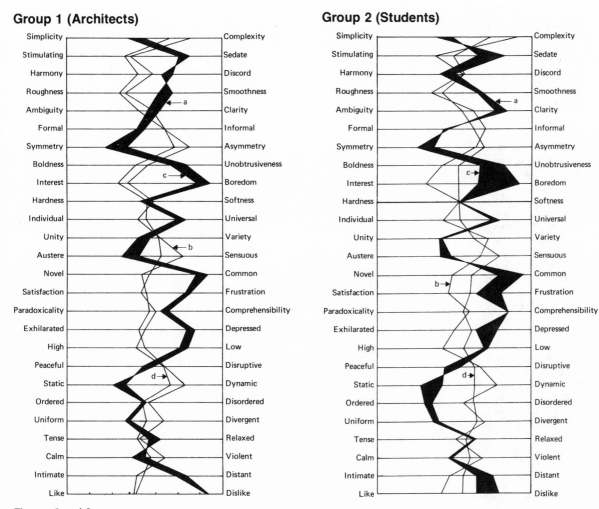

**Figures 2 and 3**
**Arithmetic mean distribution for environmental displays *a*/*b*/*c*/*d***

**Table 1**
**Analysis of Variance: Levels of Significance Between Environmental Displays**

| Attributes | Group 1 ED Comparisons | | | | | | Group 2 ED Comparisons | | | | | |
|---|---|---|---|---|---|---|---|---|---|---|---|---|
| | a–b | a–c | a–d | b–c | b–d | c–d | a–b | a–c | a–d | b–c | b–d | c–d |
| 1. Simplicity–Complexity | 0.01 | | 0.01 | 0.01 | | 0.01 | 0.01 | | | 0.01 | | 0.01 |
| 2. Stimulating–Sedate | 0.01 | | 0.01 | 0.01 | | 0.01 | 0.01 | 0.01 | 0.01 | 0.01 | 0.01 | |
| 3. Harmony–Discord | | | | | | | | | | | | |
| 4. Roughness–Smoothness | 0.01 | 0.05 | 0.01 | 0.01 | | 0.01 | 0.01 | | | 0.01 | | |
| 5. Ambiguity–Clarity | | | | | | | 0.01 | 0.01 | | | | 0.01 |
| 6. Formal–Informal | 0.01 | | 0.01 | | | 0.01 | 0.01 | 0.05 | 0.01 | | | 0.05 |
| 7. Symmetry–Asymmetry | 0.01 | | 0.01 | 0.01 | | 0.01 | 0.01 | | 0.01 | 0.01 | | 0.01 |
| 8. Boldness–Unobtrusiveness | 0.01 | | 0.01 | 0.01 | | 0.01 | 0.01 | | 0.01 | 0.01 | | 0.05 |
| 9. Interest–Boredom | 0.01 | | 0.01 | 0.01 | | 0.01 | 0.01 | 0.01 | 0.01 | 0.01 | 0.01 | |
| 10. Hardness–Softness | | | | | | | | | | | | |
| 11. Individual–Universal | 0.01 | | 0.01 | 0.01 | | 0.01 | 0.01 | | 0.01 | 0.01 | | 0.01 |
| 12. Unity–Variety | | | | | | | 0.01 | | 0.01 | 0.01 | | 0.01 |
| 13. Austere–Sensuous | 0.01 | | 0.01 | 0.01 | | 0.01 | 0.01 | | 0.01 | 0.01 | | |
| 14. Novel–Common | 0.01 | | 0.01 | 0.01 | | 0.01 | 0.01 | 0.01 | 0.01 | 0.01 | 0.01 | 0.01 |
| 15. Satisfaction–Frustration | 0.01 | | 0.01 | 0.01 | | 0.01 | 0.01 | 0.05 | 0.01 | 0.01 | | |
| 16. Paradoxicality–Comprehensibility | 0.01 | 0.01 | | | | | 0.01 | | 0.01 | 0.01 | | 0.01 |
| 17. Exhilarated–Depressed | 0.01 | | 0.01 | 0.01 | | 0.01 | 0.01 | 0.05 | 0.01 | 0.01 | 0.05 | |
| 18. High–Low | 0.01 | | 0.01 | 0.01 | | 0.01 | 0.01 | | 0.01 | 0.01 | 0.05 | 0.05 |
| 19. Peaceful–Disruptive | | | | | | | 0.01 | | 0.01 | | | 0.01 |
| 20. Static–Dynamic | 0.01 | | 0.01 | 0.01 | | 0.01 | 0.01 | | 0.01 | 0.01 | 0.05 | 0.01 |
| 21. Ordered–Disordered | | | | | | | 0.01 | | 0.01 | 0.01 | | 0.01 |
| 22. Uniform–Divergent | | | | | | | 0.01 | | 0.01 | 0.01 | | 0.01 |
| 23. Tense–Relaxed | | | 0.05 | | | | | | | | | |
| 24. Calm–Violent | 0.05 | | | | | | 0.01 | | 0.01 | 0.01 | | 0.01 |
| 25. Intimate–Distant | 0.01 | | 0.01 | 0.01 | | 0.01 | 0.01 | | 0.01 | 0.05 | | |
| 26. Like–Dislike | 0.01 | | 0.01 | 0.01 | | 0.01 | 0.01 | 0.01 | 0.01 | 0.01 | | |

tic scale could distinguish between subtle differences as well as obvious stylistic differences.

Figures 2 and 3 represent the arithmetic mean distribution for each of the sample groups. The profiles describe the polarization between EDa,c and EDb,d, and the similarity in judgmental responses of both sample groups. Based on the intensity of responses, EDa,c, which were extremely disliked, polarized to more extremes than EDb,d, which were slightly liked. The descriptors which are associated with like and dislike are indicated below. It appears that there is a more positive consensus in describing the characteristics of what is disliked than what is liked.

| *Dislike (EDa,c)* | | *Like (EDb,d)* |
|---|---|---|
| Simplicity | Common | Complexity |
| Sedate | Frustration | Stimulating |
| Symmetry | Depressed | Roughness |
| Unobtrusiveness | Static | Asymmetry |
| Boredom | Uniform | Interest |
| Universal | Distant | Sensuous |
| Austere | | Dynamic |

## The Analysis of Variance

Each of the sample groups' responses to each of the ED's was analyzed to discover which attributes appeared to distinguish between the ED's. The primary concern is to discover which of the adjective pairs can best describe the differences between all combinations of environmental displays. It is also important to know how reliable this information is and that a repetition of the study would yield the same results. The analysis of variance (AOV), then, is a statistical test for discerning where the greatest variation of responses occurs, and the level of significance is a measure of reproduceability.

From Table 1 it can be seen that the concept "simplicity–complexity" is significant in distinguishing between ED's *a,b, a,d, b,c,* and *c,d* (for Group 1); however, since ED's *a,c,* as well as *b,d,* are similar, the simplicity–complexity continuum is not sufficiently sensitive. From the analysis it is clear that verbal concepts are most appropriate for describing visual information when the features of the environment are substantially different, as in ED *a,b, a,d, b,c,* and *c,d.* Verbal concepts, or polar opposite scales do not seem to be sufficiently sensitive nor acccurate in describing environments that possess similar attribute characteristics such as ED *a,c* and *b,d.*

## Factor Analysis

*Factor analysis* is a name given to a class of techniques whose purpose consists of data reduction and summarization. It is used primarily when no a priori patterns of causality are available and when there is interest in the whole set of relationships among variables characterizing some phenomenon. The factor analytic method, then, is one of transforming a given set of variables, twenty-six attributes, into a new set of composite variables or factors that are orthogonal (uncorrelated) to each other. These factors provide the categories which form the cognitive structure of interrelationships.

First, one prepares a correlation matrix of the twenty-six attributes and their degree of interaction. In Figures 4 and 5, which show the correlation matrices, it can be observed that the attributes with the highest set of interactions for both groups were as follows: (2)

stimulation, (9) interest, (14) novel, (17) exhilarated, (20) dynamic, and (26) like. These attributes, in fact, constitute Factor 1 (Table 2). The array of twenty-six intercorrelations are reduced into smaller sets of factors.

Factor 1 is the single best summary of the relationships exhibited in the data since it accounts for the greatest amount of variance in the data structure (40.2 percent for Group 1 and for Group 2). Factor 2 can be described as the second best combination of variables which account for the proportion of variance not accounted for by Factor 1. Subsequent factors are defined similarly until all variance is exhausted.

The emerging attribute cluster patterns that discriminate between each of the factors in Group 1 (architects) are described as follows (seeTable 2):

Factor 1: interest, exhilarated, like, satisfaction, novel, dynamic, stimulating, high, sensuous, intimate.

The attributes of Factor 1 appear to connote "affective" response to the stimulus (environmental scenes). This factor appears to form the major cognitive dimension for most of the respondents.

Factor 2: relaxed, softness, comprehensibility, clarity, peaceful, ordered.

These attributes reflect the respondents' "judgments" about the stimulus.

Factor 3: uniform, unity, formal, symmetry.

These attributes appear to be more descriptive of the "spatial" meaning of the stimulus to the respondent.

The factors for Group 2 (students) are as follows:

Factor 1: like, interest, satisfaction, exhilarated, stimulating, novel, dynamic, intimate, sensuous, high.

These attributes correspond identically to Factor 1 for Group 1.

Factor 2: ordered, clarity, harmony, comprehensibility, symmetry, uniform, unity, formal.

These attributes correspond to Factor 3, Group 1, and describe the "spatial" meaning of the display.

Factor 3: tense, violent, disruptive, complexity, paradoxicality.

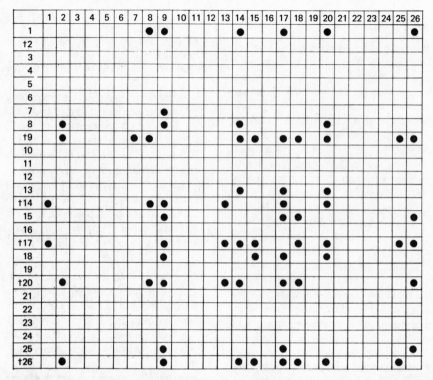

†Attributes with the highest set of intercorrelations

**Figure 4**
**Group 1: correlation matrix (attributes with a value of 0.65 or more)**

These attributes correspond to Factor 2, Group 1, and are described as "judgmental."

Of the four Environmental Displays presented, there appears to have been the greatest difference of opinion about the most preferred and the greatest agreement about the most disliked ED's. This quality of ambiguity in the environment, which was a function of the total set of responses to the total set of ED's, appears to be an environmental attribute of considerable significance. Thus it appears that on the basis of the responses of the two groups to the set of environmental displays, the salient factors in describing visual attributes are the affective meaning, evaluative meaning, and spatial meaning.

## CONCLUSION

From this study we may impute that the attributes of preferred environments appear to be "complexity," "stimulating," "sensuous," "dynamic," and so on. The less-preferred environments are described by the attributes "simplicity," "universal," "symmetry," "unobtrusiveness," and the like. It is also interesting to note that architects do not differ substantially from students when asked to rate existing environments. It is clear that there is an ambiguity inherent in our language and a strong value association with the connotative meaning of words. It is particularly important for architects to sort out this ambiguity, since we have already witnessed a "universal" approach to environmental design which

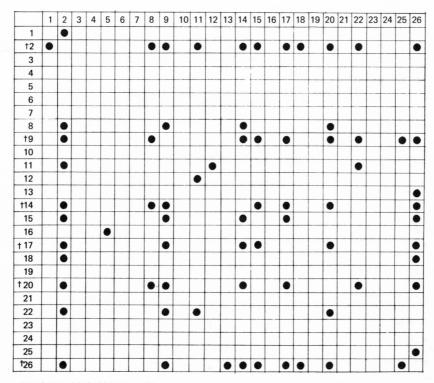

†Attributes with the highest set of intercorrelations

**Figure 5**
**Group 2: correlation matrix (attributes with a value of 0.65 or more)**

has produced boredom, frustration, unobtrusiveness, and all the other negative associations with "universal."

It may also appear to some readers that many of the responses to the turn-of-the-century street scenes in the study were more nostalgic than descriptive. However, it should be pointed out that all the dwellings were constructed by "speculative builders." Can it be possible that we will look upon scenes *a* and *c* with the same nostalgia 100 years from now as we do both *b* and *d*? Is it really a function of age or is there an association between the logic of the visual form and its complexity that accounts for the differences in perceptions of both sets of pictures?

Further, what the architects indicated as "ideal" turns out to be substantially different from their preferred rat- ings of the environmental scenes. Paradoxically, there appears to be a stronger relationship between their descriptions of the "ideal" and least preferred environments. While there is no causal explanation for this anomaly, one can advance the argument that the many heuristics (rules of thumb) in architecture have been built on contradictions such as "unity in variety" or "less is more." This suggests that the good or ideal environment consists of a balance of all attributes, which is inconsistent with the ratings reported by the architects.

The attributes "interest" and "satisfaction," two important consumer variables, are positively associated with "affective" judgments of the environmental displays described as novel, dynamic, stimulating, boldness, sensuous, and individual. Since there was a

**Table 2**
**Principal Factor Components**

| Group 1 (Architects) | | Group 2 (Students) | |
|---|---|---|---|
| Attribute | Factor loading[a] | Attribute | Factor loading[a] |
| **Factor 1 (40.2%)** | | **Factor 1** | |
| *interest*–boredom | −0.92 | *like*–dislike | −0.98 |
| *exhilarated*–depressed | −0.90 | *interest*–boredom | −0.89 |
| *like*–dislike | −0.89 | *satisfaction*–frustration | −0.87 |
| *satisfaction*–frustration | −0.84 | *exhilarated*–depressed | −0.83 |
| *novel*–common | −0.84 | *stimulating*–sedate | −0.82 |
| static–*dynamic* | 0.83 | *novel*–common | −0.81 |
| *stimulating*–sedate | −0.81 | static–*dynamic* | −0.76 |
| *high*–low | −0.79 | *intimate*–distant | −0.75 |
| austere–*sensuous* | 0.75 | austere–*sensuous* | 0.73 |
| *intimate*–distant | −0.74 | *high*–low | −0.70 |
| *boldness*–unobtrusiveness | −0.68 | *boldness*–unobtrusiveness | −0.66 |
| symmetry–*asymmetry* | 0.67 | *individual*–universal | −0.61 |
| *individual*–universal | −0.61 | uniform–*divergent* | 0.59 |
| *harmony*–discord | −0.59 | simplicity–*complexity* | 0.52 |
| *roughness*–smoothness | −0.48 | unity–*variety* | 0.45 |
| simplicity–*complexity* | 0.40 | *roughness*–smoothness | −0.45 |

[a]Positive or negative factor loadings correspond to the attributes that are italicized.

close correlation between student responses and those of the architects, the attributes appear to be meaningful. It should be recognized, however, that response information has been response defined. That is, the respondents' ratings were analyzed to provide information about the respondents and their perception, more so than identifiable characteristics of the stimulus (environmental scenes).[20] Additional techniques need to be explored, partially to test the efficacy of the semantic differential and partially to generate further insights into response patterns to visual fields.[21]

The major contribution of this research lies in its heuristic possibilities. Clearly, environmental descriptions are amenable to scientific investigation. One can reduce the terminology of environmental descriptions to a parsimonious number of factors. The future uses of descriptors will be to study the interaction between behavior occurring in an environment and the physical properties of the environment as well as its predictive and evaluative implications. Results from empirical studies in environmental perception can be of significant influence in effecting a greater visual impact of designed environments.

**Table 2**
**(continued)**

| Group 1 (Architects) | | Group 2 (Students) | |
| --- | --- | --- | --- |
| *Attribute* | *Factor loading*[a] | *Attribute* | *Factor loading*[a] |
| Factor 2 (18.1%) | | Factor 2 | |
| tense–*relaxed* | 0.75 | *ordered*–disordered | −0.76 |
| *calm*–violent | −0.73 | ambiguity–*clarity* | 0.75 |
| hardness–*softness* | 0.63 | harmony–discord | −0.72 |
| paradoxicality–*comprehensibility* | 0.60 | paradoxicality–*comprehensibility* | 0.72 |
| ambiguity–*clarity* | 0.48 | *symmetry*–asymmetry | −0.68 |
| *peaceful*–disruptive | −0.48 | *uniform*–divergent | −0.58 |
| *ordered*–disordered | −0.46 | *unity*–variety | −0.53 |
| *simplicity*–complexity | −0.45 | *formal*–informal | −0.53 |
| boldness–*unobtrusiveness* | 0.44 | *simplicity*–complexity | −0.54 |
| roughness–*smoothness* | 0.42 | *peaceful*–disruptive | −0.54 |
| | | roughness–*smoothness* | 0.53 |
| | | individual–*universal* | 0.52 |
| Factor 3 (6.6%) | | Factor 3 | |
| *uniform*–divergent | −0.79 | *tense*–relaxed | −0.82 |
| *unity*–variety | −0.75 | calm–*violent* | 0.68 |
| *formal*–informal | −0.69 | peaceful–*disruptive* | 0.61 |
| *ordered*–disordered | −0.60 | | |
| ambiguity–*clarity* | 0.55 | | |
| *peaceful*–disruptive | −0.53 | | |
| paradoxicality–*comprehensibility* | 0.43 | | |
| *symmetry*–asymmetry | −0.43 | | |
| *simplicity*–complexity | −0.42 | | |

**Note: Figures 6–9 appear on the following four pages**

Group 1

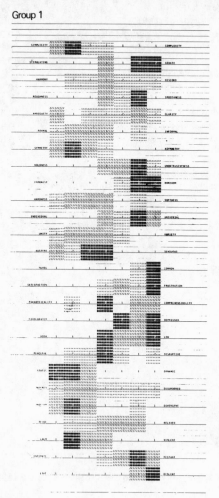

Group 2

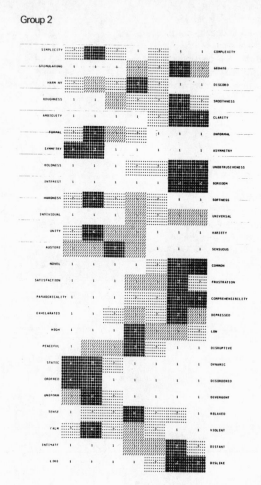

**Figure 6**
**Environmental display (EDa)**

Group 1

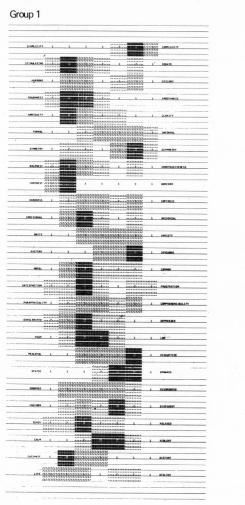

Group 2

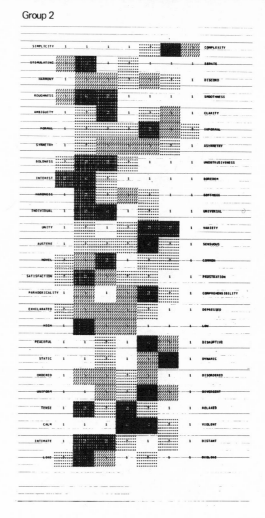

**Figure 7**
**Environmental display (ED*b*)**

Group 1

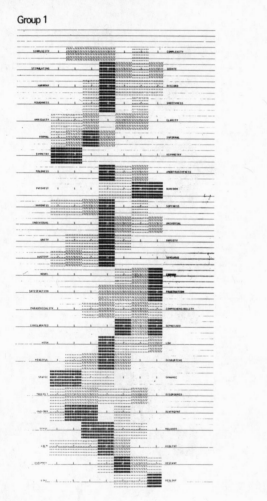

Group 2

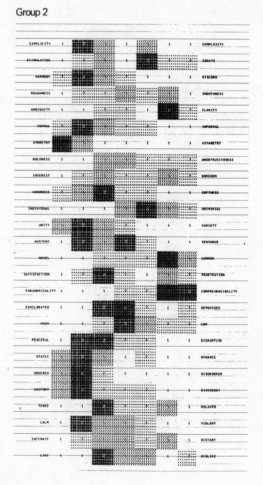

**Figure 8**
**Environmental display (EDc)**

Group 1

Group 2

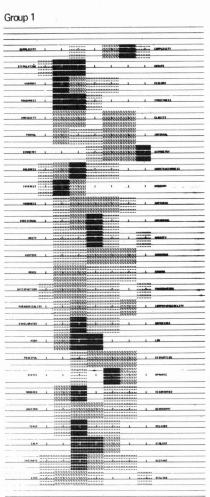

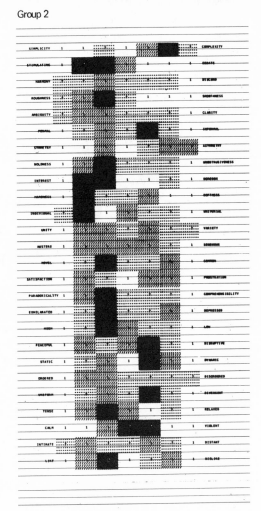

**Figure 9**
**Environmental display (ED***d***)**

## NOTES AND REFERENCES

1. Henry Fagin and Robert Weinberg, *Planning and Community Appearance,* New York: Regional Plan Association, 1958.
2. A. E. Parr, "Psychological aspects of urbanology," *Journal of Social Issues,* Vol. 22 (October 1966), 40.
3. René Dubos, "Man adapting," in W. R. Ewald, Jr., ed., *Environment for Man,* Bloomington, Ind.: Indiana University Press, 1967, 19–20.
4. Kenneth Craik, "The comprehension of the everyday physical environment," *Journal of the American Institute of Planners,* Vol. 34 (January 1968), 29–37.
5. D. E. Berlyne, "The influence of complexity and novelty in visual figures on orienting responses," *Journal of Experimental Psychology,* Vol. 55 (March 1958), 289–296.
6. D. E. Berlyne, *Conflict, Arousal and Curiosity,* New York: McGraw-Hill, 1960.
7. D. O. Hebb, *The Organization of Behavior,* New York: Wiley, 1949.
8. Carl Pfaffman, "The pleasure of sensation," *Psychology Review,* Vol. 67 (July 1960), 253–268.
9. G. Miller, E. Galanter, and K. Pribram, *Plans and the Structure of Behavior,* New York: Holt, 1960.
10. Hy Day, "Attention, curiosity and exploration," in Martin Krampen, ed., *Design and Planning,* Waterloo, Ontario: University of Waterloo Press, 1965.
11. Daniel Solomon, "The synthetic fallacy," Department of Architecture, University of California, Berkeley, 1965.
12. David Stea, "Space, territory and human movement," *Landscape* Vol. 15 (Autumn 1965), 13–16.
13. François Vigier, "An experimental approach to urban design," *Journal of the American Institute of Planners,* Vol. 31 (February 1965), 21–29.
14. Amos Rapoport and R. Kantor, "Complexity and ambiguity in environmental design," *Journal of the American Institute of Planners,* Vol. 33 (July 1967), 210–221.
15. Complexity is defined as "an intricate combination of physical elements." Ambiguity would be alternative reactions to the visual environment or associated with variability in environmental descriptions. Ambiguity thus tends to result in complexity.
16. J. Deese, *The Structure of Associations in Language and Thought,* Baltimore: The Johns Hopkins Press, 1965.
17. Charles E. Osgood, G. Suci, and P. H. Tannenbaum, *The Measurement of Meaning,* Urbana, Ill.: University of Illinois Press, 1957.
18. R. F. Terwilliger, "Free association patterns as a factor relating to semantic differential responses," *Journal of Abnormal Social Psychology,* Vol. 69 (1962), 87–94.
19. The visual mapping of the frequency distribution was accomplished by the adaption of the SYMAP graphic program which represents data as points in space (ED, *a, b, c, d*). The graphic distribution of value into ranges from white to black is represented with black corresponding to 50% or more of the total responses while white represents 10% of the response. The figure in each cell represents the percentile value from 1 to 5.
20. R. A. M. Gregson, "Aspects of the theoretical status of aesthetic response typologies," *Psychology Reports,* Vol. 5 (October 1964), 395–398.
21. D. E. Berlyne and S. Peckham, "The semantic differential and other measures of reaction to visual complexity," *Canadian Journal of Psychology,* Vol. 20, No. 2 (1966), 125–135.

This paper advocates the use of unobtrusive measures as methods for gathering information about the "fit" of the built environment. In this paper, the threats to validity that result from reactive methods such as interview and questionnaire are discussed. Unobtrusive measures, such as physical trace elements, archival records, and observational data, are evaluated as to their usefulness in environmental research in terms of their utility for architects, their relative accessibility, and their methodological shortcomings. Finally, such ethical matters as the invasion of privacy are considered.

# Unobtrusive Measures: Their Nature and Utility for Architects

**Arthur H. Patterson**

**Pennsylvania State University**

Whenever an architect creates a design that will be used, in any manner, by human beings, he is beginning a process that will have an impact upon the lives of those human beings. James Marston Fitch has stated: "every time the architect or urban designer erects a wall or paves a street, he intervenes in the behavioral modes of the population of that space. The consequences of his intervention may be major or minor, benign or malignant; they will always be real."[1]

Thus the architect must evaluate the effect of his designs. When the effect has been good, he may then incorporate the valid features into future designs. When the result has been bad, or "malignant" in Fitch's terminology, the architect must become aware of what is wrong, and correct it in future designs. An example would be the case of Pruitt–Igoe, the massive public housing project in St. Louis that has been such a clear failure. Social scientists attribute much of the social and physical blight that exists there to the project's design.[2]

Harold Proshansky has written of the need for social scientists to do research that will help provide understanding of the complex relationship of human behavior, experience, and the built environment.[3] In the same vein, Jon Lang has called for an architectural theory based on the empirical observations of architects, sociologists, and psychologists.[4] This process, in reality, contains two steps: the first is the gaining of information about the impact of the design on behavior, and the second is the using of that information in the design and use of new plans.[5]

The primary concern of this paper will be the first step of that process, the gaining of data about the impact of the design on behavior. In Alexander's terminology, the paper will be concerned with methods the architect can use to gather data on the "fits" and "misfits" in the use of the design.[6] The design should thus not be assessed in terms of the "building," but rather through the behaviors associated with it. Raymond Studer has called for a "behavior-contingent" system of design development. He states that "because units of behavior can be well defined and empirically observed, they form a reliable basis for verifying the physical results."[7]

This paper will advocate unobtrusive measures as methods of assessing behavior in order to evaluate the impact of a design upon its users. The discussion will be presented in four parts. The first will deal with why the traditional methods of evaluating designs (questionnaires and interviews) are not sufficient. The second part will present the basic unobtrusive measures, and give examples of their use. This section will rely heavily on the work of E. J. Webb, D. T. Campbell, R. D. Schwartz, and L. Sechrest, who made the seminal organizing contribution on unobtrusive measures for the social sciences.[8] The third part will deal with the specific utility of unobtrusive measures for architects. The fourth, and final, part will consider some of the ethical implications of employing these methods.

## THE REACTIVE NATURE OF QUESTIONNAIRES AND INTERVIEWS

The bulk of the social science data that has been collected by and for architects has been obtained by the use of survey techniques such as questionnaires and interviews. These paper-and-pencil and verbal reports suffer many methodological weaknesses, some of which will be discussed below. But the main problem with their use is that they have been used alone, and have rarely been validated with behavioral data. It has been suggested by several researchers that the key to a sound and practical social science lies in data obtained by multiple operations.[9,10]

What this means is that the more ways that are used to confirm the findings, the more certain one is of the validity of those findings. The use of questionnaires and interviews in studying the impact of designs, without the further confirmation of behavioral validation of the results, has left the results obtained open to many plausible, rival hypotheses. That is, there are many alternative explanations available for what was found. The architect cannot be sure whether the results obtained were due to the effect of the design, or came from some other real or artifactual variable(s). This problem is due to the many possible threats to the validity of questionnaires and interviews.

These threats to their validity generally result from the "reactive" nature of the methodology. Reactive measures are those which allow the respondent to be aware that he is being measured, or that he is an object of concern to a researcher, and which, therefore, may result in changes in the behavior of the respondent. To understand the problem, one must be familiar with

the concepts of internal and external validity. Internal validity refers to whether the researcher found what he claims to, or whether the results can be explained away as an artifact of the measurement process. This is not usually salient in true experiments, but for field studies such as this paper is concerned with, it is most important.

External validity deals with what the results mean, and to what other settings and populations they can be generalized. For the purposes of this paper, internal and external validity will be considered together. The factors which threaten one often threaten the other. For the architect who is attempting to evaluate the impact or utility of a design, the difference between the two is relatively unimportant.

### Threats to Validity That Reside in the Respondent

The basic threats to validity in the use of questionnaires and interviews (and many other reactive measures) that reside in the respondent are presented by Webb.[11] These include the awareness of being tested, the role selected by the respondent, the measurement as a change agent, and response sets. The awareness of being tested, when a reactive measure is used, results in what has been termed the "guinea pig effect."[12] As an example, the "stage" behavior that people exhibit when they realize that they are being filmed is a reaction that hardly typifies usual behavior. Another side to this problem is people's fear of being evaluated. M. S. Rosenberg has found that when people realize they are being measured, they often exhibit unusual behavior because of their concern with not appearing abnormal.[13] Rosenberg has labeled this phenomenon "evaluation apprehension."

The role selected by the respondent is another possible source of invalidity. This does not mean to imply that the respondent will be dishonest, but rather that he has numerous roles to fulfill, and the one selected may not be the appropriate one. For example, M. T. Orne has shown that the experimental situation contains many "demand characteristics," which elicit certain behavior from the respondent.[14] Often this behavior is to do what the experimenter asks, even if it is not the respondent's usual behavior. Support for this, and for evaluation apprehension, may be found in the recent work of Stephen Weber and Thomas Cook.[15] In a review of numerous laboratory experiments, they found that subjects may adopt a faithful role (attempting to "help" the researcher), and be apprehensive about how their role is being evaluated. They concluded that this had led to error in many of the experiments.

Interviewing would seem to be particularly subject to these problems. It would not appear to be unreasonable to assume that the respondent would ask himself two questions: Why have I been chosen? and What do they want from me? The reactivity of the method is apparent here.

Yet another source of invalidity is measurement as a change agent. In this case the error is not directly due to the respondent's reaction to being measured, but because an initial measurement causes changes in the respondent's behavior. The change itself is real, but it may be incorrectly attributed to other events (such as some aspect of the design), and subsequently incorrectly generalized to other settings that do not contain a prior measurement that caused the behavior change. The classic example of this are the well-known Hawthorne studies.[16] The aim of the studies was to examine the effects on production of work conditions, such as temperature and illumination, at the Hawthorne plant of the Western Electric Company. The important result was that production increased no matter what condition was varied, and it did not matter how it was varied. Whether illumination was increased or decreased, production would increase. The explanation for this is that the worker's knowledge that he was being studied, rather than the nature of the manipulation, resulted in the employee's behavior change.

There has been recent work by R. E. Lana on an analogous problem called *pretest sensitization*.[17] He finds that when the measuring process involves requiring people to respond to an experimental treatment (perhaps a new home) in a manner reflecting their attitudes, opinions, or feelings, it is almost impossible to use a pretest that will not influence the results of the posttest. The administration of the pretest (prior to the respondent's moving) will tend to sensitize him in a manner that will influence the posttest. If unobtrusive measures were used to gather the baseline data, where the respondent did not know he had been

measured, the posttest could not be affected by the pretest.

A final threat to the validity of questionnaires and interviews that lies with the respondent is the problem of response sets. There has long been a critical literature on these methods that showed consistent sources of error. L. J. Cronbach was one of the first to summarize the area.[18] Some of the response sets he presented were acquiescence sets, where the respondent more frequently picks a positive statement that disagrees with its opposite; a set to select strong statements over moderate ones; and a set to select responses on the left side of the page more than on the right side. These are not easy to control for, as there are idiosyncratic sets as well.

## Attitudes and Behavior

Undiscussed in each of the above four types of reactive error is the question: If one does validly measure the respondent's attitude with a questionnaire or interview, just what has one measured? There is some evidence that attitudes are not highly related to overt behavior.

Until recently, this problem has not been given much attention by social scientists. For the architect, where the evaluation and changes in a design are dependent upon the behavior elicited (compare Studer's behavior-contingent system), it is essential to know how the attitude measured relates to the behavior of interest.[19] I. Deutscher has pointed out that the problem of attitude–behavior inconsistency is of extreme importance when attempting to apply social science findings to social problems.[20] The lack of relationship can lead to major policy errors.

Perhaps the earliest empirical demonstration of this problem was by R. T. La Piere.[21] He wrote to 250 hotels and restaurants asking if they would serve a Chinese couple (this was in 1934), and some 92 percent replied that they would not. However, when La Piere and the couple visited the establishments, they were refused service only once. Despite methodological problems (for example, it is unlikely that the people who responded to the letter were always the same ones who actually served them), this study is an excellent example of the attitude–behavior inconsistency problem. A recent review by Alan Wicker covers 48 studies where the respondent's verbal and overt behavior responses to objects were obtained on separate occasions.[22] The measured attitudes were often unrelated or only slightly related to overt behaviors.

The problems of validity discussed above can be ameliorated by employing measures that are nonreactive. The relationship of attitudes to behavior can be better understood by validating attitude measures with unobtrusive measures of overt behavior.

## Threats to Validity That Reside in the Investigator

Before turning to the unobtrusive measures, there is yet another source of error in questionnaires and interviews that should be mentioned. This threat to validity resides in the interviewer himself. Webb reports numerous studies that show how the characteristics of the interviewer can bias the respondent's answers.[23] Such variables as the age, sex, race, social class, and even religion of the interviewer affected results.

There is work by Robert Rosenthal that indicates that researchers can influence the subject's response in the direction of the researchers' desired findings.[24] Although this can be done intentionally (by altering data), it usually results from the researcher giving off unintentional cues to the subject. Starkey Duncan has shown that these cues can be so subtle as to be paralinguistic.[25] This is a clear threat to the validity of interviews where the interviewer knows the hypothesis or the hoped-for results.

If one considers the interviewer to be part of the research instrument, and one must, the possibility of error is heightened. One can ask: to what extent is the interviewer the same instrument throughout all phases of the research? It is not unreasonable to expect him to function differently as he increases in skill, gains rapport with the respondents, becomes bored, and finally grows fatigued. Such variation will undoubtedly affect validity.

## UNOBTRUSIVE MEASURES

Architects have tried to avoid the errors resulting from the reactive nature of the methods discussed above.

Small-scale models have been "lived" in, or at least "passed through" by the use of proctoscopes. The technique was to push the proctoscope throughout the model, supposedly giving the observing architect a view of what the full-scale design would look like to the users. This is ingenious, but certainly limited in benefit and scope. At the other extreme, techniques have been developed for the total observation and evaluation of an environment, such as the Tektite 2 undersea habitat.[26] Although the techniques employed yield valuable information about specific environments, their totality requires an artificiality of setting that prevents generalization to any other situation.

What, then, are the actual types of unobtrusive measures that will be useful to architects in evaluating the impact of behavior upon design? Webb has divided the measures into three main classes: (1) physical traces, (2) archival records, and (3) observational data.[27]

## Physical Traces

Physical traces are usually divided into two types: erosion and accretion. *Erosion* is where the degree of selective wear on some material yields the measure. Erosion is a very apt measure for architects, for one can use it to check both where and how a design is used. The classic example of erosion was its use to assess exhibit popularity at Chicago's Museum of Science and Technology.[28] It was found that the tiles around the more popular exhibits would wear more rapidly than those around less popular exhibits. However, it should be noted that since most people have a right-turn response bias when entering a setting such as a museum, it is necessary to validate the finding by using a confirming measure, such as observation. Validating measures are also necessary with physical traces to determine who left the trace, and to what the trace is due.

John Simonds gives an example of using erosion to help plan a design rather than evaluate it.[29] He suggests that when planning walks or paths, especially on college campuses, they should be left out of the original design. The architect should wait, and lay down the paths along the natural lines worn in the ground by the users of the campus. This type of work, whether in planning or evaluating, can be facilitated by manipulating the material to be eroded. For example, a ground covering that was chosen to wear rapidly would save time in the measurement process. But this also allows possible bias, as people might tend to follow the now apparent path (Figure 1).

The second type of physical trace is *accretion,* where the evidence consists of some deposit of materials, remnants of past behavior. For the architect this can range from something as simple as checking oil traces to see where people park in a lot, checking window treatments for indication of varied occupancy, as in Figure 2, to examining people's trash to assess their style of life. E. C. Hughes did extensive sociological work on how janitors knew intimate details of their tenants' lives by merely observing their garbage.[30] In an industrial setting, one could tell what type of work was being performed in what sector of the building by the trash collection from the separate sectors.

Further, litter and disposal problems are apt topics for accretion measures. Even animal or human excretion may be used as an accretion measure. Dog litter can be used to tell the incidence of dogs in the setting, and where they play or are exercised. Human excre-

ment in a housing project may indicate the need and location for public bathroom facilities.

In summary, physical traces are excellent for data because the respondent does not know that he generated the data for a researcher (Figure 3). Thus the measure is nonreactive. There is a problem of ascertaining what population left the trace, but this can be handled by adhering to the principle of multiple methods. Another method can be used to confirm which population was responsible for the trace. Finally, with accretion, one must be concerned about selective survival. That is, some remnants may be allowed to survive, while others are not. The naturre of this selection process may bias the data obtained.

## Archival Records

The second type of unobtrusive measures are archival records. This measure is divided into running records and episodic records. *Running records* are the ongoing, continuing records of a society. The *episodic* records are archives that are not usually part of the public record, and are usually discontinuous in nature.

**Figure 1**

**Figure 2**

Although archival data is nonreactive, it is still open to at least two sources of bias. These are selective recording and selective survival. Selective recording has to do with what data get recorded, and thus enter the archives, and what data do not. We have the same problem with selective survival as with physical traces—only in this case it is a matter of data being expunged from the record. An example of this would be the *Congressional Record,* which purportedly records the daily activities of the Congress. However, congressmen receive proofs of the *Record,* and can make deletions and insertions. A researcher who used the *Record* as an archival source would have to be aware of this potential bias.

There are four general categories of running records. The first of these includes actuarial records, such as birth, marriage, and death. For architects, neighborhoods can be studied by who moves in and out, who marries whom, and who has children. There have been numerous studies where the style of tombstones and arrangement of plots in cemeteries were used to assess the social status of the inhabitants.[31] The Peace Corps, as part of its training, teaches volunteers to use the telephone book as a cultural resource. Certainly the same would be true for an architect who was interested in studying a community.

The second category consists of political and judicial records. A good example of this type of artifact is voting records. Although one cannot tell which way an individual voted, records are available for units as small as precincts. An early study by H. F. Gosnell divided precincts into experimental and control groups, and sent nonpartisan messages to the residents of the experimental precincts, urging them to register and vote in a forthcoming election.[32] As the votes cast were a part of the public record, after the election Gosnell could assess the effect of his messages.

Yet a third category of running records are government records other than the usual actuarial ones. The creative researcher can find an almost unlimited supply of data available to test hypotheses. For example, parking meter receipts have been used to assess the effect of a newspaper strike on a downtown shopping area.[33] There are many possible extensions of this for the study of such things as parking and transportation habits. Similarly, there has been research on the relationship of city water pressure, and a major event on television,

**Figure 3**
**Photo credit: Elliott Kaufman**

such as a Rose Bowl football game.[34] Water consumption, power consumption, and other such variables could be used by architects to study different aspects of home life.

A final category of running records are the mass media. The events recorded on television and radio, in the newspapers, and in magazines can be of great interest to the researcher. Advertisements can give examples of the cultural values and norms. News items can indicate such things as who is having social events, what types of events they are, and where they are being held. A study by G. A. Steiner indicated that when broken, television sets are repaired exceedingly rapidly in American homes.[35] How fast an appliance gets repaired is certainly an indicator of how important it is to the user. Analogously, noting what appliances get repaired at all is a measure of their use and efficiency.

The second type of archival records are the episodic and private records. These are discontinuous, and not usually part of the public record. Thus they differ from the running records in that they are not usually available over time, and are recorded only for specific instances. There are three general categories of episodic and private records, all of which can be used in place of direct observation and measurement of behavior.

The first of these categories consists of sales records. What is being sold, the volume of sales, and the current price scale—are all excellent unobtrusive measures of behavior. For example, the amount of air travel trip insurance bought can be a measure of anxiety about flying. Similarly, the amount of antacid products sold at the counter may be an indication of a lunchroom's food quality. Just as the price brought by a painting is an indication of achievement to the artist, the price brought by his designs is an indication of achievement to the architect. However, in terms of evaluation of extant designs, sales records can be more directly utilized. The amount and type of accoutrements purchased for a setting is an indication of its meaning for the user.

Industrial and institutional records form the second category of episodic and private records. These are the business and personnel records of institutions such as companies, schools, hospitals, and the military. There have been many observational studies in hospitals and schools, but few of them have employed archival data. If the role of the architect is to design wards that facilitate the patient's getting well (one of the primary functions of a hospital), then the patient discharge rates can be used as a measure of the efficacy of the design. One must be careful, of course, of unusual administrative action. A decision by hospital authorities to reduce the budget could result in an increase in discharges, and an invalid measure.

In industrial settings there are numerous archival records that could be of use in evaluating the impact of a design upon the user. The productivity of the workers, their absenteeism rates, and how far they choose to live from the site could all serve as measures of the utility of the design.

A final category of episodic archival records are personal documents. For example, letters written by individuals are usually nonreactive in nature. However, utilizing letters as research tools is usually the work of historians. But there is potential here for unobtrusively studying people's reactions to a design if the researcher is imaginative enough. Picture postcards from a setting often contain some subjective comments about the site. It is illegal to read people's mail, but it might be possible to invent a situation where the researcher was the recipient of the postcards.

In the same vein, critical letters (or positive ones) to the designer should be carefully recorded. Even though the writer is aware that he is creating the letter for review by the architect, the letter is still valuable because it is free of many of the threats to validity to which information solicited by a researcher is subject. Finally, artwork may be considered a personal document. The type of art bought or produced by an occupant for a design can be very informative as to the impact of the design upon that person.

It should be noted that the data obtained from archival records must be interpreted in relationship to the size of the population that produced the records. If comparisons are to be made between different settings, transformation may be necessary to normalize the data. Also, it should be remembered that the data, except in the case of personal documents, were produced for someone other than the researcher and recorded by someone other than the researcher. Thus the data are secondhand and may face many of the reactivity problems described for questionnaires and interviews. This can be easily controlled by emphasizing validating measures—that is, by obtaining multiple confirmations by either employing the measures over time, or utilizing other methods as well, such as observation. Despite these problems, archival records offer the architect a large body of data that is reasonably cheap and easy to obtain.

## Observation

Of the unobtrusive measures presented so far, the observational methods would appear to be the most useful to architects. Observation is the case where the researcher plays a nonintrusive role in the situation, recording data while unknown to, and unobserved by the actors. In simple observation the researcher has no control over the behavior being studied, and he plays a passive, unobserved role. In contrived observation, the researcher plays an active role in manipulating the setting to be observed, and often employs hardware to facilitate observing and recording the behavior.

Most research to date by those interested in environment–behavior relationships, including architects, has been observational in nature.[36] There is a vast literature on animal behavior from the field of ethology. Dealing with humans, Roger Barker has provided the seminal work with his research and methods for observing ecological behavior.[37] H. F. Wright has employed this observational model, with an emphasis on children's behavior.[38] The use of observation to study human behavior has been detailed in recent work by E. P. Willems and S. E. Vineberg,[39] and by the Hutts.[40] However, the observational work of those employing the Barker ecological methodology has been primarily concerned with studying behavior as it occurs in the environment, and not specifically with studying the effect of the environment on behavior.

On a more micro scale, there has been observational research concerned with the effect of the built environment. As mentioned above, institutional settings, especially schools and hospitals, have been studied extensively using unobtrusive measures.[41] On an even smaller scale, the use of the built environment in maintaining personal space has been a topic of interest, as evidenced in the work of Robert Sommer.[42] Most of the above studies have been of the simple observation type. However, there have been design evaluations that have involved manipulation and the use of hardware to facilitate the gathering of data. This is usually the case in the "total environment" studies[43] but has also been employed in much smaller-scale evaluations.[44]

Before detailing some of the methods of gaining observational data, where the researcher remains unknown and unobserved to the actors being studied, the case of participant observation should be presented. Here, the observer becomes part of what he is observing, such as in anthropological research where the researcher lives in, and becomes a part of, the culture he is studying. This method is subject to errors because of reactivity, and to instrumentation as the observer becomes biased by his experiences. Yet for architects, this method provides a chance to actually experience the design being evaluated. The potential for incorporating the data from an evaluation into future designs should be greatly facilitated if the architect has himself experienced the behavioral impact of the setting.

Webb has divided the simple and unobtrusive measures (simple only in the sense that the investigator does not intervene and no hardware is used) by the variables observed.[45] The first category is the gathering of data by the observing of exterior physical signs. In people, this can be such items as the clothing they wear, or the Sherlock Holmesian technique of ascertaining profession by calluses on the hand. In a physical setting, where and how the furnishings are arranged can be a physical sign of how the room is used by the occupants.

The expressive body movement of the actors can also be measured. When evaluating a setting, the body motion exhibited within the setting is a clue to the efficacy of the design. For example, a lounge that results in nervous or anxious behavior would appear to have design flaws. R. L. Birdwhistell's kinesics, work on nonverbal communication with the body, can be applied in the study of these types of problems.[46]

A similar measure is that of the actual physical location of people within a setting. This technique has been used extensively with animals in ethological research. The data on where people position themselves in a behavior setting, in relationship to other people and to the built environment, can be very useful in assessing the nature of the setting and the occupant's reaction to it. Sommer has presented numerous studies of this type in his work on personal space.[47]

Yet another observational technique is conversation sampling. Simply, this is unobtrusively observing what people are saying to one another. For architects, this method of gathering data can be quite useful. For example, people using or visiting a designed site often discuss their reactions to it. If observed and recorded, this data can be very fruitful because there are no threats to its validity. What the person said is usually what the person actually meant, as opposed to what is often erroneously recorded in interviews. The architect can gain much information about the use of a setting by observing that aspect of conversations.

Finally, the amount of attention paid by a person to an object can be used as an indicator of interest. With animals, where it is impossible to obtain interviews or questionnaires, the amount of time spent attending to an object has long been used as a measure. For architects interested in the visual aspects of a design, variety can be assessed by the amount of time spent passing through the design. Work of this nature has been done with museum visitors, and could easily be extended to numerous other settings, from stores to housing projects.[48] The relationship of visual features to attention is an important design question.

An important problem for observational studies is the question of timing. For relatively permanent physical signs this is not important, but for the other measures above, such as conversation or physical location, the results will be time dependent. This means that samples taken at different times will yield different results. Unless the variable under study is time itself, the researcher must be careful of this source of error.

Roger Barker and his associates have tried to handle this problem by censusing time rather than sampling it. That is, they observe during the totality of an event. An example would be their in-depth study of a boy during the course of his entire day.[49] But this is not a feasible solution for architects, except for the case of artificial situations such as the undersea habitat discussed in the article by Robert Helmreich in this book. Thus the time sampled must be chosen to best reflect the aspect of the design under study.

The second type of observation involves the intervention of the researcher, and his use of hardware, in an effort to facilitate the data-gathering process. The use of hardware in the recording of observational data has many advantages. Its use diminishes the chances of human error. It provides a permanent record for reexamination of the data. Also, this capacity to reexamine provides the opportunity to uncover valuable data not available at the first observation.

Architects have used hardware as a tool for observation. Bechtel has reviewed numerous studies where hodometers were used to record movement in a setting.[50] Also, movie cameras, and now video tape, have been used to simulate the human eye. For observational purposes, it would be more useful to turn the camera around to record the behavior exhibited in the setting under study. Audio tape recorders have been extensively used for this purpose, although video tape now provides a far richer record.

The principal benefit from the use of hardware is to reduce human observational errors. But hardware is also valuable in gaining access to areas where it would be difficult for the researcher to gain entrée. For example, within legal limits, it becomes relatively simple to use microphones and tape recorders to "bug" conversations. Or, consider the telemetry equipment used to record animal behavior such as migrations.[51] It is not unfeasible to study human movement in much the same way. Certainly telemetric data could be obtained on car movements for transportation studies.

All the above research involves a passive investigator, other than the act of installing the hardware. But what if the behavior of interest occurs so infrequently that it is difficult to study? For example, the use of fire exits in a design is exceedingly important, but a researcher would be foolish to wait around in an attempt to study their emergency use by observation. A solution would be to request the officials in charge of the setting to stage a fire drill. For even more information during the drill, the officials could be asked to block certain normal exits that would have a possibility of being cut off by a fire. This type of observer intervention provides data that would usually not be available.

Perhaps a simpler example of this technique is presented by Webb in connection with Allen Funt's Candid Camera television show.[52] Originally, Funt just filmed people in everyday situations and waited for humorous sequences to occur. But he rapidly realized that too much time was wasted in this manner and intervened by using confederates to elicit the humorous behavior. As long as the respondent does not perceive that his behavior is being manipulated, the measures taken will be nonreactive.

Some studies of behavior have manipulated micro aspects of the physical environment. For example, A. Freed and his associates observed under what circumstances students would violate a sign urging the use of an inconvenient side door rather than the usual main door of a campus building.[53] The strength of the wording of the sign was varied, along with whether or not a confederate was present to conform to or violate the sign. The use of signs to control behavior is intrinsically interesting to architects, but the method involved is of greater interest. The physical reality of an architect's design is in fact a manipulation of the environment, and thus the methods of observation used to assess the behavioral impact of environmental manipulation are of particular use to anyone concerned with environmental design.

In summary, the major values of observational measures are (1) that data are gathered firsthand, unlike archival records, and (2) that supporting data can be collected at the same time. Similarly, the individuals involved in the assessed behavior can be noted and contacted if followup information is necessary.

As we have noted, however, in simple observation there is a possibility that errors may be introduced by the observer. But through the use of hardware, the researcher can obtain richer data and also avoid instrumentation error. Furthermore, the use of hardware makes the observations both permanent and subject to in-depth analysis. One must not forget, however, that the more actively involved the researcher gets, the more he increases his chances of being perceived by those he is studying. As soon as the researcher is perceived, the value of unobtrusive measures is lost, and all the threats to validity are reinstated.

## THE UTILITY OF UNOBTRUSIVE MEASURES FOR ARCHITECTS

The utility of unobtrusive measures for architects is best understood by recalling the need for design evaluation presented at the beginning of this paper. There is little doubt that what an architect creates will have some impact on the behavior of the people who come into contact with that creation. Whether that impact has a positive or negative effect on the well-being of the users needs to be evaluated. Further, the results of this evaluation must be built into future designs. It can be reasonably argued that measuring behavior is the domain of social scientists, and thus historically has not been the concern of designers. But if architects must assess designs not in terms of "buildings" but rather through the behaviors associated with them, they must become knowledgeable about, if not sophisticated in, the use of behavioral measures.

This paper has presented unobtrusive measures as a valuable method for architects in measuring human behavior. The value lies in their nonreactivity, allowing for behavioral assessments free of the threats to validity found in the use of questionnaires and interviews. Further, unobtrusive measures are used to obtain information about actual behavior, rather than the information about attitudes toward behavior that is obtained with the paper-and-pencil and verbal methods. Finally, unobtrusive measures are relatively easy to obtain, being based upon the extant behavior of the people being studied. Empirically sound and informationally rich evaluations of the impact of a design can be made by employing a multiple-confirmation method, where unobtrusive measures are used to validate more detailed (but reactive) measures.

The architect in practice can use unobtrusive measures in both direct and indirect ways. Directly, he can utilize the measures to gain information on how to plan his design. An example of this would be John Simonds' work (mentioned earlier) on the placement of walks where the users have already worn paths on the ground.[54] Because researchers have difficulty letting people tell them what they want or need in a design, this method allows people to unknowingly show them. Or, if a design problem is similar to one already created, the architect can employ unobtrusive measures (in conjunction with other methods) to assess the design's merits and demerits, and subsequently build them into or out of the new design.

Indirectly, the architect can utilize already collected social science research on design impact if he is satisfied with the validity of the data. If unobtrusive behavioral data are used to confirm other measures, the architect can be more sure of the study's validity. For example, the Scandinavians have exercised great care in the development of their residential environment. In doing so, they have been innovative in developing methods for assessing if a design fulfilled its goals. T. Carlstein and his associates have compared survey data on activity in a neighborhood with observational (unobtrusive) data to determine the validity of the survey work.[55]

Another innovative, indirect use of an unobtrusive measure was reported by architect Louis Sauer.[56] He felt that there was a very poor match between what the architects were providing and what the people desired in the new town of Reston, Virginia. Sauer consulted the people who were in the best position to have unobtrusively sampled the conversations of prospective home buyers—the home salesmen. From the salesmen Sauer was able to gain data that were fed back into the design process.

The architect engaged in research can become actively involved in manipulating the built environment while using nonreactive measures to gather data on the effect. He can actually design and execute quasi-experiments, even without the randomization of subjects to treatments that is necessary for true experi-

ments but is so difficult to achieve in the real-world settings in which the architect works.[57] The performance of experiments allow the testing of hypotheses through the use of statistical inference, which can prove to be a powerful tool for making decisions concerning features of designs. The architect can actually build the capacity for evaluation directly into the design. D. T. Campbell has advocated an experimental approach to social reform.[58] He recommends that new programs be tried out but with built-in mechanisms of evaluation. Then good programs can be retained and ineffective ones discarded or properly modified. Among the many experimental and quasi-experimental techniques he recommends, unobtrusive measures appear to be the most appropriate for architects.

Thus the architect does not need a laboratory, nor an army of interviewers, to evaluate the impact of a design upon behavior. Unobtrusive measures, used in conjunction with other methods, can provide the valid and informational data necessary for evaluation.

## ETHICS AND UNOBTRUSIVE MEASURES

The extreme ethical position on the use of unobtrusive measures is represented in the work of E.A. Shils.[59] He would rule out any research that involved observing private behavior without the full and informed permission of the person being observed. In order to gather nonreactive data, this position is obviously unfeasible. Yet the other end of the spectrum allows measures involving trespassing and invasion of privacy. Certainly, violations of the law must also be ruled out. The solution clearly lies in a more reasonable position.

The American Psychological Association has proposed ethical standards for research with human subjects that are applicable to the use of unobtrusive measures by architects.[60] The basic premise is that if the researcher's work can contribute to human welfare, his underlying ethical imperative is to carry forward his research as best he knows how. Thus if the architect agrees that his design will have an impact on the well-being of the users, then he is ethically bound to evaluate them as best as he knows how.

But this is not a fiat. These standards are principles, and not rules. The general prohibitory ethic is that the research should not result in a negative effect upon the dignity and welfare of the subject. The standards do call for obtaining consent from subjects whenever possible. But when impossible, such as in the real-world research of concern to architects, it is required that anonymity be safeguarded.

Campbell, who has called for natural experiments to avoid problems of reactivity, presents several ethical principles for this type of research.[61] He feels that when the investigator cannot get the consent of the subjects without biasing the study, he must place a value on his research. If the research is nontrivial, then the researcher should carry it out (provided it meets the standards discussed above). This is especially true when the behavior to be observed is in the public domain, and nonresearchers also have access to it. Campbell feels that invasion of privacy can be avoided by gathering the data in such a way that the person's name cannot be linked to it.

In laboratory research there is an ethic of debriefing. That is, after the experiment the subject is told what went on in the experiment. Campbell feels that in field research it is imperative not to debrief, for the knowledge gained in debriefing would rapidly destroy any possibilities for nonreactive studies. People would soon become aware of the techniques used and become sensitive to them. If the subject's experience in the research falls within the range of his ordinary experiences, there can be no need to debrief. As ordinary experiences are the key to unobtrusive measures, there should be no ethical problem for architects.

## NOTES AND REFERENCES

1.  James M. Fitch, *American Building 2: The Environmental Forces That Shape It,* Boston: Houghton Mifflin, 1972, 163.
2.  W. L. Yancey, "Architecture, interaction, and social control: the case of a large-scale housing project," in J. Wohlwill and D. Carson, eds., *Environment and the Social Sciences: Perspectives and Applications,* Washington, D.C.: American Psychological Association, 1972, 126–136.
3.  Harold M. Proshansky, "Environmental psychology and the design professions," in Charles Burnette, Jon Lang, and David Vachon, eds., *Architecture for Human Behavior,* Philadelphia: Philadelphia Chapter/AIA, 1971, 15–22. Also in *Part One* of this book.
4.  Jon Lang, "Architecture for human behavior: the nature of the problem," in Burnette, Lang, and Vachon, *op. cit.,* 5–14. See also *Part One* of this book.
5.  Michael Brill, "Evaluating buildings on a performance

basis," in Burnette, Lang, and Vachon, *op. cit.,* 41–44; also in *Part One* of this book.
6.  Christopher Alexander, *Notes on the Synthesis of Form,* Cambridge, Mass.: Harvard University Press, 1964.
7.  Raymond G. Studer, "The dynamics of behavior-contingent physical systems," in Harold M. Proshansky, William H. Ittelson, and Leanne G. Rivlin, eds., *Environmental Psychology: Man and His Physical Setting;* New York: Holt, 1970, 73.
8.  E. J. Webb, D. T. Campbell, R. D. Schwartz, and L. Sechrest, *Unobtrusive Measures: Nonreactive Research in the Social Sciences,* Skokie, Ill.: Rand McNally, 1966.
9.  *Ibid.*
10. D. T. Campbell and D. W. Fiske, "Convergent and discriminant validation by the multitrait-multimethod matrix," *Psychological Bulletin,* Vol. 56, (1959), 81–105.
11. Webb et al., *op. cit.*
12. Claire Selltiz, Marie Jahoda, Morton Deutsch, and S. W. Cook, *Research Methods in Social Relations,* New York: Holt, 1959.
13. M. S. Rosenberg, "When dissonance fails: on eliminating evaluation apprehension from attitude measurement," *Journal of Personality and Social Psychology,* Vol. 1 (1965) 18–42.
14. M. T. Orne, "Demand characteristics and quasi-controls," in R. Rosenthal and R. Rosnow, eds., *Artifact in Behavioral Research,* New York: Academic Press, 1969, 147–177.
15. Stephen J. Weber and Thomas D. Cook, "Subject effects in laboratory research: an examination of subject roles, demand characteristics, and valid inference," *Psychological Bulletin,* Vol. 77, No. 4 (1972), 273–295.
16. F. J. Roethlisberger and William J. Dickson, *Management and the Worker,* Cambridge, Mass.: Harvard University Press, 1939.
17. R. E. Lana, "Pretest sensitization," in Rosenthal and Rosnow, *op. cit.,* 119–142.
18. L. J. Cronbach, "Response sets and test validity," *Educational and Psychological Measurement,* Vol. 6 (1946), 475–494.
19. Studer, *op. cit.*
20. I. Deutscher, "Words and deeds: social science and social policy," *Social Problems,* Vol. 13 (1966), 235–254.
21. R. T. La Piere, "Attitudes vs. actions," *Social Forces,* Vol. 13 (1934), 230–237.
22. A. W. Wicker, "Attitudes vs. actions: the relationship of verbal and overt behavioral responses to attitude objects," *Journal of Social Issues,* Vol. 25, No. 4 (1969), 41–78.
23. Webb et al., *op. cit.*
24. Robert Rosenthal, *Experimenter Effects in Behavioral Research,* New York: Appleton-Century Crofts, 1966.
25. Starkey Duncan, Jr., Milton Rosenberg, and Jonathan Finkelstein, "The paralanguage of experimenter bias," *Sociometry,* Vol. 32, No. 2 (1969), 207–219.
26. Robert Helmreich, "Evaluation of environments:

behavioral observations in an undersea habitat," in Burnette, Lang, and Vachon, *op. cit.,* 55–64; also in *Part Three* of this book.

27. Webb et al., *op. cit.*

28. *Ibid.*

29. John Ormsbee Simonds, *Landscape Architecture,* New York: F. W. Dodge Corporation, 1961, 159.

30. E. C. Hughes, *Men and Their Work,* New York: The Free Press, 1958.

31. Webb et al., *op. cit.*

32. H. F. Gosnell, *Getting Out the Vote: An Experiment in the Stimulation of Voting,* Chicago: University of Chicago Press, 1972.

33. W. A. Mindak, A. Neibergs, and A. Anderson, "Economic effects of the Minneapolis newspaper strike," *Journalism Quarterly,* Vol. 40 (1963) 213–218.

34. Webb et al., *op. cit.*

35. G. A. Steiner, *The People Look at Television,* New York: Knopf, 1963.

36. Harold M. Proshansky, William H. Ittelson, and Leanne G. Rivlin, eds., *Environmental Psychology: Man and His Physical Setting,* New York: Holt, 1970.

37. Roger G. Barker, *Ecological Psychology: Concepts and Methods for Studying the Environment of Human Behavior,* Stanford, Calif.: Stanford University Press, 1968.

38. H. F. Wright, *Recording and Analyzing Child Behavior,* New York: Harper & Row, 1967.

39. E. P. Willems and S. E. Vineberg, *Procedural Supports for the Direct Observation in Natural Settings,* Monograph, Houston, Texas: Texas Institute for Rehabilitation and Research, 1970.

40. S. J. Hutt and C. Hutt, *Direct Observation and Measurement of Behavior,* Springfield, Ill.: Charles C Thomas, 1970.

41. Proshansky, Ittelson, and Rivlin, *op. cit.*

42. Robert Sommer, *Personal Space: The Behavioral Basis of Design,* Englewood Cliffs, N. J.: Prentice-Hall, 1969.

43. Helmreich, *op. cit.*

44. Robert B. Bechtel, "Hodometer research in architecture," *Milieu,* Ser. 2, Vol. 1 (April 1967).

45. Webb et al., *op. cit.*

46. R. L. Birdwhistell, "Kinesics and communication," in E. Carpenter, ed., *Explorations in Communication,* Boston: Beacon Press, 1960, 54–64.

47. Sommer, *op. cit.*

48. Webb, et al., *op. cit.*

49. Roger G. Barker and H. F. Wright, *One Boy's Day: A Specimen Record of Behavior,* New York: Harper & Row, 1951.

50. Bechtel, *op. cit.*

51. J. R. Tester, D. B. Siniff, and C. R. Jessen, "Use of telemetry as a means of studying the spacing and behavior of animals," in A. H. Esser, ed., *Behavior and Environment: The Use of Space by Animals and Men,* New York: Plenum Press, 1971.

52. Webb et al., *op. cit.*

53. A. Freed, P. Chandler, J. Mouton, and R. Blake, "Stimulus and background factors in sign violation," *Journal of Personality,* Vol. 23 (1955), 499.

54. Simonds, *op. cit.*

55. T. Carlstein, B. Lenntorp, and Solveig Martensson, *Individers Dygnsbonor i Nagra Hushallstyper,* Institutionen for Kulturgeografi och Ekonomisk Geografi, Lunds Universitet, 1968.

56. Louis Sauer, "Programming issues in low income housing," paper presented to Division of Man–Environment Relations Colloquium Series, Pennsylvania State University, March 5, 1971.

57. D. T. Campbell and J. C. Stanley, *Experimental and Quasi-Experimental Designs for Research,* Skokie, Ill.: Rand McNally, 1966.

58. D. T. Campbell, "Reforms as experiments," *American Psychologist,* Vol. 24, No. 4 (1969), 409–429.

59. E. A. Shils, "Social inquiry and the autonomy of the individual," in D. Lerner, ed., *The Human Meaning of Social Sciences,* Cleveland: Meridian Books, 1959, 114–157.

60. S. W. Cook, "Ethical standards for research with human subjects," *APA Monitor,* (May 1972).

61. D. T. Campbell, "Prospective: artifact and control," in Rosenthal and Rosnow, *op. cit.,* 351–382.

*The concepts, technology, and methodology used to collect data with which to evaluate behavior within an undersea habitat are described and some findings indicated. Predetermined categories describing activity, communication, posture, movement, and various zones of the physical setting provide the basis for nonprofessional observers to record large amounts of highly reliable behavioral data using inexpensive, unobtrusive, portable instruments which produced data immediately available in a form that permitted a variety of statistical analyses. It is argued that the most valid way to assess environmental effects on human behavior is through the systematic, unobtrusive collection of objective data that categorizes ongoing behavior in natural settings, and that it is also imperative to analyze the environment in terms of costs and rewards anticipated by its inhabitants. This analysis should describe, in addition to the current cost–reward ratio of a setting, its change over time.*

# Evaluation of Environments: Behavioral Observations in an Undersea Habitat[1]

**Robert Helmreich**

**The University of Texas at Austin**

Man has a long history of being exposed, voluntarily or involuntarily, to extreme and stressful environments. A few examples of such settings are concentration camps, combat zones, cities under siege or air attack, Antarctic or Polar stations, space ships, and underwater habitats. Some would even add much of New York City and other urban centers to the list.

Psychologists have devoted much energy to the study of reactions to such milieux. This concentration of research effort on studies of behavior in exotic environments raises questions concerning the relevance of findings from this type of investigation to human behavior in general and to efforts to understand the overall effects of environment on man.

This discussion will focus on psychological research conducted during *Tektite 2,* a project in which teams of aquanauts lived for a total of seven months in a habitat placed on the ocean floor. The goals will be to describe a methodology for evaluating an environment and reactions in it, to provide some general conclusions from the data, and to consider the applicability of the methodology and findings to the growing field of environmental psychology.

## BACKGROUND

When a diver breathing compressed gas or air descends to depths greater than 33 feet gases dissolve in his bloodstream and tissues. This severely limits his time for work at any appreciable depth because of the need for lengthy decompression to avoid decompression sickness (the "bends"). In the early 1960's, however, the concept of saturation diving was refined, which permitted much of the continental shelf to be opened to habitation.[2] The principle behind saturation diving is very simple; after a diver has remained at a given depth for around 12 hours, the maximum possible amount of gas will have been dissolved in his system (he is "saturated"). From this time on, the amount of time required for safe decompression to atmospheric pressure remains constant. Thus, a diver can remain submerged for 12 hours, 12 days, or 12 years without paying a penalty in increased decompression time. Applying this principle, work was begun on the development of pressurized underwater habitats. While a diver is saturated, he can live safely in an underwater dwelling with its internal pressure equal to that of the water outside. For example, a habitat can be placed in 200 feet of water with an internal pressure equal to that outside (104 PSI). It can then serve as a refuge for divers working in the surrounding sea. Living in a habitat is not without its price, however. That saturated aquanaut cannot return to the surface in the event of emergency or disaffection with his environment, and he must undergo a long, gradual decompression to avoid death or disablement. As a result, the saturated aquanaut is as isolated from earth as the astronaut in space.

A number of habitats have been built and emplaced in the last 10 years. These include the U. S. Navy's *Sealab* projects and Jacques Cousteau's *Conshelf* studies. In 1969, NASA, the Department of the Interior, the U. S. Navy, and General Electric placed a habitat, *Tektite 1,* at a depth of 50 feet in Lameshur Bay, St. John, U.S. Virgin Islands. Four scientist–aquanauts spent 60 days living in the habitat and conducting research on the surrounding reef. The success of this project led to Project *Tektite 2,* a far more ambitious research endeavor.

## TEKTITE 2

*Tektite 2* was conducted during 1970 at the same Virgin Islands site as Tektite 1. Ten teams of five aquanauts, however, spent a total of 182 days living in the habitat under saturation. Each team consisted of four scientist–aquanauts who conducted a variety of research projects and an engineer who was primarily responsible for habitat operation and maintenance.

The *Tektite 2* habitat is a four-room dwelling created from two 12-foot diameter cylinders joined by a tunnel. Figure 1 shows the habitat and its layout. It was placed approximately 600 feet offshore and was connected by umbilical cables, for breathing gases, water, electricity, and communications.

An integral part of the program, funded by the Office of Naval Research and NASA, was the intensive study of the aquanauts' psychological reactions to confinement and isolation. Specific goals were to advance basic research on individual and group behavior, to provide information useful for selecting crews and manning future underwater habitats, and to obtain data applicable to problems of long-duration space flight.

The major concern in data collection was to gather data which would be highly objective and which could provide an accurate picture of both performance and adjustment in such a closed environment. A serious problem in studies of naturally occurring behavior has been that data are often collected in an anecdotal and highly subjective manner, leaving results open to criticism on grounds of unreliability and bias. The *Tektite* research was conducted at a time of serious controversy in social psychology between those who advocate experimental, laboratory studies and those who emphasize observational, naturalistic research in real-life settings. These points have been debated at length elsewhere.[3] Laboratory advocates hold that only in a controlled, experimental situation can valid conclusions about causality be drawn and that field research, by its correlational nature, can only describe relationships without isolating causal links. Those working in the "real world" argue that objective, controlled methods can be applied to natural settings and that findings can be more readily generalized to other real environments. They argue further that modern statistical techniques can provide much information about causal relations from correlational data. An additional argument is that field techniques may be the only ethical means of studying some important phenomena such as prolonged stress.

Because of this unresolved schism in the field, it became a primary goal of the behavioral research endeavor in *Tektite* to demonstrate that systematic methodology could be applied to a natural environment and that reliable, valid, and meaningful results could be obtained. To achieve this goal, two major constraints were imposed on the research design. The first was that data would be objectively coded observations of behavior and not subjective impressions of feelings, performance, or other reactions. The second was that the psychological researcher must gain his data through unobtrusive measures and must avoid interfering with ongoing behavior to give tests or to assess the psychological states of his subjects. To accomplish this

**Figure 1**

the primary method used to collect data in *Tektite 2* was the continuous monitoring of all compartments of the habitat by closed-circuit television and open microphones with continuous coding of behavior into predetermined categories on machine readable punch cards.

There were numerous advantages in using the underwater habitat as a research environment:

1. The research setting was completely real. Stress, isolation, and confinement were not simulated; accordingly, reactions to the pressures of the environment were valid indices of behavior. Closely related to this is the fact that research subjects were participating to fulfill personal, professional goals and not just to serve as psychological guinea pigs.
2. The habitat provided a relatively stable and constant environment. Unlike many field studies, all subjects could be observed under the same living conditions.
3. The number of subjects (48) and teams (10) was sufficient to allow meaningful statistical comparisons across individuals and across teams.
4. The design of the habitat provided excellent audio and video coverage. Psychologists could monitor almost all in-habitat activity.
5. An extensive battery of psychological data could be obtained on each aquanaut prior to his mission—an unusual situation in field research.
6. The natural situation provided excellent, objective criteria of performance and adjustment. These variables formed the criteria for prediction of individual reactions and the study of trends in behavior over time. Between three and five thousand observations (depending on mission length which varied from two weeks to 20 days) were taken on *each* of 50-plus variables on *each* aquanaut.

Data were collected by teams of psychological observers who were students at the University of Texas at Austin. Observers collected data 24 hours a day, standing watch in pairs for 4-hour shifts. Behavioral observation was conducted in a restricted area in a trailer located onshore and connected to the habitat by the communications umbilicus. The behavioral area was equipped with six 18-inch TV monitors—one showing each of the four compartments of the habitat, one showing the water area outside the habitat entrance and one reserve unit. Three video tape recorders were also installed enabling instantaneous recording of any signal received on the TV monitors. Three loud-speakers and two headphone jacks also permitted monitoring of in-habitat conversation.

The variables used in data collection were developed and refined from research programs conducted during the Navy's Project *Sealab* II and III and *Tektite 1*.[4] Relevant categories of behavior were specified and explicitly defined in a Behavior Observer's Manual.[5]

Primary data were recorded on punch cards using the IBM Model 3000 Information Recorder. This is a very simple, nonelectronic device, roughly 10 by 12 by 2 inches. It does no more than hold a preperforated punch card and guide template. Separate recorders were prepared with templates for recording aquanaut status, dive behavior, meal behavior, arising–retiring and sleep duration, communications with topside, and specific events such as use of leisure facilities, housekeeping, and so on. Data were recorded by using a stylus to punch holes corresponding to the various categories as indicated by the template.

The major data source was the Aquanaut Status Record, which was completed for all five aquanauts, every 6 minutes, 24 hours a day. This record showed precisely where each aquanaut was in the habitat, what he was doing, to whom he was speaking and his posture and movement. From these data, such criterion measures as time spent in various work activities, leisure behavior, and sleep behavior were formed. The categories and template used for recording the aquanauts' Status Record are shown in Figures 2 and 3, respectively. Other types of behavior were recorded each time they occurred. Table 1 lists all measures collected by direct observation.

Several points are worth noting about this method of data collection:

1. It is highly objective and highly reliable. Nonprofessional observers can be readily trained to collect data. Interrater reliability averaged between 0.89 and 0.97 across all variables.
2. Using the portable Information Recorder, data can be collected in a variety of field settings, unobtrusively and without need for electricity or bulky equipment.
3. Data are recorded in a form suitable for immediate

| Activity categories | Communication categories | Posture categories | Movement categories |
|---|---|---|---|
| 11 Direct marine science | | 11 Standing erect | |
| 0 Mar. science support | | 0 Standing slouching | 0 No movement |
| 1 Locomoting | 1 Not communicating, neither talking nor listening | 1 Standing leaning | 1 Light translational |
| 2 Habitat maintng and repair | 2 Talking with another aquanaut | 2 Sitting forward | 2 Moderate translational |
| 3 Self-maintenance | 3 Listening to aquanaut 1 | 3 Sitting upright | 3 Vigorous translational |
| 4 Maintenance of others | 4 Listening to aquanaut 2 | 4 Sitting slouching | 4 Light manipulative |
| 5 Co recreation | 5 Listening to aquanaut 3 | 5 Reclining | 5 Moderate manipulative |
| 6 Solitary recreation | 6 Listening to aquanaut 4 | 6 Squatting | 6 Vigorous manipulative |
| 7 Relaxing, resting, idling | 7 Listening to aquanaut 5 | 7 Kneeling | 7 Light expressive |
| 8 Napping, sleeping | 8 Talking or listening to topside | 8 All fours | 8 Moderate expressive |
| 9 Don't know | | 9 Lying down | 9 Vigorous expressive |

**Figure 2**

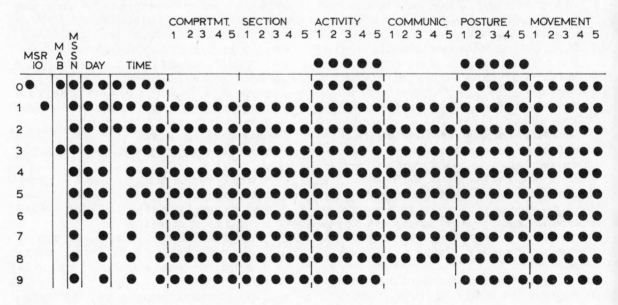

**Figure 3**

computer processing. This becomes an important consideration when large amounts of data are collected (for example, more than 200,000 cards were punched during *Tektite 2*). Transcription of written records is not only time-consuming but subject to much error.

4. Finally, and perhaps most important, using this methodology the researcher is forced to define his goals and to analyze the research setting *prior* to data collection.

It is my contention that any richness in data collected which is lost by structuring the categories of behavior observed is compensated for by the validity and reliability of measures recorded.

The results from the behavioral research were highly gratifying. There were large individual and team differences proved to be systematic and predictable. There were also highly significant relationships between in-habitat social interaction and activities over time, which provide a picture of the patterns of response to the environment. The major psychological findings have been reported elsewhere[6] and are too extensive for inclusion here. Instead, the relationships of two aspects of the data to the general field of environmental psychology will be explored.

One of the strongest conclusions to be drawn from the *Tektite* study is that aquanauts adjusted extremely well to life in the crowded, noisy, isolated habitat and worked hard and effectively despite many environmental obstacles. Although there were major individual differences in work output, even the least productive aquanaut achieved a respectable level of performance.

Figure 4 shows the average amount of time per day spent by all aquanauts in various activities. Since only time *actually* spent in work was coded, the amount of time spent productively each day is strikingly high. Indeed, several aquanauts reported that they worked more while underwater than in their normal laboratory settings.

Comcomitant with the notable productivity of the aquanauts was a generally high level of interpersonal harmony. Despite the lack of privacy and competition for limited space for both vital work and leisure, both of which provided innumerable opportunities for interpersonal conflict, there were relatively few clashes.

This success in living and working in confinement and isolation was achieved more in spite of the habitat

than because of it. The habitat was designed for use by four aquanauts; the addition of a fifth resident meant that one diver was forced to sleep on a foldup cot which could only be placed in prime work and leisure territory in the bridge compartment. This, of course, created many potential conflict situations. In addition, work space was both insufficient in size and not designed to accommodate many of the types of research conducted.

Figure 5 shows the 10 most used sections of the habitat. The figure, based on Aquanaut Status Record data, illustrates how the systematically recorded data on aquanaut location and activity can be used to provide highly accurate documentation of the usage of a facility. It should be noted that these are merely summary data and that the data are coded in such a way that a computer can also output statistics on usage at particular times of day, can trace the spatial activities of a single individual, can show the type of social interactions occurring in particular locations, and can supply data relevant to a large number of questions concerning environmental occupancy.

Turning to the data shown in the figures, it can be noted that breaking down occupancy into work and leisure categories gives a much clearer picture of the

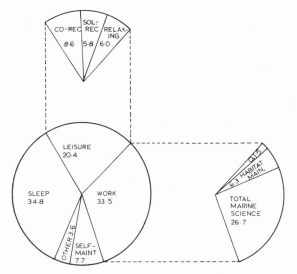

**Figure 4: Mean percentage of total mission time spent on habitat activities (all aquanauts)**

**Table 1**
**Measures Collected by Observation During *Tektite 2***

| | Frequency or Time of Collection | | Frequency or Time of Collection |
|---|---|---|---|
| **I. Aquanaut Status Record** **Variable** | | D. Posture of each aquanaut **Categories** | Every 6 minutes |
| A. Location by compartment and section of each aquanaut | Every 6 minutes | 1. Standing erect | |
| B. Activity of each aquanaut | Every 6 minutes | 2. Standing slouching | |
| **Categories of activity** | | 3. Standing leaning | |
| 1. Direct marine science | | 4. Sitting forward | |
| 2. Marine science support | | 5. Sitting upright | |
| 3. Locomoting | | 6. Sitting slouching | |
| 4. Habitat maintenance and repair | | 7. Reclining | |
| 5. Self-maintenance | | 8. Squatting | |
| 6. Maintenance of others | | 9. Kneeling | |
| 7. Corecreation | | 10. All-fours | |
| 8. Solitary recreation | | 11. Lying down | |
| 9. Relaxing, resting, idling | | **Variable** | |
| 10. Napping, sleeping | | E. Movement of each aquanaut **Categories** | Every 6 minutes |
| **Composite variables composed by grouping activity categories for summary data** | | 0. No movement | |
| 1. Total work—sum of time spent on direct marine science, marine science support, habitat maintenance, and maintenance of others | | 1. Light translational movement | |
| | | 2. Moderate translational movement | |
| | | 3. Vigorous translational movement | |
| 2. Total marine science—sum of time spent on direct marine science and marine science support | | 4. Light manipulative movement | |
| | | 5. Moderate manipulative movement | |
| 3. Total leisure—sum of time spent in corecreation, solitary recreation, and resting, relaxing, idling | | 6. Vigorous manipulative movement | |
| | | 7. Light expressive movement | |
| | | 8. Moderate expressive movement | |
| | | 9. Vigorous expressive movement | |
| C. Communication of each aquanaut | Every 6 minutes | **II. Dive Record** **Variable** | |
| **Categories** | | A. Dive start time | Each occurrence |
| 1. Not communicating | | B. Equipment used | Each occurrence |
| 2. Speaking to another aquanaut | | C. Order of egress | Each occurrence |
| 3. Listening to aquanaut 1 | | D. Dive duration | Each occurrence |
| 4. Listening to aquanaut 2 | | E. Ingress order | Each occurrence |
| 5. Listening to aquanaut 3 | | | |
| 6. jlistening to aquanaut 4 | | **III. Meal Record** **Variable** | |
| 7. Listening to aquanaut 5 | | A. Start of meal | Each occurrence |
| 8. Communicating with surface | | B. Primary cook | Each occurrence |

**Table 1**
**(continued)**

| | Frequency or Time of Collection | | Frequency or Time of Collection |
|---|---|---|---|
| C. Waiter | Each occurrence | **VI. Communication with Topside Record** | |
| D. Duration of meal | Each occurrence | **Variable** | |
| E. Primary cleanup diver | Each occurrence | A. Initiator of communication | Each occurrence |
| | | **Categories** | |
| | | 1. Topside | |
| | | 2. Aquanaut | |
| **IV. Arising–Retiring Record** | | B. Devise used | Each occurrence |
| **Variable** | | **Categories** | |
| A. Time of arising | Each occurrence | 1. Open microphone | |
| B. Time of retiring | Each occurrence | 2. Intercom | |
| C. Duration of time asleep | Every 6 minutes | 3. Telephone | |
| | | 4. Videophone | |
| | | C. Duration of conversation | Each occurrence |
| | | D. Content of communication | Each occurrence |
| **V. Specific Events Record** | | **Categories** | |
| **Variable** | | 1. Operational | |
| A. Maintenance of habitat by each aquanaut | Each occurrence | 2. Social | |
| **Categories** | | | |
| 1. Housekeeping | | | |
| 2. Habitat maintenance | | | |
| 3. Habitat repair | | | |
| 4. Baralyme change | | | |
| **Variable** | | | |
| B. Maintenance of self or other by each aquanaut | Each occurrence | | |
| **Categories** | | | |
| 1. Head usage | | | |
| 2. Use of shower | | | |
| 3. Laundry | | | |
| 4. Handling of food | | | |
| C. Use of Facilities by each aquanaut | Each occurrence | | |
| **Categories** | | | |
| 1. Watching outside TV | | | |
| 2. Watching TV tape for entertainment | | | |
| 3. Watching TV tape for training | | | |
| 4. Listening to radio | | | |
| 5. Using general leisure package | | | |
| 6. Using items from personal leisure package | | | |
| 7. Use of pressure pot | | | |
| 8. Use of winch | | | |

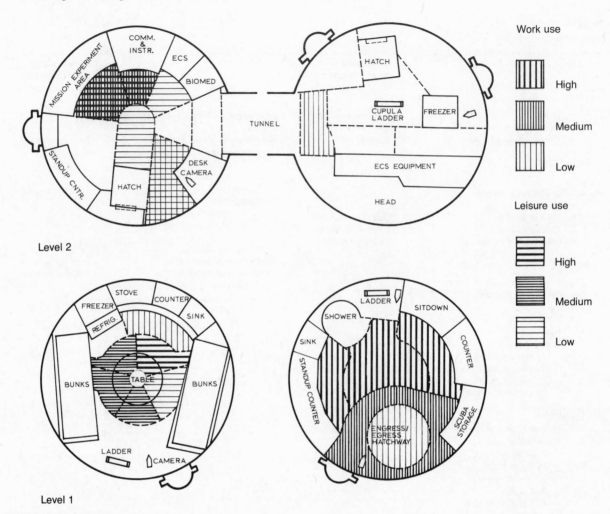

**Figure 5: Intensity of use**

utilization of the habitat than does the ranking for total use. The Wet Lab was used almost entirely for work, both research and preparation of diving equipment. It was damp, noisy, uncomfortable, and was avoided during leisure. The crew quarters (with the exception of food preparation in the kitchen area) was reserved for leisure, while the engine room was occupied only in transit and during work on life support equipment. The bridge was a mixed space, heavily used for both work and leisure. This analysis points out two major trouble spots in the habitat. The desirable space on the bridge was in demand both by those who had work to do and by those who wished to socialize. The simultaneous use of the space for work and leisure can hardly have presented an optimum work setting—especially since the modal leisure activity was conversation. An additional consideration was the fact that the fifth crew member could not spread out his bunk and retire while the space was in use—a real concern since there were large individual differences in work–sleep–leisure cycles. That this presented a problem is reflected in the fact that aquanauts sleeping on the bridge slept significantly less than those berthed in the bunks in the crew quarters. Use of the crew quarters for leisure also presented a potential disturbance for individuals. Since four bunks adjoined the table area most used for recreation, the bunk was not a silent retreat when others were up and conversing in the compartment.

Another aspect of the occupancy data suggests an environmental press. This is the fact that the most desirable spaces (in terms of total utilization) were consistently occupied by the most productive aquanauts. This could represent a territorial dominance by the most capable and motivated members of each group. However, it is also possible that the work output of nondominant group members was limited by their restriction to less choice areas.

In any case, the majority of the conflicts which did occur centered around the allocation of the limited spatial resources available in the habitat. It is also apparent that the data on space use along with other findings on aquanaut behavior could be used to design a more effective habitat environment.

Nonetheless, as emphasized earlier, the productivity and harmony of the aquanauts were outstanding despite the serious limitations and problems of the habitat and the stress, isolation, and confinement of the ocean floor setting. Such a highly positive response to a negative and stressful environment has been noted in a number of other investigations including studies of deeper, more dangerous, and more primitive underwater habitats, Antarctic stations, and space missions.[7] Indeed, a reasonable generalization from these studies would be that negative, extreme environments *facilitate* adjustment and performance—which, of course, is patently absurd. Adding to the complexity of the situation is the fact that laboratory and simulation studies of stress, isolation, and confinement indicate that man has a far lower tolerance for stress than has been repeatedly demonstrated in real-life settings. For example, small groups of subjects confined in comfortable quarters under no physical stress frequently abort their scheduled participation after one or two days, reporting the stress unbearable.[8]

In an attempt to resolve this seeming paradox, Roland Radloff and I[9] have extended J. Thibaut and H. H. Kelley's[10] formulation of social interaction into a cost–reward model of the desirability of various environments. Briefly, the model is based on the concepts of costs, rewards, and outcomes. Costs can be defined as the sum total of all stimuli which a person perceives as positive components of the total environment. The outcomes or consequences of any environment for an individual can be stated in terms of the rewards received and the costs incurred by participation. Thibaut and Kelley have proposed two standards by which the acceptability of outcomes for an individual can be judged. These are the *comparison level* (CL) and the *comparison level of alternative* CL(alt). An individual's CL is an absolute standard against which he judges the attractiveness of a situation; any environment above a person's CL is perceived as tolerable. An individual's CL(alt) is the relative standard used to judge whether or not he wishes to remain in a situation. The alternatives are other situations in which a person could be at a given time. Thus the CL defines whether a person's outcomes are better than, worse than, or equal to his expectations, while the CL(alt) indicates the relative attractiveness of other possible environments.

Figure 6 is an attempt to place various situations on a cost–reward matrix. Normally, the farther to the left and above the diagonal line, which represents the comparison level, the more desirable is the situation for a person or group. The farther to the right and below the diagonal, the less desirable are outcomes and therefore, the situation. The quality of adjustment and performance in an environment should be strongly influenced by its placement above or below the diagonal. The area below the dotted line in the lower right half of the matrix defines situations in which a person would not remain voluntarily, such as ghetto and slum environments and concentration and prison camps. Similarly, outcomes above and to the left of the upper dotted line are those which seldom occur because they yield normally, unattainably high outcomes. As an exercise, the reader may wish to try placing environments he knows on the matrix.

Note in particular the placement of circles representing *Tektite* and laboratory and simulation studies of isolation and confinement. The placement of these

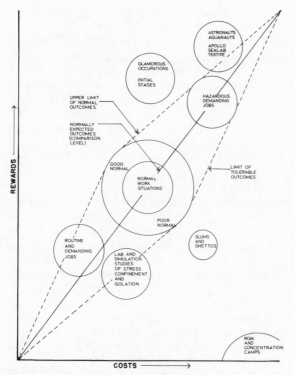

**Figure 6: The cost–reward model**

groups on the dotted lines means that *Tektite* is highly attractive, despite high costs, while simulation studies are situations of low attractiveness. In comparing the two situations within the cost–reward framework, we find that when studying groups in the laboratory or in simulation studies, we are subtracting from both sides of the equation (lower costs *and* lower rewards), thus achieving a rough level of equality between the two situations. If it were true that the only differences between simulations and naturally stressful settings were in costs incurred, then laboratory and simulation studies would have almost no value in the study of reactions to extreme environments. However, if it is recognized that many of the rewards found in the "real world" are not present in the laboratory, it would seem to redress somewhat the imbalance between the two research settings. It may be that the *ratio* of costs and rewards is more important than the absolute level in its effect on a variety of responses over a range of

cost–reward conditions. However, the noncongruence between simulation results and findings from field research suggests that the relationship may be nonlinear.

It has been suggested[11] that simulation may be a valuable tool for environmental psychologists. I would like to enter a strong warning about the utility of such studies. Because serious questions can be raised about both the validity and generality of findings from simulations, I would consider it a methodology of last resort, to be applied only when systematic data from natural settings are not available.

This leads to the final points I wish to emphasize. Foremost is the contention that the most valid way to assess environmental effects on human behavior is through the systematic, unobtrusive collection of objective data categorizing ongoing behavior in natural settings. Self-reports of participants and subjective impressions of observers will not provide the hard core of objective data needed to advance our understanding of environmental effects. The systematic observation approach to evaluation forces the investigator to define precisely the behavioral and physical parameters of the environment to be studied which should lead to better understanding of phenomena observed.

Variants of the methodology described here can be adapted to the study of most spaces, natural or manmade. Advantages include the fact that relatively unsophisticated observers can collect large amounts of highly reliable data using inexpensive, unobtrusive, portable instruments. Also, data are immediately available in a form permitting a variety of statistical analyses without a complicated transition from raw data to computer.

I also feel it imperative for the investigator to analyze the environment to be studied in terms of the costs and rewards anticipated by its inhabitants. Without consideration of both the absolute levels of costs and rewards and their ratio, interpretations of the effects of an environment are apt to be highly misleading. For example, both absolutes of cost and reward and the ratio between them are likely to be quite different if one evaluates a mental hospital ward in contrast with a similarly designed ward in a general hospital or a Naval ship of identical design. Within each pair, reactions to highly similar physical environments may be wildly divergent and might lead the designer or researcher to make unwarranted generalizations about the influence of a particular environment. The most brilliantly conceived prison may never be perceived by its residents as adequate living space while the most primitive shack inhabited by a group of scientists on the verge of a major find may be experienced as idyllic.

Another advantage of considering environments in cost–reward terms is that one can detect and assess changes in the cost and reward values of an invariant environment and can evaluate their influence. The first inhabitants of a newly created environment may gain rewards from the novelty or notoriety of the setting. These rewards may prove, however, to be transitory and a later assessment of the situation may show a very different ratio—typically, the rewards may prove to be quite labile while costs are relatively invariant.

At this point, such analyses must, of necessity, be crude and somewhat subjective. Nevertheless, attempts to place situations roughly on a cost–reward matrix and to project movement through the matrix over time will facilitate comparison of results obtained in different settings. Hopefully, as the field of environmental psychology develops, an objective system for the assessment of environmental costs and rewards will be produced which will give the student a more meaningful framework in which to place his work.

Finally, I would like to urge not only that planners routinely undertake environmental assessments prior to the execution of projects but also that they continue to evaluate the accuracy of their predictions at intervals after completion. Even doctors perform autopsies; but, then, doctors customarily bury their mistakes, while architectural and environmental blunders not only remain visible but are often replicated.

## NOTES AND REFERENCES

1. The research reported here was sponsored by the Organizational Effectiveness Research Programs, Psychological Sciences Division, Office of Naval Research under Contract No. N00014-67A-0126-0001, Contract Authority Identification Number, NR171-804 and by the National Aeronautics and Space Administration. Particular thanks are due to the aquanauts and psychological observers who made the research possible. I also appreciate the invaluable assistance of Roger Bakeman, Stephen Freeman, Daniel Gillum, Roland Radloff, and John Wilhelm who have worked on all aspects of the project.
2. G. F. Bond, "New developments in high pressure living," *Archives of Environmental Health* (1964), 310–314; J. Y. Cousteau, *World Without Sun,* New York: Harper & Row, 1965.
3. Edwins P. Willems and Harold L. Raush, eds., *Naturalistic Viewpoints in Psychological Research,* New York: Holt, 1969; and R. Radloff and R. Helmreich, *Groups Under Stress: Psychological Research in Sealab II,* New York: Appleton-Century-Crofts, 1968.
4. See Radloff and Helmreich, *op. cit.*
5. R. Helmreich, J. Lefan, and R. Mach, "Tektite 2: behavioral observer's manual," ONR Technical Report 13, Austin, Texas, 1971.
6. R. Helmreich, "The Tektite 2 human behavior program," ONR Technical Report 14, Austin, Texas, 1971; R. Bakeman and R. Helmreich, "Diagnosis and prediction: a study of daily behavioral patterns in Tektite 2," ONR Technical Report 17, Austin, Texas, 1971.
7. Radloff and Helmreich, *op. cit.;* E. K. E. Gunderson and P. D. Nelson, "Criterion measures for extremely isolated groups," *Personnel Psychology,* Vol. 19 (1966), 67–80; P. D. Nelson, "Human adaption to Antarctic station life," U. S. Naval Medical NPRU, Report 62–12, San Diego, 1962; W. M. Helvey, "Physiological and psychological problems in space flight," in *Biotechnology,* Washington, D.C.; NASA Publication SP-205, 1967.
8. W. Haythorn and I. Altman, "Personality factors in isolated environments," in M. Appley and R. Trumbell, eds., *Psychological Stress,* New York: Appleton-Century-Crofts, 1967; T. M. Fraser, "The effects of confinement as a factor in manned space flight," NASA Contractor Report 511, Washington, D.C., 1966.
9. Radloff and Helmreich, *op. cit.*
10. J. Thibaut and H. H. Kelley, *The Social Psychology of Groups,* New York: Wiley, 1959.
11. A. E. Parr, "In search of theory," in Harold M. Proshansky, William H. Ittelson, and Leanne G. Rivlin, eds., *Environmental Psychology: Man and His Physical Setting,* New York: Holt, 1970, 11–15.

*While environmental research has not involved "true" experiments, there is a growing need for control to link results of many experiments into support for design theories. In a discussion of various experimental designs, it is suggested that "quasi-experiments" are best able to deal with the complexity of variables. The author further develops evaluation of experimental design in relationship to time series. Other sources of information, such as questionnaires, behavior records, time budget measures, and observation, are discussed as supplementary souces of information for experiments the need for experimental programs to build a body of knowledge is presented in the example of experiments conducted to test the hypothesis concerning "undermanned behavioral settings. "*

# Experimental Methods in Environmental Design Research

**Robert B. Bechtel**

**Environmental Research and Development Foundation Kansas City, Missouri**

## INTRODUCTION

In the search for knowledge about human responses to the designed environment, perhaps the most restrictive and least understood method is the scientific experiment. Although "true" experiments are very few in the literature on environmental research, the word "experiment" is often used as though it were interchageable with research itself. Probably one of the reasons why experiments are so often mislabeled is that training in experimental methods is a central part of the training of psychologists but is not part of the training in the design professions, and is not emphasized in the training of sociologists, anthropologists, and other behavioral scientists.

The literature on experiments and experimental design is so voluminous that no attempt will be made to deal with it in detail.[1] Instead, the reader will be treated to a quick trip into the fundamentals with hopes that he will be either so intrigued or so mystified that he will want to carry it further.

## A DEFINITION

What is an experiment? J. Kling and L. Riggs say that it is an attempt "to control the situation in such a way that meaningful relationships can be established between antecedents and consequences."[2] The basis for the logic of most experiments goes back to John Stuart Mill:

*If an instance in which the phenomenon under investigation occurs, and an instance in which it does not occur, have every circumstance in common save one, that one occuring in the former, the circumstances in which alone the two instances differ is the effect, or the cause, or an indispensable part of the cause, of the Phenomenon.*[3]

Mill's logic can be placed in a diagram as follows:

Group A→gets the variable→Group A changes.
Group B→does not get the variable→Group B does not change.
   *Conclusion:* The variable is the cause of the change in Group A.

Likewise,

Group A→gets the variable→Group A does not change.
Group B→does not get the variable→Group B does not change.
  *Conclusion:* The variable is not the cause of any change here.

And

Group A→gets the variable→Group A changes.
Group B→does not get the variable→Group B changes.
  *Conclusion:* The variable is not the only cause of the change in Group A.

This design is really an oversimplified situation. First, it must be understood that either Group A and Group B are very much near equal on measures important to the experiment, or subjects have been randomly sampled and randomly assigned to each group. This is a cardinal rule of experiments and fulfills Mill's rule that the two circumstances must be similar in every respect save one—that of the variable introduced by the experimenter.[4] Second, the instruments used to test whether Groups A and B change must be demonstrated to be *reliable* (getting the same answers over time) and *valid* (actually measuring what they are supposed to measure), and they must be *independent*. This means that if measurement of Group A is somehow influenced by measurement of Group B (e.g., looking at each others' papers), the measures do not provide conclusive results. Likewise, measures across subjects *within* groups must be independent as well. Further, many authorities feel that the measuring instruments should be applied before and after the variable is applied to Group A, and likewise for Group B.

## EXPERIMENTAL DESIGNS

Taking the measurement problems into account, R. L. Solomon introduced one of the most elegant designs in experimental research:[5]

Group A is measured→variable *is* introduced→Group A is measured again.
Group B is measured→variable is *not* introduced→Group B is measured again.

Group C is not measured→variable *is* introduced→Group C is measured.
Group D is not measured→variable is *not* introduced →Group D is measured.

This design has the advantage of testing whether the second measures taken on Groups A and B were influenced by the first measures. This is tested by subtracting the results in Group C from Group A and Group D from Group B.

Of course, there are many more kinds of experimental designs, and these are discussed at length by D. Campbell and J. Stanley.[6] This handy little text is a sine qua non for researchers intending any sort of experiment, whether it falls into the "true" category or comes under what Campbell and Stanley call the *quasi-experiment*. A quasi-experiment is one where the experimenter cannot control all the contaminating influences. Nearly all the experiments appearing in the environmental research literature are quasi-experiments.

Campbell and Stanley disagree with the need for having premeasures like those in the Solomon design.[7] They maintain that a "true" experimental design can be achieved by the following:

Group A gets variable→Group A measured.
Group B does not get variable→Group B measured.

This means that the two groups must still be equal by measure or randomization but that premeasures are not necessary to further demonstrate that equality. And, of course, the effect of repeated measures is eliminated by not having premeasures.

Nancy Felipe and Robert Sommer did a field experiment that approximated the above design (Campbell and Stanley's type 6).[8] Subjects were hospital patients sitting out-of-doors. Both experimental and control groups were sitting alone on benches, either indoors or out-of-doors. To introduce the experimental variable, the experimenter would sit down beside the patient, and in some cases try to talk, and in others merely jangle keys. Controls were patients sitting on the benches who were not exposed to the experimenter sitting down beside them. The postmeasure for both controls and the experimental group was the time it took them to move from the bench. The design is as follows:

Patient sitting alone (Group A)→experimenter sits down→time measured until patient leaves.
Patient sitting alone (Group B)→experimenter does not sit down→time measured until patient leaves.

The results showed conclusively that patients moved away more quickly when the experimenter sat down. This design had an added sophistication by having two Group A's, one with a more obtrusive experimenter who talked and another who was less obtrusive and did not talk. This principle, varying the strength of the experimental variable, adds a further confirmation of causality. If it can be shown that the response varies with the strength of the variable introduced, the conclusion is far clearer. One criticism of this design might be that we have no assurance that the patients in Group A and B were equal and in truly equal circumstances. Yet this remains a controversy that cannot be completely settled. But inasmuch as patients in the hospital are equivalent, there is no reason to believe that any selection factor occurred—in addition to which every effort was made to find equal situations.

Often, of course, the researcher is unable to provide control groups as such and he may want to compare different methods to determine which one is the best. This can be done by a comparison group design as follows:

Group A→gets method 1→measured.
Group B→gets method 2→measured.
Group C→gets method 3→measured.
Group D→gets method 4→measured.

Since the only information needed is which method has the "best" effect, no control groups are needed. Each of the comparison groups, however, must be as statistically equivalent as possible, and this is usually accomplished by random assignment. R. Seaton and J. Collins had a basic design similar to this for simulation methods[9]:

Group A→sees real building→semantic measure.
Group B→sees color slides→semantic measure.
Group C→sees black and white slides→semantic measure.
Group D→sees model→semantic measure.

Subjects were randomly assigned to groups and then each group was assigned to one of the simulation methods. The results show that, generally speaking, the colored slide is the most equivalent to the real building. Variations on this design could be made by assigning one group to all methods and analyzing by repeated measures.[10] B. Winer argues that this is often a powerful design in that the subjects serve as their own controls. It requires, however, the specific kind of analysis of data that Winer prescribes.

A shorter variation of this design can be used. For example, when Oscar Newman compared crime rates of high-rise versus low-rise apartments and of areas with defensible versus nondefensible space, he found high-rise-nondefensible space had much higher crime rates than low-rise defensible space. His design was a simple 2-by-2 plot, which is especially amenable to such statistics as chi square.[11]

## MEASUREMENTS AND DATA

In a very real sense every time there is a design change in a building (remodeling, redecorating), a variable or set of variables is manipulated. If all other variables can be controlled, then the design change can be structured into an experimental design. More often, however, it is the case that several variables cannot be controlled and quasi-experimental designs must be used in order to study the situation. While it is true that in a quasi-experimental design the researcher cannot know the exact cause of any changes measured, he can often determine whether the general design change has produced the desired effect. In short, the quasi-experimental designs can serve the purpose of evaluation. Since evaluation is the greatest need in the field of environmental design research, the next sections of this paper will be addressed to designs for evaluation.[12]

## TIME SERIES

The quasi-experimental design chosen depends largely upon the kind of data the researcher can collect. Not all data can fit easily into the usual pre–post measurement design similar to Campbell and Stanley's design number 6.[13] It was Campbell who pointed out that with serial kinds of data collected over time, unless special time series analyses are used, the results can

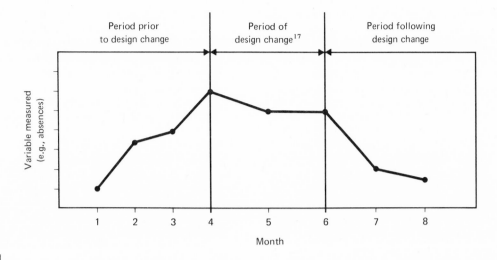

**Figure 1**

be misleading.[14] J. Gottman, R. McFall, and J. Barnett also show how several time series designs can be used to obtain useful results.[15]

The common kinds of time series data available for most researchers evaluating design change are records of things like absences, maintenance requests, complaints, incidence of crimes, illness, and other events recorded within some time frame. The advantages of these kinds of data are that the researcher does not have to collect them himself and that they have been collected usually far into the past beyond what are the usual resources for research and evaluation. The important thing is to arrange these events into those *before* the time change and those *after*. Then the data can be analyzed by the process shown in Figure 1.[16] With this design, the more intervals within the periods prior to and after the design change, the more sensitive the measurement of change.

A more powerful design is one using time-lagged multiple time series. The principle is to perform the same design change on equivalent groups *at different times* so that change can be unambiguously tied to the times that change took place. The design is shown in Figure 2.[18] What is especially powerful about this design is that when the change in introduced to Group A, Group B serves as a control, and when the change occurs in Group B, as a result of the intervention, we have further evidence that the changes are not due

to coincidence. This type of design would be especially useful in cases where the same modification was to be made in a series of buildings or in just two buildings.

## QUESTIONNAIRES

Often the researcher will want to use questionnaires that are more specific to design elements. Examples of these are Robert Sommer's "Evaluator's Cook-

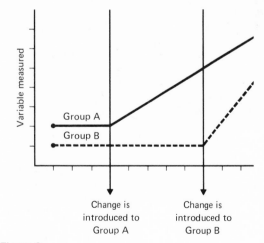

**Figure 2**

book,"[19] or for more specialized environments such as those of correctional institutions the questionnaire developed by R. Moos,[20] and for mental hospitals the questionnaires developed by J. Jackson[21] or Moos.[22] Many times researchers have used the semantic differential,[23] but if the purpose of the measure is *behavior* response, this will not do.[24] Basically, the questionnaire measures require a Solomon[25] design if one is concerned about measurement effects, or the Campbell and Stanley[26] type 6 if the researcher feels that the measurement effects are not a problem.

If the researcher does not feel that he can be certain enough of the changes expected to be measured by questionnaires, he may want to use methods that cover a wide-enough range of behavior to pick up whatever influences the design change may have on daily behavior. In that case the daily behavior records of F. Chapin and H. Hightower[27] may be used, or various other time budget measures.[28] It may also be useful to consider Roger Barker's[29] behavior-setting survey method which can be more easily tied in to some theoretical structuring of environmental factors than can other types of measures.

## THE NEED FOR EXPERIMENTAL PROGRAMS

A common problem in the presentation of experimental designs is that the novice often assumes that a single experiment is the principal vehicle by which to gain a great deal of knowledge. This is very seldom the case. The accumulation of useful knowledge in any field is a slow accretion of many experiments. Even the most critical experiment needs at least one replication. The more profitable course is for a program of experiments or investigations to pursue the variations around a hypothesis or theory.

In the field of environmental psychology there are few programs that are currently building such knowledge around a theory, but a good example of such a program is provided by Alan Wicker and his associates in their work dealing with the undermanned environment theory of Roger Barker. Barker[30] first proposed his theory upon discovering that residents of a small town in Kansas had 1.2 times as many behavior settings as a small town in England even though they

had only half the population.[31] This meant that, compared to the English town, the settings of the Kansas town were *undermanned*. Consequently, each occupant of the settings in the Kansas town had to work harder to keep the settings functioning. The situation of an undermanned setting produces many psychological and social consequences. Later research showed that the size of settings seemed to be related to the size of organizations.[32] There tended to be fewer people per behavior setting in smaller organizations than in larger ones. This can be looked at in another way: the number of behavior settings does not increase at the same rate as the number of persons when an organization gets larger.

The hypothesis states that size of behavior settings is related to the size of the organization. Barker and Paul Gump demonstrated that this was true for schools,[33] while Wicker demonstrated that this was the case for churches and cited industrial research literature that bore out the same relationship.[34]

This hypothesis has important consequences for design, especially considering that the occupants of smaller settings have more forces operating on them to participate,[35] and occupants of undermanned settings are generally more satisfied.[36] The undermanned environment theory makes it possible for the designer to deliberately induce these psychological elements in the occupants of his buildings by keeping the size of settings small.

Wicker, however, discovered that it was not solely a matter of undermanning.[37] The experiences that led to these psychological factors were more related to whether one was a *performer* in a setting rather than just a matter of having too few members. Figure 3 illustrates his discovery.

R. Petty and Wicker carried the undermanned theory further by a laboratory experiment designed to test whether undermanned groups would accept inept newcomers more readily than adequately manned groups.[38]

The simplified design was as follows:

Group A→undermanned→given inept performer→accepts.
Group B→adequately manned→given inept performer→rejects.

However, a surprise finding was that the undermanned

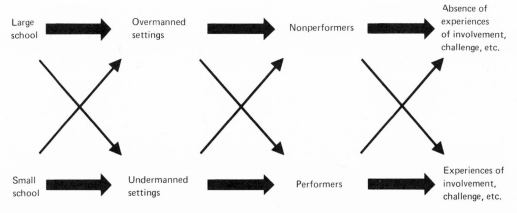

**Figure 3**

group did not *state* lower requirements for members than the adequately manned group.

In a summary of his research and the research of others, Wicker brings the undermanned environment hypothesis to a more refined state by adding the requirements of (1) *capacity* of setting, (2) determining the requirements of manning for both *performers* and *nonperformers,* (3) requiring more stringent definitions for *undermanned, adequately manned,* and *overmanned,* and by calling for more research that will (4) more carefully define the manning effects according to the task demands of the setting and that will (5) test the differential effects of degrees of manning over time.[39]

This very brief description of research in the undermanned environment theory serves only to illustrate a program of research that expands the understanding of how an increasing number of environmental conditions influence the experiences of persons in settings. As this knowledge expands the tools of the environmental designer, he will become better able to determine the kinds of experiences he wants occupants of his design to have.

## CONCLUSIONS

While the "true" experimental designs of Solomon,[40] or Campbell and Stanley's[41] type 6 are possible in some kinds of environmental research, the most common need in environmental research, that of evaluation, usu-

ally must settle for a quasi-experimental design because too many variables are outside the researcher's power to control. Nonetheless, by the careful accumulation of data from many cases, researchers can cumulatively eliminate rival hypotheses to the point where the effect of design elements on human behavior can be codified into general principles.[42] So far, the information is too scarce for most such formulations, but as time goes on attempts can be made to link results from many experiments into support for design theories.

## NOTES AND REFERENCES

1. E. G. Boring, *A History of Experimental Psychology,* 2nd ed., New York: Appleton-Century-Crofts, 1957; J. Kling and L. Riggs, *Experimental Psychology,* 3rd ed., New York: Holt, 1971; Charles E. Osgood, *Method and Theory in Experimental Psychology,* New York: Oxford University Press, 1953; B. Underwood, *Psychological Research,* New York: Appleton-Century-Crofts, 1957.
2. Kling and Riggs, *op. cit.*
3. Quoted from M. Cohen and E. Magel, *An Introduction to Logic and the Scientific Method,* New York: Harcourt, 1934, 256.
4. Underwood, *op. cit.*
5. R. L. Solomon, "An extension of control group design," *Psychological Bulletin,* Vol. 46, 1949, 137–150.
6. D. Campbell and J. Stanley, *Experimental and Quasi-Experimental Designs for Research,* Skokie, Ill.: Rand McNally, 1966.
7. *Ibid.*

8. Nancy Felipe and R. Sommer, "Invasions of personal space," *Social Problems,* Vol. 14, No. 2 (1966), 206–214.

9. R. Seaton and J. Collins, "Validity and reliability of ratings of simulated buildings," in William J. Mitchell, ed., *Environmental Design: Research and Practice: Proceedings of the EDRA3/AR8 Conference,* University of California, Los Angeles, January 1972. This is a simplification of the Seaton-Collins design. They actually had a $4 \times 4 \times 2 \times 5$ factorial design. See any standard text such as B. Winer, *Statistical Principles in Experimental Design,* 2nd ed., New York: McGraw-Hill, 1971, for explanation of the more complicated factorial designs.

10. Winer, *op. cit.*

11. Oscar Newman, *Defensible Space: Crime Prevention Through Urban Design,* New York: Macmillan, 1972.

12. Ann Ferebee, "Design for human behavior," *Design and Environment,* Vol. 2 (Winter 1971), 23.

13. Campbell and Stanley, *op. cit.*

14. D. Campbell, "Reforms as experiments," *American Psychologist,* Vol. 24, No. 4 (1969), 209–229.

15. J. Gottman, R. McFall, and J. Barnett, "Design and analysis of research using time series," *Psychological Bulletin,* Vol. 72 (1969), 29–45.

16. This diagram is adapted from Gottman, McFall, and Barnett, *op. cit.*

17. This can be eliminated so that only periods prior to and following change are analyzed.

18. From Gottman, McFall, and Barnett, *op. cit.*

19. Robert Sommer, *Design Awareness,* New York: Holt, 1972.

20. R. Moss, "The assessment of the social climates of correctional institutions," *Journal of Research on Crime and Delinquency* (July 1968), 174–188.

21. J. Jackson, "Factors of the treatment environment," *Archives of General Psychiatry,* Vol. 21 (1969), 29–45.

22. R. Moos, *Revision of the Ward Atmosphere Scales,* Technical report, Social Ecology Laboratory, Department of Psychiatry, Stanford University, June 1971.

23. Charles E. Osgood, G. Suci, and P. H. Tannenbaum, *The Measurement of Meaning,* Urbana, Ill.: University of Illinois Press, 1957.

24. Robert B. Bechtel, "Architectural space and semantic space: should the twain try to meet?" in Wolfgang Preiser, ed., *Environmental Design Research, Proceedings of the Fourth International EDRA4 Conference,* Vol. 2, Stroudsburg, Pa.: Dowden, Hutchinson & Ross, 1973.

25. Solomon, *op. cit.*

26. Campbell and Stanley, *op. cit.*

27. F. Chapin and H. Hightower, *Household Activity Systems —A Pilot Investigation,* Center for Urban and Regional Studies, University of North Carolina, Chapel Hill, 1966.

28. William Michelson, "Time budget research," in Preiser, *op. cit.*

29. Roger G. Barker, *Ecological Psychology: Concepts and Methods for Studying the Environmental Behavior,* Stanford, Calif.: Stanford University Press, 1968.

30. Roger Barker, "Ecology and motivation," *Nebraska Symposium on Motivation,* Vol. 8 (1960), 1–50.

31. Behavior settings are the natural units of behavior in community life. They comprise the stores, sidewalks, meetings, classes and all the everyday events into which people sort themselves. They are tied to a geographical place, have regular time, and have a standing pattern of behavior. See William LeCompte's paper in *Part Two.*

32. Roger G. Barker and Paul Gump, eds., *Big School, Small School,* Stanford, Calif.: Stanford University Press, 1964; E. Willems, "Sense of obligation to high school activities as related to school size and marginality of students," *Child Development,* Vol. 38 (1967), 1247–1260; Alan Wicker, "Size of church membership and members' support of church behavior settings," *Journal of Personality and Social Psychology,* Vol. 13 (1969), 278–288.

33. Barker and Gump, *op. cit.*

34. Wicker, *op. cit.*

35. W. J. Campbell, "Some effects of high school consolidation," in Barker and Gump, *op. cit.;* Paul Gump and W. Friesen "Participation in nonclass settings," in Barker and Gump, *op. cit.;* Alan Wicker, "Undermanning, performance, and students' subjective experience in behavior settings of large and small high schools," *Journal of Personality and Social Psychology,* Vol. 10 (1968), 255–261; Alan Wicker and A. Mehler, "Assimilation of new members in a large and small church," *Journal of Applied Psychology,* Vol. 55 (1971), 151–156; E. Willems, "Forces toward participating in behavior settings," in Barker and Gump, *op. cit.;* E. Willems, "Sense of obligation to high school activities as related to school size and marginality of students," *op. cit.*

36. Barker, "Ecology and motivation," *op. cit.*

37. Wicker, "Undermanning, performances and students' subjective experience," *op. cit.,* 259.

38. R. Petty and A. Wicker, "The assimilation of a new group member: a laboratory study of behavior setting theory," unpublished MS., Department of Psychology, University of Illinois, 1971.

39. Alan Wicker, "Undermanning theory and research: implications for the study of psychological and behavioral effects of excess human populations," in *Representative Research in Social Psychology,* Chapel Hill, N.C.: University of North Carolina Press (in press).

40. Solomon, *op. cit.*

41. Campbell and Stanley, *op. cit.*

42. D. Campbell, "Eliminating plausible rival hypotheses by supplementary variation," paper presented at the symposium of Methodological Problems in Cross-Cultural Research, American Psychological Association Annual Meeting, Washington, D.C., September 1967.

*The new professional who recognizes that the user is the client regardless of who pays the bill can be guided by three principles: first, the physical environment should maximize the freedom of its users to choose the way in which they want to live; second, the needs of particular user groups should be defined in terms of the underlying social meaning of behavior and attitudes in those groups rather than merely in terms of what others believe they need; and, third, the opportunities in the physical surroundings should accommodate as much as possible the needs of users. Instances in which do-it-yourself architecture has been reinforced through design or circumstances suggest a design response to the first principle.*

# Fundamental Values in Planning with the Nonpaying Client*

**John Zeisel**

**Harvard University**

## INTRODUCTION

Doctors, teachers, and architects have developed professional skills to provide services to clients who have the economic power to choose who serves them and in what way. People who cannot pay for medical care, education, and housing but who receive these services, nonetheless, have little say about how they are provided. Traditional methods are often not suited to the needs of the nonpaying clients. For example, doctors in poor urban areas cannot wait for patients in their offices. Medical problems common to the nonpaying client, such as vitamin deficiencies or poisoning from lead-based house paint, are not readily apparent, and poorer people often have great reluctance to seek out professional help. Professionals have adopted new techniques to serve nonpaying clients. Doctors go into the community, search out their patients, and work on teams with community members to overcome the forbidding image their potential patients may hold of doctors. Similarly, teachers in urban public schools are developing new ways to take into account the special needs of urban students from different cultural and

ethnic groups. To integrate what students learn with the way they live, some teachers try to spend as much time in the street as in the classroom. In housing, methods of research and community participation are being developed by architects and social scientists to make sure that housing is designed so that residents can live the way they are used to living. These professionals propose an approach in which nonpaying clients take part in the planning process, in which their needs are recognized as distinctive and newly defined, and in which services—schools, hospitals, or houses—are designed to meet those specific needs instead of to change them.

Doctors, teachers, and architects·are not alone in responding to the demands of the nonpaying client. Professionals in other fields—lawyers, politicians, businessmen, communications experts, ministers —react in different ways. Yet the new professionals share three basic values: (1) freedom for the nonpaying client to choose and control the·plans which affect him; (2) recognition of underlying social needs of the nonpaying client as the basis for service in addition to his self-perceived needs or wants; and (3) respect for the nonpaying client's needs so that the service he receives will accommodate him rather than force him to change.

How these values are translated into professional practice can be seen by analyzing in detail how one field, architecture, is reacting to a new set of requirements.

## ARCHITECTURE

Architecture is among the most irrelevant services for the nonpaying client because in the past it has truly served an aesthetic elite and because the art of architecture, its intuitive part, is so much more central to the profession than it is to either medicine or teaching.

With only intuition about his clients to guide design decisions, the architect cannot help designing for the needs of users as he sees them. Often he imposes his own values unconsciously or consciously on the people for whom he designs—behaviorally, symbolically, and aesthetically. *Behaviorally,* the designer builds for the way he himself would like to live or for the way he thinks others should live, rather than for the way others *do* live. Conflicts between the resident and his surroundings result when the planned environment does not easily adapt to his behavioral needs. *Symbolically,* the designer tells the user of an environment how to get from one place to another, how to locate someone, how to locate himself physically, or how to behave in a particular setting. When the physical cues built into a surrounding by the designer are not meaningful to the user, the user may become disoriented. *Aesthetically,* the designer often feels that he is the transmitter and interpreter of a commonly understood aesthetic style. When he designs in this style for persons familiar and comfortable with another style, a different culture, he runs the risk of robbing the user of a meaningful visual heritage. Aesthetic imposition is, of course, the least tangible form of imposition and the most easily overlooked by designers.

Today, many physical planners question whether a designer should dictate appropriate environments for behavior, whether he should be the one to define symbols to convey information, and whether he should be the transmitter of aesthetic "truths." Along with many social scientists in the field of design, these planners believe that

1. The physical environment should maximize the freedom of its users to choose the way they want to live.
2. The needs of particular user groups should be defined in terms of the underlying social meaning of behavior and attitudes in those groups rather than merely in terms of what they say they need.
3. The opportunities in the physical surroundings should accommodate as much as possible the needs of the users.

### Freedom

*The physical environment should maximize the freedom of its users to choose the way they want to live.*

Inherent in every physical environment are constraints on the behavioral and perceptual opportunities available to its users. If a large space has no walls, users may have a feeling of spaciousness, but they will find it hard to get away from others who are there. If an architect plans many walls to differentiate smaller spaces, users may feel more confined, but they can get away from one another if they want. If the architect decides that the living room is to face the street in housing with limited street frontage, other rooms, such as the kitchen, will be separated from street activity. Streets without shops maintain a strictly residential character but deny the opportunity to send children to a convenient store for daily necessities. When one is selecting a housing or office building site, opportunities for convenience in the inner city are often traded for greater personal comfort in suburban settings. The designer chooses between alternative constraints and opportunities in every design decision he makes.

When the builder was himself the user of an environment, as in most primitive societies, these choices were based on tradition. Traditional house forms evolved in response to social and cultural needs, and changed as the culture developed. Men in such societies who took the building of houses upon themselves embodied these traditions in their skills. When architecture and planning became established fields, these professionals usually reflected their clients' needs in that they

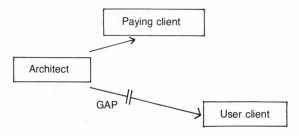

**Figure 1**

designed and built for people much like themselves. Since the industrial revolution, however, most housing and many environments have been designed and built for a client other than the user: workers' housing by the factory owner and not the worker, office buildings by a corporate board and not the secretaries, shopping centers by merchandisers and not the shoppers, hospitals by the technical staff and not the patients, schools by educators and not the students (Figure 1). The architect, paid by one client, designs for another, the user. The realization of the distinction between a paying and a user client, coupled with a commitment to maximize the user's freedom within the designed environment, led many designers to give some control over the planned surroundings to the user client.

Designers have primarily used adaptability and participation to increase user control over their planned environments. Architects, interior designers, landscape architects, and city planners are trained to design for many alternative spaces and arrangement of spaces. Today there is, as well, a trend to plan for adaptability whenever possible. Movable walls in housing, in schools, and in office buildings are commonplace. Landscape architects and recreational planners design "adventure" playgrounds, in which children can build and destroy their own recreation facilities. Bürolandschaft offices, in which there are no walls but merely movable modular partitions or desk carrels, give office workers the chance to create their own work spaces. In open-plan schools children can decide whether they want to face the window or the front of the room because their desks and chairs are on wheels. Designing simple adaptable structures also has shortcomings. Movable walls are sometimes never moved by the users once they are initially set up by the

designers. Landscaped offices can be landscaped by designers who impose themselves as much on office workers as if they had designed small enclosed cubicles. Teachers usually need special training to be able to teach children in the new setting of adaptable schools. It can be disconcerting to have a student sit with his back to you while you are lecturing the class. Despite the problems created by new forms of adaptability, designers who believe that the user should be able to control what he does within a physical setting continue to develop new forms of adaptability and to make old forms work better.

Physical planners also give users some control over their environment through user participation in both the design and the building process. City planners and architects started to work with community groups in the mid 1960's. Richard Hatch began the Architects' Renewal Committee in Harlem (A.R.C.H.) to give community members a voice in the Model Cities planning that was taking place throughout Harlem in New York City. Major U.S. housing programs, like Model Cities, made community participation a prerequisite to program funding. To help in school planning during the late 1960's and early 1970's the U.S. Department of Education began a system of community "charettes." "Charettes" bring together architects, educational specialists, community residents, teachers, and students who meet every day for several weeks to develop both an educational and architectural program for local schools. Private architectural firms, such as Arcop Associates in Montreal, hold community meetings to discuss plans for local housing, even though meetings are not required by the client. These architects realize the potential value of the user client's design input.

Although participation in the building process is not as widespread as is participation in the design process, several examples of do-it-yourself architecture exist where the planner provides a structural shell and the user client arranges the internal spaces.

Boston architect Jan Wampler's proposal for housing former residents of a shanty town in La Puntilla, San Juan, Puerto Rico, provides external walls, utilities, and a means of easily constructing internal partitions. While the architect of La Puntilla, by constructing windows and walkways, does define circulation organization, he lets the inhabitants lay out their own dwellings.

Throughout South America squatter settlements have been built up around large cities, predominately by dissatisfied urban dwellers. In Lima, Peru, the government, which has stopped sending the army periodically to rout the squatters, now offers squatters the right to settle permanently in these Barriadas. The settlers are given land title, a system of footpaths over water mains and a corehouse—a corrugated roof set on four wooden poles. As in La Puntilla the residents themselves build their own dwellings.

Buckminster Fuller's geodesic dome—now being used as roofing for restaurants, houses, sports arenas, and offices—might be seen as a technological response to this situation. It is an easily assembled shell in which any arrangement of spaces and activities is possible.

Although do-it-yourself architecture and planning definitely gives people control over their surroundings, it assumes that they have certain building skills, that the results will be more responsive to subtle needs than what the architect might be asked to do, and finally that the residents want to partake directly in the physical building of their housing. In La Puntilla and Lima the first two of these conditions are probably met. The residents of both the shanty towns of Puerto Rico and the Barriadas of Peru have demonstrated that they can construct their own simple dwellings, and from John Turner's work in South America we know that the existing Barriada dwellings are responsive to cultural differences as well as differences in family composition and size. In North American cities, however, most urban dwellers are several generations removed from a time when they possessed the manual skills to build their own homes.

While designers try to develop new ways for users to control their own environment, they often overlook the fact that even in dealing with a client who pays for and uses what is built, the architect combines personal insight into his client's needs with the information the client gives him about what he wants. He can no more depend solely on what his user client tells him than on what his paying/user client tells him. The architect must have information about the needs of users with whom he is unfamiliar. How the user client's needs are defined determines, to a large degree, how the architect responds to the user. Architects are working closely with social scientists to determine, through research, the needs of different user groups for different physical environments.

## Need

*Needs of users should be defined in terms of the underlying social meaning of behavior and perception to the user group, rather than merely in terms of what users say they need.*

"Functional" has been a catchword among designers since the turn of the century; yet the term "function" has several meanings. The Bauhaus and the modern movement in architecture used the term "function" to describe the use to which an object was put: furniture to sit on, cars to get to places in, kitchens to cook in, and streets to drive on. But, furniture is as much an expression of its owner's life style as it is a thing to sit on. Cars, for certain low-income groups, are as much a means by which men establish themselves in society as they are a form of transportation. In some cultures, kitchens have the same social impact, "latent function," for women that cars have for men: they are places for women to prove that they do their job in society well. The street has many more social functions than merely being a place to drive on.

Spaces and the behaviors that take place in them can be described in terms of both their manifest function (cars to get to places in) and their latent function (cars as a means of self-expression). While the manifest functions of most spaces and their behaviors is at least superficially similar for different societal and cultural groups, their latent functions often differ. It is therefore through identification of the latent function of a space that cultural differences between groups can be taken into account in designed physical environments. This is one of the fundamental contributions of the social sciences to research for architectural design. The use of living rooms, dining rooms and kitchens in white middle-class families, in working-class New York City Puerto Rican homes, and in moderate-income Southern black areas clearly points up the value of analyzing behavioral and perceptual data in terms of latent function. Middle-class white mothers in small urban apartments often entertain guests in the living room with their husbands. The time they spend in the kitchen is time spent away from their guests, unless a guest "helps" in the kitchen. The central social concern is how well guests get along or mix, not how much energy goes into cooking the meal. In fact, the greater the ease with which the food seems to have been prepared, the greater the praise of the hostess. A kitchen planned for this type of family is usually as compact, as efficient, as "functional" as possible. The closer it is to the living room, the more easily the hostess can join the social occasion taking place there. Also, since the living room is the symbol of sociability, the main entrance into the apartment can easily open directly into the living room, symbolizing the hospitality of the family. The apartment plan for such a middle-class family would have a closely connected living room and kitchen, and an entrance into the living room from the hallway (Figure 2).

In the homes of many working-class New York City Puerto Rican families, meals are eaten in the kitchen. The more time the lady of the house spends there the better mother she is, in the eyes of her friends and family. The living room, on the other hand, serves an important symbolic function. A study carried out in El Barrio, Puerto Rican Harlem, points out that on many living room walls in the apartments studied there are pictures of John F. Kennedy, large plaster saints, and the high school diplomas of the children. The television set in most apartments is in the living room as is a coordinated set of new living room furniture, all covered with plastic. The living room containing all of these political, religious, and economic icons of the family is, for them, a revered space, to relax away from the kitchen and for special occasions. It also provides an

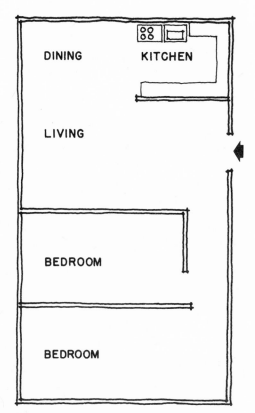

Figure 2

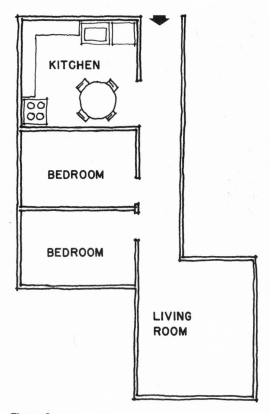

Figure 3

opportunity for the younger generation to keep out of the way of parents, and for groups of men and women to keep apart from groups of the opposite sex. In these families women and men do not always stay together during a gathering. For them there must be at least one other large space in the apartment, in addition to the kitchen. Since the living room holds a special revered meaning for the family, it is unthinkable that the entrance to the apartment be into the living room, as might be acceptable in more middle-class apartments. Also, since the lady of the house spends so much time in the kitchen during the day, it is most convenient if she has easy access to the front door, and that she be able to see which children are coming and going. The entrance to the apartment, therefore, must be separate from the living room and be closer to the kitchen than any other room. The plan for such a Puerto Rican family would have the kitchen separate from the living room, and the entrance to the apartment would be nearer to the kitchen than to any other room (Figure 3).

Finally, among moderate-income Southern blacks in South Carolina, a study found that whenever possible, the families ate in a room outside the kitchen. Instead or in addition to a matched set of living-room furniture younger families often had a matched set of dining-room furniture. If they could, they would have a separate dining room. According to the local community group, the need for a dining area, apart from the kitchen, reflects the culture of the blacks in the South, where traditional spicy and smelly foods like chitterlings, spare ribs, and fried chicken were cooked. Whereas originally a separate dining room was needed to get away from cooking smells, even as cooking habits changed, the social importance of having a separate dining area remained. The plan for this group would include a dining room separate from both living room and kitchen. The door from the living room to the dining room would be large so that guests could easily see the dining room (Figure 4).

A similar analysis of behavioral and perceptual data and their latent functional implications can be carried out for all spaces in a physical environment. Physical design implications usually can be formulated in terms of the relationship between the different spaces, as can be seen in the different relationships between living

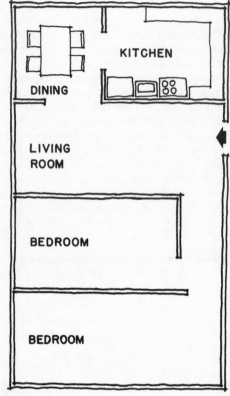

**Figure 4**

room and kitchen, and between entrance and living room in the above cases.

The underlying social impact of behaviors and spaces, their latent functions, are usually not consciously known to the residents of a particular setting. Traditional survey methods alone are seldom appropriate for discovering this type of information. Observational methods are basic to social/physical research. By observing behavior, the researcher can find out how much time middle-class white mothers spend in their kitchens as opposed to the time spent in the kitchen by working-class Puerto Rican mothers. Observing how these different groups entertain at home will allow the researcher to find out if the kitchen is a social gathering place or a place to avoid when guests are in the living room. Similarly, observing the physical setting can help

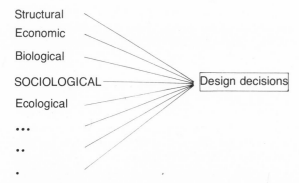

Structural
Economic
Biological
SOCIOLOGICAL
Ecological
...
..
.

Design decisions

**Figure 5**

a researcher to determine both how a space is used and its meaning to residents: in South Carolina residents had a dining table outside the kitchen door, indicating that they avoided eating in the kitchen. In Puerto Rican Harlem the living rooms were decorated with political, economic, and religious icons indicating the revered feeling residents had for this space. In whatever way the latent function of behavior, perception, and space is uncovered, the architect, planner, or designer has to translate this information into design (Figure 5). The way in which he does this depends on whether or not the designer respects and accepts the way of life of his clients, whether or not he is willing to accommodate the physical form he plans to the existing social needs of those who will use the environment.

## Fit

*The behavioral and perceptual opportunities provided by the physical surroundings should accommodate the needs of the users.*

Once the latent, as well as the manifest, function of spaces and their behaviors have been determined

through research it is not always clear how the designer should try to incorporate this information about user needs into the physical plans. Designers committed to the freedom of users and to looking for latent social structures often believe that they should respect the needs of users: that they should design a physical structure "around" a set of social needs.

The traditional architectural "program" which sets out the objectives of a plan is a good model for assuring accommodation between form and needs.

Economic and structural requirements are primary inputs: Will houses sell and will they stand up? In the 1920's biological requirements were added: Is there enough light and air in each room? Since the 1930's psychological and social criteria have been added by architects to their design programs: Will residents feel happy and be better off socially in a specific physical setting? But, while the basis for program inputs on cost, structure, and biological needs was systematic research, the basis for social and psychological program inputs was largely intuitive, ideological, and ethnocentric. Most designers felt that they knew, from their own personal experience, how people do and should live. From Le Corbusier's *Ville Radieuse* to the Goodmans' *Communitas* architects and planners have carried out almost no research to find out if their assumptions about other peoples' ways of life were justified.

A commitment to fitting social and physical structures to one another dictates as systematic an approach to research on social requirements as to research on the structural limits of materials. Five basic decision-making steps show how any design criteria are translated into design decisions (Figure 6).

In the case of structural criteria data would include the stress under which a beam of a certain length and breadth breaks. Patterns derived from many observations would be translated in this instance into a formula,

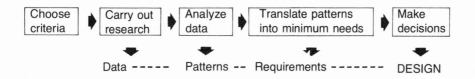

| Choose criteria | Carry out research | Analyze data | Translate patterns into minimum needs | Make decisions |

Data - - - - - Patterns - - Requirements - - - - - - - DESIGN

**Figure 6**

so that future architects would not have to repeat the same experiments whenever they wanted to choose a structural element for their housing. Patterned observations are then translated into sets of requirements the architect or planner must follow in his design. These often take the form of housing codes. Architects then use these parameters as one basis for design.

For social criteria the decision-making process is the same. Data on social phenomena are collected, predominantly on the latent function of certain behavior and perception, and analyzed in terms of the patterns that emerge. These patterns of social behavior and perception established for different social and cultural groups can then be translated into design parameters for the designer to use in making his decisions in that specific instance. The implication of a commitment to accommodation is that the physical environment should be designed to allow and facilitate those behaviors and perceptions integral to the social structure of the user group, even though these may not reflect the designers' style of life.

A study for housing carried out in South Carolina, among the working-class blacks of a moderately sized town exemplifies this approach. Preteenage children have some specific recreation patterns which could be planned for. Under the age of 6, children usually play very near their home. Mothers uniformly make rules that these children stay in the yard where mothers can keep an eye on them. In the back yard of many homes there are children's play units, including a swing, a slide, and a bar to climb (Figure 7). At the local supermarket such play units are predominantly displayed. Over the age of 6, until they reach their teenage years, children mostly ride bicycles and roller-skate in the streets and driveways near their homes. They are permitted to do so by their parents if the streets are not heavily trafficked.

In planning for these children these patterns prompted several decisions. For young children we planned no special tot-lots or playground areas near the houses. These, we felt, would quickly become the domain of the families immediately adjacent to the areas. For the bicycle and roller-skating crowd we planned two paved play areas, separated from the street by a row of poles instead of a chain so that

children would not have to get off their bikes. To make these areas and the street safer we limited access to the site by providing only one entrance, and we located the paved areas off the smaller streets. We planned many bumps in the road (known variously as "sleeping policemen" and "thank you ma'ams") to keep cars from going too fast.

All these decisions were made to respect the fact that mothers in this group want their young children to play where they can see them and that children do use the street as a playground. Every social pattern of behavior and perception can be translated into a "form requirement" the design of the physical environment has to meet if the pattern is respected. In this way just as there is an accommodation between physical and structural requirements there can be an accommodation between physical and social requirements.

**Figure 7**
**Photo credit: Brent C. Brolin**

## CONCLUSION

Among many designers and social scientists working together to solve sociophysical problems there is a common commitment to maximize the freedom of the users of an environment, to look for the underlying social meaning of behavior and perception for particular user groups, and to respect these social needs by designing environments which accommodate needs rather than conflict with them. This value orientation, coupled with a commitment to systematic sociophysical design research, is creating environments more consistently responsive to user needs than at any time since the dissolution of societies in which men built their own homes.

*An approach to the problem of developing a reasonably thorough description of behavior to be programmed for in the design of an office building is presented. The technique recognizes three categories of behavior: first, that relating to the organization to be housed—requiring an analysis of the structure of the organization as a determinate of behavior of its membership; second, that concerned with social behavior not necessarily devoted to the objectives of the organization; and, third, that manifested by the individual user—requiring an analysis of his perception of the environment, his actions within this context, and his attitudes toward it. Descriptive categories related to these behaviors and used to guide analysis of them are presented. They are organized to develop a description of the individual task, a description of the social considerations which tie individual members within an activity setting into social groups, and finally a description of the organization itself in terms of those aspects which have an effect on the behavior of individuals and on the physical environment.*

# Behavioral Analysis and Environmental Programming for Offices

Walter H. Moleski

Environmental Research Group

Philadelphia, Pennsylvania

## INTRODUCTION

In early 1971, the Environmental Research Group was asked to develop an environmental program for the interior design of a large office structure. The basis for the program was to be the incorporation of behavioral contingencies as a vital concern of the design solution. The problem was twofold: to develop a systematic way of describing the behavior across a series of occurrences in both time and space; and to systematically relate this behavior to the physical environment, developing the program requisites for that environment. To be successful, we felt that a holistic solution must be developed that would allow us to deal with all aspects of the behavioral–environmental interface. Behavior had to be researched in its actual, ecological context; it could not be researched in the laboratory setting. The significance and utility of the results would depend upon how we would analyze the complex interrelatedness of these behaviors and how we could discern the ongoing patterns and relationships of the various units which give them their character.

**Figure 1**
**Photo credit: Elliott Kaufman**

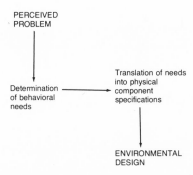

PERCEIVED
PROBLEM

Determination
of behavioral
needs

Translation of needs
into physical
component
specifications

ENVIRONMENTAL
DESIGN

**Figure 2**
**Behavioral programming process**

The success of the program would also depend upon its ability to describe the organization as an entity.

The problem of relating the behavior of the users of an environment to the design of that environment is a two-step process (Figure 2). The first step is to determine the behavioral needs of the users. The second is to translate these needs into components of the physical environment. There are some basic issues in the analysis of behavioral patterns in the context of the physical setting. Since it has been determined that behavior in relation to a physical setting is dynamically organized, and a change in any component of the setting will result in a change in the characteristic behavior of that setting,[1] an important consideration of any analysis would then be the determination of the ongoing patterns of behavior that will remain constant when the organization changes its environment either by relocating or by modifying the existing environment to the behavioral patterns; this is an essential issue in that the designer must understand what effect his manipulation of the physical elements of the environment will have on the behavior of the users. If the analysis is to lead to an environmental program, those physical elements which have an effect on the behavioral patterns must be identified and the relationship between them and the behavioral patterns must be understood. Still another important issue is the examination of all units of behavior within the setting.

To understand the behavioral components of an environmental ensemble in holistic terms, three units of behavior must be analyzed, first as separate entities and then as they interrelate. These three components

are organizational, social, and individual goal-directed behaviors.

The purpose of the analytical stage of the process is to systematically record and analyze the ongoing behavioral patterns that would be affected by design decisions. The second phase of the process would develop this behavioral analysis into an environmental program which would specify the nature of the physical environment.

As investigations began, several methods were being used to analyze office environments. These methods all failed to be holistic in approach, as each dealt with only one aspect of the organization's relation to its environment. In addition, none of them was concerned with the actual behavioral requisites of that environment. The first method, developed by the Quickborner Team (originators of office landscape planning in the late 1950's in Hamburg, Germany, led by Wolfgang Schnelle), analyzed the organizational structure in terms of its efficiency of management and decision making. Another process, developed by Warren Koepf, of Herman Miller Inc., was based upon the analysis of communication interactions and the physical requirements of tasks. A third, more complete concept was developed by Dr. Fred I. Steele,[3] in which underlying principles were based on organizational performance and considered three criteria: adaptability and problem solving, sense of identity with the organization, and reality testing of the environment.

## METHODOLOGY

Because of the complex nature of the problem with which we were concerned, no single method of data collection would have been able to generate the required data; therefore, an interrelated system comprised of interviews, user questionnaires, and structured observation techniques was employed. Each method had some inherent weakness which would tend to produce either incomplete or confounding information. The first, the structured interview conducted with the management of the corporation, has been shown in a considerable number of studies to be weak since management personnel tend to be poor judges of the attitudes, perceptions, and motivations of their employees and tend not to accurately specify the employees' environmental needs. The second method, systematic observation, has the obvious limitation of observing behavior in a probable dysfunctional environment and that "behavioral carryovers" are not necessarily ensured when the environment is changed. The third method, user questionnaire to the members of the organization, has several weaknesses; the lack of awareness of most people concerning the effect of the physical environment on their behavior, general prejudice which favors the known and the familiar, the tendency for members of a group to overemphasize their importance in terms of the function of the organization, and a failure to grasp the overall function of the larger group (Figure 3). By combining all three methods and utilizing each to gain the information that it could most effectively and appropriately elicit, a comprehensive data-gathering system was generated. Another facet of the system was that each contained some internal checks upon the information gained through other means. Initially, the investigators visited the existing location of the facility and informally observed the corporation in action. Then a series of nondirected interviews were conducted with management concerning the nature of the organization in order to form the context of the investigation. From these two activities, an investigation strategy was planned and the instruments tentatively drawn up. These instruments were planned to be free to respond to any significant areas warranting further investigation or more complete explanations to clarify a situation.

The series of structured interviews were held with both executive-level and line management-level personnel. The information sought during this time focused on the attributes of a particular work subsystem and its relationship to other subsystems and the larger organization. Questions were also directed toward broad classifications of variables and toward uncovering any dysfunction or dissatisfaction with the existing environment. Categories of information sought were organizational structure and policy, spatial description of the workflow, activity, communication, and interaction patterns, ratings of tasks performed by staff, description of perceived needs in spatial organization, ratings of the existing environment in terms of meeting these needs, indications for structuring of the existing space, perceived needs in the perceptual qualities of the space, and future trends which would affect the group's function and environment.

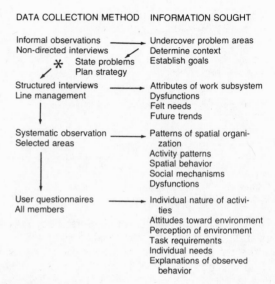

**Figure 3**
**Methodology**

The next step was the systematic observation of the environment and the behavior taking place within it. The observations lasted for a period of thirty minutes and were repeated a number of times throughout the investigation. The initial step was to map the behavior as it occurred within the setting.[4] This entailed the recording of the discrete behavioral episodes as they took place; these were then categorized and a behavioral setting inventory compiled.[5]

This inventory included both recordings of the behavior taking place and descriptions of the physical setting in which it occurred. The physical description contained patterns of spatial organization, the physical and functional distances between occupants, visibility of the occupants to each other, distractions and interferences present in the setting, boundary conditions, perceivable power cues, and the overall physical character. The activity pattern of the setting was encoded to describe what categories of activities were taking place and rated along scales of participation, tempo, and intensity. The mechanisms recorded were affective behavior, gross motor activity, manipulative activity, verbalization, thinking, variety of behavior, pressure to enter the setting, and penetration by outsiders. The social mechanisms were also recorded and rated; these included type of authority system, interdependence between this site and others, population density, occupancy time, and temporal loci of occurrence, duration, and recurrence.

The final method of gathering information utilized was the user questionnaire. These questionnaires were distributed to all members of the staff. The information sought concerned the nature of the activities pursued by the individual and his attitudes toward and perceptions of the environment and the organization. Information was also elicited concerning the individual's perceived needs. Within the first category, information included descriptions of jobs, time breakdowns of activities and task-related social participation, ratings of tasks along several adjective scales, and sociometric data about communication patterns, authority interactions, locational preferences, and workflow. In the second category, individuals were asked to rate the environment according to its physical and social attributes. A series of questions concerning how they perceived the various aspects of their environment and the organization in general were presented. The employees were asked to give their requirements for an optimum working environment and to describe any dysfunctions within their current environment and work stations. In addition, questions were asked to elicit information required for the explanation of problem areas uncovered during the first two information-gathering processes. These questions were generally concerned with employee attitudes toward working within a specific problem environment, the manner in which they performed some activity, or how they spent free time within the organizational boundaries.

The material produced by the above methods was analyzed by combining and comparing the resultant information and was mainly concerned with identifying the factors related to the behavioral–environmental interface. Any discrepancies were discussed with the people involved to ascertain the nature of the conflict. Three units of classification of the material for analysis were employed: organizational structure, spatial distribution, and job categories. In the first unit, the material was plotted according to the various components of the organization, and analysis was constructed around organizational criteria. The second unit required that the information be organized in a sociometric diagram and analyzed according to the attributes of the physical setting. In the third unit the job was broken down into job categories and analyzed by task requirements and hierarchical position. A final analysis was conducted by comparing the three units as separate bodies of information.

## RATIONALE

Several theoretical considerations strongly affect the relationship of behavior to the physical environment in a set of corporate offices. Forming the basis of our analysis, these considerations include the spatial and sociopsychological base of organizations, activity systems, behavioral settings, communication patterns, and perceptual identity within an organization.

A corporation is a complex social organization consisting of structured, functional, and social components in which people behave in an interrelated fashion according to the norms, values, and roles existing in the context of the goals of the organization and which have the acceptance of its members. A social organization is a patterning of activities which reduces the variability of human behavior by means of three types of pressures: task requirements in relation to satisfying an individual's needs; demands arising from shared values and expectations; and reinforcement of accepted rules.[6] The nature of an organization is defined, and its boundaries are determined by the relationships and patterns of behavior involved in the process of achieving its goals.[7]

An organization will establish sets of roles for its members to perform organizational tasks and to relate members to each other. These sets of role behaviors formalize the expected interdependent behavior of the members and represent standardized forms of activity.[8] Members of social organizations have strongly held expectations about their role set and the role set of others, which includes the physical setting in which the role behavior is to take place. Overtly, they will attempt to communicate their expectations for the roles to be played and will exert pressures upon the individuals involved to conform to this role set, exhibiting stress if these expectations fail to be met.[9] To ensure that these role behaviors are established, a task-oriented organization will exert influence on the behavior of the individual members by dividing the work among the members, establishing standard practices and systems of authority, providing channels of communications, and training new members.[10] By doing so, the organization develops a set of norms which make explicit the forms of behavior considered appropriate for its members and a set of values which rationalize these normative requirements. A major determinant of an organization's system of norms is the type of activity in which the organization is involved.[11]

Within the boundaries of the organization, behavior occurs which is not involved with organizational context but will nevertheless exert some influence on the physical environment. These units of behavior are the social behavior of informal groups and secondary organizations and the behavior of individuals. Because of the possibility for members of the primary organization to belong to other organizations, these overlapping secondary organizations become an adjunct component of the organizational environment. Another level of behavior within this category involves the social interactions taking place which are not concerned with the output of the organization. Since a person does not devote his entire fund of energy to the pursuit of organizational goals, the environment must allow him to pursue other behaviors than those required in organizational role performance. An individual will also attempt to organize his environment to give the maximum freedom of choice in behavior.[12] These extra-organizational behaviors must be identified and analyzed as part of the whole environmental system.

Because of the purposeful and goal-directed nature of an organization, it divides its activities into specialized subsystems to achieve optimum efficiency of means. These subsystems are in the terms of the corporation, departments, work groups, or task forces. The subsystems interrelate with each other and the relationships and linkages between them determine the nature of the organization and will affect the behavior of its members.

When considered as an ecological unit, the organization determines its environment by controlling the activities taking place within its boundaries through certain processes. An organization will distribute activities spatially and will prescribe regions for these activities to take place. It will also control behavior by segregating one behavior from another and establishing normative behavior for each setting. Ecologically, organizations also establish the rhythm and the tempo with which activities take place. Finally, the organization controls the time sequence of the activities taking place.[13] These ecological processes both temporally and spatially construct the activity system of the organization. An activity system develops when a behavioral unit such as an organization, a social group, or an individual exhibits regularities in the content and ordering of its activities in time and space.[14] The activity system consists of those discrete behavioral episodes which have meaning by being purposeful, and it is influenced by environmental constraints. Because an organization locates its activity system spatially and temporally, ongoing behavioral patterns can be studied in relationship to its physical setting.[15] This relationship between behavior and its setting can be further studied by analyzing its dynamic organization,[16] and characteristic behavioral patterns can be identified. Since the behavioral patterns must be compatible with, and are closely related to, the physical place in which they occur, components of that physical setting can be studied as to their effect on these behavioral patterns. This active and continuing process in which the components of both the physical and the behavior systems are defining and being defined by each other establishes a meaningful system of feedback between the elements of the environment.[17] It is in this manner that the physical environment supports the organizational system and the patterned behavior of its members.

## ACTIVITY SITE MODEL

The analysis of the behavior in the process taking place within the corporate environment led to the concept of activity sites as the model for developing the behavior–environment interface. This concept binds the organizational activity systems to the organizational space in which they occur. An activity site is a physical area within the organizational boundaries in which a prescribed activity recurrently and regularly takes place; this activity is purposive in that it is directed toward the achievement of organizational or corporate objectives and is controlled by organizational rules. Another facet of the concept is that because of the purposefulness of the activity, all activity sites are to some degree interrelated and are linked together to form the corporate environment.

The activity taking place within the site is patterned behavior required to carry out the continuing cycles of events to achieve the organizational goals. The behaviors can vary over a period of time, and behavior not concerned with corporate objectives may occur. The primary attribute of the activity site is the relationship between the behavioral patterns and the physical site in which they take place. Because of this interdependency, an activity site can be described in either its physical or behavioral components. A description of one set of components can be used to specify the components of the other.

Within the context of the corporate environment, the activity site can be viewed on several scales, depending upon the level of analysis. If the corporation is being studied as a totality, each department would then be considered as a separate activity site. The audit department, for example, pursues a particular system of activities in a physical setting; these are significantly different from those taking place in the accounting department or the research department. In the next lower level of analysis, the immediate environment of the work group can be considered as an activity site. At this level, scaled comparisons can be made on a more discrete level of analysis, and the behavioral components of work groups can be examined across the organization without reference to the departmental structure. The final level of analysis is the consideration of an individual's work station, whether it is a desk or a suite of offices, as a separate activity site. This scale is used to analyze the smaller-scale and individual considerations of the environment. Task activities can also be compared throughout the organization. By considering the activity sites as a system of parts, the smaller-scale activity sites can be organized hierarchically to form the corporate environment.

Another area in which the activity site concept was a tool for analysis was in the area of extraorganizational behavior or social activity taking place outside the context of the organization, consisting of informal social behaviors that occur without a formal structure of their own. These behaviors function to humanize the organization and to relieve some of the organizational stress by establishing informal contacts among members of

the organization. If an office environment is to be successful, the physical environment must be able to foster such behavior. The activity site model can be used for analysis within a context by reducing the weight of the organizational components of the model.

## RELATIONSHIP OF ANALYSIS TO PROGRAMMING

Here we are dealing with the second aspect of the problem, that of determining how behavior can be analyzed and developed into programmatic requirements for the design of the physical environment. Two design methodologies have been developed in past years in which the search for a solution to environmental problems was conceived of primarily in terms of its behavioral or sociophysical aspects. Both methodologies were steeped in the systems analysis tradition. The first was Raymond Studer's behavioral-contingent environmental design, in which he proposed that "the designer's mission is to delineate the human behavior that must be accommodated and the realization of a system of energy and matter which supports these."[18] To do this, he developed a design methodology in which the initial step is the delineation of the behavioral system. The next step is the specification of the characteristics of the required physical support system. Only after these two steps are accomplished can the physical system be realized.

In another article, Michael Brill[19] describes several levels on which specifications for environmental performance may be developed. The one which applies to the problem in which we are interested and which permits the widest range of solution was the specification of environmental objectives. These objectives were described by performance characteristics which included nine scales of sociophysical considerations, including levels of privacy, social interaction, formality, familiarity, accessibility, legibility, diversity of activities, adaptability, and comfort. An environment to be designed can be described in these nonhardware terms, and a number of solutions can then be proposed which would satisfy the specified performance.

While agreeing with these two approaches, we nevertheless felt that something was lacking in each of them when considered for our purposes. The Studer paradigm lacked a realistic way in which the behavior system could be translated into a physical system. Brill's method was vague concerning what generates the need for the performance requirements. It was felt that criteria were needed for determining at what level the physical environment had to perform in order to support the behavioral system of the organization. It is not, however, a simple step to go from the behavioral description of the environment to the physical environment. An intermediary step is needed which contains elements having both social and physical attributes to describe the performance of the environment in supporting behavior. This is where Brill's model develops its significance, in that he presents a clear concept for developing performance characteristics. Guided by this approach, our investigators constructed a model having three components: (1) a description of the behavioral system of the environment; (2) a definition of performance of the environment in sociophysical terms; and (3) a specification of the physical components of the environment (Figure 4).

## ANALYTICAL PROGRAMMING MODEL

The activity site concept was developed to relate behavioral and physical components. By doing so, it enabled us to analyze the behavioral system and to develop sociophysical performance characteristics for the supporting physical system.

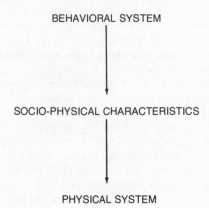

BEHAVIORAL SYSTEM

SOCIO-PHYSICAL CHARACTERISTICS

PHYSICAL SYSTEM

**Figure 4**
**Analytical programming process**

The model which we developed for the functional analysis of behavior by activity sites and for specification of the physical components of the environment consists of three interrelated parts. The first is a system of behavioral descriptors used to describe those elements of the activity system having an effect on design decision making. Other aspects of behavior were present but either had no effect on the design of the environment or were idiosyncratic regarding individual users and would not affect the ongoing behavioral patterns. By systematically describing the behavioral component of the activity site, using descriptive dimensions to follow, the second element of the model, the performance characteristics of the activity site, is developed. To support an activity, the physical component must perform in a specifiable manner. By analyzing the behavior as described in the first element, the performance requirements of the environment are generated. To satisfy the performance characteristics of the ensemble, a physical support system can be developed to accommodate the behavioral pattern. Research has shown that the physical environment has some effect on the behavioral patterns in the setting, and manipulation of the physical setting will change the characteristic behavior.[20]

To further understand the concept of the behavioral analysis, performance, and physical-setting dependency, it is necessary to discuss the dynamics of the system which it constructs. Each of its three elements, behavior, performance, and physical subsystems, must be considered as whole entities comprised of interrelated descriptors. Any manipulation within a subsystem will change the nature of the whole. All the behavioral descriptors come into play in determining the performance characteristics; no one single descriptor has the power to completely control any one performance characteristic. Each performance characteristic is dependent upon a number of behavioral descriptors, and the performance will vary according to the magnitude of the behavioral descriptors. The descriptors, however, can be weighted to achieve optimization of the ensemble, and tradeoffs can be made to bring the system into congruence. There is no single direct translation between a physical descriptor and a physical component. The role of the performance characteristics is to permit the generation of a number of alternative ways in which the physical elements can be manipulated. Finally, the behavioral–physical system is dynamically organized, so that any change in the ensemble would result in a change in the characteristic behavior pattern. To achieve balance in the behavioral system, one may make a change in the physical, social, or organizational structures which define the setting in order to achieve the necessary congruity within the activity site. To describe the behavioral components of the activity sites we found it necessary to develop a systematic method which would be capable of describing behavior over a number of different sites. We termed this method of description a genotypic function typology. This term refers to the activity performed by a unit of the organization as part of its function within the larger organization. The typology divides behavior into three subsets: task, social, and organizational behavior (Figure 5).

What we have termed task-related descriptors include those behavioral components created by the task itself, as performed by the individual or workgroup. A simple, concise *definition of the activity* taking place gives a very general indication of the ongoing behavior within the activity site, and this constitutes the initial step. Then, the following descriptors are used to characterize each task; each descriptor can be given rank and scale values as to its hierarchical importance within the system:

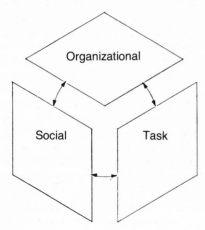

**Figure 5**
**Activity site model**

The *level of activity* is the specification of the amount of physical activity actually required to perform the task. Two types of activity must be considered: gross motor activity and the manipulative activities involving fine muscle control.

The *level of thinking* describes both the type and the intensity of thinking required for the performance of the task. Here it is necessary to determine whether the occupant is involved in problem solving, decision making, or rote mental activity. An intensity dimension is required, as well as a dimension of differentiation in thinking activities.

The *level of routineness* present describes the amount of repetition in the performance of a task over a period of time and whether the task is varied in nature.

The *level of attention* indicates the type, as well as the intensity, of selective attention which must be maintained by the performer.

The *orientation of the performer* involves a description of the central focus which must be maintained to accomplish the task; it can be a physical or a nonphysical element.

The *volume of work* refers to the actual amount of work which is completed by the performer during a specified temporal period.

The social considerations of the activity system describe those elements which tie individual members within the activity site together into social groups. In this way, the first level of the social structure is formed.

The *amount of social structure and the formalized role systems* discernible within the group provide the initial dimension. This has reference to the presence of behavioral patterns which are anchored in the attitudes, perceptions, beliefs, and motivations of the inhabitants of a social space. The formalized role system is the explicit formulation of rules which define the interdependent behaviors.

A second criterion involves the *interactions related to the task which are required for its performance.* This becomes a description of the communications patterns serving to form individuals into groups. These exist along two dimensions: type and intensity. Another characteristic of these interactions is that they are purposeful in that they exist because of the needs of the activity. In sites where a low level of task-related interaction is required to perform the task, a second level of social interaction takes place which serves to link the group together.

The *communication networks* that tie one group to another constitute additional criteria. These criteria permit the examination of the links existing between groups or between individuals on several levels, such as frequency, mode, and purpose.

The *level of supervision* required to ensure that organizational objectives are being met describes the exercise of authority within the site and and the amount of choice afforded an occupant in selecting a behavior pattern.

The *social focus of the performers* in the sites simply describes the group in terms of its type and size within the larger setting.

Organizational considerations of the genotypic function of the site are those components that describe the organizational behavior. Since the organization effectively controls much of the behavior which takes place, it is necessary to categorize those aspects of the organization which have an effect on the behavior of individuals and on the physical environment. The organization is the larger form of social structure uniting the smaller groups.

The *value system as held by the leaders of the group* describes the ideological justifications and aspirations of those who have control of the system. This buttresses the authority structure and the behavior of the system. Such a dimension can be described on a continuum from pragmatic to transcendental.

The *system norms* make explicit the forms of behavior which are appropriate for members. These are accepted by the members as being relevant and desirable. These can be scaled along three standards: the acceptance of appropriate behavior, the commonal-

ity of the acceptance, and the awareness of group support for this acceptance.

The *outcome of the activity* provides a measure regarding whether the activity is immediately and directly involved in the primary product of the organization, or whether it is involved in influencing other subsystems.

The *type of reward system* describes how the members receive their rewards for task performance. Two types of reward systems are the expressive cycle and the instrumental cycle. The expressive cycle refers to rewards based on personal fulfillment of the individual in the performance of his role; the instrumental cycle refers to rewards based on pay and other external considerations.[21]

The *type of authority system* describes how management expresses its control over its members. Theory X refers to the reliance on authority as the primary means of control, and it is reductive in intent. Theory Y relies upon the motivation of the performers for control and is developmental in intent.[22]

## ACTIVITY SITE LINKAGE CONSIDERATIONS

Since an organization must divide itself into functional subsystems and will distribute activities within its boundaries, the organizational environment will consist of a myriad of activity sites linked together by various ties. The type of links existing between activity sites and the strength of these links is a function of the type of activity that takes place within the sites. Some linkages are networks that span the entire organization, while others will only connect several sites together.

The most common linkage is the *communication network,* which ties one site to another by the flow of information required to perform the task of that site. These networks are usually established across the organization in relationship to its character and the nature of the activities. Two types of communication networks exist normally within a corporate environment, a formal one which is defined by organizational policy and an informal one which develops outside that policy. The character and function of the information can be analyzed by the direction of its flow.

The characteristics of some activity systems require that other forms of connection take place between sites. One classification is *functional connections of work flow, material flow, and paper flow*. In a situation where the activity is part of a larger ongoing system or material that was utilized was produced within another site, or a large volume of work passed between sites, the most important locational criterion was the ease with which the work or material flowed between sites.

Because of the organizational goals or values, other activity sites were located by *considerations of status*. To increase the status of an activity site to reach some organizational objects, it was located within the perceptual sphere of a high status site so that it may share its perceptual identity. In addition, activity sites were connected by *power networks,* which were generated by the hierarchical organizational structure.

The final means of locating activity sites within the organizational territory was the *compatibility of activities,* physical settings, or populations. This category of linkage operated when there were no other available criteria to locate the sites. It was also used to modify the strength of other connections. Two sites have a communication requirement that represents a tie between them; however, if the activity patterns are incompatible, some dysfunction may result if it is not taken into consideration.

The linkage elements can be analyzed as to their character and strength, and weighting can be given to each. This then can be utilized to establish the geographic distribution of the activity sites across the organization, and these relationships can be described by either mathematical matrices or sociograms.

## NONORGANIZATIONAL SETTINGS

In settings which are not involved in carrying out purposeful behavior for the organization, this three-part descriptive system could also be used to describe the behavior of those sites by merely eliminating the nonrelevant organizational factors. These informal settings do not have an organizational substructure of their own and they comprise the extrasocial environment which is not limited by the boundaries set by the organization. For the environment to fulfill all the needs of the users, these overlapping social settings must be included in the design and their performance can

be specified in the same manner as that of the activity sites.

## SOCIOPHYSICAL PERFORMANCE DESCRIPTIONS

The sociophysical performance characteristics are those elements which define the performance of the environment in terms that have both physical and social connotations. These performance elements serve as a translating function permitting the nonphysical behavioral components to be developed into a physical setting (Figure 6). The advantage of systematically describing the performance of the site allows the designer a choice of alternatives in satisfying those requirements and holistically developing design concepts to unify the organizational environment. This structuring of alternatives also permits the designer to evaluate his decision along a consistent set of dimensions and to predict the success or failure of the design solution.

The performance required to support the activity patterns is determined by scaling the requirements along various continuums which are measures of environ-

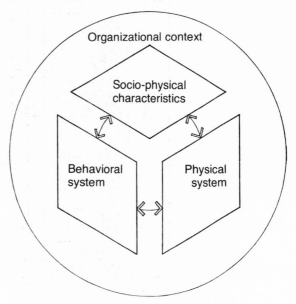

**Figure 6**
**Analytical programming model**

mental properties. These continuums are nonvalue scales, and do not indicate that one end of the scale or the other is more or less desirable. For example, there is nothing to indicate that privacy is more desirable than communality. It only becomes desirable when it is applied to some context.

In a particular activity site, some of the scales may also be irrelevant as indicated by a particular behavioral pattern. In such cases it is simple to disregard those scales for that site. The scales need not possess equal weight for all sites, as this will be indicated by the analysis of the behavioral description. The weighting that is noted relative to performance characteristics can be used to guide the manipulation of the physical components. The performance characteristics themselves will have various implications for the physical system; some will refer more strongly to spatial configurations, others to the environmental components. Some will have implications for all aspects of the physical environment, while others will affect only a single aspect.

The sociophysical scales utilized in the programming for this project are listed below, including the primary physical variable for each (Figures 7 and 8):

The *privacy* scale is a measure of how much choice an individual has in being observed within his work

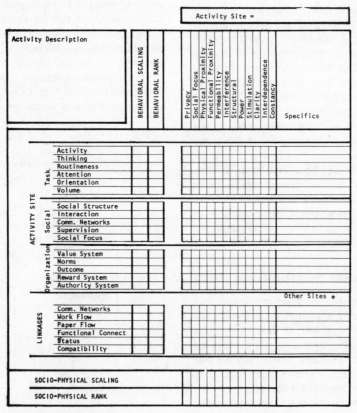

* See matrices for relationships.

**Figure 7**
**Matrix 1: behavioral system to sociophysical characteristics**

site by others. This is scaled along a dimension from open to closed. The physical variable is the amount of separation between the occupants of the site.

The *social focus* scale is the degree to which a setting encourages or discourages interaction between occupants of a site, and its dimension is along a sociopetal–sociofugal scale.[23] The physical variable is the positioning of the individuals and the location of barriers within the setting.

The *physical proximity* characteristic describes the requirements for distancing between individuals. This is based on the concept of personal space,[24] and the performance is, of course, based on connotations of distance.

The *functional proximity* scale measures the degree of closeness which must be achieved in order to perform the organizational tasks. The dimension is again a close–distant scaling of environmental components. The physical variable is the arrangement of facilities in reference to the tasks being performed.

The *permeability* scale is the indication of the amount of restriction required to permit entrance into the setting. Accessibility and inaccessibility are the terms for this scale, and the physical variable is the delineation of boundaries around a site.

The *interference* scale refers to the number of other activities taking place within a setting before the distraction generates a dysfunction. The measure is according to the levels of activity, and the physical element is the integration or segregation of a setting in terms of the overall organizational environment.

The *structural* component is the degree of explicitness with which messages are encoded in the environment concerning the rules of behavior. The scaling of this dimension is along a continuum of formal–informal. The physical variable is the level of perceptual messages within the environment.

The *power* scale is the level of power cues in an environment which indicates the members of the authority structure. The dimension is rated from overt to covert, and the physical variable is the use of status and power symbols to encode the setting.

The *environmental stimulation* scale is the level of perceptual stimulation which a site develops to support a given activity; it is scaled along a monotonous–exciting continuum.

The *clarity* scale gives the indication of whether a site should have clear messages of the intended usage of the setting, and this is described along a scale of ambiguity to legibility. The physical variable is the inclusion of spatial cues to identify the use of the environment, as well as the mood of the environment.

The *interdependence* scale measures the degree to which the setting affects the behavior in other settings. This is measured along a range from influential to noninfluential. The physical variable is the location of the site and its function in relation to other sites.

| | | Privacy | Social Focus | Physical Proximity | Functional Proximity | Permeability | Interference | Structural | Power | Stimulation | Power | Stimulation | Clarity | Interdependence | Constancy | PHYSICAL SCALING | PHYSICAL RANK |
|---|---|---|---|---|---|---|---|---|---|---|---|---|---|---|---|---|---|
| | SOCIO-PHYSICAL SCALING | | | | | | | | | | | | | | | | |
| | SOCIO-PHYSICAL RANK | | | | | | | | | | | | | | | | |
| Spatial Configuration | Scale | | | | | | | | | | | | | | | | |
| | Positioning | | | | | | | | | | | | | | | | |
| | Visibility through | | | | | | | | | | | | | | | | |
| | Physical definition | | | | | | | | | | | | | | | | |
| | Networks/Linkages | | | | | | | | | | | | | | | | |
| | Boundary | | | | | | | | | | | | | | | | |
| Environ. Components | Arrangement | | | | | | | | | | | | | | | | |
| | Organization | | | | | | | | | | | | | | | | |
| | Traffic | | | | | | | | | | | | | | | | |
| | Location | | | | | | | | | | | | | | | | |
| Attributes | Thermal | | | | | | | | | | | | | | | | |
| | Acoustics | | | | | | | | | | | | | | | | |
| | Lighting | | | | | | | | | | | | | | | | |
| | Color | | | | | | | | | | | | | | | | |
| | Materials | | | | | | | | | | | | | | | | |
| | Texture | | | | | | | | | | | | | | | | |
| | Style | | | | | | | | | | | | | | | | |
| Perceptual Quality | Graphics | | | | | | | | | | | | | | | | |
| | Status Consideration | | | | | | | | | | | | | | | | |
| | Symbols | | | | | | | | | | | | | | | | |
| | Image | | | | | | | | | | | | | | | | |
| | Mood | | | | | | | | | | | | | | | | |

**Figure 8**
**Matrix 2: sociophysical characteristics to physical system**

The *constancy* scale measures the capacity of a setting to adapt to change and is scaled along a continuum of adaptability and fixity. The physical variable is the performance of the components and the flexibility of their usage.

## PHYSICAL SYSTEM SPECIFICATIONS

It is easily demonstrated that by analyzing the sociophysical performance characteristics of the setting, the designer can more systematically explore alternatives to achieve the required performance. The primary physical variables above imply only the context in which a manipulation takes place and not the manner in which it takes place. The separation between occupants required to gain privacy may develop in many ways, a few of which are the erection of walls around the individual, isolation of an individual spatially, use of devices such as white sound, positioning of an individual in the environment, and placement of perceptual cues in the environment; the designer is free to choose which is the most appropriate solution to the problem. We found it useful to establish four major categories of possibilities which the designer could manipulate to satisfy the behavioral requirements of the activity site in terms of the physical environment. These general categories are spatial configuration, environmental components, environmental attributes, and environmental perceptual elements, all of which are familiar to designers.

The spatial configuration category describes the large-scale elements which control the overall environmental envelope and includes the spatial characteristics of the site: the scale and size, the positioning of space-containing large-scale elements, the visibility through the space, its physical definition, communication networks, and the boundary characteristics. The environmental components include those lesser-scale elements which occupy the space and which occupants use with a lesser degree of fixity than the larger ones. These characteristics include the arrangement of the space-occupying elements, the organization of work areas, control of circulation and traffic, location of individuals, and the generation of social spaces. The environmental attributes are those elements which give the activity site its overall character and mood and include such elements as lighting, color, use of materials, texture, and style. The perceptual elements are those characteristics of the activity site which encode it and which transmit messages to the participants. These can be as simple as the use of graphic materials to indicate direction, or as subtle as the use of spatial location to denote position in the hierarchical structure of an organization.

## CONCLUSION

It must be emphasized that the role of the physical system in a balanced environmental system is to support the behavioral system. The physical environment cannot be considered as the sole determinant of the behavioral system, since this precludes many aspects of the man–environment interface. Foremost of these is the fact that man is a goal-directed organism and will thus organize his environment to accomplish his goals. It also eliminates the role of an individual's perceptions, attitudes, and motivations in the selection of a behavioral pattern to be employed. The role of the designer is to develop a physical system that will support the desired behavioral pattern, with the system being open enough to permit individual behavior to take place. To be successful, this physical system must be in accordance with the accepted belief system of the occupants and must be structured to fit the expectations and the behavioral repertoire of the individual and of the social organization.

## NOTES AND REFERENCES

1. Harold M. Proshansky, William H. Ittelson, and Leanne G. Rivlin, "The influence of the physical environment on behavior: some basic assumptions," in Proshansky, Ittelson, and Rivlin, eds., *Environmental Psychology: Man and His Physical Setting,* New York: Holt, 1970.
2. R. Propst, *The Office: A Facility Based on Change,* Ann Arbor, Mich.: Herman Miller, 1968.
3. F. I. Steele, "Architecture and organizational health," in John Archea and Charles Eastman, eds., *EDRA2: Proceedings of the Second Annual Environmental Design Research Association Conference,* Pittsburgh, Pa., October 1970, 252–272.
4. William H. Ittelson, Leanne G. Rivlin, and Harold M. Proshansky, "The uses of behavioral maps in environmental psychology," in Proshansky, Ittelson, and Rivlin, *op. cit.*
5. Roger G. Barker, *Ecological Psychology: Concepts and Methods for Studying the Environment of Human*

*Behavior,* Stanford, Calif.: Stanford University Press, 1968.

6. D. Katz and R. Kahn, *The Social Psychology of Organizations,* New York: Wiley, 1966.
7. R. Kahn, D. Wolfe, R. Quinn, J. Snoek, and R. Rosenthal, *Organizational Stress: Studies in Role Conflict and Ambiguity,* New York: Wiley, 1964.
8. Katz and Kahn, *op. cit.*
9. Kahn et al., *op. cit.*
10. Herbert A. Simon, *Administrative Behavior,* New York: The Free Press, 1945.
11. Katz and Kahn, *op. cit.*
12. Harold M. Proshansky, William H. Ittelson, and Leanne G. Rivlin, "Freedom of choice and behavior in a physical setting," in Proshansky, Ittelson, and Rivlin, *op. cit.*
13. Amos H. Hawley, *Human Ecology: A Theory of Community Structure,* New York: Ronald Press, 1950.
14. F. Stuart Chapin, Jr., and Richard K. Brail, "Human activity systems in metropolitan United States," *Environment and Behavior,* Vol. 1 (December 1969), 107–130.
15. Barker, *op. cit.*
16. Proshansky, Ittelson, and Rivlin, *op. cit.*
17. *Ibid.*
18. Raymond G. Studer, "Some aspects of the man-designed environment interface," in *Response to Environment,* Raleigh, N.C.: Student Publication of the School of Design, North Carolina State University, 1969.
19. Michael Brill, "A systems approach to environmental design," *Environment: Planning and Design* (January-February 1970).
20. Proshansky, Ittelson, and Rivlin, *op. cit.*
21. Katz and Kahn, *op. cit.*
22. D. McGregor, *The Human Side of Enterprise,* New York: McGraw-Hill, 1960.
23. Humphry Osmond, "Function as the basis of psychiatric ward design," in *Mental Hospitals,* Vol. 8 (April 1957), 23–29.
24. Edward T. Hall, *The Hidden Dimension,* Garden City, N.Y.: Doubleday, 1966.

*Lack of formal evaluation is seen as a major block to the development of anything like a science of design. Evaluations presently made are independent of the design process and its assumptions about the uses of the building. The use of the performance concept for the design and procurement of buildings is seen as a "natural" for the development of formal evaluation procedures because of information recording at four critical and linked levels: objectives, activities, environmental characteristics, and hardware solutions. Any useful performance-based evaluation process must work at all four levels; therefore, we must be able to measure the degree of success or failure for each of them. The state-of-the-art is seen as preventing this at three critical points: perceiving environments holistically but measuring (and therefore evaluating) them parametrically; an inadequate set of measures for the psychosocial variables; and a design process very much in need of redesign itself.*

# Evaluating Buildings on a Performance Basis

**Michael Brill**

**State University of New York at Buffalo**

Building, the major industry in this nation, is run very much like a candy store.[1] It has an almost flat learning curve because it has no way to evaluate its performance and few mechanisms to incorporate and diffuse new experience. At this point in time, there is no process of evaluating explicitly developed and formally used in the building industry.

For instance, no architect I know of *records* his design assumptions ("If I shape the space *this* way, people will behave *that* way") and then goes back to the building a year after occupancy to ascertain whether or not his assumptions were correct. Worse yet, these untested assumptions are *reused* again and again as part of the architect's design repertoire. In other words, each building is a poorly planned "experiment" whose "hypotheses" are neither explicitly stated nor tested. Ray Bauer, commenting on the state-of-the-art of social indicators, has said that with our present evaluative measuring tools we cannot even be sure whether things are getting better or worse. The same holds true for our evaluations of the built environment.

There are two basic aspects to evaluation: (1) gaining information about the usefulness of buildings, and (2) using that information in the design and use of new buildings. This paper will attempt to cover both aspects but with a clear emphasis on the design process. I also speak from a particular point of view—that the *performance concept* can and should be used as an evaluation mechanism.

## THE PERFORMANCE CONCEPT

Before discussing evaluation, let us be reasonably precise about the performance concept—especially its use in performance specifications. *Performance specifications* state in precise terms the characteristics desired by users of a product or system's performance without regard to the specific means to be employed in achieving the results. Such specifications have recently come into use as mechanisms for procuring building subsystems *and* evaluating their performance.

Performance specifications do not describe dimensions, materials, finishes, or methods of manufacture—they describe the performance the user/consumer requires.

In normal use, traditional, or "prescriptive," specifications are a way of assuring that what is procured will be identical to some "model" which has given satisfactory performance in the past. Prescriptive specifications often prescribe the materials of which the object is to be made, the dimensions it must have, the finishes and the shapes, how it shall be installed, and in many cases who shall make it.

For example, in specifying a 10-inch brick cavity wall with running bond, we will accept as a solution *only* a 10-inch brick cavity wall with running bond. Yet we have selected that specification, whether we know it or not, on a *performance* basis. Actually, we wish a wall which has the following characteristics:

1. A certain amount of stability against lateral and vertical forces.
2. A certain amount of sound attenuation and other acoustic qualities.
3. A certain amount of thermal insulation.
4. A certain color and texture.
5. A certain amount of surface imperviousness to weather.

We have found, in the past, that a certain solution (a brick wall) will do this specific job, and when we are faced with the same problem, we draw on our experience and select that solution again. And yet, we are really seeking a certain level of *performance. Every conventional material specification is based on an implicit performance specification.* Prescriptive specifications are only a convenience. They are also a constraint to innovation in that only a very narrow range of solutions to any one problem is acceptable at any given time—even though many solutions are available which would give equal (or better) performance.

## CATEGORIES OF EVALUATION

There are many ways to develop a system of evaluations. They fall into one of four categories and may be diagrammed as shown in the flow diagram in Figure

1.[2] In the design process, the goals, or *objectives,* of the building to be designed are described. Each objective probably requires a set of *activities* to be performed by men, equipment, or environments to achieve this objective. Each activity requires that some desired *environmental characteristics* be present to enable the activity to be performed. Each environmental characteristic is supplied and controlled by some *hardware solution.*

The concept of environmental characteristics is the critical one. These are the qualities, or characteristics, which the environment must supply in order for the human user to perform the activity. These are always described in performance terms. For example, if we were designing a space which contains reading and writing as its primary activities (perhaps a library reading room), one of the critical environmental characteristics is adequate illumination. Notice we are *not* saying we need lighting fixtures, but illumination. There are many solutions to the need for illumination, including lighting fixtures as well as windows, illuminated texts, candles, or some unknown device. *All* are acceptable as long as the desired environmental characteristic is supplied. Notice that in the diagram there are two sets of arrows—the diagram "works" in both directions. As we move from objectives to solutions, we are in a design mode. As we move from solutions to objectives we are using the building to achieve objectives, or evaluating it in terms of the causal links between categories.

The evaluation of solutions without reference to the design process which generated them is seen (by this author) to be a "dead end." We argue that much of the experimentation in the subjective evaluations now being explored by many researchers will be of little value because they are essentially "unhinged" from the design process. Understanding people's responses to spatial qualities and configurations without regard to or knowing the goals of the system and the activities to be carried out does not increase our capacity to

**Figure 1**

design. Looking at pictures of houses, using semantic differentials, and many other of the recently popular techniques are not going to yield useful information for designers because we never deal with, or learn about, the causal relationship between object and response. None of it is really replicable experience, and little of it is wholly understandable in terms of the design process. Ray Studer's work in behavior-contingent systems[3] and that of Tom Markus[4] in model building is still the only major work linked directly to a design process of the future. However, the authors of both admit that the complexity of these models precludes useful answers for quite some time.

However, many people *are* involved in the process of evaluating buildings subjectively *because it is something we can do* ("meanwhile") fairly easily and does not require a heavy research base of investment. I do not discount the value of such work,[5] but it must be understood as largely external to the design process, and requiring the further development of some fundamental "connective tissue" to be useful to designers.

## A PROCESS OF PERFORMANCE-BASED EVALUATION

Because the needs of the user form the brief for procurement on a performance basis, because these users' needs are based explicitly on objectives and activities, and because all of this is *recorded* before design and construction, performance procurement is an ideal context in which to initiate *formal* evaluation processes useful for an ongoing system of design.

To be more explicit, a performance specification contains at least the three kinds of information necessary to understand *(requirement),* measure *(criteria),* and evaluate *(test)* the presence of the environmental characteristic. This information exists for each and every requirement. A performance specification would contain, for example:

1. A *requirement:* "control air motion."
2. A *criterion:* "this subsystem in use shall distribute air to the space such that air motion in the occupied zone shall be no less than 20 FPM nor more than 50 FPM. The occupied zone is all space from the finished floor to 78 inches above the finished floor excepting spaces closer than 2 inches to a partition."

3. A *test:* "field measurement or system prototype."[6] This information is only that part which appears in the procurement document, the performance specification. Objectives and activities are described to generate the requirement and criterion, which constitute a specific environmental characteristic. It is obvious from this example that the capability for a process of evaluation is automatically "built into" a performance procurement by the presence of a formal criterion and test method. More significantly, most environmental characteristics can be evaluated *before* construction through simulation, when design can still be modified. We argue that the utility of evaluation is dependent on its utility in an ongoing design process. Therefore, only if we can evaluate and measure whether objectives are being reached and only if we can evaluate and measure the success of activities, can we have this kind of useful process.

## THE STATE-OF-THE-ART OF PERFORMANCE-BASED EVALUATION

What is the *state-of-the-art* in the measurement of objectives and activities? As with the field of social indicators the measures we have for these are very crude but not entirely useless. For example, one of the objectives in an office environment is to be able to secure information from unauthorized persons.[7] The evaluation of this objective's being met deals with the level of security which can be attained and still permit relatively free flow of this information to authorized persons. It must also recognize that nothing is 100 percent secure and that any break in security must be known.

The evaluation criteria for the objective of *security* developed here were

1. Any kind of confidential information must be able to be secured, and *at* the work station.
2. The method of securing and the method of authorized retrieval must take no more than one minute by any 100-pound adult female.
3. Any successful unauthorized retrieval must take at least ten minutes and destroy some visually apparent part of the system or otherwise generate a signal that a breach of security has taken place.

This example is one of many being developed by many researchers in the field of performance design and performance evaluation.

There exist three major problems which presently inhibit the development of a broadly used system of evaluation on a performance basis:

1. *Parametric versus holistic design:* The basic problem that researchers face is that objectives, activities, and environmental characteristics are almost always conceived of, researched, recorded, and used parametrically, rather than holistically. For example, we perform experiments in which we try to understand acoustic phenomena, others to understand spatial perception, others to understand privacy, and still others to understand air movement and many other parameters of which the environment is made. In these experiments, we try to hold everything constant (as independent variables) and examine one, or a small number, of parameters. There is an underlying assumption that we can resynthesize this fragmented information into some whole. But efforts at resynthesis are notable failures. We recognize this as a basic problem since perceptions and behaviors are responses to a *holistic* (rather than parametric) environment. Right now, we are still dependent on that very fragile thing, the genius of the designer, to organize these parameters into a working whole.

2. *Poor measures:* Another major problem in this development is the inability of the behavioral sciences to measure (in Lord Kelvin's terms) with a "number that means something." The argument for a sociological versus a psychological approach to appraisal, while relevant, seems slightly premature in view of the fact that neither discipline is able to "deliver the goods" necessary to a formal, measured evaluation. We are able now to measure, with accuracy, the physiological aspects of satisfaction but only very poorly the psychological and sociological aspects.

3. *Design methodology:* A final problem is one endemic to the design professions. It is highly probable that the design process itself is one which cannot accommodate much new information—especially of the precision and volume likely to be generated in the next decade. The entire history of the design process has shown a contraction of scope every time new information has been introduced, leading us once again to a period of flamboyance, love of ambiguity, and neomysticism

in design—a deliberate denial of "hard" information, of design as problem solving, of design as control. On the other hand, much of the new thrust in design methodology research is a recognition of the need for a new design process.

In summation, the present processes of design and building are operating essentially *without* any formal evaluation procedures. We argue that the use of the performance concept allows such evaluation to take place as a natural outgrowth of procurement. Further, we have said that evaluation of hardware solutions alone, without reference to the objectives and activities of the building, does not lead to an informed design.

## NOTES AND REFERENCES

1. An old friend of mine, George Borowsky, a planner, drove me to the Franklin Institute conference (see Preface) and said, "Mike, what's the talk going to be like? Should I stay?" I said, "No, you don't want to stay. Mine is one of those talks that starts out by saying that building, America's biggest industry, is run very much like a candy store." He said, "That's not even true. At least if I walk into a candy store and ask for cinnamon gum drops, both the candy store owner and I know what we mean." He's right. Even that level of knowledge does not really exist in the industry that provides us with our built environment.

2. I am indebted to Dr. Thomas Markus at the University of Strathclyde in Scotland for his insights into these issues.

3. Raymond G. Studer "The dynamics of behavior-contingent physical systems," in Harold M. Proshansky, William H. Ittleson and Leanne G. Rivlin, eds., *Environmental Psychology: Man and His Physical Setting,* New York: Holt, 1970, 56–75.

4. Thomas Markus, "Optimization by evaluation in the appraisal of building," in John Archea and Charles Eastman, eds., *EDRA2: Proceedings of the Second Annual Environmental Design Research Association Conference,* Pittsburgh, Pa., October 1970, 77–93.

5. Work done by the following falls in these "unhinged from design" areas of evaluation: Tom Davis at SUNY Central, BOSTI in Buffalo, Haviland/Bednar at RPI (supported by Davis), Sanoff in North Carolina, OSTI's "resident ethnographer" concept for the defunct HUD in-cities program, etc.

6. From the performance specification for federal office buildings developed by the author's team at the National Bureau of Standards.

7. From the work done by the author and Terry Collison for the Hauserman Corporation's Office Interior System program of research and development.

As interest in building evaluation grows, the problems that accompany it must be brought to light. Difficulties inherent in evaluation studies are as follows: the lesser importance of the built environment relative to other factors in user satisfaction; the primitivism of theoretical notions about man–environment relations; the large degree of personal variation found in response to the built environment; the .eed to specify whose satisfaction is being talked about; the need to specify the point of time at which the evaluation is made; and the establishment of the proper unit to evaluate. The authors point out that if evaluation studies are to be worthwhile, they must produce information that architects can use to improve their work. To do so, evaluations must specify the users' characteristics in greater detail and must take into consideration what the users think about the environment. Since the management and maintenance systems of the building contribute significantly to user satisfaction, they must be included in any evaluation study. The actual process of building must be studied by the architect, and the social and behavioral sciences must produce more sophisticated theory and information if evaluation is to be successful.

# Building Evaluation, User Satisfaction, and Design*

**Robert Gutman and Barbara Westergaard**

**Rutgers University**

It is common knowledge that architects have become increasingly concerned with building evaluation in recent years. The growth of this concern probably stems from the architect's new interest in the user; instead of measuring his building against aesthetic standards, he now wants to measure it against utilitarian standards.[1]

At first glance the idea of building evaluation seems fairly clear cut. What one wants to determine is how well the building fulfills the functions it was intended to serve.[2] To find this out, one determines the degree of user satisfaction. We have worded this in a simple fashion, but we would like to argue that even sophisticated notions of building evaluation turn out on closer examination to be based on slippery concepts. Before developing the argument, though, we'd like to explain how we happened to become involved in building evaluations, because we think the way we were led to the field is in itself instructive.

Some time ago the senior author became interested in Louis Kahn's Richards building at the University of Pennsylvania medical school. The building intrigued him because it was at once hailed in architectural circles as the most important post-World War II American building—"one of the greatest buildings of modern times"[3]—and denounced in scientific circles as a disaster—"an edifice which has . . . seriously impeded the progress of medical science. . . . We can even discuss the problem of disassembly and crating for transmission to the Smithsonian."[4] He was curious to learn more about a building that could be both an architectural monument and an impossible environment for scientific research (Figures 1 and 2).

Our first forays into the history of the building produced some shocks: many of the most famous features of this building apparently resulted from the client's decision to cut costs and not from the architect's design intentions. At the same time our interviews with occupants and former occupants of the building revealed at once that the scientists' attitudes toward it as a place to work were not quite as one-sided as legend had it.

Some seven years after the completion of the Richards building another laboratory was built for the

*Built Environment Research Paper 17, Rutgers University.

**Figure 1**

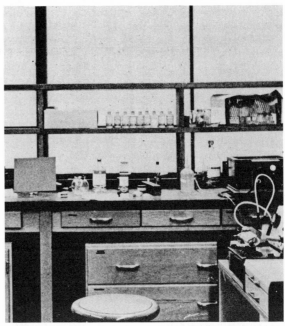

**Figure 2**

**Figure 3**

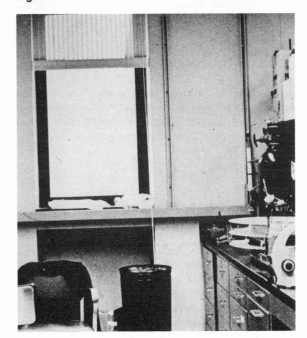

**Figure 4**

medical school. This building was of no architectural distinction whatever but was reputed to be a highly successful laboratory (Figures 3 and 4). Working in it were many scientists who had previously worked in the Richards building. Some of them had also been active on the program committees for the second building. Legend even had it that the program was conceived as a reaction against the Richards building. But, again, as we began talking to scientists who worked in this second building, it soon became apparent that their attitudes were not so clear-cut either.

Thus gradually we were led into an attempt to evaluate the two buildings. What is it that makes a good laboratory building? Which of these two was a better laboratory building? Why? Because we did not know the degree to which the problems in each of these two buildings were unique to these two, we were led to add a third and eventually a fourth building to the study. During the course of more than a year's research in which we tried many different approaches to evaluation, the difficulty mentioned at the beginning of this paper gradually forced itself to our attention: the current approach to building evaluation is simplistic.

In one sense there is nothing new about building evaluation. Architects have been evaluating their buildings all along, if by evaluation we mean the comparison of an object to some standard of excellence. The tradition of architectural criticism, after all, involves judging a building against the critic's aesthetic standards. The judgment is of course subjective and the standards usually left unstated. What is different about the current concept of evaluation is that now we want our measures to be objective and our standards explicit.

## USER SATISFACTION

Making standards explicit unfortunately does not make them either way easy to define or easy to measure. In some rare cases we may want to find out how well a building fulfills a narrow, quantifiable intention. If, for example, a factory building were to be judged in terms of the output that could be produced during a given period of time at a given cost, it would be relatively easy to decide whether factory A or factory B was the better building.[5] Unfortunately, we are usually interested, not in output per unit of time, but in determin-

ing whether the occupants of a building are satisfied with it. How is one to measure the users' satisfaction? And even if one could measure user satisfaction with precision, a methodological problem remains that is perhaps more serious. How are we to separate out the influence of the building itself on factory output or user satisfaction from all the other influences on these same variables—especially when it seems to be the case that the built environment is one of the less important influences on user satisfaction?

Most evaluation studies are done either by or for architects; so it is not surprising that one would never gather from perusing them that the built environment is a relatively small factor in determining user satisfaction. We are all aware of the architect's tendency to believe in architectural determination—that is, to believe that his success or failure on a project will determine the happiness, social cohesion, productivity, or what have you of the building's occupants. The evidence against this belief is now overwhelming, and architects' tenacity in maintaining it undoubtedly reflects the individual architect's need to justify his work.[6]

The facts seem to be that job satisfaction, for example, is determined largely by factors other than the physical working conditions—by salary, the intrinsic interest of the job, office morale, and so on.[7] The same is apparently true of housing. We all know the studies done in both England and America that show that houses condemned as slums by municipal housing authorities were highly regarded by their inhabitants because of the rewarding social conditions of the neighborhood.[8] People are highly adaptable and can make do with an enormous range of physical conditions. Furthermore, they do not usually leave their surroundings alone. If they do not like their physical environment, they will probably try either to leave it or to modify it until it no longer annoys them. Even under highly restricted conditions, most people attempt to make their living conditions as personal as possible.[9]

The fact that the built environment plays a relatively unimportant part in determining people's satisfaction is not, however, a reason to stop worrying about it. In the first place, although people are tolerant of wide ranges of conditions, there are extremes in which the environment can make a difference. Just because, for example, it has been found that high density does not automatically produce social disorganization[10] does not mean that density can be increased indefinitely without producing ill effects. As a first step it is important to learn what the thresholds of acceptable variation are.

In the second place, to say that people are highly adaptable to seemingly uncomfortable conditions is not an argument for ignoring their preferences. Office workers may adjust to spaces that have been built on the assumption that they can be treated like machines, but this does not mean that spaces suitable for machines are therefore what *should* be provided.

In the third place, although the physical environment may be found to be a smaller influence on such major goals as happiness and social cohesion than is thought by many architects, it may have a much greater influence on more specific events, such as accident and crime rates.[11] In other words architects may have been looking in the wrong place for the effects of their work and ignoring the areas where they can make a real difference.

Finally, just because the built environment is less important than other factors in determining satisfaction does not mean it is of no importance at all. If the purpose of evaluation studies is to provide feedback for the architect so that he can do better next time round, then whatever information can be passed on to him is of value. However small the impact of the built environment may be, it is after all the area over which the architect has some control.

## THEORY AND EVALUATION

Another fundamental difficulty in evaluation studies is that our theoretical notions about the interaction between man and the built environment are so primitive. This makes it difficult to explain the effect the environment has on the individual, even in those cases where a clear effect can be discerned. We have already mentioned the relatively small role the built environment plays in determining user satisfaction and the relatively large role played by cultural, social, and personal factors. But we would like to be able to specify how much of a role is played by each of these factors and under what conditions. Only then can we define the characteristics of a building that must be studied in an evaluation and the behavior that is likely to be influenced.

The fact that we do not know the mechanisms by which the environment influences people means that we are forced to take at face value their statements of satisfaction and dissatisfaction. Yet it seems clear that a large amount of displacement occurs in attitudes toward the built environment. That is, attitudes toward the physical environment suffer from a halo effect; they depend not just on the physical environment but on the other characteristics of the respondent or of his situation. Many of our informants mentioned to us that when a scientist's work is going well, when research grants are coming in, when he feels secure in his faculty status, he is more willing to accept existing conditions. The same man in the midst of a frustrating experiment will find many things wrong with his physical environment that never bothered him when his work was going well.

Another source of distortion grows out of the fact that often deficiencies in the environment became apparent or bothersome only when they are pointed out. In this area there is an enormous differencce between asking people what is on their mind and presenting them with a questionnaire that contains queries about specific aspects of the environment. Thus we found that our respondents, when questioned, indicated many negative feelings that as far as we could tell had actually disturbed them hardly at all.

Furthermore, some people simply complain more than other people. Chronic complainers may be displacing other feelings, but no matter what psychological mechanism is operating, in any evaluation study involving only a few buildings, their presence or absence is a distorting factor. The end result of an evaluation may thus hang on whether the building happens to be peopled by a large number of complainers or noncomplainers.

There also seems to be considerable variation in people's expectations as to how closely the environment should be tailored to their desires. Most discussions of this phenomenon, which is usually referred to as *environmental fit,* have assumed that the basic problem is minimizing the lack of congruence, or "slack," between expectations and spatial requirements.[12] In fact, people differ in their tolerance toward slack. For reasons we cannot yet fathom, it seems that some users anticipate a certain amount of slack between their desires and what the environment provides, whereas others demand a close fit.

What theory there is that relates man to the built

environment has been developed by behavioral scientists interested in architecture and environmental phenomena and by designers, architects, planners, and critics interested in the social or behavioral significance of space. Ideas developed by the former group include such concepts as proxemics, personal space, and territoriality; those developed by the latter group include such concepts as sacred space, pattern language, existential space, and the third environment.[13] Most of these concepts have enjoyed considerable popularity, yet they are inadequate for helping us understand the intellectual, emotional, and cultural processes that are involved in the human response to the environment.

The major drawback to using these concepts is that they lack explanatory power. That is, they do not really help us predict the ways in which people will respond to the environment. Concepts like personal space or territoriality point to presumed basic needs and are intended to have implications for the design of the environment. In fact, however, these concepts do not help us design the environment more than knowing that men need food to survive enables the nutritionalist to prescribe a diet or the chef to prepare a menu. What does knowing that a man needs personal space to maintain his psychological health tell the architect who is about to design the man's house?

## PERSONAL VARIATIONS IN USER SATISFACTION

A third major difficulty in user satisfaction surveys is caused by the large degree of personal variation found in responses to the built environment. Part of this variation is apparently due to differences in perception. Each person possesses his own structure for viewing the environment, and even such seemingly simple concepts as near and far, warm and cold, have entirely different meanings to different individuals. Consequently, if the user is asked whether his needed facilities are close to his desk or not, his answer will depend on what he thinks of as "close." But even if one assumes that different users perceive the same environment, differences in preferences remain. The Richards building has large windows. Some of our respondents liked the resulting light, and others, doing similar research, did not. Furthermore, different users assign different priorities to various properties. For one

scientist, having a window in his laboratory is more important than the quality of his equipment (always, of course, up to a point); for a second, the sole criterion of building adequacy is whether it can house his equipment; for a third, the most important quality a laboratory can have is privacy, and so on. It is not clear to us to what degree these variations in subjective response are a function of personality, cultural, or organizational variables among users. But whatever their source, they make it difficult to generalize about the acceptability of a given set of physical conditions.

## WHOSE SATISFACTION?

A fourth major difficulty in evaluation research is the need to specify whose satisfaction is being talked about. There are two aspects to this problem. One is that the common assumption in today's evaluation studies is that the user's satisfaction is to be taken as the standard against which buildings are measured. We would certainly agree that it is time the design professions took more notice of the needs of the users, but it is naïve to assume that they are the only people whose satisfaction matters. There are many people who do not actually work inside a building whose attitude or professional duties will influence the physical conditions faced by the users. In many institutions the board of trustees approves appropriations for new buildings; its opinions may carry some weight. The financial vice president of a university expects a building to meet certain criteria, which will not necessarily be compatible with the users' criteria. So will the insurance agent, the fire marshal, the head of the campus security staff, the chief of the university maintenance staff, the head of the institution that lends funds, the members of the community who must look at the building on their way to work. Now it might be argued that all these criteria are secondary; what really counts is the user's satisfaction, and his demands should take precedence. But the matter is not so simple. One may agree, for example, that a scientific lab should not be built to suit the security staff, but if the building is so difficult to police that expensive equipment keeps disappearing, it is the users who will suffer. If a laboratory that pleases its users is so expensive that money is drained away from other parts of the university, how are competing values to be reconciled? Obviously, if the viewpoints conflict, any choice be clear that the definition of a satisfactory building cannot depend on an examination of the users alone. In any case decisions made by other groups will influence the way the occupants can use their building.

The other aspect of the problem is deciding which users are to be considered. Even the people who actually work inside the building have different expectations, and their varying demands may conflict. The head of a department evaluates his building from a point of view that may diverge from that of other senior professors. Judging from our experience, he will be more inclined to worry about changes in types of experiments and therefore in room use or about facilities for group activities or storage for shared materials. His viewpoint will undoubtedly diverge from the viewpoint held by junior professors, technical staff, secretaries, and so on. How are these divergent viewpoints to be reconciled? Obviously, if the viewpoints conflict, any choice among them involves a tradeoff, and an evaluation study ought at least to be able to say that although scientists found this laboratory highly successful on these grounds, the same characteristics displeased the technicians for the following reasons.

## MORE DIFFICULTIES
## IN EVALUATING BUILDINGS

A fifth major difficulty with evaluation studies involves the need to specify the point of time at which the evaluation is being made. The time that elapses between programming and occupancy makes it almost certain that many of the initial users will be different from those for whom the building was intended. This is obviously the case for new campuses where programs are often completed before staff is hired, but for most institutions the turnover is such that a building's first occupants will differ from those for whom the programming committee planned. As time goes on the staff continues to change, and later users of the building will be different from the initial users. What satisfied one group of users will not necessarily satisfy the next group.

There is a tendency in evaluation studies to consider all users interchangeable so that the results of a study can be generalized to all scientists or all office workers. We find this assumption dubious, particularly for laboratories. The popularity of different types of research changes with time, and since the physical requirements of different sciences vary widely, the adequacy of the labs will change.

Not only do users change, the buildings themselves change. Most institutional buildings undergo more or less continual modification. The Richards building has changed so much that we would not be surprised if on its fiftieth anniversary we were to learn that the University of Pennsylvania had applied for a grant to restore the building to its original condition as a historical monument. Changes of course are not uniform throughout a building. They are least likely to occur in the basic structure, more likely to occur in the partition systems, and most likely to occur in the services. Presumably modifications represent attempts to make the building satisfy the current users more completely, but they mean that the results of an evaluation study are only valid for the time at which it was made.

The fact of continual modification also suggests that one of the most important physical factors influencing user response is the ease with which a building can be modified. But, *pace* the architectural magazines, this criterion cannot be studied as an independent architectural characteristic. Indeterminate buildings or buildings planned for change have been popular concepts among architects recently. The architect may indeed intend his building to be easily adaptable to changing needs, but whether in fact it is frequently modified is less likely to depend on the architect's intentions than on the attitude of the administration toward spending money on building changes, the prestige of the department involved, and so on.

In fact it seems clear that one property of the environment that has been neglected in evaluation studies, which has apparently a significant bearing on the user's satisfaction, is the kind of maintenance provided with a building.[14] We would include under maintenance the willingness of the relevant administration to pay for renovations. Thus it is not the frequency of equipment breakdown that seems to matter but the speed of repair. It is not the potential flexibility of a building but the willingness of the administration to pay for alterations. This is another, and important, argument against thinking of evaluation as an activity concerned solely with a physical object. Rather, evaluation must look at the physical object as part of a social system.

Even when the users remain the same, the time at which a study is made will influence the results. For one thing subjective responses are highly unstable over time, presumably because these responses are in such large measure not really responses to the environment itself. Apparently attitudes vary with the season,[15] and one investigator has claimed that user satisfaction shows a general tendency to decrease with time.[16]

A sixth major difficulty with evaluation studies is finding the proper unit to evaluate. "The building" may exist for the financial vice president, but the areas of interest to the scientist are likely to be more circumscribed. When he thinks about the environment in which he works, he may be thinking only of his particular laboratory and office, perhaps also of the ground floor lobby, the elevator, and the fifth floor corridor. The head of a department may worry about a considerably greater area, but his attitudes toward the place he performs his experiments and the places his colleagues perform theirs may differ considerably. Even buildings made up of repeated identical spaces are likely to become increasingly differentiated over time, and it may therefore be preferable to concentrate on the relatively fixed aspects of a building. In any case because different parts of the buildings, once occupied, acquire distinctive features, it would be a mistake to generalize from judgments about different parts of a building to the building as a whole. And if evaluation studies are to make any practical difference to the architect, it is important to be clear (and explicit) about which environment the users are relating to.

If the objective characteristics of the built environment are to be related to measures of behavior or satisfaction, they must be defined precisely. We have found it useful to think in terms of the following properties: amenity properties, ambient properties, symbolic properties, communication properties, and sensory properties.[17] For those characteristics we have defined as amenity and ambient properties, precise definition is relatively unproblematic. With sufficient resources to obtain the necessary instruments it is relatively easy to measure objectively such characteristics as light levels, humidity, number of feet of uninterrupted bench space, and so on. Unfortunately, it is just in those areas of most interest to architects that the measures become less satisfactory. For example, we have been unable to develop an efficient means for measuring the communication properties of the buildings we have studied, although various indirect means used in other studies may be informative (for example, comparing perimeters as a measure of compactness, calculating the average distance of laboratories from offices or library, clocking the time spent getting from room to room, etc.[18]). Data about the symbolic content and the sensory qualities of the environment are highly subjective. These of course are the properties that architects tend to think of when they discuss the influence of their work on those who use it, but it seems to us virtually impossible to "measure" these properties independently of the specific responses of particular users.

But if building evaluation is to be a worthwhile undertaking, it must produce information that architects and other participants in the building process can use to improve their work. We have suggested that the whole idea needs considerable thought and considerable study before its results are meaningful. But does this mean that we should abandon the whole enterprise? No; simply because current evaluations tend to be characterized by sloppy or naive thinking is by no means reason to abandon the enterprise. On the contrary, *more,* not less, attention should be paid to it if we are to improve the current level of the built environment.[19]

We see no reason why it should not be possible to develop standards of building performance that would deal with the behavioral impact of buildings. But first it is necessary to abandon some of the current habits of building evaluation. In the first place the standards cannot be derived directly from information about user satisfaction. We have discussed some of the reasons why this is so, and why it would be misleading to compare buildings in terms of the quantity of negative comments expressed by the occupants. Nor can the environment being judged be defined in the conventional terms of the design profession. As an example, consider again that popular architectural concept, the "flexible" building. We maintain there is no such thing as a flexible building independent of the particular institution that permits and pays for the changes that built-in flexibility supposedly encourages.

## STEPS TOWARD MORE MEANINGFUL EVALUATIONS

As a first step toward more meaningful evaluations, we suggest that user characteristics be specified in greater detail. How much detail depends of course on the type of organization using the building, but as an example of the kinds of variables we have in mind, here are some of the questions we have begun to ask about our laboratory users. What are the cultural norms of these groups? What is the position of each person in the hierarchy of this group? What are the ideas current among medical biologists about the best ways to organize labs? What is the nature of the social organization specific to a department or lab team? What experience has the individual had in other labs? What personality factors are operating that influence the individual's sensitivity to aesthetic as oposed to utilitarian concerns or the relative emphasis he places on opportunities for community and privacy?

What we are suggesting by this list of questions is that if the concern with user satisfaction is genuine, then the work of developing standards must take into account the way in which the users themselves think about the environment. How exactly this is to be done in the course of design practice and what the connection should be between the user's conceptualization and the way the architect organizes his material to find design solutions are indeed baffling problems. On the other hand, until these problems are faced, it is doubtful that architects can produce buildings that work any better than those they are building now.

We would also like to stress again that a concern for systems of managing and maintaining buildings can contribute as much to user satisfaction as do the objective characteristics of the physical environment itself. To put it another way, it is important to extend the concept of performance standards to include the managerial services usually provided in institutional buildings.

We believe that success in this type of research demands the inauguration of other projects. For example, although we remain convinced that depth studies of particular buildings and their users are important for generating concepts, developing models, and testing research methods, certain issues require large-scale comparative studies in which, say, fifty laboratory buildings and their users are investigated with respect to a small number of variables. Only then can the large number of nonenvironmental variables and the high degree of personal variability be controlled sufficiently to find out what, if any, behavioral effects are produced by the environment itself.

It is also imperative that the actual process of building, from the planning stages through final construction, be studied. Our limited historical venture has shown that some of the shortcomings apparent in all three buildings we studied most closely resulted from budgetary cutbacks decided on by the client. Thus it is not enough to discuss the intentions of the designer or the needs of the client. Furthermore, in order to understand how it is that apparently routine failures crop up so often in finished buildings, it is necessary to see what actually happens in planning and construction. Apparently, for example, engineers are often uncertain about the kind of ambient environment that will result from combining a particular set of physical characteristics. Much reliance is placed on the fact that equipment manufacturers guarantee their products. Thus the need to examine in advance possible thermal problems is lessened for both architects and engineers if they can count on the fact that the furnace manufacturer guaranteed certain results from his product. Finally, it is impossible to deal with the reconciliation of competing values and criteria unless the actual nature of decision making in the design and building industries is understood.

There has been much talk about the need for the design professions to restructure their view of the building process, to change their attitude and approach to their work, to stop acting like the romantically inclined artists of the nineteenth century, and so on. It is easy to castigate the architects, but success depends also on progress in the social and behavioral sciences. The field needs desperately to develop both more sophisticated theory and more information about the terms in which the users think about their environment. Research on environmental assessment takes place in a context of many disciplines. Without collaborative effort from the behavioral sciences environmental assessment will remain in its present primitive state.

## NOTES AND REFERENCES

The research on which this paper is based was funded in part by a grant from the National Science Foundation. Our study of biomedical research laboratories is part of a larger Rutgers–Princeton University project concerned with developing concepts and techniques for assessing various types of built environments. We are grateful for the advice of Klaus Gartler, Robert Geddes, Suzanne Keller, Llonas Miller, Martin Silverman, Philip Steadman, and Maury Wolfe.

1. See Alan Lipman's paper, "The architectural belief system and social behavior" which appears in *Part One* of this volume.

2. We do not mean here the currently popular "architect's intentions." By "the functions it was intended to serve" we are referring to what the client or program committee has indicated as the purpose the building is to achieve.

3. Vincent Scully, *Louis I. Kahn*, New York: Braziller, 1962 27.

4. Personal correspondence from a scientist who had worked in the Richards building.

5. Despite the fact that, compared to other evaluation attempts, this one is relatively unproblematic, it has not to our knowledge been studied. The effect of physical working conditions (light, temperature, etc.) on productivity was for a time a favorite topic of industrial psychologists. The most commonly cited work growing out of this tradition is *Management and the Worker* (F. J. Roethlisberger and William J. Dickson, Cambridge, Mass.: Harvard University Press, 1939), which records the results of the Hawthorne experiments. But what is of interest here is the shift in focus of this project from a concern for physical factors to a concern for social factors.

6. See Lipman, *op. cit.*

7. See, for example, F. J. Langdon, *Modern Offices: A User Survey*, Ministry of Technology, Building Research Station, National Building Studies, Research Paper 41, London: H.M.S.O., 1966, 6; or S. A. Stouffer, *The American Soldier: Measurement and Prediction*, Vol. 1, Princeton, N.J.: Princeton University Press, 1949, 337–361.

8. See Marc Fried and Peggy Gleicher, "Some sources of residential satisfaction in an urban slum," *Journal of the American Institute of Planners*, Vol. 27 (1961), 305–315; Herbert J. Gans, *The Urban Villagers*, New York: The Free Press, 1963; Chester W. Rapkin, "Social values and housing orientation," *Journal of Social Issues*, Vol. 19 (April 1963), 113–131; M. Young and P. Wilmott, *Family and Kinship in East London*, New York: The Free Press, 1957.

9. We all know the stories of soldiers decorating the insides of their lockers. One can sense the strength of this tendency to personalize space by observing the efforts of administrators of institutional buildings to suppress it. In prestige offices, workers may be forbidden to hang pictures unless they have been passed by an "aesthetics committee." College administrators may try, in the interest of economy, to prevent students from altering their rooms. An interesting example of the consequences of such restrictions is reported by Sim Van der Ryn and Murray Silverstein in *Dorms at Berkeley: An Environmental Analysis*, Berkeley, Calif.: Center for Planning and Development Research, University of California, 1967.

10. See, for example, John Cassel, "Health consequences of population density and crowding," in R. Gutman, ed., *People and Buildings*, New York: Basic Books, 1972, 250–268, or Robert C. Schmitt, "Implications of density

in Hong Kong," *Journal of the American Institute of Planners*, Vol. 29 (1963), 210–217.

11. See James Marston Firtch, "The social consequences of architectural intervention," in *American Building 2: The Environmental Forces That Shape It*, Boston: Houghton Mifflin, 1972, and Oscar Newman, "Alternatives to fear," *Progressive Architecture*, Vol. 53 (October 1972), 92–105.

12. See Christopher Alexander, *Notes on the Synthesis of Form*, Cambridge, Mass.: Harvard University Press, 1964, 15–45.

13. For proxemics, see Edward T. Hall, *The Hidden Dimension*, Garden City, N.Y.: Doubleday, 1966; for personal space, Robert Sommer, "Studies in personal space," *Sociometry*, Vol. 22 (September 1959), 247–260; for territoriality, Stanford M. Lyman and Marvin B. Scott, "Territoriality: a neglected sociological dimension," in R. Gutman, ed., *People and Buildings*, New York: Basic Books, 1972; for sacred space, Mircea Eliade, *Images and Symbols*, by Philip Mairet, New York: Sheed and Ward, 1969; for pattern language, Christopher Alexander, Sara Ishikawa, and Murray Silverstein, *A Pattern Language Which Generates Multi-Service Centers*, Berkeley, Calif.: Center for Environmental Structure, 1968; for existential space, Christian Norberg-Schulz, *Existence, Space and Architecture*, New York: Praeger, 1971; for the third environment, James Marston Fitch, "The aesthetics of function," in R. Gutman, ed., *People and Buildings*, New York: Basic Books, 1972, 4–16.

14. An interesting example of this is described in "Building appraisal: St. Michael's Academy, Kilwinning," *Architects' Journal*, Vol. 151 (January 7, 1970), 9–50. Here the heating system of the school in question was faulty, but on closer examination the difficulty turned out to lie not in architectural or engineering deficiences but in maintenance deficiencies; the janitor did not receive new filters regularly.

15. William Michelson, "Space as a variable in sociological inquiry: serendipitous findings on macro-environment," 1969, 14–21 (mimeographed).

16. David Canter, "Royal hospital for sick children, Yorkhill, Glascow, by Baxter, Clark and Paul, a psychological analysis," *Architects' Journal*, Vol. 156 (September 6, 1972), 544.

17. For discussion of these properties see Robert Gutman, "Library architecture and people," in Ernest R. De Prospo, Jr., ed., *The Library Building Consultant: Role and Responsibility*, New Brunswick, N.J.: Rutgers University Press, 1969, and Robert Gutman et al., "Social functions of a built environment," (in press).

18. Such measures have been used in studies in other types of buildings. See, for example, "Building appraisal: St. Michael's Academy, Kilwinning," *op. cit.;* David K. Trites, "Radial nursing units prove best in controlled study," *Modern Hospital*, Vol. 112 (April 1969), 94–99.

19. For an example of a modestly scaled evaluation program that attempted to feed its findings directly into the design

process, see the work on old people's homes done by the British Ministry of Housing and Local Government, *Flatlets for Old People,* London: H.M.S.O., 1958; *More Flatlets for Old People,* London H.M.S.O., 1962; *Grouped Flatlets for Old People:* London: H.M.S.O., 1966. Here sociological study of old people's homes led to specific design recommendations. These recommendations were used in the program for buildings at Stevenage. After these buildings were occupied, they were evaluated, particularly in relation to the design recommendations, and further recommendations resulted, which will presumably be used next time around.

**PART FOUR
CONCLUSION**

**Photo credit: Mitchell Payne**

# CONCLUSION

Through their introductions and the selection of papers the editors of this book have attempted to give some structure to the consideration of how architects may regain some appreciation of the fundamental service which they may offer their clients. In a time when the focus of their efforts has become confused by the increasingly complex task of building for a many-faceted, highly technological society, this appears to be a necessary task.

No simple reductionism is intended. Rather, a general updating of a humanistic orientation which has always been professed within the discipline of architecture is sought. The essential art in architecture is not misunderstood. It is the preconditions to that art that are being questioned: the lack of objective information, appropriate attitudes, adequate understanding, and responsible consideration for the effects of built environments on the people who use them.

The editors, and probably all the contributors to this book, believe that any creative expression that is truly helpful to mankind will grow most readily out of a cultivated knowledge and an inquiring empathy.

It has been noted that the role of the professional in today's society is changing, that the architect's belief system as to the effect of his work on human behavior does not rest on a firm foundation of facts, and that such facts as there are have not been gathered into a useful theory of man–environment relations. It has been suggested that if the profession would recognize the habits, needs, and desires of building users as primary determinants in design, it will need to know more about the relationships between the designed environment, and human behavior and thought than it does at present. Moreover, if the profession is to use this information creatively, it must be organized in a way which lends itself to such use. The design process, it has been said, is presently largely mimetic; typological solutions are adjusted to new situations and approaches to designing are imitated. The emphasis in teaching, as in practice, has been on the formal generation of the product with little attention to the understanding of the human problems involved.

Yet there is evidence that researchers and designers alike can get caught up with their questions and instruments or the internal aesthetics of the theories or procedures with which they are concerned, forgetting that the whole purpose of their efforts is to enhance human life.

Neither the behavioral scientist nor the architect can afford to merely pay lip service to the idea of cooperation if either is to be judged well by the public that supports them. There must be a systematic merging of information relating behavior to the design of environments. It is essential that architects make clear the character of the information that they can use in design and that scientists work to assure its quality and availability.

There must also be a change in attitude within the profession toward questions of architectural criticism and evaluation. A system which brooks no criticism by peers and makes almost no effort to scientifically evaluate its product in human terms is intolerable. Improvement depends on critical and constructive assessment of experience and on learning from one another's mistakes. If improvement across the entire scope of the built environment is to be made in this way, architectural awards must not continue to be made only on the basis of photographs and only by professionals. The architect must be judged on his success in realizing a program by those who must use his building and in terms of his own explicitly stated intentions. Given better definition of need, better information, and improved tools of representation and synthesis, the architect can continue his art of social expression.

It was not intended that this be a how-to-do-it book. It is instead an effort to bring an organized awareness to the reader in order that he may be encouraged to utilize the work of others to forward his own thinking. By bringing together papers which present polemic, scientific, and theoretical aspects of anthropology, sociology, and psychology as they relate to architectural programming, design, and evaluation, the editors hope to encourage their practical evaluation and synthesis into a more useful form. However, a general plea is entered for the development of descriptive conventions to enable the sharing of behavioral information and the consequent systemization of knowledge into well-founded theory to guide design.

Many architects, well settled in their atheoretical ways of thinking about architecture and design, may find it difficult to broaden the scope of their concern to consider factors and methods largely neglected in the past. Traditionally unaccustomed to dealing with the subjects this book addresses, they may be tempted to dismiss it and the thoughts expressed herein as one aspect of a passing phase of criticism of the profession. Certainly this is an attitude that is prevalent in a number of schools today. However, there are very real demands which will make it increasingly difficult to maintain this attitude.

Not the least of these is the greater sophistication of the client and the practical demands of marketing professional services to people not accustomed to purchasing them in the traditional role of patron. Similarly, the very complexity of design problems demands that the representation of information for design as well as methods of designing and the quality of the information used be improved. Financial pressures on schools of architecture now forcing greater teaching loads onto the faculties also require that new pedagogical tools of a complementary nature be developed. Learning almost entirely by firsthand tutorial experience is no longer possible and must be augmented by carefully prepared information and preorchestrated learning experiences.

In all these efforts it is essential to become explicit in the expression of intentions, accurate and objective in the description of facts, flexible and systematic in their organization, clear and relevant in communication, efficient and timely in applications, controlled and appropriate in the effects achieved, and broadly sensitive in evaluation. Such dimensions as these can provide a rational measure of success in designing for human behavior, but the ultimate measure must be the quality of the lives of all involved. The editors have faith that all our lives can be enhanced if the architect can focus on man and go on to offer a fundamental service to humanity through the environment he designs.

The following paper by Stuart Rose of the American Institute of Architects in Washington brings this book to a close with a somewhat tongue-in-cheek treatise in which he asks the profession to test some of the ideas presented here and to provide the feedback necessary for progress.

# Arm Folding and Architecture: the Allied Arts

**Stuart W. Rose**

**Continuing Education Programs
American Institute of Architects**

*How willing are architects to change their habits of designing? A link between architect and researcher is needed if the quality of research is to be improved. We need a coordinated information system which will provide for easy dissemination of this information. We need opportunities to attempt new approaches to designing without messing up a project. The A.I.A. is developing procedures that will provide for both these needs. The architect, himself, should also be conducting research on his own buildings and processes of designing.*

Please . . . fold your arms in front of you and sit for a moment before reading further.

How does it feel? Natural? Warm? Comfortable?

Now . . . please fold your arms in front of you the other way. The arm previously on top should now be on the bottom. Having any problems? How does it feel? Unnatural? Uncomfortable?

*The research findings of several studies over the past twenty years show that the second way you folded your arms is not only better for your health, but will enable you to be more productive in the use of your arms.*

Are you really going to change your arm-folding behavior? As you found, doing things a new way is difficult—even painful—besides being awkward. If my livelihood depended on how well I fold my arms, I'd stay with the first way despite the research findings which say I should change. If I feel awkward the new way, I'm liable to do a terrible arm-folding job and jeopardize my livelihood. The risk of doing it awkwardly and poorly, the new way, is very high. And the amount of practice and patience and discomfort will be enormous. I simply don't feel the need—or benefits—of changing the way I now fold my arms. Do you?

I've always found comfort the way I naturally fold them . . . and reasonably good results. I'm sure there's always room for improvement, but for now I'm staying on firm, known, comfortable ground.

Besides, if I change which arm is on top, I have to change my cigarette-holding hand. And that may affect my smoking habit, which is really playing with fire! The need for other changes if I accomplish this one might make things unbearable. I'm quite nervous and afraid . . . and skeptical . . . of what might happen. I'll take my chances and fold them the way I have been.

Let's look at what's happened.

Several researchers conducted arm-folding research for twenty years. After investing a lot of their energy, and the funds and energy of others, they have, first, finally informed you about the fruits of their labors and, second, been rejected. Most of us don't like being rejected. We need to reduce this dissonance to be comfortable and live with ourselves. One way of reducing it is to discredit the rejector: "The arm-folding practitioners don't care about the quality of their activity; they're only interested in money!"

The same holds true from the practitioners' viewpoint: "Those researchers are in ivory towers; they're not living in the real world; they'd never make it on the outside!"

Neither viewpoint is healthy for the arm-folding professionals or for the state of their art. Both viewpoints and the phenomena that cause them are quite natural. While nothing is really evil, nothing constructive is happening. What seems needed in arm folding (and architecture) is a link which causes the research results to be transferred into practice, provides feedback to the researchers, and establishes an interdependent relationship between the two roles. Then both would feel useful and needed, which is a warmer, more reinforcing relationship as well as more productive in advancing the state of the art

This book is concerned with "designing for human behavior." Practitioners: do you feel that you are doing your best to design for the best possible behavioral results? I believe you do. Now . . . how much of what you read here, in this book, do you feel you *will* use in your daily practice? Researchers: on the basis of these papers, how much do you feel you will influence practitioners to do better in designing for human behavior? Nothing? A little? A lot? I think a little. How much arm-folding change do you think I caused?

We've all had training throughout our lives. This has had a strong influence on the habits we now have. Folding our arms one way is no more of a habit and certainly no easier to change than the way we design for human behavior. Changing that habit will be very difficult. There is a lot of risk. An entire project, upon which our livelihood and professional image depends, could be jeopardized. And how can we be sure that the risk will, in fact, be worth whatever benefits may be achieved? Can we be certain that there even will be benefits, just because the researchers say so? I can't, for the most part.

But, I can for some parts, I tried them. . . and many of them really worked! And as I tried them a second and third time, I got better and also more comfortable with doing things the new way. As a matter of fact, the new ways became no longer new but were now just a part of me.

And, you can be sure that when I tried a new way of doing something, there was as little risk involved as possible. Off in a corner, I could dabble and play

with the method. Then I tried it on some projects, usually old completed ones, to see what would happen. But none of this was on an official basis or as a replacement for what was normal practice. Only when my confidence had been developed, would I begin to try it "for real."

What would be the elements of a more formal and widespread approach to diffusing new approaches to designing for human behavior? First, I must have a description, preferably as recent and concise as possible, of the new findings. But that's not so easy to get, is it? Who could I call or to whom could I jot a note and receive, say, new methods for evaluating social behavior in office settings as a function of layout? We do need places, or a system of places, from which we can easily get either the information we seek or at least a direct reference to that information. The only source I know of presently is the Director of Research at A.I.A., and yet even his system is not nearly as comprehensive and easily operated as he would like.

Second? I suspect two things are needed. . . . the time to "play" or "dabble" and perhaps someone with experience to help out when needed . . . a friendly helper or guide who's available on request. This phase is being helped to a limited degree by the Architectural Training Laboratory program developed by the A.I.A. Each lab represents a safe—no risk—environment in which new behaviors are tried and a guide is available to help as needed. However, one- or two-day durations do not allow for as much play and repetition as would be desirable. What is needed is a more continuous form of opportunity. Perhaps a cadre of researchers throughout the country can set up a "friendly guide service" to assist practitioners as they dabble and need help. For now, there is very little help available.

A system of the nature described above will be prerequisite to facilitating this kind of continuous retraining that can significantly improve the state of our art.

Let's assume I've seen the light and have developed confidence and have retrained myself to fold my arms the other way. The result, as the research stated, was true. I'm now more productive in the use of my arms (and I really feel healthy!). Applying this new capability, I've found some useful results. I wonder if anyone else has also found useful results. I'd sure like to compare notes with them, build on some of their experiences, and throw in whatever I can to help them.

The initial research on arm folding was, necessarily,

funded as a research project to develop a useful new approach with applicability in a variety of situations. Such research is generally referred to as "basic" research. Because it cannot often be economically tied to a budget of an application project, it is usually performed with independent support by universities, government, foundations, or sometimes by larger firms.

While we've discussed the transfer of basic research findings into application or practice, the practitioner also may conduct research. Using some methods generated by basic research, practitioners may experiment with a variety of problems on a project. As solutions to those problems are a viable part of a commission, such research may be justifiably funded within the project budget.

Space planning based on behavioral criteria is inherent in virtually all projects. What arrangement of furnishings and spaces will contribute to a healthier home life for the particular family? What office layout will improve employee morale and efficiency? What classroom arrangement will enhance the learning rate of students? How can I *know* when behavior will be better or worse? How can I test—or experiment—to be certain I'm doing the best design . . . before the project is built? Where can I learn of other studies of relationships between behavior and layout? If I wish to conduct experiments, how can I learn to do them properly, so that the results are accurate? Who can I call to get help setting up an experiment that achieves what is needed and stays within the project budget and schedule? How do I tell others what I've done so they can benefit from my activity?

This "applied" research can be conducted on virtually every aspect of a project. In behavior areas, what space is best? What colors? What forms? What textures? What scale? What circulation pattern? What lighting? What climate? What materials? What image, or character, should be generated by the design? As designers, we make judgmental decisions constantly. Most of us had training at a university which caused us to make decisions without adequate data or precise data, by being asked to work on hypothetical "problems" or projects. Rarely were we obligated to work on actual projects and forced to seek out as much precise data as possible. Methods for fusing "hard" data into our design decisions have not been extensively built into our professional training. The question

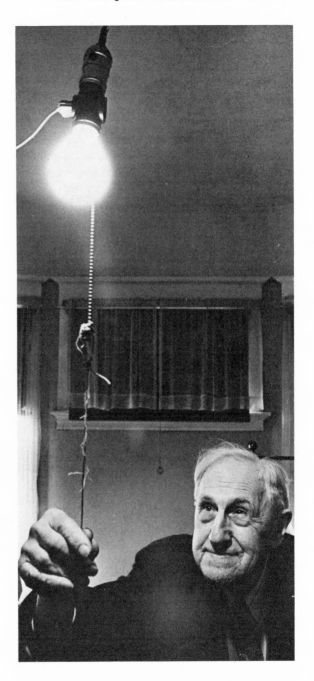

**Photo credit: City**

is not: What color will *work* best?" but: What color must be here to achieve the best behavioral results? And "How do I *know* that this is the *best* behavior and that the color *will* do the job!"

You've probably browsed through or read some of the papers in this book. Have any aroused your curiosity? Do you feel as though one or two describe something that would be useful to you? Don't stop there! Try it. Play with it in some corner. Get the "feel" of it. Is it becoming a good feeling or more comfortable as you continue to dabble with it? Do you understand it a little better now? Will it help you—perhaps—to do something better than you're now doing it? How could you try it out on a project, but with no risk? How could you get hold of a "friendly helper" who has more experience with the approach? (You could go to the horse's mouth, actually . . . these horses love to talk!) I've developed a few methods myself; it felt very satisfying to see them actually put to use and see them improve a situation. That was a warm, healthy, and very productive experience for both the practitioners and myself. It seems that this kind of relationship is more constructive to our professional activity than the first one described.

Meanwhile, keep trying to fold your arms the other way, and. . . .

**PART FIVE
BIBLIOGRAPHY**

# Designing for Human Behavior: A Reference Bibliography

The growth of interest in the relationship between human behavior, attitudes, and values, and the designed environment has been accompanied by a proliferation of literature on the subject. Hopefully, selecting and organizing a subset of this literature of the greatest interest to architects will aid the flow of information between professionals and researchers. It must not be thought that the references collected here present a unified theory of architecture. Indeed a perusal of only a few of them will quickly indicate the inconsistencies and contradictions which exist in our current thinking on the social and psychological aspects of architecture. Nevertheless, these books and articles do represent the current state-of-the-art and the basis for a reconsideration of architectural and designing theory.

The categories into which the references have been divided approximate the outline of the book. An attempt has been made to place each title into the category most appropriate to its content and aim. However, the organization is somewhat arbitrary and many of the references could easily have been placed in a different category.

Jon Lang
Walter Moleski
David Vachon

## INTRODUCTION

### Criticisms of the Present "Built-Form" and the Present Status of Architectural Philosophy

Alexander, Christopher, "A city is not a tree," *Architectural Forum,* Vol. 122 (April 1965), 58-62; (May 1965); 58-61.

————, "Major changes in environmental form required by social and psychological demands," *Ekistics,* Vol. 28 (August 1969), 78–85.

Boughey, Howard N., Jr., *Blueprints for Behavior: The Intentions of Architects to Influence Social Action Through Design,* Ph. D. dissertation, Princeton University, 1968; Ann Arbor, Mich.: University Microfilm No. 69, 1969.

Broady, Maurice, *Planning for People: Essays on the Social Context of Planning,* London: Bedford Square Press of the National Council of Social Services, 1968.

Chombart de Lauwe, Paul, *Famille et habitation,* Paris: Centre National de la Recherche Scientifique, 1959.

Fitch, James Marston, "The future of architecture," *The Journal of Aesthetic Education,* Vol. 4 (January 1970), 85–103.

Gans, Herbert J., *People and Plans: Essays on Urban Problems and Solutions,* Part 1, "Environment and behavior," New York: Basic Books, 1968, 1–52.

Gropius, Walter, *Scope of Total Architecture,* New York: Macmillan, Collier Books, 1962 (Harper & Row, 1943).

Gutman, Robert, ed., *People and Buildings,* New York: Basic Books, 1971.

————, "The sociological implications of programming practices," *Building Research,* Vol. 6 (April–June 1969), 26–27.

Hall, Edward T., "What is quality?" *AIA Journal,* Vol. 40 (July 1963), 44–48.

Jones, Barclay G., "Design from knowledge not belief," *AIA Journal,* Vol. 38 (December 1962), 104–105.

Lipman, Alan, "The architectural belief system and social behavior," *The British Journal of Sociology,* Vol. 20 (June 1969), 190–204.

Michelson, William, "Most people don't want what architects want," *Transaction,* Vol. 5 (July–August 1968), 37–43.

Montgomery, Roger, "Comment on 'Fear and house-as-haven in the lower class'," *Journal of the American Institute of Planners,* Vol. 32 (January 1966), 31–37.

Parr, A. E., "Lessons of an urban childhood," *The American Montessori Bulletin,* Vol. 7, No. 4.

———, "Psychological aspects of urbanology," *Journal of Social Issues,* Vol. 22 (October 1966), 39–45.

Pawley, Martin, *Architecture Versus Housing,* New York: Praeger, 1971.

Perin, Constance, *With Man in Mind,* Cambridge, Mass.: The MIT Press, 1970.

Rainwater, Lee, "Fear and house-as-haven in the lower class," *Journal of the American Institute of Planners,* Vol. 32 (January 1966), 23–31.

Rapoport, Amos, "Whose meaning in architecture?" *Arena/Interbuild,* Vol. 14 (October 1967), 44–46.

### Emerging Models of the Designing Process

Alexander, Christopher, and Barry Poyner, "The atoms of environmental structure," in Gary Moore, ed., *Emerging Methods in Environmental Design and Planning,* Cambridge, Mass.: The MIT Press, 1970, 308–321.

Broadbent, Geoffrey, "Systems and environmental design," in John Archea and Charles Eastman, eds., *EDRA2: Proceedings of the Second Annual Environmental Design Research Association Conference,* Pittsburgh, Pa., October 1970, 145–155.

Corkill, Philip A., and Robert F. Guenther, "Systematic approaches to design," *AIA Journal,* Vol. 50 (December 1968), 75–77.

Esherick, J., "Problems of the design of a design system," in J. C. Jones and D. C. Thornley, eds., *Conference on Design Methods,* New York: Macmillan, Inc., 1943.

Horowitz, Harold, "The program's the thing," *AIA Journal,* Vol. 47 (May 1967), 94–100.

Markus, Thomas A., "The role of building performance measurement and appraisal in design method," *Architects' Journal,* Vol. 146 (December 20, 1967), 1567–1573.

Roe, P. H., G. N. Sonlis, and V. K. Handa, *The Discipline of Design,* Boston: Allyn and Bacon, 1967.

Sanoff, Henry, *A Systematic Approach to Design,* Raleigh, N.C.: Design Research Laboratory, School of Design, North Carolina State University, April 1969.

Studer, Raymond G., "The dynamics of behavior-contingent physical systems," in A. Ward and G. Broadbent, eds., *Design Methods in Architecture,* London: Lund Humphries, 1970, 59–70; also in Harold M. Proshansky, William H. Ittelson, and Leanne G. Rivlin, eds., *Environmental Psychology: Man and His Physical Setting,* New York: Holt, 1970, 56–76.

———, and David Stea, "Architectural programming and human behavior," *Journal of Social Issues,* Vol. 22 (October 1966), 127–136.

Swinburne, Herbert H., "Change is the challenge," *AIA Journal,* Vol. 47 (May 1967), 83–90.

Van der Ryn, Sim, "Searching for a science of design: problems and puzzles," *AIA Journal,* Vol. 45 (January 1966), 37–42.

### Social and Psychological Factors in Architecture and the Potential Contribution of the Behavioral Sciences to Architectural Theory and Designing

Bayes, Kenneth, *The Therapeutic Effect of the Environment on Emotionally Disturbed and Mentally Subnormal Children,* London; The Gresham Press, 1967.

———, and Sandra Franklin, *Designing for the Handicapped,* London: George Gibson, 1971.

Broady, Maurice, "Social theory in architectural design," *Arena, Journal of the Architectural Association,* Vol. 81 (1966) 149–154.

Brolin, Brent C., and John Zeisel, "Mass housing, social research and design," *Architectural Forum,* Vol. 129 (July–August 1968), 66–71.

Canter, David, ed., *Architectural Psychology,* London: RIBA, 1970.

Carson, Daniel H., "The interaction of man and his environment," in *SER2: School Environments Research: Environmental Evaluations,* Ann Arbor, Mich.: University of Michigan Press, 1965, 13–52.

Chein, Isadore, "The environment as a determinant of behavior," *Journal of Social Psychology,* Vol. 39 (1954), 115–127.

Chombart de Lauwe, Paul H., "The sociology of housing: methods and prospects of research," *International Journal of Comparative Sociology,* Vol. 2 (March 1961), 22–41.

Craik, Kenneth H., "Environmental psychology," in *New Directions in Psychology 4,* New York: Holt, 1970, 1–121.

Dubos, René, "Our buildings shape us," in *So Human an Animal,* New York: Scribner's Sons, 1968, 160–181.

Esser, Aristide, *Environment and Behavior,* New York: Clifton Press, 1971.

Fitch, James Marston, *American Building 2: The Environmental Forces That Shape It,* Boston: Houghton Mifflin, 1972.

Foster, George M., *Applied Anthropology,* Boston: Little, Brown, 1969.

Good, Lawrence R., Saul M. Segal, and Alfred P. Bay, *Therapy by Design, Implications of Architecture for Human Behavior,* Springfield, Ill.: Charles C Thomas, 1965.

Gutman, Robert, *People and Buildings,* New York: Basic Books, 1972.

———, "What schools of architecture expect from sociology," *AIA Journal,* Vol. 49 (March 1968), 70–76.

Griffen, William V., Joseph H. Mauritzen, and Joyce V. Kasmar, "The psychological aspects of the architectural environment: a rewiew," *American Journal of Psychiatry,* Vol. 125 (February 1969), 1057–1062.

Hole, W. Vere, "User needs and the design of houses—the current and potential contribution of the sociological studies," in *The Social Environment and Its Effect on the Design of the Building and Its Immediate Surroundings,* CIB Symposium W. 45, Stockholm, October 1969, 117–124.

Honikman, Basil, ed., *AP 70 Proceedings of the Architectural Psychology Conference at Kingston Polytechnic, 1970,* London: RIBA, 1971.

Izumi, Kyoshi, "Psychosocial phenomena and building design," *Building Research,* Vol. 2 (July–August 1965), 9–11.

Michelson, William, *Man and His Urban Environment: A Sociological Approach,* Reading, Mass.: Addison-Wesley, 1970.

Moller, Clifford B., *Architectural Environment and Our Mental Health,* New York: Horizon Press, 1968.

Norberg-Schulz, Christian, *Intentions in Architecture,* Cambridge, Mass.: The MIT Press, 1965.

Proshansky, Harold M., William H. Ittelson and Leanne G. Rivlin, eds., *Environmental Psychology: Man and His Physical Setting,* New York: Holt, 1970.

Rapoport, Amos, "The design professionals and the behavioral sciences," *Architectural Association Quarterly,* Vol. 1 (Winter 1968–69), 20–24.

———, *House Form and Culture,* Englewood Cliffs, N.J.: Prentice-Hall, 1969.

Rasmussen, Steen Eiler, *Experiencing Architecture,* 2nd ed., Cambridge, Mass.: The MIT Press, 1962 (originally published 1959).

Rusch, Charles W., "On the relation of form to behavior," *Design Methods Group Newsletter,* Vol. 3 (October 1969).

Searles, Harold F., *The Non-Human Environment in Normal Development and Schizophrenia,* New York: International Universities Press, 1960.

Stinger, Peter, "Architecture, psychology, the game's the same," in David V. Canter, ed., *Architectural Psychology,* London: RIBA, 7–11.

Taylor, Calvin W., "The new psychology for urban design," *Consulting Engineer,* Vol. 32 (March 1969), 152–157.

Wells, B. W. P., "Towards a definition of environmental studies: a psychologist's contribution," *Architects' Journal* (September 1965), 677–683.

Willmott, Peter, "Social research and new communities," *Journal of the American Institute of Planners,* Vol. 33 (November 1967), 387–398.

Wirth, Louis, "Housing as a field of sociological research," in Albert J. Reiss, Jr., ed., *Louis Wirth on Cities and Social Life,* Chicago: Phoenix Books, 1964.

Wohlwill, Joachim F., "The emerging discipline of environmental psychology," *American Psychologist,* Vol. 25 (April 1970), 303–312.

## ENVIRONMENTAL PERCEPTION AND COGNITION

### *"Basic Design" and Architectural "Form"*

Arnheim, Rudolph, *Art and Visual Perception,* Berkeley, Calif.: University of California Press, 1954.

————, "From function to expression," *Journal of Aesthetics and Art Criticism,* Vol. 23 (Fall 1964), 29–42.

De Sausmarez, Maurice, *Basic Design: The Dynamics of Visual Form,* New York: Van Nostrand Reinhold, 1964.

Isaac, A.R.G., *Approach to Architectural Design,* Toronto: University of Toronto Press, 1971.

Jones, Peter Lloyd, "The failure of basic design," *Leonardo,* Vol. 2 (April 1969), 155–160.

Kepes, Gyorgy, *Language of Vision,* Chicago: Paul Thiebold, 1964.

Orvik, Otto G., et al., *Art Fundamentals, Theory and Practice,* Dubuque, Iowa: William C. Brown, 1968.

Prak, Luning, "Formal and symbolic aesthetics," in *The Language of Architecture,* The Hague: Mouton, 1968, 3–13.

### *Meaning and Symbolism*

Bachelard, Gaston, *The Poetics of Space,* Boston: The Beacon Press, 1969.

Birren, Faber, *Light, Color and Environment,* New York: Van Nostrand Reinhold, 1969.

Boulding, Kenneth E., *The Image,* Ann Arbor, Mich.: University of Michigan Press, 1961.

Choay, Françoise, *The Modern City: Planning in the Nineteenth Century,* New York: Braziller, 1969.

Constantine, Mildred, and Egbert Jacobson, *Sign Language for Buildings and Landscape,* New York: Van Nostrand Reinhold, 1961.

Gibson, James J., "Meaning," in *Perception of the Visual World,* Boston: Houghton Mifflin, 1950, 197–213.

Hershberger, Robert G., "Architecture and meaning," *Journal of Aesthetic Education,* Vol. 4 (October 1970), 37–55.

Jenks, Charles, and George Baird, eds., *Meaning in Architecture,* New York: Braziller, 1969.

Ogden, Charles K., and I. A. Richards, *The Meaning of Meaning: A Study of the Influence of Language upon Thought and the Science of Symbolism,* New York: Harcourt, 1923.

Ruesch, Jurgen, and Weldon Kees, *Non-Verbal Communications: Notes on the Visual Perception of Human Relations,* Berkeley, Calif.: University of California Press, 1956.

### *Environmental Cognition*

Appleyard, Donald, "Styles and methods of structuring a city," *Environment and Behavior,* Vol. 2 (June 1970), 100–117.

————, "Why buildings are known; a predictive tool for architects and planners," *Environment and Behavior,* Vol. 1 (December 1969), 131–156.

Best, Gordon A., "Direction finding in large buildings," in David V. Canter, ed., *Architectural Psychology,* London: RIBA, 1970, 72–75.

"Cognitive mapping," in William J. Mitchell, ed., *Environmental Design: Research and Practice: Proceedings of the EDRA3/AR8 Conference,* University of California, Los Angeles, January 1972, 1.1.1–1.4.9.

*Environment and Behavior,* Vol. 2 (June 1970); whole issue.

Lynch, Kevin, *The Image of the City,* Cambridge, Mass.: The MIT Press, 1960.

Moore, Gary T., "Conceptual issues in the study of environmental cognition," in William J. Mitchell, ed., *Environmental Design: Research and Practice: Proceedings of the EDRA3/AR8 Conference,* University of California, Los Angeles, January 1972; 30.1.1–30.1.3.

Piaget, Jean, and Barbara Inhelder, *The Child's Conception of Space,* tr. by F. G. Langdon and J. L. Lunzer, New York: Norton, 1967 (originally published 1948).

Stea, David, "Environmental perception and cognition: towards a model for 'mental maps'," in Gary Coates and Kenneth Moffat, eds., *Response to Environment,* Raleigh, N.C.: Student Publication of the School of Design, North Carolina State University, 1969, 62–75.

Strauss, Anselm L., *Images of the American City,* New York: The Free Press, 1961.

## Perception, Cognition and Affect

Allport, F. H., *Theories of Perception and the Concept of Structure,* New York: Wiley, 1955.

Balint, Michael, "Friendly expanses—horrid empty spaces," *International Journal of Psychoanalysis,* Vol. 36 (1955), 225–241.

Berlyne, D. E., *Conflict, Arousal and Curiosity,* New York: McGraw-Hill, 1960.

Bruner, Jerome, Jacqueline Goodnow, and George Austin, *A Study of Thinking,* New York: Wiley, 1956.

Canter, David V., "An intergroup comparison of the connotative dimensions in architecture," *Environment and Behavior,* Vol. 1 (June 1969), 37–48.

Dewey, John, *Art as Experience,* New York: Putnam, Capricorn Books, 1958 (originally published 1934).

Fiske, D. W., and S. R. Maddi, *Functions of Varied Experience,* Homewood, Ill.: Dorsey Press, 1961.

Fitch, James Marston, "Experimental bases for aesthetical decision," *Annals of the New York Academy of Science,* Vol. 128 (1965), 706–714; also in Harold M. Proshansky, William H. Ittelson and Leanne G. Rivlin, eds., *Environmental Psychology: Man and His Physical Setting,* New York: Holt, 1970, 76–84.

Gibson, James J., *The Senses Considered as Perceptual Systems,* Boston: Houghton Mifflin, 1966.

Ittelson, William, "Perception of the large scale environment," paper presented to the New York Academy of Sciences, April 13, 1970.

Jones, Barclay G., "Prolegomena to the study of the esthetic effects of cities," *Journal of Aesthetics and Art Criticism,* Vol. 18 (June 1960), 419–429.

Kavolis, Vytautas Martynas, *Artistic Expression: A Sociological Analysis,* Ithaca, N.Y.: Cornell University Press, 1968.

Michelson, William, "An empirical analysis of urban environmental preferences," *Journal of the American Institute of Planners,* Vol. 32 (November 1966), 355–360.

Rapoport, Amos, "The study of spatial quality," *Journal of Aesthetic Education,* Vol. 4 (October 1970), 81–95.

————, and Ron Hawkes, "The perception of urban complexity," *Journal of the American Institute of Planners,* Vol. 36 (March 1970), 106–111.

————, and Robert Kantor, "Complexity and ambiguity in environmental design," *Journal of the American Institute of Planners,* Vol. 33 (July 1967), 210–221.

Sanoff, Henry, "House form and preference," in John Archea and Charles Eastman, eds., *EDRA2; Proceedings of the Second Annual Environmental Design Research Association Conference,* Pittsburgh, Pa., October 1970.

Santayana, George, *The Sense of Beauty,* New York: Dover, 1955 (New York: Scribner's Sons, 1901).

Southworth, Michael, "The sonic environment of cities," *Environment and Behavior,* Vol. 1 (June 1969), 49–70.

Valentine, Charles Wilfred, *Introduction to the Experimental Psychology of Beauty,* London: Methuen, 1962 (originally published 1919).

Vitz, Paul C., "Affect as a function of stimulus variation," *Journal of Experimental Psychology,* Vol. 71 (January 1966), 74–79.

Winkel, Gary, Roger Malek, and Philip Thiel, "The role of personality differences in the judgment of roadside quality," *Environment and Behavior,* Vol. 1 (December 1969), 199–223.

## SPATIAL BEHAVIOR

### Behavior Settings and Activity Patterns

Barker, Roger G., *Ecological Psychology; Concepts and Methods for Studying the Environment of Human Behavior,* Stanford; Calif.: Stanford University Press, 1968.

————, ed., *The Stream of Behavior,* New York: Appleton-Century-Crofts, 1963.

Brown, Lawrence A., John Holmes, and John F. Jakubus, "Urban activity systems in a planning context," in John Archea and Charles Eastman, eds., *EDRA2: Proceedings of the Second Annual Environmental Design Research Association Conference,* Pittsburgh, Pa., October 1970, 102–110.

Chapin, Stuart F., Jr., "The study of urban activity patterns," in *Urban Land Use Planning,* 2nd ed., Urbana, Ill.: University of Illinois Press, 1965, 221–253.

Goffman, Erving, *Behavior in Public Places,* New York: The Free Press 1963.

Gump, Paul V., "Milieu, environment and behavior," *Design and Environment,* Vol. 2 (Winter 1971), 48–50, 60.

"The interface between behavior and milieu in a total institution," in William J. Mitchell, ed., *Environmental Design: Research and Practice: Proceedings of the EDRA3/AR8 Conference,* University of California, Los Angeles, January 1972, 4.1.1–4.5.1.

Watson, Donald A., "Modelling the activity system," in Henry Sanoff and Sidney Cohn, eds., *EDRA1: Proceedings of the First Annual Environmental Design Research Association Conference,* Raleigh, N.C., 1970, 318–327.

### Ergonomics and Anthropometrics

"Biometric design: designing for human use," *Architectural and Engineering News,* Vol. 11 (February 1969), 29–43.

Dreyfuss, Henry, *The Measure of Man: Human Factors in Design,* 2nd ed., New York: Whitney Library of Design, 1967.

Kira, Alexander, *The Bathroom: Criteria for Design,* Ithaca, N.Y.: Center for Housing and Environmental Studies, Cornell University, 1966.

Le Corbusier (Jeanneret-Gris, Charles Edouard), *The Modulor, a Harmonious Measure to the Human Scale, Universally Applicable to Architecture and Mechanics,* by Peter de Francia and Anna Bostock, Cambridge, Mass.: Harvard University Press, 1954 (originally published 1951).

Morgan, Clifford T., et al., *Human Engineering: Guide to Equipment Design,* New York: McGraw-Hill, 1963.

Murrell, K. F. H., *Ergonomics; Man in His Working Environment,* London: Chapman & Hall, 1965.

Ramsey, Charles G., and Harold R. Sleeper, *Architectural Graphic Standards,* ed. by Joseph N. Boaz, New York: Wiley, 1970.

### Personal Space, Territoriality, and Proxemic Theory

Ardrey, Robert, *The Territorial Imperative,* New York: Atheneum, 1966.

De Long, Alton J., "Dominance-territorial relations in a small group," *Environment and Behavior,* Vol. 2 (September 1970), 170–191.

Hall, Edward T., *The Hidden Dimension,* Garden City, N.Y.: Doubleday, 1966.

————, *The Silent Language,* Garden City, N.Y.: Doubleday, 1959.

Lipman, Alan, "Territoriality: a useful architectural concept?" *RIBA Journal,* Vol. 77 (February 1970), 68–70.

Little, Kenneth B., "Personal space," *Journal of Experimental Social Psychology,* Vol. 1 (1965), 237–241.

Lyman, Stanford M., and Marvin B. Scott, "Territoriality: a neglected sociological dimension," *Social Problems,* Vol. 15 (Fall 1967), 236–249.

"Personal space," in William J. Mitchell, ed., *Environmental Design; Research and Practice: Proceedings of the EDRA3/AR8 Conference,* University of California, Los Angeles, January 1972, 2.1.1.–2.4.8.

Rapoport, Amos, "The personal element in housing: an argument for open-ended design," *RIBA Journal,* Vol. 75 (July 1968), 300–307.

Sommer, Robert, *Personal Space; The Behavioral Basis of Design,* Englewood Cliffs, N.J.: Prentice-Hall, 1969.

————, and Franklin D. Becker, "Territorial defense and the good neighbor," *Journal of Personality and Social Psychology,* Vol. 11 (February 1969), 85–92.

Stea, David, "Space, territory and human movement," *Landscape,* Vol. 15 (Autumn 1965), 13–16.

Suttles, Gerald D., *The Social Order of the Slum: Ethnicity and Territoriality in the Inner City,* Chicago: University of Chicago Press, 1968.

Webber, Melvin M., "Culture, territoriality and the elastic mile," *Papers of the Regional Science Association,* Vol. 13 (1964), 59–69.

### Spatial Organization, Architecture, and Social Interaction

Blake, Robert R., et al., "Housing architecture and social interaction," *Sociometry,* Vol. 19 (June 1956), 133–139.

Chermayeff, Serge, and Christopher Alexander, *Community and Privacy,* Garden City, N.Y.: Doubleday, 1963.

Cooper, Clare, *Some Social Implications of House and Site Plan Design at Easter Village: A Case Study,* Berkeley, Calif.: Institute of Urban and Regional Development, Center for Planning and Development Research, University of California, 1965.

Festinger, Leon, and Harold H. Kelley, *Changing Attitudes through Social Contact; An Experimental Study of a Housing Project,* Ann Arbor, Mich.: Research Center for Group Dynamics, Institute for Social Research, University of Michigan, 1951.

————, Stanley Schachter, and Kurt Back, *Social Pressures in Informal Groups; A Study of Human Factors in Housing,* New York: Harper & Row, 1950.

Gans, Herbert J., "Planning and social life: Friendship and neighbor relations in suburban communities," *Journal of the American Institute of Planners,* Vol. 27 (May 1961), 134–140.

Gutman, Robert, "Site planning and social behavior," *Journal of Social Issues,* Vol. 22 (October 1966), 103–115.

Hall, Edward T., "The maddening crowd: space and its organization as a factor in mental health," *Landscape,* Vol. 12 (Autumn 1962), 26–30.

Hazard, John N., "Furniture arrangements as a symbol of judicial roles," *ETC: A Review of General Semantics,* Vol. 19 (July 1962), 181–188.

Ittelson, William H., Harold M. Proshansky, and Leanne G. Rivlin, "Bedroom size and social interaction of the psychiatric ward," *Environment and Behavior,* Vol. 2 (December 1970), 255–270.

Katz, Robert D., "Relationship of density to livability," *Building Research,* Vol. 1 (January–February 1964), 15–18.

Keller, Suzanne, *The Urban Neighborhood: A Sociological Perspective,* New York: Random House, 1968.

Lansing, John B., Robert W. Marans, and Robert B. Zehner, *Planned Residential Environments,* Ann Arbor, Mich.: Survey Research Center, Institute for Social Research, University of Michigan, 1970.

Lipman, Alan, "Building design and social interaction," *Architects' Journal,* Vol. 147 (January 3, 1968), 23–30.

Madge, John, "Privacy and social interaction," *Transactions of the Bartlett Society,* Vol. 3 (1964–65), 121–141.

Roscow, Irving, "The social effects of the physical environment," *Journal of the American Institute of Planners,* Vol. 27 (May 1961), 127–133.

Schmidt, Robert, "Density, health and social disorganization," *Journal of the American Institute of Planners,* Vol. 32 (January 1966), 38–40.

Sommer, Robert, *Personal Space: The Behavioral Basis of Design,* Englewood Cliffs, N.J.: Prentice-Hall, 1969.

Srivastava, Rajendra K., and Lawrence Good, "Patterns of group interaction in three architecturally different psychiatric treatment sections," *Milieu,* Ser. 1, Vol. 4 (January 1968), 1–10.

Westin, A., *Privacy and Freedom,* New York: Ballantine, 1970.

Willis, Margaret, "Designing for privacy: 1, What is privacy? 2, Overlooking; 3, Personal relationships," *Architects' Journal,* Vol. 137 (May 29, 1963), 1137–1141; (June 5, 1963), 1181–1187; (June 12, 1963), 1231–1236.

## LIFE STYLE, SOCIAL STATUS, AND THE DESIGNED ENVIRONMENT

Belcher, John C., "Differential aspirations for housing between blacks and whites in rural Georgia," *Phylon,* Vol. 31 (Fall 1970), 231–243.

Bell, Wendell, "Social class, life style and suburban residence," in William M. Dobriner, ed., *The Suburban Community,* New York: Putnam, 1958, 225–247.

Bensman, Joseph, and Arthur J. Vidich, "The new middle classes: their culture and life styles," *Journal of Aesthetic Education,* Vol. 4 (January 1970), 23–39.

Beyer, Glen, *Housing and Personal Values,* Ithaca, N.Y.: Cornell University, Agricultural Experiment Station, Memoir 364, 1959.

Cooper, Clare, "Fenced back yard—unfenced front yard—enclosed porch," *Journal of Housing,* Vol. 24 (June 1967), 268–274.

Dean, John P., "Housing design and family values," in W. L. C. Wheaton and G. Milgram, eds., *Urban Housing,* New York: The Free Press, 1966, 127–138.

Ellis, William R., "Planning, design, and black community style: the problem of occasion—adequate space," in William J. Mitchell, ed., *Environmental Design:*

Research and Practice: Proceedings of the EDRA3/AR8 Conference, University of California, Los Angeles, January 1972, 6.12.1–6.12.10.

Feldman, Arnold S., and Charles Tilly, "The interaction of social and physical space," *American Sociological Review,* Vol. 25 (December 1960), 877–884.

Hartman, Chester, "Social values and housing orientations," *The Journal of Social Issues,* Vol. 19 (April 1963), 113–131.

Hole, W. Vere, and J. J. Attenburrow, *Houses and People: A Review of User Studies at the Building Research Station,* London: H.M.S.O., 1966.

Manning, Peter, *Office Design,* Liverpool University Department of Building Science, 1965.

Milgram, Stanley, "The experience of living in cities," *Science,* Vol. 167 (March 13, 1970).

Rainwater, Lee, "Fear and house-as-haven in the lower class," *Journal of the American Institute of Planners,* Vol. 32 (January 1966), 23–31.

Schermer, George, Associates, *More than Shelter: Social Needs in Low and Moderate Income Housing,* Washington, D.C.: GPO, Research Report 0.8, National Commission on Urban Problems, 1968.

Van der Ryn, Sim, and Murray Silverstein, *Dorms at Berkeley: An Environmental Analysis,* Berkeley, Calif.: Center for Planning and Development Research, 1967.

Wilner, Daniel M., Rosabelle Price Walkley, and Thomas C. Pinkerton, *The Housing Environment and Family Life,* Baltimore: The Johns Hopkins Press, 1960.

## STUDYING HUMAN BEHAVIOR AND ARCHITECTURAL DESIGNING AND RESEARCH

### General

Canter, David, "On appraising building appraisals," *The Architects' Journal,* Vol. 148 (August 21, 1968), 339–341.

Daley, Janet, "Psychological research in architecture—the myth of quantifiability," *Architects' Journal,* Vol. 148 (August 21, 1968), 339–341.

Festinger, Leon, and Daniel Katz, eds., *Research Methods in the Behavioral Sciences,* New York: Holt, 1953.

Hyman, Ray, *The Nature of Psychological Inquiry,* Englewood Cliffs, N.J.: Prentice-Hall, 1964.

Noble, John, and Joan Ach, "Appraisal of user requirements in mass housing," *Architects' Journal,* Vol. 144 (August 24, 1966), 479–486.

Perin, Constance, "Concepts and methods for studying environments in use," in William J. Mitchell, ed., *Environmental Design: Research and Practice: Proceedings of the EDRA3/AR8 Conference,* University of California, Los Angeles, January 1972, 13.6.1–13.6.10.

Rapoport, Amos, "An approach to the study of environmental quality," in Henry Sanoff and Sidney Cohn, eds., *EDRA1: Proceedings of the First Annual Environmental Design Research Association Conference,* Raleigh, N.C., 1970, 1–13.

Sanoff, Henry, *Techniques of Evaluation for Designers,* Raleigh, N.C.: Design Research Laboratory, School of Design, North Carolina State University, 1968.

Selltiz, Claire, Marie Jahoda, Morton Deutsch, and S. W. Cook, *Research Methods in Social Relations,* New York: Holt, 1959.

Sommer, Robert, "The new evaluator cookbook," *Design and Environment,* Vol. 2 (Winter 1971), 35–37, 59.

Wheeler, Lawrence, *Behavioral Research for Architectural Planning and Design,* Terre Haute, Ind.: Ewing Miller Associates, 1967.

———, and Ewing H. Miller, "Human factors analysis," in William Dudley Hunt, Jr., *Comprehensive Architectural Services: General Principles and Practice,* Washington, D.C.: American Institute of Architects, 1965, 194–200.

### Experimentation: What It Is and Its Uses in Architectural Research

Anderson, Barry F., *The Psychology Experiment; An Introduction to Scientific Methods,* Belmont, Calif.: Wadsworth, 1966.

Bechtel, Robert, "Hodometer research in architecture," *Milieu,* Ser. 2, Vol. 1 (April 1967), whole issue.

Buckley, Walter, ed., *Modern Systems Research for the Behavioral Scientist; a Sourcebook,* Chicago: Aldine-Atherton, 1968.

————, *Sociology and Modern Systems Theory,* Englewood Cliffs, N.J.: Prentice-Hall, 1967.

Payne, Ifan, "Pupillary responses to architectural stimuli," in David V. Canter, ed., *Architectural Psychology,* London: RIBA, 1970, 35–39.

Sidman, Murray, *Tactics of Scientific Research,* New York: Basic Books, 1966.

Stevens, Stanley S., ed., *Handbook of Experimental Psychology,* New York: Wiley, 1951.

Winkel, Gary, and Robert Sasanoff, "An approach to an objective analysis of behavior in architectural space," Architectural Development Series, College of Architecture and Urban Planning, University of Washington, Seattle, 1966.

Zajonc, Robert B., *Social Psychology: An Experimental Approach,* Belmont, Calif.: Wadsworth, 1966.

### Empirical Nonexperimental Approaches, Unobtrusive Measures

Barker, Roger G., *Ecological Psychology: Concepts and Methods for Studying the Environment of Human Behavior,* Stanford, Calif.: Stanford University Press, 1968.

Bechtel, Robert B., "Footsteps as a measure of human preference," Environmental Research Foundation, Topeka, Kan., May 1967.

Byers, Paul, "Still photography in the systematic recording and analysis of behavioral data," *Human Organization,* Vol. 23 (Spring 1964).

Duffy, Francis, "A method of analyzing and charting relationships in the office," *Architects' Journal,* Vol. 149 (March 12, 1969), 693–699.

Halprin, Lawrence, "Motation," *Progressive Architecture,* Vol. 46 (July 1965), 126–133.

Ittelson, William H., Leanne G. Rivlin, and Harold M. Proshansky, "The use of behavioral maps in environmental psychology," in Proshansky, *Environmental Psychology: Man and His Physical Setting,* New York: Holt, 1970.

Preiser, Wolfgang E., "The use of ethological methods in environmental analysis: a case study," in William J. Mitchell, ed., *Environmental Design: Research and Practice: Proceedings of the EDRA3/AR8 Conference,* University of California, Los Angeles, January, 1972, 3.2.1–3.2.10.

Webb, Eugene J., D. T. Campbell, R. D. Schwartz, and L. Sechrest, *Unobtrusive Measures; Nonreactive Research in the Social Sciences,* Skokie, Ill.: Rand McNally, 1966.

### The Use of Surveys, Questionnaires, and Scales in the Assessment of Attitudes and Values

Canter, David V., "The subjective assessment of the environment," *Building Performance Research Unit,* University of Strathclyde, Glasgow, 1969.

Hershberger, Robert G., "Towards a set of semantic scales to measure the meaning of architectural environments," in William J. Mitchell, ed., *Environmental Design: Research and Practice: Proceedings of the EDRA3/AR8 Conference,* University of California, Los Angeles, January 1972, 6.4.1.–6.4.10.

Kendall, Patricia A., and Paul Lazarsfeld "Problems of Survey Analysis" in Robert K. Merton and Paul Lazarsfeld, eds., *Continuities and Social Research,* New York, The Free Press, 1950, 133–167.

McKechnie, George, "Measuring environmental disposition with the environmental response inventory," in John Archea and Charles Eastman, eds., *EDRA2: Proceedings of the Second Annual Environmental Design Research Association Conference,* Pittsburgh, Pa. October 1970, 320–326.

"Methods for Investigating Imagery and Meaning," William J. Mitchell, ed., *Environmental Design: Research and Practice: Proceedings of EDRA3/AR8 Conference, University of California, Los Angeles, January 1972, 6.1.1–6.1.10*

Michelson, William, "Analytical Sampling for Design Information: A Survey of Housing Experience" in Henry Sanoff and Sidney Cohn, eds., *EDRA1: Proceedings of the First Annual Environmental Design Research Association Conference,* Raleigh, N.C. 1970, 183–197.

Osgood, Charles E., G. Suci, and P. Tannenbaum, *The Measurement of Meaning,* Urbana, Ill.; University of Illinois Press, 1957.

Parten, Mildred Bernice, *Surveys, Polls and Samples: Practical Procedures,* New York: Cooper Square, 1966 (originally published 1950).

Ravetz, Alison, "The use of surveys in the assessment of residential design," *Architectural Research and Teaching,* Vol. 1 (April 1971), 23–31.

Sanoff, Henry, *Techniques of Evaluation for Designers,* Raleigh, N.C.: Design Research Laboratory, School of Design, North Carolina State University, 1968.

### General References

Berelson, B., and G. A. Steiner, *Human Behavior; An Inventory of Psychological Findings,* New York: Harcourt, 1964.

Blalock, Hubert, Jr., *Causal Inferences in Non-Experimental Research,* Chapel Hill, N.C.: University of North Carolina Press, 1961.

Miller, G., E. Galanter, and K. Pribram, *Plans and the Structure of Behavior,* New York: Holt, 1960.

Sellitz, Claire, Marie Jahoda, Morton Deutsch, and S. W. Cook, *Research Methods in Social Relations,* New York: Holt, 1959.

Willems, E. P., and H. L. Rausch, eds., *Naturalistic Viewpoints in Psychological Research,* New York: Holt, 1969.